Trends in Digital Signal Processing

About the Series

A. G. Constantinides, Series Editor

Digital Signal Processing (DSP) is an area which either implicitly or explicitly forms the fundamental bedrock of a very wide range of applications and needs in our modern society. The broadening of the theoretical developments coupled with the accelerated incorporation of DSP to an ever wider range of applications highlights the need to have a rapid-reaction focus for the dissemination of the various advancements. The series is aimed at providing such a focus.

Pan Stanford Series on Digital Signal Processing — Volume 1

Trends in Digital Signal Processing

A Festschrift in Honour of A. G. Constantinides

edited by

Yong Ching Lim
Hon Keung Kwan
Wan-Chi Siu

PAN STANFORD PUBLISHING

Published by

Pan Stanford Publishing Pte. Ltd.
Penthouse Level, Suntec Tower 3
8 Temasek Boulevard
Singapore 038988

Email: editorial@panstanford.com
Web: www.panstanford.com

British Library Cataloguing-in-Publication Data
A catalogue record for this book is available from the British Library.

Trends in Digital Signal Processing: A Festschrift in Honour of A. G. Constantinides

ISBN 978-981-4669-50-4 (Hardcover)
ISBN 978-981-4669-51-1 (eBook)

Printed in Singapore

Reviews

"*This book is a very valuable addition to the signal processing literature. All chapters are written by internationally acclaimed researchers in the field addressing hot topics of current interest. Many of these renowned experts carry the technical DNA inherited from Prof. Constantinides, a living proof of how outstanding genetic information can lead to fruitful contributions to society development.*

"*The book includes eighteen survey chapters on the general areas of digital filters and transforms, signal processing, and communications, beautifully written by the technical heirs of Prof. Constantinides and his contemporary colleagues. Indeed this book reflects some of the many advances that Prof. Constantinides and his generation brought about to the ubiquitous DSP technology that benefits the current generation.*"

Prof. Paulo S. R. Diniz
Federal University of Rio de Janeiro, Brazil

"*A fitting tribute to a world-renowned pioneer in digital filter design, DSP, and communications, this book offers panoramic views of the past, present, and future of the theory and applications of these fields. The continual evolutions in time-interleaved A/D converters, all-pass filters, and multi-rate filters have pushed the envelopes of their applications, ranging from wireless communications to human face recognition and seismic signal processing. Authored by leading researchers in these fields, this book provides valuable insights into what have been made possible and potential future developments.*"

Prof. Yih-Fang Huang
University of Notre Dame, USA

"Professor Constantinides has made worldwide impact on DSP through his novel contributions to this area. With his unique energy, he has successfully pushed forward DSP scientists in the fields of education, research, and services. His personal inspiration to attract young scientists to work on DSP, especially in Europe, already started in the seventies with the establishment of the European Association for Signal Processing and the European Journal for Signal Processing *as well as the organization of the first international series of meetings on DSP."*

Prof. Tapio Saramäki
Tampere University of Technology, Finland

"This festschrift covers a number of most recent and important DSP research works, including DSP theories, filter designs, and applications, and is very valuable for the DSP community."

Prof. Soo-Chang Pei
National Taiwan University, Taiwan

Contents

PART III SIGNAL PROCESSING

PART V FINALE

Foreword

This book honors the illustrious career of Anthony Constantinides. It was inspired by the occasion of his seventieth birthday, on which many of his friends, colleagues, and former students gathered at Imperial College in London to reminisce about the past, to talk about the future, and generally to celebrate this special event.

Professor Constantinides is one of the pioneers of digital signal processing, with many firsts to his name. He was the first to formulate the fundamental concepts of direct methods for digital filter design and to place these on a firm analytical basis. He also initiated the first international gathering of researchers in the world in this field, and published one of its very first textbooks: his celebrated *Introduction to Digital Filtering* (Wiley, 1975), based in part on his lecture notes from one of the earliest courses offered in the field. These activities were instrumental in spreading the "gospel" of digital signal processing throughout the world and were very influential in bringing it to the forefront in the signal processing community.

Beyond his contributions to digital signal processing, Prof. Constantinides has continued to lead the way into new fields, from image processing to wireless communications, and has even made contributions to the archaeology of ancient Greece. Moreover, he has provided vision and leadership in establishing a world-class curriculum and supportive research environment in signal processing at Imperial College, one of the world's leading academic institutions, as well as in advising other universities worldwide in curricular and other matters. These activities are coupled with his supervision, training and nurturing of well over 100 PhD students, an astonishing contribution to scholarship and to human capital. Many of these and the 400 MSc students educated by him have become internationally recognized scholars, researchers, and industrial leaders currently occupying pre-eminent positions throughout the world. Collectively, his students represent a very significant force in advancing the knowledge and technology of our field.

Over the decades, Prof. Constantinides has also become the connector of a vital and far-flung community of countless friends and colleagues, who span both the globe and the discipline. This book is a product of that community, which offers it as a tribute to the remarkable influence that he has had, and continues to have, on so many of us.

H. Vincent Poor
Princeton, New Jersey

PART I

INTRODUCTION

Chapter 1

Introduction

Yong Ching Lim,[a] Hon Keung Kwan,[b] and Wan-Chi Siu[c]
[a] School of Electrical and Electronic Engineering,
Nanyang Technological University,
50 Nanyang Avenue, Singapore, 639798, Singapore
[b] Department of Electrical and Computer Engineering,
University of Windsor, Windsor, Ontario N9B 3P4, Canada
[c] Centre for Multimedia Signal Processing,
Department of Electronic and Information Engineering,
The Hong Kong Polytechnic University, Hong Kong
elelimyc@pmail.ntu.edu.sg, kwan1@uwindsor.ca, enwcsiu@polyu.edu.hk

This festschrift is published in honor of Emeritus Professor Anthony George Constantinides, a pioneer and a world leader in digital signal processing (DSP). The publication of this festschrift is made possible by the contributions of the authors, and the founder and CEO of Pan Stanford Publishing who was a student of Prof. Constantinides.

It was the morning of the twenty-fifth day of January 2013. Prof. Constantinides, many of his ex-PhD students, including three of us, his friends, and colleagues, gathered in the Department of Electrical and Electronic Engineering, Imperial College, while attending the 2013 Constantinides International Workshop on Signal Processing. The Workshop was specially organized to celebrate the seventieth birthday of Prof. Constantinides. One of the decisions made during the Workshop was the publication of this festschrift.

Trends in Digital Signal Processing: A Festschrift in Honour of A. G. Constantinides
Edited by Yong Ching Lim, Hon Keung Kwan, and Wan-Chi Siu
Copyright © 2016 Pan Stanford Publishing Pte. Ltd.
ISBN 978-981-4669-50-4 (Hardcover), 978-981-4669-51-1 (eBook)
www.panstanford.com

Prof. Constantinides has made a wide range of contributions in digital signal processing since its beginning in the 1960s. In those days, digital techniques for processing signals were only applicable for very low-frequency applications where inductors and capacitors would be too bulky to be practical. Today, DSP is ubiquitous. His fundamental contributions in digital filters have attracted and inspired many electrical engineers, including the three of us, who chose to complete our PhD theses with Prof. Constantinides as our supervisor.

This festschrift is divided into five parts: (I) Introduction, (II) Digital Filters and Transforms, (III) Signal Processing, (IV) Communications, and (V) Finale. The festschrift starts with a foreword by Prof. Vicent Poor and ends with closing remarks by Prof. Lajos Hanzo. Chapter 1 in Part I gives an introduction to the festschrift.

There are six chapters in Part II, Digital Filters and Transform. It starts with Chapter 2 on the design of digital filters to seamlessly merge the outputs of a bank of analog-to-digital converters (ADCs) producing an equivalent ADC operating at extremely high sampling rate. In many real-time signal processing applications, the maximum sampling rate is limited by the sampling rate of the ADC. It is possible to use a bank of ADC operating at a time-interleaved manner to sample an input signal at a rate much higher than that can be achieved by a single ADC. This type of ADC bank is called a TIADC (time-interleaved ADC). As a result of mismatches between different sub-ADC outputs, the quality of the raw TIADC output is unacceptably poor if it is not properly processed. Chapter 2 presents a review of filtering techniques that minimize spurious frequencies caused by sub-ADC mismatches.

Chapter 3 describes a specific class of multirate filters that are extremely efficient for the implementation of very wideband digital filters for modern software-defined radio applications. They have the capability to optimize the sample rate while processing signals. This results in many advantages. It has the advantage of cost and computational complexity reduction, improved performance, and reduced chip size, power, and weight over other systems.

Constantinides transformation, the all-pass transformation that transforms any digital lowpass filter into any multi-band digital filter has been widely adopted. Chapter 4 has been written as a tribute to Prof. Constantinides who introduced the all-pass-based frequency transform digital filters. It reviews how all-pass filters can be exploited to design efficient structures for adaptive notch filters. It also includes recent extensions of the technique to complex adaptive notch filters.

A sparse FIR filter is a digital filter that contains a considerable number of zero coefficients; since arithmetic operations (and consequently circuit components) corresponding to zero coefficients are not required, such type of digital filters offer an efficient approach for implementation. Recent advances in sparse FIR filter design are inspired by sparse coding in which some classical sparse coding methods have been applied to solve the design problems. Due to the inherent differences between these two classes of problems, more sophisticated l_0 and l_1 optimization techniques have been developed lately. In Chapter 5, several state-of-the-art design methods are reviewed. Some of these methods are computationally efficient, while others explore more sophisticated design strategies. The effectiveness of these methods is evaluated by filter design examples.

Echo cancellation is an old filtering problem that is still new today for its increasing applications. The special nature of echo cancellation requires a practical echo canceller to have a very high degree of sparsity. Proportionate normalized least mean squares and its extension, affine projection algorithm, are two of the well-known techniques in sparse adaptive filtering. In Chapter 6, a compressed sensing motivated sparsity-promoting mechanism induced via properly constraining or regularizing the l_1 norm or approximating the l_0 norm solution is described.

Chapter 7 starts with a classic review on some basic requirements of a transform that allows the complete recovery of a signal from its version in the transform domain. The chapter subsequently introduces the work by Constantinides and Siu on the minimum number of multiplications for the computation of discrete Fourier transform using the number theoretic transform. These form some solid foundation and basic initiatives for further research investigations in the area, which include the discovery of newer integer cosine kernels possibly for future video coding standards, and new learning-based approaches for super-resolution videos via the discrete cosine transform. They are key topics on applying hi-tech to modern video surveillance systems.

There are six chapters in Part III, Signal Processing. Fourier representation is the most commonly used representation for the analysis of periodic signals. Nevertheless, the Fourier approach is not the only approach. Presented in Chapter 8 is an interesting non-Fourier alternative representation of periodic sequences using Ramanujan sums, an integer-valued sequence named after the early twentieth century Indian number theoretician. The Ramanujan sums are defined for all integers not less than unity. The periodic components can be identified by performing integer-valued orthogonal projections on the original signal.

Over the past decade, most of the published literature on kernel-based adaptive filtering and machine learning for signal processing applications focused on learning strategies such as least squares, least mean square, and recursive least squares. Results on non-homogeneous function estimation are relatively lacking. To fill this void, Chapter 9 presents the application of high-dimensional kernels such as hypercomplex-valued and vector-valued kernels for non-homogeneous function estimation. The extent to which such multivariate mappings provide enhanced learning capability over standard, single-kernel, approaches is also established.

Accurate signal time delay estimation is important in determining the direction-of-arrival of a signal. In an absolutely noise-free scenario, signal time delay can be estimated to infinite precision using only three data points. In real-life application, noise is always present and the optimum strategy depends on the nature of the signal and the noise characteristics of the environment. Chapter 10 presents an information-theoretic based technique for linear microphone arrays time delay estimation assuming speech-shaped signal distributions. The analysis performed depicts that the marginal mutual information criterion does not depend on the underlying assumption for the distribution of speech as long as it belongs to the generalized Gaussian distribution.

Face recognition is a convenient and effective identification technique in a variety of applications such as access control, border crossing, and security surveillance. Although there exist highly accurate face recognition systems in controlled environments, accuracy of face recognition is extremely degraded in unconstraint conditions, such as poor illumination and partial occlusion. In Chapter 11, the state-of-the-art techniques employing human physiological characteristics to overcome these two challenging degradations are studied. These techniques include illumination-insensitive preprocessing, illumination-invariant descriptors, and block-based recognition strategies to suppress the lighting effect. Also, local-based face recognition techniques are applied to deal with occlusion.

Chapter 12 presents a novel system for semantic and content-based access to audiovisual information by combining semantic content search and enrichment with state-of-the-art visual content analysis. On one hand, it performs analysis of the metadata and the text accompanying films for detecting interesting objects or events, as well as the enrichment of these through thematic thesauri and ontologies; on the other hand, it uses local visual feature detectors to detect film frames that show historic locations and monuments. Experimental results on films are shown to demonstrate the performance of the proposed approach.

A complex architecture can be decomposed into its constituents to make it simple, analytically tractable, and capable to be reconstructed, resulting in a holistic representation that is fully descriptive in an elegant and uniform manner using mathematical modeling tools. Since the days at Imperial (1994–1997), Prof. Tetsuya Hoya has engaged in a number of research topics, including graph theoretic representation of image data, data pruning, neural network learning models, and artificial mind system. Chapter 13 presents a review on his research activities on modeling complex systems, with a reminiscence of the days in the past and suggestions on future directions.

There are four chapters in Part IV, Communications. Chapter 14 presents a class of low-complexity detectors applicable to both code division multiple access (CDMA) and multiple-input multiple-output (MIMO) communications. The presented detectors have a complexity that grows only linearly with the number of users/space multiplexed data streams and yet perform very close to their optimum counterparts. The presented algorithms make use of Markov chain Monte Carlo (MCMC) simulation techniques to search for a subset of important samples from the data signal space whose use is sufficient for a near optimum performance of the receiver. The detail of implementation of the MCMC detector in hardware is also presented and shown to be amenable to low-complexity logic and parallelism.

Information transmitted over wireless networks can be accessed by unauthorized users (eavesdroppers). Traditionally, ensuring that only the legitimate receiver will be able to decipher the transmitted information has been achieved by cryptographic approaches operating at various layers of the network protocol stack. Cryptography makes it difficult for the unauthorized user to decrypt the message contained in the packets. Physical (PHY) layer approaches have recently received significant attention as means of achieving secure wireless communications without relying on cryptography. By exploiting the characteristics of the wireless channel, PHY layer approaches provide the packet to the unauthorized user under such conditions, that the unauthorized user would not even be able to recover the message in the packet even if he knew the encoding/decoding scheme. Chapter 15 investigates the secrecy capacity of a system consisting of a transmitter, a destination, and an eavesdropper, all having multiple antennas.

While the classical radio frequency–based satellite navigation systems such as GPS, GLONASS, and BeiDou provide excellent services on open space areas directly under the clear blue sky, it is unsuitable for providing location information in indoor environments. Chapter 16 considers factors influencing the redesign of radio frequency based localization systems to meet challenges of new indoor localization applications areas such as the "Internet of Things." Radio frequency localization systems are often faced with the need to make trade-offs between accuracy and bandwidth. The cost of implementation is also an important factor in applications that require the deployment of a very large number of "smart dust" nodes.

Location information in Wi-Fi networks can be very useful to both businesses and consumers. In Chapter 17, four classification and prediction techniques for a powerful localization method called fingerprinting are studied using randomly generated data and data from real environments. It has been found that the Support Vector

Machine classifier and the k-Nearest Neighbor classifier perform well in all the tests. Furthermore, all techniques under study demonstrate diminishing improvement in the probability of correct prediction as the number of measurements used for training or prediction increases.

Finally, in Part V, Chapter 18 addresses the following questions: How is our world better served by DSP technologies and their innovative solutions? How do DSP technologies expressed in complex symbols and the sophisticated simulations that cover a wide spectrum of core components in hardware and software systems affect our daily activities? What is the impact of digital filtering techniques and complicated transformation equations, large varieties and many variations in signal processing, and the huge cloud in communications networks of people and data on our society?

The book front cover contains a photo of the PCB of the 14-bit 4 × 400 mega-sample-per-second time-interleaved analog-to-digital converter with details published in Y. C. Lim, Y. X. Zou, J. W. Lee, S. C. Chan, Time-interleaved analog-to-digital converter compensation using multichannel filters, *IEEE Trans. CAS-1*, vol. CAS-I-56, no. 10, pp. 2234–2247, Oct. 2009.

PART II

DIGITAL FILTERS AND TRANSFORMS

Chapter 2

A Review on Time-Interleaved Analog-to-Digital Converters and Mismatch Compensation Techniques

Saihua Xu and Yong Ching Lim

School of Electrical and Electronic Engineering, Nanyang Technological University,
50 Nanyang Avenue, Singapore, 639798, Singapore
shxu@ntu.edu.sg, elelimyc@pmail.ntu.edu.sg

Time interleaving a parallel array of slow analog-to-digital converters (ADCs) is an effective approach to achieve high sampling rate within a given process technology. The resulting system is a time-interleaved ADC (TIADC). In this chapter, we first review the parallel architecture of a TIADC and its associated speed improvement. Despite the speed advantage, various technology-dependent imperfections cause component mismatches among the sub-ADCs and distort the output signal leading to degraded system performance. In particular, the effects of offset, gain, timing, and frequency response mismatches in both the time and frequency domain are explained. Followed by that is a review of the techniques published in the literature for estimating and correcting the mismatch errors.

Trends in Digital Signal Processing: A Festschrift in Honour of A. G. Constantinides
Edited by Yong Ching Lim, Hon Keung Kwan, and Wan-Chi Siu
Copyright © 2016 Pan Stanford Publishing Pte. Ltd.
ISBN 978-981-4669-50-4 (Hardcover), 978-981-4669-51-1 (eBook)
www.panstanford.com

2.1 Introduction

Digital signal processing (DSP) finds its application in a wide range of advanced systems such as audio processing, image and video processing, telecommunications, sonar and radar processing, and sensor technology. The rapid evolution of digital integrated circuit (IC) technology together with parallel computing architecture has made DSP systems faster and less expensive over the past decades. To fully exploit the advantages of DSP systems, real-world signals need to be transformed into discrete, binary coded samples to be processed by sophisticated software algorithms. Therefore, the availability of high-speed and high-resolution ADCs is essential to the success of these advanced systems. For instance, in the telecommunication area, high speed ADCs allow direct conversion of signals at radio frequencies (RF), eliminating the need for analog down conversion stages.

In turn, the continuous development of these advanced systems has consistently pushed the boundaries of the ADCs. For a single-chip ADC, flash ADCs have the highest speed at the expense of large area, high power dissipation, and limited resolution. It has been pointed out that the speed of sampling is limited by the comparator ambiguity, which is related to the speed of the device technology used to fabricate the ADC [116]. Downscaling of the device technology leads to speed improvement but makes circuit design difficult.

In order to achieve high conversion rate while maintaining reasonable increase of area and power dissipation within a given device technology, a time-interleaved ADC (TIADC) scheme has been proposed by Black and Hodge [5] and widely used since then. A TIADC consists of several slow sub-ADCs sampling at interleaved time instants as if they were effectively a single ADC operating at a much higher speed. In spite of the significant speed advantage, TIADCs have a major drawback that any mismatch between the sub-ADC channels generates undesirable distortions in the output spectrum and significantly degrades the performance of the TIADC such as the spurious-free dynamic range (SFDR) and the signal-to-noise-and distortion ratio (SINAD) [1].

The organization of this chapter is as follows. Section 2.2 gives an introduction of the architecture of a TIADC system. Four types of mismatch errors that exist in a TIADC, namely, offset, gain, timing, and frequency response mismatch are then investigated in Section 2.3. The behavior of the mismatch errors in both the time domain and frequency domain are recapitulated. Section 2.4 surveys the techniques proposed by various researchers over the past 20 years to estimate and compensate for the mismatches. Section 2.5 concludes the chapter.

2.2 TIADC Architecture

In this section, we briefly review the sampling process by an ideal single ADC and an ideal TIADC. Throughout this chapter, we use the variables Ω and ω to denote the continuous-time and the discrete-time frequency variable. The symbols $x_a(t)$ and $x[n]$ denote the continuous-time and the discrete-time signals respectively. $X_a(j\Omega)$ and $X(e^{j\Omega T_s})$ represent the Fourier transform of $x_a(t)$ and $x[n]$, respectively. The notations and operations used in this chapter are listed in Table 2.1 for ease of reference.

2.2.1 *Ideal ADC*

An ideal ADC performs two basic functions on an analog signal: (1) samples the analog signal at uniform time intervals and hold it for a specified time and (2) converts the held signal into finite number of discrete levels. As shown in Fig. 2.1, an ideal ADC operating at the rate of f_s is equivalently modeled by a uniform sampler with sampling frequency of f_s and a quantizer.

Ignoring the quantization effect, the ideal output sequence $\ddot{x}[n]$ is obtained by sampling the analog input signal $x_a(t)$ uniformly at time

Figure 2.1 An ideal ADC is modeled by a uniform sampler and a quantizer.

Table 2.1 Definitions of notations

Notation	Definition
Ω	Continuous-time angular frequency
ω	Discrete-time angular frequency, $\omega = \Omega T_s$
M	Number of parallel sub-ADC channels in the TIADC system
f_s	Aggregated sampling rate of the TIADC
T_s	Sampling period of the TIADC, $T_s = 1/f_s$
Ω_s	Aggregated sampling rate of the TIADC in radians per second
o_m	DC offset of the m-th sub-ADC
g_m	Gain of the m-th sub-ADC
τ_m	Time skew error of the m-th sub-ADC in seconds
r_m	Time skew error of the m-th sub-ADC normalized with respect to T_s, i.e. $r_m = \tau_m/T_s$
$\Omega_{m,BW}$	Cut-off frequency of the sample-and-hold circuit of the m-th sub-ADC
Ω_0	Bandwidth of the analog input signal $x_a(t)$
$x_a(t)$	Continuous-time or analog signal
$X_a(j\Omega)$	Continuous-time Fourier transform (CTFT) of $x_a(t)$
$x[n]$	Discrete-time signal
$X(e^{j\Omega T_s})$	Discrete-time Fourier transform (DTFT) of $x[n]$
$\ddot{x}[n]$	Ideally sampled sequence of $x_a(t)$
$\ddot{X}(e^{j\Omega T_s})$	DTFT of $\ddot{x}[n]$
$g * f$	Convolution of function g and f
$[]^*$	Complex conjugate of $[]$
$[]^T$	Transpose of $[]$
$\langle k \rangle M$	k modulo M operation
$\mathbb{Z}$	Space of all integers, $\dots, -1, 0, 1, \dots$

instants $t = nT_s$, $n \in \mathbb{Z}$, where $\mathbb{Z}$ is the space containing all integers.

$$\ddot{x}[n] = x_a(nT_s), \, n \in \mathbb{Z} \qquad (2.1)$$

where $T_s = 1/f_s$ is the sampling period of the ADC. In the frequency domain, the Fourier transforms of $x_a(t)$ and $\ddot{x}[n]$ are related according to

$$\ddot{X}\left(e^{j\Omega T_s}\right) = \frac{1}{T_s} \sum_{k=-\infty}^{\infty} X_a\left(j\left(\Omega - \frac{2\pi k}{T_s}\right)\right), \qquad (2.2)$$

where Ω denotes the continuous-time frequency variable in radians per second (rad/s). Suppose the analog input signal $x_a(t)$ has a frequency spectrum shown in Fig. 2.2a, then the spectrum of the uniformly sampled sequence $\ddot{x}[n]$ will be that shown in Fig. 2.2b. Throughout this chapter, it is assumed that (1) the analog input

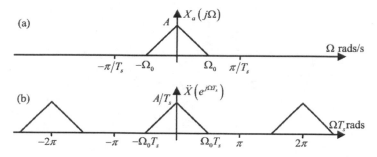

Figure 2.2 Spectrum of (a) the analog bandlimited signal $x_a(t)$ and (b) the uniformly sampled sequence $\ddot{x}[n]$.

signal $x_a(t)$ has finite energy and is bandlimited to Ω_0 rad/s, and (2) The Nyquist criterion is fulfilled so that no aliasing occurs, i.e., $\Omega_0 \leq \pi/T_s$. From Eq. (2.2), the spectrum of $\ddot{x}[n]$ is periodic with a period of 2π with respect to ΩT_s. Therefore, if the above two assumptions are valid, the analog signal $x_a(t)$ can be uniquely recovered from $\ddot{x}[n]$ by considering only one period of $\ddot{X}(e^{j\Omega T_s})$

$$\ddot{X}\left(e^{j\Omega T_s}\right) = \frac{1}{T_s} X_a\left(j\Omega\right), \ |\Omega| \leq \pi/T_s. \tag{2.3}$$

2.2.2 *Ideal TIADC*

The concept of a TIADC operating at an overall sampling rate of f_s is illustrated in Fig. 2.3. The architecture consists of M sub-ADCs working in a round-robin manner. The detailed structures of the sub-ADCs are not of concern as long as the sub-ADCs are identical. The M sub-ADCs sample and convert the analog input signal at a rate of f_s/M according to the M clock signals $(\phi_0, \phi_1, \ldots, \phi_{M-1})$ which are usually generated by a multiphase clock generator. Each clock signal is delayed from the precedent one by T_s seconds, where $T_s = 1/f_s$ is the sampling period of the overall system. Thus, the M sub-ADCs operate at interleaved sampling times as if they were a single ADC operating at a full sampling rate f_s. Digital outputs from all M sub-ADC channels are combined by the digital multiplexer to form the complete digital stream with data rate of f_s samples per second.

Time interleaving is an effective way to implement a high-sampling-rate ADC without placing too much burden on current

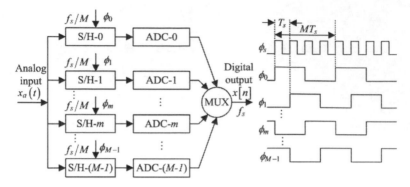

Figure 2.3 System architecture of an M-channel TIADC and the M clock signals driving the sub-ADC channels.

device technology. However, TIADCs suffer from errors caused by the mismatches among the sub-ADC channels, which would not be a problem in a single ADC. The TIADC architecture in Fig. 2.3 also includes M sample-and-hold (S/H) circuits in front of the M sub-ADCs. These are sometimes called track-and-hold rather than sample-and-hold in the literature. Usually the S/H circuits can be lumped into the sub-ADCs and they are shown explicitly here for the ease of illustration of bandwidth mismatch and the corresponding correction techniques, which will be covered in the subsequent sections. The S/H circuits in an M-channel TIADC must have M-times wider bandwidth than that is required by single channel conversion at f_s/M; otherwise, the high frequency components of the input signal will be attenuated.

2.3 Sources of Mismatch Errors and Their Effects

An ideal TIADC consists of M sub-ADC channels with identical characteristics. However, this can never be achieved in practice. Any mismatch between the sub-ADCs introduces unwanted aliasing images and distortion tones in the TIADC output spectrum leading to degraded SFDR and effective resolution of the system. Detailed analysis of the mismatch errors and how they affect the system

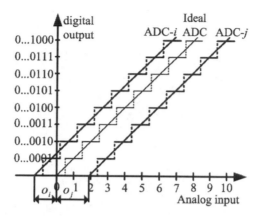

Figure 2.4 Transfer characteristics of different ADCs experiencing different offset voltages.

performance has been discussed in the literature [15, 22, 24, 32, 43, 44, 64, 78, 95, 111, 112, 120] and are summarized here.

2.3.1 *Offset Mismatches*

Each sub-ADC has a constant DC value from the ideal ground level, which may be attributed to the DC offset of op-amp and comparator, charge injection of the switch, etc. The DC value can be different for different sub-ADCs leading to a mismatch in the offset voltage. This is illustrated in Fig. 2.4, where ADC-i and ADC-j with different offset voltages experience different transfer characteristics. Denote the DC offset in the m-th sub-ADC channel as o_m. In the time domain, DC offset is equivalent to adding a constant voltage o_m to the m-th channel output. The offset mismatch is independent of the input signal and manifests at the output stream of the TIADC as a periodic additive noise with the pattern of $\{o_0, o_1, \ldots, o_{M-1}, o_0, o_1, \ldots, o_{M-1}, \ldots\}$.

2.3.2 *Gain Mismatches*

The gain from analog input to digital output may also be different for different sub-ADCs leading to gain mismatch. Gain mismatch among different channels are attributed to different gains of the

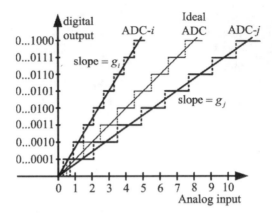

Figure 2.5 Transfer characteristics of different ADCs experiencing different gains.

sample and hold amplifier (SHA), inequality of passive components, etc. The gain of an ADC is represented by the slope of the best fit line to the ADC transfer characteristic as shown in Fig. 2.5. An ideal ADC has unity gain. Denote the gain in the m-th channel as g_m. In the time domain, the effect of gain mismatch is equivalent to multiplying the ideally sampled sequence by a periodic pattern $\{g_0, g_1, \ldots, g_{M-1}, g_0, g_1, \ldots, g_{M-1}, \ldots\}$ and thus behaves like amplitude modulation. The maximum error due to gain mismatch occurs at the peaks of the input signal.

2.3.3 Timing Mismatches

Ideally, the sampling instants of the M sub-ADCs are equally spaced apart by T_s seconds. In practice, channel-m samples the input signal at $t = kMT_s + mT_s + \tau_m, k \in \mathbb{Z}$, where τ_m is the time skew which represents the deterministic deviation between the ideal and real sampling instants in channel-m. There is also another kind of timing error, which is the stochastic deviation from each ideal sampling point named clock jitter. Clock jitter affects the performance of a single ADC system as well and tends to spread out the effect on the whole output spectrum by raising the noise floor. In the context of TIADC, timing mismatch refers to the mismatch in the deterministic time skew τ_m. Possible sources contributing to the timing mismatch

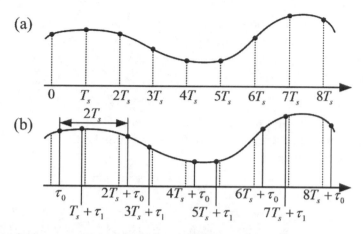

Figure 2.6 An example of a two-channel TIADC. (a) Ideal sampling instants (dashed line). (b) Real sampling instants (solid line). Time skew is the deterministic deviation between the ideal sampling instants and the real sampling instants.

include imperfections of the multiphase clock generation circuit, asymmetric distribution of the clock path, different transistor gate delay, and parasitic effects. TIADC in the presence of timing skew errors produces a periodically nonuniformly sampled sequence. This is illustrated in Fig. 2.6 with an example of a two-channel TIADC. The effect of the timing mismatch in time domain is like phase modulation. The maximum of the error introduced by timing mismatch occurs when the input signal has the largest slew rare.

2.3.4 Frequency Response Mismatches

In addition to the offset, gain, and timing mismatches introduced above, a TIADC may also experience frequency response mismatch. The input behavior of each sub-ADC channel can be characterized by a linear system, of which the frequency response may differ from that of other sub-ADCs. A special case of frequency response that is widely studied is the bandwidth mismatch. The S/H circuit in the sample mode can be approximated by a first-order RC circuit constituted of the on-resistance of the MOS sampling switch and the hold capacitance. Due to the fabrication process imperfections, components mismatch is inevitable resulting in mismatched bandwidths. Denote the bandwidth of the S/H in the m-th channel as $\Omega_{m,BW}$ rad/s, the channel transfer function is then

$$H_{A,m}(j\Omega) = \frac{1}{1 + j\Omega/\Omega_{m,BW}}. \qquad (2.4)$$

It has been derived in [64] that for an input signal with frequency Ω_{in}, bandwidth mismatch introduces additional gain and timing mismatches given by

$$g_{m,BW} = 1 \Big/ \sqrt{1 + (\Omega_{in}/\Omega_{m,BW})^2} \qquad (2.5)$$

$$\tau_{m,BW} = -\arctan(\Omega_{in}/\Omega_{m,BW})/\Omega_{in}. \qquad (2.6)$$

$g_{m,BW}$ and $\tau_{m,BW}$ depend on the input frequency Ω_{in} and are different from the gain and time skew discussed in Sections 2.3.2 and 2.3.3. Time skew τ_m introduces a linear phase mismatch while the time skew due to finite bandwidth, $\tau_{m,BW}$, introduces nonlinear phase mismatch. Bandwidth mismatch causes more severe errors at higher input frequency. A more complicated model that considers the transient effects of the S/H is given by [100].

$$H_{A,m}(j\Omega) = \frac{1}{1 + j\Omega/\Omega_{m,BW}} \frac{1 - e^{-(\Omega_{m,BW}T_s + j\Omega T_s)}}{1 - e^{-(\Omega_{m,BW}T_s + jM\Omega T_s)}}. \qquad (2.7)$$

Time skew can be regarded as a special case of channel frequency response. An amount of τ_m deviation from the ideal sampling edge is equivalent to sampling a time shifted version of the input signal, $x_a(t + \tau_m)$, at the ideal sampling instants, i.e., the channel transfer function is $H_{A,m}(j\Omega) = e^{j\Omega\tau_m}$.

2.3.5 *Effect of the Mismatches in the frequency domain*

In order to get a clear picture of how the combined mismatches interact and affect the frequency spectrum of the TIADC output, a simple mathematical model of the m-th sub-ADC channel as shown in Fig. 2.7 is assumed. The effects of gain, time skew and frequency response mismatch in channel-m are modeled by the linear system $H_{A,m}(j\Omega)$. Offset mismatch cannot be modeled by $H_{A,m}(j\Omega)$ and is represented by the addition of a DC voltage o_m.

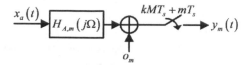

Figure 2.7 An equivalent model of the m-th sub-ADC channel. The input signal first passes through the linear system $H_{A,m}(j\Omega)$ modeling the gain, timing and frequency response mismatches. It is then added to the offset o_m and finally sampled with a sampling interval of MT_s. The sampling instants are delayed by mT_s with respect to that of channel-0.

Neglecting the quantization noise, the output sequence of the m-th sub-ADC channel is then written as

$$y_m(t) = \sum_{k=-\infty}^{\infty} (x_a(t) * h_{A,m}(t) + o_m) \cdot \delta(t - kMT_s - mT_s), \quad (2.8)$$

where $h_{A,m}(t)$ is the continuous-time impulse response of $H_{A,m}(j\Omega)$, $\delta(t)$ is the Dirac delta function and "$*$" denotes the convolution operation. The TIADC output is obtained by summing the output sequence of all the M sub-ADC channels. Because the input signal is bandlimited and Nyquist criterion is fulfilled, the TIADC output spectrum is periodic with period Ω_s. Therefore, it suffices to consider only one period of the output spectrum, from 0 to Ω_s

$$Y(j\Omega) = \frac{1}{T_s} \sum_{k=0}^{M-1} \left[A_k \left(j \left(\Omega - \frac{k\Omega_s}{M} \right) \right) X_a \left(j \left(\Omega - \frac{k\Omega_s}{M} \right) \right) \right]$$
$$+ 2\pi B_k \delta \left(j \left(\Omega - \frac{k\Omega_s}{M} \right) \right), \quad (2.9)$$

where

$$A_k(j\Omega) = \frac{1}{M} \sum_{m=0}^{M-1} H_{A,m}(j\Omega) e^{-j\frac{2\pi km}{M}} \quad (2.10)$$

$$B_k = \frac{1}{M} \sum_{m=0}^{M-1} o_m e^{-j\frac{2\pi km}{M}}. \quad (2.11)$$

Several observations can be made from Eqs. (1.9–1.11):

(i) The gain, timing, and frequency response mismatches interact with each other and generate spectral components which are copies of the input signal weighted by $A_k(j\Omega)/T_s$ and shifted by integer multiples of the channel sampling rate, i.e., $k\Omega_s/M$, $k = 0, \ldots, M-1$, whereas offset mismatch creates spectral lines with magnitudes of $2\pi B_k/T_s$ located at $k\Omega_s/M$, $k = 0, \ldots, M-1$.

(ii) The desired signal term is $A_0(j\Omega)X_a(j\Omega)$, where $A_0(j\Omega) = 1/M \sum_{m=0}^{M-1} H_{A,m}(j\Omega)$ is a frequency-dependent gain term introduced to the original signal.

(iii) The *distortion weighting coefficient* sets $A_k(j\Omega)$ and B_k are discrete Fourier transforms (DFTs) of the channel mismatch parameters $H_{A,m}(j\Omega)$ and o_m, respectively and are periodic with period M with respect to k.

(iv) Using the DFT property, the spectral lines introduced by DC offset mismatch have the symmetric property that $[B_k]^* = B_{-k} = B_{M-k}$. The distortion coefficients A_k introduced by gain mismatch have the same property that $[A_k]^* = A_{-k} = A_{M-k}$. For timing mismatch and frequency response mismatches, it is easy to verify that $A_k(-j\Omega) = [A_{M-k}(j\Omega)]^*$. The distortions introduced by the gain mismatch have the same magnitude for each pair of negative and positive frequency components, whereas this is not true for the distortions introduced by timing and frequency response mismatches. To get a straightforward view, the output spectrum of a four-channel TIADC assuming a sinusoidal input signal $x_a(t) = a \cdot \sin(\Omega_{in}t)$ is shown in Fig. 2.8. The amplitude of the input signal is omitted for simplicity. Fig. 2.8a plots the spectrum when only offset and gain mismatch are present. The distortion coefficients are independent of the input frequency. The output spectrum in the presence of timing and frequency response mismatches is shown in Fig. 2.8b.

If all the channels have identical frequency characteristic $\bar{H}_A(j\Omega)$ and identical offset voltage $\bar{o}$, the coefficient sets $A_k(j\Omega)$ and B_k are reduced to

$$A_k(j\Omega) = \frac{1}{M}\bar{H}_A(j\Omega)\sum_{m=0}^{M-1} e^{-j\frac{2\pi km}{M}} = \begin{cases} \bar{H}_A(j\Omega), k = 0, M, 2M, \ldots \\ 0, \text{otherwise} \end{cases}$$

(2.12)

$$B_k = \frac{1}{M}\bar{o}\sum_{m=0}^{M-1} e^{-j\frac{2\pi km}{M}} = \begin{cases} \bar{o}, k = 0, M, 2M, \ldots \\ 0, \text{otherwise} \end{cases}.$$

(2.13)

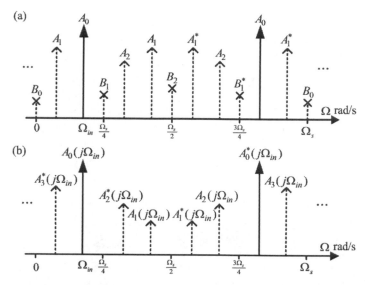

Figure 2.8 Output spectrum of a four-channel TIADC over $[0, \Omega_s]$ assuming a sinusoidal signal with frequency Ω_{in}. Solid line: desired signal components. Dashed line: spectral images and distortion tones caused by mismatches. (a) Gain and offset mismatches. The distortion pair introduced by gain mismatch is symmetric about $k\Omega_s/M$, $k = 1, \ldots, M-1$. (b) Timing and frequency response mismatch. The distortion coefficients are frequency dependent and the distortion pair is in general not symmetric about $k\Omega_s/M$, $k = 1, \ldots, M-1$.

In this case, the aliasing components no longer exist and the output spectrum is the same as that of a single ADC with frequency characteristic $\bar{H}_A(j\Omega)$ and DC offset $\bar{o}$.

The distortion components introduced by the mismatches degrade the performance of the TIADC such as the SINAD and SFDR. The SINAD due to individual mismatch errors can be explicitly derived using either the given mismatch parameters or parameter distributions [32, 43, 44, 78, 95, 111, 120]. Assume the same input signal $x_a(t) = a \cdot \sin(\Omega_{in}t)$ and ignore the quantization noise. If the offset values are explicitly known, the SINAD due to offset mismatch only is calculated as

$$\text{SINAD} = 10 \log_{10} \left(\frac{a^2/2}{\frac{1}{M} \sum_{m=0}^{M-1} o_m^2} \right). \tag{2.14}$$

If the channel offsets o_m, $m = 0, \ldots, M - 1$ are M independent, identically distributed (i.i.d.) random variables with zero mean and standard deviation σ_o, the expected SINAD is [32, 111, 120]

$$\text{SINAD} = 20 \log_{10} \left(a \Big/ \left(\sqrt{2}\sigma_o \right) \right). \qquad (2.15)$$

The SINAD due to offset mismatch is independent of the number of interleaving channels and can be improved by 6 dB for every doubling of the amplitude of the input signal or halving of the offset mismatch. When gain mismatch is the sole mismatch source and the gain values are available, the SINAD is

$$\text{SINAD} = 10 \log_{10} \left(\frac{\left(\sum_{m=0}^{M-1} g_m \right)^2}{M \sum_{m=0}^{M-1} g_m^2 - \left(\sum_{m=0}^{M-1} g_m \right)^2} \right). \qquad (2.16)$$

Suppose the channel gain g_m, $m = 0, \ldots, M - 1$ are M i.i.d. random variables with mean μ_g and standard deviation σ_g, the expected SINAD is [32, 111, 120]

$$\text{SINAD} \approx 20 \log_{10} \left(\mu_g / \sigma_g \right) - 10 \log_{10} \left(1 - 1/M \right). \qquad (2.17)$$

The SINAD due to gain mismatch is affected by the number of interleaving channels, but the effect is very limited. When M is increased from two to infinity, the SINAD degrades by 3 dB only. With known timing mismatch, the SINAD due to timing mismatch can be calculated according to

$$\text{SINAD} = 10 \log_{10} \left(\frac{\left| \sum_{m=0}^{M-1} e^{j\Omega_{in}\tau_m} \right|^2}{M^2 - \left| \sum_{m=0}^{M-1} e^{j\Omega_{in}\tau_m} \right|^2} \right). \qquad (2.18)$$

Suppose the time skew τ_m, $m = 0, \ldots, M - 1$ are M i.i.d. Gaussian random variables with zero mean and standard deviation σ_τ, the expected SINAD is approximated by [32, 43, 44, 111, 120]

$$\text{SINAD} \approx -20 \log_{10} \left(\Omega_{in}\sigma_\tau \right) - 10 \log_{10} \left(1 - 1/M \right). \qquad (2.19)$$

The excepted SINAD does not depend on the actual distribution of the offset and gain mismatch, only their respective means and standard deviations, whereas the distribution of the timing mismatch is necessary to calculate the SINAD. The distortion caused by timing mismatch becomes more severe as the input frequency increases. For every decade increase in the input frequency or the time skew standard deviation, the SINAD drops by 20 dB. SINAD analysis when bandwidth mismatch is present is provides in [95] by using the first-order model in Eq. (2.4)

$$H_{A,m}(j\Omega) = \frac{1}{1 + j\Omega/\Omega_{m,BW}} = \frac{1}{1 + (j\Omega/\Omega_{ref})(1 + \varepsilon_m)} \quad (2.20)$$

where Ω_{ref} represents the reference bandwidth and $\varepsilon_m = \Omega_{ref}/\Omega_{m,BW} - 1$ is the deviation of m-th channel bandwidth from the reference value. By assuming ε_m, $m = 0, \ldots, M - 1$ are M i.i.d. Gaussian random variables with zero mean and standard deviation σ_ε, the expected SINAD due to bandwidth mismatch is derived as

$$\text{SINAD} \approx 10\log_{10}\left(1 + \left(\Omega_{in}/\Omega_{ref}\right)^2\right) - 20\log_{10}\left(\sigma_\varepsilon \Omega_{in}/\Omega_{ref}\right)$$
$$- 10\log_{10}\left(1 - 1/M\right). \quad (2.21)$$

Similar to the case of timing mismatch, SINAD due to bandwidth mismatch is inversely proportional to the square of the input frequency, as expected.

The mismatch effects in a TIADC when the sampling sequence of the sub-ADCs is randomly selected have been studied from a probabilistic viewpoint [22, 24]. It has been concluded that randomization improves the SFDR by transforming the mismatch images into a more noise-like distortion but has no effect on the SINAD because the total distortion power remains unchanged.

Some works in the literature [3, 65, 107, 108] investigate the influence of the mismatch in the static nonlinearities, which are usually characterized by integral nonlinearity (INL) and differential nonlinearity (DNL). Static nonlinearity mismatches are not covered in this work because their impacts are minor ones compared to the mismatches mentioned above. Other significant error sources such as clock jitter, thermal noise, and comparator ambiguity, which do not have anything to do with the parallel structure of the TIADC and are inherent to all ADC structures, are not covered either.

2.4 Mismatch Estimation and Compensation

The mismatches caused by component inequalities among different sub-ADC channels can be reduced by laser trimming technology.

However, fabrication process can be rather costly and time consuming; component matching becomes more difficult to achieve with ever shrinking IC technologies and increasing clock speed. Further, the mismatch parameters are drifting due to temperature variation or component aging. Trimming cannot track variations over time. Post-fabrication calibration methods that relax the stringent requirements on the IC technologies have been proposed by a number of researchers to attenuate the spurious spectral components. It can be done by either adding extra analog circuitry to the ADC's front end or post-processing the digital samples. The variations of the mismatch parameters due to environmental change are usually very slow and thus can be tracked and corrected by adaptive algorithms. In this section, the correction and identification methods for each of the four types of mismatches, namely offset, gain, timing, and frequency response mismatches, are reviewed.

2.4.1 *Identification and Correction of Offset Mismatch*

Identification of the DC offset value in each sub-ADC is fairly easy. The offset may be estimated by calculating the mean value of a batch of sub-ADC output samples [7] or measured at the digital output with zero input signal [63, 96]. Either analog or digital method may be employed for offset correction. Analog correction can be done by for example, connecting an auxiliary capacitor storing the offset voltage to the input of the respective sub-ADC. Alternatively, digital correction method may be employed where the estimated offset value is subtracted from the output samples of the corresponding sub-ADC. Analog method does not reduce the signal range whereas digital method is more robust. A self-calibration method for time-interleaved pipeline ADC that measures the offset and gain mismatch parameters using analog circuitry was presented in [37]. The authors of [72] have employed a digital averaging method to alleviate the effect of mismatch in a two-channel TIADC where the output of each channel is delayed by one sample and added to the other channel. The proposed method does not require the mismatch parameters to be explicitly measured. However, the digital averaging technique has a low pass transfer characteristic with bandwidth equal to half of the Nyquist frequency. The mismatch estimation method presented in [28] requires an extra reference ADC. During the calibration phase, identical clock and calibration signals are applied to one of the sub-ADCs and the reference ADC. With two calibration signals, the input–output relationship of the two ADCs forms four equations from which the offset and gain are calculated using simple algebra.

Background adaptive methods which do not interrupt the normal operation of the TIADC and are able to track slowly varying mismatches have been presented in [12, 13, 29]. The analog background calibration method demonstrated in [12, 13] requires $M+1$ conversion ADCs and a reference ADC for an M-channel TIADC. At any time, M sub-ADCs do the conversion while the extra sub-ADC, denoted as ADC-i, and the reference ADC are fed identical calibration signals. A least mean square (LMS) loop as shown in Fig. 2.9 was employed to track and correct the offset in ADC-i over time. The offset in ADC-i was updated according to

$$o_i [n + 1] = o_i [n] + \mu \cdot \text{sgn} [e_i [n]], \qquad (2.22)$$

where $\text{sgn}[e_i[n]]$ is a function that compares the error signal with zero and μ is the step size which controls the convergence rate. In steady-state, the average difference between the outputs of the reference ADC and ADC-i is added to ADC-i input so the offset of ADC-i equals that of the reference ADC. When the calibration is done, another sub-ADC in the M-channel array is selected for calibration and ADC-i is switched back to perform normal conversion. Some disadvantages of this method include the need of two extra ADCs and generation of pattern noise due to periodically swapped in/out of sub-ADCs. A digital background calibration method for a two-channel TIADC which eliminates these problems has been introduced in [12, 29]. The same LMS algorithm as that shown in Fig. 2.9 was employed except that the error was between the output of the two sub-ADCs and the accumulator output was added to the digital code of the corresponding sub-ADC. One drawback associated with offset estimation methods in [12, 13, 29] is that the input signal cannot have frequency components located at $kf_s/M, k \in \mathbb{Z}$ because signal at these frequencies after being sampled by different sub-ADCs appear as different DC voltages and cannot be distinguished from the offset.

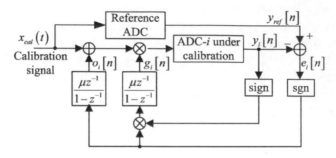

Figure 2.9 The LMS loop for analog background tracking and correction of the offset and gain mismatch in [13].

The problem associated with frequency component at kf_s/M, $k \in \mathbb{Z}$ has been overcome in [6, 14, 48, 74, 75] where the input signal was randomly chopped by multiplying it with an uncorrelated pseudo random sequence consisting of only two values, $+1$ and -1. We denote this sequence as *PRN[n]* in this chapter. The analog signal after chopping becomes a white signal with zero mean and thus has little information at DC. The offset value was then obtained by averaging [14, 48, 74, 75] or low pass filtering [6] and subtracted from the sub-ADC output code. The input signal is recovered by multiplying the offset removed sub-ADC output sequence with the same pseudo random sequence. The techniques presented in [34, 76, 101] have exploited existing system hardware to correct for offset mismatch of the TIADC used in a communication system. The signal presented at the ADC input has a wide-band spectral content and no DC content in the digital communication system [34]. The output samples averaged over time corresponds to the offset value and an LMS algorithm was employed for offset correction. A similar approach can be found in [101]. In [76], the polarity of the transmitted signal tone was modulated by a known pseudo random sequences, *PRN[n]*, and the offset was obtained by correlating the receiver signal with the same pseudo random sequence.

A fast Fourier transform (FFT)-based offset correction method has been presented in [77]. The method calculates the FFT of a batch of output samples and measures the *distortion weighting coefficients* B_k, $k = 0, \ldots, M - 1$, from which the offset mismatches o_m, $m = 0, \ldots, M - 1$ are obtained and removed from the output samples. The FFT of the new data is evaluated again. This process continues until the power of the mismatch distortions falls below some threshold. In [41], rather complicated functions in terms of the input signal and the slope of the signal were used to approximate the error distortions using a least-squares formulation. A blind estimation method has been demonstrated in [23] where the analog input signal was assumed to be quasi-stationary and offset values were estimated by iteratively minimizing a cost function parameterized on the DC offsets. The approaches in [23, 41, 77] require a substantial amount of computation due to the repetitive FFT evaluation, complicated error model, or gradient searching.

2.4.2 *Identification and Correction of Gain Mismatch*

Gain matching was improved offline by using components with better matching, careful layout design or hardware sharing in [7, 63]. In the parallel pipeline ADC structure presented in [63], the hardware for the most significant bit (MSB) was shared, whereas the hardware for least significant bits (LSBs) was interleaved, eliminating mismatches associated with hardware for the MSB. The MSB hardware, however, must operate at the full speed of the TIADC.

Background methods for gain calibration have been presented in [6, 12, 13, 18, 29, 34, 48, 66, 69, 101]. Gain mismatch correction was done using an LMS adaptive loop similar to that for offset correction shown in Fig. 2.9 [12, 13]. The gain in ADC-i, was updated according to

$$g_i \, [n + 1] = g_i \, [n] + \mu \cdot \text{sign} \, [y_i \, [n]] \cdot \text{sgn} \, [e_i \, [n]] , \qquad (2.23)$$

where sign$[y_i[n]]$ represents the sign bit of the output sample of ADC-i, $y_i [n]$, and is used to simplify system implementation. The negative feedback loop forces the gain of ADC-i equal to that of the reference ADC in steady state. Figure 2.10 shows the digital background calibration method presented in [12, 29]. A pseudo random sequence which is uncorrelated with the input signal, *PRN[n]*, after a 1-bit digital-to-analog converter (DAC) is added to the input of the ADC-i. A variable gain is applied at the output of ADC-i for gain correction. The same random sequence is subtracted from the gain corrected digital output to restore the original signal.

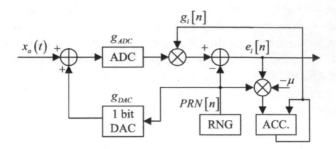

Figure 2.10 The LMS loop for digital background tracking and correction of the gain mismatch in [29].

The variable gain in the ADC-i is updated adaptively using an LMS algorithm according to

$$g_i[n+1] = g_i[n] - \mu \cdot PRN[n] \cdot e_i[n]. \qquad (2.24)$$

The error signal $e_i[n]$ consists of two parts: One is the input signal multiplied by the gain of ADC-i, g_{ADC}, and the variable gain, $g_i[n]$; the other is the $PRN[n]$ multiplied by ($g_{DAC}\, g_{ADC}\, g_i[n] - 1$). An accumulator in the feedback loop calculates the correlation between $PRN[n]$ and $e_i[n]$ and the result is used to control $g_i[n]$. In the long run, the term related to the product of the input signal and $PRN[n]$ zeros out and if the algorithm converges, the variable gain applied at the digital output will make the overall gain in that channel equal to $1/g_{DAC}$, i.e., $g_{DAC}\, g_{ADC}\, g_i[n] = 1$.

In [6], the input was randomly chopped and transformed into a wide band noise. The gain was estimated from the sub-ADC output after applying a small known DC voltage after the chopper and before the sub-ADC input. The authors of [48] demonstrated that multiplying the digital output of a two-channel TIADC with a chopping signal that alternates between +1 and −1 at the sampling rate causes the signal and image to switch position in the spectrum. The product of the chopped output and the TIADC output accumulated over time is a DC term proportional to the relative gain between the two channels. A direct extension of the chopper-based method to a four-channel TIADC was demonstrated in [66]. A related technique estimates and compensates for the gain mismatch by applying the Hadamard transform to the TIADC output was presented in [69]. In the case of a two-channel TIADC, the gain estimation methods of [48] and [69] are equivalent as the Hadamard transform of order 2 has the same function as a chopper. A problem associated with the techniques of [48, 66, 69] is that when the input signal has components at $kf_s/2M$, $k \in \mathbb{Z}$ the product of the TIADC output and the chopped output is a DC term even when there is no gain mismatch. Therefore, notch filters with sharp cutoff producing nulls at $kf_s/2M$, $k \in \mathbb{Z}$ are necessary.

Gain mismatch of the TIADC in a digital communication system was corrected using an LMS adaptive loop in [34, 101]. The correlation between the channel output and the slicer error in that channel was used to update the variable gain connected to the output of the sub-ADC. In [18], the input signal was multiplied by a pseudo random sequence alternating between 0 and 1. The digital output was correlated with the product of the same random sequence and the sign of the input in the background to extract the gain. An FFT-based method was found in [77] and a blind adaptive method was found in [23]. Randomizing the selection of the sub-ADCs for each sample transforms the offset and gain mismatch induced tones into noise-like distortions and has been employed to improve the SFDR performance [4, 17, 50].

2.4.3 *Identification and Correction of Timing Mismatch*

The distortion power introduced by the timing mismatch increases as the input frequency increases. Timing mismatch caused by the multi-phase clock generator may be controlled by careful circuit design prior to fabrication [7]. However, the improvement of the accuracy is very limited and time skew variations due to environmental change cannot be tracked. The techniques for timing mismatch correction so far may be classified into two broad categories: One is analog or mixed signal correction [16, 30, 31, 33, 35, 36, 38, 79–82, 106, 117, 118] and the other is digital interpolation [8–11, 19–21, 23, 25, 26, 39, 40, 45, 46, 49, 51–60, 66, 68, 69, 73, 83–85, 91, 92, 98, 99, 103, 113, 114, 121, 122]. Digital techniques have drawn tremendous research interest recently because of their independence of the process technology and superior accuracy.

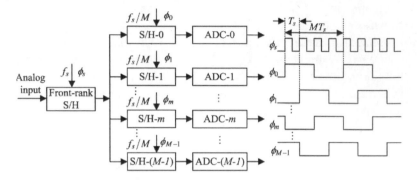

Figure 2.11 A two-rank S/H system to avoid timing mismatch caused by nonideal sampling instants. ϕ_s is the clock signal driving the front-rank S/H. $\phi_m, m = 0, \ldots, M - 1$ are the clock signals driving the second-rank S/Hs.

2.4.3.1 Correction of timing mismatch

Mismatch in the time skews was avoided by using a single front-rank S/H in front of all the interleaving channels [12, 13, 29–31, 37, 63, 79, 96]. Poulton et al. have proposed a 1 GHz 6-bit ADC system consisting of a front-rank GaAs S/H operating at 1 GHz and four 250 MHz silicon digitizers [79]. In a two-rank S/H system, the single full speed S/H operating at f_s acquires samples on the analog input and the second-rank S/H circuits reacquire and digitize the held sample. Second-rank S/H's go from track to hold during the hold time of the first-rank S/H when the voltage at the input of the second-rank S/H's is kept constant. Therefore, the timing mismatch caused by the nonideal sampling instants has no effect. The two-rank S/H structure and the clock signals driving the respective S/H's are shown in Fig. 2.11. During the track period, i.e., when clock ϕ_s is high, at least $M/2$ second-rank S/H's load the first-rank S/H. An improved two-rank S/H circuit has been introduced in [30, 31] where the duty cycle of the channel sampling clock is designed to be less than $1/M$. Thus, no more than one sub-ADC loads the front-rank S/H at any given time instant. Despite the clear advantage offered by the two-rank S/H scheme, the requirement that the front-rank S/H must operate at the full sampling rate imposes stringent constraints on the settling time of the S/H, making the circuit design a great challenge in practice. Therefore, the number of channels that may be interleaved is limited.

Mixed-signal approaches that detect the timing information from the output samples using digital processing and adjust the analog circuitry to eliminate the effect of timing mismatch can be found in the literature [16, 33–36, 38, 44, 80–82, 106, 117, 118]. Variable delay circuits were included in the clock distribution path to adjust the sampling clock of each channel in the foreground [44, 80–82]. A special phase where a known signal is injected for time skew identification is needed at startup or when the time skews change due to environmental variations. Background methods that estimate and correct for the timing mismatch at the same time by employing an LMS-based algorithm have been presented in [16, 33–36, 38, 117, 118]. The estimated timing information is used to adaptively adjust the digitally controlled delay units connected to the clock buffers until the mismatch is minimized. A method that simultaneously alleviates the effect of timing and bandwidth mismatches has been introduced in [106]. The S/H in each conversion channel introduces nonlinear phase mismatch. The timing mismatch in each channel is removed by tuning the transfer characteristics of the S/H on the analog side such that the linear phase term of the S/H counteracts the timing mismatch in that channel.

Including tunable delay units in the clock path may complicate the hardware implementation and introduce random jitter. Using analog circuits for mismatch correction has several drawbacks such as low accuracy and difficulty in porting to other process technologies. Another option to calibrate the timing mismatch without adjusting the sampling clock is by processing the TIADC raw output in the digital domain to interpolate the sample values that would have been captured at the ideal sampling instants [8–11, 19–21, 23, 25, 26, 39, 40, 45, 46, 49, 51–60, 66, 68, 69, 73, 83–85, 91, 92, 98, 99, 103, 113, 114, 121, 122]. Digital processing offers guaranteed accuracy, great reliability, and flexibility and becomes faster and less expensive as the process technology downscales.

A well-known theorem for the reconstruction of a bandlimited continuous-time signal $x_a(t)$ from its nonuniform samples by Yao and Thomas [119] is that if a bandlimited continuous-time signal, $x_a(t)$, is sampled at an irregular grid $\{t_k, k \in \mathbb{Z}\}$ with an average rate exceeding the Nyquist rate, then $x_a(t)$ is uniquely determined by its nonuniform samples $x_a(t_k)$ according to

$$x_a(t) = \sum_{k=-\infty}^{\infty} x_a(t_k) \frac{G(t)}{G'(t)(t - t_k)}, \qquad (2.25)$$

where

$$G(t) = (t - t_0) \prod_{k=-\infty, k\neq 0}^{\infty} (1 - t/t_k). \qquad (2.26)$$

$G'(t_k)$ is the derivative of $G(t)$ evaluated at $t = t_k$, and t_0 can be chosen to be zero. In the case of a TIADC, $t_k = kT_s + \tau_{\langle k \rangle M}$ where $\langle k \rangle M$ denotes k modulo M operation. By incorporating Eq. (2.25) and the periodical sampling pattern of the TIADC, Eldar and Oppenheim [26] first derived a continuous-time synthesis filter bank and then an equivalent discrete-time synthesis filter bank to interpolate the uniform samples. The ideal filter derived has a piecewise constant frequency response and can achieve perfect reconstruction. However, the practical case of designing casual filters of finite order was not addressed. The techniques for reconstructing the uniform samples presented in [26, 52–54, 68, 73, 83] have the form of a multirate filter bank structure [105] as shown in Fig. 2.12a. The discrete-time sequence $\ddot{x}[n]$ represents the samples of the analog input signal $x_a(t)$ taken uniformly at rate f_s. The analysis filter bank consists of the discrete-time filters $H_{A,m}(e^{j\Omega T_s}) = e^{jr_m\Omega T_s}$, $m = 0, \ldots, M - 1$, which represent the time skews in the sub-ADC channels. $H_{A,m}(e^{j\Omega T_s})$ is the discrete-time equivalent of $H_{A,m}(j\Omega)$ and r_m is the time skew normalized with respect to the overall sampling period, i.e., $r_m = \tau_m/T_s$; The term $e^{jm\Omega T_s}$ models the uniform delay among the channel sampling clocks. The output of the M sub-ADC channels are the M sequences after the M-fold down-sampler. The reconstruction is performed by the right half of the multirate filter bank, including the M-fold up-sampler, the delay term $e^{-jm\Omega T_s}$ and the synthesis filter bank $H_m(e^{j\Omega T_s})$ where $m = 0, \ldots, M-1$. If no compensation is performed to correct for the timing mismatch, i.e., $H_m(e^{j\Omega T_s}) = 1$, the delay term together with the up-sampler and the adder is equivalent to a digital multiplexer and the output sequence $y[n]$ represents the raw TIADC output. The underlying principle of the multirate filter

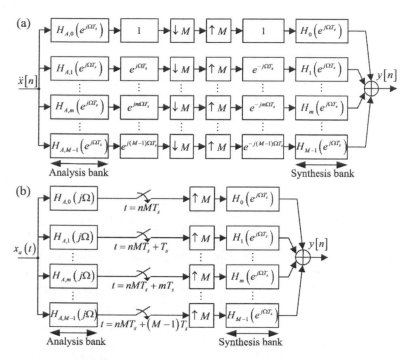

Figure 2.12 (a) An all digital multirate filter bank structure for the reconstruction of uniform samples from TIADC output. The analysis bank models the TIADC timing mismatch. The synthesis filter bank performs the reconstruction. (b) An equivalent hybrid model with continuous-time analysis bank and discrete-time synthesis bank.

bank approach can be summarized as follows: the output of each sub-ADC channel is an undersampled and thus aliased version of the analog input signal $x_a(t)$; when the subsequences are interpolated to the full sampling rate f_s, i.e., up-sample by M, and summed to form the final output, the aliasing terms persist due to the mismatch; synthesis filter banks are designed to shape the spectral characteristics of the output of the sub-ADCs in such a way that the aliasing components are minimized as much as possible while the signal is retained as much as possible when the filter outputs are summarized together. The analysis filter bank in Fig. 2.12a does not exist in actual implementation. An equivalent hybrid model with continuous-time analysis bank modeling the sampling process and discrete-time synthesis bank modeling the reconstruction is shown in Fig. 2.12b. The time skew in each channel is represented by the continuous-time transfer function $H_{A,m}(j\Omega) = e^{j\Omega\tau_m}$.

Ignoring the quantization effect, and using the same derivation as that in Section 2.3.5, the Fourier transform of the final output sequence $y[n]$ can be written as

$$Y\left(e^{j\Omega T_s}\right) = \frac{1}{T_s} \sum_{k=0}^{M-1} V_k\left(j\Omega\right) X_a\left(j\left(\Omega - \frac{2\pi k}{MT_s}\right)\right), \qquad (2.27)$$

where

$$V_k\left(j\Omega\right) = \frac{1}{M} \sum_{m=0}^{M-1} e^{-j\frac{2\pi km}{M}} e^{j\left(\Omega - \frac{2\pi k}{MT_s}\right)\tau_m} H_m\left(e^{j\Omega T_s}\right). \qquad (2.28)$$

When $k = 0$, $V_0(j\Omega)$ represents the frequency-dependent gain imposed on the input signal. For all the other cases where $k = 1, \ldots, M - 1$, $V_k(j\Omega)$ represents the gain of the aliasing component. We call them *signal function* and *aliasing function* respectively. The case where $V_0(j\Omega) = ce^{-jd\Omega T_s}$ and $V_{k\neq0}(j\Omega) = 0$ over the frequency range $|\Omega| \le \pi/f_s$ is called *perfect reconstruction* (PR) [105] where c is a constant and d represents an integer delay. In the PR condition, the output is simply a delayed and scaled version of the ideally sampled sequence, i.e., $y[n] = c\ddot{x}[n-d]$. In [52–54], digital fractional delay filters with different gain constants were employed as the synthesis filters. The frequency response of the synthesis filter has the form of $H_m(e^{j\Omega T_s}) = a_m ce^{-j\Omega T_s(r_m+d)}$. The gain constant a_m was chosen such that the *signal function* $V_0(j\Omega) = ce^{-jd\Omega T_s}$ and *aliasing function* $V_{k\neq0}(j\Omega) = 0$. The digital fractional delay filters, $e^{-j\Omega T_s(r_m+d)}$, $m = 0, \ldots, M - 1$ were approximated by finite impulse response (FIR) filters. Oversampling is required by the proposed method; $x_a(t)$ has to be bandlimited by $\Omega_0 \le \pi(M + 1)/2MT_s$ for odd M and $\Omega_0 \le \pi/2T_s$ for even M. In [83], the linear phase term $e^{j\Omega T_s(r_m+m)}$ modeling the non-ideal sampling instants was approximated by FIR filters using truncation and represented in polyphase matrix form. The FIR synthesis filters were derived using the PR condition in polyphase term [105]. Oversampling, either by sampling considerably faster than the Nyquist rate or by using additional channels in the filter bank, is required to alleviate the effects of inaccuracies in approximating the analysis filter bank.

Similar approximation can be found in [73] and the design of the synthesis filter bank was viewed as a communication equalization problem. The authors of [68] assumed a stationary known input spectrum and designed compensation system in the form of a Wiener filter using a statistically optimal LMS criterion. If infinite order is allowed for the filters in [83] and [68] and if the input is restricted to be a bandlimited signal in [68], the methods of [83] and [68] achieves PR and are equivalent to the ideal filters derived in [26]. The compensation structures in [48, 49, 66] take the form of multirate filter banks as well. Either closed-form [48, 49] or approximated solutions [66] were obtained. The methods in [54, 68, 83] are able to deal with timing mismatch in a more general form of periodic nonuniformly sampling scheme where $P > M$ sub-ADC channels operate at f_s/M resulting in an overall sampling rate of $P f_s/M$. The resulting sequence is periodic with period MT_s and contains P samples per period. In this case, Eq. (2.28) is modified to

$$V_k\left(j\Omega\right) = \frac{1}{M}\sum_{p=0}^{P-1}e^{j\left(\Omega - \frac{2\pi k}{MT_s}\right)t_p} H_m\left(e^{j\Omega T_s}\right), \qquad (2.29)$$

where t_p denotes the deviation of the sampling instants of channel-p from that of channel-.

In [55–60], signal reconstruction was performed by employing a discrete-time periodic time-varying FIR filter according to

$$y\left[n\right] = \sum_{p=-N}^{N} x\left[n - p\right]g_n\left[p\right], \qquad (2.30)$$

where $x[n]$ is the nonuniformly sampled sequence; $g_n[p]$ represents the impulse response of the time-varying filter where the subscript n implies the time-varying nature. The filter is also periodic with period M, i.e., $g_n[p] = g_{n+M}[p]$ for each n. Utilizing this periodicity, the time-varying filter reconstruction system can be represented by an equivalent all-digital multirate filter bank structure shown in Fig. 2.12a. The analysis filter bank in this case does not represent the time skew mismatch. Instead, it incorporates the coefficients of the time-varying filter and has the following expression:

$$G_m\left(e^{j\Omega T_s}\right) = \sum_{p=-N}^{N} g_m\left[p\right]e^{-j\Omega T_s\left(p-r_{m-p}\right)} \qquad (2.31)$$

The synthesis filters, $H_m(e^{j\Omega T_s})$, $m = 0, \ldots, M-1$ are equal to 1. The time-varying filters $g_n[p]$, $m = 0, \ldots, M-1$ were optimally designed in a minimax sense such that the *signal function* $V_0(j\Omega)$ and the *aliasing function* $V_{k\neq 0}(j\Omega)$ approximate 1 and 0, respectively. The resulting filter order is lower than that in [73] and [83] if the same level of reconstruction accuracy was to be achieved. The least squares design, which minimizes the average error power, was also presented. An improved structure that avoids online filter design when the sampling pattern varies due to environmental variations in a two-channel TIADC was proposed in [58, 60]. The design employed the Farrow structure [27] where the coefficients $g_1[p]$ were expressed in polynomials of r_1 where r_1 represents the time skew in channel-1 with reference to channel-0. The resulting filter was implemented as a linear combination of a small number of fixed sub-filters weighted by different powers of r_1. Therefore, when r_1 varies, it suffices to adjust the coefficients corresponding to r_1. The possibility of the straightforward extension to the M-periodic case was discussed in [59]. However, it leads to the use of polynomials in multiple variables, r_m, $m = 1, \ldots, M - 1$ which increases the design complexity rapidly as M grows.

The compensation methods reported in [69, 98, 99] utilized a common model where the TIADC output is decomposed into a signal that is caused by the timing mismatch, i.e., the error signal and a signal which is free from timing mismatch, i.e., the desired signal. The compensation was achieved by, in either frequency domain [69, 98] or discrete-time domain [99], reproducing the error signal and subtracting it from the TIADC output to obtain the desired signal. In the case of a two-channel TIADC as presented in [98], the time skew term $e^{jr_m\Omega T_s}$, $m = 0, 1$ was approximated using the first two terms of the Taylor series expansion and the error spectrum was reproduced by applying a differentiator, $j\omega$, to the TIADC output followed by frequency shifting of π. In [99], the signal $x_a(t)$ at the nonuniformly sampling instance $(mT_s + r_mT_s)$ was expressed as a polynomial of r_m using Taylor series expansion about the ideal sampling instant mT_s. The implementation structures of [98] and [99] consist of FIR filters approximating the ideal differentiator and time-varying multipliers corresponding to different powers of r_m. For a better performance, more stages that correct for higher order terms may be used and the number of FIR filters comprised in each stage scales linearly with the number of correction stages. The methods in [98, 99] are suboptimal ones due to the use of Taylor series expansion. In [69], Hadamard transform, which is an orthogonal transform separating the desired signal from the aliasing image, was employed to generate the pseudo aliasing images. The resulting implementation structure comprises only a fixed FIR filter and a few general multipliers for arbitrary number of interleaving channels.

A TIADC with timing mismatch is a linear time-varying system and the input–output relation may be represented as a system of linear equations

$$\mathbf{x} = \mathbf{A}\ddot{\mathbf{x}}, \tag{2.32}$$

where $\mathbf{x} = [x[0], \ldots, x[N-1]]^T$ and $\ddot{\mathbf{x}} = [\ddot{x}[0], \ldots, \ddot{x}[N-1]]^T$ are the output vector and input vector, respectively, and the elements in matrix $\mathbf{A}$ are the coefficients of the FIR time-varying filters approximating the timing mismatch $e^{jr_m\Omega T_s}$. Reconstruction of the uniform samples is possible with extremely high computational complexity by inverting $\mathbf{A}$. Utilizing Eq. (2.32), the authors of [10] have developed a constrained least squares formulation by incorporating the bandlimited constraint of the input signal. Certain amount of oversampling is mandatory and the inversion of large dimension matrix leads to considerable amount of computation. Alternatively, an iterative framework where the reconstruction is performed in a sample by sample manner using Richardson iteration may be found in [103].

The uniform samples may be estimated by using a weighted combination of the neighboring nonuniform samples [51, 121]. A multichannel Lagrange polynomial interpolation framework having low computational complexity and simple implementation structure was developed in [121]. The weighting of each nonuniform sample was computed using the Lagrange interpolation formula and the estimated time skew values. In [51], the sample time error was corrected by employing a linear casual interpolation method based on an iterative algorithm called "Neville's method." Jenq has demonstrated a frequency domain approach that recovers spectral information at discrete frequency points of a uniformly sampled signal based on points in the nonuniformly sampled spectrum [45, 46]. The method requires the processing of a batch of time domain samples to obtain the information at one point in the nonuniformly sampled spectrum, thus preventing its usage in real-time applications.

It has been demonstrated that the impact of mismatch errors can be alleviated by spectral shaping methods that do not rely on the accurate estimation of time skews [22, 24, 97, 109, 110]. One way to shape the spectrum of the TIADC is through randomizing the sampling sequence of the sub-ADCs [22, 24, 97]. In a normal TIADC, only one sub-ADC is available at each sampling instants. Extra sub-ADCs need to be introduced to the interleaved structure in order to enable randomization. Both theoretical derivation and simulation results have shown that as the number of additional sub-ADCs increases, the degree of randomness is increased and the spurious images are transformed into a more noise-like distortion. The SFDR is improved but the SINAD remains unchanged though since the total noise power remains the same. A 3 dB improvement in the SINAD can be obtained by doubling the oversampling ratio and using a low pass filter. A simple sorting algorithm was employed in [109] to control the sampling sequence of the sub-ADCs such that the spurious images residing at the higher frequency band near $\Omega_s/2$ have greater power. The out-of-band mismatch spurs were then suppressed by a low pass filter leading to both improved SFDR and SINAD. A method that combines both randomization and the sorting algorithm was presented in [110]. The mismatch distortions are therefore flattened and shaped.

The time skew may vary over time due to environmental variations and component aging. In that case, the compensation structures have to be redesigned to cope with the changes in the time skew values. It is desirable that the redesign of the compensation system is avoided or at least can be done easily online so that the operation of the TIADC is not halted. The filter coefficients were updated whenever a new estimate of the time skew is available by storing several coefficient sets in a look up table (LUT) [48, 49] or using an adaptive filter bank [66]. In [54, 58–60, 103], Farrow-based structure [27] where the coefficients of the correction filters are expressed as polynomials of the time skew values were employed. For the time-varying filter structure in [58–60], the Farrow structure is limited to small number of interleaving channels and small time skews due to the high design complexity. The solutions in [98] and [99] are based on Taylor expansion with respect to the time skews. The compensating structures consist of fixed FIR filters approximating the ideal differentiator and time-varying multipliers corresponding to different powers of the time skew values. When the time skews change, it suffices to adjust the values of the multipliers which correspond to the time skews [54, 58–60, 98, 99, 103].

2.4.3.2 Identification of time skews

The time skews must be known beforehand when designing the re-construction filters using the aforementioned techniques. A known signal may be incorporated to facilitate the direct measurement of the time skew parameters [42, 44, 47, 51]. In the foreground detection schemes presented in [44, 47], a known sinusoidal signal was applied and the time skews were extracted from the timing mismatch induced image tones in the output spectrum using inverse DFT (IDFT). The normal operation of the TIADC must be stopped during the foreground detection. The authors of [51] proposed a background time skew estimation technique in which a ramp signal having known slope and period T_s was mixed with the input signal. Deviation from the ideal sampling instant causes a fixed DC voltage at the sub-ADC output from which the timing information is measured. Several drawbacks associated with this method include accurate test signal generation, reduced system dynamic range and extra hardware. The scheme of [42] utilized the ramp signal for time skew estimation as well. An extra reference ADC and complex channel switching were required. The authors of [33–36] have demonstrated a background time skew detection scheme catered for the digital communication system where the analog input is a wideband signal with no DC content. The time skew in ADC-i was estimated using a time function that is the correlation between the samples of ADC-$(i\text{-}1)$ after the slicer and the samples of ADC-i before the slicer. The difference in the time function between two adjacent channels is proportional to the time skew mismatch.

Time skew mismatch between two adjacent channels was detected by counting the zero-crossings between their adjacent samples [38, 117, 118]. The principle of the time skew detection is based on the observation that the probability of zero-crossing between two adjacent samples is proportional to the sampling interval between the two channels. The detection scheme is sensitive to comparator offset and requires the input signal to be narrowband and asynchronized to the sampling clocks. A background method which employs an extra single-bit calibration ADC was presented in [16]. The SINAD of the TIADC achieves its maximum when the cross-correlation between the output of each sub-ADC and the calibration ADC is maximized. An LMS-based algorithm was used to adjust the control voltage applied to the delay line attached to the clock buffer so that the correlation is maximized at convergence. One drawback is that certain types of input signal would prevent the algorithm from converging and the time skew cannot be properly estimated and compensated.

Foreground estimation methods usually offer superior accuracy due to dedicated characterization and calibration hardware. Therefore, they are suitable for applications where high resolution is required and system stoppage is tolerable. On the other hand, when the mismatches are time-varying or continuous system operation is mandatory, blind methods are preferred. For the blind methods proposed so far, these are usually achieved at the cost of higher computational complexity, being limited to smaller number of channels, and certain restrictions on the input signal [8, 9, 11, 19–21, 23, 25, 39, 40, 49, 66, 69, 84, 85, 91, 92, 113, 114, 122]. For instance, blind recovery methods presented in [8, 9, 11, 19, 39, 40, 84, 85, 113, 114] require the input signal to be oversampled.

An expectation-maximize algorithm was employed in [8] to iteratively produce the maximum likelihood estimates of gain and timing parameters. The input signal is restricted to stationary bandlimited zero-mean Gaussian process. Time skews were estimated by minimizing the out-of-band energy of the reconstructed signal parameterized on the time skews using a least squares formulation [9, 11]. Several iterations may be needed to improve the estimation accuracy for large time skews. The techniques can be implemented using adaptive filtering scheme such as recursive least squares (RLS) or LMS algorithm. Considerable amount of computation is required for the methods presented in [8, 9, 11].

Small amount of oversampling ensures that there exists a frequency band around the zero frequency where no aliasing component appears for a two-channel system [39] and only three aliasing components appear for a four-channel system [40]. These spectral properties were then exploited to derive a synthesis filter bank parameterized on the time skews using adaptive null-steering algorithm. The techniques in [39, 40] have reduced computational complexity but are restricted to system with few sub-ADCs.

Blind identification methods presented in [84, 85, 113, 114] have exploited the spectral information in the signal free band centered at $\Omega_s/2$ resulted from oversampling. By expressing the spectral content at K discrete frequency points in the signal free region in terms of the input spectrum and the *distortion weighting function* $A_k(j\Omega)$, $A_k(j\Omega)$ was obtained using a least squares method and the timing skews were thus identified [113]. This method requires the evaluation of FFT of a batch of output samples to gather the spectral information. Adaptive algorithms were adopted in [84, 85, 114]. The time skew estimate in a two-channel TIADC was updated using a LMS algorithm so that the difference between the actual error signal in the signal free region obtained by high pass filtering and the reproduced error signal parameterized on the estimate is minimized [84]. Signal reconstruction was performed using the same model as that presented in [98]. An extension to the identification of both gain and timing mismatch in an arbitrary number of channels has been provided in [114]. The method presented in [85] employed a filtered-error LMS algorithm leading to reduced implementation complexity compared to that of [114]. Taylor series approximation was used in [84, 85, 114] and thus the estimation accuracy was limited. In [122], the input signal needs to have certain spectrum sparsity to ensure that there exist some alias free frequency points in the output spectrum. The phase information of the output digital sub-band spectra of the sub-ADCs at the alias free frequency points was exploited to estimate the time skews. The estimation accuracy improves with higher sparsity.

The methods in [19–21, 23, 25] was based on the observation that the signal changes more on average if the time interval between samples is longer and vice versa. Time skews were estimated by calculating the mean square difference of the output samples between two adjacent sub-ADCs [19–21]. The algorithm gives a bias in the estimate and the accuracy is affected by the uncorrected gain and offset mismatches. Further, the algorithm only works well for signals bandlimited to about one-third of the Nyquist frequency. Time skews were found iteratively by minimizing a cost function that involves the evaluation of the cross-correlation between adjacent channels and the autocorrelation of each channel [23, 25]. The channel outputs are reconstructed using the estimates obtained in previous iteration. The methods are computationally very demanding because of the FFT and inverse FFT (IFFT) calculation of large data blocks involved in each iteration for data reconstruction.

With a wide sense stationary (WSS) input signal, the output resulted from an ideal ADC is WSS and wide sense cyclostationary (WSCS) from a TIADC with mismatch errors. The iterative methods presented in [91, 92] estimate the time skew by minimizing the sum of squares of the Fourier series coefficients of the output autocorrelation function such that the WSS property of the reconstruction signal is restored gradually. The synthesis filter bank needs to be redesigned for each new estimate leading to high computational complexity. Therefore, real-time implementation is limited to relatively low sampling rate or small number of channels.

The authors in [48, 49] have demonstrated a chopper-based time skew estimation technique for a two-channel TIADC. Chopping the TIADC output and delaying it by $\pi/2$ causes the signal and image to switch position in the spectrum. The product of the chopped and un-chopped output accumulated over time produces a DC term proportional to the relative time skew between the two channels. Estimation and correction were performed simultaneously using an adaptive LMS algorithm. The input signal must satisfy the requirement that it should not overlap with its image and therefore is bandlimited to $\Omega_s/4$. In the four-channel case presented in [66], channel-1 output is combined with the output of channel-0 and channel-2 separately to obtain two sequences which, after being correlated with their respective chopped output, are summed and averaged over time to produce the time skew of channel-1. The time skews of channel-2 and channel-3 with reference to channel-0 and channel-1, respectively, were estimated using the method in [49]. The estimation takes longer time as the convergence of the time skews in different channels are achieved in order. Further, the number of channels is limited to radix of two. A related correlation based estimation method that employs the Hadamard transform has been reported in [69]. The aliasing signals obtained by applying the Hadamard transform to the TIADC output, after being differentiated were correlated with the original sequence to estimate the time skews in all channels at the same time. Extension to arbitrary number of channels is straightforward by extending the Hadamard transform. The methods in [48, 49, 66, 69] have a common limitation of frequency null at $kf_s/2M, k \in \mathbb{Z}$.

2.4.4 *Correction of Frequency Response Mismatch*

Frequency response mismatch such as the mismatch in the bandwidths of the S/H circuits introduces additional gain and timing mismatches that are frequency dependent. The spectral images caused by frequency response mismatch reside at the same locations as those caused by the static gain and timing mismatches. The effect of the frequency response mismatch becomes more prominent at higher frequencies. Correcting only for static gain and timing mismatches is not able to achieve good accuracy and hence high resolution over a wide frequency range. Frequency-dependent mismatch correction is thus important for achieving high-resolution or/and high-speed and has been studied in various research works [2, 61, 62, 67, 70, 71, 86–90, 93–94, 100–102, 104, 115]. Among these compensation techniques, [88, 89, 100, 101] correct for the bandwidth mismatch, while [2, 61, 62, 67, 70, 71, 86, 87, 90, 93, 94, 102, 104, 115] deal with the general frequency response mismatch. One way to avoid performance degradation caused by bandwidth mismatch is to design S/H circuits with bandwidths much higher than the maximum input frequency. However, high bandwidth places great burden on the circuit design and cannot suppress high frequency noise. Hence, digital correction is more preferable.

The S/H circuit of each sub-ADC channel was modeled as a first-order RC low pass filter [88, 89, 100]. The authors of [100] have derived an equivalent transfer function shown in Eq. (2.7) for the S/H circuit. The synthesis filter bank was designed based on the analysis of the *signal function* and *aliasing function* for a single tone sinusoidal input signal. Bandwidths of the S/H circuits need to be known *a priori* to design the reconstruction filter. The correction structure for a two-channel TIADC demonstrated in [88] admits the multirate filter bank structure as well. By using a first-order approximation of the inverse of the aliasing component matrix and further rearrangement, the design complexity was reduced to a single FIR filter. The semiblind background estimation scheme of the relative bandwidth mismatch in a two-channel TIADC presented in [89] complements the work in [88]. The scheme requires the input signal has no spectral content near the zero frequency and has some spectral content in a high frequency band just below $\Omega_s/2$ symmetric to the signal free band. The second condition can be guaranteed by injecting a test signal near $\Omega_s/2$. A transfer function relating the image spectra at the low pass band of the two sub-ADCs was derived and parameterized on the relative bandwidth mismatch to the first order. Utilizing the transfer function and a stochastic gradient algorithm, the estimate was updated such that the image spectra at the low pass band in the two channels are approximated as much as possible. The correction structure is the same as that in [88] except that they are approximated to the first order of the bandwidth mismatch and adaptive to the variations in bandwidth mismatch. Generalization to arbitrary number of channels was not addressed. Bandwidth mismatch in a communication receiver where the transmitted data has zero mean and white spectrum has been corrected using an adaptive M-periodic time-varying feedforward equalizer [101]. The coefficients of the equalizer were updated so that slicer error is driven to zero by a LMS loop.

Frequency response mismatch correction was performed in the frequency domain in [2]. The spectrum of each sub-ADC output was multiplied by the respective frequency-dependent correction coefficient and summed together to form the corrected output spectrum. The frequency-dependent correction coefficients were designed such that the aliasing components over the frequency band of interest are cancelled. The algorithm involves the calculation of DFTs of the sub-ADC outputs and is therefore not suitable for real-time processing. The method presented in [90] compensates for the general frequency response mismatch (including static gain and timing mismatch) using the multirate filter bank approach where the *signal function* and *aliasing function* on a dense grid of frequency points spanning over the band of interest were controlled simultaneously. The optimization was performed in a weighted least square (WLS) sense. The method requires the inversion of a matrix of size $MN \times MN$ with N being the length of each FIR filter in the synthesis filter bank. The multichannel filtering approach in [67] is to estimate the value of an ideal sample using a weighted combination of the output samples from all the sub-ADCs sampling in the neighborhood of the ideal sample. Unlike the case of a filter bank approach where each synthesis filter only filter samples from one sub-ADC, the FIR compensation filters in the multichannel filtering approach take samples from all the sub-ADCs, hence the name "multichannel." The compensation filters were designed such that the difference between the ideal and estimated frequency responses evaluated on a dense frequency grid is minimized in a WLS sense. Solving the problems of [67] requires the inversion of M separate matrix, each with size $N \times N$, where N is the filter length. It was reported in [67] that for the same filter length, the filters designed using the methods in [90] and [67] were identical and the multichannel filtering approach required less computational effort and is numerically more robust. A special characterization stage where the gain and phase change induced by each sub-ADC are measured at the optimization frequency points is necessary at system startup or when the frequency responses vary.

Similar to the time skew correction technique in [98], magnitude response mismatch correction was performed by first reproducing the image spectrum and then subtracting it from the TIADC output spectrum [70, 71]. The error spectrum was obtained by applying a frequency-dependent scaling function $A_{k\neq0}(j\Omega)/A_0(j\Omega)$ to the TIADC output followed by frequency shifting of $2\pi k/M$ where $k = 1, \dots, M - 1$. Implementation of the correction structure requires $(M - 1)$ FIR filters and $(M - 1)$ time-varying multipliers switching at the overall data rate. Phase response mismatch, however, was not treated. The compensation structures in [70, 71, 98, 99] have been generalized to a unified model [115]. The authors described a general input–output relationship in a TIADC and demonstrated that the error signal arise from frequency response mismatch can be reproduced using the output samples and proper filtering. The correction structure can be implemented in various forms and able to achieve any desired reconstruction accuracy by cascading more stages of the correction filters assuming the error due to filter design is negligible. The model is not limited to TIADCs and can be applied to the correction of general time-varying systems.

A straightforward extension from the timing mismatch correction in [57] to the more general frequency response mismatch correction has been presented in [61]. The estimation of channel frequency response mismatch was, however, not mentioned. Exact models describing the channel transfer function is usually not available. In [67] and [90], the need for an accurate model was avoided by characterizing the responses of the sub-ADCs at discrete frequency points. Polynomial models that approximate the frequency characteristic in terms of polynomials in the frequency ω or the mismatch parameters have been adopted in a number of research works [62, 93, 94, 102, 104]. Polynomial models are simple and can achieve desired accuracy by including higher order terms. In [62], the channel frequency responses were expressed in terms of polynomials of $j\omega$. The resulting compensation structure has a cascaded from where the residue error is reduced successively and becomes higher power terms of $j\omega$ with diminishing coefficients. The structure makes use of a number of fixed digital filters approximating different orders of $j\omega$, and a few variable multipliers corresponding to the coefficients in the polynomial model. Only the values of the variable multipliers need to be adjusted whenever the channel frequency responses vary.

Another technique that approximates the channel frequency responses of a TIADC with a linear periodic time-varying FIR filter and treats the reconstruction as a linear inverse problem of a time-varying system shown in Eq. (2.32) has been demonstrated in [102, 104]. The matrix **A** in this case consists of the coefficients of the FIR filters approximating the channel transfer functions of the sub-ADCs. An iterative correction framework employing Gauss–Seidel iteration was presented. Compared the Richardson iteration used in [103], Gauss–Seidel iteration converges much faster, usually in two or three iterations. Farrow-based filters where the filter coefficients are expressed in terms of polynomials of a single mismatch parameter have been adopted to cope with variations in the channel frequency response. Farrow filter implementation is available when the mismatch only depends on a single parameter such as the time skew or bandwidth. When multiple sources of mismatch are present, cascading the correction structure to deal with different types of mismatches is necessary.

Extension of the gain and timing mismatch correction in [91, 92] to the frequency response mismatch for a two-channel TIADC was demonstrated in [93, 94]. The magnitude and phase responses were modeled as polynomials in ω. The polynomial parameters were estimated iteratively by minimizing the norm of a cyclic correlation function of the signal reconstructed using the estimates from previous iteration [93]. An analytic approach that avoids matrix inversion and time-frequency transformation and is thus numerically less intensive has been reported in [94].

The coefficients of the time-varying compensation filter were updated using a M-periodic LMS algorithm so that the difference between the TIADC output and the output of a low-resolution ADC was minimized [86]. Eventually, the reconstructed signal using the time-varying filter will experience the same frequency response as that of the reference ADC. The approach requires an extra reference ADC working at the overall sampling rate. The method in [87] corrects for the frequency response mismatch in a two-channel TIADC and is an extension of the work in [85]. The frequency-dependent scaling function $A_1(j\Omega)/A_0(j\Omega)$ was approximated by polynomial of $j\omega$. A filtered-error LMS algorithm that updates the estimates of the polynomial parameters by minimizing the difference between the residue error and the reproduced error in the signal free region was employed.

2.5 Conclusion

In this chapter, we reviewed the architecture of a TIADC as an effective means to achieve high sampling speed with reasonable increase in area and power dissipation within a given device technology. Unfortunately, fabrication imperfections give rise to mismatches among the sub-ADC channels leading to deteriorated TIADC performance. In particular, four types of mismatch errors— offset, gain, timing, and frequency response mismatches—were studied and their impacts in both the time and frequency domain were analyzed. After that, the research work dealing with channel mismatch compensation carried out over the past 20 years was reviewed.

The problem of channel mismatch compensation consists of two parts: One is to estimate the mismatches with good accuracy and the other is to design the reconstruction system correcting for the mismatch errors. Out of the four types of mismatches, identification and correction of offset and gain mismatches are relatively easy. The correction system can be as simple as an adder and a multiplier in the signal path. In many cases, offset in each sub-ADC can be estimated by averaging the output samples and the gain can be obtained by calculating the correlations between the subsequences.

Timing mismatch introduces linear phase mismatch. Frequency response mismatch causes frequency-dependent gain mismatch and nonlinear phase mismatch, which are more challenging to identify and correct. Among the numerous techniques proposed, offline calibration methods achieve high reconstruction fidelity because of dedicated characterization stage and calibration setup but are not adaptive to the changes in the mismatch errors. Offline methods find their use in measurement application but are not suitable for communication systems. On the other hand, blind methods impose certain requirements on the input signal and need high computation efforts in exchange for continuous system operation even when the mismatches drift due to environmental variations.

The research effort in the future will be toward finding accurate and reliable online identification methods for timing and frequency response mismatches while maintaining reasonable computational and implementation complexity. The correction system needs to achieve high reconstruction accuracy over the frequency band of interest. When the mismatch errors change, the correction system has to be adaptive to the variations without redesign of the entire system.

References

1. *IEEE Standard for Terminology and Test Methods for Analog-to-Digital Converters*, IEEE Standard 1241-2010, January 2011.

2. Asami, K. (2005). Technique to improve the performance of time-interleaved A–D converters, *Proc. IEEE Int. Test Conf. (ITC)*, Paper 34.1.

3. Asami, K., Suzuki, H., Miyajima, H., Taura, T., and Kobayashi, H. (2008). Technique to improve the performance of time-interleaved A-D converters with mismatches of non-linearity, *Proc. 17th Asian Test Symp. (ATS)*, pp. 105–110.

4. Bemardinis, G., Malcovati, P., Maloberti, F., and Soenen, E. (2002). Dynamic stage matching for parallel pipeline A/D converters, *Proc. IEEE Int. Symp. Circuits Syst. (ISCAS)*, **1**, pp. 905–908.

5. Black, Jr., W. C., and Hodges, D. A. (1980). Time interleaved converter arrays, *IEEE J. Solid-State Circuits*, **SC-15**(6), pp. 1022–1029.

6. Cabrini, A., Maloberti, F., Rovatti, R., and Setti, G. (2006). On-line calibration of offset and gain mismatch in time-interleaved ADC using a sampled-data chaotic bit-stream, *Proc. IEEE Int. Symp. Circuits Syst., (ISCAS)*, pp. 3398–3401.

7. Conroy, C. S. G., Cline, D. W., and Gray, P. R. (1993). An 8-b 85-MS/s parallel pipeline A/D converter in 1-µm CMOS, *IEEE J. Solid-State Circuits*, **28**(4), pp. 447–454.

8. Divi, V., and Wornell, G. W. (2004). Signal recovery in time-interleaved analog-to-digital converters, *Proc. IEEE Int. Conf. Acoustics Speech Signal Process. (ICASSP)*, pp. 593–596.

9. Divi, V., and Wornell, G. W. (2006). Scalable blind calibration of timing skew in high-resolution time-interleaved ADCs, *Proc. IEEE Int. Symp. Circuits Syst. (ISCAS)*, pp. 3390–3393.

10. Divi, D., and Wornell, G. W (2008). Bandlimited signal reconstruction from noisy periodic nonuniform samples in time-interleaved ADCs, *Proc. IEEE Int. Conf. Acoustics Speech Signal Process. (ICASSP)*, pp. 3721–3724.

11. Divi, V., and Wornell, G. W. (2009). Blind calibration of timing skew in time-interleaved analog-to-digital converters, *IEEE J. Sel. Topics Signal Process.*, **3**(3), pp. 509–522.

12. Dyer, K. C., Fu, D., Hurst, P. J., and Lewis, S. H. (1998). A comparison of monolithic background calibration in two time-interleaved analog-to-digital converters, *Proc. IEEE Int. Symp. Circuits Syst. (ISCAS)*, **1**(1), pp. 13–16.

13. Dyer, K. C., Fu, D., Lewis, S. H., and Hurst, P. J. (1998). An analog background calibration technique for time-interleaved analog-to-digital converters, *IEEE J. Solid-State Circuits*, **33**(12), pp. 1912–1919.

14. Eklund, J.-E., and Gustafsson, F. (2000). Digital offset compensation of time-interleaved ADC using random chopper sampling, *Proc. IEEE Int. Symp. Circuits Syst. (ISCAS)*, **3**, pp. 447–450.

15. El-Chammas, M., and Murmann, B. (2009). General analysis on the impact of phase-skew in time-interleaved ADCs, *IEEE Trans. Circuits Syst. I, Reg. Papers*, **56**(5), pp. 902–910.

16. El-Chammas. M., and Murmann, B. (2011). A 12-GS/s, 81-mW 5-bit time-interleaved flash ADC with background timing skew calibration, *IEEE J. Solid-State Circuits*, **46**(4), pp. 838–847.

17. El-Sankary, K., Assi, A., and Sawan, M. (2003). New sampling method to improve the SFDR of time-interleaved ADCs, *Proc. Int. Symp. Circuits Syst. (ISCAS)*, **1**, pp. 833–836.

18. El-Sankary, K., and Sawam, M. (2006). A background calibration technique for multibit/stage pipelined and time-interleaved ADCs, *IEEE Trans. Circuits Syst. II, Exp. Briefs*, **53**(6), pp. 448–452.

19. Elbornsson, J., and Eklund, J.-E. (2001). Blind estimation of timing errors in interleaved AD converters, *Proc. IEEE Int. Conf. Acoustics Speech Signal Process. (ICASSP)*, **6**, pp. 3913–3916.

20. Elbornsson, J., Gustafsson, F., and Eklund, J.-E. (2002). Amplitude and gain error influence on time error estimation algorithm for time interleaved A/D converter system, *Proc. IEEE Int. Conf. Acoustics Speech Signal Process. (ICASSP)*, **2**, pp. 1281–1284.

21. Elbornsson, J., Folkesson, K., and Eklund, J.-E. (2002). Measurement verification of estimation method for time errors in a time interleaved A/D converter system, *Proc. IEEE Int. Symp. Circuits Syst. (ISCAS)*, **3**, pp. 129–132.

22. Elbornsson, J., Gustafsson, F., and Eklund, J.-E. (2003). Analysis of mismatch noise in randomly interleaved ADC system, *Proc. IEEE Int. Conf. Acoustics Speech Signal Process. (ICASSP)*, **6**, pp. 277–280.

23. Elbornsson, J., Gustafsson, F., and Eklund, J.-E. (2004). Blind adaptive equalization of mismatch errors in a time-interleaved A/D converter system, *IEEE Trans. Circuits Syst. I, Reg. Papers*, **51**(1), pp. 151–158.

24. Elbornsson J., and Gustafsson, F., and Eklund, J.-E. (2005). Analysis of mismatch effects in a randomly interleaved A/D converter system, *IEEE Trans. Circuits Syst. I, Reg. Papers*, **52**(3), pp. 465–476.

25. Elbornsson, J., Gustafsson, F., and Eklund, J.-E. (2005). Blind equalization of time errors in a time-interleaved ADC system, *IEEE Trans. Signal Process.*, **53**(4), pp. 1413–1424.

26. Eldar, Y. C., and Oppenheim, A.V. (2000). Filterbank reconstruction of bandlimited signals from nonuniform and generalized samples, *IEEE Trans. Signal Process.*, **48**(10), pp. 2864–2875.

27. Farrow, C. W. (1988). A continuously variable digital delay element, *Proc. IEEE Int. Symp. Circuits Syst. (ISCAS)*, **3**, pp. 2641–2645.

28. Ferragina, V., Fornasari, A., Gatti, U., Malcovati, P., and Maloberti, F. (2004). Gain and offset mismatch calibration in time-interleaved multipath A/D sigma-delta modulators, *IEEE Trans. Circuits Syst. I, Reg. Papers*, **51**(12), pp. 2365–2373.

29. Fu, D., Dyer, K. C., Lewis, S. H., and Hurst, P. J. (1998). A digital background calibration technique for time-interleaved analog-to-digital converters, *IEEE J. Solid-State Circuits*, **33**(12), pp. 1904–1911.

30. Gupta, S. K., Choi, M., Interfield, M. A., and Wang, J. (2006). A 1 GS/s 11b time-interleaved ADC in 0.13 μm CMOS, *IEEE Int. Solid-State Circuits Conf., Dig. Tech. Papers*, pp. 2360–2369.

31. Gupta, S. K., Inerfield, M. A., and Wang, J. (2006). A 1-GS/s 11-bit ADC with 55-dB SNDR, 250-mW power realized by a high bandwidth scalable time-interleaved architecture, *IEEE J. Solid-State Circuits*, **41**(12), pp. 2650–2657.

32. Gustavsson, M., Wikner, J. J., and Tan, N. N. (2002). Overview of high-speed A/D converter architectures, in *CMOS Data Converters for Communications*, Chapter 3 (Kluwer Academic Publishers, New York) pp. 61–86.

33. Haftbaradaran, A., and Martin, K. W. (2005). A background compensation technique for sample-time errors in time-interleaved A/D converters, *Proc. 48th IEEE Int. Midwest Symp. Circuits Syst. (MWSCAS)*, **2**, pp. 1011–1014.

34. Haftbaradaran, A., and Martin, K. W. (2006). Mismatch compensation techniques using random data for time-interleaved A/D converters, *Proc. Int. Symp. Circuits Syst. (ISCAS)*, pp. 3402–3405.

35. Haftbaradaran, A., and Martin, K. W. (2007). A sample-time error compensation technique for time-interleaved ADC systems, *Proc. IEEE Custom Integrated Circuits Conf. (CICC)*, pp. 341–344.

36. Haftbaradaran, A., and Martin, K. W. (2008). A background sample-time error calibration technique using random data for wide-band high-resolution time-interleaved ADCs, *IEEE Trans. Circuits Syst. II, Exp. Briefs*, **55**(3), pp. 234–238.

37. Hakkarainen, V., Sumanen, L., Aho, M., Waltari, M., and Halonen, K. (2003). A self-calibration technique for time-interleaved pipelined ADCs, *Proc. IEEE Int. Symp. Circuits Syst. (ISCAS)*, **1**, pp. 825–828.

38. Huang, C.-C., Wang, C.-Y., and Wu, J.-T. (2011). A CMOS 6-bit 16-GS/s time-interleaved ADC using digital background calibration techniques, *IEEE J. Solid-State Circuits*, **46**(4), pp. 848–858.

39. Huang, S., and Levy, B. C. (2006). Adaptive blind calibration of timing offset and gain mismatch for two-channel time-interleaved ADCs, *IEEE Trans. Circuits Syst. I, Reg. Papers*, **53**(6), pp. 1278–1288.

40. Huang, S., and Levy, B. C. (2007). Blind calibration of timing offsets for four-channel time-interleaved ADCs, *IEEE Trans. Circuits Syst. I, Reg. Papers*, **54**(4), pp. 863–876.

41. Hummels, D. M., McDonalds, II, J. J., and Irons, F. H. (1996). Distortion compensation for time-interleaved analog to digital converters, *Proc. IEEE Instrum. Meas. Conf. (IMTC)*, **1**, pp. 728–731.

42. Iroaga, E., Murmann, B., and Nathawad, L. (2005). A background correction technique for timing errors in time-interleaved analog-to-digital converters, *Proc. IEEE Int. Symp. Circuits Syst. (ISCAS)*, **6**, pp. 5557–5560.

43. Jenq, Y.-C. (1988). Digital spectra of nonuniformly sampled signals: Fundamentals and high-speed waveform digitizers, *IEEE Trans. Instrum. Meas.*, **37**(2), pp. 245–251.

44. Jenq, Y.-C. (1990). Digital spectra of nonuniformly sampled signals: A robust sampling time offset estimation algorithm for ultra high-speed waveform digitizers using interleaving, *IEEE Trans. Instrum. Meas.*, **39**(1), pp. 71–75.

45. Jenq, Y.-C. (1997). Perfect reconstruction of digital spectrum from nonuniformly sampled signals, *IEEE Trans. Instrum. Meas.*, **46**(3), pp. 649–652, June 1997.

46. Jenq, Y.-C. (1997). Perfect reconstruction of digital spectrum from nonuniformly sampled signals, *Proc. IEEE Instrum. Meas. Technol. Conf. (IMTC)*, **1**, pp. 624–627.

47. Jenq, Y.-C. (2008). Improving timing offset estimation by alias sampling, *IEEE Trans. Instrum. Meas.*, **57**(7), pp. 1376–1378.

48. Jamal, S. M., Fu, D., Chang, N. C.-J., Hurst, P. J., and Lewis, S. H. (2002). A 10-b 120-Msample/s time-interleaved analog-to-digital converter with digital background calibration, *IEEE J. Solid-State Circuits*, **37**(12), pp. 1618–1627.

49. Jamal, S. M., Fu, D., Singh, M. P., Hurst, P., and Lewis, S. (2004). Calibration of sample-time error in a two-channel time-interleaved analog-to-digital converter, *IEEE Trans. Circuits Syst. I, Reg. Papers*, **51**(1), pp. 130–139.

50. Jin, H., Lee, E. K. F., and Hassoun, M. (1997). Time-interleaved A/D converter with channel randomization, *Proc. IEEE Int. Symp. Circuits Syst. (ISCAS)*, **1**, pp. 425–428.

51. Jin, H., and Lee, E. K. F. (2000). A digital-background calibration technique for minimizing timing-error effects in time-interleaved ADC's, *IEEE Trans. Circuits Syst. II, Analog Digit. Signal Process*, **47**(7), pp. 603–613.

52. Johansson, H., and Löwenborg, P. (2001). Reconstruction of nonuniformly sampled bandlimited signals using digital fractional delay filters, *Proc. IEEE Int. Symp. Circuits Syst. (ISCAS)*, **2**, pp. 593–596.

53. Johansson, H., and Löwenborg, P. (2002). Reconstruction of a class of nonuniformly sampled and decimated bandlimited signals, *Proc. IEEE Int. Symp. Circuits Syst. (ISCAS)*, 2, pp. 604–607.

54. Johansson, H., and Löwenborg, P. (2002). Reconstruction of nonuniformly sampled bandlimited signals by means of digital fractional delay filters, *IEEE Trans. Signal Process.*, **50**(11), pp. 2757–2767.

55. Johansson, H., and Löwenborg, P. (2004). Reconstruction of nonuniformly sampled bandlimited signals using time-varying discrete time FIR filters, *Proc. 12th European Signal Processing Conf.*, pp. 97–100.

56. Johansson, H., and Löwenborg, P. (2004). Reconstruction of periodically nonuniformly sampled bandlimited signals using time-varying FIR filters, presented at the International Workshop on Spectral Methods Multirate Signal Processing.

57. Johansson, H., and Löwenborg, P. (2006). Reconstruction of nonuniformly sampled bandlimited signals by means of time-varying discrete-time FIR filters, *EURASIP J. Appl. Signal Process.*, **2006**, Article ID 64185, pp. 1–18.

58. Johansson, H., Löwenborg, P., and Vengattaramane, K. (2006). Reconstruction of two-periodic nonuniformly sampled signals using polynomial impulse response time-varying FIR filters, *Proc. IEEE Int. Symp. Circuits Syst. (ISCAS)*, pp. 2993–2996.

59. Johansson, H., Löwenborg, P., and Vengattaramane, K. (2006). Reconstruction of M-periodic nonuniformly sampled signals using multivariate polynomial impulse response time-varying FIR filters, presented at the 14th European Signal Processing Conference.

60. Johansson, H., Löwenborg, P., and Vengattaramane, K. (2007). Least-squares and minimax design of polynomial impulse response FIR filters for reconstruction of two-periodic nonuniformly sampled signals, *IEEE Trans. Circuits Syst. I, Reg. Papers*, **54**(4), pp. 877–888.

61. Johansson, H., and Löwenborg, P. (2008). A least-squares filter design technique for the compensation of frequency-response mismatch errors in time interleaved A/D converters, *IEEE Trans. Circuits Syst. II: Exp. Briefs*, **55**(11), pp. 1154–1158.

62. Johansson, H. (2009). A polynomial-based time-varying filter structure for the compensation of frequency-response mismatch errors in time-interleaved ADCs, *IEEE J. Sel. Topics Signal Process.*, **3**(3), pp. 384–396.

63. Kim, K. Y., Kusayanagi, N., and Abidi, A. A. (1997). A 10-b, 100-MS/s CMOS A/D converter, *IEEE J. Solid-State Circuits*, **32**(3), pp. 302–311.

64. Kurosawa, N., Kobayashi, H., Maruyama, K., Sugawara, H., and Kobayashi, K. (2001). Explicit analysis of channel mismatch effects in time-interleaved ADC systems, *IEEE Trans. Circuits Syst. I, Fundam. Theory Appl.*, **48**(3), pp. 261–271.

65. Kurosawa, N., Kobayashi, H., and Kobayashi, K. (2001). Channel linearity mismatch effects in time-interleaved ADC systems, *Proc. IEEE Int. Symp. Circuits Syst. (ISCAS)*, **1**, pp. 420–423.

66. Law, C. H., Hurst, P. J., and Lewis, S. H. (2010). A four-channel time-interleaved ADC with digital calibration of interchannel timing and memory errors, *IEEE J. Solid-State Circuits*, **45**(10), pp. 2091–2103.

67. Lim, Y. C., Zou, Y. X., Lee, J. W., and Chan, S. C. (2009). Time-interleaved analog-to-digital-converter compensation using multichannel filters, *IEEE Trans. Circuits Syst. I, Reg. Papers*, **56**(10), pp. 2234–2247, Oct 2009.

68. Marelli, D., Mahata, K., and Fu, M. (2009). Linear LMS compensation for timing mismatch in time-interleaved ADCs, *IEEE Trans. Circuits Syst. I, Reg. Papers*, **56**, no.11, pp. 2476–2486.

69. Matsuno, J., Yamaji, T., Furuta, M., and Itakura, T. (2013). All-digital background calibration technique for time-interleaved ADC using pseudo aliasing signal, *IEEE Trans. Circuits Syst. I, Reg. Papers*, **60**(5), pp. 1113–1121.

70. Mendel, S., and Vogel, C. (2006). A compensation method for magnitude response mismatches in two-channel time-interleaved analog-to-digital converters, *Proc. 13th IEEE Int. Conf. Electron. Circuits Syst. (ICECS)*, pp. 712–715.

71. Mendel, S., and Vogel, C. (2007). On the compensation of magnitude response mismatches in M-channel time-interleaved ADCs, *Proc. IEEE Int. Symp. Circuits Syst. (ISCAS)*, pp. 3375–3378.

72. Nakamura, K., Hotta, M., Carley, L. R., and Allstot, D. J. (1995). An 85 mW, 10 b, 40 Msample/s CMOS parallel-pipelined ADC, *IEEE J. Solid-State Circuits*, **30**(3), pp. 173–183.

73. Namgoong, W. (2002) Finite-length synthesis filters for non-uniformly time-interleaved analog-to-digital converter, *Proc. IEEE Int. Symp. Circuits Syst. (ISCAS)*, **4**, pp. 815–818.

74. Ndjountche, T., and Unbehauen, R. (2000). Design techniques for high-speed sigma-delta modulators, *Proc. 43rd IEEE Midwest Symp. Circuits Syst. (MWSCAS)*, **2**, pp. 916–919.

75. Ndjountche, T., and Unbehauen, R. (2001). Adaptive calibration techniques for time-interleaved ADCs, *Electron. Lett.*, **37**(7), pp. 412–414.

76. Oh, Y., and Murmann, B. (2006). System embedded ADC calibration for OFDM receivers, *IEEE Trans. Circuits Syst. I, Reg. Papers*, **53**(8), pp. 1693–1703.

77. Pereira, J. M. D., Girão, P. M. B. S., and Serra, A. M. C. (2004). An FFT-based method to evaluate and compensate gain and offset errors of interleaved ADC systems, *IEEE Trans. Instrum. Meas.*, **53**(2), pp. 423–430.

78. Petraglia, A., and Mitra, S. K. (1991). Analysis of mismatch effects among A/D converters in a time-interleaved waveform digitizer, *IEEE Trans. Instrum. Meas.*, **40**(5), pp. 831–835.

79. Poulton. K, Corcoran, J. J., and Hornak, T. (1987). A 1-GHz 6-bitADC system, *IEEE J. Solid-State Circuits*, **SC-22**, pp. 962–970.

80. Poulton, K., Knudsen, K. L., Kerley, J., Kang, J., Tani, J., Cornish, E., and VanGrouw, M. (1997). An 8-GSa/s 8-bit ADC system, *Symp. VLSI Circuits, Dig. Tech. Papers*, pp. 23–24.

81. Poulton, K., Neff, R., Muto, A., Liu, W., Burstein, A., and Heshami, M. (2002). A 4 GSample/s 8b ADC in 0.35 μm CMOS, *IEEE Int. Solid-State Circuits Conf., Dig. Tech. Papers*, **1**, pp. 166–457.

82. Poulton, K., Neff, R., Setterberg, B., Wuppermann, B., Kopley, T., Jewett, R., Pernillo, J., Tan, C., and Montijo, A. (2003). A 20 GS/s 8b ADC with a 1 MB memory in 0.18 μm CMOS, *IEEE Int. Solid-State Circuits Conf., Dig. Tech. Papers*, pp. 318–319.

83. Prendergast, R. S., Levy, B.C., and Hurst, P. J. (2004). Reconstruction of band-limited periodic nonuniformly sampled signals through

multirate filter banks, *IEEE Trans. Circuits Syst. I, Reg. Papers*, **51**(8), pp. 1612–1622.

84. Saleem, S., and Vogel, C. (2007). LMS-based identification and compensation of timing mismatches in a two-channel time-interleaved analog-to-digital converter, presented at the 25th IEEE Norchip Conference.

85. Saleem, S., and Vogel, C. (2010). On blind identification of gain and timing mismatches in time-interleaved analog-to-digital converters, *Proc. 33rd Int. Conf. Telecommun. Signal Process. (TSP)*, pp. 151–155.

86. Saleem, S and Vogel, C. (2010). Adaptive compensation of frequency response mismatches in high-resolution time-interleaved ADCs using a low-resolution ADC and a time-varying filter, *Proc. IEEE Int. Symp. Circuits Syst. (ISCAS)*, pp 561–564.

87. Saleem, S and Vogel, C. (2011). Adaptive blind background calibration of polynomial-represented frequency response mismatches in a two-channel time-interleaved ADC, *IEEE trans. Circuits Syst. I, Reg. Papers*, **58**(6), Jun. 2011.

88. Satarzadeh, P., Levy, B. C., and Hurst, P. J. (2007). Bandwidth mismatch correction for a two-channel time-interleaved A/D converter, *Proc. IEEE Int. Symp. Circuits Syst. (ISCAS)*, pp. 1705–1708.

89. Satarzadeh, P., Levy, B. C., and Hurst, P. J. (2009). Adaptive semiblind calibration of bandwidth mismatch for two-channel time-interleaved ADCs, *IEEE Trans. Circuits Syst. I, Reg. Papers*, **56**(9), pp. 2075–2088.

90. Seo, M., Rodwell, M. J. W., and Madhow, U. (2005). Comprehensive digital correction of mismatch errors for a 400-Msamples/s 80 dB SFDR time-interleaved analog-to-digital converter, *IEEE Trans. Microw. Theory Tech.*, **53**(3), pp. 1072–1082.

91. Seo, M., Rodwell, M. J. W., and Madhow, U. (2005). Blind correction of gain and timing mismatches for a two-channel time-interleaved analog-to-digital converter, *Proc. 39th Asilomar Conf. Signals System Comput.*, pp. 1121–1125.

92. Seo, M., Rodwell, M. J. W., and Madhow, U. (2006). Blind correction of gain and timing mismatches for a two-channel time-interleaved analog-to-digital converter: Experimental verification, *Proc. IEEE Int. Symp. Circuits Syst. (ISCAS)*, pp. 3394–3397.

93. Seo, M., Rodwell, M., and Madhow, U. (2007). Generalized blind mismatch correction for a two-channel time-interleaved A-to-D converters, *Proc. IEEE Int. Conf. Acoustics Speech Signal Process. (ICASSP)*, **3**, pp. 1505–1508.

94. Seo, M., and Rodwell, M. (2007). Generalized blind mismatch correction for a two-channel time-interleaved ADC: Analytic approach, *Proc. IEEE Int. Symp. Circuits Syst. (ISCAS)*, pp. 109–112.

95. Sin, S.-W., Chio, U.-F., U, S.-P., and Martins, R. P. (2008). Statistical spectra and distortion analysis of time-interleaved sampling bandwidth mismatch, *IEEE Trans. Circuits Syst. II, Exp. Briefs*, **55**(7), pp. 648–652.

96. Sumanen, L., Waltari, M., and Halonen, K. A. I. (2001). A 10-bit 200-MS/s CMOS parallel pipeline A/D converter, *IEEE J. Solid-State Circuits*, **36**(7), pp. 1048–1055.

97. Tamba, M., Shimizu, A., Munakata, H., and Komuro, T. (2001). A method to improve SFDR with random interleaved sampling method, *Proc. Int. Test Conf. (ITC)*, pp. 512–520.

98. Tertinek, S., and Vogel, C. (2007). Reconstruction of two-periodic nonuniformly sampled band-limited signals using a discrete-time differentiator and a time-varying multiplier, *IEEE Trans. Circuits Syst. II, Exp. Briefs*, **54**(7), pp. 616–620.

99. Tertinek, S., and Vogel, C. (2008). Reconstruction of nonuniformly sampled bandlimited signals using a differentiator-multiplier cascade, *IEEE Trans. Circuits Syst. I, Reg. Papers*, **55**(8), pp. 2273–2286.

100. Tsai, T. H., Hurst, P. J., and Lewis, S. H. (2006). Bandwidth mismatch and its correction in time-interleaved analog-to-digital converters, *IEEE Trans. Circuits Syst. II, Exp. Briefs*, **53**(10), pp. 1133–1137.

101. Tsai, T.-H., Hurst, P. J., and Lewis, S. H. (2009). Correction of mismatches in a time-interleaved analog-to-digital converter in an adaptively equalized digital communication receiver, *IEEE Trans. Circuits Syst. I, Reg. Papers*, **56**(2), pp. 307–319.

102. Tsui, K. M., and Chan, S. C. (2010). Iterative correction of frequency response mismatches in time-interleaved ADCs: A novel framework and case study in OFDM systems, *Proc. Int. Conf. Green Circuits Syst. (ICGCS)*, Shanghai, pp. 253–258.

103. Tsui, K. M., and Chan, S. C. (2011). A versatile iterative framework for the reconstruction of bandlimited signals from their nonuniform sample, *J. Signal Process. Syst.*, **62**(3), pp. 459–468.

104. Tsui, K. M., and Chan, S. C. (2011). New iterative framework for frequency response mismatch correction in time-interleaved ADCs: Design and performance analysis, *IEEE Trans. Instrum. Meas.*, **60**(12), pp. 3792–3805.

105. Vaidyanathan, P. P. (1993) Maximally decimated filter banks, in *Multirate Systems and Filter Banks* (Prentice-Hall, Englewood Cliffs), Chapter 5, pp. 188–285.

106. Vogel, C., Draxelmayr, D., and Kuttner, F. (2004). Compensation of timing mismatches in time-interleaved analog-to-digital converters through transfer characteristic tuning, *Proc. 47th IEEE Midwest Symp. Circuits Syst. (MWSCAS)*, **1**, pp. 341–344.

107. Vogel, C., and Kubin, G. (2004). Analysis and compensation of nonlinearity mismatches in time-interleaved ADC arrays, *Proc. IEEE Int. Symp. Circuits Syst. (ISCAS)*, **1**, pp. 593–596.

108. Vogel, C., and Kubin, G. (2005). Modeling of time-interleaved ADCs with nonlinear hybrid filter banks, *AEU—Int. J. Electron. Commun.*, **59**(5), pp. 288–296.

109. Vogel, C., Draxelmayr, D., and Kubin, G. (2005). Spectral shaping of timing mismatches in time-interleaved analog-to-digital converters, *Proc. IEEE Int. Symp. Circuits Syst. (ISCAS)*, **2**, pp. 1394–1397.

110. Vogel, C., Pammer, V., and Kubin, G. (2005). A novel channel randomization method for time-interleaved ADCs, *Proc. IEEE Instrum. Meas. Technol. Conf. (IMTC)*, **1**, pp. 150–155.

111. Vogel, C. (2005). The impact of combined channel mismatch effects in time-interleaved ADCs, *IEEE Trans. Instrum. Meas.*, **54**(1), pp. 415–427.

112. Vogel, C., and Johansson, H. (2006). Time-interleaved analog-to-digital converters: Status and future directions, *Proc. IEEE Int. Symp. Circuits Syst. (ISCAS)*, pp. 3386–3389.

113. Vogel, C. (2006). A frequency domain method for blind identification of timing mismatches in time-interleaved ADCs, *Proc. 24th Norchip Conf.*, pp. 45–48.

114. Vogel, C., Saleem, S., and Mendel, S. (2008). Adaptive blind compensation of gain and timing mismatches in M-channel time-interleaved ADCs, *Proc. 15th IEEE Int. Conf. Electron Circuits Syst. (ICECS)*, pp. 49–52.

115. Vogel, C., and Mendel, S. (2009). A flexible and scalable structure to compensate frequency response mismatches in time-interleaved ADCs, *IEEE Trans. Circuits Syst. I, Reg. Papers*, **56**(11), pp. 2463–2475.

116. Walden, R. H. (1999). Analog-to-digital converter survey and analysis, *IEEE J. Sel. Areas Commun.*, **17**(4), pp 539–550.

117. Wang, C.-Y., and Wu, J.-T. (2006). A background timing-skew calibration technique for time-interleaved analog-to-digital converters, *IEEE Trans. Circuits Syst. II, Exp. Briefs*, **53**(4), pp. 299–303.

118. Wang, C.-Y., and Wu, J.-T. (2009). A multiphase timing-skew calibration technique using zero-crossing detection, *IEEE Trans. Circuits Syst. I, Reg. Papers*, **56**(6), pp. 1102–1114.

119. Yao, K., and Thomas, J. (1967). On some stability and interpolatory properties of nonuniform sampling expansions, *IEEE Trans. Circuit Theory*, **CT-14**(4), pp. 404–408.

120. Yu, B., and Black, Jr., W.C. (2001). Error analysis for time-interleaved analog channels, *Proc. IEEE Int. Symp. Circuits Syst. (ISCAS)*, **1**, pp. 468–471.

121. Zou, Y. X., Zhang, S. L., Lim, Y. C., and Chen, X. (2011). Timing mismatch compensation in time-interleaved ADCs based on multichannel Lagrange polynomial interpolation, *IEEE Trans. Instrum. Meas.*, **60**(4), pp. 1123–1131.

122. Zou, Y. X., and Xu, X. J. (2012). Blind timing skew estimation using source spectrum sparsity in time-interleaved ADCs, *IEEE Trans. Instrum. Meas.*, **61**(9), pp. 2401–2412.

Chapter 3

How to Perform Very Wideband Digital Filtering in Modern Software Defined Radios

Fred Harris, Elettra Venosa, and Xiaofei Chen

San Diego State University, Department of Electrical and Computer Engineering, 5500 Campanile Drive, San Diego, California 92182-1309, USA

fred.harris@sdsu.edu, evenosa@spacemicro.com, chenxiaofei_sdsu@yahoo.com

This chapter describes a particular class of multirate filters and the potential that they bring to communication systems and in particular to modern wideband software radios. Multirate filters have the capability of optimizing the sample rate while processing signals and this characteristic provides many advantages to digital systems. Cost and computational complexity reduction, improved performance and reduced chip size, power and weight are just some of them.

Practical implementation of wideband digital filters in modern radios is currently limited by the hardware clock rate. The maximum hardware processing speed limits the bandwidth that can be processed digitally. When the input bandwidth increases, the sample rate increases and the processing speed should increase conse-quently. The most modern field programmable gate array (FPGA)

Trends in Digital Signal Processing: A Festschrift in Honour of A. G. Constantinides
Edited by Yong Ching Lim, Hon Keung Kwan, and Wan-Chi Siu
Copyright © 2016 Pan Stanford Publishing Pte. Ltd.
ISBN 978-981-4669-50-4 (Hardcover), 978-981-4669-51-1 (eBook)
www.panstanford.com

chips that are used for state-of-the-art digital telecommunication applications have a maximum clock speed of only a few GHz.

Perfect reconstruction (PR) non-maximally decimated filter banks (NMDFBs) are a special class of multirate filters that solve this problem by reducing the sampling rate of the signal before processing it. When the signal sample rate is reduced as desired the clock speed is not a limitation anymore.

In this chapter, we will describe the theoretical architecture of PR NMDFBs, we will explain how they work and how they can be implemented on hardware. We will focus on their capability of performing digital wideband filtering and we will propose some of the newest and most significant application s of PR NMDFBs in communication systems.

3.1 Introduction

Signal processing is the art of representing, manipulating and transforming wave shapes and the information content that they carry by means of hardware and/or software devices. Until 1960s almost entirely continuous time, analog technology was used for performing signal processing. The evolution of digital systems along with the development of important algorithms such as the wellknown fast Fourier transform (FFT), by Cooley and Tukey in 1965, caused a major shift to digital technologies giving rise to new digital signal processing architectures and techniques. The key difference between analog processing techniques and digital processing techniques is that while the first one processes analog signals, which are continuous functions of time; the second one processes sequences of values. The sequences of values, called digital signals, are series of quantized samples (discrete time signal values) of analog signals.

The link between the analog signals and their sampled versions is provided by the sampling process. When sampling is properly applied, it is possible to reconstruct the continuous time signal from its samples preserving its information content. Thus, the selection of the sampling rate is crucial: An insufficient sampling frequency causes surely, irrecoverable loss of information, while a more than necessary sampling rate causes useless overload on the digital systems. The Nyquist sampling theorem states that the minimum sampling frequency for a band-limited low-pass signal is twice its bandwidth. However this is only a theoretical limit. In reality faster sampling rates are needed [6, 7].

The string of words multirate digital signal processing indicates the operation of changing the sample rate of digital signals, one or multiple times, while processing them. The sampling rate changes can occur at a single or multiple locations in the processing architecture. When the multirate processing applied to the digital signal is a filtering then the digital filter is named multirate filter; a multirate filter is a digital filter that operates with one or more sample rate changes embedded in the signal processing architecture. The opportunity of selecting the most appropriate signal sampling rate at different stages of the processing architecture, rather than having a single (higher) sampling rate, enhances the performance of the system while reducing its implementation costs. However, the analysis and design of multirate systems could result complicated because of the fact that they are time-varying systems. It is interesting to know that the first multirate filters and systems were developed in the context of control systems. The pioneer papers on this topic were published in the second half of 1950s [41, 42]. Soon the idea spilled in the areas of speech, audio, image processing [43, 44] and communication systems [6–7]. Today, multirate structures seem to be the optimum candidates for cognitive and software-defined radio [7, 27, 28, 38], which represents the frontier of innovation for the upcoming communication systems.

One of the wellknown techniques that find its most efficient application when embedded in multirate structures is the polyphase decomposition of a prototype filter. The polyphase networks, of generic order M, originated in the late 1970s from the works by Bellanger et al. [45, 46]. The term polyphase is the aggregation of two words: poly, that derives from the ancient Greek word *polys*, which means many, and phase. When applied to an M-path partitioned filter these two words underline the fact that, on each path, each aliased filter spectral component, experiences a unique phase rotation due to both their center frequencies and the time delays, which are different in each path because of the way in which the filter has been partitioned. When all the paths are summed together the undesired spectral components, having phases with opposite polarity, cancel each other while only the desired components, which experience the same phase on all the arms of the partitions, constructively add up. By applying appropriate phase rotators to each path, we can arbitrarily change the phases of the spectral components selecting the spectral component that survives as a consequence of the summation. It is interesting to know that the first applications of the polyphase networks were in the areas of real-time implementation of decimation and interpolation filters, fractional sampling rate changing devices, uniform DFT filter banks as well as perfect reconstruction analysis/synthesis systems. Today polyphase filter banks, embedded in multirate structures, are used in many modern DSP applications as well as in communication systems where they represent, according to the author's belief, one of the most efficient options for designing fully digital radios.

The twentieth century saw the explosion of hardware-defined radio as a means of communicating all forms of data, audible and visual information over vast distances. These radios have little or no software control. Their structures are fixed in accordance with the applications; the signal modulation formats, the carrier frequencies, and bandwidths are only some of the factors that dictate the radio structures. The smallest change to one of these parameters could imply a replacement of the entire radio system. A consequence of this is, for example, the fact that a television receiver purchased in France does not work in England. The reason, of course, is that the different geographical regions employ different modulation standards for the analog TV as well as for digital TV. Then, the citizens cannot use the same TV for receiving signals in both countries; they need to buy a new television for each country in which they decide to live. Sometimes, even if the communication devices are designed for the same application purposes and they work in the same geographical area, they are not able to communicate between each other. One of the most evident examples of this is that the city police car radio cannot communicate directly with the city fire truck radio, or with the local hospital ambulance radio even if they have the common purpose of helping and supporting the citizen. Also, the city fire truck radio cannot communicate with the county fire truck radio, or with the radios of the fire truck operated by the adjacent city, or by the state park service, or the international airport. None of these services can communicate with the National Guard, or with the local Port Authority, or with the local Navy base, or the local Coast Guard base, or the US Border Patrol, or US Customs Service. In a hardware-defined radio, if we decide to change one of the parameters of the transmitted signal, like bandwidth or carrier frequency (for example because the carrier frequency we want to use is the only one available at that particular moment), most likely we will need to change the transmitter. On the other side, every time we want to receive a signal having different bandwidth or center frequency, we need to change the receiver. Hardware defined transmitter and receiver devices are not flexible at all. They operate over particular, well-defined, bandwidths and center frequencies and we must modify their structure every time we change even one of the transmitting and receiving signal parameters.

In 1991, Joe Mitola coined the term software-defined radio. It was referred to a class of reprogrammable (and reconfigurable) devices. At that time it was not clear at which level the digitization should occur to define a radio as software but the concept sounded pretty interesting, and the dream of building a completely reconfigurable radio device involved scientists from all over the world. Today the exact definition of software-defined radio is still controversial, and no consensus exists about the level of reconfigurability needed to qualify a radio as software.

Figure 3.1 shows, in a simple block diagram, all the possible places in which the digitization can occur in a radio receiver. The dual block diagram can be portrayed for the radio transmitter. Current radios, often referred to as digital, after shifting the signals to baseband or to intermediate frequency (IF), digitize them and assign all the remaining tasks to a digital signal processor. One of the main reasons for shifting the signals to a lower frequency, before digitizing them, is to reduce their maximum frequency so that a smaller number of samples can be processed for preserving the information content.

Implementation of ideal software radios requires digitization at the antenna with a minimum radio frequency (RF) section,

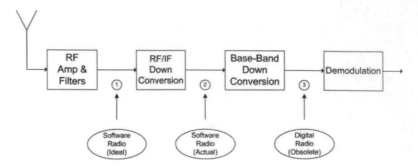

Figure 3.1 Simple block diagram indicating all the possible places in which the digitization can occur in a radio receiver.

allowing complete flexibility in the digital domain. Then it requires the design and implementation of high performance analog-to-digital converters (ADCs) and digital-to-analog converters (DACs), of flexible and efficient DSP-based modem architectures and the design of flexible, digitally controlled, RF front-ends for handling a wide range of power levels, carriers, bandwidths, and modulation formats. These issues have not been solved yet in the commercial systems due to technology limitations and cost considerations.

In this chapter, we address the problem of designing an efficient DSP-based modem for SDRs. The modem we propose is based on PR-NMDFBs and it is able to handle high sample rates removing the current limitations on the bandwidth of the signal that can be processed digitally. We first demonstrate the capability of these engines of performing very wide band filtering and then we show how this capability can solve the SDR paradigm. In particular, this chapter is organized in seven main sections. Section 3.1 introduces the motivations of this chapter. Section 3.2 describes the theoretical model of NMDFBs and the mathematics behind them. The PR property is described in Section 3.3 and also suggestions on how to verify it in NMDFB chains are provided in the same section. Section 3.4 describes their practical implementation on digital circuits. Section 3.5 describes the wideband filtering processing through NMDFBs while some design suggestions are given in Section 3.6. Some examples of applications for communication systems are provided in Section 3.7.

3.2 NMDFBs Model

The theoretical model of NMDFBs has been presented in the past [23, 24]. For clarity we represent the basic block diagram Fig. 3.1. This block diagram is composed by three main parts:

- the analysis filter bank also referred to as analysis channelizer, which is composed of a filter bank and a vector of down samplers followed by a vector of complex heterodynes
- the intermediate processing matrix, which is a matrix of complex rotators
- the synthesis filter bank also referred to as synthesis channelizer, which is the dual of the analysis filter bank and it is composed by a vector of complex heterodynes followed by an up converter and a filter bank

The Z-transforms of the band pass filters composing the bank in the analysis channelizer are denoted as $H_m(Z)\, m = 0, 1, \ldots, M - 1$. They all have equal bandwidth, and each of them is centered on digital frequency $\theta_m = \frac{2\pi}{M}m$, $m = 0, 1, \ldots, M - 1$. Those filters are created by appropriately partitioning a low-pass prototype filter (LPPF) that is designed according to the required specifications. Let $h(n)$ be the impulse response of the low-pass prototype filter. The mth band pass filter is its heterodyned version and can be represented as $h_m(n) = h(n)\,e^{j\frac{2\pi}{M}mn}$, whose Z-transform is $H_m(Z) = H(e^{-j\frac{2\pi}{M}m}Z) = H\left(W_M^m Z\right)$, and $W_M \overset{\text{def}}{=} e^{-j\frac{2\pi}{M}}$.

Similar reasoning can be done for the synthesis filter bank whose low-pass prototype impulse response is indicated as $g(n)$. The mth filter in the synthesis bank is a heterodyned version of the low-pass prototype filter, $g_m(n) = g(n)\,e^{j\frac{2\pi}{M}mn}$, and its Z-transform is $G_m(Z) = G\left(W_M^m Z\right)$.

In the analysis filter bank a down sampling operation by a factor D, which is a generic integer that divides M, follows each band pass filter. After the down sampling operation a set of complex rotators whose values are $e^{-j\frac{2\pi}{M}mnD}$ is applied to the signal.

With these definitions, the output signal of the mth band pass filter in the analysis bank (see Fig. 3.2) is $v_m(n) = x(n) * h_m(n)$. The decimation by D causes D-fold aliases and can be written as $x_m(n) =$

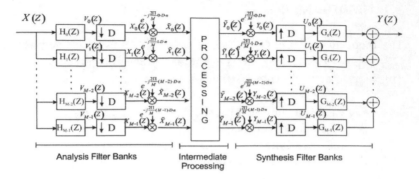

Analysis Filter Banks   Intermediate Processing   Synthesis Filter Banks

Figure 3.2 Analysis/synthesis filter bank model with intermediate processing matrix.

$v_m (Dn)$ for $n = 0, 1, \ldots, \infty$. The Z-transform of signal presented at the input to the intermediate processing matrix denoted as $\tilde{X}_m (Z)$ can be expressed as

$$\tilde{X}_m (Z) = \frac{1}{D} \sum_{d=0}^{D-1} X\left(Z^{1/D} W_D^d W_M^{-m}\right) H\left(Z^{1/D} W_D^d\right) \qquad (3.1)$$

Denote the intermediate processing transfer function for the mth filter in the bank to be $K_m(Z)$, for $m = 0, 1, \ldots M-1$. Thus, the input to the mth filter in the synthesis filter bank is $\tilde{Y}_m (Z) = K_m(Z)\tilde{X}_m (Z)$. Heterodyning $\tilde{Y}_m (Z)$ by $e^{j\frac{2\pi}{M}mnD}$ we obtain $Y_m (Z) = \tilde{Y}_m \left(Z W_M^{mD}\right)$ which can be expressed as

$$Y_m (Z) = \frac{1}{D} K\left(Z W_M^{mD}\right) \sum_{d=0}^{D-1} X\left(Z^{1/D} W_D^d\right) H\left(Z^{1/D} W_D^d W_M^m\right).$$

Signal $U_m (Z)$ is obtained by up sampling $Y_m (Z)$ by D, i.e., $U_m (Z) = Y_m \left(Z^D\right)$ and the final output of the SFBs $Y(Z)$ is

$$Y(Z) = \frac{1}{D} \sum_{d=0}^{D-1} X(Z W_D^d) \sum_{m=0}^{M-1} K(Z^D W_M^{mD}) H(Z W_D^d W_M^m) G(Z W_M^m) \qquad (3.2)$$

3.2.1 *Non-Maximally Decimated Filter Banks and Perfect Reconstruction Property*

Equation (3.2) can be compactly expressed in matrix form. Let us define the following column vectors:

$$\mathbf{G}(\mathbf{Z}) = \left[G\left(Z W_M^0\right) \dots G\left(Z W_M^{M-1}\right)\right]^T$$

$$\mathbf{H}(\mathbf{Z}) = \left[H\left(Z W_M^0 W_D^0\right) \dots H\left(Z W_M^{M-1} W_D^0\right)\right]^T$$

$$\bar{\mathbf{X}}(\mathbf{Z}) = \left[X\left(Z W_D^1\right) \dots X\left(Z W_D^{D-1}\right)\right]^T$$

$$\mathbf{X}(\mathbf{Z}) = \left[X\left(Z W_D^0\right), \bar{\mathbf{X}}(\mathbf{Z})\right]^T$$

We also define matrices:

$$\mathbb{H}(\mathbf{Z}) = \begin{bmatrix} H\left(Z W_M^0 W_D^0\right) & \cdots & H\left(Z W_M^0 W_D^{D-1}\right) \\ \vdots & \ddots & \vdots \\ H\left(Z W_M^{M-1} W_D^0\right) & \cdots & H\left(Z W_M^{M-1} W_D^{D-1}\right) \end{bmatrix}_{M \times D}$$

$$= \left[\mathbf{H}_{M \times 1} | \bar{\mathbb{H}}_{M \times (D-1)} \right]_{M \times D}$$

$$\mathbb{K}(\mathbf{Z}) = diag\left(K\left(Z^D W_M^{0D}\right), \dots, K\left(Z^D W_M^{(M-1)D}\right)\right)$$

$$= \begin{bmatrix} K\left(Z^D W_M^{0D}\right) & \cdots & 0 \\ \vdots & \ddots & \vdots \\ 0 & \cdots & K(Z^D W_M^{(M-1)D}) \end{bmatrix}_{M \times M}$$

Then, the matrix representation of Eq. (3.2) can be written as

$$Y(\mathbf{Z}) = \frac{1}{D} \mathbf{G}_{1 \times M}^T(\mathbf{Z}) \mathbb{K}_{M \times M}(\mathbf{Z}) \mathbb{H}_{M \times D}(\mathbf{Z}) \mathbf{X}_{D \times 1}(\mathbf{Z})$$

$$= \frac{1}{D} \mathbf{T}_{1 \times D}^{\mathbb{K}}(\mathbf{Z}) \mathbf{X}_{D \times 1}(\mathbf{Z}) \tag{3.3}$$

where $\mathbf{T}_{1 \times D}^{\mathbb{K}}(\mathbf{Z}) \overset{def}{=} \mathbf{G}_{1 \times M}^T(\mathbf{Z}) \mathbb{K}_{M \times M}(\mathbf{Z}) \mathbb{H}_{M \times D}(\mathbf{Z}) = \left[T_s^{\mathbb{K}}(Z) \mathbf{T}_A^{\mathbb{K}}(Z)\right]$ is the total transfer function for the M-path, decimate by D, AFBs and SFBs, $T_s^{\mathbb{K}}(Z) \overset{def}{=} \mathbf{G}_{1 \times M}^T(\mathbf{Z}) \mathbb{K}_{M \times M}(\mathbf{Z}) \mathbf{H}_{M \times 1}(\mathbf{Z})$ is the desired signal transfer function, whereas $\mathbf{T}_A^{\mathbb{K}}(Z) \overset{def}{=} \mathbf{G}_{1 \times M}^T(\mathbf{Z}) \mathbb{K}_{M \times M}(\mathbf{Z}) \bar{\mathbb{H}}_{M \times (D-1)}(\mathbf{Z})$ is the undesired aliasing transfer function.

We then rewrite Eq. (3.3) as

$$Y(\mathbf{Z}) = \frac{1}{D} T_s^{\mathbb{K}}(Z) X(Z) + \frac{1}{D} \mathbf{T}_A^{\mathbb{K}}(Z) \bar{X}(Z) \tag{3.4}$$

If the aliasing transfer function $\mathbf{T}_A^{\mathbb{K}}(Z) = \mathbf{0}_{1 \times (D-1)}$, the aliasing energy would be completely canceled:

$$\sum_{m=0}^{M-1} K\left(Z^D W_M^{mD}\right) H\left(Z W_D^d W_M^m\right) G\left(Z W_M^m\right) = 0,$$

$$\forall d = 1, \ldots, D - 1$$

Thus, the aliasing cancelation condition becomes

$$\sum_{m=0}^{M-1} H\left(Z W_D^d W_M^m\right) G\left(Z W_M^m\right) = 0, \forall d = 1, \ldots, D-1$$

Because the AFBs and SFBs are essentially the modulated version of their baseband low-pass prototype filter, we can remove the constant modulation W_M^m as well as the summation over m. Therefore, the condition that ensures aliasing cancelation is

$$H\left(Z W_D^d\right) G(Z) = 0, \forall d = 1, \ldots D-1 \qquad (3.5)$$

Note that, Eq. (3.5) holds regardless of the intermediate processing block.

Examine the first term in Eq. (3.4), the condition for producing a distortionless response for input signal $X(Z)$ is

$$T_s^{\mathbb{K}}(Z) = \sum_{m=0}^{M-1} K(Z^D W_M^{mD})\, H(Z W_M^m)\, G(Z W_M^m) = Z^{-n_D}$$

where n_D is a positive integer representing the total delay introduced by the analysis/synthesis chain, plus the intermediate processing. We do not require the intermediate processing matrix $\mathbb{K}_{M \times M}$ to participate in distortionless response, thus setting it to identity $\mathbb{K}_{M \times M} = \mathbb{I}_{M \times M}$, the distortion-less condition then becomes

$$\sum_{m=0}^{M-1} H\left(Z W_M^m\right) G(Z W_M^m) = Z^{-n_D} \qquad (3.6)$$

Therefore, in the absence of the intermediate processing matrix $\mathbb{K}_{M \times M}$, the perfect reconstruction condition for a NMDFB has to simultaneously satisfy Eqs. (3.5) and (3.6).

3.2.2 *Low-Pass Prototype Filter Design*

In general, the choices for the low-pass prototype filter in the analysis and synthesis engines, $H(Z)$ and $G(Z)$ are not unique. The non-maximally decimation property offers certain degrees of freedom for designing those filters. The goal is to cancel the aliasing and to verify the PR property. From Eq. (3.5), it can be seen that as long as

$H\left(Z\,W_D^d\right)$ and $G(Z)$, $\forall d = 1 \ldots D - 1$ do not share common pass band and certain part of their transition bands, the aliasing energy can be made arbitrarily small by increasing the prototype filters' stop-band performance (near perfect reconstruction). Furthermore Eq. (3.6) is satisfied when the composite response of $H\,(Z)$ and $G\,(Z)$ forms a Nyquist channel. One option for that is to design both $H\,(Z)$ and $G\,(Z)$ to be identical square root raised cosine (SRRC) filters. In our observation, if channelization [27, 28] is the desired operation this is a good option for designing $H\,(Z)$ and $G\,(Z)$ which gives a paraunitary filter bank. The square root raised cosine filters appear frequently in communications serving as a pair of fixed shaping and matched filter for the purpose of suppressing noise injected in between transmitter and receiver and maximizing the signal to noise ratio.

However, SRRC filters have poor stop-band performance [6]; thus another valid option is to let the analysis prototype filter $H(Z)$ be any Nyquist pulse and the synthesis prototype filter $G(Z)$ be designed via Remez algorithm satisfying Eqs. (3.5) and (3.7)

$$H(Z)\,G(Z) = H^{NYQ}(Z), \tag{3.7}$$

where $H^{NYQ}(Z)$ is any Nyquist pulse.

Summarizing, the design strategy for the analysis/synthesis low-pass prototype filters should give considerations to both in-band aliasing error described in Eq. (3.5), and distortionless condition described in Eq. (3.6). The in-band aliasing error can be bounded using proper filter design specification. The distortionless condition is met by forcing the product $H(Z)\,G(Z)$ to be a Nyquist pulse.

3.3 PR Property

In the previous section we have specified the mathematical conditions for designing NMDFBs with perfect reconstruction property. In this section we would like to give a more intuitive explanation on how to design analysis/synthesis chains with PR property and why this property is so important.

Nyquist filter presents the interesting property of having a band edge gain equal to 0.5 (or -6 dB). By using this filter as prototype in the analysis and/or synthesis channelizers, we place M of them across the whole spanned spectrum with each filter centered on kf_S/M. All adjacent filters exhibit -6 dB overlap at their band-edges. The channelizer working under this configuration is able to collect all the signal energy across its full operating spectrum range even if signals occupy more than one adjacent channel or it resides in the channel's overlapping transition bandwidths.

Nyquist pulse is the name given to the wave shapes $f(n)$ required to communicate over band-limited channels with no inter-symbol interference (ISI). When sampled at equally spaced time increments they have to verify the requirement of Eq. (3.8), which is known as Nyquist pulse criterion for zero ISI.

$$f(n) = \begin{cases} 0 \text{ if } n \neq 0 \\ 1 \text{ if } n = 0 \end{cases} \tag{3.8}$$

There are infinite such functions that satisfy this set of restrictions and this is why, ideally, we have infinite options for designing the low-pass prototype filters in PR channelizers. The one with minimum bandwidth is the ubiquitous $\sin(x)/x$, which is variously known as the cardinal pulse when used for band limited interpolation and the Nyquist pulse when used in pulse shaping. The transform of this wave shape, $R(f)$, is the unit area rectangle with spectral support $1/T$ Hz. Unfortunately this waveform is non-causal and further it resides on an infinite support. If the pulse resided on a finite support we could delay the response sufficiently for it to be causal. We have to form finite support approximations to the $\sin(x)/x$ pulse. The first approximation to this pulse is obtained by convolving the rectangular spectrum, $R(f)$, with an even symmetric, continuous spectrum $W(f)$ with finite support α/T. The convolution between $R(f)$ and $W(f)$ in the frequency domain is equivalent to a product in the time domain between the $r(t)$ and $w(t)$, where $w(t)$ is the inverse transform of $W(f)$. The effect of the spectral convolution is to increase the two-sided bandwidth from $1/T$ to $(1 + \alpha)/T$. The excess bandwidth α/T is the cost we incur to form filters on finite support. The term α is called the roll-off factor and is typically on the order of 0.5 to 0.1 with many systems using values of $\alpha = 0.2$. The transition bandwidth caused by the convolution is seen to exhibit odd symmetry about the half amplitude point of the original rectangular spectrum. This is a desired consequence of requiring even symmetry for the convolving spectral mass function. When the windowed signal is sampled at the symbol rate $1/T$ Hz, the spectral component residing beyond the $1/T$ bandwidth folds about the frequency $\pm 1/2T$ into the original bandwidth. This folded spectral component supplies the additional amplitude required to bring the spectrum to the constant amplitude of $R(f)$.

Following this reason, we note that the significant amplitude of the windowed wave shape is confined to an interval of approximate width $4T/\alpha$ so that a filter with $\alpha = 0.2$ spans approximately $20T$, or 20 symbol durations. We can elect to simply truncate the windowed impulse response to obtain a finite support filter, and often choose the truncation points at $\pm 2T/\alpha$. A second window, a rectangle, performs this truncation. The result of this second windowing operation is a second spectral convolution with its transform. This second convolution induces pass-band ripple and out-of-band side-lobes in the spectrum of the finite support Nyquist filter. The description of this band-limited spectrum normalized to unity pass-band gain is presented in Eq. (3.3)

$$
H_{NYQ}(w) = \begin{cases} 1 & \text{for } \dfrac{|w|}{w_{SYM}} \le (1-\alpha) \\[2mm] 0.5 * \left\{ 1 + \cos\left\{ \dfrac{2\pi}{\alpha} \left[\dfrac{w}{w_{SYM}} - (1-\alpha) \right] \right\} \right\} & \text{for } (1-\alpha) \le \dfrac{|w|}{w_{SYM}} \le (1+\alpha) \\[2mm] 0 & \text{for } \dfrac{|w|}{w_{SYM}} \ge (1+\alpha) \end{cases}
$$

$$(3.9)$$

The continuous time domain expression for the cosine-tapered Nyquist filter is shown in Eq. (3.10). Here we see the windowing operation of the Nyquist pulse as a product with the window that is the transform of the half-cosine spectrum.

$$
h_{NYQ}(t) = f_{SYM} \frac{\sin(\pi f_{SYM} t)}{(\pi f_{SYM} t)} \frac{\cos(\pi \alpha f_{SYM} t)}{[1 - (2\alpha f_{SYM} t)^2]}
$$

$$(3.10)$$

Since the Nyquist filter is band limited, we can form the samples of a digital filter by sampling the impulse response of the continuous filter. Normally this involves two operations. The first is a scaling factor applied to the impulse response by dividing by the sample rate, and the second is the sampling process in which we replace

__78__ _How to Perform Very Wideband Digital Filtering in Modern Software Defined Radios_

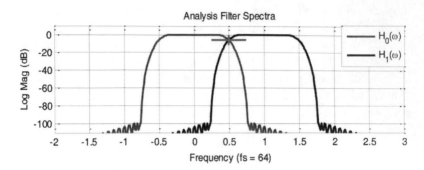

Figure 3.3 Spectra of analysis low-pass prototype filter and its heterodyned version.

t with nT_s or n/f_s. The sample rate must exceed the two-sided bandwidth of the filter that, due to the excess bandwidth, is wider than the symbol rate. It is standard to select the sample rate f_s to be an integer multiple of the symbol rate f_{SYM} so that the filter operates at M-samples per symbol. It is common to operate the filter at 4 or 8 samples per symbol.

When building analysis/synthesis chains that verify the property, the composite response of the two engines has to be a Nyquist pulse. As mentioned before, there are many possibilities for obtaining that. If wideband channelization is the goal, probably the selection of two SRRC filters in both the analysis and synthesis (in the transmitter and in the receiver) are a good option. If channelizers are used for other purposes inherent to communication systems, i.e. synchronization or channel equalization, a good option is to choose one of the low-pass prototype filters to be a Nyquist pulse and the other low-pass prototype filter to have a wider band which entirely covers the Nyquist filter band without affecting its PR property. This option is shown in Figs. 3.3 and 3.4. Which of the two prototype filter should be selected to be the Nyquist is application dependent.

3.4 Practical Implementation of PR-NMDFBs

The direct implementation of the theoretical model shown in Fig. 3.2 is impractical because building all the band pass filters for the

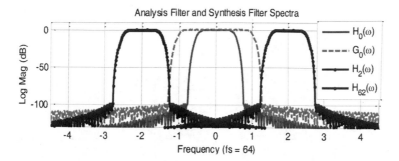

Figure 3.4 Spectra of analysis Nyquist filters with overlapped, in red dotted line, the synthesis low-pass prototype filter, which entirely covers its bandwidth.

analysis/synthesis filter banks is computationally prohibitive. Thus, in the next sections, we present and comment on the generalized polyphase implementation for the analysis and synthesis filter banks.

3.4.1 *Polyphase Analysis Channelizer*

In the analysis filter bank, the down sampling operation can be transferred to the input side of AFB via Noble identity [6, 7]. This leads to the polyphase implementation. The M-path partition of the mth analysis filter bank can be written as

$$H_m(Z) = H\left(ZW_M^m\right) = \sum_{k=0}^{M-1} Z^{-k} W_M^{-km} E_k\left(Z^M\right), \qquad (3.11)$$

where $E_k\left(Z^M\right)$ is the kth polyphase component obtained from the 2-D partition of the prototype low-pass filter $H(Z)$.

By using the Noble Identity to transfer the down-sampling operation through filter $H_m(Z)$, we obtain the polyphase form of $H_m(Z)$, denoted as $H_m^P(Z)$, which can be written as follows:

$$H_m^P(Z) = \sum_{k=0}^{M-1} Z^{-k} W_M^{-km} E_k\left(Z^{M/D}\right) \qquad (3.12)$$

Here we require that M is an integer multiple of D. Note that, the complex rotator W_M^{-km} in Eq. (3.12) can be implemented via IFFT simultaneously servicing all M channels [6, 7]. Also note from Fig.

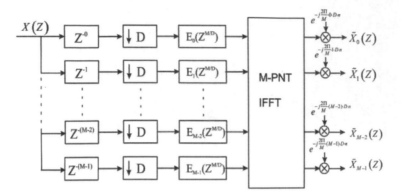

Figure 3.5 Generalized M-path, decimation by D, polyphase analysis channelizer.

3.2 that a complex heterodyne $e^{-j\frac{2\pi}{M}mnD}$ is applied to the mth analysis filter bank. The complete block diagram of a generalized M-path, decimation by D, polyphase analysis channelizer is shown in Fig. 3.5. In the case of $D = M/2$, the complex rotators $e^{-j\frac{2\pi}{M}mnD}$, followed by each polyphase component vanish if m is even; or they reduce to $(-1)^n$ when m is odd [25]. This phase rotation array can be offset by using a two-state circular shift buffer [27, 28] at the input to the FFT. In the first state (Flag = 0), all channels are weighted by 1, thus an M-point IFFT is performed. In the second stage (Flag = 1), all odd channels are weighted by -1, and even channels are weighted by 1. This phase offset can be absorbed by switching the upper half outputs with the bottom half outputs. Similar arrangement can be made for other decimation factors to avoid the complex shifters.

Based on Fig. 3.5, and following the just addressed comments, the block diagram for the M-Path, decimation by $D = M/2$ polyphase analysis channelizer used in [25, 27, 28] is represented in Fig. 3.6. Notice that we have again used the Noble Identity to further exchange the $D = M/2$ down sampler with delay element resulting in a two-port input commutator.

When the input commutator is so designed, the $M/2$ addresses to which the new $M/2$ input samples are delivered have to be first vacated by their former contents, the $M/2$ previous input samples. All the samples in the two-dimensional filter undergo a serpentine

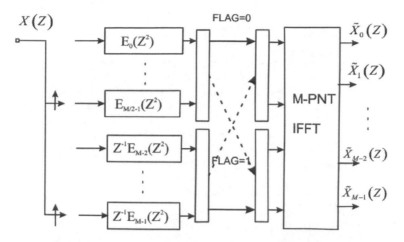

Figure 3.6 *M*-Path, decimation by $D = M/2$ polyphase analysis channelizer.

shift of $M/2$ samples with the $M/2$ samples in the bottom half of the first column sliding into the $M/2$ top addresses of the second column while the $M/2$ samples in the top half of the second column slide into the $M/2$ addresses in the bottom half of the second column, and so on. This is equivalent to performing a linear shift through the prototype one-dimensional filter prior to the polyphase partition. In reality, we do not perform the serpentine shift but rather perform an addressing manipulation that swaps two memory banks.

After each $M/2$-point data sequence is delivered to the partitioned M-stage polyphase filter, the shifted time origin of the input samples in the M-path filter has to be aligned with the stationary time origin of the IFFT phase rotators. We can understand the problem by visualizing, in Fig. 3.7, a single cycle of a sine wave extending over M samples being inserted in the input data register, the first column of the polyphase filter in segments of length $M/2$. We can assume that the data in the first $M/2$ addresses are phase aligned with the first $M/2$ samples of a single cycle of the sine wave offered by the IFFT.

When the second $M/2$ input samples are delivered to the input data register the first $M/2$ input samples shift to the second half of the M-length array. Its original starting point is now at address $M/2$ but the IFFT's origin still resides at address 0. The shift of the

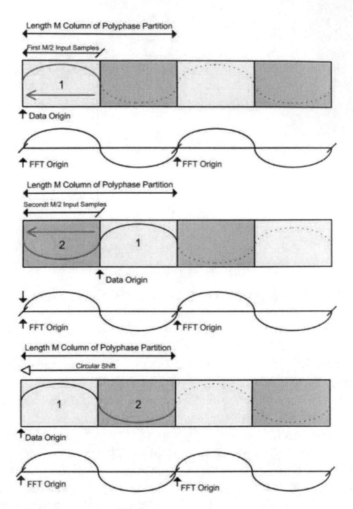

Figure 3.7 Phase reversal of M-point sinusoid input to $M/2$ path polyphase filter.

origin causes the input sine wave in the register to have the opposing phase of the sine wave formed by the IFFT; in fact the data shifting into the polyphase filter stages causes a frequency dependent phase shift: Odd-indexed frequency terms experience a phase shift of π radians for each successive N/2 shift of input data. This π radiants phase shift is due to the fact that the odd-indexed frequencies alias to the half sample rate when the input signal is down sampled by

$M/2$ while, when down sampled $M/2$-to-1, the sinusoids with an even number of cycles in the length M array alias to DC. We can compensate for the alternating signs in successive output samples by applying the appropriate phase correction to the spectral data as we extract successive time samples from the odd-indexed frequency bins of the IFFT. As mentioned before, the phase correction here is trivial and it is performed by the two-state circular shift buffer, but for other down-sampling ratios, the residual phase correction would require a complex multiply at each transform output port. The two-state circular shift buffer of the polyphase filter output data is implemented as an address-manipulated data swap. This data swap occurs on alternate input cycles and a simple two-state machine determines for which input cycle the output data swap is applied.

3.4.2 *Polyphase Synthesis Channelizer*

The polyphase synthesis channelizer is the dual system of the polyphase analysis channelizer and its high level block diagram is shown in Fig. 3.8. The M-path polyphase partition of the synthesis filter for the mth channel can be written as

$$G_m(Z) = G\left(Z W_M^m\right) = \sum_{k=0}^{M-1} Z^{-k} W_M^{-km} F_k\left(Z^M\right), \qquad (3.13)$$

where $F_k\left(Z^M\right)$ is the kth polyphase component.

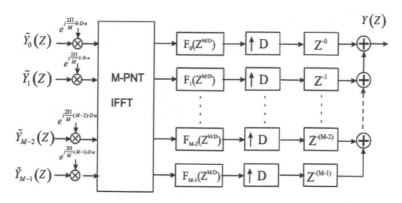

Figure 3.8 Generalized M-path, up sample by D, polyphase synthesis channelizer.

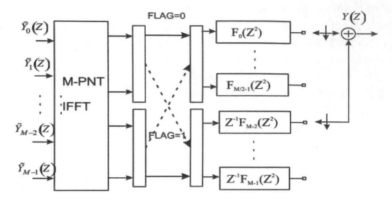

Figure 3.9 M-path, up sample by $D = M/2$, polyphase synthesis channelizer.

Sliding the up sampling operation through the partitioned filter $G_m(Z)$, we obtain the polyphase representation $G_m^p(Z)$.

$$G_m^p(Z) = \sum_{k=0}^{M-1} Z^{-k} W_M^{-km} F_k\left(Z^{M/D}\right) \tag{3.14}$$

Again, an IFFT block is placed in front of the synthesis polyphase filter servicing all M channels. Setting $D = M/2$ and carrying out similar arrangement as for the polyphase analysis channelizer, we obtain the efficient implementation of the synthesis engine, which is shown in Fig. 3.9 [25, 27, 28].

The polyphase implementation significantly reduces the computation complexity of the analysis/synthesis filter bank and allows building realizable systems.

Examining the polyphase forms shown in Figs. 3.5 to 3.9, in each analysis/synthesis bank operation interval, D samples from the incoming serial signal are processed; M samples are generated in the intermediate processing stage; and D output data samples are produced. Although the incoming signal seems to be partitioned into length D segments, the entire process is still continuous. Moreover, by varying decimation factor D, we acquire the capability of deciding how frequently the intermediate processing elements are applied. This flexibility is important since building block filters with time varying update support is one of our goals.

3.5 Spectral Shaping Approximation via Intermediate Processing Elements

An M-path non-maximally decimated analysis/synthesis filter bank chain acquires the perfect reconstruction property when the composite response of the low-pass prototype filters is a Nyquist pulse and the intermediate processing matrix, $\mathbb{K}_{M \times M}$, is an identity matrix.

Because the analysis filter banks are essentially a bank of digital band pass filters centered on multiples of $\frac{2\pi}{M}$, their outputs offer access to the frequency domain. At the output of the analysis channelizer, we have access to all the channels that are shifted to base band at a reduced sample rate. If we modify gain and phase of those channels as desired, we acquire the capability of approximating any desired spectral shape.

Following is a theoretical description of the spectral approximation capability through a matrix of complex rotators placed in between the analysis and synthesis engines. Given the discrete time Fourier transform (DTFT) of an arbitrary signal spectrum $S(\omega)$ and its corresponding finite time duration or truncated impulse response $s(n)$, $n = 0, 1, \ldots N_{\max}$, the goal is to synthesize or approximate it via an M-path PR-MNDFB. Let us consider the frequency domain and time domain filtering models shown in Fig. 3.10. In Fig. 3.10a, the input signal $x(n)$ is passed through an M-path, decimation by D, analysis/synthesis chain between which there is a diagonal IPE matrix $\mathbb{K}_{M \times M}$, whose $(m, m)^{\text{th}}$ entry is a complex scalar denoted as K_m, for $m = 0, 1, \ldots, M - 1$. In Fig. 3.10b, the same input signal, $x(n)$, is fed into an FIR filter $S(Z) = \mathcal{Z}\{s(n)\}$, and then delayed by n_D, where n_D is the total delay introduced by the M-path, decimation by D, analysis/synthesis chain. Using Eq. (3.4), the Z-transform of the output signal $y^f(n)$ corresponding to Fig. 3.10a is $Y^f(Z) = T_s^{\mathbb{K}}(Z) X(Z) + \mathbf{T}_A^{\mathbb{K}}(Z) \tilde{X}(Z)$. As mentioned earlier, the aliasing energy can be made arbitrarily small by increasing the filter's stop band attenuation. We now assume the aliasing energy is small and ignore it in the following analysis. Therefore, we rewrite $Y^f(Z)$ as

$$Y^f(Z) = T_s^{\mathbb{K}}(Z) X(Z). \qquad (3.15)$$

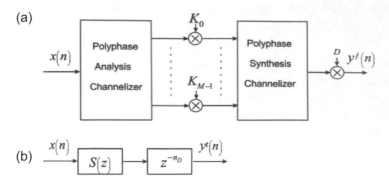

Figure 3.10 (a) Filtering model through PR-NMDFBs. (b) Standard time domain filtering model.

The Z-transform of the output signal $y^t(n)$ corresponding to the time domain filtering model shown in Fig. 3.10b can be written as

$$Y^t(Z) = S(Z) Z^{-n_D} X(Z) \tag{3.16}$$

The difference between the two filtering models can be defined as

$$E(Z) = \left[T_s^{\mathbb{K}}(Z) Z^{n_D} - S(Z) \right] X(Z) Z^{-n_D}. \tag{3.17}$$

Following Eq. (3.17), we can further define the error transfer function to be

$$T_{\mathcal{E}}(Z) = T_s^{\mathbb{K}}(Z) Z^{n_D} - S(Z) = \sum_{m=0}^{M-1} K_m H^{NYQ} \left(Z W_M^m \right) Z^{n_D} - S(Z). \tag{3.18}$$

Since the goal is to use PR analysis/synthesis chain with intermediate processing matrix to approximate at best the arbitrary spectrum $S(\omega)$, the error transfer function $T_{\mathcal{E}}(Z)$ must be reduced to zero or, if acceptable by the application requirements, close to zero. Recall that n_D is total delay of the Nyquist pulse $H^{NYQ}(Z W_M^m)$. Thus, term $H^{NYQ}(Z W_M^m) Z^{n_D}$ is the zero phase version of the chosen Nyquist pulse that has a real spectrum that we denote as $\tilde{H}^{NYQ}(Z W_M^m)$. We can further split Eq. (3.18) into real and imaginary parts as shown in

Eq. (3.19).

$$T_{\mathcal{E}}(\omega) = \left[\sum_{m=0}^{M-1} Re\{K_m\} \, \tilde{H}^{NYQ}(\omega - \omega_m) - Re\{S(\omega)\} \right]$$

$$+ j \left[\sum_{m=0}^{M-1} Im\{K_m\} \, \tilde{H}^{NYQ}(\omega - \omega_m) - Im\{S(\omega)\} \right] \quad (3.19)$$

Eq. (3.19) suggests the real and imaginary part of K_m can be independently designed based on the real and imaginary part of the target spectrum $S(\omega)$. In addition, $\tilde{H}^{NYQ}(\omega - \omega_m)$, is also a design parameter, since any waveforms satisfying Nyquist channel condition can be used to design the analysis/synthesis low-pass prototype filters.

In the next section, we explore two of the most significant options for approximating desired spectral shapes through PR-NMDFBs.

3.5.1 *Piecewise Constant Spectral Approximation*

Let us select the Nyquist pulse to be a *sinc* function. The magnitude response of the *sinc* pulse covers $\frac{1}{M}$ of the total bandwidth, and overlaps with its adjacent neighbors at its half power transition band, i.e., $\tilde{h}^{NYQ}(n) = \frac{1}{M} sinc\left(\frac{1}{M}n\right)$, for $-n_d \leq n \leq n_d$. For simplicity of analysis, we assume the magnitude response of the *sinc* pulse is a perfect rectangular window:

$$\tilde{H}^{NYQ}(\omega - \omega_m) = \begin{cases} 1, & \omega \in \left[\omega_m - \frac{\pi}{M}, \omega_m + \frac{\pi}{M}\right], \quad m = 0, 1, \ldots, M-1 \\ 0, & \text{Otherwise} \end{cases}.$$

Examine Eq. (3.18) and consider that the chosen Nyquist pulse only covers the mth band, i.e., $[\omega_m - \frac{\pi}{M}\omega_m + \frac{\pi}{M}]$. Therefore, the error transfer function for the mth band is

$$T_{E,m}(\omega) \stackrel{\text{def}}{=} K_m \tilde{H}^{NYQ}(\omega - \omega_m) - S(\omega), \quad \text{for } \omega \in \left[\omega_m - \frac{\pi}{M}, \omega_m + \frac{\pi}{M}\right]$$
$$(3.20)$$

Using midpoint approximation method, we let

$$K_m = S(\omega_m), \quad (3.21)$$

which results in a piecewise constant approximation of the given spectrum $S(\omega)$.

Now we want to evaluate the precision of our approximation. In order to do this, we assume the given spectrum $S(\omega)$ is an analytic function, and twice differentiable. Therefore, we may expand it using Taylor series around frequency ω_m for $\omega \in [\omega_m - \frac{\pi}{M}\omega_m + \frac{\pi}{M}]$ such that

$$S(\omega) = S(\omega_m) + \dot{S}(\eta)(\omega - \omega_m) \qquad (3.22)$$

for some $\eta \in [\omega_m - \frac{\pi}{M}\omega_m + \frac{\pi}{M}]$. Using Eqs. (3.20)–(3.22) and the zero phase property of the chosen Nyquist pulse, we can write the error transfer function, $T_{\mathcal{E},m}(\omega)$, as

$$T_{\mathcal{E},m}(\omega) = \left[S(\omega_m) - S(\omega_m) - \dot{S}(\eta)(\omega - \omega_m) \right] = \dot{S}(\eta)(\omega - \omega_m) \qquad (3.23)$$

Therefore, we arrive at the inequality:

$$|T_{\varepsilon,m}(\omega)| \leq \mathop{\text{Max}}_{\omega \,\in\, [\omega_m \frac{\pi}{M} \pm \frac{\pi}{M}]} |\dot{S}(\omega)| \cdot \frac{\pi}{M} = B_{\varepsilon,m} \qquad (3.24)$$

which is the maximum gain distortion due to the piecewise constant approximation. Because the low energy section of $S(\omega)$ is more sensitive to the phase distortion, the upper bound for the maximum phase distortion can be obtained by considering the smallest magnitude response within region $\omega \in \left[\omega_m - \frac{\pi}{M}, \omega_m + \frac{\pi}{M}\right]$. Let us define $\gamma_{s,m} \equiv \mathop{Min}_{\omega \,\in\, [\omega_m \frac{\pi}{M} \pm \frac{\pi}{M}]}$, the maximum phase distortion ϕ_m can be readily obtained as

$$\phi_m \leq \operatorname{atan}\left(\frac{B_{E,m}}{\sqrt{(\gamma_{s,m})^2 - (B_{E,m})^2}}\right), \quad \text{for } \gamma_{s,m} > B_{E,m}. \qquad (3.25)$$

Note that, if $\gamma_{s,m} \leq B_{E,m}$ the phase distortion is from $-\pi$ to π. However, this also implies that the target spectrum $S(\omega)$ has significant attenuation at ω_m and the signal around frequency ω_m may not have significant value.

Also, note from Eqs. (3.24) and (3.25) that the gain and phase distortion is related to the first derivative of the target spectrum and the filter bank's path number M. This implies that a fast variation in the target spectrum causes/increases both magnitude and phase distortion. However, increasing the path number M can always help in reducing the magnitude and phase errors.

A qualitative diagram of the piecewise constant approximation is given in Fig. 3.11. In our case the curve we want to approximate is the desired spectrum and we approximate it in the channelized domain

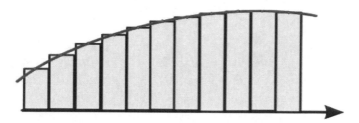

Figure 3.11 Qualitative diagram showing a piecewise constant approximation of the blue line.

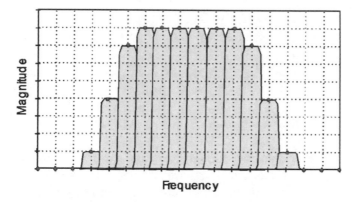

Figure 3.12 Qualitative diagram showing the piecewise constant approximation in the channelized domain.

by applying the appropriate complex rotators at the output of the analysis channelizer. The complex rotators change phase and gain of the channels as described. This process is qualitatively described in Fig. 3.12.

3.5.2 *Straight Line Spectral Approximation*

An immediate improvement over the piecewise constant approximation is to let Nyquist pulse, $\tilde{H}^{NYQ}(\omega)$, have a triangular magnitude response, which yields linear interpolation between adjacent filter banks. We then define the Nyquist pulse as

$$\tilde{h}^{NYQ}(n) = \frac{1}{M}sinc^2\left(\frac{1}{M}n\right), \ \text{for} - n_d \leq n \leq n_d$$

$$\tilde{H}^{NYQ}(\omega - \omega_m) = \begin{cases} 1 - \left| \frac{\omega - \omega_m}{2\pi/M} \right|, & \omega \in [\omega_m - \frac{2\pi}{M}, \omega_m + \frac{2\pi}{M}] \\ 0, & \text{Otherwise} \end{cases}.$$

Due to the underlying triangular pulse shape, the approximated spectrum by the complex elements K_m, K_{m+1} for $\omega \in [\omega_m \omega_{m+1}]$, can be written as $\{(\omega_{m+1} - \omega) \cdot K_m + \omega \cdot K_{m+1}\}$. Using Eq. (3.18), and only considering region $\omega \in [\omega_m \omega_{m+1}]$, we can define the error transfer function on the interval $\omega \in [\omega_m \omega_{m+1}]$ as

$$T_{\mathcal{E},m}(\omega) \overset{\text{def}}{=} (\omega_{m+1} - \omega) \cdot K_m + \omega \cdot K_{m+1} - S(\omega). \tag{3.26}$$

Set $K_m = S(\omega_m)$ and $K_{m+1} = S(\omega_{m+1})$, and expand $S(\omega)$ using Taylor series around $\omega = \omega_m$, we find

$$S(\omega) = S(\omega_m) + \dot{S}(\omega_m)(\omega - \omega_m) + \frac{1}{2}\ddot{S}(\eta)(\omega - \omega_m)^2 \tag{3.27}$$

for some $\eta \in [\omega_m \omega_{m+1}]$.

The maximum gain within region $[\omega_m \omega_{m+1}]$ can be bounded by

$$|T_{\mathcal{E},m}(\omega)| \leq \underset{\omega \in [\omega_m, \omega_{m+1}]}{\text{Max}} |\ddot{S}(\omega)| \cdot \frac{1}{2} \cdot \left(\frac{\pi}{M}\right)^2 = B_{\mathcal{E},m}. \tag{3.28}$$

And the bound for the maximum phase error can be obtained via Eq. (3.25).

Notice that the magnitude and phase distortion are directly proportional to the 2nd derivative of the target spectrum, and inversely proportional to M^2, the squared number of paths of the analysis/synthesis chain.

A qualitative diagram of the straight line approximation is given in Fig. 3.13. As mentioned before, the curve we want to approximate is the desired spectrum and we approximate it in the channelized domain by applying the appropriate complex rotators at the output of the analysis channelizer. The complex rotators change phase and gain of the channels as described. This process is qualitatively described in Fig. 3.14.

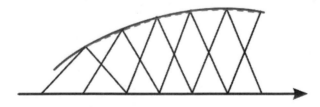

Figure 3.13 Qualitative diagram showing a straight line approximation of the blue line.

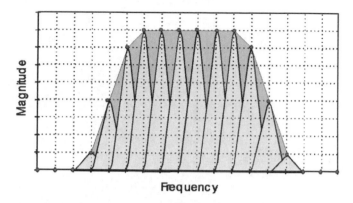

Figure 3.14 Qualitative diagram showing the straight line approximation in the channelized domain.

3.6 Design Options

Many options are available to us to achieve the PR property in NMDFBs. As long as the composite analysis-synthesis channel response is a Nyquist pulse, the signal at the output of the chain is perfectly reconstructed. The simplest option for achieving the PR property is to design two square root Nyquist filters in both the analysis and synthesis channelizers. However, a smarter choice, if the final task is not channelization but spectral shape approximation, i.e., wideband digital filtering, is to use a Nyquist pulse in the analysis channelizer and a wideband filter in the synthesis channelizer. The pass-band of the wider filter must be designed to completely cover the Nyquist pulse so that the PR property is preserved. When the rectangular window is selected as a Nyquist pulse, piecewise constant approximation of the desired spectral shape is performed and the error between the approximated and the desired spectrum is directly proportional to the first derivative of the desired spectrum. As mentioned before, an immediate improvement over the piecewise constant approximation is to let the Nyquist pulse in the analysis channelizer have a triangular magnitude response; this yields a linear interpolation between adjacent filter banks with an error, which is directly proportional to the second derivative of the desired spectrum. However, even though this

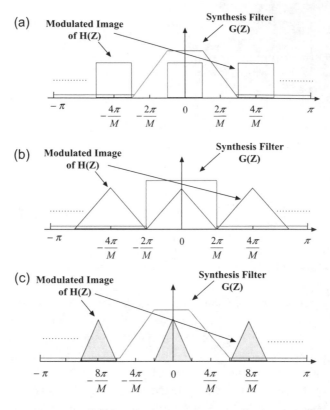

Figure 3.15 (a) $D = \frac{M}{2}$ rectangular design. (b) $D = \frac{M}{2}$ triangular design. (c) $D = \frac{M}{4}$ triangular design.

design provides a better spectral approximation, it requires a larger (non-critical) decimating factor with a consequent increase in the required computational speed. In fact, the triangular pulse is given by the convolution of two rectangular pulses and its bandwidth is twice the bandwidth of a rectangular pulse. Figures 3.15a–c provide the pictorial views, in the frequency domain, of those two different options. In particular Figs. 3.15a and 3.15b show the rectangular and triangular design options in the *M*:2 case. It is clear, from Fig. 3.15b that the *M*:2 decimation is not a feasible option in the triangular design case (we would need an infinitely long wideband filter). A better condition for this option is shown in Fig. 3.15c. The decimation factor here is *M*:4 and this selection would provide us enough room to design the wideband synthesis filter. However, as we will demonstrate in the next sections, also a decimation by M:3 is sufficient to use the triangular design option and to achieve linear interpolation performance.

3.6.1 *Rectangular Low-Pass Prototype Filter Design*

The analysis and synthesis filter banks have been extensively studied in the past [8, 13]. In the most standard maximally decimated bank, each analysis band pass filter is critically down sampled. The major benefit provided by the analysis/synthesis chain is the possibility of introducing intermediate processing stages between the analysis and synthesis banks. Those stages do operate at lowered sampling rate, thus guaranteeing computational efficiency. The perfect reconstruction property ensures that no signal loss occurs during the processing. Despite the efficiency they provide, critically down sampling filter banks introduce aliasing due to the folding of the channel transition bands. It is not easy to design critically decimated M-path perfect reconstruction filter bank with nearly perfect aliasing cancelation. Communication signals arc extremely fragile and sensitive to various types of distortion. Maximally decimated filter banks would introduce additional distortion with consequent performance losses. Therefore they are not an option to be considered for communication applications.

PR NMDFBs offer the option of applying intermediate processing elements while avoiding the aliasing problem due to the in-band folding of adjacent channels. In this section, we describe two options to achieve the PR property in NMDFBs and the constraint that they impose on the decimation factor. We decide to provide design examples in order to better clarify the theoretical concepts. In the following the design of $M = 64$ path analysis/synthesis perfect reconstruction filter bank with rectangular low-pass prototype filter design is proposed. As specified before, the selection of the prototype filter affects the decimation factor. In particular, the rectangular design, which has a rectangular Nyquist pulse in the analysis bank and a wideband pulse in the synthesis bank allows us to decimate the signal by a factor $D = \frac{M}{2}$ We design the 64-path NMDFB, decimation by 32, for a 100 dB dynamic range system. Our designs have been tested in Matlab. The analysis low-pass prototype filter can be designed as a windowed *sinc* function, with normalized bandwidth equal to $\frac{1}{M} = \frac{1}{64}$. The synthesis LPPF has to verify the following requirements:

- Its pass band has to cover the analysis prototype filter and it has to reject the modulated images of the analysis prototype filter.
- The nearest modulated image of the analysis prototype filter is located at $H\left(Z W_{32}^1\right) = H\left(Z W_{64}^2\right)$ (same as the negative frequency direction). Therefore, the pass band edge of the synthesis prototype filter is $\frac{\pi}{64}$, and its stop band edge is $\frac{3\pi}{64}$.

If we normalize each channel spacing to be one, i.e., $f_s = 64$, then the low-pass prototype filter pass band is from 0 to 0.5, and its stop band will be from 1.5 to 32.

Figure 3.16 shows the magnitude response of the designed analysis and synthesis prototype filters. In particular, the upper

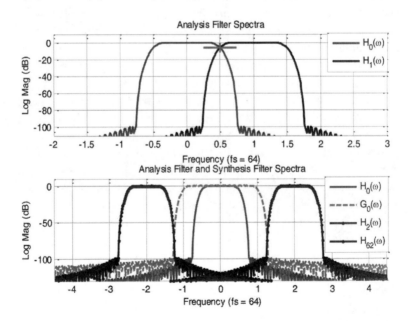

Figure 3.16 64-Path, decimation by 32, rectangular shaped design.

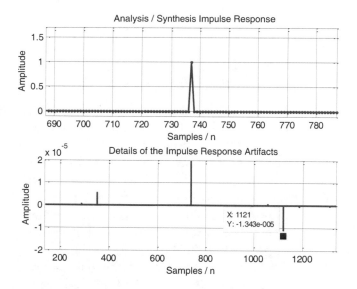

Figure 3.17   Impulse response of the analysis and synthesis filter bank.

subplot of Fig. 3.16 shows the magnitude response of the designed analysis filter $H_0(\omega)$ along with its frequency shifted version $H_1(\omega) = H_0(\omega - \frac{2\pi}{64})$. The two responses overlap at their half-power point and they are even symmetric around $\omega = \frac{\pi}{64}$, which makes them Nyquist pulse. The lower subplot of Fig. 3.16 shows the magnitude response of the designed synthesis filter (in dotted red line). We can see its pass band fully covers $H_0(\omega)$, while rejecting all other modulated images. The pass band of this synthesis is from 0 to 0.725, and its stop band from 1.275 to 32. The length of this filter is 769 taps, same as the analysis prototype filter.

Figure 3.17 shows the impulse response of the designed analysis/synthesis filter bank. Since it is a perfect reconstruction filter bank, the ideal output is simply the delayed version of the input impulse. In this case, as shown in the upper subplot, the total latency is 736 samples, which equals to the composite latency of analysis and synthesis prototype filter subtracted by 32. The subtraction by 32 is due to the polyphase implementation. The zoomed lower subplot shows the artifacts in the impulse response due to the reconstruction error and in-band aliasing. We can see that the biggest artifact has an amplitude of -1.343×10^{-5}, which is -97 dB.

3.6.2 *Triangular Low-Pass Prototype Filter Design*

The second option, in which a triangular pulse is used to achieve the PR property, allows us to design the banks with a decimation factor, $D = \frac{M}{3}$. The design of 60-path, decimated by 3, analysis/synthesis chain with triangular low-pass prototype filter is presented in this section. It has been found that any smaller decimation factor will cause aliasing and signal distortion. The analysis prototype filter has a bandwidth of $\frac{3\pi}{M}$. This filter can be generated, in Matlab, by windowing a squared *sinc* function. The proposed filter is shown in Fig. 3.18. In particular, in the upper subplot, the impulse response of the filter is shown. In the middle subplot, the frequency response of the filter is plotted. Here the scale on the Y axes is linear and the adjacent channel is also visualized to demonstrate the PR property.

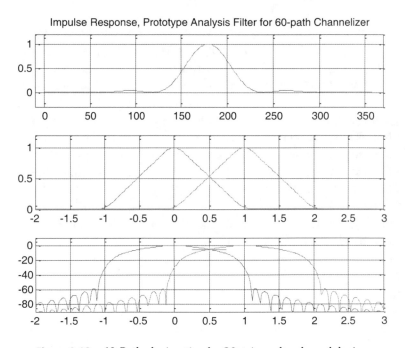

Figure 3.18   60-Path, decimation by 20, triangular shaped design.

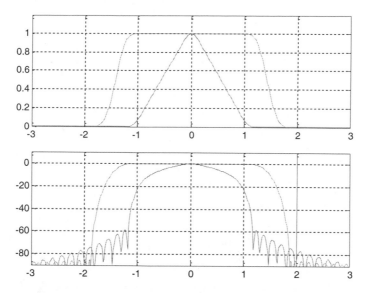

Figure 3.19 Analysis and synthesis prototype filters for a 60-path channelizer.

It is, in fact, clear from this figure that the filter responses overlap at their 0.5 gain point. In the lower subplot of Fig. 3.18 the same frequency responses are presented on a logarithmic scale.

Figure 3.19 shows the frequency view of the analysis low-pass prototype filter with overlapped frequency response of the synthesis low-pass prototype filter in both linear scale (upper subplot) and logarithmic scale (lower subplot).

To test the efficacy of the proposed design, we decided to pass a QAM constellation through the analysis/synthesis chain and look at the output. Figure 3.20 shows the constellation at the input of the analysis channelizer (after the shaping filter has been applied), while Fig. 3.21 shows the same constellation after the signal is passed through the processing chain, which also applies a frequency domain matched filter.

It is worth specifying that the length of the wideband synthesis filter is significantly reduced in the $D = \frac{M}{3}$ case compared to the $D = \frac{M}{2}$ case. This is because the modulated image of the analysis filter is further apart from its baseband copy. This allows having wider

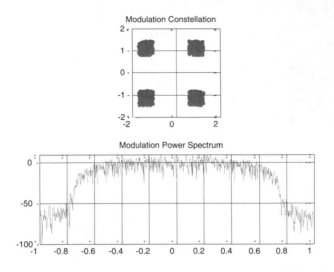

Figure 3.20   Shaped constellation diagram in input to the PR NMDFB.

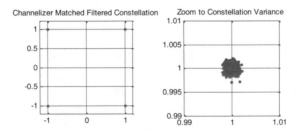

Figure 3.21 Signal constellation at the output of the PR NMDFB with applied frequency domain matched filter.

synthesis filter's transition bandwidth. However, the $D = \frac{M}{3}$ design needs to process data faster than the $D = \frac{M}{2}$ design.

3.7 Application Example

Multiple are the applications in which polyphase filter banks have already been utilized and multiple are the research topics open for finding novel and efficient applications of polyphase filter banks. In this chapter we focus on novel applications of PR NMDFBs in

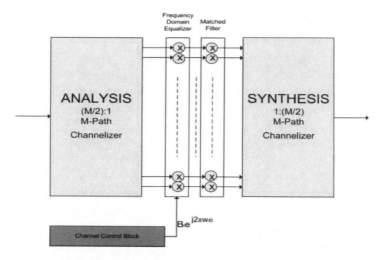

Figure 3.22 High level block diagram of proposed architecture for performing matched filtering and wireless channel equalization in the channelized domain.

communication systems. In particular we describe how to perform matched filtering and wireless channel equalization digitally, in very wideband systems. The results proposed here are preliminary and extended versions of the described approaches have being explored.

As shown in Fig. 3.22, the proposed equalizer architecture is formed by a 64-path PR non-maximally decimated (64:2) analysis-synthesis chain to which two sets of multiplier arrays have been added. This is a simplified block diagram in which the analysis and the synthesis can be built as depicted in Figs. 3.6 and 3.9 respectively. As anticipated, the analysis filter bank disassembles the input spectrum while simultaneously shifting its fragments to baseband. The dimensionality of such an engine should be designed according to the input signal and the available hardware resources. Also, workload issues help in the proper selection of the number of paths.

Once the signal fragments are at baseband and their sample rate has been properly decreased (it is now commensurate to the new reduced bandwidth) we can equalize them via intermediate processing elements. The equalization process is performed in the channelized domain by applying appropriate complex scalars to the output ports of the analysis channelizer. The complex scalars adjust the gain and phase of each channelizer channel undoing the effect of the wireless channel. The complex multipliers are selected according to the prior knowledge of the multipath channel which is provided to the system by a channel probe block. This scheme reproduces more standard equalizing schemes, thus channel knowledge is fundamental for adjusting the intermediate processing elements appropriately. They have to approximate the inverse channel response.

Before synthesizing the equalized spectral fragments we also perform matched-filtering on the signal in the channelized domain. This is done by applying the appropriate complex weights, which approximate the matched filter frequency response, to a set of intermediate processing elements. At the output of the synthesis channelizer, additional post processing may be applied to the filtered signal which might include arbitrarily interpolation to obtain two samples per symbol [28].

Figure 3.23 shows the impulse response, and the analysis filter spectra of the designed channelizer based on the triangular shaped spectral design. As expected the channelizer's overall impulse response is a Nyquist pulse. We emphasize the importance of requiring the analysis filter spectra to be a triangle. Figure 3.24 shows the transmitted QPSK signal constellation and its power spectrum. In the absence of channel and noise, the received and demodulated QPSK signal via the designed channelizer is shown in Fig. 3.25, where we can see that the channelizer has successfully accomplished perfect reconstruction as well as frequency domain matched filter tasks.

In Fig. 3.26 we apply a channel whose distortion profile is also displayed in the same figure. We can see, from the distortion profile, the channel causes sharp notches to the received signal which is considered to be a bad channel. A FIR equalizer usually does not perform well in this situation. Figure 3.27 demonstrates the distorted signal constellation as well as finer resolution detail of the distorted power spectrum.

Assuming the receiver has perfect knowledge about the channel, we then apply the equalization as the frequency domain inverse of the probed channel via the equalizer multiplier array. The equalized

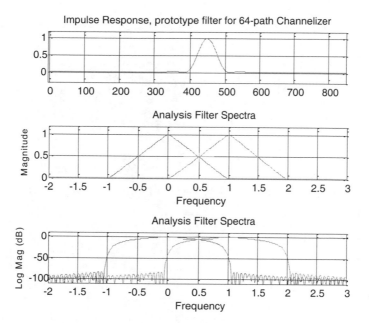

Figure 3.23 Channelizer prototype filter design.

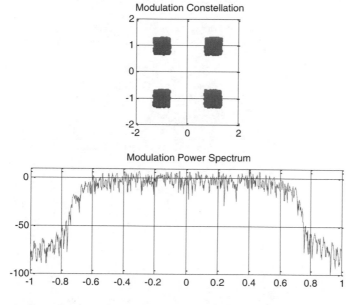

Figure 3.24 Transmitted signal constellation and spectrum.

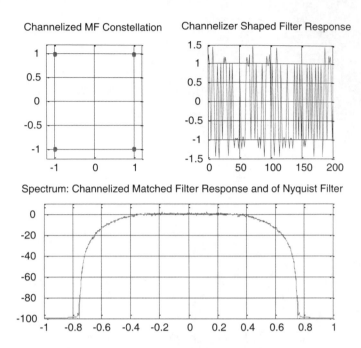

Figure 3.25 Demodulated signal without channel and noise.

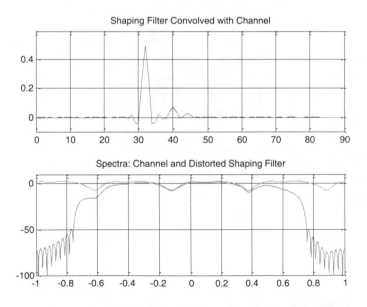

Figure 3.26 Channel distortion profile.

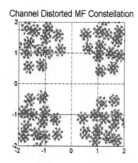

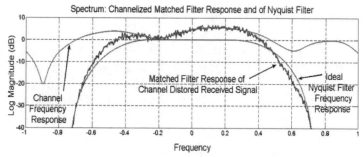

Figure 3.27 Received constellation and power spectrum.

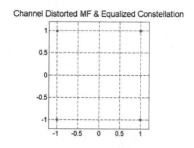

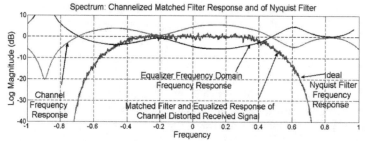

Figure 3.28 Equalized and matched filtered results.

results are explicitly shown in Fig. 3.28. We can see the channel introduced constellation dispersion has been significantly shrunk. The lower subplot of Fig. 3.28 shows spectrum of the channel (pink line), the equalization multiplier array response (black line), and the equalized and matched filtered signal spectrum. We can see from the spectra, the channel distortion has been dramatically mitigated.

3.8 Conclusions

In this chapter, we have presented a solution for solving the software-defined radio paradigm. One of the main problems in implementing fully digital radios is the capability of handling high sample rates. The signal sample rate increases when its bandwidth increases. In software radios we want to sample as wide bands as possible so that we can process them in the digital domain. The digital domain offers better performance and more flexibility than the analog domain. Different signals for different applications can lie in the received bandwidth. The digital modem, driven by a cognitive engine, will process them accordingly.

When the sample rate is high, even the simplest FIR filtering becomes a problem due to the hardware limitation of the current digital chips. To solve this issue we propose a wideband filtering method based on PR-NMDFBs. By having a matrix of complex intermediate elements between the analysis and synthesis channel-izers any filter frequency response can be well approximated. At the output of the analysis channelizer the sample rate is reduced at minimum thus the hardware clock speed does not represent a limitation anymore. After the signal has been filtered in the channelized domain it can be reconstructed and its sample rate can be increased as desired by the synthesis channelizer. No energy is lost in this process given the PR property.

At the end of this chapter, we give an example on how to utilize PR-NMDFBs for matched filtering and wireless channel equalization. This example gives the reader a hint on why PR-NMDFBs can represent the future of software-defined radios.

References

1. A. V. Oppenheim and R. W. Schafer, *Digital Signal Processing*, Englewood Cliffs, NJ, Prentice-Hall, 1975.

2. R. van Nee and R. Prasad, *OFDM Wireless Multimedia Communication*, Artech House Boston London, 2000.

3. D. Falconer S. L. Ariyavisitakul, A. Benyamin-Seeyar, and B. Eidson, Frequency domain equalization for single-carrier broadband wireless systems, *Communications Magazine, IEEE*, **40**(4), 58–66, April 2002.

4. J. Mitola, Cognitive radio architecture evolution, *Proceedings of IEEE*, **97**(4), April 2009.

5. J. G. Proakis and D. G. Manolakis, *Digital Signal Processing*, Prentice-Hall, 1996.

6. F. J. Harris, *Multirate Signal Processing for Communication Systems*, Prentice Hall, Upper Saddle River, New Jersey, 2004.

7. E. Venosa, F. Harris, and F. Palmieri, *On Software Radio: Sampling Rate Selection, Design and Synchronization*, Springer Science + Business Media, LLC, New York, NY, in press.

8. P. P. Vaidyanathan, Theory and design of a 4-channel maximally decimated quadrature mirror filters with arbitrary M having the perfectreconstruction property *IEEE Transaction on Acoustics, Speech and Signal Processing*, **ASSP-35**(4), April 1987.

9. T. A. Ramstad, Cosine-modulated analysis-synthesis filter bank with critical sampling and perfect reconstruction, *Proceedings of the International Conference on Acoustics, Speech and Signal Processing*, pp. 1789–1792, 1991.

10. Y. Lin and P. P. Vaidyanathan, Linear phase cosine modulated maximally decimated filter banks with perfect reconstruction, *IEEE Transactions on Signal Processing*, **43**, pp. 2525–2539 1995.

11. M. Vetterli and D. Le Gall, Perfect reconstruction FIR filter banks: Some properties and factorizations, *IEEE Transactions on Acoustics, Speech, and Signal Processing*, **37**(7), 1057–1071, July 1989.

12. V. Jain and R. Crochiere, A novel approach to the design of analysis/Synthesis filter banks *IEEE International Conference on Acoustics, Speech, and Signal Processing*, **8**, 228–231, April 1983, doi: 10.1109/ICASSP.1983.1172208.

13. P. P. Vaidyanathan, *Multirate Systems and Filter Banks* Prentice Hall Signal Processing Series, Englewood Cliffs, NJ 1993.

14. G. Strang and T. Nguyen, *Wavelets and Filter Banks* Wellesley College 2nd ed., 1996.

15. N. J. Fliege, *Multirate Digital Signal Processing*, Wiley, Chichester, UK, 1994.

16. P. N. Heller, T. Karp, and T. Q. Nguyen, A general formulation of modulated filter banks, *Signal Processing, IEEE Transactions on*, **47**(4), pp. 986–1002, April 1999.

17. T. Q. Nguyen, Near-perfect-reconstruction pseudo-QMF banks, *Signal Processing, IEEE Transactions on*, **42**(1), pp. 65, 76, January 1994.

18. S. S. Yin, S. C. Chan, and K. M. Tsui, On the design of nearly-PR and PR FIR cosine modulated filter banks having approximate cosinerolloff transition band *Circuits and Systems II: Express Briefs, IEEE Transactions on*, **55**(6), pp. 571, 575, June 2008.

19. G. Doblinger, A fast design method for perfectreconstruction uniform cosinemodulated filter banks *Signal Processing, IEEE Transactions on*, **60**(12), pp. 6693, 6697, December 2012.

20. T. D. Tran, M-channel linear phase perfect reconstruction filter bank with rational coefficients, *Circuits and Systems I: Fundamental Theory and Applications, IEEE Transactions on*, **49**(7), 914, 927, July 2002.

21. R. B. Casey and T. Karp, Performance analysis and prototype filter design for perfect-reconstruction cosine-modulated filter banks with fixed-point implementation *Circuits and Systems II: Express Briefs, IEEE Transactions on*, **52**(8), 452, 456, August 2005.

22. H. Bolcskei and F. Hlawatsch, Oversampled cosine modulated filter banks with perfect reconstruction, *Circuits and Systems II: Analog and Digital Signal Processing, IEEE Transactions on*, **45**(8), 1057–1071, August 1998.

23. Z. Cvetkovic and M. Vetterli, Oversampled filter banks, *Signal Processing, IEEE Transactions on*, **46**(5), 1245, 1255, May 1998.

24. H. Bolcskei, F. Hlawatsch, and H. G. Feichtinger, Frame-theoretic analysis of oversampled filter banks, *Signal Processing, IEEE Transactions on*, **46**(12), 3256–3268, December 1998.

25. T. Karp and N. J. Fliege, Modified DFT filter banks with perfect reconstruction, *Circuits and Systems II: Analog and Digital Signal Processing, IEEE Transactions on*, **46**(11), 1404–1414, November 1999.

26. J. M. de Haan, *Filter Bank Design for Subband Adaptive Filtering* Phd thesis, Department of Telecommunications and Signal Processing, Blekinge Institute of Technology, Sweden, 2001.

27. F. Harris, X. Chen, E. Venosa and B. D. Rao, Wideband 160-channel polyphase filter bank cable TV channeliser, *Signal Processing, IET,* **5**(3), 325–332, June 2011.

28. F. Harris, E. Venosa, X. Chen and B. D. Rao, Polyphase analysis filter bank down-converts unequal channel bandwidths with arbitrary center frequencies *Analog Integrated Circuits and Signal Processing,* **71**(3), 481–494, 2012.

29. A. Viholainen, J. Alhava, and M. Renfors, Efficient implementation of $2\times$ oversampled exponentially modulated filter banks *Circuits and Systems II: Express Briefs, IEEE Transactions on,* **53**(10), 1138, 1142, October 2006.

30. D. Pinchon, and P. Siohan, Oversampled paraunitary DFT filter banks: A general construction algorithm and some specific solutions *Signal Processing, IEEE Transactions on,* **59**(7), 3058, 3070, July 2011.

31. T. Tanaka, A direct design of oversampled perfect reconstruction FIR filter banks *Signal Processing, IEEE Transactions on,* **54**(8), 3011, 3022, August 2006.

32. L. Chai, J. Zhang, and Y. Sheng, Optimal design of oversampled synthesis FBs with lattice structure constraints *Signal Processing, IEEE Transactions on,* **59**(8), 3549, 3559, August 2011.

33. Y. C. Lim and Y. Lian, Frequency-response masking approach for digital filter design: Complexity reduction via masking filter factorization, *Circuits and Systems II: Analog and Digital Signal Processing, IEEE Transactions on,* **41**(8), 518, 525, August 1994.

34. Y. C. Lim and R. Yang, On the synthesis of very sharp decimators and interpolators using the frequency-response masking technique, *Signal Processing, IEEE Transactions on ,* **53**(4), 1387–1397, April 2005.

35. L. Rosenbaum, P. Lowenborg, H. Johansson, Cosine and sine modulated FIR filter banks utilizing the frequency-response masking approach, *Circuits and Systems, 2003. ISCAS '03. Proceedings of the 2003 International Symposium on,* **3**, III-882, III-885 25–28, May 2003.

36. Z. U. Sheikh, H. Johansson, Efficient wide-band FIR LTI systems derived via multi-rate techniques and sparse bandpass filters *Signal Processing, IEEE Transactions on,* **60**(7), 3859, 3863, July 2012.

37. F. Harris, E. Venosa, C. Xiaofei, and B. Rao, Variable bandwidth M-path filter with fixed coefficients formed by M-path polyphase filter engines, *Circuit Theory and Design (ECCTD), 2011 20th European Conference on,* pp. 5,8, 29–31, August 2011.

38. F. Harris and W. Lowdermilk, Software defined radio: A chapter, *IEEE Instrumentation and Measurement Magazine*, February 2010.

39. L. R Rabiner and B. Gold, *Theory and Application of Digital Signal Processing*, Prentice-Hall, Englewood Cliffs 1975.

40. F. Harris, Performance and design of Farrow filter used for arbitrary resampling, *Digital Signal Processing Proceedings, 1997 (DSP 97), 13th International Conference on*, **2**, 595–599, 2–4, July 1997.

41. G. M. Kranc, Input-output analysis of multirate feedback systems, *IRE Transaction on Automatic Control*, **AC-2**, 21–28, 1956.

42. E. I. Jury and F. J. Mullin, The analysis of sampled-data control systems with a periodically time-varying sampling rate, *Automatic Control, IRE Transactions on*, **AC-4**, 15–21, 1959.

43. P. Vary and U. Heutev, A short-time spectrum analyzer with polyphase-network and DFT, *Signal Processing*, **2**(1), 55–65, January 1980.

44. R. W. Shafer and L. R. Rabiner, Design of digital filter banks for speech analysis, *Bell System Technical Journal*, **50**, 3097–3115, December 1971.

45. M. Bellanger, G. Bonnerot, and M. Coudreuse, Digital filtering by polyphase network: Application to sample-rate alteration and filter bank, *IEEE Transaction on Acoustic, Speech and Signal Processing*, **24**(2), 109–114, April 1976.

46. M. Bellanger and J. Daguet, TDM-FDM transmultiplexer: Digital polyphase and FFT, *IEEE Transaction on Communications*, **22**(9), 1199–1205, September 1974.

Chapter 4

A Survey of Digital All-Pass Filter-Based Real and Complex Adaptive Notch Filters

P. T. Wheeler,[a] J. A. Chambers,[a] and P. A. Regalia[b]

[a] *EESE, Loughborough University, UK*
[b] *EECS, National Science Foundation, Arlington, Virginia, USA*
p.wheeler2@lboro.ac.uk, j.a.chambers@lboro.ac.uk, regalia@cua.edu

4.1 Introduction

As a tribute to the pioneer, Professor Tony Constantinides, of all-pass transformation based digital filter design, this article, jointly authored by one of his former PhD students and another international researcher in the field, reviews how all-pass filters can also be exploited to design efficient structures for adaptive notch filters.

Initially, real second-order all-pass adaptive notch filters are considered in terms of their z-domain transfer functions and the implications of using equation-error[a] and output-error learning

---

[a] We adopt the term "equation-error" to represent algorithms which are not proper gradient descent procedures, although some authors apply the term "instrumental variable", which is the case in Ljung (1977).

Trends in Digital Signal Processing: A Festschrift in Honour of A. G. Constantinides
Edited by Yong Ching Lim, Hon Keung Kwan, and Wan-Chi Siu
Copyright © 2016 Pan Stanford Publishing Pte. Ltd.
ISBN 978-981-4669-50-4 (Hardcover), 978-981-4669-51-1 (eBook)
www.panstanford.com

algorithms are discussed. Useful characteristics such as orthogonal bandwidth and notch frequency parameters are highlighted together with numerical advantages resulting from structurally all-pass designs. Comparative evaluations in the context of single and multiple frequency tracking, through cascading adaptive notch filters, are included.

More recent extensions of these designs to complex adaptive notch filters are also described together with learning schemes for both the bandwidth and notch frequency parameters. Analysis is included to confirm the convergence properties of these schemes and further performance evaluations in terms of objective statistical measures such as bias and variance are used to support the advantage of exploiting of all-pass structures in complex adaptive notch filter design.

This chapter is structured as follows: Section 4.2 provides an analysis of four real adaptive notch filters. Section 4.3 shows the development of two of these structures into a form capable of tracking complex sinusoid signals. Section 4.4 investigates tracking complex-valued chirp signals with the two structures. Section 4.5 investigates adapting the notch bandwidth parameter in one of these structures. Section 4.6 concludes this chapter.

4.2 Evaluation of Four Adaptive Notch Filters

The background behind the first section of this chapter is that over the last three decades various structures have been proposed to perform adaptive notch filtering; however, a critical comparison of the key important approaches has not been performed for tracking multiple real sinusoid signals (RSSs). Hence, as a structure may excel under certain conditions, but may be weak in other scenarios; we believe it is timely to undertake this study.

Therefore, we consider four structures due to Chambers and Constantinides (1990), Regalia (1991), Cho et al. (1989) and Kwan and Martin (1989). We evaluate their performance in tracking two and three sinusoid signals and estimate their accuracies statistically. These four structures all utilise the normalised least mean square

(NLMS) type of learning algorithm, thereby permitting a fair comparative study.

In the past real designs have been created with constrained poles and zeros, either through "all-pass decompositions" Chambers and Constantinides (1990), Regalia (1991), Cho et al. (1989), or by" direct coefficient scaling' (DCS) Kwan and Martin (1989). In this investigation only one approach uses DCS, which is Kwan and Martin (1989), and historically, all-pass variations have been developed more recently than DCS methods. Generally, all-pass designs are computationally simpler and usually deliver superior tracking performance, when compared to structures based on DCS; so naturally are currently the preferred choice. One further observation is that DCS solutions alter the magnitude response of a filter, whilst an all-pass solution passes all frequencies unaltered.

When tracking multiple sinusoid signals either equation-error or output-error solutions are available, which take the form of cascading DCS or all-pass structures. Hence Fig. 4.1 shows diagrammatically the difference between equation-error and output-error cascade structures.

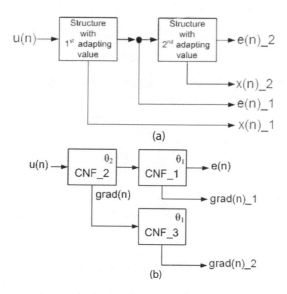

Figure 4.1 The difference between (a) an equation-error approach and (b) an output-error approach, for tracking two sinusoid signals.

An equation-error approach utilises a local error $e(n)$, and filter regressor signal term $x(n)$ for each notch filter in the cascade. Therefore, in the equation-error approach, each notch filter is tracking an individual frequency, which is being fed from the output of the previous notch filter, where the previous notch filter is assumed to have removed the frequency it has tracked from the input to the next notch filter in the chain. In Fig. 4.1a, the local errors are shown as $e(n)\_1$ and $e(n)\_2$; then the regressor terms used in the frequency updates are defined as $x(n)\_1$ and $x(n)\_2$.

On the other hand, an output-error approach minimises some function of the 'overall' error $e(n)$, which is typically the squared error, and creates a gradient term $grad(n)$ for each arm of the structure, which is shown as $grad(n)\_1$ and $grad(n)\_2$: in Fig. 4.1b.

Such gradient terms will generally need higher complexity for their realisation than an equation-error structure; however, as will be shown in the later simulations, output-error approaches yield improved performance for multiple sinusoid tracking.

In the next part of this section, we show the synthesis of the four structures.

4.2.1 Synthesising the Four Structures

Now to introduce the notch filters under study, initially for Regalia's and Chambers and Constantinides' approaches, a notch filter is produced as shown in Fig. 4.2; therefore, the notch transfer function

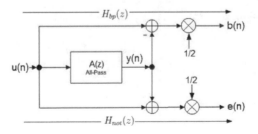

Figure 4.2 A block diagram showing how a notch filter is produced using an all-pass structure; herein the bandpass output is denoted as $b(n)$, and the notch output is denoted as $e(n)$.

for these structures is

$$H_{not}(z) = \frac{1}{2}[1 + A(z)].$$ (4.1)

Then moving on, the four methods are summarised in the following four parts of this section.

4.2.1.1 Chambers and Constantinides' NFB all-pass structure

First, Chambers and Constantinides' NFB approach has the following notch transfer equation:

$$H_{not}(z) = \frac{(1+\alpha)}{2} \frac{1 - 2\beta z^{-1} + z^{-2}}{1 - (1+\alpha)\beta z^{-1} + \alpha z^{-2}};$$ (4.2)

herein, α is the pole radius squared, and $\beta = \cos \omega_0$. Then, β is updated by applying the NLMS equation as follows:

$$\beta(n) = \beta(n-1) - \mu \frac{e(n)grad(n)}{\psi(n)},$$ (4.3)

where $\psi(n) = \psi(n-1)\gamma + (1-\gamma)grad(n)^2$, and the gradient term: $grad(n)$, may be implemented as shown in Fig. 4.3.

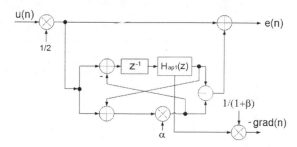

Figure 4.3 Chambers and Constantinides' NFB structure with output-error gradient term.

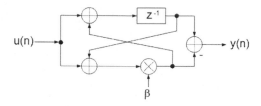

Figure 4.4 The all-pass filter $H_{ap1}(z)$ included in Fig. 4.3

4.2.1.2 Regalia's all-pass solution

The second structure: Regalia's all-pass method, contains $x(n)$ which is a regressor term.

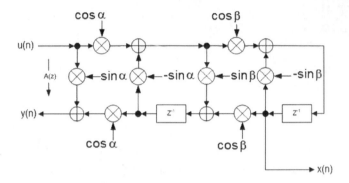

Figure 4.5 The implementation of the all-pass filter A(z) in Regalia's approach.

The notch transfer function of this structure is the same as Chambers and Constantinides' NFB approach, which is included as equation (4.2).

In Regalia's structure, r is the pole radius, therefore $\alpha = r^2$; and $\beta = -\cos \omega_0$.

The parameter β is updated by applying the NLMS equation as follows:

$$\beta(n) = \beta(n-1) - \mu \frac{e(n)x(n)}{\psi(n)}; \qquad (4.4)$$

herein, $\psi(n) = \psi(n-1)\gamma + (1-\gamma)(x(n))^2$.

4.2.1.3 Cho, Choi and Lee's all-pass method

The transfer function for Cho, Choi and Lee's structure is

$$H(z) = \frac{1 + \beta(1+k_1)z^{-1} + k_1 z^{-2}}{1 + \beta(1+a_1)z^{-1} + a_1 z^{-2}}; \qquad (4.5)$$

herein $a_1 = \alpha k_1$, $k_1 = 1$ and $\beta = -\cos \omega_0$.

Then to implement the update the following parameters are calculated: $A(n) = 2.x(n-1)$, $B(n) = x(n-2) + x(n-1)$, $C(n) = \gamma C(n-1) + A(n).B(n)$, $D(n) = \gamma D(n-1) + A(n)^2$, wherein $x(n)$ is the regressor term. Please note that as shown above, an additional delay

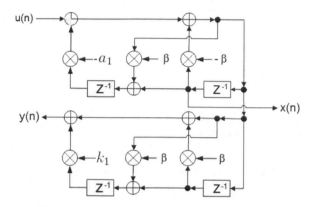

Figure 4.6   Cho, Choi and Lee's all-pass structure.

is required to generate the $B(n)$ parameter; also observe that no adaptation gain is used in this implementation, although the authors recommend applying a forgetting factor γ of 0.5. Also, upper case letters are used to follow the convention in Cho et al. (1989), as they correspond to calculating parameters which form the reflection coefficients.

These parameters then adapt β via the update

$$\beta = -\frac{C(n)}{D(n)}. \tag{4.6}$$

4.2.1.4 Kwan and Martin's DCS solution

The notch transfer function for Kwan and Martin's structure is

$$H_{not}(z) = \frac{2-\alpha}{2} \frac{1 - \frac{2(2-\alpha-\beta^2)}{2-\alpha}z^{-1} + z^{-2}}{1 - (2-\alpha-\beta^2)z^{-1} + (1-\alpha)z^{-2}}, \tag{4.7}$$

wherein $r = \sqrt{1-\alpha}$, and $\beta = \sqrt{1-r^2 - 2r\cos\omega_0}$, herein ω_0 is the notch frequency. The sensitivity output $s'(n)$, which equates to the gradient with the adjustment $grad(n) = \frac{2s'(n)}{\alpha}$, updates the tracking

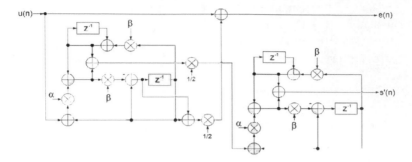

Figure 4.7 Kwan and Martin's DCS structure implemented to track a single sinusoid signal, which is created from two bi-quads, although the second bi-quad may be simplified slightly.

parameter β via the normalised least mean square (NLMS) update as follows:

$$\beta(n) = \beta(n-1) - \mu\frac{e(n)grad(n)}{\psi(n)}; \qquad (4.8)$$

herein, μ is the adaptation gain, and $\psi(n) = \psi(n-1)\gamma + (1 - \gamma)grad(n)^2$, where $0 \ll \gamma < 1$, which is the forgetting factor.

Observe that all functions admit orthogonal tuning, as the bandwidth and tracking parameters are clearly separable for all four of these structures; thus α tunes the frequency of the notch and β the bandwidth.

Please note that the estimated bias and variance in the frequency estimates presented in this chapter have been calculated from the final 200 values in each simulation, i.e. when the solutions have fully converged, although complex-valued chirp signals should be considered differently, and most of their range should be considered, with the exception of when the estimate is initially locating the target signal.

In the next section, we present the results obtained from tracking multiple RSSs. These results are presented in Figs. 4.8 and 4.9 and Tables 4.1 and 4.2, where the first set of results is for tracking two sinusoids, and the second set of results is for tracking three sinusoids. Please note that the results in this section have been obtained using an ensemble average of ten trials, which has been found sufficient to obtain statistically stable results.

4.2.2 Tracking Two Real Sinusoid Signals

To compare these four structures, initially we consider tracking a single frequency ω_0, for a RSS of the form

$$u(n) = S\sin(\omega_0 n + \phi) + w(n), \tag{4.9}$$

where S defines the SNR, which is a scale factor, ϕ is a random phase uniformly distributed over $(0, 2\pi)$, and the term $w(n)$ is zero mean unity variance white noise.

The results in Table 4.1 correspond to the use of two notch filters that are initialised at 0.6283 and 0.6912 radians, with target frequencies of $\omega_1 = 0.8796$ and $\omega_2 = 0.7540$. These signals have amplitudes of 1 and 0.01, and the variance of the noise added to the signals was 0.01, which corresponds to signal to noise ratios (SNR) of 17 and -3 dB. To facilitate consistency throughout these results, α the notch bandwidth parameter has been set to 0.9025, which is equivalent to the pole radius parameter r, in two of these structures. Also note that we optimised the performance of each algorithm through the adaptation gains (μ), to gain similar initial convergence, whilst ensuring convergence to a satisfactory solution.

Table 4.1 Results for tracking two RSSs, wherein $\Delta\omega_1$ and $\Delta\omega_2$ are sample biases and σ_1^2 and σ_2^2 are the sample variances, and a † labels a value smaller than 0.00005

Method	$\Delta\omega_1$	$\Delta\omega_2$	σ_1^2	σ_2^2
Chambers and Constantinides	0.0011	0.000†	3.556 exp -4	2.491 exp -5
Regalia	0.0018	0.0002	2.743 exp -3	1.553 exp -4
Cho, Choi and Lee	-0.0005	0.0001	1.034 exp -3	3.224 exp -4
Kwan and Martin	0.0002	0.000†	3.426 exp -4	2.699 exp -5

Next we consider the results, and in Fig. 4.8 observe that Regalia's approach does not fully converge to the solution, and if the sample range is extended the value stabilises at approximately 0.9.

It should also be clarified that frequency values in simulations are presented in terms of radians; please also note that the key shown in Fig. 4.8 also applies to Fig. 4.9. Therefore, the tracking performance of each structure simulated is recorded in the following colours:

Chambers and Constantinides (1990) is presented in blue, Regalia (1991) is shown as red, Cho et al. (1989) is displayed as black, and Kwan and Martin (1989) is shown in green.

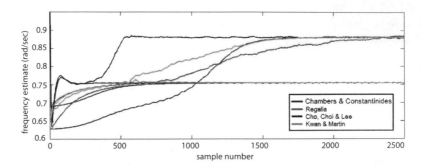

Figure 4.8   The results for tracking two real sinusoids, which correspond to the data in Table 4.1.

Notice all structures quickly lock onto the frequency ω_2: 0.7540, whereas there is more variation in the time to lock onto the second frequency; interestingly, ω_2 is tracked by the first notch filter in the cascade; however, sometimes Kwan and Martin's DCS method tracks ω_1 first: 0.8796, and when this occurs its convergence is poor. Analysing the results further shows that Cho, Choi and Lee's structure converges the fastest, with Chambers and Constantinides' solution providing the second quickest convergence; however, Chambers and Constantinides' structure also achieves the least overall variance in its final solution.

4.2.3 *Tracking Three Real Sinusoid Signals*

The results collated in Table 4.2 are provided for three cascaded notch filters that were initialised to 1.131, 1.257 and 1.382 which correspond to the target frequencies, and then the frequency at 1.131 instantaneously hops to 1.508 at sample number 1000. These signals have amplitudes of 1.24, 1.02 and 1.00, the noise was added to yield SNRs of 4.1, 2.4 and 2.2 dB.

Table 4.2 Results for tracking three real sinusoid signals, wherein $\Delta\omega_1$–$\Delta\omega_3$ are the sample biases and σ_1^2–σ_3^2 are the sample variances

Method	$\Delta\omega_1$	$\Delta\omega_2$	$\Delta\omega_3$	σ_1^2	σ_2^2	σ_3^2
C & C[a]	0.000†	0.000†	−0.001	$1.72\exp-4$	$2.01\exp-4$	$1.29\exp-4$
Regalia	0.020	0.009	0.005	$2.43\exp-3$	$1.43\exp-3$	$1.84\exp-3$
C, C & L[b]	−0.001	0.008	0.011	$9.66\exp-4$	$3.82\exp-3$	$3.20\exp-3$
K & M[c]	0.000†	0.000†	−0.001	$8.93\exp-5$	$1.29\exp-4$	$1.48\exp-4$

[a]Chambers and Constantinides.
[b]Cho, Choi and Lee.
[c]Kwan and Martin.

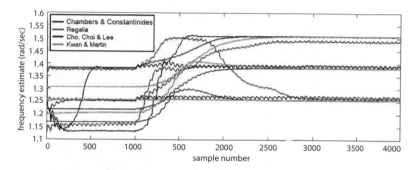

Figure 4.9 The results for tracking three real sinusoids, which correspond to the data in Table 4.2.

The results from tracking three RSSs show that Kwan and Martin's structure converges to the most accurate solution, with Chambers and Constantinides' solution being a close second; however, Chambers and Constantinides solution converges more quickly than Kwan and Martin's structure. Again, Cho, Choi and Lee's solution converges quickly, although it also shows the most variance σ^2 in its final solution: when considering both frequencies.

Next, we consider the computational complexity of the four structures, which is embodied in Table 4.3.

Table 4.3 The complete complexity of the four real structures required at one time sample, whilst tracking one and two real sinusoid signals

The complexity of the four structures whilst tracking a single sinusoid			
Method	Divisions	Multiplications	Additions
Chambers and Constantinides (1990)	2	9	9
Regalia (1991)	1	15	10
Cho et al. (1989)	1	15	17
Kwan and Martin (1989)	3	14	12
The complexity of the four structures whilst tracking two sinusoids			
Method	Divisions	Multiplications	Additions
Chambers and Constantinides (1990)	4	20	24
Regalia (1991)	2	27	19
Cho et al. (1989)	2	30	32
Kwan and Martin (1989)	6	36	27

Table 4.3 clarifies that Kwan and Martin's solution is the most complex, and also confirms that the equation-error approaches simplify the computational complexity when tracking multiple sinusoids.

Now to complete this section, a table of signal to noise improvement ratio (SNR_IR) for the structures evaluated is included on the next page, using $\alpha = 0.9025$, which is equivalent to r, and this table shows that the structure due to Chambers and Constantinides yields the highest SNR_IR.

Table 4.4 SNR improvement ratio expressions for the real structures under evaluation

Paper	Chambers & Constantinides	Kwan & Martin	Cho, Choi & Lee	Regalia
Calculation	$\dfrac{2}{1-\alpha}$	$\dfrac{2}{1-r^2}$	$\dfrac{1+\alpha}{1-\alpha}$	$\dfrac{2}{1-r^2}$
SNR_IR	20.51	10.78	19.51	10.78

4.2.4 *Summary*

In our analysis of the real structures, the structure proposed by Chambers and Constantinides (1990) appears to provide the most robust overall solution, whilst Regalia (1991) is a simple solution, although it fails to converge under certain conditions; Cho et al. (1989) provides a powerful solution, but it shows erratic initial convergence and shows the most variance in its final solution. The DCS solution by Kwan and Martin (1989) is computationally complex and does not enjoy the potential numerical robustness of all-pass realisations. It should be noted that when tracking a single RSS, equation-error approaches generally outperform output-error variance minimisation methods, since the basin of attraction is wider for an equation-error approach; however, this wider basin of attraction appears to be a disadvantage when multiple frequencies are tracked.

When tracking four RSSs, if robustness is considered, Chambers and Constantinides (1990) is the most reliable method, followed by Regalia (1991), then Cho et al. (1989) and Kwan and Martin (1989) fails to converge most often: although this result has not formally been included in this chapter, it has been published in Wheeler and Chambers (2012).

Next, we move onto the topic of complex adaptive notch filters.

4.3 Evaluating the Two Complex Adaptive Notch Filters

There is a need for complex adaptive notch filters (CANF) as many systems are now commonly functioning with complex signals particularly in radar, sonar, and communications, e.g. in-phase and quadrature (I&Q) sampling in sensors or in modulators/demodulators.

In this section two CANFs are considered, where the first is by Wheeler and Chambers (2013) and the second by Regalia (2010). These CANFs have the advantage that being developed from an all-pass design based on a structurally lossless prototype, which is canonic in the number of multipliers and delay elements, they can also be easily expanded to facilitate the tracking of multiple complex sinusoid signals (CSS)s. The development of the output-error learning algorithm is included from Wheeler and Chambers (2013), and Regalia (2010) is also summarised in this section, which is an equation-error design.

We highlight some of the first references to complex adaptive filtering as Widrow (1975), Shynk (1986), and Pei and Tseng

(1994). Also, it should be duly noted that Regalia has written a comprehensive monograph (Regalia, 1995) that provides an excellent foundation to the subject of IIR Adaptive Filtering.

Next, we show how the NFB structure from Chambers and Constantinides (1990) can be developed into a form capable of tracking CSSs, and then we compare its performance to the approach in Regalia (2010), where the strengths and weaknesses of both approaches are highlighted.

4.3.1 *Filter Realisation*

To develop the NFB structure from Chambers and Constantinides (1990) into a complex form, initially a standard first order real all-pass filter is considered, whose z-domain transfer function is

$$A(z) = \frac{z^{-1} - \alpha}{1 - \alpha z^{-1}}, \qquad (4.10)$$

where $0 \ll \alpha < 1$ and is a real coefficient. The all-pass structure is modified via a frequency mapping to the following form

$$A(z) = \frac{z^{-1}\beta - \alpha}{1 - \alpha z^{-1}\beta}, \qquad (4.11)$$

wherein it should be observed that an additional phase parameter β has been introduced. This value equates to $\beta = e^{j\theta}$, where θ is the complex phase shift angle which is equivalent to the frequency being tracked. Then the CANF is synthesised as shown in Fig. 4.10a, together with Regalia's structure in Fig. 4.10b, and its z-domain transfer function becomes

$$C(z) = \frac{E(z)}{U(z)} = \frac{1}{2}\{1 - A(z)\} = \frac{1}{2}\frac{(1+\alpha)(1 - z^{-1}\beta)}{1 - \alpha z^{-1}\beta}. \qquad (4.12)$$

Herein, as before α controls the notch bandwidth of the filter, and is fixed during the learning process for stability reasons. Whilst the β parameter, controls the notch frequency, which is adapted during learning. It should be noted that for such a complex first order notch filter the notch in the frequency response is not symmetric, but this is not considered further in this chapter.

The input to the gradient output of the z-domain transfer function, which is required later in developing the learning algorithm, is given as

$$\frac{GRAD(z)}{U(z)} = \frac{1}{2}\frac{(1+\alpha)(-jz^{-1}\beta)}{1 - \alpha z^{-1}\beta}. \qquad (4.13)$$

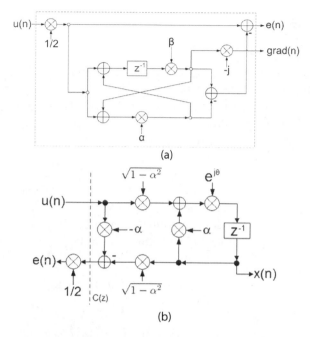

(a)

(b)

Figure 4.10 Complex adaptive notch filter structures, wherein (a) is Wheeler and Chambers' structure, and (b) is Regalia's structure.

In the next section, the development of the learning algorithm utilised to control β, or equivalently θ, is shown.

4.3.2 *The Learning Algorithm*

Now to derive the output-error based learning algorithm for Wheeler and Chambers' scheme, the cost function (J) is defined as

$$J = |e(n)|^2 = e(n)e^*(n), \qquad (4.14)$$

where |.| and (.)* denote the modulus and conjugate of a complex quantity. An update for the unknown parameter θ can be derived from J via the LMS type algorithm; the update equation derivation begins as

$$\theta(n+1) = \theta(n) - \frac{\mu}{2} \nabla J |_{\theta(n)=\theta(n+1)}, \qquad (4.15)$$

wherein μ is the adaptation gain. By differentiating (4.14) gives

$$\nabla J = e(n)\nabla e^*(n) + \nabla e(n)e^*(n), \qquad (4.16)$$

Thus, (4.15) becomes

$$\theta(n+1) = \theta(n) - \mu\, Re(e^*(n)\nabla e(n)); \qquad (4.17)$$

herein the signal $\nabla e(n) = grad(n)$ as shown in Fig. 4.10. The non-quadratic nature of the cost function J in (4.14) with respect to θ in $\beta = e^{j\theta}$, requires us to adopt a normalised LMS type update for θ.

The normalised LMS algorithm includes a recursive calculation of the gradient energy ψ, and this calculation is

$$\psi(n+1) = \psi(n)\gamma + (1-\gamma)(grad(n).grad^*(n)), \qquad (4.18)$$

wherein the γ term is the forgetting factor, which is a value between zero and one. The parameter γ is chosen to be ≥ 0.97 in the simulations in this section. The initialising value for $\psi_0 = 1.0$. Then updating (4.17) with (4.18) yields the final update equation for the updated θ to be

$$\theta(n+1) = \theta(n) - \mu\, Re\{e(n).grad(n)/\psi_n\}. \qquad (4.19)$$

For comparison purposes, the update for Regalia's structure is

$$\theta(n+1) = \theta(n) + \mu\, Im\{e(n).x^*(n)/\psi_n\}; \qquad (4.20)$$

herein, $\psi(n+1) = \psi(n)\gamma + (1-\gamma)(x(n).x^*(n))$, where $Re\{.\}$ and $Im\{.\}$ denote the real and imaginary parts of complex numbers.

In the next part of this chapter, we describe the methods required to track multiple CSSs with the two approaches.

4.3.3 *Tracking Two Complex Sinusoid Signals*

To track two CSSs with these structures, the equation-error approach is required for Regalia's method, which is shown in Fig. 4.10(a), and the output-error approach is required for Wheeler and Chambers' scheme, which is shown in Fig. 4.10(b). In the output-error approach, an additional complex notch filter structure: CNF_3, is required to generate the gradient value for CNF_2. This requires only two additional significant multipliers as shown in Fig. 4.10(a), which are for the α and β multiplications.

Both structures are easily expanded to track more than two frequencies; however, in this section we only consider the tracking of two CSSs. To preserve the stability of the notch structures, we fix α to 0.8 in our simulations. Also, the adaptation gain μ is chosen to be small enough to avoid instability in the learning algorithm in these experiments.

Next, simulation results are provided to compare the two approaches.

4.3.4 *Simulation Results and Comparison*

To compare Regalia's and Wheeler and Chambers' structures, initially we consider tracking a single frequency ω_0, for a CSS of the form

$$u(n) = Se^{j(\omega_0 n + \phi)} + w_j(n); \tag{4.21}$$

herein $w_j(n)$ is zero mean unity variance complex white noise. In this section of the chapter, as in Regalia (2010), the results have been achieved by utilising a SNR of 0 dB.

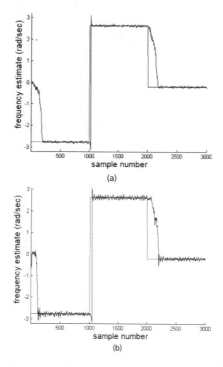

Figure 4.11 A comparison for tracking one complex sinusoid signal with: (a) Wheeler and Chambers' structure, and (b) Regalia's structure.

Both Figs. 4.11 and 4.12 include a target signal which is frequency hopping. This target signal (shown in red) is first initialised, then instantaneously hops every 1000 samples in Fig. 4.11. However, Fig. 4.12 differs slightly from Fig. 4.11 as there are two signals, where the first value hops at 1000 samples, and the second value hops at 1500 samples.

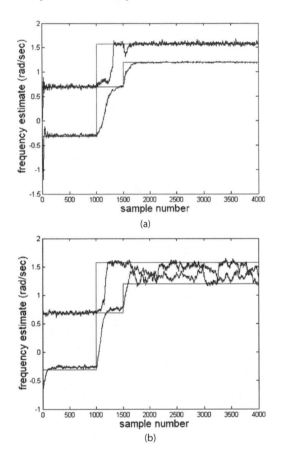

(a)

(b)

Figure 4.12 A comparison for tracking two complex sinusoid signals with: (a) Wheeler and Chambers' structure, and (b) Regalia's structure.

Figure 4.11(a) was produced with $\mu = 0.15$ and $\gamma = 0.97$, whilst Fig. 4.11(b) was achieved with $\mu = 0.05$ and $\gamma = 0.8$, and in both simulations θ_0 was initialised as -1.26.

Therefore, Fig. 4.11 demonstrates that Wheeler and Chambers' solution performs as well as, or better than the Regalia's as there are visible convergence improvements in these results. One example of the improved performance is, in Fig. 4.11(a), the faster convergence to the final frequency following the final hop at sample number 2000.

It should be noted that adding the term ψ to Regalia (2010) improves the performance of Regalia's structure further, thus implementing an NLMS-type of learning algorithm, which facilitates a fair comparison with Wheeler and Chambers' method.

We now compare the ability of both structures to track the frequencies of two CSSs. The parameters that facilitated the results in Fig. 4.12(a) are $\mu = 0.08$ and $\gamma = 0.99$, then for Fig. 4.12(b) $\mu = 0.02$ and $\gamma = 0.8$, these values have been found empirically to yield optimum results with equivalent tracking performance. From Fig. 4.12b observe when the target frequencies are closer together, Regalia's structure fails to converge, and this effect worsens if you decrease the value of α further below 0.8. When the values become close together at sample number 1500, Regalia's structure clearly does not converge in the remaining 2500 samples; this result is a consequence of not using an output-error based learning algorithm in Regalia (2010).

The average estimated frequency errors and the variances in the frequency estimates are shown in Table 4.5 for the results presented in Fig. 4.12(a) and Fig. 4.12(b). In this scenario, Wheeler and Chambers' scheme delivers a stronger performance than Regalia's, which is confirmed by the reduction in error and variance presented in Table 4.5.

Please note that the research in this section has previously been published in Wheeler and Chambers (2013).

Table 4.5 The results for tracking two complex sinusoid signals, wherein $\Delta\omega_1$ and $\Delta\omega_2$ are sample biases and σ_1^2 and σ_2^2 are the sample variances

Method	$\Delta\omega_1$	$\Delta\omega_2$	σ_1^2	σ_2^2
Wheeler and Chambers' method	−0.0014	+0.0001	0.0030	0.000775
Regalia's approach	+0.0235	−0.0176	0.0075	0.0145

4.3.5 *Summary*

Two complex adaptive notch filters have been compared, where Wheeler and Chambers' method is an output-error approach, whilst Regalia applies an equation-error approach. It was shown that generally, an output-error approach will facilitate more reliable tracking than an equation-error approach for real and complex signals; however, output-error approaches are slightly more computationally complex. For practical applications the low complexity and robustness of both structures are indeed very attractive.

In the next section, tracking a complex-valued chirp signal is considered.

4.4 Tracking a Complex-Valued Chirp Signal

First in this section, we analyse the convergence of Wheeler and Chambers' approach, before comparing this method against Regalia's for tracking a complex-valued chirp signal (CVCS).

4.4.1 *Convergence of the Update of the Frequency Parameters*

To demonstrate the convergence of Wheeler and Chambers' scheme, consider the adaptation algorithm applied to a general parameter θ, which is

$$\theta(n+1) = \theta(n) - \mu \, Re\left[\frac{e^*(n)grad(n)}{\psi(n)}\right], \qquad (4.22)$$

where we are analysing the angle parameter θ, with a fixed α; herein, $grad(n)$ is the gradient shown in Fig. 4.10a, which is calculated as the derivative of the output-error $e(n)$, with respect to θ; and $\psi(n) = \psi(n-1)\gamma + (1-\gamma)(grad(n).grad^*(n))$. Now building upon the approaches in Regalia (2010) and Ljung (1977), where Ljung (1977) shows that for sufficiently slow adaptation, the evolution of the adaptation algorithm is weakly linked to an ordinary differential equation of the form

$$\frac{d\theta}{dt} = E\left\{Re\left[\frac{e^*(n)grad(n)}{\Psi}\right] |\theta\right\}. \qquad (4.23)$$

Herein as notationally emphasised, the expectation on the right-hand side is evaluated for a fixed θ. Also, to proceed we make the assumption that the normalisation term $\psi(n)$ is a constant, which we denote Ψ.

From (4.11) the transfer functions $G(z)$ and $F(z)$ linking the input to the notch output and the filter regressor are given as

$$G(z) = \frac{1+\alpha}{2} \frac{1 - e^{j\theta}z^{-1}}{1 - \alpha e^{j\theta}z^{-1}} \quad F(z) = \frac{1+\alpha}{2} \frac{-j e^{j\theta}z^{-1}}{1 - \alpha e^{j\theta}z^{-1}}.$$

Then we may define the expectation $E\{\frac{e^*(n)grad(n)}{\psi}\}$ as the inner product

$$E\left\{\frac{e^*(n)x(n)}{\Psi}\right\} = \frac{1}{2\pi} \int_{-\pi}^{\pi} S_u(\omega) G(e^{j\omega}) F^*(e^{j\omega}) d\omega, \qquad (4.24)$$

where, $S_u(\omega)$ is the power spectral density of the input defined in (4.28), which is: $S_u(\omega) = 2\pi A_m^2 \delta(\omega - \omega_0) + \sigma^2$, herein ω_0 is the unknown frequency, which gives us the expectation

$$E\left\{\frac{e^*(n)x(n)}{\Psi}\right\} = \frac{A_m^2}{\Psi} G(e^{j\omega_0}) F^*(e^{j\omega_0})$$

$$+ \frac{\sigma^2}{2\pi\Psi} \int_{-\pi}^{\pi} G(e^{j\omega}) F^*(e^{j\omega}) d\omega,$$

wherein

$$G(e^{j\omega_0}) F^*(e^{j\omega_0}) = \frac{(1+\alpha)^2}{4} \frac{(1 - e^{j(\omega_0 - \theta)})(-j e^{-j(\omega_0 - \theta)})}{|1 - \alpha e^{j(\omega_0 - \theta)}|^2}. \qquad (4.25)$$

The real part of this equation then becomes

$$Re\left(E\left\{\frac{e^*(n)x(n)}{\Psi}\right\}\right) = \frac{A_m^2(1+\alpha)^2}{4\Psi} \frac{\sin(\omega_0 - \theta)}{|1 - \alpha e^{j(\omega_0 - \theta)}|^2}$$

$$+ \frac{\sigma^2(1+\alpha)^2}{8\pi\Psi} \underbrace{\int_{-\pi}^{\pi} \frac{\sin(\omega_0 - \theta)}{|1 - \alpha e^{j(\omega_0 - \theta)}|^2} d\omega}_{=0};$$

$$(4.26)$$

herein the noise-induced term vanishes, as this is the integral over one period of a function, which is odd about $\omega_0 = \theta$. Therefore, the associated differential equation becomes

$$\frac{d\theta}{dt} = \frac{A_m^2(1+\alpha)^2}{4\Psi} \frac{\sin(\omega_0 - \theta)}{|1 - \alpha e^{j(\omega_0 - \theta)}|^2}. \qquad (4.27)$$

Then convergence of θ to ω_0 from (4.27) is shown by choosing a Lyapunov function of the continuous variable t

$L(t) = [\omega_0 - \theta(t)]^2$, to obtain $\frac{dL(t)}{dt}$

$$= \frac{dL}{d\theta}\frac{d\theta}{dt} = -\frac{A_m^2(1+\alpha)^2}{2\Psi}\frac{(\omega_0 - \theta)\sin(\omega_0 - \theta)}{|1 - \alpha e^{j(\omega_0 - \theta)}|^2} < 0,$$

for $\theta \neq \omega_0$.

Now assuming $(\omega_0 - \theta)$ is restricted to the principle range $-\pi \leq \omega_0 - \theta \leq \pi$, which implies that $L(t)$ is monotonically decreasing, then $\theta(t)$ converges to ω_0 as desired. However, if $|\omega_0 - \theta| > \pi$, then θ converges to $\omega_0 + 2\pi k$: for an appropriate integer k; since θ intervenes through the filter computations purely from the factor $\beta = e^{j\theta(n)}$, a modulo-2π ambiguity in θ is unavoidable.

Please note that a similar proof for Regalia's scheme was first included in Regalia (2010). Since we have confirmed mathematically that Wheeler and Chambers' approach converges, tracking CVCS signals is investigated next and compared against Regalia's approach.

4.4.2 Comparison of Two Methods for Tracking a CVCS

In Regalia (2010), Regalia demonstrated that the complex version of his design is capable of tracking a CVCS, which in this case is a quadratically varying frequency of the form

$$u(n) = A_m e^{j\phi(n)} + b(n), \qquad (4.28)$$

wherein A_m is a scale factor, which can be taken as real, as if A_m were complex its phase angle would be absorbed into ϕ, leaving behind a real-valued scale factor; $b(n)$ is a white complex circular Gaussian noise process, and $\phi(n)$ is defined as

$$\phi(n) = \phi_2 n^2 + \phi_3 n^3, \qquad (4.29)$$

where the values used to create the CVCS in Fig. 4.13 are: $\phi_2 = -0.004$ and $\phi_3 = 1.2 \times 10^{-6}$. In Regalia (2010), Regalia demonstrates the ability of his design to track a CVCS, which we include in this section as Fig. 4.13(a); however, we apply the NLMS update, with an adaptation gain (μ) of 0.08, and $\gamma = 0.8$.

Equivalently, a comparable result may be produced with Wheeler and Chambers' structure, and this result is shown in Fig. 4.13(b), which was achieved by using the following parameters: $\mu = 0.15$, $\gamma = 0.8$ and $\alpha = 0.9$ in both Fig. 4.13(a) and 4.13(b).

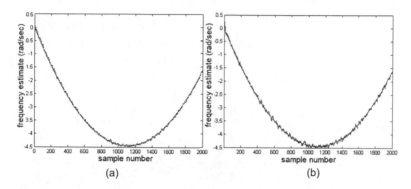

(a)   (b)

Figure 4.13 Tracking a complex-valued chirp signal with the two notch filter structures, which are: (a) Wheeler and Chambers' structure, and (b) Regalia's structure.

Please note that the learning parameters used were the optimum settings found empirically to achieve the best tracking performance with minimum variance; when tracking this CVCS the variance has been estimated from the 50th to the final sample.

It is clearly visible when comparing Fig. 4.13(a) and 4.13(b) that Wheeler and Chambers' structure produces slightly superior results as compared to Regalia's structure; this improvement is also clarified by Table 4.6. Also observe that Table 4.6 contains a full gradient term for β, which provides a slight improvement; this can be derived in a similar way to the full gradient term for α, which is shown in Section 4.5 of this chapter.

Table 4.6 Comparison of methods for tracking a CVCS

Method	σ^2
Wheeler and Chambers' structure - Fig. 4.13(a)	0.0017
Full gradient for β within Wheeler and Chambers' structure	0.0016
Regalia's method - Fig. 4.13(b)	0.0026

Please note that the research in this section shall be published in Wheeler and Chambers (2014).

4.4.3 *Summary*

First, the convergence of the update of the frequency parameters was proven for Wheeler and Chambers' approach; a similar proof is available for Regalia's scheme in Regalia (2010).

Then the strong performance of both Regalia's and Wheeler and Chambers' structures for tracking a CVCS has been demonstrated, which also included a result for the full gradient term for Wheeler and Chambers' approach.

Next, we discuss the method for updating the bandwidth parameter for Wheeler and Chambers' approach.

4.5 Bandwidth Parameter Adaptation in a Complex Adaptive Notch Filter

In this section we consider the update of the bandwidth parameter; therefore, first to demonstrate the effect of adapting the bandwidth parameter for a frequency hopping CSS, consider Fig. 4.14

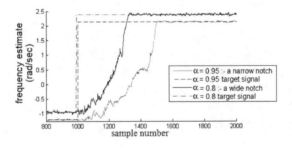

Figure 4.14   The effect of different values of α when tracking a CSS.

Observe in Fig. 4.14 that the 'wide notch' locates the target signal quickly but has significant noise on the estimate, whilst the 'narrow notch' is slow to locate the target signal but has much less noise on the estimate, thus highlighting the benefits of adapting the bandwidth parameter.

Little research has been published to date on updating the bandwidth parameter of any notch filter, although notable references are Knill and Constantinides (1993), Mvuma, Nishimura and Hinamoto (2002), Punchalard, Lertvasana and Chumchu (2003), and Levin and Ionnou (2008). Unfortunately, these works do not show in detail why a steepest ascent rather than descent approach is required for adapting the notch bandwidth parameter.

A significant point to note is that when updating the notch bandwidth parameter (α) a direction of ascent must be applied. This has been implemented previously by other researchers; however, has not been fully explained, which is the case in Mvuma, Nishimura and Hinamoto (2002). To minimise the output mean square error (MSE) the expected result was for α to be adapted with a direction of descent, although if a steepest descent approach is applied, then α converges to minus one.

To provide an explanation for this, if we assume a single CSS input with noise as in Mvuma, Nishimura and Hinamoto (2002), whilst β is fixed at the exact correct frequency, then only noise will be output from the CANF. Therefore, the CANF will become as wide as possible to minimise the noise output, thus producing essentially an all-stop response, which reduces the noise variance.

Now to demonstrate the effect of α increasing observe Fig. 4.15, where the integral defined in (4.30) and (4.31), also clearly increases. Considering this integral implies that a method of steepest ascent should be used to update α, which allows the transfer function to approach the perfect notch case, where the perfect case

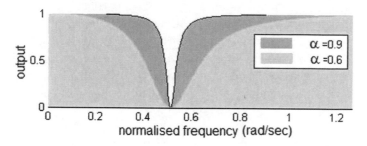

Figure 4.15 The magnitude response of the notch filter as a function of two values of the bandwidth parameter.

is when the CSS has been removed, thus leaving purely white noise at the CANF's output.

The equation that defines the noise variance (σ^2) at the CANF output signal is found from the power spectral density, which is

$$\sigma^2 = \frac{1}{2\pi} \int_{-\pi}^{\pi} P(\omega)d\omega; \tag{4.30}$$

herein $P(\omega)$ is the power spectral density of the CANF output signal. This expression may also be re-arranged as follows:

$$\sigma^2 = \frac{\sigma_N^2}{2\pi} \int_{-\pi}^{\pi} |C(\omega)|^2 d\omega, \tag{4.31}$$

where $C(\omega) = C(z)$ by applying the transformation $z = e^{j\omega}$ as in (4.12); the last term σ_N^2 is defined as the input noise variance. This implies that a steepest ascent algorithm should be applied in α's update. Thus, the update equation for α is

$$\alpha(n+1) = \alpha(n) + \mu_\alpha Re(e^*(n).grad\_\alpha(n)/\psi_\alpha(n)). \tag{4.32}$$

Within this equation, the term $\psi_\alpha(n)$ is again a recursive calculation of gradient energy, and the gradient of the output MSE with respect to α is $grad\_\alpha(n)$. Note that stability of the CANF is preserved by limiting the maximum value of $\alpha(n)$, and therefore a similar analysis as in Section 4.4 is unnecessary, where $\alpha(n) = \max(0.995, 4.32)$.

Next we derive an update equation for α, since the correct form of the learning algorithm has been identified.

4.5.1 *The Full Gradient Term for the Update of α*

Wheeler and Chambers stated that: initially, a partial gradient result was investigated, which was the method applied for adapting β in Wheeler and Chambers (2013). Unfortunately, the performance was poor for this partial gradient approach; therefore, by removing the assumption that α is fixed in the denominator, a full gradient term can be derived as follows. This process begins with the z-domain transfer function for this CANF, which is

$$C(z) = \frac{E(z)}{U(z)} = \frac{1}{2} \frac{(1+\alpha)(1-z^{-1}\beta)}{(1-\alpha z^{-1}\beta)} \tag{4.33}$$

$$= \frac{1}{2}(1+\alpha)(1-z^{-1}\beta)(1-\alpha z^{-1}\beta)^{-1}, \tag{4.34}$$

which may be manipulated to the form

$$\frac{\partial}{\partial \alpha} = \frac{1}{2}(1 - z^{-1}\beta)\left[\frac{z^{-1}\beta(1+\alpha) + (1-\alpha z^{-1}\beta)}{(1-\alpha z^{-1}\beta)^2}\right]. \qquad (4.35)$$

Then the full gradient term can be derived to be

$$\frac{GRAD\_\alpha(z)_{full}}{U(z)} = \frac{1}{2}\left[\frac{(1+z^{-1}\beta)}{(1-\alpha z^{-1}\beta)} \times \frac{(1-z^{-1}\beta)}{(1-\alpha z^{-1}\beta)}\right]. \qquad (4.36)$$

To implement this expression a second filter is required, which along with the gradient term derived in (4.36) can now be implemented as shown in Fig. 4.16.

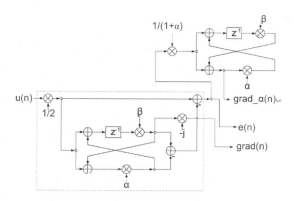

Figure 4.16 A structure capable of implementing the full gradient term for updating α, wherein the original structure which only updates β is shown by the dashed line.

Moving on, as the update has been derived, the next section of this chapter discusses the results achieved from adapting α.

4.5.2 *Simulations and Results*

This section contains the results achieved for updating the bandwidth parameter in three scenarios, which are: (1) tracking a single frequency hopping CSS, (2) tracking two frequency hopping CSSs, whilst updating a bandwidth parameter for each CSS being tracked, and (3) tracking a CSS and a CVCS, whilst updating a bandwidth parameter for each signal being tracked. The first set of results presented is for tracking a single frequency hopping CSS.

4.5.2.1 Tracking a single CSS whilst also updating α

First, the results for tracking a single CSS whilst updating α, are summarised in Table 4.7. Please note that within these results, the first value in Tables 4.7–4.8 is for the original approach from Wheeler and Chambers (2013), where α is fixed at 0.8.

Table 4.7 Comparison of methods for adapting α whilst tracking a single CSS, with a final value of -0.48; $\Delta\omega$ is the sample bias in the estimated frequency and σ^2 the sample variance

Method	$\Delta\omega$	σ^2
Fixed notch bandwidth: $\alpha = 0.8$	0.0006	1.5448e-05
Adapting α via the full gradient term	0.0001	5.8668e-07

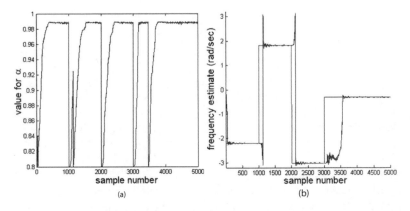

(a) (b)

Figure 4.17 The full gradient approach for adapting α as in Wheeler and Chambers (2013), whilst following a hopping CSS which is tracked by β, wherein (a) shows the adaptation of α in this CANF, and (b) shows the tracking performance of the CANF.

Table 4.7 demonstrates that updating α whilst tracking a single CSS, does indeed generate improvements in the overall performance with all three methods for adapting α. It should also be noted that the best results are achieved by applying constraints to the adaptation of α. These constraints are: limiting α's range, only adapting α once the target frequency has been located, and resetting

α if there is a large variation in $e(n).e^*(n)$, which may be detected by using the following update:

$$\psi_e(n+1) = \gamma \psi_e(n) + (1 - \gamma)e(n).e^*(n).$$

Next, the results for tracking two CSSs whilst updating α are summarised.

4.5.2.2 Tracking two CSSs, whilst adapting individual α values for each CSS being tracked

This section includes the results for tracking two CSSs whilst updating a value of α for each CSS tracked; to illustrate the additional complexity required to implement the full gradient approach when tracking two CSSs, the complete structure necessary is shown in Fig. 4.18.

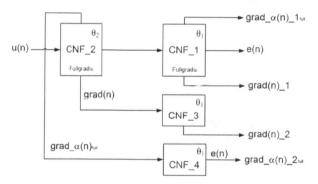

Figure 4.18 The structure capable of tracking two CSSs, whilst adapting unique α values for each CSS with the full gradient approach.

Please note that within Fig. 4.18 CNF_1 and CNF_2 are effectively double CANF structures as shown in Fig. 4.16 as they derive the full gradient term for α.

The results are now detailed in Table 4.8, where the result 'Adapting α via the full gradient term' is included as Fig. 4.19, which was produced with: $\mu_\beta = 0.1$, $\mu_\alpha = 0.001$; γ was set to 0.8 for the adaptation of α, and 0.9 for the adaptation of β. This result demonstrates that adapting multiple values of α does indeed improve the performance of a CANF: when tracking multiple CSSs,

Table 4.8 Comparison of methods for adapting two α values as in Wheeler and Chambers (2013), whilst tracking two CSS, wherein $\Delta\omega_1$ and $\Delta\omega_2$ are sample biases and σ_1^2 and σ_2^2 are the sample variances, and a † labels a value smaller than 0.00005

Method	$\Delta\omega_1$	$\Delta\omega_2$	σ_1^2	σ_2^2
Fixed notch bandwidth: $\alpha = 0.8$	0.0001	0.000†	0.0032	0.0013
Adapting α via the full gradient term	0.000†	−0.0001	2.51e-04	1.06e-04

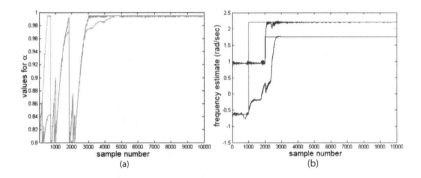

(a)   (b)

Figure 4.19 Tracking two frequencies whilst adapting separate α values with the full gradient approach as in Wheeler and Chambers (2013), wherein (a) shows the adaptation of both α values in this CANF, and (b) shows the tracking performance of the CANF.

although, consequently this increases the computational complexity of the solution.

The final set of results investigates tracking a CVCS and a frequency hopping CSS.

4.5.2.3 Tracking a CVCS and a frequency hopping CSS

This section contains the results for tracking a CVCS and a frequency hopping CSS simultaneously. First, with a fixed value of α; then α is adapted, which is shown in Table 4.9 on the next page.

Within Table 4.9, please recall that the variances σ_1^2 and σ_2^2 are calculated for as much of the CVCS as possible, which in this result is from 2500–4000 samples.

Table 4.9 Comparison of the variances with a fixed then adapting α values, whilst tracking a chirp and a hopping CSS

Method	CVCS_1[a]		CVCS_2[b]	
	σ_1^2	σ_2^2	σ_1^2	σ_2^2
Fixed notch bandwidth: $\alpha = 0.8$	7.02e-04	5.76e-04	7.75e-04	8.17e-04
Adapting α via the full gradient term	8.96e-06	6.45e-05	3.13e-05	1.62e-04

CVCS_1[a]: $\phi(n) = 0.1e - 06(n)^3 - 0.0005(n)^2$.
CVCS_2[b]: $\phi(n) = 0.3e - 06(n)^3 - 0.002(n)^2 + 2(n)$.

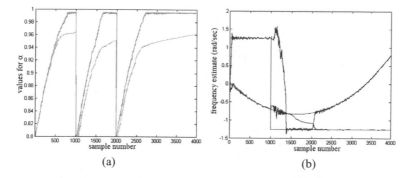

(a)   (b)

Figure 4.20 Tracking a CVCS and a hopping CSS simultaneously, whilst adapting values of α for each signal, wherein (a) shows the adaptation of both α values in this CANF, and (b) shows the tracking performance of the CANF.

Figure 4.20 was generated with: $\mu_\beta = 0.1$, $\mu_\alpha = 0.001$, $\gamma_\beta = 0.9$ and $\gamma_\alpha = 0.8$. Table 4.9 and Fig. 4.20 demonstrate that adapting α generates a significant improvement to both signals.

Next, the computational complexity for CANFs is formally considered.

4.5.3 *Computational Complexity of the Algorithms Used to Track CSSs*

This section contains the number of calculations required to track CSSs, first with Regalia's approach, then with Wheeler and Chambers' method; in addition, the calculations required for adapting α in Wheeler and Chambers' approach are detailed.

Table 4.10 The computational complexity required to track CSSs in the configurations considered in this chapter, at one time sample

The complexity required to track a single CSS			
Method	Divisions	Multiplications	Additions
Regalia: fixed α	1	11	8
Wheeler and Chambers: fixed α	2	10	8
Wheeler and Chambers: adapting α	4	19	15
The complexity required to track two CSSs			
Method	Divisions	Multiplications	Additions
Regalia: fixed α	2	22	16
Wheeler and Chambers: fixed α	4	24	21
Adapting one α value[a]	6	33	28
The complexity for adapting two values of α whilst tracking two CSSs			
Method	Divisions	Multiplications	Additions
Adapting two α values	8	43	42

[a]Denotes a result where within CNF_1 a single value of α is updated for the complete structure, thus reducing the overall complexity: For further information, see Wheeler and Chambers (2013).

Table 4.10 demonstrates that Regalia's approach is slightly less computationally complex than Wheeler and Chambers' method; if the notch bandwidth parameter is updated for tracking multiple CSSs, this can double the complexity of the design.

Please note that the research in this section has previously been published in Wheeler and Chambers (2013) and Wheeler and Chambers (2014).

4.5.4 *Summary*

In this section, we have demonstrated that a method of steepest ascent is required for the adaptation of the bandwidth parameter α and have proven that the performance of the CANF can be significantly improved, if both the notch bandwidth and frequency parameters are updated simultaneously, in all three scenarios which were considered.

In addition, we have shown the computational complexity of the CANF structures described in this section. Next, overall conclusions are provided for this chapter.

4.6 Overall Conclusions

In this chapter we have demonstrated that DCS solutions are generally more complex than all-pass structures, and that all-pass structures also provide superior performance to DCS methods in adaptive notch filtering. We also compared the performances of four real second-order all-pass adaptive notch filter structures, including considering their computational complexities, and highlighted the strengths and weaknesses of each of the four structures.

We showed how the structure from Chambers and Constantinides (1990) can be developed into a form capable of tracking CSSs, which is published in Wheeler and Chambers (2013). Then we compared Regalia's equation-error approach, and Wheeler and Chambers' output-error approach. Noting that when tracking a single sinusoid signal, equation-error approaches generally outperform output-error variance minimisation methods, since the basin of attraction is wider for an equation-error approach; however, this wider basin of attraction appears to be a disadvantage when multiple frequencies are tracked.

The convergence of Wheeler and Chambers' scheme was analysed; then we demonstrated the strong performance of both Regalia (2010) and Wheeler and Chambers (2013) CANFs for tracking a CVCS.

We described why a method of steepest ascent is required for the adaptation of the notch bandwidth parameter α and demonstrated that the performance of the CANF can be significantly improved if both the notch bandwidth and frequency parameters are updated simultaneously in three scenarios.

The computational complexities of Regalia's and Wheeler and Chambers' CANFs have been included in this chapter, along with the additional complexity required to adapt the notch bandwidth parameter in Wheeler and Chambers' approach. The inclusion of the computational complexity demonstrated that although the performance of this CANF structure can be significantly improved by adapting the notch bandwidth parameter, this may double the complexity of the design, which may be significant in real-time processing.

All the authors dedicate this chapter to the pioneer of digital signal processing, Professor Tony Constantinides.

References

1. J. A. Chambers and A. G. Constantinides. Frequency tracking using constrained adaptive notch filters synthesized from allpass sections, *Proc. Inst. Elect. Eng. F*, vol. 137, pp. 475–481, Dec. 1990.

2. N. I. Cho, C.-H. Choi, and S. U. Lee. Adaptive line enhancement using an IIR lattice notch filter, *IEEE Trans. Acoust., Speech, Signal Process.*, vol. 37, no. 4, pp. 585–589, Apr. 1989.

3. K. M. Knill and A. G. Constantinides. Least-mean square adaptation of the orthogonal block adaptive line enhancer, Signals, Systems and Computers, 1993 Conference Record of the Twenty-Seventh Asilomar Conference, pp. 663–667, vol. 1, 1–3 Nov. 1993.

4. T. Kwan and K. Martin. Adaptive detection and enhancement of multiple sinusoids using a cascade IIR filter, *IEEE Trans. Circuits Syst.*, vol. 36, no. 7, pp. 937–947, Jul. 1989.

5. J. Levin and P. Ioannou. Multirate adaptive notch filter with an adaptive bandwidth controller for disk drives, *American Control Conference*, 2008, pp. 4407–4412, 11–13 June 2008.

6. L. Ljung. Analysis of recursive stochastic algorithms, *Automatic Control, IEEE Transactions on*, vol. 22, no. 4, pp. 551–575, Aug. 1977.

7. A. Mvuma, S. Nishimura, and T. Hinamoto. Adaptive optimization of notch bandwidth of an IIR filter used to suppress narrow-band interference, *Circuits and Systems, ISCAS* 2002. in the IEEE International Symposium on, pp. V-341–V-344 vol. 5, May 2002.

8. S.-C. Pei and C.-C. Tseng. Complex adaptive IIR notch filter algorithm and its applications, *IEEE Trans. Circuits Syst. II*, vol. 41, no. 2, pp. 158–163, Feb. 1994.

9. R. Punchalard, W. Lertvasana, and P. Chumchu. Convergence speed improvement for a variable step-size plain gradient algorithm by using variable notch bandwidth technique, *Image and Signal Processing and Analysis, ISPA* 2003. in the 3rd International Symposium on, pp. 788–792 vol. 2, 18–20 Sept. 2003.

10. P. A. Regalia. An improved lattice-based adaptive IIR notch filter, *IEEE Trans. Signal Process.*, vol. 39, pp. 2124–2128, Sep. 1991.

11. P. A. Regalia. Adaptive IIR Filtering in Signal Processing and Control. New York: Marcel Dekker, 1995.

12. P. A. Regalia. A Complex Adaptive Notch Filter, *Signal Proc. Letters, IEEE*, vol. 17, pp. 937–940, Nov. 2010.

13. J. J. Shynk. A complex adaptive algorithm for IIR filtering, *IEEE Trans. Acoust. Speech, Signal Proc.*, vol. ASSP-34, pp. 1342–1344, Oct. 1986.

14. P. T. Wheeler and J. A. Chambers. Real Adaptive Notch Filter Analysis and a New Structure Developed for Tracking Complex Sinusoidal Signals, *in the 9th IMA International Conference on Mathematics in Signal Processing*, 17–20 Dec. 2012.

15. P. T. Wheeler and J. A. Chambers. Complex adaptive notch filter structure for tracking multiple complex sinusoidal signals, *Electronics Letters*, vol. 49, no. 3, pp. 179–181, 31 Jan. 2013.

16. P. T. Wheeler and J. A. Chambers. Simultaneous Adaptation of Bandwidth and Frequency Parameters within a Complex Notch Filter, *Intelligent Signal Processing Conference*, London, 2–3 Dec. 2013.

17. P. T. Wheeler and J. A. Chambers. Tracking Complex-Valued Multi-component Chirp Signals Using a Complex Notch Filter with Adaptive Bandwidth and Frequency Parameters, to appear in the ICASSP Conference, Florence, 4–9 May 2014.

18. B. Widrow, J. McCool, and M. Ball. The complex LMS algorithm, *Proc. IEEE*, vol. 63, pp. 719–720, Apr. 1975.

Chapter 5

Recent Advances in Sparse FIR Filter Design Using l_0 and l_1 Optimization Techniques

Aimin Jiang[a] and Hon Keung Kwan[b]

[a] College of Internet of Things Engineering,
Hohai University, Changzhou, Jiangsu 213022, China
[b] Department of Electrical and Computer Engineering,
University of Windsor, Windsor, Ontario N9B 3P4, Canada
jiangam@hhuc.edu.cn, kwan1@uwindsor.ca

A digital filter is a tool to extract useful information and remove undesired signal components from input sequences. It plays an important role in various applications of communications and signal processing [1, 2]. In general, digital filters are classified into two categories according to the duration of their impulse responses, *finite-duration impulse response* (FIR) and *infinite-duration impulse response* (IIR). Compared to IIR filters, FIR filters have several advantages:

(1) As all poles of an FIR filter are fixed at the origin, its frequency response is determined by its zeroes. Thereby, there is no stability concern for the FIR filter design.

Trends in Digital Signal Processing: A Festschrift in Honour of A. G. Constantinides
Edited by Yong Ching Lim, Hon Keung Kwan, and Wan-Chi Siu
Copyright © 2016 Pan Stanford Publishing Pte. Ltd.
ISBN 978-981-4669-50-4 (Hardcover), 978-981-4669-51-1 (eBook)
www.panstanford.com

(2) Using (anti-)symmetric structures, one can readily achieve exactly linear phase over the whole frequency band $[0, \pi)$. However, except in some special cases, it is difficult to design an IIR filter with a linear phase over $[0, \pi)$.

(3) A lot of FIR filter design problems can be equivalently formulated as convex optimization problems, which means that their globally optimal solutions can be attained by various optimization techniques. However, if both magnitude and phase responses are under consideration, in general, it is hard to transform an IIR filter design problem into an equivalent convex optimization problem and, thus, globally optimal solutions cannot be definitely achieved.

Since the 1960s, many efforts have been devoted to the design of linear-phase FIR filters [1, 2]. A linear-phase FIR filter demonstrates a symmetric or anti-symmetric structure. Therefore, the number of free variables of the corresponding design problem is reduced by about one half. Moreover, as the group delay of a linear-phase FIR filter is constant over $[0, \pi)$, its frequency response can be simplified as a trigonometric function of filter coefficients, such that original complex design problems could be simplified as real ones. On the other hand, in order to achieve linear phase over the whole frequency band $[0, \pi)$, the group delay of a linear-phase FIR filter can only be set approximately equal to $N/2$, where N denotes the filter order. If a lower group delay is required in some scenario of signal processing, the filter length has to be decreased. However, sometimes this is not achievable because of the strict design specifications. In this situation, a general FIR filter with nonlinear phase response is more useful to meet the design requirements. Therefore, general FIR filter designs are also well studied lately.

5.1 Classical FIR Filter Designs

The first FIR filter design technique is the Fourier series method [1, 2], in which a desired frequency response is first expanded as its Fourier series and then truncated to a finite length. To reduce the Gibbs' oscillations near the cutoff frequencies, a smooth time-limited window is generally multiplied with the coefficients of the Fourier series. Another class of methods utilizes the frequency sampling technique [1] to design FIR filters. The desired frequency response is uniformly sampled on a number of discrete frequency points, and then the inverse discrete Fourier transform (IDFT) is applied to obtain the discrete-time impulse response. Both design approaches aforementioned can be implemented very efficiently. Nevertheless, their performance is inferior to that of design methods using optimization techniques.

Lately, optimization methods have been widely used in the design of FIR filters. In general, a classical FIR filter design problem can be cast as

$$\min_{\mathbf{h}} \quad J(\mathbf{h}) \tag{5.1a}$$

$$\text{s.t.} \quad g_i(\mathbf{h}) \leq 0, \quad i = 1, \ldots, K \tag{5.1b}$$

$$p_j(\mathbf{h}) = 0, \quad j = 1, \ldots, L, \tag{5.1c}$$

where $\mathbf{h} = [h_0 \ h_1 \ \ldots \ h_N]^T$ represents filter coefficients to be optimized, the objective function $J(\mathbf{h})$ denotes an approximation error evaluated under some optimization criterion, and $g_i(\mathbf{h})$ and $p_j(\mathbf{h})$ are various constraints imposed on time or frequency domain.

For instance, if $J(\mathbf{h})$ is chosen as the maximum approximation error over the union of frequency bands of interest, denoted by Ω_I, the minimax (or Chebyshev) design problem is accordingly expressed by

$$\min_{\mathbf{h}} \quad \max_{\omega \in \Omega_I} \quad W(\omega) \left| H(e^{j\omega}) - D(\omega) \right|, \tag{5.2}$$

where $W(\omega)$ is a nonnegative weighting function defined on Ω_I and $D(\omega)$ denotes the ideal frequency response to approximate. In Eq. (5.2), $H(e^{j\omega})$ represents the frequency response of an FIR filter, which is computed from the transfer function $H(z)$ defined by

$$H(z) = \sum_{n=0}^{N} z^{-n} h_n = \varphi_N^T(z) \mathbf{h}, \tag{5.3}$$

where $\varphi_N(z) = [1 \ z^{-1} \ \ldots \ z^{-N}]^T$. By introducing a slack variable δ, problem (5.2) can be further written by

$$\min_{\mathbf{h}} \quad \delta \tag{5.4a}$$

$$\text{s.t.} \quad W(\omega) \left| H(e^{j\omega}) - D(\omega) \right| \leq \delta, \quad \forall \omega \in \Omega_I. \tag{5.4b}$$

In practical designs, constraint (5.4b) can be implemented on a set of discretized frequency points sampled over Ω_I. Then, problem (5.4) becomes a second-order cone program (SOCP) [3]. For a linear-phase FIR filter, both $H(e^{j\omega})$ and $D(\omega)$ in (5.4b) are replaced by their (ideal) magnitude responses and, accordingly, (5.4b) is converted to a set of linear inequality constraints. The most well-known minimax design method was proposed in 1972 by Parks and McClellan [4] for the linear-phase FIR filter design. By virtue of the alternation theorem, there always exists an optimal design with equiripple magnitude response for the weighted minimax design problem. Using the Remez exchange algorithm, the optimal design of (5.4) can be efficiently and reliably attained. In [5], Rabiner formulated the same design problem as a linear program (LP) and applied the simplex method to solve it.

In contrast to the minimax design, the weighted least-squares (WLS) criterion is also widely used in practice. The WLS design problem is formulated as

$$\min_{\mathbf{h}} \int_{\omega \in \Omega_I} W(\omega) \left| H(e^{j\omega}) - D(\omega) \right|^2 d\omega. \qquad (5.5)$$

For a general FIR filter design, (5.5) can be further cast as an SOCP problem [3], while the linear-phase FIR filter design in the WLS sense can be solved by eigenvalue decomposition [6].

5.2 Sparse FIR Filter Designs

The above discussion shows that classical FIR filter designs focus on how to minimize an approximation error in some optimization sense, which guarantees that the filtering performance of an FIR filter designed by classical optimization-based design methods maximally satisfies practical requirements. Furthermore, many classical design problems (for example, (5.4) and (5.5)) are inherently convex optimization problems, such that they can be efficiently and reliably solved by well-developed numerical solvers with little programming effort [7]. However, classical design methods seldom take into account the implementation efficiency during the design stage. Consequently, a great deal of effort has been made to develop efficient algorithms for low complexity FIR filter designs.

For example, in [8–11], filter coefficients are represented by a sum of signed power-of-two (SPT) terms. Then, the implementation complexity of an FIR filter with SPT coefficients is determined by the number of adders, which can be minimized during the design process. If subexpressions are extracted and shared among filter coefficients, the implementation complexity of an FIR filter can be further reduced [12–15]. Various discrete optimization techniques (*e.g.*, branch-and-bound techniques and evolutionary algorithms) have been employed in these design methods to handle discrete filter coefficients. Another way to efficiently implement an FIR filter is to force a considerable number of filter coefficients equal to 0, such that corresponding circuit components or arithmetic operations are no longer required. Sparse FIR filters can be applied in various practical applications, such as channel shortening equalizers [16].

A sparse FIR filter design problem is generally cast as

$$\min_{\mathbf{h}} \quad \|\mathbf{h}\|_0 \tag{5.6a}$$

$$\text{s.t.} \quad J(\mathbf{h}) \leq \delta \tag{5.6b}$$

$$g_i(\mathbf{h}) \leq 0, \quad i = 1, \ldots, K \tag{5.6c}$$

$$p_j(\mathbf{h}) = 0, \quad j = 1, \ldots, L, \tag{5.6d}$$

where $\|\cdot\|_0$ represents l_0 (quasi-)norm which counts the number of nonzero elements of a vector. A typical sparse FIR filter design problem is given below:

$$\min_{\mathbf{h}} \quad \|\mathbf{h}\|_0 \tag{5.7a}$$

$$\text{s.t.} \quad W(\omega) \left| H(e^{j\omega}) - D(\omega) \right| \leq \delta(\omega), \quad \forall \omega \in \Omega_I. \tag{5.7b}$$

Here, the weighted absolute frequency response error is upper bounded by $\delta(\omega)$, which is originally minimized as the objective function in (5.4a). Similarly, the WLS-error-constrained design problem can be written by

$$\min_{\mathbf{h}} \quad \|\mathbf{h}\|_0 \tag{5.8a}$$

$$\text{s.t.} \quad \int_{\omega \in \Omega_I} W(\omega) \left| H(e^{j\omega}) - D(\omega) \right|^2 d\omega \leq \delta. \tag{5.8b}$$

Ideally, one can locate the optimal solutions to design problems shown above by an exhaustive search. However, the resulting computational cost is extremely high. To overcome this difficulty, a number of global optimization design methods were proposed to improve the computational efficiency. In [17], a mixed integer linear programming (MILP) method was developed for the design of sparse FIR filters. The objective function is composed by two terms, corresponding to the costs of arithmetic operations and delay, which are both related to the sparsity of filter coefficients. Another MILP design approach was proposed in [18], where auxiliary binary variables are introduced to indicate the existence of nonzero filter coefficients. Both design problems formulated in [17] and [18] can be solved by any MILP package. In essence, sparse FIR filter designs are combinatorial optimization problems. Thus, traditional combinatorial optimization techniques can also be employed to solve this class of design problems. For instance, a branch-and-bound method was presented in [19], where the depth-first search is employed to gradually locate zero coefficients. Although these approaches employ effective searching techniques, their computational complexity is so formidable that they are unsuitable to large-scale design problems or for some situations in which design specifications change over time.

Note that constraints (5.7b) and (5.8b) can both be written in a general form

$$\|\mathbf{d} - \mathbf{Fh}\|_2 \leq \upsilon. \tag{5.9}$$

For the peak-error-constrained design problem (5.7), $\mathbf{d}$, $\mathbf{F}$, and υ are defined by

$$\mathbf{d} = W(\omega) \begin{bmatrix} \text{Re}\,\{D(\omega)\} \\ \text{Im}\,\{D(\omega)\} \end{bmatrix} \tag{5.10}$$

$$\mathbf{F} = W(\omega) \begin{bmatrix} \text{Re}\,\{\varphi_N(e^{j\omega})\} \\ \text{Im}\,\{\varphi_N(e^{j\omega})\} \end{bmatrix} \tag{5.11}$$

$$\upsilon = \delta(\omega) \tag{5.12}$$

and, for the WLS-error-constrained design problem (5.8), they are computed by

$$\mathbf{d} = \mathbf{A}^{-\frac{1}{2}}\mathbf{b} \tag{5.13}$$

$$\mathbf{F} = \mathbf{A}^{\frac{1}{2}} \tag{5.14}$$

$$\upsilon = \left(\delta - c + \mathbf{b}^T\mathbf{A}^{-1}\mathbf{b}\right)^{\frac{1}{2}} \tag{5.15}$$

where

$$\mathbf{A} = \int_{\omega \in \Omega_l} W(\omega) \mathrm{Re} \left\{ \varphi_N(e^{j\omega}) \varphi_N^H(e^{j\omega}) \right\} d\omega \qquad (5.16)$$

$$\mathbf{b} = \int_{\omega \in \Omega_l} W(\omega) \mathrm{Re} \left\{ D^*(e^{j\omega}) \varphi_N(e^{j\omega}) \right\} d\omega \qquad (5.17)$$

$$c = \int_{\omega \in \Omega_l} W(\omega) \left| D(e^{j\omega}) \right|^2 d\omega. \qquad (5.18)$$

Then, sparse FIR filter design problems (5.7) and (5.8) seem similar to the sparse coding problem, an important l_0-norm optimization problem in sparse representation [20] or compressive sensing [21], which is generally formulated as follows:

$$\min_{\mathbf{x}} \quad \|\mathbf{x}\|_0 \qquad (5.19a)$$

$$\text{s.t.} \quad \mathbf{y} = \mathbf{D}\mathbf{x} \text{ or } \|\mathbf{y} - \mathbf{D}\mathbf{x}\|_2 \leq \nu. \qquad (5.19b)$$

However, it has to be emphasized that these two classes of problems inherently differ from each other due to the following reasons:

(1) In the sparse coding problem, $\mathbf{D}$ is generally an over-complete matrix of finite size. In other words, it has more columns than rows. Nevertheless, in the peak-error-constrained sparse FIR filter design problem (5.7), each element of $\mathbf{F}$ is essentially a function with respect to ω. In the WLS-error-constrained design problem (5.8), $\mathbf{F}$ is a square matrix.

(2) In practice, $\mathbf{D}$ can be predefined (*e.g.*, wavelet or DCT) or learned from a set of measurements $\{\mathbf{y}_l\}$. However, in sparse FIR filter designs, $\mathbf{F}$ is determined by (5.11) or (5.14).

(3) For sparse coding, optimal solutions can be guaranteed by various sufficient conditions imposed on spark, mutual coherence (MC), or restricted isometry property (RIP) of $\mathbf{D}$ [22–25]. These conditions ensure the equivalence of l_0-norm minimization problems and their l_1-norm counterparts. In contrast, for sparse FIR filter designs, $\mathbf{F}$ generally does not satisfy these sufficient conditions. This implies that optimal solutions are hard to attain in sparse FIR filter designs.

Lately, a large number of algorithms, such as orthogonal matching pursuit (OMP) [26] and basis pursuit (BP) [27], have been proposed to efficiently tackle the sparse coding problem (5.19).

Considering the similarity between sparse coding and sparse FIR filter designs, a straightforward way to solve sparse filter design problems is to make full use of those pursuit or convex relaxation algorithms. However, in view of their distinctions aforementioned, researchers have to develop more sophisticated techniques. We shall review some typical approaches in the following subsections.

5.2.1 *Hard Thresholding Method*

In sparse coding, l_1-norm is widely used as a convex relaxation of l_0-norm. In the same way, Lu et al. proposed in [28] a hard thresholding method to tackle sparse FIR filter design problems. However, slightly different to that of (5.7a) and (5.8a), the approximation error of an FIR filter is combined with the sparsity of filter coefficients and minimized using this approach. The major steps of the hard thresholding method are given as follows:

(1) Solve an augmented design problem as follows:

$$\min_{\delta, \mathbf{h}} \quad \delta + \mu \, \|\mathbf{h}\|_1 \tag{5.20a}$$

$$\text{s.t.} \quad W(\omega) \left| H(e^{j\omega}) - D(\omega) \right| \le \delta, \quad \forall \omega \in \Omega_I, \tag{5.20b}$$

where parameter μ is used to control the relative importance between peak error and l_1-norm of filter coefficients. As (5.20) is a convex optimization problem, its optimal solution $(\delta^*, \mathbf{h}^*)$ can be efficiently and reliably attained.

(2) Rearrange elements of $\mathbf{h}^*$ in a nondescending order according to their magnitudes, i.e., $\left| h_{(0)}^* \right| \le \left| h_{(1)}^* \right| \le \cdots \le \left| h_{(N)}^* \right|$, and choose $\mathcal{Z} = \{(0), \ldots, (L)\}$ where L is the desired number of zero coefficients.

(3) Solve the following minimax design problem to achieve the final solution

$$\min_{\delta, \mathbf{h}} \quad \delta \tag{5.21a}$$

$$\text{s.t.} \quad W(\omega) \left| H(e^{j\omega}) - D(\omega) \right| \le \delta, \quad \forall \omega \in \Omega_I \tag{5.21b}$$

$$h_n = 0, \quad \forall n \in \mathcal{Z}, \tag{5.21c}$$

where $\mathcal{Z}$ is the set containing all the indices of zero coefficients located in the preceding step.

Compared to other design methods, the hard thresholding method is very efficient since it only has to solve two SOCP problems (or two LP problems for linear-phase FIR filter design). When μ is sufficiently small, the optimal solution to (5.20) is close to the one of classical minimax design problem (5.4). Simulations show that, in this situation, the hard thresholding method works as well as other design methods to be described later. As μ becomes larger, δ^* also becomes larger. Then, the optimal solution to the original peak-error-constrained design problem (5.7) could be extremely sparse. In this situation, simply replacing l_0-norm by l_1-norm hardly yields better designs than other approaches using more sophisticated optimization techniques. However, because the hard thresholding method is of computational efficiency, its design result can be used to arrive at an initial solution for other iterative design methods.

5.2.2 *Minimum 1-Norm Method*

In 2010, Baran et al. proposed in [29] another l_1-norm-based design method, which aims to solve (5.7). The original design method is developed for linear-phase FIR filters. However, it is also applicable to the design of general FIR filters. The major steps of this approach is as follows:

(1) Replace l_0-norm by l_1-norm in the objective function of (5.7), and solve the resulting convex optimization problem. Let the optimal solution be $\mathbf{h}^*$.
(2) Rearrange elements of $\mathbf{h}^*$ in a nondescending order according to their magnitudes, i.e., $\left| h_{(0)}^* \right| \leq \left| h_{(1)}^* \right| \leq \cdots \leq \left| h_{(N)}^* \right|$.
(3) Use the bisection search to determine a maximal J, such that $\delta_{\mathcal{Z}}^* \leq \max_{\omega \in \Omega_l} \delta(\omega)$ where $\delta_{\mathcal{Z}}^*$ is the optimal objective function value of (5.21) with $\mathcal{Z} = \{(0), (1), \ldots, (J)\}$.

The minimum 1-norm method and the hard thresholding method have some properties in common. First, both methods utilize l_1-norm to replace l_0-norm. As l_1-norm can only lead to a solution which contains a number of coefficients with small magnitude, the operation of hard thresholding has to be applied to attain a sparse filter. This technique is very computationally efficient for locating zero coefficients. However, it is worth noting that once l_1-norm design problems are solved, the order of nullifying coefficients is accordingly fixed. That is, if $h_{(i)}^*$ is set to zero, $\left\{ h_{(j)}^* \right\}_{j=0}^{i-1}$ are all zero coefficients. One can only adjust $|\mathcal{Z}|$ to control the number of zero coefficients or make approximation error of the designed FIR filter sufficiently small. In practice, this strategy could impair their capability of achieving optimal designs. As an attempt to obtain better designs, more sophisticated searching techniques have to be developed.

5.2.3 *Successive Thinning Method*

In the same paper [29], Baran et al. also proposed the successive thinning method, which dynamically updates the order of nullifying coefficients. The major steps of this approach is summarized as follows:

(1) Initialize $\mathcal{N}^{(0)} = \left\{ 0, 1, \dots, \frac{N}{2} \right\}$ and $\mathcal{Z}^{(0)} = \emptyset$;
(2) Repeat for $i = 1, 2, \dots$

    (a) Select an index $n^{(i)} \in \mathcal{N}^{(i-1)}$ according to some predefined selection rule;
    (b) Update

$$\mathcal{N}^{(i)} = \mathcal{N}^{(i-1)} - \left\{ n^{(i)} \right\}$$
$$\mathcal{Z}^{(i)} = \mathcal{Z}^{(i-1)} + \left\{ n^{(i)} \right\}.$$

The most important step in the successive thinning method is how to choose the index $n^{(i)}$ of a new zero coefficient from the index set $\mathcal{N}^{(i-1)}$ in each iteration. The successive thinning method provides two heuristic options, i.e., *minimum-increase rule* or *smallest-coefficient rule*. The minimum-increase rule determines $n^{(i)}$ in the way described below:

(1) In the ith iteration, solve (5.21) to obtain $\delta_j^{(i)}$ using $\mathcal{Z}_j^{(i)} = \mathcal{Z}^{(i-1)} + \left\{ n_j \right\}$ for $\forall n_j \in \mathcal{N}^{(i-1)}$;
(2) Choose $n^{(i)}$ as the index merging which with $\mathcal{Z}^{(i-1)}$ yields the minimum increase on peak error, that is,

$$n^{(i)} = \arg \min_{n_j} \delta_j^{(i)}. \tag{5.22}$$

Note that to choose $n^{(i)}$ the minimum-increase rule has to exhaustively examine all indices in $\mathcal{N}^{(i-1)}$. This examining procedure is further nested in the outer iteration.

The second option is the smallest-coefficient rule, which chooses $n^{(i)}$ as follows:

(1) In the ith iteration, solve (5.21) with $\mathcal{Z}^{(i-1)}$ to obtain $\mathbf{h}^{(i)}$;
(2) Choose $n^{(i)}$ corresponding to the coefficient with the smallest magnitude among $\{ h_n^{(i)} : n \in \mathcal{N}^{(i-1)} \}$, that is,

$$n^{(i)} = \arg \min_{n \in \mathcal{N}^{(i-1)}} \left| h_n^{(i)} \right|. \qquad (5.23)$$

In each outer iteration, the smallest-coefficient rule needs to solve only one minimax design problem. Thus, its computational complexity is much lower than that of the minimum-increase rule.

Both selection rules abandon the fixed order of nullifying coefficients. Instead, in each outer iteration, index $n^{(i)}$ of the new zero coefficient is determined by index sets $\mathcal{Z}^{(i-1)}$ and $\mathcal{N}^{(i-1)}$ which are obtained in the previous iteration, such that the most suitable index could be picked out. In this way, sparser FIR filters can be attained by the successive thinning method. Another noticeable feature of the successive thinning method is that it follows the greedy strategy to expand index set $\mathcal{Z}^{(i)}$ of zero coefficients. Namely, once one coefficient is set equal to zero in current iteration, it is never turned back to a nonzero value. The greedy strategy is adopted by a variety of sparse coding algorithms. It guarantees that the iterative procedure definitely converges to a final solution. However, in practice, the greedy strategy lacks the flexibility of searching locally optimal designs.

5.2.4 *Iterative Shrinkage/Thresholding (IST) Method*

Jiang et al. proposed in [30] an iterative method to solve the peak-error-constrained sparse FIR filter design problem (5.7). For the convenience of succeeding discussion, constraint (5.7b) is discretized over Ω_I, yielding a set of second-order cone constraints

$$\| \mathbf{d}_k - \mathbf{F}_k \mathbf{h} \|_2 \le \upsilon_k, \quad k = 1, \dots, K \qquad (5.24)$$

where $\mathbf{F}_k$, $\mathbf{d}_k$ and υ_k are defined by substituting $\omega_k \in \Omega_I$ into (5.10)–(5.12), respectively. The IST method starts from a given initial point

$\mathbf{h}^{(0)}$. Then, in the succeeding iterations, constraint (5.24) is replaced by

$$\left\| \mathbf{h} - \mathbf{b}_k^{(i)} \right\|_2^2 \leq u_k^{(i)}, \quad k = 1, \ldots, K \tag{5.25}$$

where

$$\mathbf{b}_k^{(i)} = \mathbf{F}_k^T \mathbf{v}_k^{(i)} + \mathbf{h}^{(i-1)}$$

$$u_k^{(i)} = \frac{1}{c_k} v_k^2 - \mathbf{v}_k^{(i)T} \left(c_k \mathbf{I} - \mathbf{F}_k \mathbf{F}_k^T \right) \mathbf{v}_k^{(i)}$$

$$\mathbf{v}_k^{(i)} = \frac{1}{c_k} \left(\mathbf{d}_k - \mathbf{F}_k \mathbf{h}^{(i)} \right).$$

In the above equations, $\mathbf{h}^{(i-1)}$ represents a solution obtained in the previous iteration, and constant c_k is chosen such that $c_k \geq \lambda_{\max} \left(\mathbf{F}_k^T \mathbf{F}_k \right)$ for $k = 1, \ldots, K$ where $\lambda_{\max}(\cdot)$ denotes the maximum eigenvalue of a symmetric matrix. Note that the feasibility domain defined by (5.25) is completely contained within the original one defined by (5.24). This modification results in a simplified design problem

$$\min_{\mathbf{h}} \quad \|\mathbf{h}\|_0 \tag{5.26a}$$

$$\text{s.t.} \quad \left\| \mathbf{h} - \mathbf{b}_k^{(i)} \right\|_2^2 \leq u_k^{(i)}, \quad k = 1, \ldots, K. \tag{5.26b}$$

To proceed, the Lagrangian dual problem of (5.26) is constructed as follows:

$$\max_{\lambda, \mathbf{z}} \quad \lambda^T \mathbf{p}^{(i)} - \mathbf{1}^T \mathbf{z} \tag{5.27a}$$

$$\text{s.t.} \quad \frac{\left(\lambda^T \mathbf{q}_n^{(i)} \right)^2}{\mathbf{1}^T \lambda} \leq 1 + z_n, \quad n = 0, \ldots, N \tag{5.27b}$$

$$\lambda \geq 0 \tag{5.27c}$$

$$\mathbf{z} \geq 0 \tag{5.27d}$$

where $\lambda \in \mathbb{R}^K$ are Lagrangian multipliers associated with (5.25), $\mathbf{z} \in \mathbb{R}^{N+1}$ are auxiliary variables, each entry of $\mathbf{p}^{(i)}$ is computed by

$$p_k^{(i)} = \sum_{n=0}^{N} \left(b_{k,n}^{(i)} \right)^2 - u_k^{(i)}$$

and $\mathbf{q}_n^{(i)}$ is defined by

$$\mathbf{q}_n^{(i)} = \left[b_{1,n}^{(i)} \ b_{2,n}^{(i)} \ \cdots \ b_{K,n}^{(i)} \right]^T.$$

Problem (5.27) is a convex optimization problem, which can be efficiently and reliably solved. Let $(\lambda^{(i)}, \mathbf{z}^{(i)})$ be the optimal solution to (5.27). Then, the primal solution $\mathbf{h}^{(i)}$ is recovered by

$$
\begin{aligned}
h_n^{(i)} &= \frac{\lambda^{(i)T} \mathbf{q}_n^{(i)}}{\mathbf{1}^T \lambda^{(i)}} \cdot \left\| z_n^{(i)} \right\|_0 \\
&= \begin{cases}
\frac{\lambda^{(i)T} \mathbf{q}_n^{(i)}}{\mathbf{1}^T \lambda^{(i)}}, & \frac{\left(\lambda^{(i)T} \mathbf{q}_n^{(i)}\right)^2}{\mathbf{1}^T \lambda^{(i)}} > 1 \ \left(\text{or } z_n^{(i)} > 0\right) \\
0, & \frac{\left(\lambda^{(i)T} \mathbf{q}_n^{(i)}\right)^2}{\mathbf{1}^T \lambda^{(i)}} \leq 1 \ \left(\text{or } z_n^{(i)} = 0\right),
\end{cases}
\end{aligned}
\tag{5.28}
$$

which is to be used in the next iteration. The major steps of the IST method are summarized as follows:

(1) Initialize $\mathbf{h}^{(0)}$;
(2) Repeat for $i = 1, 2, \ldots$

    (a) Construct subproblem (5.26) using $\mathbf{h}^{(i-1)}$;
    (b) Solve the Lagrangian dual problem (5.27) to obtain $(\lambda^{(i)}, \mathbf{z}^{(i)})$;
    (c) Restore the primal solution $\mathbf{h}^{(i)}$ by (5.28) using $(\lambda^{(i)}, \mathbf{z}^{(i)})$.

The remaining question is why the IST method resorts to the dual problem (5.27) instead of the primal problem (5.26). In general, the optimal objective value of the dual problem (5.27) only provides a lower bound of that of the primal problem (5.26). However, the following theorem demonstrates that by solving the convex optimization problem (5.27) one can obtain an optimal solution to (5.26).

Theorem 5.1. *In each iteration i, let* $\mathcal{Z}^{(i)} = \left\{ n : h_n^{(i)} = 0 \right\}$. *If*

$$
\frac{\left(\lambda^{(i)T} \mathbf{q}_n^{(i)}\right)^2}{\mathbf{1}^T \lambda^{(i)}} \neq 1, \ \forall n \in \mathcal{Z}^{(i)},
\tag{5.29}
$$

$\mathbf{h}^{(i)}$ *is the optimal solution to (5.26) and the duality gap between (5.26) and (5.27) is zero.*

Similar strategy can also be applied to solve the WLS-error-constrained design problem (5.8) [31]. However, because there is only one second-order cone constraint, the design method is accordingly simplified. The major steps of the IST method for (5.8) are as follows:

(1) Initialize $\mathbf{h}^{(0)}$;
(2) Repeat for $i = 1, 2, \ldots$

    (a) Use the similar technique aforementioned to construct a subproblem

$$\min_{\mathbf{h}} \quad \|\mathbf{h}\|_0 \tag{5.30a}$$

$$\text{s.t.} \quad \left\|\mathbf{h} - \mathbf{b}^{(i)}\right\|_2^2 \le u^{(i)} \tag{5.30b}$$

    (b) Solve the subproblem above by *the successive activation method*.

Here, the successive activation method is developed to tackle the simplified subproblem (5.30). Its main steps are shown below:

(1) Rearrange elements of $\mathbf{b}^{(i)}$ in a nonascending order according to their magnitudes, *i.e.*, $\left|b_{(0)}^{(i)}\right| \ge \ldots \ge \left|b_{(N)}^{(i)}\right|$, and set $n = 0$;

(2) If $\sum_{j=n+1}^{N} \left|b_{(j)}^{(i)}\right|^2 \le u^{(i)}$, specify $h_{(n)}^{(i)}$ as any value within the interval $\left[b_{(n)}^{(i)} - \Delta u^{(i)}, b_{(n)}^{(i)} + \Delta u^{(i)}\right]$ where $\Delta u^{(i)} = \sqrt{u^{(i)} - \sum_{j=n+1}^{N} \left|b_{(j)}^{(i)}\right|^2}$ and return $\mathbf{h}^{(i)}$;

(3) Choose $h_{(n)}^{(i)} = b_{(n)}^{(i)}$, set $n = n + 1$, and go to the second step.

Note that, although it still needs to iteratively construct a subproblem, the IST method proposed for the WLS-error-constrained design problem does not directly deal with the Lagrangian dual problem of (5.30). Since in each iteration the successive thinning method only involves scalar operations, the IST method is computationally efficient. Another point needs to be mentioned is that for the peak-error-constrained design problem optimal solutions can be achieved in each iteration only when condition (5.29) is satisfied. In contrast, this optimality condition is always satisfied for the WLS-error-constrained design problem, such that the resulting solution obtained is always locally optimal.

    Compared to the successive thinning method, in each iteration the IST method aims to find a new index set of zero coefficients by solving the subproblems which are driven by the sparsity of an FIR filter. This is different to the greedy strategy to expand $\mathcal{Z}$ in the

Table 5.1 Specifications of Example 1

Filter order	$N = 100$
Passband cutoff frequency	$\omega_P = 0.0436\pi$
Stopband cutoff frequency	$\omega_S = 0.0872\pi$
Passband ripple	Within ± 0.3 dB of unity
Stopband attenuation	$\delta(\omega) \leq -50$ dB

successive thinning method. In this way, the IST method provides a more flexible way to locate zero coefficients.

To demonstrate the advantage of this design strategy, we conclude the discussion of this subsection by an example of designing a lowpass linear-phase FIR filter. The specifications are given in Table 5.1.

The magnitude responses of FIR filters designed by the successive thinning method and the IST method are depicted in Fig. 5.1 Apparently, both design methods achieve sparse FIR filters with similar magnitude responses. However, FIR filter designed by the

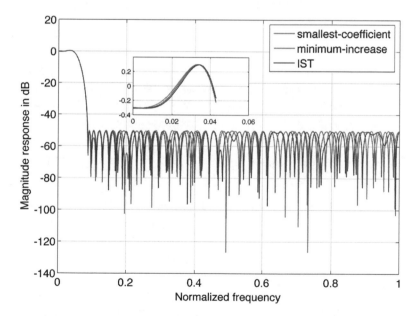

Figure 5.1 Magnitude responses of sparse FIR filters designed by the successive thinning method and the IST method.

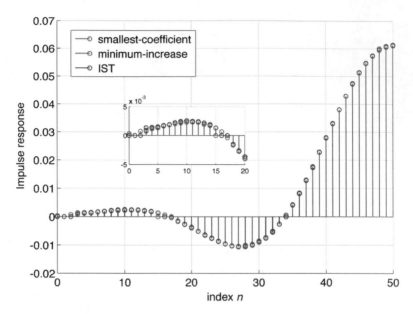

Figure 5.2 Impulse responses of sparse FIR filters designed by the successive thinning method and the IST method.

IST method only has 89 nonzero coefficients, while the successive thinning method can only reduce the number of nonzero coefficients to 93. Impulse responses of FIR filters designed in this example are shown in Fig. 5.2 Due to the symmetric structure of a linear-phase FIR filter, only one half of filter coefficients are depicted in Fig. 5.2.

5.2.5 *Joint Optimization of Coefficient Sparsity and Filter Order*

Sparse FIR filter design methods aforementioned assume that the predefined filter order is sufficient large such that there always exist sparse solutions given other design specifications. However, in practice it is unclear so far what the best value of this predefined order is. In general, a larger N leads to more zero coefficients. However, it does not mean that the corresponding implementation cost always decreases with the growth of N. On the other hand, the filtering performance of an FIR filter is affected by its filter order. For instance, a higher filter order for a linear-phase FIR filter leads to a higher group delay, which is inappropriate in many situations. In view of these considerations, filter order is jointly optimized in [32] with the sparsity of an FIR filter.

Compared to the traditional sparse FIR filter design problem (5.7), the joint optimization problem is cast as

$$\min_{\mathbf{h}} \quad (1 - \lambda) \|\mathbf{h}\|_0 + \lambda \rho(\mathbf{h}) \tag{5.31a}$$

$$\text{s.t.} \quad W(\omega) \left| H(e^{j\omega}) - D(\omega) \right| \leq \delta, \quad \forall \omega \in \Omega_I \tag{5.31b}$$

where $\rho(\mathbf{h})$ is a regularization term to penalize a large filter order. In practice, there are various ways to construct $\rho(\mathbf{h})$. In [32], $\rho(\mathbf{h})$ is defined as follows for the ease of the development of design methods

$$\rho(\mathbf{h}) = \left\| \begin{bmatrix} |h_N| \\ |h_N| + |h_{N-1}| \\ \vdots \\ |h_N| + |h_{N-1}| + \cdots + |h_0| \end{bmatrix} \right\|_0. \tag{5.32}$$

Note that if $\lambda = 0$ the above problem reduces to (5.7), while setting $\lambda = 1$ yields a design problem which aims to find the minimum filter order of an FIR filter that satisfies the given specifications.

Two design methods are developed in [32] to tackle (5.31). In the first approach, an upper bound of $\rho(\mathbf{h})$ is derived

$$\rho(\mathbf{h}) = \sum_{m=0}^{N} \left\| \sum_{i=0}^{m} |h_{N-i}| \right\|_0$$

$$\leq \sum_{m=0}^{N} \sum_{i=0}^{m} \| |h_{N-i}| \|_0 \tag{5.33}$$

$$= \sum_{n=0}^{N} (n+1) \|h_n\|_0$$

which is substituted to the objective function of (5.31), yielding a weighted l_0-norm minimization problem

$$\min_{\mathbf{h}} \quad \sum_{n=0}^{N} (1 + \lambda n) \|h_n\|_0 \tag{5.34a}$$

$$\text{s.t.} \quad W(\omega) \left| H(e^{j\omega}) - D(\omega) \right| \leq \delta, \quad \forall \omega \in \Omega_I. \tag{5.34b}$$

Essentially, in (5.34) different coefficients bear different weights. More specifically, larger weights are specified on filter coefficients with smaller indices, such that they are more likely to be nullified when minimizing the upper bound, yielding an FIR filter with a lower order. In the second approach, a more accurate problem formulation is derived by introducing a set of auxiliary variables $\{y_n\}_{n=0}^{N+1}$, which satisfy $y_n = y_{n+1} + |h_n|$ and $y_{N+1} = 0$. In this way, (5.31) is reformulated as

$$\min_{\mathbf{h}, \mathbf{y}} \quad (1 - \lambda) \|\mathbf{h}\|_0 + \lambda \|\mathbf{y}\|_0 \tag{5.35a}$$

$$\text{s.t.} \quad W(\omega) \left| H(e^{j\omega}) - D(\omega) \right| \leq \delta, \quad \forall \omega \in \Omega_I \tag{5.35b}$$

$$|h_n| = y_n - y_{n+1}, \quad n = 0, \dots, N. \tag{5.35c}$$

To proceed, constraints (5.35c) are relaxed to

$$|h_n| \leq y_n - y_{n+1}, \quad n = 0, \dots, N \tag{5.36}$$

such that the feasibility domain defined by (5.35b) and (5.36) is a convex set. Although these relaxed inequality constraints define a larger feasibility domain, Theorem 5.2 given below guarantees that optimal solutions to (5.35) can always be achieved by optimal solutions to the following relaxed design problem

$$\min_{\mathbf{h}, \mathbf{y}} \quad (1 - \lambda) \|\mathbf{h}\|_0 + \lambda \|\mathbf{y}\|_0 \tag{5.37a}$$

$$\text{s.t.} \quad W(\omega) \left| H(e^{j\omega}) - D(\omega) \right| \leq \delta, \quad \forall \omega \in \Omega_I \tag{5.37b}$$

$$|h_n| \leq y_n - y_{n+1}, \quad n = 0, \dots, N. \tag{5.37c}$$

Theorem 5.2. *Problems (5.35) and (5.37) have the same minimum objective function value. Any optimal solution to (5.37) can be transformed to an optimal solution to (5.35).*

In [32], the iterative-reweighted-least-squares (IRLS) algorithm is applied to tackle both (5.34) and (5.37). The basic idea of the IRLS algorithm is that the solution to an l_0-norm minimization problem can be obtained by its l_1-norm relaxation. Moreover, by defining a diagonal matrix $\mathbf{H} = \text{diag}(|h_0|, |h_1|, \dots, |h_N|)$, $\|\mathbf{h}\|_1$ can be rewritten as $\mathbf{h}^T \mathbf{H}^{-1} \mathbf{h}$. In practice, as $\mathbf{H}$ is unknown, $\mathbf{H}^{-1}$ has to be approximated by another diagonal matrix $\mathbf{W}^{(i)}$, where each diagonal element is computed by

$$W_n^{(i)} = \left(|h_n^{(i-1)}| + \sigma \right)^{-p}, \quad n = 0, 1, \dots, N. \tag{5.38}$$

In the above equation, σ is a small constant used to avoid the division by zero, and $p \geq 1$ aims to accelerate the convergence of the iterative procedure. Similar technique is also applied to handle $\|\mathbf{y}\|_0$ in the objective function of (5.37).

Reweighting technique is also utilized by the design approach in [33]. However, similar to (5.20), a regularized design problem is considered in [33]. In each iteration, the following design problem is solved:

$$\min_{\mathbf{h},\delta} \quad \delta + \mu \left\| \mathbf{W}^{(i)}\mathbf{h} \right\|_1$$

$$\text{s.t.} \quad W(\omega)\left| H\left(e^{j\omega}\right) - D(\omega)\right| \le \delta, \quad \forall \omega \in \Omega_I$$

$$\delta \le \gamma$$

$$h_n = 0, \quad \forall n \in \mathcal{Z}^{(i-1)},$$

where $\mathbf{W}^{(i)}$ is updated using (5.38) with $p = 1$. The above formulation implies that [33] still uses the greedy strategy to expand the index set of zero coefficients. Therefore, its performance is similar to that of the successive thinning method.

In summary, the IST method and the joint optimization method both adopt a dynamic design strategy, which presents two important features. First, the order of nullifying coefficients is varied from one iteration to the next. Second, zero (nonzero) coefficients in the current iteration could be turned to nonzero (zero) ones in the next iteration. Due to these characteristics, both methods are more flexible to attain sparser designs.

To conclude this subsection, we present two numerical examples to demonstrate the effectiveness of the joint optimization method. In the first example, a set of lowpass FIR filters are designed using specifications given in Table 5.2. Design results obtained by the joint optimization method are compared to those attained by the hard thresholding method and the minimum 1-norm method. Since the joint optimization method and the minimum 1-norm method both need $\delta(\omega)$ to construct peak error constraints, for a fair comparison

Table 5.2 Specifications of Example 2

Initial filter order	$N = 200$
Passband cutoff frequency	$\omega_P = 0.0436\pi$
Stopband cutoff frequency	$\omega_S = 0.0872\pi$
Number of zero coefficients specified for the hard thresholding method	$4 \sim 20$

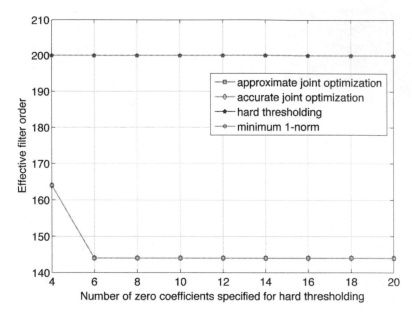

Figure 5.3 Variation of effective filter order with respect to the number of zero coefficients specified for the hard thresholding method.

we first utilize the hard thresholding algorithm to design an FIR filter. Its maximum magnitude approximation error is then used as $\delta(\omega)$. The desired number of zero coefficients specified for the hard thresholding method is listed in Table 5.2. The variations of effective filter order and the number of nonzero coefficients with respect to the desired number of zero coefficients are illustrated in Figs. 5.3 and 5.4, respectively. Figure 5.3 shows that the hard thresholding method and the minimum 1-norm method are unable to attain an FIR filter with a lower order, even if the initial order N is sufficiently large for the given specifications. In contrast, by introducing the regularization term $\rho(\mathbf{h})$ the joint optimization method is capable of finding a filter order more suitable than the initial value. Figure 5.4 demonstrates that both the hard thresholding method and the joint optimization method can achieve consistent design results under various specifications. More specifically, they can obtain sparser designs while increasing the desired number of zero coefficients

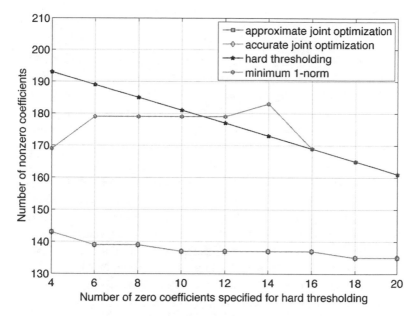

Figure 5.4 Variation of the number of nonzero coefficients with respect to the number of zero coefficients specified for the hard thresholding method.

specified for the hard thresholding method and, accordingly, the upper bound of approximation error $\delta(\omega)$.

As mentioned before, if parameter λ used in (5.31a) is set to 1, the joint optimization method is able to estimate the minimum filter order, given a set of design specifications. To comprehensively evaluate this capability, we present at the end of this section another example, which consists of three sets of lowpass filter designs using different passband cutoff frequency ω_P, transition bandwidth $\Delta\omega$, and desired maximum approximation error $\delta_d = \max_{\omega \in \Omega_l} \delta(\omega)$. The detailed specifications are given in Table 5.3.

Table 5.3   Specifications of Example 3

Initial filter order	$N = 80$
Passband cutoff frequency	$\omega_P \in [0.1\pi, 0.6\pi]$
Transition bandwidth	$\Delta\omega \in [0.05\pi, 0.15\pi]$
Desired maximum approximation error	$\delta_d \in [0.001, 0.01]$

In the first set of designs, we fix $\Delta\omega$ and δ_d to 0.1π and 0.01, respectively, and then design FIR filters with various $\omega_P \in [0.1\pi, 0.6\pi]$. For comparison, we also design for each ω_P an FIR filter with the minimum order required for the given specifications. In practice, there is no systematic way to definitely determine the minimum filter order so far. Thereby, starting from an initial value, we gradually decrease the filter order and then solve the minimax design problem (5.4) until peak error constraint is violated at some specific frequency points. To save unnecessary computation, the starting point of searching the minimum filter order is chosen as the effective filter order of FIR filter designed by the accurate joint optimization method. Figure 5.5 demonstrates the variation of filter order and the number of nonzero coefficients with respect to ω_P.

Similarly, in the second set of designs, we choose $\omega_P = 0.45\pi$ and $\delta_d = 0.01$. The transition bandwidth $\Delta\omega$ varies between 0.05π and 0.15π. Using these parameters, a set of FIR filters are designed by the joint optimization method and, given any triplet $(\omega_P, \Delta\omega, \delta_d)$, the minimum filter order is also attained by the exhaustive search employed in the first set of designs. Figure 5.6 shows the design results.

In the third set of designs, ω_P and $\Delta\omega$ are chosen equal to 0.3π and 0.1π, respectively. The allowable maximum approximation error δ_d is set to different values uniformly sampled within $[0.001, 0.01]$. The variation of filter order and the number of nonzero coefficients with respect to δ_d is depicted in Fig. 5.7

It is demonstrated by simulation results that the accurate joint optimization method can approach optimal solutions to the design problem (5.37), given any triplet $(\omega_P, \Delta\omega, \delta_d)$. This complies with the fact that when $\lambda = 1$ (5.37) is an accurate formulation of the design problem with the objective to minimize filter order, while (5.34) is just an approximate formulation that encourages coefficient sparsity by preferentially setting coefficients with smaller indices equal to zero. On the other hand, forcing coefficients equal to zero renders the reduction on the objective function value of (5.34a), while the effect of coefficient sparsity is completely removed from (5.37a). Thereby, the approximate joint optimization method is expected to achieve equivalent or better

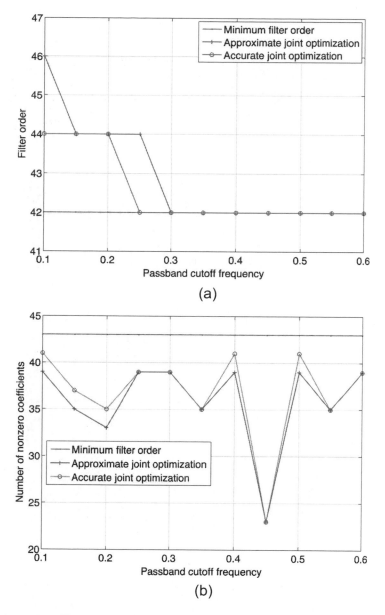

Figure 5.5 Variation of effective filter order and the number of nonzero coefficients with respect to ω_P. The transition bandwidth and the desired maximum approximation error are chosen as $\Delta\omega = 0.1\pi$ and $\delta_d = 0.01$.

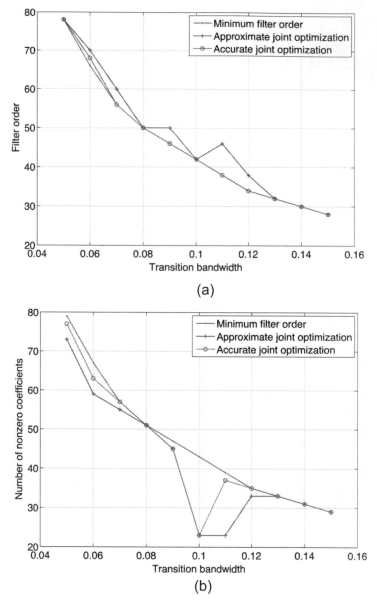

Figure 5.6 Variation of effective filter order and the number of nonzero coefficients with respect to $\Delta\omega$. The passband cutoff frequency and the desired maximum approximation error are chosen as $\omega_P = 0.45\pi$ and $\delta_d = 0.01$.

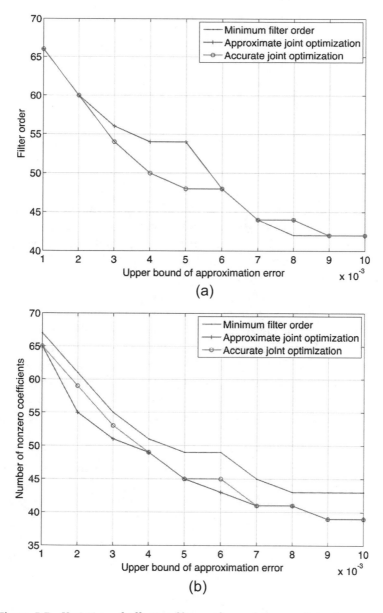

Figure 5.7 Variation of effective filter order and the number of nonzero coefficients with respect to δ_d. The passband cutoff frequency and the desired maximum approximation error are chosen as $\omega_P = 0.3\pi$ and $\Delta\omega = 0.1\pi$.

designs in terms of the number of nonzero coefficients. This is also confirmed by design results presented in this example.

5.3 Summary

As a sparse FIR filter contains a considerable number of zero coefficients, circuit components or arithmetic operations corresponding to zero coefficients are no longer required in practical implementation, thus leading to a low implementation complexity. In principle, the design of a sparse FIR filter is a combinatorial optimization problem. Its optimal solutions can be attained by exhaustive search, whose computational complexity could, however, be prohibitively high in practical designs. Thus, the development of more efficient design techniques draws much attention. It is noticed that the design of a sparse FIR filter is highly related to sparse coding, which has been extensively exploited lately. Actually, recent advances in the design of sparse FIR filters are inspired by the development of sparse coding. Some classical sparse coding methods (e.g., OMP, BP) could be applied to solve some sparse FIR filter design problems. However, there are inherent differences between these two classes of problems. Therefore, more sophisticated l_0 and l_1 optimization techniques have to be developed. In this chapter, we have reviewed several state of the art design mehods. Some of them are of computational efficiency, for example, the hard thresholding method and the minimum 1-norm method. Some other design methods explore more sophisticated design strategies. Generally speaking, the dynamic design strategy is required to obtain satisfactory results.

References

1. V. Cappellini, A. G. Constantinides, and P. Emiliani, *Digital Filters and their Applications*, London, New York, Academic Press, 1978.
2. A. Antoniou, *Digital Signal Processing: Signals, Systems, and Filters*, Chicago, London, Toronto, McGraw-Hill, 2006.

3. K. M. Tsui, S. C. Chan, and K. S. Yeung, Design of FIR filters with prescribed flatness and peak error constraints using second-order cone programming, *IEEE Trans. Circuits Syst. II*, 52, 601–605, 2005.

4. T. W. Parks and J. H. McClellan, Chebyshev approximation for non-recursive filters with linear phase, *IEEE Trans. Circuit Theory*, CT-19, 189–194, Mar. 1972.

5. L. R. Rabiner, Linear programming design of finite impulse response (FIR) filters, *IEEE Trans. Audio Electroacoust.*, AU-20, 280–288, 1972.

6. P. P. Vaidyanathan and T. Q. Nguyen, Eigenfilters: A new approach to least-squares FIR filter design and applications including Nyqvist filters, *IEEE Trans. Circuits Syst.*, 34, 11–23, January 1987.

7. T. N. Davidson, Enriching the art of FIR filter design via convex optimization, *IEEE Signal Process. Mag.*, 27, 89–101, May 2010.

8. D. Li, Y. C. Lim, Y. Lian, and J. Song, A polynomial-time algorithm for designing FIR filters with power-of-two coefficients, *IEEE Trans. Signal Process.*, 50, 1935–1941, August 2002.

9. Y. C. Lim, R. Yang, D. Li, and J. Song, Signed power-of-two term allocation scheme for the design of digital filters, *IEEE Trans. Circuits Syst. II, Analog Digit. Signal Process.*, 46(5), 577–584, May 1999.

10. Q. Zhao and Y. Tadakoro, A simple design of FIR filters with power-of-two coefficients, *IEEE Trans. Circuits Syst.*, 35(5), 566–570, May 1988.

11. Y. C. Lim and S. R. Parker, FIR filter design over a discrete power-of-two coefficient space, *IEEE Trans. Accoust., Speech, Signal Process.*, ASSP-31(3), 583–591, June 1983.

12. D. Shi and Y. J. Yu, Design of linear phase FIR filters with high probability of achieving minimum number of adders, *IEEE Trans. Circuits Syst. I*, 58, 126–136, January 2011.

13. Y. J. Yu and Y. C. Lim, Design of linear phase FIR filters in subexpression space using mixed integer linear programming, *IEEE Trans. Circuits Syst. I*, 54, 2330–2338, October 2007.

14. F. Xu, C.-H. Chang, and C.-C. Jong, Contention resolution algorithm for common subexpression elimination in digital filter design, *IEEE Trans. Circuits Syst. II, Exp. Briefs*, 52, 695–700, October 2005.

15. R. I. Hartley, Subexpression sharing in filters using canonic signed digit multipliers, *IEEE Trans. Circuits Syst. II, Analog Digit. Signal Process.*, 43(10), 677–688, October 1996.

16. A. Chopra and B. L. Evans, Design of sparse filters for channel shortening, in *Proc. IEEE Int. Con. Accost., Speech, Signal Process.*, 2010, pp. 1518–1521.

17. J. T. Kim, W. J. Oh, and Y. H. Lee, Design of nonuniformly spaced linear-phase FIR filters using mixed integer linear programming, *IEEE Trans. Signal Process.*, 44, 123–126, January 1996.

18. O. Gustafsson, L. S. DeBrunner, V. DeBrunner, and H. Johansson, On the design of sparse half-band like FIR filters, in *41st Asilomar Conf. Signal, Syst., Comp.*, Pacific Grove, USA, November 2007, pp. 1098–1102.

19. Y.-S. Song and Y. H. Lee, Design of sparse FIR filters based on branch-and-bound algorithm, in *Proc. 40th Midwest Symp. Circuits Syst.*, vol. 2, Sacramento, USA, August 1997, pp. 1445–1448.

20. M. Elad, *Sparse and Redundant Representations: From Theory to Applications in Signal and Image Processing*. New York, USA: Springer, 2010.

21. Y. C. Eldar and G. Kutyniok, *Compressive Sensing: Theory and Applications*. New York, USA: Cambridge University Press, 2012.

22. E. J. Candes and T. Tao, Decoding by linear programming, *IEEE Trans. Inf. Theory*, 51, 4203–4215, December 2005.

23. J. A. Tropp, Greed is good: Algorithmic results for sparse approximation, *IEEE Trans. Inf. Theory*, 50, 2231–2242, October 2004.

24. D. L. Donoho, M. Elad, and V. N. Temlyakov, Stable recovery of sparse over complete representations in the presence of noise, *IEEE Trans. Inf. Theory*, 52, 6–18, January 2006.

25. E. Candies, The restricted isometry property and its implications for compressed sensing, *Competes Rendus Mathematique*, 346, 589–592, 2008.

26. Y. Pati, R. Rezaiifar, and P. Krishnaprasad, Orthogonal matching pursuit: Recursive function approximation with applications to wavelet decomposition, in *Asilomar Conf. Signals, Systems, and Computers*, Pacific Grove, CA, USA, Nov. 1993.

27. S. Chen, D. L. Donoho, and M. Saunders, Atomic decomposition by basis pursuit, *SIAM J. Sci. Comput.*, 20, 33–61, 1998.

28. W.-S. Lu and T. Hinamoto, Digital filters with sparse coefficients, in *Proc. IEEE Int. Symp. Circuits Syst.*, Paris, France, May 2010, pp. 169–172.

29. T. Baran, D. Wei, and A. V. Oppenheim, Linear programming algorithms for sparse filter design, *IEEE Trans. Signal Process.*, 58, 1605–1617, Mar. 2010.

30. A. Jiang, H. K. Kwan, and Y. Zhu, Peak-error-constrained sparse FIR filter design using iterative SOCP, *IEEE Trans. Signal Process.*, 60, 4035–4044, Aug. 2012.

31. A. Jiang and H. K. Kwan, WLS design of sparse FIR digital filters, *IEEE Trans. Circuits Syst. I*, 60, 125–135, January 2013.

32. A. Jiang, H. K. Kwan, Y. Zhu, X. Liu, N. Xu, and Y. Tang, Design of sparse FIR filters with joint optimization of sparsity and filter order, *IEEE Trans. Circuits Syst. I*, 62, 195–204, January 2015.

33. C. Rusu and B. Dumitrescu, Iterative reweighted l_1 design of sparse FIR filters, *Signal Process.*, 92, 905–911, April 2012.

Chapter 6

Sparse Models in Echo Cancellation: When the Old Meets the New

Yannis Kopsinis, Symeon Chouvardas,
and Sergios Theodoridis

Department of Telecommunications and Informatics, University of Athens, Greece
kopsinis@ieee.org

6.1 Introduction

Echo cancellation, which is a key ingredient towards high-quality communications, appears to be a very challenging filtering task due to a number of inherent peculiarities. Figure 6.1 depicts a schematic representation of the echo cancellation problem. In an ideal communication setting, the loudspeaker at the far-end would either exclusively transmit the voice of the person at the near-end or nothing if this person is silent. This should be the case irrespective of whether the person at the far-end is speaking or not. However, in realistic conditions, this is not true; the far-end speech signal travels through the communication channel and it is transmitted via the loudspeaker in the near-end room. Due to the room impulse response and delays in the communication line, the microphone

Trends in Digital Signal Processing: A Festschrift in Honour of A. G. Constantinides
Edited by Yong Ching Lim, Hon Keung Kwan, and Wan-Chi Siu
Copyright © 2016 Pan Stanford Publishing Pte. Ltd.
ISBN 978-981-4669-50-4 (Hardcover), 978-981-4669-51-1 (eBook)
www.panstanford.com

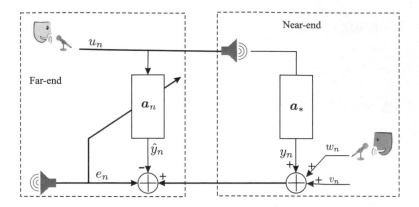

Figure 6.1 Schematic representation of the echo cancellation problem.

at the near-end captures a filtered version of the far-end speech, which is transmitted back to the far-end in the form of annoying echo. In wired communications, even when a room is not involved in echo generation, known as acoustic echo, electrically induced echo appears due to unbalanced coupling between the 2-wire and 4-wire circuits. The echo cancellation task aims at estimating the impulse response corresponding to the echo path. Doing so, the echo can be reproduced at the far-end and be subtracted from the received signal. In this way, the received signal is cleansed from the echo before its transmission through the loudspeaker.

In mathematical terms, the signal, y_n received at the far-end at time instance n is given by the typical linear regression model

$$y_n = u_n^T a_* + w_n + v_n, \quad \forall n \in \mathbb{N}, \tag{6.1}$$

where, $a_* \in \mathbb{R}^L$ is the L component long impulse response of the echo path, $u_n = [u_n, u_{n-1}, \ldots, u_{n-L+1}]^T \in \mathbb{R}^L$ is the input vector to the system at time instance n, comprising L successive samples of the far-end speech signal and w_n, v_n are the near-end speech sample and the background noise sample, respectively, at time n. The superscript $(\cdot)^T$ denotes vector transposition and the pair (y_n, u_n) is referred to as *data pair*. Echo cancellation is characterized by certain properties underling the echo path, the input signal and the noise:

(a) The unknown system a_* is time-varying, i.e., its entries may exhibit slow variations over time or it even change abruptly.

Moreover, a_* is sparse, i.e., most of its entries are zeros. In addition to that, the echo path impulse response is usually about 128 ms or longer. Such a value, even for moderate sampling rates of 8192 Hz, corresponds to a_* comprising more than 800 components.

(b) The input signal u_n, $n \in \mathbb{N}$ is the far-end speech signal, which is highly correlated, non-stationary and it also exhibits strong magnitude fluctuations allowing to get, from time to time, very small values.

(c) The overall noise comprises the background noise v_n and a highly disturbing term corresponding to the near-end speech signal w_n.

The characteristics above pose a number of difficulties to conventional system identification techniques and special treatment is needed. First of all, it is clear that adaptive filtering is required in order to cope with the time-varying nature of the echo path. Accordingly, convergence speed is a primal figure of merit, which it might be compromised due to the long impulse response of the echo paths and the highly correlated input signal. The appropriate exploitation of the sparsity attribute and/or the concurrent processing of many successive data pairs can lead to convergence speed enhancements at the cost of extra computational complexity. However, it is a big asset to keep computational complexity low due to the recommendations for low cost implementation, low battery consumption, and online/real-time operation. Finally, extra care is needed in order to be robust against the disruption caused be the near-end speech signal.

All the factors above build a rather hostile environment rendering the development of efficient echo-cancellers an open research field and the echo-cancellation problem the ideal "arena" for fair evaluation of different adaptive learning approaches. The better known methods suitable for echo-cancellation are the normalized least means squares (NLMS) and the affine projection algorithm (APA) both fused with the sparsity-promoting *proportionate update* philosophy (Benesty and Gay, 2002; Paleologu et al., 2010). The advent of compressed sensing allowed the incorporation in NLMS and APA of an alternative, sparsity-promoting mechanism mainly induced via properly constraining or regularizing the ℓ_1 norm or approximates of the ℓ_0 norm of the solution. This approach has not yet being evaluated in realistic echo-cancellation simulation setups. In this chapter, the two sparsity-inducing mechanisms are studied performance-wise and then merged under a set-theoretic adaptive filtering framework, known as adaptive projected subgradient method (APSM). Moreover, robust implementations in order to cope against the near-end speech disturbances are given and evaluated.

6.2 Sparse Adaptive Filtering: The Proportionate Updating Approach

Adaptive filtering and learning is among the most widely employed signal processing tasks in numerous applications, such as echo cancellation, channel equalization, prediction, etc. (Sayed, 2003; Haykin, 1996). The least means squares (LMS) algorithm and its normalized version (NLMS) are considered "classical" in the adaptive filtering community, offering robust performance with a very low computational complexity profile. However, the convergence speed of the LMS might be considered to be rather slow, for certain applications. As an alternative, the APA, which is essentially a generalization of NLMS, has gained much attention. It processes multiple data vectors in each adaptation step, achieving faster convergence rates, albeit at the expense of increased computational cost and potential instabilities, due to the matrix inversions involved.

As discussed before, the unknown parameter vector, $\boldsymbol{a}_*$, to be learned in echo cancellation is sparse. Motivated by that, the first instances of sparsity promoting online learning algorithms, which trace back well before compressed sensing, were developed for echo cancellation, e.g., Homer et al. (1998) and Sugiyama et al. (1996). The landmark of sparsity aware echo canceller was developed in 2000 by Duttweiler (Duttweiler, 2000), which is referred to as proportionate normalized least means squares (PNLMS). Since then, this basic scheme was improved (Benesty and Gay, 2002) and extended to the APA rationale (Paleologu et al., 2010). The fundamental idea behind the proportionate updating approach is to update each coefficient with a different step size, which is made proportional to the magnitude of the respective estimated coefficient. Accordingly, large coefficients, which are likely to correspond to non-zero components of the true parameter vector, are updated faster increasing convergence speed.

APA algorithm is concurrently processing the q lately obtained data pairs at each iteration. Denote by $U_n = [u_n, u_{n-1}, \cdots, u_{n-q+1}] \in \mathbb{R}^{L \times q}$ and $y_n = [y_n, y_{n-1}, \cdots, y_{n-q+1}]^T \in \mathbb{R}^q$, the matrix and the vector comprising the q latest input vectors and observations respectively. Then the APA adaptation formula at time n can be derived by minimizing the following constrained minimization task:

$$\min_{a_n} \|a_n - a_{n-1}\|_{Q_n^{-1}}^2, \quad \text{s.t.} \quad y_n = U_n^T a_n, \tag{6.2}$$

where a_{n-1} is the estimate at the previous time step, $Q_n \in \mathbb{R}^{L \times L}$ a diagonal, positive definite matrix and $\|a_n - a_{n-1}\|_{Q_n^{-1}}^2$, with $\|x\|_{Q_n^{-1}} = \sqrt{x^T Q_n^{-1} x}$ is a metric to compute the distance (discrepancy) between two successive estimates. Several variants of the APA differ only on the selection of matrix Q_n. In the standard APA case (Sayed, 2003), Q_n is set equal to the identity matrix, I, whereas in the proportionate APA (PAPA), $Q_n = G_n = \text{diag}(g_n)$, where $g_n(i) = \left(\frac{1-k}{2L} + (1+k) \frac{|a_{n-1}(i)|}{2\|a_{n-1}\|_1} \right)$, $i = 1, \ldots, L$, where diag denotes diagonal matrix and the ℓ_1 norm $\|x\|_1$ equals to $\sum_{i=1}^L |x(i)|$. Parameter $k \in [-1, 1]$ determines the extent to which the sparsity is taken into consideration and it is user defined (the larger the k the sparser the solution tend to be).

According to (6.2), APA in each adaptation step aims at finding a tentative estimate a_n which, without being far apart from the previous estimate a_{n-1}, satisfies the constraint equation $y_n = U_n^T a_n$. In order to geometrically interpret the function of the APA, one has to realize that there are infinitely many vectors a_n, which comply with the constraints $y_n = U_n^T a_n$. In particular, potential solutions are all those vectors lying on the $L - q$-dimensional plane H_n:

$$H_n := \{x \in \mathbb{R}^L : U_n^T x - y_n = 0\} \tag{6.3}$$

The minimization task (6.2), among all the points on H_n, selects the one that is closer to a_{n-1} with respect to the metric distance $\|a_n - a_{n-1}\|_{Q_n^{-1}}^2$. When $Q_n = I$, this distance is the Euclidean one and a_n is given by the orthogonal projection of a_{n-1} onto H_n. When Q_n equals to the diagonal matrix G_n, then

$$\|a_n - a_{n-1}\|^2_{G_n^{-1}} = \sum_{i=1}^{L} d_n^2(i)g_n^{-1}(i), \qquad (6.4)$$

where $d_n(i) = |a_n(i) - a_{n-1}(i)|$. In words, $d_n(i)$ is the amount of adaptation that the ith component admits at time instance n. From (6.4), it becomes apparent that the contribution to the overall distance of the adjustment of each component is *weighted* by the value $g_n^{-1}(i)$. Note that since $g_n^{-1}(i)$ is inversely proportional to $|a_{n-1}(i)|$, when the latter is zero (or has values very close to zero) then $g_n^{-1}(i)$ admits its maximum value (or values relatively large). Accordingly, the closer to zero the ith component is, the greater its significance in the formation of the total distance becomes. Put in other words, even small updates of such components can lead to large increments of the overall distance. Conversely, the large-magnitude components can be adapted gently without affecting much the overall distance, since the corresponding values of $g_n^{-1}(i)$ tend to be small. This behavior is particularly favorable in the echo cancellation case, where a_* is sparse allowing the proportionate APA to update the large components, which is likely to be the components corresponding to the true non-zero elements of a_*, much faster than the standard APA, leading to faster convergence. This point is further discussed in Section 6.4.

The APA algorithm (Sayed, 2003) equipped with a step size $\mu \in$ (0, 2) and a regularization parameter δ for increased stability (see Benesty et al. (2011) and Paleologu et al. (2011) for a thorough discussion), is given by

$$a_n = a_{n-1} + \mu G_n U_n (\delta I + U_n^T G_n U_n)^{-1} e_n, \qquad (6.5)$$

where $e_n = y_n - U_n^T a_{n-1}$. The exact solution of (6.2) corresponds to $\mu = 1$ and $\delta = 0$. The incorporation of the step size μ allows to control the convergence behavior of the algorithm, namely, for large μ, to achieve fast convergence albeit with a relatively high steady-state error or, for small μ, to attain low error values after convergence at the expense of a slower convergence speed.

When $q = 1$ then APA reduces to the NLMS and to the improved proportionate NLMS (IPNLMS) for $Q_n = I$ and $Q_n = G_n$, respectively.

6.3 Sparse Adaptive Filtering: Sparsity-Induced Regularization/Thresholding Approach

Recently, motivated by advances in Compressed Sensing, the regularization with specially chosen penalties have been proposed as a promising alternative to proportionate updating for sparsity promotion. The resulted approach applied to the APA algorithm (for $q = 1$ the corresponding NLMS versions stem directly), hereafter referred to as *sparse-APA* (*sparse-NLMS*), at each time step, aims at solving the following constrained minimization task:

$$\min_{a_n} \|a_n - a_{n-1}\|_2^2 + \lambda P(a_n), \quad \text{s.t.} \quad y_n = U_n^T a_n, \qquad (6.6)$$

where $P(a_n)$ is a penalty function, which favors sparse solutions by taking large values when a_n is not sparse. The optimal choice would be to use the ℓ_0 pseudo-norm, $P(a_n) = \|a_n\|_0$, which directly measures the number of the non-zero components of a_n, the so called, sparsity level. However, such a choice is not handy due to the fact that it is a non-differentiable function. On the contrary, approximates of the ℓ_0 norm taking the form $P(a_n) = \sum_{i=1}^{L} p(|a_n(i)|)$ are employed in practice, where p is a non-negative, non-decreasing and differentiable function on $(0, \infty)$ (Chen et al., 2009; Gu et al., 2009; Taheri and Vorobyov, 2014; Gui and Adachi, 2013; Meng et al., 2011; Su et al., 2012). Parameter λ regularizes the effect of the penalty function to the overall cost, and the larger it is, the sparser the solutions of (6.6) tend to be.

Several variants of the sparse APA/NLMS result using different p functions, where some indicative and popular examples are listed in Table 6.1 together with their corresponding derivatives.

The abbreviations correspond to zero-attracting (ZA), reweighted zero-attracting (RZA) (Chen et al., 2009) and smooth ℓ_0

Table 6.1 Penalty functions and their derivatives

Sparse APA	$p(|a(i)|)$	$p'(a(i))$
ZA-APA	$|a(i)|$	$\text{sgn}(a(i))$
RZA-APA	$\log(1 + \tilde{\varepsilon}|a(i)|)$	$\dfrac{\tilde{\varepsilon}\,\text{sgn}(a(i))}{1 + \tilde{\varepsilon}|a(i)|}$
Sℓ_0	$\left(1 - e^{-\beta|a(i)|}\right)$	$\beta\,\text{sgn}(a(i))e^{-\beta|a(i)|}$

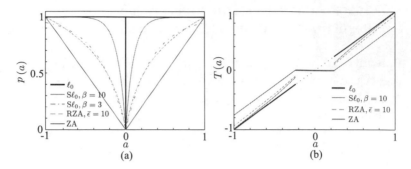

Figure 6.2 Penalty functions and the corresponding thresholding operators.

(Sℓ_0) (Gu et al., 2009; Su et al., 2012; Shi and Shi, 2010; Di Lorenzo et al., 2012).

Plots of these penalty functions are shown in Fig. 6.2a. Observe that that ZA penalty is the only convex one, whereas RZA and Sℓ_0 are more elaborated compared to it. They are non-convex and involve additional parameters such as $\bar{\epsilon}$ and β, which affect the curvature of the penalty functions. The larger the $\bar{\epsilon}$ and β are the closer the RZA and Sℓ_0 are getting to the ℓ_0 penalty, which is shown with thick solid line.

Under the assumption that the sparsity characteristics are approximately preserved from time instance $n-1$ to n, $P(a_n)$ can be replaced by $P(a_{n-1})$ leading to a closed form solution for the sparse APA adaptation step e.g., (Meng et al., 2011; Lima et al., 2014):

$$\bar{a}_n = a_{n-1} + \mu U_n(\delta I + U_n^T U_n)^{-1} e_n \tag{6.7}$$

$$a_n = \bar{a}_n - \lambda F(a_{n-1}) + \lambda U_n(\delta I + U_n^T U_n)^{-1} U_n^T F(a_{n-1}), \tag{6.8}$$

where $F(a_{n-1}) = \sum_{i=1}^{L} p'(|a_{n-1}(i)|)$, where p' stands for derivative. As shown in (6.5), both a step size $\mu \in (0, 2)$ and a regularization parameter δ have been introduced for stability issues with the exact solution of (6.6) corresponding to $\delta = 0$ and $\mu = 1$. Moreover, for $q = 1$ the sparse-NLMS algorithm stems directly. Note that sparse-APA comprises two stages in each adaptation step, where the first one, (6.7), is the adaptation step of the conventional APA/NLMS algorithms and then sparsity is imposed via the second update stage, (6.8).

Following similar reasoning, in Chen et al. (2009), Gu et al. (2009) and Taheri and Vorobyov (2014), sparse-LMS rather than NLMS were developed resulting in the simpler form:

$$\bar{a}_n = a_{n-1} + \mu u_n e_n \tag{6.9}$$

$$a_n = \bar{a}_n - \lambda F(a_{n-1}). \tag{6.10}$$

There are two differences between the sparse-LMS with (6.7) and (6.8), when $q = 1$. First, the normalization factor $(\delta + u_n^T u_n)$ is absent and second, the second additive term of (6.8) has been omitted. The sparsity inducing effect of (6.10) is clear. Advising Table 6.1, the components of the term $\lambda F(a_{n-1})$ have all the same sign with that of a_{n-1} acting as a zero attractor, meaning that for λ properly small, (6.10) tends to bring all the components closer to zero. In the case of ZA, the attraction to zero is uniform for all components, whereas in the RZA and smooth ℓ_0 the attraction to zero is stronger for the small components and weaker for the large ones. The sparse-LMS is in general inferior to the sparse-NLMS and optimized μ values can be very small rendering their optimization cumbersome. Besides, the second term of (6.8) in sparse-APA/NLMS does not offer significant improvements to justify the extra computational burden. So it is recommended to use the standard normalized NLMS with only the zero attracting term, $-\lambda F(a_{n-1})$ in the sparsification step.

Following alternative routes, Murakami et al. (2010) builds upon the idea of proximal forward-backward splitting in order to substitute the zero attracting step, (6.10), in APA, NLMS, and/or their proportionate versions with a time-varying soft thresholding operator. Recently, all the sparse LMS variants discussed so far where derived via the online convex optimization (OCO) framework (Hu and Chklovskii, 2014). In the same framework, a sparse LMS equipped with a fixed soft-thresholding operator was proposed.

$$\bar{a}_n = a_{n-1} + \mu u_n e_n \tag{6.11}$$

$$a_n = \text{Thres}(\bar{a}_n, \rho), \tag{6.12}$$

where, the thresholding operator Thres($\cdot$) acts component-wise,

$$\text{Thres}(\bar{a}_n(i), \rho) = \begin{cases} 0, & |\bar{a}_n(i)| \leq \rho, \\ \bar{a}_n(i) - \rho \text{sgn}(\bar{a}_n(i)), & |\bar{a}_n(i)| > \rho \end{cases}, \forall i$$

6.4 Adaptive Sparsity Promotion: A Geometrical Point of View

Both proportionate updating and sparsity-promoting regularization approaches aim at producing solutions that are compressible, i.e., most of the components assume values very close to zero. Truly sparse solution, i.e., most of the components being exactly zero, cannot be guaranteed unless thresholding operation is involved such as in (6.12). In any case, the two sparsity-promoting mechanisms are largely different as it is geometrically demonstrated with the aid of Fig. 6.3. For simplicity, the $q = 1$, i.e., the NLMS case, with $\mu = 1$ and $\delta = 0$ is considered. Moreover, in the scenario shown any type of noise is absent. The true unknown vector, $\boldsymbol{a}_* \in \mathbb{R}^2$ is sparse comprising only one non-zero component lying, therefore, on one of the axes. Assume also that the time of reference is $n - 2$ and the update iterations up to the time instance n are examined. The data pairs $(y_i, \boldsymbol{u}_i)$, $i = n - 1$, n, form two hyperplanes, which due to the absence of noise, i.e., $y_i = \boldsymbol{u}_i^T \boldsymbol{a}_*$, $\forall i$, pass through $\boldsymbol{a}_*$. Figure 6.3a displays with solid and dashed lines the updating steps realized by the conventional and the proportionate NLMS respectively. As it was described in Section 6.2, adapted here to the $q = 1$ case, the conventional NLMS, in each step, among the infinite number of

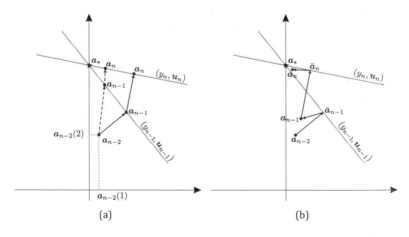

Figure 6.3 Geometric interpretation: (a) Proportionate NLMS. (b) Sparse NLMS.

solutions, a, complying with the constraint $y_i = u_i^T a$ chooses the one with the minimum Euclidean distance from the estimate in the previous step. This corresponds to the orthogonal projection of the previous estimate onto the current hyperplane. On the contrary, proportionate updating favors the faster updating of the large components resulting in oblige projections. Indeed, the value of the coordinate $a_i(1)$, $i = n - 1$, n, does not change significantly from one step to the next since it is much smaller than $a_i(2)$.

Figure 6.3(b) shows the two-step updating approach of the sparse NLMS. In the first step, i.e., (6.7), as in conventional NLMS, the Euclidean projection onto the corresponding hyperplane is performed. In the second step, the components of the $\bar{a}_i$ are shrunk according to the specific penalty function used.

6.5 Sparse Adaptive Filtering: Set Theoretic Approach

In this section, a set-theoretic based adaptive filtering approach, referred to as APSM (Yamada and Ogura, 2004; Slavakis et al., 2006; Theodoridis et al., 2011), will be employed in order to incorporate the two different sparsity promotion mechanisms discussed before in a unified framework. Former attempts to this were made before in Murakami et al. (2010) and Chouvardas et al. (2012). The proposed method is more general providing certain convergence guarantees.

Moreover, the approach to be followed is different compared to other state-of-the-art sparsity promoting set-theoretic methods, such as Lima et al. (2014).

A key point of the set-theoretic estimation rationale is to associate each data pair with a closed convex set such that all the constructed sets to contain the unknown vector. In the absence of noise, as shown in Fig. 6.3, if each data pair is represented by a hyperplane, then the request above is fulfilled[a] and a_* will be found in the common intersection of all the hyperplanes. In the presence of noise, however, the true vector a_* would not lie on the hyperplanes because in this case $u_i^T a_* - y_i \neq 0$, $\forall i$. In such cases, a popular choice, as shown in Fig. 6.4, is to replace the hyperplanes with *hyperslabs*

---

[a]The set of all points lying on a hyperplane is convex.

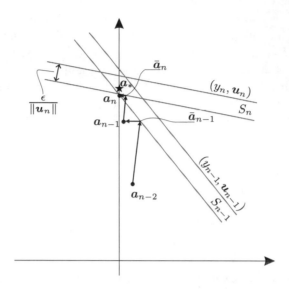

Figure 6.4   Geometric illustration of the APSM adaptation steps.

defined as:

$$S_n := \left\{ \boldsymbol{x} \in \mathbb{R}^L : |\boldsymbol{u}_n^T \boldsymbol{x} - y_n| \le \epsilon \right\}, \qquad \forall n \in \mathbb{N}, \tag{6.13}$$

for some user-defined tolerance $\epsilon \ge 0$ and for $\boldsymbol{u}_n \ne \boldsymbol{0}$. The parameter ϵ determines, essentially, the width of the hyperslabs. Note that in case of bounded noise, a parameter ϵ, which guarantees that the true solution will be included inside all the hyperlsabs, can be found. When the noise is not bounded, e.g., it is normal distributed, then one can choose an ϵ large enough to guaranteed that the vast majority of hyperslabs contain $\boldsymbol{a}_*$. As time evolves, new hyperslabs are formed and the true solution, $\boldsymbol{a}_*$, is contained in their common intersection. The objective of the adaptive set-theoretic algorithms is to converge to any vector that belongs to this common intersection. In APSM this is carried out via a series of projections, not necessarily Euclidean, onto the formed convex sets as it will be discussed next.

The metric projection, with respect to any positive definite weighting matrix $\boldsymbol{Q}_n^{-1}$, of a point $\boldsymbol{a}_n$ onto a hyperslab S_i, is given by (Yukawa and Yamada, 2009; Chouvardas et al., 2012):

$$P_{S_i}^{(\boldsymbol{Q}_n^{-1})}(\boldsymbol{a}_n) = \boldsymbol{a}_n + \beta_i \boldsymbol{Q}_n \boldsymbol{a}_n, \tag{6.14}$$

where

$$\beta_i = \begin{cases} \dfrac{e_i(\boldsymbol{a}_n) - \text{sgn}(e_i(\boldsymbol{a}_n))\epsilon}{\|\boldsymbol{a}_n\|_{\boldsymbol{Q}_n}^2 + \delta}, & \text{if } |e_i(\boldsymbol{a}_n)| > \epsilon, \\ 0, & \text{otherwise} \end{cases} \qquad (6.15)$$

the error function $e_i(\boldsymbol{a}_n) = y_i - \boldsymbol{u}_i^T \boldsymbol{a}_n$ and the $\text{sgn}(\cdot)$ stands for the sign function. When $\delta = 0$, the metric projection $P_{S_i}^{(\boldsymbol{Q}_n^{-1})}(\boldsymbol{a}_n)$ maps $\boldsymbol{a}_n$ to the unique point $\boldsymbol{a}_o \in S_i$ of the hyperslab S_i, which minimizes the metric distance of $\boldsymbol{a}_n$ from S_i, i.e., $\boldsymbol{a}_o = \min_{\boldsymbol{a} \in S_n} \|\boldsymbol{a}_n - \boldsymbol{a}\|_{\boldsymbol{Q}_n^{-1}}$. In APSM, the function of δ is similar to the regularization parameter in APA. For a geometrical point of view regarding regularization in APSM as well as for more APSM-suited regularization strategies the interested reader is referred to Kopsinis et al. (2014). In a similar to the generalized APA case, (6.2), when $\boldsymbol{Q}_n = \boldsymbol{I}$ the metric projection becomes the Euclidean (orthogonal) projection. When $\boldsymbol{Q}_n$ is set equal to the diagonal matrix, $\boldsymbol{G}_n$ used in the IPAPA, then oblique projections onto the hyperlsabs are performed sharing with IPAPA the same sparsity inducing properties according to the discussion in Section 6.2. Apart from the two aforementioned choices, the use of other properly selected positive definite matrices $\boldsymbol{Q}_n$, offers a large generalization potential to the APSM approach allowing to incorporate adaptation characteristics found in a number of diverse algorithms such as transform-domain adaptive filters, Newton and quasi-Newton adaptive filter, Krylov-proportionate adaptive filters, (e.g., Yukawa and Yamada (2009), Yukawa et al. (2007), and references therein).

Starting from an arbitrary $\boldsymbol{a}_0 \in \mathbb{R}^L$ and using $\boldsymbol{Q}_n = \boldsymbol{G}_n$ in order to encourage sparse solutions via the proportionate updating mechanism, the APSM recursion is given by the two steps below:

$$\bar{\boldsymbol{a}}_n = \boldsymbol{a}_{n-1} + \mu_n \frac{1}{q} \left(\sum_{i=n-q+1}^{n} \left(P_{S_i}^{(\boldsymbol{G}_n^{-1})}(\boldsymbol{a}_{n-1}) - \boldsymbol{a}_{n-1} \right) \right) \qquad (6.16)$$

$$\boldsymbol{a}_n = T(\bar{\boldsymbol{a}}_n) \qquad (6.17)$$

where q is the number of lately received hyperslabs that APSM takes into account at each time instance. Operator $T(\cdot)$ incorporates a priori knowledge, regarding the unknown vector, in the form of projections or various types of non-expansive mappings (Slavakis and Yamada, 2013; Kopsinis et al., 2011). In our case here, it can be exploited in order to incorporate the second sparsity promotion mechanism, which is performed by the regularized/thresholding-based sparse-APA/LMS algorithms discussed in 6.3. In order to do so, a generalized thresholding operator proposed in Kopsinis et al. (2012) and Slavakis et al. (2013) can be used:

Given an estimate K of the true sparsity level $K_* = \|a_*\|_0$, the generalized thresholding (GT) operator $T_{\text{GT}}^{(K)} : \mathbb{R}^L \to \mathbb{R}^L$ is defined as follows: for any $a \in \mathbb{R}^L$, the output $z := T_{\text{GT}}^{(K)}(a)$, is obtained coordinate-wise as follows:

$$z(l) := \begin{cases} a(l), & l \in J_a^{(K)}, \\ \text{shr}(a(l)), & l \notin J_a^{(K)}, \end{cases} \tag{6.18}$$

where $J_a^{(K)}$ contains all those indices, which correspond to the K largest, in absolute value, components of the vector a, and shr denotes a user-defined shrinkage function required to satisfy some mild properties (Slavakis et al., 2013). In simple words, GT identifies, first, the K largest in magnitude components of a living them unaltered, while applies the shrinkage function to the rest of them.

A systematic way to build the shrinkage functions related to the sparsity promoting penalties discussed in Section 6.3, is via the minimization of the univariate *penalized least-squares* cost function

$$\text{shr}(a) = \min_{\theta} \left\{ \frac{1}{2}(a - \theta)^2 + \lambda p(|\theta|) \right\}, \tag{6.19}$$

where examples of penalty functions $p(|\cdot|)$ have been listed in Table 6.1. Then, in general, there is a thresholding operator $S(.)$, for which $S(a)$ is the unique optimal solution to the minimization task in (6.19) (Antoniadis, 2007). Examples of penalty functions and the associated thresholding operators are given in Figs. 6.2a and 6.2b respectively.

A method for constructing thresholding operators, which leads to a minimum (either global or local) of (6.19) for any non-negative, non-decreasing and differentiable penalty function for which $-\theta - \lambda p'(\theta)$ is strictly unimodal is given in Antoniadis and Fan (2001). According to that, the thresholding operator is given by:

$$S(a) = \begin{cases} 0, & \text{if } |a| \le P_0, \\ \text{sgn}(a)\theta_0, & \text{otherwise,} \end{cases} \tag{6.20}$$

where $P_0 := \min_{\theta \geq 0}(\theta + \lambda p'(\theta))$ and θ_0 is the largest solution of the equation $\theta + \lambda p'(\theta) = |a|$. Unfortunately, this equation does not admit a close form solution for all the penalty functions of interest, since the derivative of the $p'(\cdot)$ is a function of the unknown θ. This is the case for the non-convex penalties considered in this chapter.[a] In order to alleviate this obstacle, in this chapter, we propose the following. Note that $\hat{\theta} + \lambda p'(|a|) = |a| + \mathcal{O}(\lambda p'(|a|))$ (Antoniadis, 2007), i.e., when $p'(\theta)$ is substituted with $p'(|a|)$, leading in such a way to closed form solution, then the error is of the order of $\lambda p'(|a|)$. When the penalty function is concave, which is the case, e.g., for both RZA and Sℓ_0, then $p'(|z|) \to 0$ as $|z| \to 0$, rendering this approximation of θ_0, denoted hereafter by $\tilde{\theta}_0$, accurate for large enough $|z|$.

As an example, for the case of the smooth ℓ_0 penalty, the quantities P_0 and θ_0 in (6.20) are given by

$$P_0 = \begin{cases} \lambda\beta, & \lambda\beta^2 \leq 1, \\ \dfrac{1}{\beta}\left(1 + \ln(\lambda\beta^2)\right) & \text{otherwise.} \end{cases} \tag{6.21}$$

and $\theta_0 = |a| - \lambda\beta e^{-\beta|a|}$.

6.5.1 *Adaptive Thresholding*

The type of generalized threshold discussed so far has a shape which is fixed and dependent on parameters K, λ and on some auxiliary parameters of the penalty function, e.g., $\tilde{\epsilon}$ and β. Among these parameters, λ is much harder to be tuned for optimized performance. This is also true in the case of sparse-APA/NLMS algorithms. Parameter λ inherently determines the number of coefficients that will get values either equal to zero or very close to zero. There is not, however, any rule for tuning this parameter effectively and one has to rely on cross-validation. As an alternative here, we replace λ with a varying parameter λ_n, which is adaptively tuned in a way that guarantees that in each iteration a fixed number of components of the estimate is exactly zero. This leads to generalized thresholding operators, which are varying with time. Such an option is theoretically supported by the APSM (Kopsinis

---

[a]In Slavakis et al. (2013), the penalty $p(|a|) = |a|^{0.5}$ leading to closed form solution of the equation $\theta + \lambda p'(\theta) = |a|$ was adopted.

et al., 2011). Say that $L - \bar{K}$ components are to be set to zero in each iteration. Note that parameter $\bar{K}$ need to be larger than K, otherwise the GT is reduced to a simple hard-thresholding operator.

As long as the tentative estimates, $\boldsymbol{a}_n$, are getting close to $\boldsymbol{a}_*$, the smaller in magnitude a component of $\boldsymbol{a}_n$ is the more likely it gets to correspond to an actual zero value of the true vector. Building upon the intuition above, it is the $L - \bar{K}$ smaller in magnitude components of $\boldsymbol{a}_n$, which will be selected and set to zero in each iteration. In order for this to happen, λ_n should be adapted in a way that P_0 in (6.20) equals to $\xi_{\boldsymbol{a}_n}^{(\bar{K})} - \varrho$, with ϱ being an arbitrarily small number and $\xi_{\boldsymbol{a}}^{(\bar{K})}$ stands for the $\bar{K}$-th largest component, in magnitude, of the vector $\boldsymbol{a}$. As an example, take the smooth ℓ_0 case for which, as shown in (6.21), P_0 is computed via two relations depending on the $\lambda_n \beta^2$ product. Solving both equations for λ_n and setting $P_0 = \xi_{\boldsymbol{a}_n}^{(\bar{K})} - \varrho$ we get:

$$\lambda_n = \begin{cases} \dfrac{\xi_{\boldsymbol{a}_n}^{(\bar{K})} - \varrho}{\beta}, & \text{if } \lambda_n \beta^2 \leq 1, \\ \dfrac{1}{\beta^2} e^{\beta(\xi_{\boldsymbol{a}_n}^{(\bar{K})} - \varrho) - 1} & \text{otherwise.} \end{cases} \quad (6.22)$$

As a result, two λ_n values are computed; however, there is no ambiguity since it can be easily shown that only one of them would comply with the corresponding $\lambda_n \beta^2$ constrain. The shape of GT with adaptive $T_{S\ell_0}(z)$ is shown in Fig. 6.2. In order to keep the tuning of the proposed algorithm simple, probably sacrificing slightly performance, in the simulations that will follow $\bar{K}$ is set equal to $L - 1$. In other words, in each iteration only one component will get to zero exactly.

With respect to the step-size μ_n of APSM, it can take any value in $(0, 2)$. Moreover, when $q > 1$, convergence acceleration can be succeeded paying for some extra computational cost by setting $\mu_n \in (0, 2\mathcal{M}_n)$, with

$$\mathcal{M}_n := \begin{cases} \dfrac{\sum_{i=n-q+1}^{n} \| P_{S_i}^{(Q_n^{-1})}(\boldsymbol{a}_{n-1}) - \boldsymbol{a}_{n-1} \|_{Q_n^{-1}}^2}{\| \sum_{i=n-q+1}^{n} P_{S_i}^{(Q_n^{-1})}(\boldsymbol{a}_{n-1}) - \boldsymbol{a}_{n-1} \|_{Q_n^{-1}}^2}, & \sum_{i=n-q+1}^{n} P_{S_i}^{(Q_{n-1}^{-1})}(\boldsymbol{a}_{n-1}) \neq \boldsymbol{a}_{n-1}, \\ 1, & \text{otherwise.} \end{cases}$$

$$(6.23)$$

With respect to the theoretical properties of the GT-based APSM, it has been proved that under mild assumptions, it leads to a sequence of estimates $(a_n)_{n \in \mathbb{N}}$ whose set of cluster points is non-empty, each one of them is guaranteed to be, at most, K-sparse, and located arbitrarily close to an intersection of an infinite number of hyperslabs S_n (Slavakis et al., 2013). Note that this result is valid even though the fixed-point set of the operator $T_{\mathrm{GT}}^{(K)}$ is non-convex.

6.6 Robust Online Learning: The Double-Talk Scenario

An important aspect in echo cancellation problems is the degradation of the echo canceler during "double-talk," i.e., when the near-end speech is present. This can be partly tackled by using a double-talk detector (DTD), which pauses the update of the adaptive filter when the near-end speech is active. Unfortunately, the DTD cannot detect immediately the presence of the near-end signal and, consequently, the performance of the echo canceler might get significantly degraded.

In order to deal with the double-talk, a route to follow is to resort to the algorithmic family of robust adaptive filtering. In one way or another, robust adaptive filters reduce the contribution of the error, e_n, when they detect that it takes an excessively large value. Robust adaptive filters applied to echo cancellation have been proposed in Gansler et al. (2000), Rey Vega et al. (2009), etc. In the sequel, we will present an APSM-based algorithm for echo cancellation in double-talk environments.

The robust APSM discussed here is slightly different to the one proposed in the previous sections. Without going into many details, we exploit a special case of the APSM algorithm, described in Slavakis et al. (2012), which is suitable for minimizing convex, yet not necessarily differentiable, cost functions. Our main concern is to reduce the effect of the double talk in the echo canceler. In order to achieve this, we resort to the Huber cost function (Huber, 2011). The Huber loss, employed in robust adaptive filtering via the APSM (see, for example, (Chouvardas et al., 2011)), takes the form:

$$
\mathcal{L}_n(a) := \begin{cases} 0, & |y_n - a^T u_n| \leq \epsilon \\ 1/2(y_n - a^T u_n)^2 - \epsilon^2/2, & \epsilon < |y_n - a^T u_n| \leq c \\ c|y_n - a^T u_n| - c^2/2 - \epsilon^2/2, & c < |y_n - a^T u_n|, \end{cases}
$$

$$(6.24)$$

where ϵ and c are user-defined thresholds. The physical reasoning behind this cost function is discussed next. If the error is less or equal than ϵ, then the function scores a zero loss. This branch acts similarly to a hyperslab, where the points lying inside a hyperslab are not updated. If $\epsilon < |y_n - \boldsymbol{a}^T \boldsymbol{u}_n| \leq c$, then the estimate scores a non-zero penalty, with a square dependence on the error. Whenever an outlier hits, e.g., the observed signal is contaminated by near-end speech, leading to relatively large error values, this branch of the cost function might get excessively large values leading to potential divergence of the adaptive algorithm. Parameter c determines the larger error value, which is can be safely assumed not to be the result of an outlier. Finally, in the case where $c < |y_n - \boldsymbol{a}^T \boldsymbol{u}_n|$, the cost function now exhibits a linear dependence to the error. In such a way, the contribution of large errors to the adaptation step is reduced leading to a more robust behavior.

The goal of the algorithm is to minimize asymptotically the cost functions. The recursion employed in order to achieve the aforementioned goal is:

$$\boldsymbol{a}_{n+1} = \boldsymbol{a}_n - \mu_n \sum_{j=n-q+1}^{n} \omega_j \frac{\mathcal{L}_j(\boldsymbol{a}_n)}{\|\mathcal{L}'_j(\boldsymbol{a}_n)\|^2 + \delta_j} \mathcal{L}'_j(\boldsymbol{a}_n), \qquad (6.25)$$

where $\mathcal{L}'_n(\boldsymbol{a}_n)$ is the subgradient of the loss function given by

$$\mathcal{L}'_n(\boldsymbol{a}) := \begin{cases} 0, & |y_n - \boldsymbol{a}^T \boldsymbol{u}_n| \leq \epsilon \\ -\boldsymbol{u}_n(y_n - \boldsymbol{a}^T \boldsymbol{u}_n), & \epsilon < |y_n - \boldsymbol{a}^T \boldsymbol{u}_n| \leq c \\ -c\boldsymbol{u}_n \mathrm{sign}(y_n - \boldsymbol{a}^T \boldsymbol{u}_n), & c < |y_n - \boldsymbol{a}^T \boldsymbol{u}_n|, \end{cases} \qquad (6.26)$$

It is worth pointing out that the regularization parameter, here, is allowed to be time-varying. This further aids the capability of the algorithm to deal with outliers via the approach described next. First, if the error is smaller or similar to c then we choose a small value for δ_n, in a similar way as in the NLMS. On the contrary, if an excessively large error value occurs, then this is an indication that the measurement probably contains an outlier, e.g., near-end speech, and the value of δ_n is increased so as to reduce its influence in the updated estimate. We have observed through experimentation that if one chooses a large $\delta_n \; \forall |e_j(\boldsymbol{a}_n)| > c$ then the convergence speed of the algorithm is decreased; to that end, the larger δ_n is incorporated if $\forall |e_j(\boldsymbol{a}_n)| > Bc$, where $B > 1$ is a user defined parameter.

6.7 Experimental Validation

In all the simulation examples, the input is a real voice signal sampled at 8 KHz, which is shown in the lower part of Fig. 6.5. Moreover, the SNR is fixed to 20 dB and all the curves are the result of the ensemble average of 20 independent realizations. In Figs. 6.5 and 6.6, the unknown echo path $\boldsymbol{a}_*$ exhibits an abrupt change when the half of the total number of observations have been received. In the first half, $\boldsymbol{a}_*$ has $L = 1024$ coefficients, whereas only $S = 100$ among them are non-zeros. In each independent realization, the positions of the non-zero components are picked at random and their values are drawn from a normal distribution $\mathcal{N}(0, 1)$. In the second half, $\boldsymbol{a}_*$ is chosen to be the fourth echo path listed in the ITU-T recommendation G.168-2002 regarding digital network echo cancellers. This echo path comprises 128 non-zero components and in order to comply with the impulse response length adopted in the first half of the experiment, it is zero-padded with 1024–128 = 896 zeros. In both cases, the norm of the unknown vector was normalized to one.

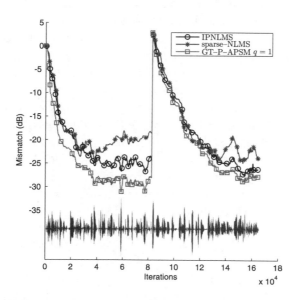

Figure 6.5 Performance evaluation in the case of $q = 1$.

The performance of the lowest complexity variants, corresponding to $q = 1$, of the major algorithms discussed in Sections 6.2, 6.3, and 6.5, namely the IPNLMS, the sparse-NLMS and the APSM supplied with both proportionate and generalized thresholding-based sparsity promotion (GT-P-APSM, $q = 1$) is evaluated in Fig. 6.5. Similarly, in Fig. 6.6, the $q = 5$ case was examined corresponding to the IPAPA and sparse-APA algorithms. In both cases, the thresholding in sparse-NLMS and in the APSM is the one corresponding to the smooth ℓ_0 norm penalty function with parameter $\beta = 10$. As discussed in Section 6.5, APSM requires an estimate K of the true sparsity level, K_*. Here, $K = 150$ was selected, i.e., an overestimation of the true sparsity level of the two adopted echo path impulse responses. The sparse-NLMS algorithm requires a cross validation-based fine-tuning of the regularization parameter λ resulting to the value $4 \cdot 10^{-7}$. On the contrary, in APSM the adaptive thresholding approach was followed, which, as it was described in Section 6.5.1, allows the adaptive estimation of λ in each iteration without needing any fine-tuning. The regularization parameter in δ in IPNLMS and IPAPA was set equal to the optimized values derived in Benesty et al. (2011) and Paleologu et al. (2011), referred hereafter as $\bar{\delta}$. For the APSM and the sparse-NLMS/APA, the corresponding value was optimized. In APSM it turned out that a good choice, not necessarily the optimum one is to set its regularization parameter equal to 3 up to 5 times the quantity $q\bar{\delta}$ without being particularly sensitive to the exact value chosen. Here, $\delta = 3q\bar{\delta}$ was chosen. For the smooth-NLMS and the smooth-APA the values $L\bar{\delta}$ and $3L\bar{\delta}$, respectively, performed best. Moreover, as it has been reported elsewhere, e.g., in Kopsinis et al. (2011), APSM exhibits relatively low sensitivity in the tuning of parameter ϵ determining the width of the hyperslabs and any value between σ_n, which is used here, and $\sqrt{2}\sigma_n$ with σ_n being the noise variance, is a valid choice. Finally, the step sizes of the different algorithms were given such a value in order all of them to exhibit similar convergence speeds. This is translated to the values 0.3, 1, and 1 for the IPNLMS, smooth-NLMS and $q = 1$ APSM, respectively, and to the values 0.1, 0.3, and 0.4 for the IPAPA, smooth-APA and $q = 5$ APSM, respectively.

Comparing IPNLMS with sparse-NLMS in Fig. 6.5, it is apparent that in this realistic setting the classical algorithm for echo

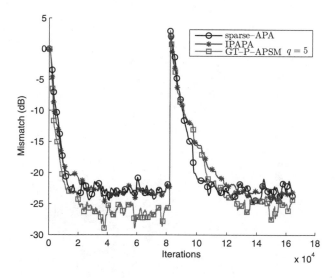

Figure 6.6 Performance evaluation in the case of $q = 5$.

cancellation based on proportionate updating outperforms the newly proposed approach although the latter has exhibited very strong performance and sparsity promoting characteristics. The correlated and highly variant input signal is to blame for this performance degradation. The APSM-based approach is benefited by the robustness of the proportionate updating and its performance is further enhanced by the thresholding-based sparsity promoting mechanism showing enhanced performance, especially in the first half of the experiment. In the $q = 5$ case (Fig. 6.6), the performance of the sparse-APA is significantly improved reaching this of the IPAPA and the APSM-based approach still reaches lower error floors.

In the last experiment depicted in Fig. 6.7, the robust versions of the algorithms are evaluated in a double-talk scenario. The only difference compared to the simulation setup discussed before is that the abrupt change of the echo path impulse response is realized earlier for better visualization. Moreover, the time instances where double-talk appears are denoted by vertical bars in horizontal axis. The double-talk appears for 100 samples each time assuming that in the meantime the DTD will have detected it and freeze further adaptation. We compare the performance of the APSM

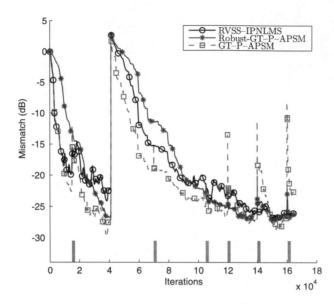

Figure 6.7 Performance evaluation in the presence of near-end speech.

employing the Huber cost function (Section 6.6), the non robust APSM presented here (Section 6.3) and the robust NLMS algorithm, proposed in Rey Vega et al. (2009). In a nutshell, the latter algorithm computes recursively an approximate value of $\mathbb{E}\|a_n - a_{n-1}\|^2$, denoted by $\hat{\delta}_n$, and scales properly the error if an outlier is detected. It is worth pointing out (see Rey Vega et al., 2009) that use of this statistical approximation leads to degraded performance in time-varying scenarios; to that end, one should resort to ad hoc methodologies proposed in Rey Vega et al. (2008), which have been incorporated in the example here in order to allow this algorithm to track the abrupt change. The parameters for the APSM algorithm are chosen as follows: $q = 1$, $\epsilon = 2 * \sigma_n^2$, $\mu = 1.5$, $c = 70 * \sigma^2$. As we have already mentioned in Section 6.6 the parameter δ_n is allowed to be time-varying and it is error dependent. In this experiment, if $|e_n(a_n)| \leq 15c$ then it equals to $\delta_n = 7 * 10^{-9}$, whereas if $|e_n(a_n)| > 15c$ then $\delta_n = 7 * 10^{-7}$. Moreover, the proportionate weights are chosen according to the rule presented in Section 6.2 and for the sparsification we employ is the generalized thresholding as in the non-robust case. For the robust NLMS we set the step-size equal to 1, we initialize $\hat{\delta}_0 = \frac{\sigma_d^2}{\sigma_x^2 L}$, where σ_d^2, σ_x^2 are the variances of the output/input respectively. From Fig. 6.7 it can be seen that the non-robust APSM undergoes large variations when the double-talk is present, especially after its convergence. Finally, the robust APSM exhibits performance similar to that of the robust NLMS.

References

1. Antoniadis, A. (2007). Wavelet methods in statistics: Some recent developments and their applications, *Statistics Surveys* **1**, pp. 16–55.

2. Antoniadis, A., and Fan, J. (2001). Regularization of wavelet approximations, *J. American Statistical Association* **96**, pp. 939–967.

3. Benesty, J., and Gay, S. L. (2002). An improved PNLMS algorithm, in *IEEE International Conference on Acoustics, Speech, and Signal Processing (ICASSP)*, vol. 2.

4. Benesty, J., Paleologu, C., and Ciochina, S. (2011). On regularization in adaptive filtering, *IEEE Transactions on Audio, Speech, and Language Processing* **19**, 6, pp. 1734–1742.

5. Chen, Y., Gu, Y., and Hero, A. O. (2009). Sparse LMS for system identification, in *Proceedings of the IEEE ICASSP*, pp. 3125–3128.

6. Chouvardas, S., Slavakis, K., Kopsinis, Y., and Theodoridis, S. (2012). A sparsity promoting adaptive algorithm for distributed learning, *Signal Processing, IEEE Transactions on* **60**, 10, pp. 5412–5425.

7. Chouvardas, S., Slavakis, K., and Theodoridis, S. (2011). Adaptive robust distributed learning in diffusion sensor networks, *IEEE Transactions on Signal Processing* **59**, 10, pp. 4692–4707.

8. Di Lorenzo, P., Barbarossa, S., and Sayed, A. (2012). Sparse diffusion LMS for distributed adaptive estimation, in *2012 IEEE International Conference on Acoustics, Speech and Signal Processing (ICASSP)*, pp. 3281–3284.

9. Duttweiler, D. L. (2000). Proportionate NLMS adaptation in echo cancelers, *IEEE Trans. Speech Audio Processing* **8**, pp. 508–518.

10. Gansler, T., Gay, S. L., Sondhi, M., and Benesty, J. (2000). Double-talk robust fast converging algorithms for network echo cancellation, *Speech and Audio Processing, IEEE Transactions on* **8**, 6, pp. 656–663.

11. Gu, Y., Jin, J., and Mei, S. (2009). L0 norm constraint LMS algorithm for sparse system identification, *Signal Processing Letters, IEEE* **16**, 9, pp. 774–777.

12. Gui, G., and Adachi, F. (2013). Improved least mean square algorithm with application to adaptive sparse channel estimation, *EURASIP Journal on Wireless Communications and Networking* **2013**, 1, p. 18.

13. Haykin, S. (1996). *Adaptive Filter Theory*, 3rd ed. (Prentice-Hall, New Jersey).

14. Homer, J., Mareels, I., Bitmead, R., Wahlberg, B., and Gustafsson, F. (1998). Lms estimation via structural detection, *Signal Processing, IEEE Transactions on* **46**, 10, pp. 2651–2663, doi:10.1109/78.720368.

15. Hu, T., and Chklovskii, D. (2014). Sparse lms via online linearized bregman iteration, in *Acoustics, Speech and Signal Processing (ICASSP), 2014 IEEE International Conference on*, pp. 7213–7217.

16. Huber, P. J. (2011). *Robust Statistics* (Springer).

17. Kopsinis, Y., Chouvardas, S., and Theodoridis, S. (2014). Sparsity-aware learning in the context of echo cancelation: A set theoretic estimation approach, in *Signal Processing Conference (EUSIPCO), 2014 Proceedings of the 22nd European*, pp. 1846–1850.

18. Kopsinis, Y., Slavakis, K., and Theodoridis, S. (2011). Online sparse system identification and signal reconstruction using projections onto weighted ℓ_1 balls, *IEEE Trans. Signal Proc.* **59**, 3, pp. 905–930.

19. Kopsinis, Y., Slavakis, K., Theodoridis, S., and McLaughlin, S. (2012). Generalized thresholding sparsity-aware algorithm for low complexity online learning, in *Acoustics, Speech and Signal Processing (ICASSP)* (IEEE), pp. 3277–3280.

20. Lima, M., Ferreira, T., Martins, W., and Diniz, P. (2014). Sparsity-aware data-selective adaptive filters, *Signal Processing, IEEE Transactions on* **62**, 17, pp. 4557–4572.

21. Meng, R., de Lamare, R., and Nascimento, V. (2011). Sparsity-aware affine projection adaptive algorithms for system identification, in *Sensor Signal Processing for Defence (SSPD 2011)*, pp. 1–5.

22. Murakami, Y., Yamagishi, M., Yukawa, M., and Yamada, I. (2010). A sparse adaptive filtering using time-varying soft-thresholding techniques, in *Acoustics Speech and Signal Processing (ICASSP), 2010 IEEE International Conference on*, pp. 3734–3737.

23. Paleologu, C., Benesty, J., and Ciochin, S. (2011). Regularization of the affine projection algorithm, *IEEE Transactions on Circuits and Systems II: Express Briefs* **58**, 6, pp. 366–370.

24. Paleologu, C., Ciochina, S., and Benesty, J. (2010). An efficient proportionate affine projection algorithm for echo cancellation, *Signal Processing Letters, IEEE* **17**, 2, pp. 165–168.

25. Rey Vega, L., Rey, H., Benesty, J., and Tressens, S. (2008). A new robust variable step-size nlms algorithm, *Signal Processing, IEEE Transactions on* **56**, 5, pp. 1878–1893.

26. Rey Vega, L., Rey, H., Benesty, J., and Tressens, S. (2009). A family of robust algorithms exploiting sparsity in adaptive filters, *IEEE Transactions on Audio, Speech, and Language Processing* **17**, 4, pp. 572–581.

27. Sayed, A. H. (2003). *Fundamentals of Adaptive Filtering* (John Wiley & Sons, New Jersey).

28. Shi, K., and Shi, P. (2010). Convergence analysis of sparse LMS algorithms with l1-norm penalty based on white input signal, *Signal Process.* **90**, 12, pp. 3289–3293.

29. Slavakis, K., Bouboulis, P., and Theodoridis, S. (2012). Adaptive multiregression in reproducing kernel hilbert spaces: The multiaccess mimo channel case, *IEEE Transactions on Neural Networks and Learning Systems* **23**, 2, pp. 260–276.

30. Slavakis, K., Kopsinis, Y., Theodoridis, S., and McLaughlin, S. (2013). Generalized thresholding and online sparsity-aware learning in a union of subspaces, *Signal Processing, IEEE Transactions on* **61**, 15, pp. 3760–3773, doi:10.1109/TSP.2013.2264464.

31. Slavakis, K., and Yamada, I. (2013). The adaptive projected subgradient method constrained by families of quasi-nonexpansive mappings and its application to online learning, *SIAM Journal on Optimization* **23**, 1, pp. 126–152.

32. Slavakis, K., Yamada, I., and Ogura, N. (2006). The adaptive projected subgradient method over the fixed point set of strongly attracting non-expansive mappings, *Numerical Functional Analysis and Optimization* **27**, 7&8, pp. 905–930.

33. Su, G., Jin, J., Gu, Y., and Wang, J. (2012). Performance analysis of l_0 norm constraint least mean square algorithm, *Signal Processing, IEEE Transactions on* **60**, 5, pp. 2223 –2235.

34. Sugiyama, A., Sato, H., Hirano, A., and Ikeda, S. (1996). A fast convergence algorithm for adaptive fir filters under computational constraint for adaptive tap-position control, *Circuits and Systems II: Analog and Digital Signal Processing, IEEE Transactions on* **43**, 9, pp. 629–636, doi:10.1109/82.536759.

35. Taheri, O., and Vorobyov, S. A. (2014). Reweighted l1-norm penalized LMS for sparse channel estimation and its analysis, *Signal Processing* **104**, 0, pp. 70 – 79.

36. Theodoridis, S., Slavakis, K., and Yamada, I. (2011). Adaptive learning in a world of projections, *Signal Processing Magazine, IEEE* **28**, 1, pp. 97–123.

37. Yamada, I., and Ogura, N. (2004). Adaptive projected subgradient method for asymptotic minimization of sequence of nonnegative convex functions, *Numerical Functional Analysis and Optimization* **25**, 7&8, pp. 593–617.

38. Yukawa, M., Slavakis, K., and Yamada, I. (2007). Adaptive parallel quadratic-metric projection algorithms, *IEEE Trans. Audio, Speech, and Signal Processing* **15**, 5, pp. 1665–1680.

39. Yukawa, M., and Yamada, I. (2009). A unified view of adaptive variable-metric projection algorithms, *EURASIP Journal on Advances in Signal Processing* **2009**, p. 34.

Chapter 7

Transform Domain Processing for Recent Signal and Video Applications

Wan-Chi Siu

Centre for Multimedia Signal Processing,
Department of Electronic and Information Engineering,
The Hong Kong Polytechnic University, Hong Kong
enwcsiu@polyu.edu.hk

Orthogonality and cyclic convolution structure are two interesting properties of many transforms that allow complete recovery of a signal from its version in the transform domain. In this chapter, we start by visiting some very fundamental requirements of a transform with these properties and naturally formulate the discrete Fourier transform (DFT) and the number theoretic transform (NTT). We then highlight the fastest way to realize the DFT using the NTT and develop the discrete cosine transform (DCT), integer cosine transform (ICT) with the kernel (1,2,1) in H.264/HEVC standards and our most recently suggested kernel (5,7,3) for video coding. We shall also discuss our recent work on using DCT techniques for fast and quality super-resolution videos. We have a strategy on using academic research results to underpin industrial research and

Trends in Digital Signal Processing: A Festschrift in Honour of A. G. Constantinides
Edited by Yong Ching Lim, Hon Keung Kwan, and Wan-Chi Siu
Copyright © 2016 Pan Stanford Publishing Pte. Ltd.
ISBN 978-981-4669-50-4 (Hardcover), 978-981-4669-51-1 (eBook)
www.panstanford.com

development, which are mostly related to modern video surveillance with big data and Internet of things. With this strategy in mind, we will end the chapter with brief ideas on new trends and future hi-tech applications.

7.1 Introduction

7.1.1 *DSP Operation Basis: Cyclic Convolutions and Discrete Fourier Transforms*

For many years digital signal processing (DSP) techniques (Cappellini, Constantinides, and Emiliani, 1978; Bogner and Constantinides, 1975; Cappellini and Constantinides, 1980; Oppenheim and Schafer, 1975; Peled and Liu, 1975; Rader, 1968; McClellan and Rader, 1979; Nussbaumer, 1981) have been extensively studies because of their importance in a wide range of hi-tech applications such as image/video processing (Tekalp, 1995; Chen, Koc, and Liu, 2002) and coding in JPEG/MPEG/H.264/HEVC, video super-resolution, speech processing, surveillance, pattern recognition, robot vision, radar processing, biomedical engineering and many others. The most basic structure of a digital filter is linear convolution, while the cyclic convolution gives a link between digital filter and DFT. Digital filtering and DFT are two most important topics of digital signal processing techniques. There are many good books on DSP include those classic ones written by Cappellini, Constantinides, Bogner, Oppenheim, Gold, Rader, etc., and the newer ones written by (Mitra, 2010; Proakis and Manolakis, 2007). In this chapter, we start with a review on some basic properties of the cyclic convolution and its relation with a transform with perfect reconstruction. Orthogonal properties have also been stressed, which are extremely useful in most parts of this chapter. We review the development of the NTT and its use for the realization of the discrete Fourier transform. As proposed by Siu and Constantinides (Siu and Constantinides, 1983; Siu and Constantinides, 1984a; Siu and Constantinides, 1984b; Siu and Constantinides, 1984c; Siu and Constantinides, 1985) that theNTT can possibly be used as an effective means to realize the discrete Fourier transform. This gives the least number of multiplications reported in the literature required for the realization of discrete Fourier transform. We subsequently discuss the development of discrete cosine transform and the newest ICT kernel IK(5,7,3) proposed by Wong and Siu (Wong and Siu, 2009; Wong and Siu, 2011a; Wong and Siu, 2011b) in 2011, and the most recent approaches (Huang, Hung, and Siu, 2014; Hung and Siu, 2013; Hung and Siu, 2014a; Hung and Siu, 2014b) on using the DCT for image interpolation/super-resolution.

Every linear digital filter can be described by the linear convolution sum. For the implementation of these filters (Peled and Liu, 1975), transform techniques have very often been used to carry out the computation. Most fast convolution algorithms such as those based on fast Fourier transform (FFT) (Cooley and Tukey, 1965; Brigham, 1974), apply only to periodic functions and are able to compute cyclic convolutions effectively. Hence, in order to take advantage of various fast cyclic convolution algorithms to speed-up the calculation of digital filtering processes, methods like the overlap-add and overlap-save (Peled and Liu, 1975) can be employed to effect the computations. Furthermore, the discrete Fourier transform can also be converted into a cyclic convolution form when the transform length, N is a prime number (Rader, 1968). It is evident, therefore, that the cyclic convolution is a very basic and essential operation in digital signal processing.

It is almost self-evident to state that if an efficient method for computing the DFT is developed, then there is a high likelihood that the same technique may be used to compute the cyclic convolutions and vice versa. There is therefore a parallel development between the computation of cyclic convolutions and discrete Fourier transforms.

We gave some contributions contributions (Chan and Siu, 1992; Lun and Siu, 1993, Wong and Siu, 1991) and are of course well aware of the conventional fast algorithms for computing DSP with FFT (Cooley and Tukey, 1965; Brigham, 1974), Winograd Fourier transform algorithms (WFTA) (Cooley and Tukey, 1965), polynomial transforms (PT) (Nussbaumer, 1981), and others (Brigham, 1974; Winograd, 1975; Pollard, 1971; Rader, 1972; Agarwal and Burrus, 1974; Rayner, 1976). In order to save space, we will not mention all these techniques even though they are very useful.

7.1.2 *Number Theoretic Transforms*

The NTT we mentioned relies heavily on number theory in mathematics. The number theoretic transform is defined on finite fields or rings of real integers (Pollard, 1971; Rader, 1972; Agarwal and Burrus, 1974; Rayner, 1976; Siu, 1982; Agarwal, Burrus, 1975; Britanak, Yip and Rao, 2007; Chan and Siu, 1997; Chan and Siu, 1993; Cham, 1989; Malvar, 2001; Hallapuro, Karczewicz, and Malvar, 2002; Bjontegaard, 1997; Bjontegaard, 1999). The transform involves no complex-number multiplications and has properties similar to those of the discrete Fourier transform. Thus, it can be used as a method for fast and error free calculation of cyclic convolutions applicable for example to the implementation of digital signal processors.

Of the various versions of the NTT proposed, the Fermat number transform (FNT), which has been thoroughly investigated by Agarwal and Burrus (Agarwal and Burrus, 1974), and the Mersenne number transform (MNT), which was introduced by Rader (Rader, 1972) are the most promising cases. Since the transform length N of the Fermat number transform must be a power of two, a fast implementation for it similar to the Fast Fourier Transform with radix two is possible.

In Section 7.4, we suggest the use of the number theoretic transforms to compute the discrete Fourier transform. By noting the symmetry of the NTT, we show that the number of multiplications per point for the DFT for a real sequence length of P is less than 1 (actually $(1 - 1/P)$). This is the least number of multiplications that has ever been reported for the computation of DFTs.

7.2 Theory of a General Transform

In this section, we start our discussion with the development of the general structure of transforms with the convolution property and then present the number theoretic transforms modulo an integer as a practical scheme for calculating cyclic convolutions. It is possible to obtain a number theoretic transform that involves no multiplications and no round-off errors in the calculation. The ease of implementation of the transform often depends on the choice of modulus (M), root of unity (α) and the order (N) of the transform. This chapter also includes the conditions for the existence of the number theoretic transform and the discussions on the constraints and advantages of using NTTs for digital signal processing.

7.2.1 *Circular Convolution Property*

In this section, we discuss the essential requirements for transforms to have the circular convolution property, as the discrete Fourier transform has. The circular convolution property of a transform means that the transform of the cyclic convolution of two sequences is equal to the product of their individual transforms. Consider two sequences

$$\tilde{\mathbf{x}} = \mathbf{x}^T = [x\,(0)\,, x\,(1)\,, \ldots, x\,(N-1)]$$

$$\tilde{\mathbf{h}} = \mathbf{h}^T = [h\,(0)\,, h\,(1)\,, \ldots, h\,(N-1)],$$

where $N =$ length of the sequences

For the cyclic convolution of these two sequences, we can write

$$\tilde{\mathbf{y}} = \tilde{\mathbf{x}} \otimes^c \tilde{\mathbf{h}} \text{ and}$$

$$y(m) = \sum_{n=0}^{N-1} x(m-n)h(n) \tag{7.1}$$

where $m = 0, 1, \ldots, N-1$.

The symbol $\otimes^c$ means circular convolution. This definition assumes the sequences are periodically extended with period N.

Consider an $N \times N$ non-singular matrix $\mathbf{T}$ whose elements are, $t_{k,n}$ where $k,n = 0,1,\ldots,N-1$ respectively. Let also

$$\tilde{\mathbf{y}} = \mathbf{y}^T = [y\,(0)\,, y\,(1)\,, \ldots, y\,(N-1)]$$

Let us use matrix $\mathbf{T}$ to transform $\mathbf{x}$ and $\mathbf{h}$ into a new domain and let capital letters denote the transformed sequences, we obtain

$$\mathbf{X} = \mathbf{Tx}; \mathbf{H} = \mathbf{Th}; \mathbf{Y} = \mathbf{Ty} \tag{7.2}$$

$\mathbf{T}$ is now defined to have the property that

$$\mathbf{Y} = \mathbf{X} \otimes \mathbf{H} \tag{7.3}$$

where $\otimes =$ term by term multiplication

The individual terms in Eq. (7.3) can be written as

$$Y(k) = X(k) H(k),$$

where

$$X(k) = \sum_{\ell=0}^{N-1} t_{k,\ell} x(\ell)$$

and

$$H(k) = \sum_{n=0}^{N-1} t_{k,n} h(n) \text{ for } k = 0, 1, \dots, N-1$$

Hence,

$$Y(k) = \sum_{\ell=0}^{N-1} t_{k,\ell} x(\ell) \sum_{n=0}^{N-1} t_{k,n} h(n)$$

$$= \sum_{n=0}^{N-1} \sum_{\ell=0}^{N-1} x(\ell) h(n) t_{k,\ell} t_{k,n}$$

However, $Y(k)$ can also be expressed by putting Eq. (7.1) in the transform domain:

$$Y(k) = \sum_{m=0}^{N-1} t_{k,m} y(m)$$

$$= \sum_{m=0}^{N-1} t_{k,m} \sum_{n=0}^{N-1} x(m-n) h(n)$$

Let $\ell = m - n$; hence, $m = \ell + n$, where $\ell = 0, 1, \dots, N-1$, we get

$$Y(k) = \sum_{n=0}^{N-1} \sum_{\ell=0}^{N-1} x(\ell) h(n) t_{k,\ell+n} \tag{7.4}$$

Equation (7.4) must be equivalent to Eq. (7.4); therefore,

$$t_{k,\ell+n} = t_{k,\ell} t_{k,n} \tag{7.5}$$

where $k, \ell, n = 0, 1, \dots, N-1$ respectively.

The properties of the t's give the essential features of the transforms having the convolution property; hence, it is necessary to elaborate Eq. (7.5) in more details.

(i) It is clear from Eq. (7.5) that

$$t_{k,1+1} = t_{k,1}t_{k,1}$$

and

$$t_{k,2} = t_{k,1}^2;\ t_{k,3} = t_{k,2+1} = t_{k,1}^3;\ \ldots \tag{7.6}$$

Therefore, in general

$$t_{k,n} = t_{k,1}^n \tag{7.7}$$

(ii) From Eq. (7.5), it is also clear that

$$t_{k,\ell+0} = t_{k,\ell}t_{k,0}$$

Hence

$$t_{k,0} = 1 \tag{7.8}$$

(iii) For the cyclic property of $\ell + n$,

$$t_{k,i+N} = t_{k,i}$$

From Eq. (7.5) again,

$$t_{k,i+N} = t_{k,i}t_{k,N} = t_{k,i}t_{k,1}^N$$

Hence

$$t_{k,1}^N = 1 \tag{7.9}$$

Note that

$$t_{k,nN} = t_{k,\underbrace{n+n+\ldots}_{N}} = t_{k,n}^N$$

Interchange n and N,

$$t_{k,nN}\ \text{also}\ = t_{k,N}^n = t_{k,0}^n = 1\ \text{(cyclic property)}$$

Therefore

$$t_{k,n}^N = 1 \tag{7.10}$$

This shows that $t_{k,n}$'s are N^{th} roots of unity.

(iv) For **T** to be nonsingular, $\mathbf{T}^{-1}$ must exist, and $t_{k,1}$'s should be distinct.

(v) **T** can now be written in the following form:

$$
T = \begin{bmatrix}
1 & t_{0,1} & t_{0,1}^2 & \cdots & t_{0,1}^{N-1} \\
1 & t_{1,1} & t_{1,1}^2 & \cdots & t_{1,1}^{N-1} \\
\cdot & \cdot\cdot & & \cdots & \cdot\cdot \\
1 & t_{N-1,1} & t_{N-1,1}^2 & \cdots & t_{N-1,1}^{N-1}
\end{bmatrix}
$$

$$
= \begin{bmatrix}
1 & \alpha_{0,1} & \alpha_0^2 & \cdots & \alpha_0^{N-1} \\
1 & \alpha_1 & \alpha_1^2 & \cdots & \alpha_1^{N-1} \\
\cdot & \cdot\cdot & \cdot\cdot & \cdots & \cdot\cdot \\
1 & \alpha_{N-1} & \alpha_{N-1}^2 & \cdots & \alpha_{N-1}^{N-1}
\end{bmatrix} \tag{7.11}
$$

where α's are N^{th} root of unity.

To make a further development of point (v), Eq. (7.11) shows that

$$
t_{k,1}^N = 1
$$

That is $t_{1,1}^N = 1; t_{2,1}^N = 1;\dots t_{N-1,1}^N = 1$

It is essential that $t_{k,1}$'s are distinct roots of unity. Note that in a certain field, for $t_{1,1}^N = 1$, there are only N distinct N^{th} roots of unity, where N is the least positive integer such that $t_{1,1}^N = 1$.

For the sake of simplicity and without loss of generality, let

$$
t_{k,1} = t_{1,1}^k \tag{7.12}
$$

Let also $\alpha = t_{1,1}$ and combine Eqs. (7.11) and (7.7). We find

$$
t_{k,n} = t_{1,1}^{kn} = \alpha^{kn} \tag{7.13}
$$

Inverse Transform: In order to transform the result back to the original domain, we have to find $\mathbf{T}^{-1}$. Let $t_{k,n}^{-1}$ be the elements of $\mathbf{T}^{-1}$ and have the following form:

$$
t_{k,n}^{-1} = N^{-1}\alpha^{-kn}m, \text{ where } k = 0, 1, \dots, N-1
$$

Let us prove the validity of this assumption.

Since

$$
X(k) = \sum_{n=0}^{N-1} t_{k,n}x(n) = \sum_{n=0}^{N-1} \alpha^{kn}x(n)
$$

now

$$
x(n) = \sum_{\ell=0}^{N-1} N^{-1}\alpha^{-\ell n}X(\ell)
$$

Hence

$$X(k) = \sum_{n=0}^{N-1} \alpha^{kn} \sum_{\ell=0}^{N-1} N^{-1} \alpha^{-\ell n} X(\ell)$$

$$X(k) = \sum_{\ell=0}^{N-1} X(\ell) \left(N^{-1} \sum_{n=0}^{N-1} \alpha^{(k-\ell)n} \right) \tag{7.14}$$

Let us consider the term $N^{-1} \sum_{n=0}^{N-1} \alpha^{(k-\ell)n}$. Due to the circular property, the value of $(k - \ell)$ should modulo N.

(i) If $(k - \ell) = 0 \bmod N$, then

$$\alpha^{k-\ell} = 1$$

Therefore

$$N^{-1} \sum_{n=0}^{N-1} \alpha^{(k-\ell)n} = 1$$

$$\text{for} \quad (k - \ell) = 0$$

(ii) If $(k - \ell) \neq 0 \bmod N$, then

$$\alpha^{k-\ell} \neq 1$$

That is

$$\alpha^{k-\ell} - 1 \neq 0 \tag{7.15}$$

Multiply the expression $N^{-1} \sum_{n=0}^{N-1} \alpha^{(k-\ell)n}$ by $(\alpha^{(k-\ell)} - 1)$; hence, we get,

$$N^{-1}(\alpha^{k-\ell} - 1) \sum_{n=0}^{N-1} \alpha^{(k-\ell)n} = N^{-1} \sum_{n=0}^{N-1} \alpha^{(k-\ell)(n+1)} - N^{-1} \sum_{n=0}^{N-1} \alpha^{(k-\ell)n}$$

$$= N^{-1} \sum_{n=1}^{N} \alpha^{(k-\ell)n} - N^{-1} \sum_{n=0}^{N-1} \alpha^{(k-\ell)n}$$

$$= N^{-1} \left(\sum_{n=1}^{N-1} \alpha^{(k-\ell)n} + \alpha^{(k-\ell)N} \right.$$

$$\left. - \sum_{n=1}^{N-1} \alpha^{(k-\ell)n} - 1 \right)$$

$$= N^{-1}[\alpha^{(k-\ell)N} - 1]$$

$$= 0 \text{ for } \alpha^{N} = 1 \tag{7.16}$$

Since $(\alpha^{k-\ell} - 1) \neq 0$, we conclude that

$$\sum_{n=0}^{N-1} \alpha^{(k-\ell)n} = 0, \quad \text{for } (k-\ell) \neq 0 \qquad (7.17)$$

Hence, from (i) and (ii), it is clear that $N^{-1} \sum_{n=0}^{N-1} \alpha^{(k-\ell)n}$ plays the same role as the Kronecker delta function. Cases (i) and (ii) are the conditions for a perfect reconstruction of a transform and are also called the orthogonal conditions. These can be summarized as

$$\delta_{k,\ell} = N^{-1} \sum_{n=0}^{N-1} \alpha^{(k-\ell)n} = \begin{cases} 1 & \text{if}(k-\ell) = 0 \mod N \\ 0 & \text{otherwise} \end{cases}. \qquad (7.18)$$

Therefore, Eq. (7.14) reduces to

$$X(k) = \sum_{\ell=0}^{N-1} X(\ell) N^{-1} \sum_{n=0}^{N-1} \alpha^{(k-\ell)n}$$
$$= X(k).$$

Possible Transforms with Perfect Reconstruction:
At this juncture, we must stress that the derivation is not only valid for the real and complex number systems, but this also works very well for other arithmetic systems, say the modulo arithmetic system. In the latter case, even though Eq. (7.17) is true, for $(\alpha^{k-\ell} - 1) \neq 0$, we still cannot conclude that Eq. (7.18) is valid. Some other conditions may have to be imposed to confirm the validity of the transform (see below). However, if there is no simpler means available, one can check the transform against Eq. (7.18), which is a more rigid condition for its existence.

The following points give a short summary of what we have discussed so far:

(1) The structures of the elements of the transform matrix **T** and its inverse **T**$^{-1}$ are given by

(a) $t_{m,n} = \alpha^{kn}$ and
(b) $t_{k,n}^{-1} = N^{-1}\alpha^{-kn}$, where $n,k = 0, 1, \ldots, N-1$ respectively.

(2) The existence of an $N \times N$ transform having the cyclic convolution property with perfect reconstruction property depends on

(i) the existence of an α that is a root of unity of order N

(ii) the existence of N^{-1} and

(iii) the validity of

$$N^{-1} \sum_{n=0}^{N-1} \alpha^{nm} = \begin{cases} 1 & \text{if } m = 0 \mod N \\ 0 & \text{otherwise} \end{cases} \tag{7.19}$$

Conditions (i) and (ii) are the basic requirements for the existence of a transform having cyclic convolution property. Recall the arithmetic systems that we are using, the complex number field with the root of unity, $\alpha = e^{-j(2\pi/N)}$ may form a transform having the cyclic convolution property with perfect reconstruction. This is the kernel of the DFT and it is straightforward to check that the DFT satisfies all requirements in (i), (ii) and (iii) in Eq. (7.20).

On the other hand, in a finite field or ring of integers modulo an integer M, we may also find a transform with cyclic convolution property if the system satisfies (i), (ii), and (iii) in Eq. (7.20).

7.3 Transform in a Ring of Integers Modulo an Integer, *M*

In order to fulfill the requirements in Eq. (7.20) for cyclic convolution we may use modulo arithmetic in a ring of integers. Let M be the base modulo arithmetic, N be the order of the transform (the smallest N to satisfy Eq. (7.20), and α be a root of unity of order N modulo M. Hence, $\alpha^N = 1 \mod M$ or in the notation of number theory,

$$<\alpha^N> = 1 \mod M,$$

Relation between α and M: Consider now Eq. (7.20), and let α and M have the highest common factor, q. That is, $(\alpha, M) = q$.

Hence, $\frac{\alpha^N}{M} = \text{product} \dots \text{remainder}$.

Therefore, we can write

$$\alpha^N = \text{product} . M + \text{remainder}$$
$$(p) \qquad\qquad (r)$$

But q is the common factor of α and M; it follows that

$$(\alpha')^N q^N = (q . M') p + r$$

or

$$[(\alpha')^N q^{N-1} - M'.p]q = r$$

Hence, q must also be a factor of r and the remainder r can never be 1. This implies that

$$\alpha^N \neq 1 \bmod M, \text{ if}(\alpha, M)' \neq 1.$$

The implication from this result is that in order to have $\alpha^N = 1 \bmod M$, α and M must be relatively prime. That is

$$(\alpha, M) = 1 \tag{7.20}$$

Existence of N^{-1}: We have also pointed out that in order to form the inverse transform, N^{-1} must exist in mod M. Let us discuss the relationship of N and M for the existence of N^{-1}. Let $(N,M) \neq 1 = q$ and x be an integer.

$$\frac{N.x}{M} = \text{product (p)} + \text{remainder}$$

$$N.x = M.p + \text{remainder}(r)$$

$$q(N'.x - M'.p) = r$$

Since q is a factor of r, r can never be 1. This implies that there is no inverse for N. Hence, for the existence of an inverse for N,

$$(N, M) = 1 \tag{7.21}$$

From Eq. (7.18), it is clear that the next condition to be considered for the existence of the transform is that $N^{-1} \sum_{n=0}^{N-1} \alpha^{nm} = 0$ for $m \neq 0$ mod N. For the transform in a ring of integers modulo an integer M, and with the root of integer, this condition can be simplified to the following form:

$$((\alpha^{m-1}), M) = 1; \text{ for } m = 1, 2, \ldots, N - 1 \tag{7.22}$$

Equation (7.23) can be obtained from the fact that the product of $(\alpha^{k-\ell} - 1)$ and $\sum_{n=0}^{N-1} \alpha^{(k-\ell)n}$ of Eq. (7.16) is always zero. Hence, if $(\alpha^{k-\ell} - 1)$'s are relatively prime to M, it is impossible to form a product of $(\alpha^{k-\ell} - 1)$ and a number, say x to be a multiple of M, unless x is a multiple of M. This implies that if all $(\alpha^{k-\ell} - 1)$'s are relatively prime to M, $\sum_{n=0}^{N-1} \alpha^{(k-\ell)n}$ must be zero.

From the above discussion, it is obvious that for forming a proper number theoretic transform, $\{\alpha, M, N\}$ should be chosen on the ring of integers under the following conditions:

(i) $(\alpha, M) = 1$
(ii) $(N, M) = 1$ and
(iii) $< \sum_{n=0}^{N-1} \alpha^{nm} = 0 >_M$, for $M \neq 0$

(7.24)

or

(iii) can be written as
(iv) $((\alpha^{m-1}), M) = 1$

7.3.1 *Mersenne Number and Fermat Number Transforms*

In order to make the number theoretic transform more attractive, it should be computationally efficient. The transform should involve only simple arithmetic manipulations. It is desirable for the power of α, the root of unity to have a simple binary representation using very few bits. It is obvious that the best choice of α is 2. To facilitate modulo arithmetic, M should also be represented by simple binary word as well. It seems that the best choice of M is 2 raised to a certain power. However, this is contrary to Eq. (7.24) (i) if we also choose α to be 2 or powers of 2. Furthermore, this choice also gives rise to sequence length problems. The choice of N depends very much on the choice of α and M. If $\alpha = 2$, it is also desirable for N to be a power of 2 so that FFT-type of algorithms may be used for fast computation.

Mersenne Number Transform: Let $M = 2^P - 1$, where P is a prime number and $\alpha = 2$. Numbers of the form $2^k - 1$ are traditionally called Mersenne numbers; hence, this transform is called a Mersenne number transform. Now, let us define the Mersenne number transform as

$$X(k) = \sum_{n=0}^{N-1} x(n) 2^{nk}, \text{ where } k = 0, 1, \ldots, N-1. \quad (7.25)$$

To find the transform length N, we may write

$$M = 2^P - 1; \text{ hence,}$$

$$<2^P = 1>_M$$

This implies that the length $N = P$. Hence, we may write the Mersenne number transform pair as

$$X(k) =< \sum_{n=0}^{P-1} x(n)2^{nk} >_M \qquad (7.26)$$

and

$$X(n) =< \frac{1}{p} \sum_{k=0}^{P-1} x(k)2^{-nk} >_M, \qquad (7.27)$$

where $n, k = 0, 1, \ldots, P - 1$

This transform requires very simple arithmetic operations. The addition of two numbers modulo M $(= 2^P - 1)$ is simply ones-complement addition in a P-bit word. This is a good transform, but it is restricted to have short transform length which is equal to P, i.e., $N = P$.

Fermat Number Transform (FNT): For Fermat number transforms, we have $M = F_t = 2^{2^t} + 1$ and α is usually chosen to be 2 or a power of 2. We can write the Fermat number transform pair as

$$X(k) =< \sum_{n=0}^{N-1} x(n)\alpha^{nk} >_{F_t} \qquad (7.28)$$

and

$$x(n) = < \frac{1}{N} \sum_{k=0}^{N-1} x(k)\alpha^{-nk} >_{F_t} \qquad (7.29)$$

for $k, n = 0, 1, \ldots, N - 1$

To find the possible values of the transform length N, we recall $< \alpha^N >_{F_t} = 1$. From Eq. (7.22),

$$N|[(p_1 - 1), (p_2 - 1), \ldots, (p_\ell - 1)] \text{ of } F_t.$$

All F_1, F_2, F_3 and F_4 are primes; hence, for F_t, where $t = 1, 2, 3,$ or 4,

$$N| (F_t - 1), \text{ or } N|2^{2^t}$$

We can therefore have a FNT with a transform length as long as $N = 2^{2^t}$.

However, the major restriction comes from a basic property of number theory. After finding $N = 2^{2^t}$, we have to choose an α that satisfies the equation $\alpha^N = 1 \bmod F_t$. In the case, α is actually the primitive root of F_t and it is defined as the integer which can generate the largest order. As we mentioned before, the most desirable value for α is 2. However, if we make a detailed examination of the possible values of α with $N = 2^{2^t}$, it shows that 2 is not primitive root of F_t.

Example 1

Let $t = 2$. $F_t = 2^{2^t} + 1 = 17$. The expected largest order is $(F_t - 1) = 16$. If $\alpha = 2$, we get:

n	2^1	2^2	2^3	2^4	2^5	2^6	2^7	2^8
Residue	2	4	8	16	15	13	9	1

This shows that 2 is not a primitive root of F_2. It is a generator of the cyclic group listed above. If $\alpha = 3$

n	3^1	3^2	3^3	3^4	3^5	3^6	3^7	3^8	3^9	3^{10}	3^{11}	3^{12}	3^{13}	3^{14}	3^{15}	3^{16}
Residue	3	9	10	13	5	15	11	16	14	8	7	4	12	2	6	1

This shows that 3 is a primitive root of order $N(= 2^{2^2} = 16)$, which is the largest possible transform length. Practically, the Fermat number transform is one of the most interesting form of the NTT, which also approaches practical uses; especially it is used to combine with other prime factor algorithms to form an efficient composite algorithm. Let us conclude this section with an example using the Fermat number transform.

Example 2

Cyclic Convolution using FNT. Consider the cyclic convolution of the sequences

$$\tilde{\mathbf{x}} = \mathbf{x}^T = [0, 1, 3, -2]$$

$$\tilde{\mathbf{h}} = \mathbf{h}^T = [2, 0, 0, 1]$$

(a) By direct calculation
$$y(0) = 0.2 + 1.1 + 3.0 + (-2).0 = 1$$
$$y(1) = 0.0 + 1.2 + 3.1 + (-2).0 = 5$$

$$y(2) = 0.0 + 1.0 + 3.2 + (-2).1 = 4$$
$$y(2) = 0.1 + 1.0 + 3.0 + (-2).2 = -4$$

(b) By Fermat number transform

Choose $M = F_2 = 2^{2^t} = 2^{2^2} = 17$, for $t = 2$. The maximum transform length with powers of 2 as root of unity is $\alpha = 2t+1 = 8$, or $<2^8 = 1>_{17}$.

For this example, $N = 4$ and $\alpha = 2^2 = 4$ is chosen. The transformation matrix **T** is given by

$$\mathbf{T} = \begin{bmatrix} 1 & 1 & 1 & 1 \\ 1 & 4 & 4^2 & 4^3 \\ 1 & 4^2 & 4^4 & 4^6 \\ 1 & 4^3 & 4^6 & 4^9 \end{bmatrix} = \begin{bmatrix} 1 & 1 & 1 & 1 \\ 1 & 4 & -1 & -4 \\ 1 & -1 & 1 & -1 \\ 1 & -4 & -1 & 4 \end{bmatrix}$$

Note that $4^{-1} = 4^{-1}4^4 = -4$

$$\mathbf{T}^{-1} = 4^{-1} \begin{bmatrix} 1 & 1 & 1 & 1 \\ 1 & 4^{-1} & 4^{-2} & 4^{-3} \\ 1 & 4^{-2} & 4^{-4} & 4^{-6} \\ 1 & 4^{-3} & 4^{-6} & 4^{-9} \end{bmatrix} = \begin{bmatrix} 1 & 1 & 1 & 1 \\ 1 & -4 & -1 & 4 \\ 1 & -1 & 1 & -1 \\ 1 & 4 & -1 & -4 \end{bmatrix}$$

Therefore,

$$\mathbf{X} = \mathbf{T.x} = \begin{bmatrix} 1 & 1 & 1 & 1 \\ 1 & 4 & -1 & -4 \\ 1 & -1 & 1 & -1 \\ 1 & -4 & -1 & 4 \end{bmatrix} \begin{bmatrix} 0 \\ 1 \\ 3 \\ 2 \end{bmatrix} = \begin{bmatrix} 2 \\ 9 \\ 4 \\ -15 \end{bmatrix} = \begin{bmatrix} 2 \\ 9 \\ 4 \\ 2 \end{bmatrix} \text{ mod } 17$$

$$\mathbf{H} = \mathbf{T.h} = \begin{bmatrix} 1 & 1 & 1 & 1 \\ 1 & 4 & -1 & -4 \\ 1 & -1 & 1 & -1 \\ 1 & -4 & -1 & 4 \end{bmatrix} \begin{bmatrix} 2 \\ 0 \\ 0 \\ 1 \end{bmatrix} = \begin{bmatrix} 3 \\ -2 \\ 1 \\ 6 \end{bmatrix} \text{ mod } 17$$

$$\mathbf{Y} = \mathbf{X \cdot H} \begin{bmatrix} 6 \\ -18 \\ 4 \\ 12 \end{bmatrix} = \begin{bmatrix} 6 \\ -1 \\ 4 \\ -5 \end{bmatrix} \text{ mod } 17.$$

Taking the inverse transform, we have

$$\mathbf{y} = -4 \begin{bmatrix} 1 & 1 & 1 & 1 \\ 1 & -4 & -1 & 4 \\ 1 & -1 & 1 & -1 \\ 1 & 4 & -1 & -4 \end{bmatrix} \begin{bmatrix} 6 \\ -1 \\ 4 \\ -5 \end{bmatrix} = \begin{bmatrix} 1 \\ 5 \\ 4 \\ -4 \end{bmatrix} \text{ mod } 17.$$

7.4 Very Fast Discrete Fourier Transform Using Number Theoretic Transform

In the previous sections, we have shown that number theoretic transforms can be used to implement cyclic convolutions very effectively. It is the purpose of this section to show that the same basic structures can be used to implement the discrete Fourier transform.

In this section, it is shown that NTT can be used to compute DFT very efficiently (Siu and Constantinides, 1983). By noting some simple properties of the number theory and the DFT, the total number of real multiplications for a length-q DFT is reduced to $(q - 1)$, where q is a prime number. This requires less than one real multiplication per point. For a proper choice of transform length and NTT, the number of shift-adds per point is approximately the same as the number of additions required for FFT algorithms.

Theory: Let g be a primitive root that generates all nonzero elements inside the field modulo q. Consider now an N-point discrete Fourier transform,

$$Y(k) = \sum_{n=0}^{N-1} x(n)\, W_0^{nk}, \qquad (7.30)$$

where $k = 0, 1, \ldots, N - 1$ and $W_0 = e^{-j(2\pi/N)}$

If N is a prime number q, then Eq. (7.30) can be reordered by Rader's Algorithm (Rader, 1968) in the following form, which is essentially going to map k to $<g^k>_q$ and n to $<g^{-n}>_q$ in major part of the computation, where g a primitive root of q.

$$Y(0) = \sum_{n=0}^{q-1} x(n) \qquad (7.31)$$

And

$$Y(<g^k>_q) = x(0) + \sum_{n=1}^{q-1} x(<g^{-n}>_q) W_0^{<g^{k-n}>_q}, \qquad (7.32)$$

$$\text{for } k = 1, 2, \ldots, q - 1$$

We can write Eq. (7.32) as

$$Y(<g^k>_q) = x(0) + X(<g^k>_q), \qquad (7.33)$$

where

$$X(< g^k >_q) = \sum_{n=1}^{q-1} x(< g^{-n} >_q) W_0^{<g^{k-n}>_q},$$ (7.34)

for $k = 1, 2, \ldots, q - 1$

Equation (7.34) represents a backward circular convolution of length-$(q - 1)$. That is

$$\{x(g^{-1}), x(g^{-2}), \ldots x(g^{-q+1})\} \otimes^c \{W_0^{g^0}, W_0^{g^1}, \ldots W_0^{g^{q-2}}\},$$ (7.35)

where $\otimes^c$ means circular convolution and the subscripts and indices are modulo q. Let us now define

$$X_k = X(< g^{k+1} >_q)$$ (7.36)

$$W_n = W_0^{<g^n>_q}$$ (7.37)

$$x_n = x(< g^{-(n+1)} >_q),$$ (7.38)

for $k, n = 0, 1, \ldots, q - 2$

Hence, Eqs. (7.34) and (7.35) become

$$X_k = \sum_{n=0}^{q-2} x_n W_{k-n}$$

for $k = 0, 1, \ldots, q - 2$ (7.39)

$$\{x_0, x_1, \ldots x_{q-2}\} \otimes^c \{W_0, W_1, \ldots W_{q-2}\}$$ (7.40)

The number theoretic transform can now be applied to compute the cyclic convolution sum of these two sequences. Thus, we can write

$$X'_m = < \sum_{n=0}^{q-2} x_n \alpha^{mn} >_M$$ (7.41)

and

$$W'_m = < \sum_{n=0}^{q-2} W_n \alpha^{mn} >_M,$$ (7.42)

for $m = 0, 1, \ldots, q - 2$

The results can then be obtained by the inverse transform of the products, $X'_m W'_m$'s. That is

$$X_k = < \frac{1}{q-1} \sum_{m=0}^{q-2} X'_m W'_m \alpha^{-mk} >_M,$$ (7.43)

for $m = 0, 1, \ldots, q - 2.$

Recall that all W_m's are complex numbers; hence, apparently the total number of multiplications for a real sequence of length-q (to find all $X_{m'} W_{m''}$s) for this method is $2(q - 1)$. However, the sequence $\{W_0^{g^0}, W_0^{g^1}, \ldots W_0^{g^{q-2}}\}$ can actually be written as

$$\{W_0^{g^0}, W_0^{g^1}, \ldots, W_0^{g^{\frac{q-1}{2}-1}} \ W_0^{g^{0*}}, W_0^{g^{1*}}, \ldots, W_0^{g^{\frac{q-1}{2}-1*}}\}, \qquad (7.44)$$

where * denotes complex conjugates.

Therefore, the sequence $\{W_0, W_1, \ldots, W_{q-2}\}$ can be written as

$$\{W_0, W_1, \ldots W_{\frac{q-1}{2}-1}, W_0^*, W_1^*, \ldots W_{\frac{q-1}{2}-1}^*\}. \qquad (7.45)$$

Note also that $\text{Real}(W_n) = \text{Real}(W_n^*)$ and $\text{Imag}(W_n) = -\text{Imag}(W_n^*)$.

Hence

$$\text{Real}(W_{n+\frac{q-1}{2}}) = \text{Real}(W_n) \qquad (7.46)$$

$$\text{Imag}(W_{n+\frac{q-1}{2}}) = -\text{Imag}(W_n) \qquad (7.47)$$

$$\text{for } n = 0, 1, \ldots (\frac{q-1}{2} - 1)$$

In view of these relationships, Eq. (7.42) can be written as

$$W_m' = \ < \sum_{n=0}^{\frac{q-1}{2}-1} W_n \, \alpha^{mn} + \sum_{n=\frac{q-1}{2}}^{q-2} W_n \, \alpha^{mn} >_M \qquad (7.48)$$

$$= \ < \sum_{n=0}^{\frac{q-1}{2}-1} W_n \, \alpha^{mn} + \sum_{n=0}^{\frac{q-1}{2}-1} W_{n+\frac{q-1}{2}} \, \alpha^{(n+\frac{q-1}{2})m} >_M \qquad (7.49)$$

and since $\alpha^{(q-1)/2} = -1$, we can write

$$W_m' = \ < \sum_{n=0}^{\frac{q-1}{2}-1} W_n \, \alpha^{mn} + (-1)^m \sum_{n=0}^{\frac{q-1}{2}-1} W_{n+\frac{q-1}{2}} \, \alpha^{mn} >_M \qquad (7.50)$$

On combining Eqs. (7.46), (7.47), and (7.50), it is clear that

$$\text{Real}(W_m') = \ \text{Real}\left(< 2 \sum_{n=0}^{\frac{q-1}{2}-1} W_n \, \alpha^{mn} >_M \right) \text{ for } m = \text{even}$$

$$= 0 \text{ for } m = \text{odd} \qquad (7.51)$$

$\text{Imag}(W'_m) = 0$ for $m = $ odd for $m = $ even

$$= \text{Imag}\left(< 2 \sum_{n=0}^{\frac{q-1}{2}-1} W_n\, \alpha^{mn} >_M \right) \text{ for } m = \text{even}$$

(7.52)

Equations (7.51) and (7.52) are very important in practical implementations. This is not primarily due to the fact that the number of shift-adds (α multiplications if α is a simple combination of power of 2), either the MNT or FNT, reduces by a factor of 2 for the calculation of W'_m's, since all W'_m's should be pre-calculated before realization; it is due, however, to the fact that the total number of real multiplications forming $X'_m W'_m$'s reduces from $(2q-2)$ to $(q-1)$. This gives less than one (actually $1 - 1/p$) multiplication per point for the DFT of a real sequence of length-q. The number of additions required in this technique is evaluated below.

The shift-adds required to compute W'_m's are not counted since these quantities can be pre-calculated and stored in the program for a software implementation. The total number of shift-adds required for transforming $\{x_0, x_1, \ldots, x_{q-2}\}$ to $\{x'_0, x'_1, \ldots, x'_{q-2}\}$ is $(q-1)(q-2)$. However, if we choose $(q-1)$ to be highly composite, an FFT-type of algorithm can be applied to effect the transformation. In particular if $(q-1)$ is a power of 2, the total number of shift-adds is equal to $(q-1)\log_2(q-1)$.

Example 3

To illustrate the idea let us consider the DFT of the sequence $\{x(0), x(1), x(2), x(3), x(4)\}$, i.e., $N = q = 5$. In this case the 2 is a primitive root that is used to generate elements inside the field modulo 5. Hence, the mapping for $\{x(n)\}$ in Eqs. (7.34) and (7.35) is given by

$$\{x_n : n = 1, 2, 3, 4\} = \{x(<g^{-n}>_M), : n = 1, 2, 3, 4\}$$
$$= \{x(3), x(4), x(2), x(1)\} \text{ and}$$
$$\{W_0^{g^n}, : n = 0, 1, 2, 3\} = \{W_0^1\ W_0^2, W_0^4, W_0^3\}.$$

Hence, Eq. (7.35) becomes

$$\{x(3), x(4), x(2), x(1)\} \otimes \{W_0^1\ W_0^2, W_0^4, W_0^3\}$$

$$\{x(3), x(4), x(2), x(1)\} \otimes \{W_0^1\ W_0^2, W_0^{1^*}, W_0^{2^*}\} \quad (7.53)$$

This convolution sum can be computed by NTT. Now let us use an FNT to make the calculation. Let $M = F_4 = 2^{16} + 1$, $\alpha = 2^8$ and of course $N = 4$. Hence

$$
\begin{bmatrix} x_0' \\ x_1' \\ x_2' \\ x_3' \end{bmatrix} = < \begin{bmatrix} 1 & 1 & 1 & 1 \\ 1 & 2^8 & -1 & -2^8 \\ 1 & -1 & 1 & -1 \\ 1 & -2^8 & -1 & 2^8 \end{bmatrix} \begin{bmatrix} x(3) \\ x(4) \\ x(2) \\ x(1) \end{bmatrix} >_M \qquad (7.54)
$$

$$
\begin{bmatrix} W_0'' \\ W_1'' \\ W_2'' \\ W_3'' \end{bmatrix} = < \begin{bmatrix} 1 & 1 & 1 & 1 \\ 1 & 2^8 & -1 & -2^8 \\ 1 & -1 & 1 & -1 \\ 1 & -2^8 & -1 & 2^8 \end{bmatrix} \begin{bmatrix} W_0^1 \\ W_0^2 \\ W_0^{1*} \\ W_0^{2*} \end{bmatrix} >_M \qquad (7.55)
$$

where $W_0 = e^{-j(2\pi/5)}$

In order to use modulo arithmetic, the W_0 terms have to be normalized to integer values. Multiplying these terms by 90 and rounding off the results to integers, we obtain

$$
\begin{bmatrix} W_0'' \\ W_1'' \\ W_2'' \\ W_3'' \end{bmatrix} = \begin{bmatrix} -90 & + & j0 \\ 0 & + & j38229 \\ 202 & + & j0 \\ 0 & + & j26964 \end{bmatrix}
$$

This expression may be compared with Eqs. (7.51) and (7.52) for agreement. Hence, for the computation $X_m' W_m''$, for $m = 0,1,2,3$ a total number of four real multiplications is sufficient. This is also the total number of multiplications required for a 5-point DFT. As we introduced, this requires the 4/5 (or generally $(N-1)/N$ multiplications per points, which is the smallest number of multiplications that has ever reported in the literature for the realization of the discrete Fourier Transform. The total number of real shift-adds required is $2(4)\log_2(4) - (5-3)/2 = 15$. The major disadvantages of the method using NTT to calculate DFT are that special arithmetic (modulo arithmetic) and normally relatively large word lengths may have to be used for the major part of the calculation, a fact common to all number theoretic transforms.

7.5 Discrete Cosine Transform

The DCT (Britanak, Yip and Rao, 2007; Chan and Siu, 1997; Chan and Siu, 1993) and the subsequent the ICT (Cham, 1989; Malvar,

2001) have been used as the major kernel for transform coding. The desirable properties of a transform for such an application include energy compaction, de-correlation and simplicity. Most transforms have the former two properties; however, the DCT is a simple transform that processes both very good properties of energy compaction and de-correlation. In this section, we will start with a simplified derivation of the DCT, which avoids sharp discontinuity. We will then develop the ICT systematically in one-dimensional form. The ICT has received great attention in the recent years. Combining with ICT and quantization, the ICT can be implemented without any multiplication, just using additions and shifts.

Simplified Derivation of the Discrete Cosine Transform and Fast Algorithm

Let us derive the discrete cosine transform from the frequency domain of a signal. This derivation is simple and reflects directly that the DCT is a form of representation of the signal in the frequency domain. We start with the representation of the signal without discontinuity, and subsequently use the discrete Fourier transform as a vehicle for the development. Consider again a sequence as shown in Fig. 7.1a, which is represented by $\{x(n): n = 0, 1, \ldots N - 1g$, where N is the length of the sequence. If we are going to find the frequency spectrum of the signal, usually we will take the discrete Fourier transform of the signal. The transformation process will consider the signal to be periodic and the values of the periodic sequence will repeat itself at a distance of N as shown in Fig. 7.1c. In order to avoid sudden discontinuity, the original sequence can be extended to double its length by a mirror reflection of the signal to the right hand side using the edge of the last point as the mirror position. This mirror-extended signal can then be considered as a periodic sequence as shown in Fig. 7.1d to be transformed into the frequency domain. Note that the period of the sequence is now $2N$, and this new sequence does not contain any artificial discontinuity.

Mathematically, the mirror extended sequence can be written as

$$y(n) = x(n) + x(2N - 1 - n), \text{ where} n = 0, 1, \ldots, 2N - 1. \quad (7.56)$$

Example 3.6: Let us consider $N = 4$; hence, the sequence becomes $\{x(n): n = 0, 1, 2, 3\}$. From Eq. (7.56), we have

$$y(n) = x(n) + x(7 - n) \quad (7.57)$$

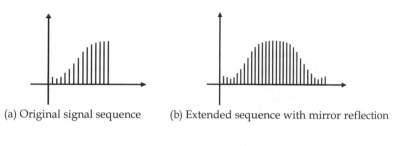

(a) Original signal sequence   (b) Extended sequence with mirror reflection

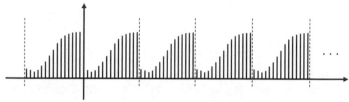

(c) Periodic sequence resulting from the original signal sequence

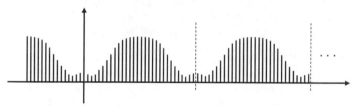

(d) Periodic sequence resulting from the extended sequence

Figure 7.1   Formation of periodic sequence.

We can write

$$\{y(0), y(1), y(2), y(3), y(4), y(5), y(6), y(7)\}$$
$$= \{x(0), x(1), x(2), x(3), x(3), x(2), x(1), x(0)\}$$

Or

$$y(n) = x(n) \quad 0 \leq n \leq N - 1 \tag{7.58}$$

$$= x(2N - 1 - n) \quad N \leq n \leq 2N - 1 \tag{7.59}$$

This becomes a length-8 sequence as shown in Fig. 7.2.

The formation of an extended sequence is extremely important, since it eliminates artificial sharp discontinuities. If we transform these sharp discontinuities into the transform domain, they spread

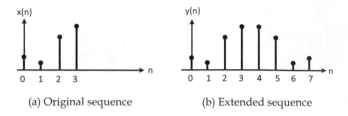

Figure 7.2 Sequence extension.

the errors evenly across the whole spectrum of the transform, thus increasing the correlation among coefficients in the transform domain. This is against the de-correlation requirement of a transform that is suitable for coding. It is also very important to point out that the periodicity requirement is usually the assumption that is innate in the transform of sampled signals.

Let us use the DFT to convert the $2N$-sequence as shown in Eq. (7.56) into the frequency domain. We have

$$Y(k) = \sum_{n=0}^{2N-1} y(n) W^{nk} \tag{7.60}$$

$$= \sum_{n=0}^{2N-1} [x(n) + x(2N - 1 - n)] W^{nk} \, .$$

$$\text{for } k = 0, 1, \ldots, 2N - 1 \text{ and } W = e^{-j\frac{2\pi}{2N}}$$

Note that k has a value between 0 and $2N - 1$.
Now expand Eq. (7.60), we have

$$Y(k) = \sum_{n=0}^{N-1} x(n) W^{nk} + \sum_{n=N}^{2N-1} x(2N - 1 - n) W^{nk}$$

For the second term in the RHS, let $m = (2N - 1 - n)$. Hence, $n = 2N - 1 - m$, For the limits of the summation, when $n = N$, $m = N - 1$, and when $n = (2N - 1)$, $m = 0$. Note that m is dummy variable and this second term can be written back in terms of n after the substitution. We then have

$$Y(k) = \sum_{n=0}^{N-1} x(n) W^{nk} + \sum_{n=0}^{N-1} x(n) W^{(2N-n-1)k}$$

$$= \sum_{n=0}^{N-1} x(n) \left[W^{nk} + W^{-(n+1)k} \right],$$

for $k = 0, 1, \ldots, 2N - 1$ and $W^{2N} = 0$.

Extracting $W^{-\frac{k}{2}}$ out from the RHS, we have

$$Y(k) = W^{-\frac{k}{2}} \left[\sum_{n=0}^{N-1} x(n) W^{nk+\frac{k}{2}} + \sum_{n=0}^{N-1} x(n) W^{-nk-\frac{k}{2}} \right]$$

$$= w^{-\frac{k}{2}} \left[\sum_{n=0}^{N-1} x(n) e^{-j\frac{2\pi}{4N}k(2n+1)} + \sum_{n=0}^{N-1} x(n) e^{j\frac{2\pi}{4N}k(2n+1)} \right]$$

Hence

$$Y(k) = W^{-\frac{k}{2}} \sum_{n=0}^{N-1} 2x(n) \cos \frac{\pi}{2N} k(2n+1), \qquad (7.61)$$

for $k = 0, 1, \ldots, 2N - 1$.

In Eq. (7.61), the term $W^{-(k/2)}$ has fixed values for different k. If N is fixed, the values of $W^{-(k/2)}$ are constants irrespective to the sampled signal $\{x(n)\}$ being considered. Hence, this factor gives no significant effect to the spectrum of the transformed results. Let us define

$$Y(k) = 2W^{-\frac{k}{2}} X'(k), \qquad (7.62a)$$

where

$$X'(k) = \sum_{n=0}^{N-1} x(n) \cos \frac{2\pi}{4N} k(2n+1), \qquad (7.62b)$$

for $k = 0, 1, \ldots, 2N - 1$.

Or from Eq. (7.62a)

$$X'(k) = \frac{1}{2} W^{\frac{k}{2}} Y(k), \quad \text{for } k = 0, 1, \ldots, 2N - 1. \qquad (7.62c)$$

Normally, for a sequence with length-$2N$, we have also $2N$ transformed coefficients in the transform domain. Let us recall the symmetric properties of the DFT. If the values of $y(n)$ are real numbers, the real part of the $Y(k)$ is an even function and the imaginary part of $Y(k)$ is an odd function, where, of course, i.e.,

$$Yr(2N - k) = Yr(k) \text{ and } Yi(2N - k) = -Yi(k)$$

where $Y(k) = Y_r(k) + jY_i(k)$ and for $k = 0, 1, \ldots, N - 1$

Hence, there are redundant terms in Eq. (7.62). Let us state without proof two properties of Eq. (7.62a) and give a numerical example as shown below.

Property 1: When $k = N$, we have $X'(k) = X'(N) = 0$

Property 2: $X'(2N - k) = -X'(k)$, or $X'(N + k) = -X'(N\text{-}k)$

Example 5

Let $\{x(n)\} = \{1,2,5,6,2,8\}$.

We have $\{y(n)\} = \{1,2,5,6,2,8,8,2,6,5,2,1\}$

We can find $\{X'(k)\} = \{24, -7.0203, -1.7321, -4.2426, 6, -2.7777,$

$$0, 2.777, -6, 4.2426, 1.7321, 7.0203\}$$

Hence, the first N terms are sufficiently enough to represent the sequence of signal in the transform domain.

Now let us define the **DCT** of $x(n)$ for k, which ranges from 0 to $N - 1$ (not from 0 to $2N - 1$) as shown below:

$$X(k) = \begin{cases} \frac{1}{2} w^{\frac{k}{2}} Y(k) & 0 \le k \le N\text{-}1 \\ 0 & \text{otherwise} \end{cases} \tag{7.63}$$

or

$$X(k) = \sum_{n=0}^{N-1} x(n) \cos \frac{2\pi}{4N} k(2n + 1), \tag{7.64}$$

for $k = 0, 1, \ldots, N - 1$

Fast Algorithm for Computing the DCT: Surprisingly we end up with a real transform that involves no complex number operations. This implies that the required computation could be simple. This simple derivation can also be used as a means to give a fast algorithm for the computation of the DCT by making use of the discrete Fourier transform. The following three steps show the way to compute the DCT via the discrete Fourier transform.

1. Find $y(n) = x(n) + x(2N - 1 - n)$ from Eqs. (7.58) and (7.59).
2. Find the DFT of $y(n)$, $Y(k) = \text{DFT}\{y(n)\}$ from Eq. (7.60).
3. Find the required result from Eq. (7.62),

$$X(k) = \begin{cases} \frac{1}{2}w^{k/2}\,Y(k) & 0 \le k \le N - 1 \\ 0 & \text{otherwise} \end{cases}$$

The second step requires the computation of the discrete Fourier transform that can easily be obtained via an FFT algorithm, since many efficient FFT algorithms are available.

7.5.1 *Length-4 DCT*

In order to let the reader to see the structure of DCT at this early stage, let us substitute $N = 4$ to Eq. (7.64) to form the kernel of the length-4 DCT. This example is also useful for the discussion of the inverse DCT in the next section. From Eq. (7.64), for $N = 4$, we have

$$\mathbf{X} = \begin{bmatrix} \mathbf{X}_0 \\ \mathbf{X}_1 \\ \mathbf{X}_2 \\ \mathbf{X}_3 \end{bmatrix} = \begin{bmatrix} a & a & a & a \\ b & c & -c & -b \\ a & -u & -a & a \\ c & -b & b & -c \end{bmatrix} \begin{bmatrix} x_0 \\ x_1 \\ x_2 \\ x_3 \end{bmatrix} \tag{7.65}$$

where $a = 0.5000$, $b = \frac{1}{\sqrt{2}}\cos\frac{\pi}{8} = 0.6533$, and $c = \frac{1}{\sqrt{2}}\cos\frac{3\pi}{8} = 0.2706$

Equation (7.65) can be factorized as follows:

$$\mathbf{X} = \begin{bmatrix} X_0 \\ X_1 \\ X_2 \\ X_3 \end{bmatrix} = \begin{bmatrix} 1 & 1 & 1 & 1 \\ 1 & \frac{c}{b} & -\frac{c}{b} & -1 \\ 1 & -1 & -1 & 1 \\ \frac{c}{b} & -1 & 1 & -\frac{c}{b} \end{bmatrix} \begin{bmatrix} x_0 \\ x_1 \\ x_2 \\ x_3 \end{bmatrix} \otimes \begin{bmatrix} a \\ b \\ a \\ b \end{bmatrix} \tag{7.66}$$

where $\otimes$ means term by term multiplication
or

$$\mathbf{X} = \begin{bmatrix} \mathbf{X}_0 \\ \mathbf{X}_1 \\ \mathbf{X}_2 \\ \mathbf{X}_3 \end{bmatrix} = \begin{bmatrix} 1 & 1 & 1 & 1 \\ 1 & d & -d & -1 \\ 1 & -1 & -1 & 1 \\ d & -1 & 1 & -d \end{bmatrix} \begin{bmatrix} x_0 \\ x_1 \\ x_2 \\ x_3 \end{bmatrix} \otimes \begin{bmatrix} a \\ b \\ a \\ b \end{bmatrix}, \tag{7.67}$$

where $d = \frac{c}{b} = \frac{0.2706}{0.6533} = 0.4142$

7.5.2 *Inverse DCT*

In the derivation of DCT, we started with a $2N$-point DFT of the sequence $\{y(n)\}$ as in Eq. (7.60):

$$Y(k) = \sum_{k=0}^{2N-1} y(n)W^{nk} \text{ for } W = e^{-j\frac{2\pi}{2N}} \qquad (7.68)$$

What is $\{x(n)\}$? $\{x(n)\}$ is just the beginning part of $\{y(n)\}$. Hence, if we can find $\{y(n)\}$, we just take the beginning half of $\{y(n)\}$, which is actually $\{x(n)\}$, as shown in Fig. 7.2

Hence, we make use of $\{y(n)\}$ to find $\{x(n)\}$. Let us start to look for the inverse transform of $Y(k)$, which is the forward transform result of $\{y(n)\}$.

$$y(n) = \frac{1}{2N} \sum_{k=0}^{2N-1} Y(k)W_i^{nk} \text{ for } W_i = e^{-(-j\frac{2\pi}{2N})} = e^{j\frac{2\pi}{2N}} = W^{-1}$$

$$(7.69)$$

Recall Eq. (7.62a), $Y(k) = 2W^{-\frac{k}{2}}X'(k)$, the inverse DFT of $Y(k)$ can be written as

$$y(n) = \frac{1}{2N} \sum_{k=0}^{2N-1} 2W^{-\frac{k}{2}}X'(k)W_i^{nk} \text{ for } W_i = e^{j\frac{2\pi}{2N}} = W^{-1} \quad (7.70)$$

Note that Eq. (7.70) is in terms of $X'(k)$, not $X(k)$. The term $X'(k)$ has been defined in Eq. (7.62) for $k = 0, 1, \ldots, 2N - 1$.

Let us group W terms in Eq. (7.70).

$$y(n) = \frac{1}{N} \sum_{k=0}^{2N-1} W^{-\frac{k}{2}}X'(k)W^{-nk} \text{ for } W_i = W^{-1}$$

$$= \frac{1}{N} \sum_{k=0}^{2N-1} X'(k)W^{-(n+\frac{1}{2})k}, \qquad (7.71)$$

where $n = 0, 1, \ldots, 2N - 1$

Expending Eq. (7.71)

$$y(n) = \frac{1}{N}X'(0) + \frac{1}{N}\left(\begin{array}{l} \sum_{k=1}^{N-1} X'(k)W^{-(n+\frac{1}{2})N} + X'(N)W^{-(N+\frac{1}{2})N} \\ + \sum_{k=N+1}^{2N-1} X'(k)W^{-(n+\frac{1}{2})k} \end{array} \right)$$

Since $X'(k)W^{-(n+\frac{1}{2})N} = 0$ as in the example, we have

$$y(n) = \frac{1}{N}X'(0) + \frac{1}{N}\left(\sum_{k=1}^{N-1} X'(k)W^{-(n+\frac{1}{2})k} + \sum_{k=N+1}^{2N-1} X'(k)W^{-(n+\frac{1}{2})k}\right)$$

Let us arrange the last term of the equation in line with the second last term. Let $m = 2N - k$, then $k = 2N - m$. When $k = N+1$, $m = N-1$; and when $k = 2N-1$, $m = 1$. Note again m is a dummy variable. Hence,

$$y(n) = \frac{1}{N}X'(0) + \frac{1}{N}\left(\begin{array}{l}\sum_{k=1}^{N-1} X'(k)W^{-(n+\frac{1}{2})k} \\ + \sum_{k=N-1}^{1} X'(2N-k)W^{-(n+\frac{1}{2})(2N-k)}\end{array}\right)$$

Recall the symmetric property in Example 5: $X'(2N - k) = -X'(k)$.

$$y(n) = \frac{1}{N}X'(0) + \frac{1}{N}\left(\sum_{k=1}^{N-1} X'(k)W^{-(n+\frac{1}{2})k} - \sum_{k=1}^{N-1} X'(k)W^{-(n+\frac{1}{2})(2N-k)}\right)$$

$$= \frac{1}{N}X'(0) + \frac{1}{N}\sum_{k=1}^{N-1} X'(k)\left(e^{j\frac{2\pi}{2N}(n+\frac{1}{2})k} - e^{-j\frac{2\pi}{2N}(n+\frac{1}{2})(k-2N)}\right)$$

$$= \frac{1}{N}X'(0) + \frac{1}{N}\sum_{k=1}^{N-1} X'(k)\left(e^{j\frac{2\pi}{2N}(n+\frac{1}{2})k} - e^{-j\frac{2\pi}{2N}(n+\frac{1}{2})k}e^{j(2n+1)\pi}\right)$$

$$= \frac{1}{N}X'(0) + \frac{1}{N}\sum_{k=1}^{N-1} X'(k)\left(e^{j\frac{2\pi}{2N}(n+\frac{1}{2})k} + e^{-j\frac{2\pi}{2N}(n+\frac{1}{2})k}\right)$$

We also have

$$y(n) = \frac{1}{N}X'(0) + \frac{1}{N}\sum_{k=1}^{N-1} X'(k)\left(e^{j\frac{2\pi}{2N}(n+\frac{1}{2})k} + e^{-j\frac{2\pi}{2N}(n+\frac{1}{2})k}\right)$$

Substitute $X'(k)$ with $X(k)$ since only the first N terms of $X'(k)$ are needed.

Hence,

$$y(n) = \frac{1}{N}X(0) + \frac{2}{N}\sum_{k=1}^{N-1} X(k)\cos\left(\frac{2\pi}{2N}(n+\frac{1}{2})k\right)$$

for $n = 0, 1, \ldots, 2N - 1$

Taking half of $\{y(n)\}$, it gives $\{x(n)\}$ as we said:

$$x(n) = \frac{1}{N}X(0) + \frac{2}{N}\sum_{k=1}^{N-1} X(k)\cos\left(\frac{2\pi}{4N}(2n+1)k\right)$$

for $n = 0, 1, \ldots, N-1$

For conventional practice, we usually write

$$x(n) = \frac{2}{N}\sum_{k=0}^{N-1} c(k)X(k)\cos\left(\frac{2\pi}{4N}(2n+1)k\right), \qquad (7.72)$$

$$\text{where } c(k) = \begin{cases} \frac{1}{2}, & k = 0 \\ 1, 1 \le k \le N-1 \end{cases}$$

Hence, the DCT pair can then be written as

Forward DCT:

$$X(k) = \sum_{n=0}^{N-1} x(n)\cos\frac{2\pi}{4N}k(2n+1), \qquad (7.73)$$

for $k = 0, 1, \ldots, N-1$

Inverse DCT:

$$x(n) = \frac{2}{N}\sum_{k=0}^{N-1} c(k)X(k)\cos\frac{2\pi}{4N}k(2n+1), \qquad (7.74)$$

$$\text{where } c(k) = \begin{cases} \frac{1}{2}, & k = 0 \\ 1, & 1 \le k \le N-1 \end{cases}$$

Scaling Factors of DCT

Equations (7.73) and (7.74) are unsymmetrical, which sometimes will make the realization difficult. To make them symmetrical, we simply redefine both the DCT and IDCT as shown below:

$$X(k) = c'(k)\sum_{n=0}^{N-1} x(n)\cos\frac{2\pi}{4N}k(2n+1) \qquad (7.75)$$

$$x(n) = \sum_{k=0}^{N-1} c'(k)X(k)\cos\frac{2\pi}{4N}k(2n+1), \qquad (7.76)$$

where

$$c'(k) = \begin{cases} \sqrt{\frac{1}{N}}, & k = 0 \\ \sqrt{\frac{2}{N}}, & 1 \le k \le N-1 \end{cases}$$

7.6 Integer Cosine Transform

7.6.1 *Length-4 DCT Again*

Let us develop the Integer DCT (IDCT) via a length-4 DCT, which is the simplest way to grab ideas.

Example 6

Consider a length-4 DCT

$$X(k) = \sqrt{\frac{1}{2}} C(k) \sum_{n=0}^{3} x(n) \cos \frac{2\pi(2n+1)k}{16} \text{ for } C(k) = \begin{cases} 1/\sqrt{2} & \text{for } k = 0 \\ 1 & \text{otherwise} \end{cases}$$

Expanding this equation, we have

$$X(0) = \quad \tfrac{1}{2}x(0) \quad + \quad \tfrac{1}{2}x(1) \quad + \quad \tfrac{1}{2}x(2) \quad + \quad \tfrac{1}{2}x(3)$$
$$X(1) = \tfrac{1}{\sqrt{2}}x(0)\cos 2\pi\theta + \tfrac{1}{\sqrt{2}}x(1)\cos 2\pi 3\theta + \tfrac{1}{\sqrt{2}}x(2)\cos 2\pi 5\theta + \tfrac{1}{\sqrt{2}}x(3)\cos 2\pi 7\theta$$
$$X(2) = \tfrac{1}{\sqrt{2}}x(0)\cos 2\pi 2\theta + \tfrac{1}{\sqrt{2}}x(1)\cos 2\pi 6\theta + \tfrac{1}{\sqrt{2}}x(2)\cos 2\pi 10\theta + \tfrac{1}{\sqrt{2}}x(3)\cos 2\pi 14\theta$$
$$X(3) = \tfrac{1}{\sqrt{2}}x(0)\cos 2\pi 3\theta + \tfrac{1}{\sqrt{2}}x(10)\cos 2\pi 9\theta + \tfrac{1}{\sqrt{2}}x(2)\cos 2\pi 15\theta + \tfrac{1}{\sqrt{2}}x(3)\cos 2\pi 21\theta$$

where

$$\theta = \frac{2}{16} = \frac{1}{8}$$

Or in matrix form with rounding, we have

$$\begin{bmatrix} X(0) \\ X(1) \\ X(2) \\ X(3) \end{bmatrix} = \begin{bmatrix} 0.5000 & 0.5000 & 0.5000 & 0.5000 \\ 0.6533 & 0.2706 & -0.2706 & -0.6533 \\ 0.5000 & -0.5000 & -0.5000 & 0.5000 \\ 0.2706 & -0.6533 & 0.6533 & -0.2706 \end{bmatrix} \begin{bmatrix} x(0) \\ x(1) \\ x(2) \\ x(3) \end{bmatrix}$$

We can also write

$$\mathbf{X} = \mathbf{H_4 x}$$

where

$$\mathbf{X} = \begin{bmatrix} X_0 \\ X_1 \\ X_2 \\ X_3 \end{bmatrix} = \begin{bmatrix} a & a & a & a \\ b & c & -c & -b \\ a & -a & -a & a \\ c & -b & b & -c \end{bmatrix} \begin{bmatrix} x_0 \\ x_1 \\ x_2 \\ x_3 \end{bmatrix} \qquad (7.77)$$

and

$$\mathbf{H_4} = \begin{bmatrix} a & a & a & a \\ b & c & -c & -b \\ a & -a & -a & a \\ c & -b & b & -c \end{bmatrix} \qquad (7.78)$$

where

$$a = 0.5000, b = \frac{1}{\sqrt{2}} \cos \frac{\pi}{8} = 0.6533, c = \frac{1}{\sqrt{2}} \cos \frac{3\pi}{8} = 0.2706$$

Let us study the structure of the elements of the kernel matrix $\mathbf{H}_4$. Only *three different elements* are available within the matrix. Note also that the inverse DCT transform kernel is equal to the transpose of the forward kernel. That is,

$$\mathbf{H}_4^{-1} = \mathbf{H}_4^T = \begin{bmatrix} a & b & a & c \\ a & c & -a & -b \\ a & -c & -a & b \\ a & -b & a & -c \end{bmatrix}, \tag{7.79}$$

where $a = 0.500$, $b = 0.6533$ and $c = 0.2706$.

Equation (7.77) can be factorized as shown below:

$$\mathbf{X} = \begin{bmatrix} X_0 \\ X_1 \\ X_2 \\ X_3 \end{bmatrix} = \begin{bmatrix} 1 & 1 & 1 & 1 \\ 1 & \frac{c}{b} & -\frac{c}{b} & -1 \\ 1 & -1 & -1 & 1 \\ \frac{c}{b} & -1 & 1 & -\frac{c}{b} \end{bmatrix} \begin{bmatrix} x_0 \\ x_1 \\ x_2 \\ x_3 \end{bmatrix} \otimes \begin{bmatrix} a \\ b \\ a \\ b \end{bmatrix}, \tag{7.80}$$

where $\otimes$ means term by term multiplication.

Or

$$\mathbf{X} = \begin{bmatrix} X_0 \\ X_1 \\ X_2 \\ X_3 \end{bmatrix} = \begin{bmatrix} 1 & 1 & 1 & 1 \\ 1 & d & -d & -1 \\ 1 & -1 & -1 & 1 \\ d & -1 & 1 & -d \end{bmatrix} \begin{bmatrix} x_0 \\ x_1 \\ x_2 \\ x_3 \end{bmatrix} \otimes \begin{bmatrix} a \\ b \\ a \\ b \end{bmatrix}, \tag{7.81}$$

where $d = \frac{c}{b} = \frac{0.2706}{0.6533} = 0.4142$

$$\text{Or, } \mathbf{X} = \mathbf{H}' \times \mathbf{S}, \tag{7.82}$$

where

$$\mathbf{H}' = \begin{bmatrix} 1 & 1 & 1 & 1 \\ 1 & d & -d & -1 \\ 1 & -1 & -1 & 1 \\ d & -1 & 1 & -d \end{bmatrix}$$

and

$$\mathbf{S} = \begin{bmatrix} a \\ b \\ a \\ b \end{bmatrix} \text{ and } \mathbf{S} \text{ is the scaling factor.}$$

7.6.2 *Orthogonal Requirement for Length-4 DCT*

Let us apply the orthogonal property in Eq. (7.18) to the length-4 DCT kernel. Again we have two cases

(i) $\phi_i \cdot \phi_j = 0$ for $i \neq j$. It is interesting to point out and the reader is invited to check that the dot product of between two rows in Eq. (7.77) is zero for all $i \neq j$. For example for rows 2 and 3, we have $[bc \ -c \ -b] \cdot [a \ -a \ -a \ a]^T = 0$. Hence, this part of the property does not cast any condition on the choice of (a, b, c) in Eq. (7.77), but confirms partly the DCT is orthogonal.

(ii) $\phi_i \cdot \phi_j = \phi_j \cdot \phi_i = 1$ for $i = j = 0, 1, 2, 3$. The first and the third rows give the condition that

$$4a^2 = 1 \tag{7.83a}$$

and the second and the fourth rows give the following condition:

$$2(b^2 + c^2) = 1 \tag{7.83b}$$

More generally, the condition to recover the original signal is that

$$\phi_i^2 = \text{const, where const is a constant.}$$

This is because the final results can always be scaled up or down to suit for the required condition. Hence, we can equate Eqs. (7.83a) and (7.83b).

$$2a^2 = b^2 + c^2 \tag{7.84}$$

In order to form an integer transform, the values of (a, b, c), i.e., 0.5, $\frac{1}{\sqrt{2}} \cos \frac{\pi}{8}$ and $\frac{1}{\sqrt{2}} \cos \frac{3\pi}{8} = (0.5, 0.6533, 0.4142)$, have to be modified to have integer values for the basis transform kernel. Since the transform kernels in Eq. (7.81) involve variable d only and its value is 0.4142, it is a natural choice to make d equal 0.5

i.e.,

$$d = \frac{c}{b} = 0.5$$

or

$$c = 0.5b$$

From the orthogonal requirement in Eq. (7.85), we have

$$2a^2 = b^2 + (0.5b)^2.$$

Hence,

$$8a^2 = 5b^2$$

a is originally equal to 0.5; let us retain this value for a; hence,

$$b = \sqrt{\frac{8a^2}{5}} = \underline{\sqrt{\frac{2}{5}}}$$

Hence, parameters (a, b, c) become $(\frac{1}{2}, \sqrt{\frac{2}{5}}, \sqrt{\frac{1}{10}})$ and the length-4 integer transform of x becomes

$$\mathbf{X} = \begin{bmatrix} 1 & 1 & 1 & 1 \\ 1 & \frac{1}{2} & -\frac{1}{2} & -1 \\ 1 & -1 & -1 & 1 \\ \frac{1}{2} & -1 & 1 & -\frac{1}{2} \end{bmatrix} \begin{bmatrix} x_0 \\ x_1 \\ x_2 \\ x_3 \end{bmatrix} \otimes \begin{bmatrix} a \\ b \\ a \\ b \end{bmatrix}$$

Integer Cosine Transform:
It is desirable to have the kernels H' and H'^{-1} consisting integer values only, so we scale up row one and row three of H' by 2. This requires element one and three of the scaling matrix be scaled down by $1/2$. Hence, we have

$$\mathbf{X} = \begin{bmatrix} 1 & 1 & 1 & 1 \\ 2 & 1 & -1 & -2 \\ 1 & -1 & -1 & 1 \\ 1 & -2 & 2 & -1 \end{bmatrix} \begin{bmatrix} x_0 \\ x_1 \\ x_2 \\ x_3 \end{bmatrix} \otimes \begin{bmatrix} a \\ \frac{1}{2}b \\ a \\ \frac{1}{2}b \end{bmatrix}, \text{ or } \mathbf{X} = \mathbf{H'S} \quad (7.85)$$

where $\mathbf{H''} = \begin{bmatrix} 1 & 1 & 1 & 1 \\ 2 & 1 & -1 & -2 \\ 1 & -1 & -1 & 1 \\ 1 & -2 & 2 & -1 \end{bmatrix}$ is the integer kernel, and $\mathbf{S} = \begin{bmatrix} a \\ \frac{1}{2}b \\ a \\ \frac{1}{2}b \end{bmatrix}$

is the scaling vector.

Let us code without proof that the inverse transform of the length-4 Integer DCT can be written as $H''^{-1} = \begin{bmatrix} 1 & 2 & 1 & 1 \\ 1 & 1 & -1 & -2 \\ 1 & -1 & -1 & 2 \\ 1 & -2 & 1 & -1 \end{bmatrix}$

Advantages: Equation (7.85) is the simplest form of the DCT-like kernel, which contains integer elements only, and they are obviously rational numbers. If elements of x are also integers (like those in videos (in 2D)), there will not be any rounding error for any number of forward and inverse processing. This is certainly the advantage of this formulation. The scaling part involves simply term-by-term multiplications that can be absorbed inside the post-transformation processing, and of course before the inverse transform. For example, video coding standards such as H.264/AVC and HEVC combine the scaling of the integer kernels and the quantization/dequantization process together to form the corresponding scaling matrices (called the "multiplication matrix" and the "rescaling matrix") (Hallapuro, Karczewicz, and Malvar, 2002).

7.6.3 *New Integer Cosine Kernels*

Let us denote the integer version of a length-4 DCT-like kernel mentioned in this chapter as IK(a, b, c). Its complete form is

$$
\mathbf{H}_{\text{DCT-like}} =
\begin{bmatrix}
a' & a' & a' & a' \\
b' & c' & -c' & -b' \\
a' & -a' & -a' & a' \\
c' & -b' & b' & -c'
\end{bmatrix}
\tag{7.86}
$$

where a, b, and c are all positive integers. We will also denote it in Table 7.1, etc., as (a, b, c) for the sake of simplicity and if there is no ambiguity. The IK(1,2,1) discussed in the above section has been used in H.264/AVC, as the major default integer kernel. In this case, $a = 1$, $b = 2$, and $c = 1$ (Malvar, 2001) for Eq. (7.86).

Or

$$
IK(1, 2, 1) =
\begin{bmatrix}
a' & a' & a' & a' \\
b' & c' & -c' & -b' \\
a' & -a' & -a' & a' \\
c' & -b' & b' & -c'
\end{bmatrix}
=
\begin{bmatrix}
1 & 1 & 1 & 1 \\
2 & 1 & -1 & -2 \\
1 & -1 & -1 & 1 \\
1 & -2 & 2 & -1
\end{bmatrix}
$$

Actually, there could be a large number of kernels available in the literature (Hallapuro, Karczewicz and Malvar, 2002; Wong and Siu, 2011a; Wong and Siu, 2011b). Sample kernels include

IK(1,2,1) Used in MPEG/H.264
IK(2,3,1) Adopted by AVS-M
IK(5,7,3) Proposed by Wong and Siu in 2011
IK(7,9,4) Adopted by AVS-M

For example, the IK(5,7,3) can be written as

$$
IK(5, 7, 3) = \begin{bmatrix} a' & a' & a' & a' \\ b' & c' & -c' & -b' \\ a' & -a' & -a' & a' \\ c' & -b' & b' & -c' \end{bmatrix} = \begin{bmatrix} 5 & 5 & 5 & 5 \\ 7 & 3 & -3 & -7 \\ 5 & -5 & -5 & 5 \\ 3 & -7 & 7 & -3 \end{bmatrix}
$$

Note that the quality of these kernels depends on (i) simplicity and (ii) the closeness of the elements to the real DCT kernel elements. For simplicity, we mean the use of simple integer values for (a,b,c). Besides "0," the simplest integers are "1" and "2." Hence, the kernel (1,2,1) should be the simplest kernel. Closeness refers to how close (a,b,c) are equal to $(0.5000, \frac{1}{\sqrt{2}} \cos \frac{\pi}{8}, \frac{1}{\sqrt{2}} \cos \frac{3\pi}{8})$ as in Eq. (7.78). Note that these kernels can be normalized to obtain their orthonormal kernels, which allow perfect reconstruction as we discussed.

The way to find new kernels: Our objective is to find DCT-like kernels that have closer property with the DCT kernel in Eq. (7.79). One possible way (Bjontegaard, 1997) is to scale up the floating-point DCT kernel by a scalar α and then round the scaled result so as to preserve the characteristics of DCT. This is a systematic approach to find DCT-like kernels. During the kernel searching process, the similarity between the newly found kernel and the DCT Kernel can be indirectly measured by the *Kernel Percentage Error* (*KPE*) as shown below:

$$
\text{KPE} = \left| \frac{\sqrt{\frac{1}{2}\left[\left(\frac{c'}{b'}\right)^2 + 1\right]} + \frac{c'}{b'}}{\sqrt{\frac{1}{2}\left[\left(\frac{c}{b}\right)^2 + 1\right]} + \frac{c}{b}} - 1 \right|, \tag{7.87}
$$

where b and c are coefficients of the DCT Kernel in Eq. (7.79), and b' and c' are coefficients of the possible DCT-like kernel in Eq. (7.86). Let us highlight some details on the meaning and derivation of Eq. (7.87).

The Kernel Percentage Error (KPE): The ratios among coefficients of the normalized version of a DCT-like kernel can be considered as features to represent this kernel, and can also be used to measure how far it deviates from the DCT Kernel. Let us normalize the integer

DCT-like kernel with respect to a' in Eq. (7.86), and from Eq. (7.84), we have

$$\mathbf{H} = \begin{bmatrix} A & A & A & A \\ B & C & -C & -B \\ A & -A & -A & A \\ C & -B & B & -C \end{bmatrix}, \qquad (7.88)$$

where $A = a' = a = 0.5$, $Bb'/a' = b'/[2(b'^2 + c'^2)]^{1/2}$, and $C = c'/a' = c'/[2(b'^2 + c'^2)]^{1/2}$.

Coefficients b' and c' are the positive integers of the DCT-like kernel $(a'b'c')$. The two ratios A/B and C/B can be regarded as features extracted from the DCT-like kernel. They can be represented in terms of b and c as shown below:

$$\begin{cases} \text{ratio1} = \frac{A}{B} = \dfrac{0.5}{b' / \left[2\left(b'^2 + c'^2\right)\right]^{\frac{1}{2}}} = \sqrt{\frac{1}{2}\left[\left(\frac{c'}{b'}\right)^2 + 1\right]}' \\[3mm] \text{ratio2} = \dfrac{C}{B} = \dfrac{c' / \left[2\left(b'^2 + c'^2\right)\right]^{\frac{1}{2}}}{b' / \left[2\left(b'^2 + c'^2\right)\right]^{\frac{1}{2}}} = \dfrac{c'}{b'} \end{cases} . \qquad (7.89)$$

Similarly, we can also derive the ratios for the DCT Kernel

$$\begin{cases} \text{ratio1}_{\text{DCT}} = \dfrac{A}{B} = \sqrt{\frac{1}{2}\left[\left(\frac{c}{b}\right)^2 + 1\right]} \\[3mm] \text{ratio2}_{\text{DCT}} = \dfrac{C}{B} = \dfrac{c}{b} \end{cases}, \qquad (7.90)$$

where b and c are the coefficients of the DCT Kernel. The percentage error can be calculated as follows:

$$\text{KPE} = \frac{|\text{ratio1} - \text{ratio1}_{\text{DCT}}| + |\text{ratio2} - \text{ratio2}_{\text{DCT}}|}{\text{ratio1}_{\text{DCT}} + \text{ratio2}_{\text{DCT}}} \qquad (7.91)$$

By substituting Eqs. (7.89) and (7.90) in Eq. (7.91), we obtain the KPE as shown below

$$KPE = \left| \frac{\sqrt{\frac{1}{2}\left[\left(\frac{c}{b}\right)^2 + 1\right]} + \frac{c}{b}}{\sqrt{\frac{1}{2}\left[\left(\frac{c_{\text{DCT}}}{b_{\text{DCT}}}\right)^2 + 1\right]} + \frac{c_{\text{DCT}}}{b_{\text{DCT}}}} - 1 \right|. \qquad (7.92)$$

We have to emphasize that a kernel must be simple so that it leads to small dynamic ranges of intermediate results, in order to keep the

Table 7.1   The DCT-like kernels found by the up-scaling method

Kernel	KPE	Description
IK(2,3,1)	8.55%	Adopted by AVS-M[a]
IK(3,4,2)	9.41%	New Kernel
IK(4,5,2)	1.53%	Adopted by AVS-M
IK(5,6,2)	8.55%	New Kernel
IK(5,7,3)	1.55%	New Kernel
IK(6,8,3)	4.19%	New Kernel
IK(7,9,4)	3.28%	Adopted by AVS-M
...		
IK(13,17,7)	0.26%	Proposed by Bjontegaard (Bjontegaard, 1997), once adopted by the H.264/AVC (Bjontegaard, 1999)
...		

[a]The AVS stands for the Audio Video Standard. It is an audio-video coding standard initiated by the government of P. R. China. AVS-M is a part of the AVS which mainly targets at the application of mobile video.

computational complexity at a reasonable level. Through a computer search by setting α from 1.00 to 50.00 with step 0.01, a number of integer kernels have been found (Wong and Siu, 2011a; Wong and Siu, 2011b) which have relatively small KPE as shown in Table 7.1. There are some new kernels as a result of this search, while others were proposed in the literature quite some time ago before. The first few small-scale kernels have the advantage of simplicity, while as the scale of kernel increases the similarity also increases. It is interesting to note when α is around 26.00, the similarity measure of the scaled kernel IK(13,17,7) reaches the maximum. This is also one of the most famous DCT-like kernels, once adopted during the H.264/AVC standardization process proposed by Bjontegaard (Bjontegaard, 1997). The multiplication factors and rescaling factors have been calculated according to (Hallapuro, Karczewicz, and Malvar, 2002) and the results are shown in Table 7.1.

These kernels can be used separately in video coding standards, or future standards. However, it is good to point out that a combination of these kernels can be used for video coding which forms possible effective ways of video coding in the future direction.

Roughly speaking the IK(5,7,3) requires word-lengths of 3 more bits as compared to IK(1,2,1) and the IK(13,17,7) also requires word-lengths of 3 more bits as compared to IK(5,7,3) for a practical realization, even though the coding efficiency is improved by 2.52% for employing the dual-kernel MB-AKM{(1,2,1) and (5,7,3)}and improved by 3.18% for employing the dual-kernel MB-AKM{(1,2,1) and (13,17,7)}. Computational complexity is not an issue at all if we use software with sufficiently large word-lengths and/or registers in the CPU. However, for dedicated hardware realization, every bit is expensive. This will make MB-AKM{(1,2,1) and (5,7,3)} be a better choice compared with the MB-AKM{(1,2,1) and (13,17,7)}. This point is very much application specific, and we would leave it to readers/users for making their judgment.

7.7 Application to Interpolation and Super-Resolution Videos/Images

7.7.1 *Interpolation*

Video enlargement is important for video inspection and coding in Scalable Video Coding (SVC), which is also the major study of this section. For real-time applications, conventional polynomial-based interpolation methods such as bilinear and bicubic interpolation are often used due to their computational simplicity (Hou and Andrews, 1978; Keys, 1981). Since edges are visually attractive to human perceptual system, some edge-directed interpolation methods have been developed to address the edge reconstructions (Wang and Ward, 2007; Yang, Kim and Jeong, 2008; Hong, Paik, Kim and Lee, 1996). The intuitive way is to explicitly estimate the edge orientation and then interpolate along the edge orientation (Wang and Ward, 2007; Yang, Kim and Jeong, 2008; Hong, Paik, Kim and Lee, 1996). One major improvement to the explicit methods is to adaptively fuse the results of several estimates of different edge orientations (Min and Nguyen, 2008; Zhang and Wu, 2006). Super-resolution aims to produce a high-resolution (HR) image from one to several observed low-resolution (LR) images by up-sampling, deblurring and denoising, and its methods can be classified into single-image super-resolution (only one LR image is observed) (Dong, Zhang, Shi, and Wu, 2011; Sun, Xu, and Shum, 2011; Gao, Zhang, Tao, and Li, 2012) and multi-frame super-resolution (Farsiu, Elad, and Milanfar, 2006; Woods, Galatsanos, and Katsaggelos, 2006; Nguyen,

Milanfar, and Golub, 2001). There are two major categories of SR algorithms: They are the reconstruction-based and learning-based algorithms. The super-resolution methods can also be classified as blind (Woods, et al., 2006; Nguyen, et al., 2001) and non-blind methods (Dong, Zhang, Shi and Wu, 2011; Sun, Xu and Shum, 2011; Gao, Zhang, Tao and Li, 2012, Farsiu, Elad and Milanfar, 2006). Based on our experience on image interpolation (Hung and Siu, 2012a) and super-resolution (Hung and Siu, 2012b), we have done some interesting work on using the DCT for image/video enlargement.

7.7.2 Methodology

Let us start to recall the DCT pairs, and a hybrid algorithm (Wu, Yu, and Chen, 2010) relating the transform domain and spatial domain for interpolation. The 2D DCT transform pair can be written as

Forward 2-D DCT,

$$X(k_2, k_1) = \frac{2C(k_2)C(k_1)}{N}$$

$$\sum_{n_2=0}^{N-1} \sum_{n_1=0}^{N-1} x(n_2, n_1) \cos \frac{2\pi}{4N}(2n_1+1)k_1 \cos \frac{2\pi}{4N}(2n_2+1)k_2$$

where

$$C(k_2), C(k_1) = \begin{cases} 1/\sqrt{2} & \text{for } k_2 k_1 = 0 \\ 1 & \text{otherwise} \end{cases},$$

and the inverse 2-D DCT can be written as

$$x(n_1, n_2) = \frac{2}{N} \sum_{k_2=0}^{N-1} \sum_{k_1=0}^{N-1} C(k_1)C(k_2)X(k_1, k_2)$$

$$\cos \frac{2\pi(2n_1 + 1)k_1}{4N} \cos \frac{2\pi(2n_2 + 1)k_2}{4N}$$

The important point here is that DCT is separable, which means that the DCT terms can be grouped or separately computed and this property has been used in the rest part of this book.

7.7.3 Video Up-Sampling with the Transform Domain

Assume that the low-resolution (LR) image block is obtained by a direct down-sampling of the high-resolution image (HR) in the DCT domain as shown in Fig. 7.3.

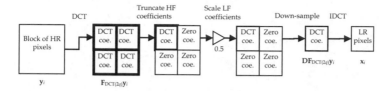

Figure 7.3 Graphical illustration of the dyadic down-sampling process in the block DCT domain (Hung and Siu, 2014b).

Let us move directly using a hybrid model in both spatial and transform domains for interpolation. This is a major part of this section, which is to make use of both the advantages of the transform domain enlargement and spatial domain interpolation for up-sampling an image or video frame.

Let the low-resolution image block be **x**, and the ground high-resolution image block be **y** and its interpolated one be **y**′. If **x** is a block of 8×8 ($= N \times N$) pixels and then **y** and **y**′ have a dimension of 16×16 pixels. We then have (note subscript N^2 is used to emphasize its size only),

$$\mathbf{x}_{N^2} = \begin{pmatrix} x_{00} & x_{01} & \cdot\cdot \\ x_{10} & x_{11} & \cdot\cdot \\ \cdot\cdot & \cdot\cdot & \cdot\cdot \end{pmatrix}, \text{ and its DCT form is}$$

$$\mathbf{X}_{N^2} = DCT(x_{N^2}) = \begin{pmatrix} X_{00} & X_{01} & \cdot\cdot \\ X_{10} & X_{11} & \cdot\cdot \\ \cdot\cdot & \cdot\cdot & \cdot\cdot \end{pmatrix} \qquad (7.93)$$

Let us append zeros to $\mathbf{X}_{N^2}$ for forming a $4N^2$ matrix in the transform domain, we have

$$\mathbf{Y}_{4N^2} = \begin{pmatrix} \mathbf{X}_{N^2} & \mathbf{0}_{N_2} \\ \mathbf{0}_{N_2} & \mathbf{0}_{N_2} \end{pmatrix}, \text{ where, } \mathbf{0}_{N^2} = \begin{pmatrix} 0 & 0 & \cdot\cdot \\ 0 & 0 & \cdot\cdot \\ \cdot\cdot & \cdot\cdot & \cdot\cdot \end{pmatrix} \qquad (7.94)$$

Its inverse transform $DCT^{-1}(\mathbf{Y}_{4N^2}) = \mathbf{y}_{4N^2}$ becomes the interpolated results of **x** (or $\mathbf{x}_{N^2}$), which can interpolate **x** perfectly with smooth regions.

In order to interpolate edges better, we can use a fix tap Wiener filter in the spatial domain (Wu, Yu, and Chen, 2010) to interpolate

x. Hence, we have

$$
\mathbf{y}_{4N^2} = \begin{pmatrix}
x_{00} & y_{01} & x_{01} & \cdots \\
y_{10} & y_{11} & y_{12} & \cdots \\
x_{01} & x_{21} & x_{11} & \cdots \\
\cdots & \cdots & \cdots & \cdots \\
y_{(2N-1)0} & y_{(2N-1)1} & \cdots & y_{(2N-1)(2N-1)}
\end{pmatrix}
\tag{7.95}
$$

Let us take DCT of $\mathbf{y}_{4N^2}$. We have

$$
\mathbf{Y}_{4N^2} = DCT(\mathbf{y}_{4N^2}) = \begin{pmatrix}
Y_{00} & Y_{00} & Y_{01} & \cdots \\
Y_{10} & Y_{11} & Y_{12} & \cdots \\
\cdots & \cdots & \cdots\cdots & \\
Y_{(2N-1)0} & Y_{(2N-1)1} & \cdots & Y_{(2N-1)(2N-1)}
\end{pmatrix}
\tag{7.96}
$$

Divide this frequency domain into four parts: the low-low, low-high, high-low and high-high parts ($\mathbf{Y}_i$, where $i = 0, 1, 2$ and 3), each with a dimension of N^2. We then have

$$
\mathbf{Y}_{4N^2} = \begin{pmatrix}
\mathbf{Y}_0 & \mathbf{Y}_1 \\
\mathbf{Y}_2 & \mathbf{Y}_3
\end{pmatrix}
\tag{7.97}
$$

Note that $\mathbf{Y}_1$, $\mathbf{Y}_2$, and $\mathbf{Y}_3$ are high frequency blocks in the transform domain generated by the spatial interpolation, which can enhance sharp edges. An almost ground true $\mathbf{Y}_0$ is available, which is $\mathbf{X}_{N^2}$ in Eq. (7.93). Hence, combining the advantages of the spatial and transform domain properties, we can form the interpolated image by making use of $\mathbf{X}_{N^2}$, $\mathbf{Y}_1$, $\mathbf{Y}_2$, and $\mathbf{Y}_3$ as shown below.

$$
\mathbf{Y}'_{4N^2} = \begin{pmatrix}
\mathbf{X}_{N^2} & \mathbf{Y}_1 \\
\mathbf{Y}_2 & \mathbf{Y}_3
\end{pmatrix},
\tag{7.98}
$$

and its inverse DCT gives the, interpolated result $\mathbf{y}'_{4N^2} = DCT^{-1}(\mathbf{Y}'_{4N^2})$. This approach makes use of the advantages of both transform and spatial domain processing.

(i) Non-Iterative Algorithm

Recall the hybrid video interpolation approach in (Wu, Yu, and Chen, 2010) which is restricted mainly to use simple Wiener filter. In this section, we introduce the use of some training image pairs to learn the 2D 64×16 tap Wiener filter, in order to replace the original 1D 6-tap Wiener filter used in the hybrid DCT-Wiener filter. The much higher tap 2D Wiener filter can significantly minimize the reconstruction errors at the expense of a little computation power, equivalent to the computation power of 2D 8 × 8 DCT transformation. Experimental results show that using this 2D Wiener filter in the hybrid DCT-Wiener filter (Wu, Yu, and Chen, 2010) provides 0.293 dB improvement on average. Let us label this as the hybrid DCT-2D Wiener filter (**DCT-2DWF**).

Formation of a 2D 64 × 16 tap Universal Wiener filter: In this approach the 2D Wiener filter (64 × 16) directly outputs a 64 × 1 vector (HR block) from an input 16 × 1 vector (LR block). It can be explained as concatenating a set of pixel-based 2D Wiener filters (1 × 16) (Hou and Andrews, 1978) using the same input vector (instead of different input vector for each pixel output in (Hou and Andrews, 1978)). The design is novel and more efficient. Moreover, the degradation matrix that relates the HR image and LR image can be easily derived from the 2D Wiener filter, as shown in point (ii) below. In order to make this approach more convincing, we have conducted some simple experimental work for analysis and to compare the results for up-sampling performance using the universal Wiener filter (just trained by the Lena image) and an adaptive Wiener filter (ADF) (trained by the original HR image) using the same filter size of 64 × 16. Since the output of the Wiener filter **H** are 8 × 8 blocks, we also tested the difference of using overlapping filters on the same pixel locations. To facilitate the overlapping option, we shifted the locations of blocks for 16 times to obtain 16 results of the up-sampled HR image by the 2D Wiener filter. Eventually, the 16 images are averaged to obtain the final image. Table 7.2 concludes that the 1D 6-tap Wiener filter (used in H.264 standard) is not optimized for the DCT decimated signals. The universal 2D Wiener filter with overlapping option performs only 0.13 dB worse than the optimized Adaptive Wiener filter. The results verify the benefit and reason for choosing the (overlapping) universal Wiener filter for DCT up-sampling. This algorithm should be useful for fast image interpolation and image prediction in scalable video coding. It is not sufficient to do training just making use of the Lena image. More advanced work can be found in (Hung and Siu, 2014a).

(ii) Iterative Algorithm
An *iterative* hybrid DCT-2D Wiener filter framework, which progressively improves the estimated HR image in both spatial and

Table 7.2 The PSNR (dB) of the universal Wiener filter and adaptive Wiener filter

Images	1D 6-tap Wiener filter (Park, Park, and Oh, 2003)	Universal 2D Wiener filter - no over lapping	Universal 2D Wiener filter - overlapping	Adaptive 2D Wiener filter - no overlapping	Adaptive 2D Wiener filter- over- lapping
Boat	27.730	30.356	30.640	30.533	**30.641**
Splash	35.713	39.662	40.080	**40.942**	40.431
Flin	23.124	27.366	28.040	27.587	**28.052**
MRI	31.546	35.122	35.553	**36.224**	35.561
Light-house	24.842	26.690	27.101	27.050	**27.156**
Man	28.836	31.509	31.772	31.631	**31.758**
Average	*28.632*	*31.784*	*32.198*	***32.328***	*32.267*

frequency domains is shown in Fig. 7.4. We can use the learnt 2D Wiener filter to approximate the degradation matrix, which relates the LR and HR images in the spatial domain. Hence, we can set up an iterative algorithm to improve the HR image progressively by forcing the estimated HR image to match with the observed LR image in the spatial domain. Then, during the iteration, we force the low-frequency DCT components of the estimated HR image to match with that of the observed LR image in the frequency domain. This iterative hybrid scheme is novel and can further improve the PSNR of the hybrid DCT-2D Wiener filter (**DCT-2DWF**) by 0.3 dB on average in our preliminary tests.

Some details: For the sake of simplicity, let us consider a LR image $\mathbf{x}''(256 \times 256)$, and we want to interpolate it to become an HR image $\mathbf{y}''(512 \times 512)$. We partition the LR and HR images into 4×4 and 8×8 blocks to vectorize the blocks. Then, the vectors are grouped into the matrices: LR image $\mathbf{x}$ (16×4096) and HR image $\mathbf{y}$ (64×4096).

(1) Calculation of 2D 64×16 tap Universal Wiener filter:

$$\mathbf{H} = \mathbf{y}\mathbf{x}^T (\mathbf{x}\mathbf{x}^T)^{-1}, \tag{7.99}$$

where the Lena image ($\mathbf{y}$ and $\mathbf{x}$) is used to learn this 2D Wiener filter $\mathbf{H}$. Note that the Wiener filter's coefficients are universal for every image; thus they are not required to be encoded in video coding applications. On the contrary, some algorithms (Bjontegaard, 1999; Hou and Andrews, 1978) use the non-universal Wiener filter, for which the coefficients are required to be encoded for each frame.

(2) Up-sampling by 2D 64 × 16 tap University Wiener filter:

$$\hat{\mathbf{y}} = \mathbf{H}\mathbf{x} \qquad (7.100)$$

where $\hat{\mathbf{y}}$ is the up-sampled HR image from the observed LR image $\mathbf{x}$, which can be any images other than the Lena image. In our experiments, we used six other images to verify the performance of the learnt 2D Wiener filter.

(3) Approximation of degradation matrix in the spatial domain:

$$\hat{\mathbf{y}} = \mathbf{H}\mathbf{x}$$
$$\mathbf{H}^T\hat{\mathbf{y}} = \mathbf{H}^T\mathbf{H}\mathbf{x} \qquad (7.101)$$
$$(\mathbf{H}^T\mathbf{H})^{-1}\mathbf{H}^T\hat{\mathbf{y}} = \mathbf{x}$$

Hence, the degradation matrix, which degrades the estimated HR image $\hat{\mathbf{y}}$ to the observed LR image $\mathbf{x}$, is given by

$$\mathbf{D} = (\mathbf{H}^T\mathbf{H})^{-1}\mathbf{H}^T.$$

(4) Iterative improvement of the estimated HR in the time domain by the maximum-likelihood estimation (back-projection) (Hou and Andrews, 1978):

$$\hat{\mathbf{y}}^{n+1} = \hat{\mathbf{y}}^n - \lambda\mathbf{D}^T(\mathbf{D}\hat{\mathbf{y}}^n - \mathbf{x}), \qquad (7.102)$$

where n is the iteration index.

During the iteration, we hope to find a solution of the HR image, $\hat{\mathbf{y}}^n$, whose degraded version, $\mathbf{D}\hat{\mathbf{y}}^n$, can match with the observed ground truth LR image $\mathbf{x}$ in the spatial domain. To achieve this, the difference between the degraded image and the ground truth LR image, $\mathbf{D}\hat{\mathbf{y}}^n - \mathbf{x}$, is projected onto the estimate of the HR image. At the same time, during the iterations we replace the low-frequency DCT components of the estimated HR image $\hat{\mathbf{y}}^n$ by the DCT components of the observed ground truth LR image $\mathbf{x}$. Hence, our iterative hybrid DCT-2D Wiener filter finds a solution of the HR image, which can best match the observed LR image in both spatial and frequency domains, which is a novel idea. As shown in Fig. 7.4, the HR image is

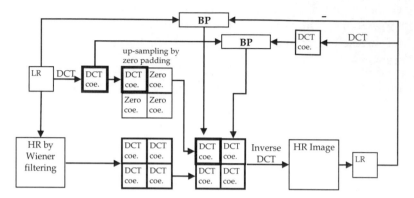

Figure 7.4 Iterative algorithm with both spatial and transform domains processes.

iteratively improved by comparing its degraded LR version with the observed LR image in the spatial domain, where the low-frequency DCT components of the HR image is replaced by the frequency component of the observed LR image. That is, we further enforce the low-frequency DCT components of the estimated HR image $\hat{\mathbf{y}}^n$ to match with that in the observed LR image $\mathbf{x}$ during the iterations. Hence, Eq. (7.102) formulates this final iterative hybrid DCT-2D Wiener filter approach.

Testing Results: Grey scale images (512×512) of various contents (Fig. 7.5) were used to verify the performance of this novel iterative hybrid DCT-2D Wiener filter approach. The HR images were DCT-decimated by two times in both dimensions to generate the LR images. The step size in Eq. (7.102) was set to $\lambda = 0.1$ and the number of iterations in Eq. (7.102) was fixed to 4 iterations for all validating images. Some intermediate results this algorithm are shown on the last two to three columns of Table 7.3. The table shows that this algorithm outperforms the state-of-the-art algorithms (Park, Park, and Oh, 2003; Wu, Yu, and Chen, 2010) by 0.549 dB and 0.365 dB on average. Good visual improvement (see Hung and Siu (2014a)) has also been achieved compared with other algorithms in the literature.

Table 7.3 The PSNR (dB) of the validating images

Images	DCT up-sampling (Park, Park, and Oh, 2003)	Hybrid DCT-WF (Wu, Yu, and Chen, 2010)	Proposed 2D Wiener filter	Proposed hybrid DCT-2DWF	Proposed iterative hybrid DCT-2DWF
Boat	30.415	30.429	30.640	30.772	**30.843**
Splash	39.780	40.022	40.080	40.202	**40.241**
Flin	27.458	27.924	28.040	28.295	**28.520**
MRI	35.242	35.470	35.553	**35.694**	35.643
Lighthouse	26.831	26.877	27.101	27.254	**27.312**
Man	31.539	31.650	31.772	31.911	**32.000**
Average	*31.878*	*32.062*	*32.198*	*32.355*	*32.427*

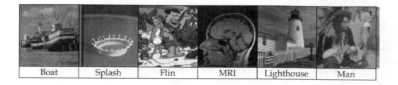

| Boat | Splash | Flin | MRI | Lighthouse | Man |

Figure 7.5 The validating images for testing.

7.8 Conclusion

A review of the basic theory of the transform domain processing allows us to have a deeper understanding of the critical issues of modern DSP. This will facilitate us to make new discoveries. We have discussed our new iterative hybrid DCT-adaptive Wiener filter approach that shows very promising results as an up-sampling algorithm for the DCT-decimated image and video sequence. There are a lot of interesting works that can be done. It is good to study (i) the sensitivity of the training image used, (ii) the optimal number of taps of the 2D Wiener filter, (iii) the convergence of the iterative scheme in Eq. (7.102), (iv) the design of the iterative time-frequency algorithm in Eq (7.102) and (v) the computation reduction for real-time applications. Note also that these formulations should be extremely useful to spatial scalability for SVC in surveillance systems, since these allows us to accurately estimate high frequency DCT components; hence, reduce error signals.

Non-dyadic Interpolation: It is interesting to extend the above ideas into non-dyadic interpolation. It is very often to enlarge an image proportionally, from N^2 into $(N + i)^2$ sizes, where i is an integer. This is shown in Fig. 7.6. For video monitor in computer systems, this is done via the video scaler which uses a comprehensive video processing chip (Altera, 2010; LogicCORE, 2010) to resize the input image or video signals, which makes use of FIR design (Gryskiewlcz, et al. 2000; Chen, et al., 2000) with algorithms such as the traditional Bilinear, Bicubic, Lanczos interpolation. Obviously, we can also use the DCT for the enlargement. However, both the DCT and these video scaler approaches will make the interpolated image blurry. Figure 7.6 shows an example (interpolation from 8×8 to 10×10) of the spatial interpolation. It is clear that the interpolation

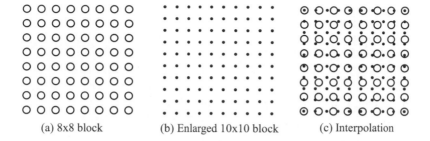

(a) 8x8 block   (b) Enlarged 10x10 block   (c) Interpolation

Figure 7.6   Non-dyadic interpolation.

can be done by a Winner filter using techniques as suggested in the previous sections. It is also true that the ground true 8×8 image in the transform domain ($\mathbf{X}_{N^2}$) is available, such that the interpolated image in the transform domain using this hybrid techniques can be formed,

$$\mathbf{Y}'_{4N^2} = \begin{pmatrix} \mathbf{X}_{N^2} & \mathbf{Y}_1 \\ \mathbf{Y}_2 & \mathbf{Y}_3 \end{pmatrix},$$

where $\mathbf{Y}_1$, $\mathbf{Y}_2$, and $\mathbf{Y}_3$ are the extension parts of the spatially interpolated image in the transform domain. The dimension of $\mathbf{Y}_1$, $\mathbf{Y}_2$, and $\mathbf{Y}_3$ are $i \times N$, $N \times i$, and $i \times i$, respectively.

Can edges be further enhanced in the spatial domain with certain edge operators? What is the best specific Wiener filter for this application? Should further intensity equalization be used between $\mathbf{x}$ and $\mathbf{y}$ before entering into the transform domain step? What modifications of the iterative algorithm are required? A large number of open questions remain to be answered.

Newer directions: Transforms and transform domain properties are the basis of our study. The usefulness of DFT is self-evident. DCT and integer DCT are extremely useful for modern image/video coding and super-resolution videos. They are included in our bigger scope of studies on visual surveillance, which obviously include the above topics, but also our other works such as image segmentation (Gao, Siu and Hou, 2001; Kwok, Siu and Constantinides, 1998), object recognition (Chau and Siu, 2004), tracking (Yam, Siu, Law and Chan, 2010) and scene analytics. Can we detect or track an object without decoding image sequences transmitted from multiple sources or from a storage device.

This is a difficult topic, since the residual signals in the DCT domain do not relate too much to the real object/scene, and these are residues between the predicted object/scene and the actual object/scene. Our approach, say for example (Yam, Siu, Law, and Chan, 2010), for moving object identification, is to separate the background firstly. We can then find a foreground object, identify it and track it temporally. A good way to do this is to make use of the HOG (Histogram of Oriented Gradients) to form the features vector for matching. Most of the sequences are coded in MPEG standards (or HEVC). For fast tracking or identification, we do not want to decode the sequence, but work on the available data say for example the motion vectors and residual signals. Motion vectors can be part of the feature vector, but it just gives a rough idea on motion activities of the block. No shape and contents of the object are included in an encoded video sequence. Hence, residual signals in the hybrid video coding scheme should be valuable to us.

Learning based approach has been initially proposed and used in our most recent image interpolation and super-resolution algorithms (Huang and Siu, 2015a; Huang and Siu, 2015b) with great success, which can represent the possibility of getting good breakthroughs. Via learning we can obtain parameters of models that reflect more truly the characteristics of real images/videos to perform regression. If the regression models are built via training off-line, the approach can be done in real-time with excellent quality. Interestingly this class of approaches can further be investigated and expanded to other areas. For example, regular video coding has almost come to its compression limit using conventional hybrid video coding models such as those in MPEG, H.264 and HEVC. However, if we just turn the problem around and make it content dependent and learning based, there is plenty of room for improvement. It relies on the initial learning such that the codec can make intelligent decision on classification. Early classification in the processing stage is an important step since it possibly gives us the optimal path to select the correct coding mode (or to select a regressive model in interpolation), such that it makes the prediction accurate, and subsequently it can reduce the codes required to code the difference. For designing a really highly efficient codec, this becomes content-based design and eventually come up with different dictionaries for various applications. SVM (Support Vector Machine) and neural network with deep learning are obviously good choices for learning and classification. However, we do not restrict just to use SVM or neural networks even though we currently also make use of them. As another approach, say for example, our initial finding shows that random forests techniques are extremely useful as a learning tool to build a dictionary set and subsequently to do up-sampling by classification and regression, say for example The learning can be continued in the user stage, such that the approach can be adaptive to changing environment. Learning in this way is better for image interpolation, video coding, object recognition, tracking, etc. making or not to make use of transform techniques, because most of the previous studies were too ideal, such as with clear pictures, well-defined objects, self-added noise, etc. In real applications, images are blurred and noisy, the objects are unclear and obstructed, lighting conditions are changing and there are so many conditions that we cannot identify in a single algorithm or even a set of rules; therefore learning is the best approach, or at least one of the best approaches as a basic tool for signal and information processing and applications.

Acknowledgment

This work was supported in part by the Center for Signal Processing, the Hong Kong Polytechnic University, and the Research Grant Council of the Hong Kong SAR Government under B-Q38S. Thanks are given to my students and colleagues Junjie Huang, Xuefei Yang, Bochuen Do and Wai-Lam Hui, for their assistance in the preparation of this manuscript.

References

1. Agarwal, R. C., and Burrus, C. S., Fast convolution using Fermat number transform with applications to digital filtering, *IEEE Trans. Acoust. Speech Signal Process.*, vol. ASSP-22, pp. 87–97, 1974.

2. Agarwal, R. C., and Burrus, C. S., Number theoretic transforms to implement fast digital convolution, *Proc. IEEE* , vol. 63, pp. 550–560, 1975.

3. Altera, Enabling improved image format conversion with FPGAs, White Paper, 2010.

4. Bjontegaard, G., Coding improvement by using 4×4 blocks for motion vectors and transform, ITU-T Q.15/SG16, Doc. Q15-C-23, December 2–5, 1997.

5. Bjontegaard, G., H.26L test model long term number 1 (TML-1) draft 2, ITU-T SG16/Q15, Doc. Q15-H-36d2, August 3–6, 1999.

6. Bogner, R. E., and Constantinides, A. G., *Introduction to Digital Filtering* (John Wiley & Sons, 1975).

7. Brigham, E. O., *The Fast Fourier Transform,* Prentice Hall, Inc., 1974.

8. Britanak, V., Yip, P. C., and Rao, K. R., *Discrete Cosine and Sine Transforms: General Properties, Fast Algorithms and Integer Approximations,* Academic Press, 2007.

9. Cappellini, V., and Constantinides, A. G., *Digital Signal Processing,* Academic Press, 1980.

10. Cappellini, V., Constantinides, A. G., and Emiliani, P., *Digital Filters and their Applications,* Academic Press, 1978.

11. Cham, W. K., Development of integer cosine transforms by the principle of dyadic symmetry, *IEE Proceedings I Commun. Speech Vision*, vol. 136, no. 4, pp. 276–282, 1989.

12. Chan, Y.-H., and Siu, W.-C., On the realisation of discrete cosine transform using the distributed arithmetic, *IEEE Trans. Circuits Systems*, vol. 39, no. 9, pp. 705–712, September, 1992.

13. Chan, Y. H., and Siu, W. C., Mixed-radix discrete cosine transform, *IEEE Trans. Signal Process.*, vol. 41, no. 11, pp. 3157–3161, 1993.

14. Chan, Y. L., and Siu, W. C., Variable temporal-length 3-D discrete cosine transform coding, *IEEE Trans. Image Process.*, vol. 6, no. 5, pp. 758–763, 1997.

15. Chen, J., Koc, U.-V., and Liu, K. J. R., *Design of Digital Video Coding Systems,* Marcel Dekker, Inc., 2002.

16. Chen, T.-C., et al., Variable-size spatial and temporal video scaler, US Patent, No. 6108047, August, 2000.

17. Cooley, J. W., and Tukey, J. W., An algorithm for the machine calculation of complex Fourier series, *Math. Comput.*, vol. 19, pp. 297–301, 1965.

18. Dong, W., Zhang, L., Shi, G., and Wu, X., Image deblurring and super-resolution by adaptive sparse domain selection and adaptive regularization, *IEEE Trans. Image Process.*, vol. 20, no. 7, pp. 1838–1857, 2011.

19. Farsiu, S., Elad, M., and Milanfar, P., Video-to-video dynamic super-resolution for grayscale and color sequences, *EURASIP J. Appl. Signal Process.*, Article ID 61859, pp. 1–15, 2006.

20. Gao, X., Zhang, K., Tao, D., and Li, X., Joint learning for single-image super-resolution via a coupled constraint, *IEEE Trans. Image Process.*, vol. 21, no. 2, pp. 469–480, 2012.

21. Gryskiewlcz, P. S., et al., Adaptive video scaler, US Patent, No. 6937291 B1, August 2000.

22. Hallapuro, A., Karczewicz, M., and Malvar, H. S., Low complexity transform and quantization—Part I: Basic implementation, Doc. JVT-B038, Geneva, CH, January 29 –February 1, 2002.

23. He, H., and Siu, W.-C., Single image super-resolution using Gaussian process regression, *Proceedings of the IEEE International Conference on Computer Vision and Pattern Recognition (CVPR2011)*, 20–25 June 2011, Colorado, USA, pp. 449–456, 2011.

24. Hong, K. P., Paik, J. K., Kim, H. J., and Lee, C. H., An edge-preserving image interpolation system for a digital camcorder, *IEEE Trans. Consumer Electron.*, vol. 42, no. 3, pp. 279–284, 1996.

25. Hou, H. S., and Andrews, H. C., Cubic splines for image interpolation and digital filtering, *IEEE Trans. Acoust., Speech, Signal Process.*, vol. ASSP-26, no. 6, pp. 508–517, 1978.

26. Huang, J.-J., Hung, K.-W., and Siu, W.-C., Hybrid DCT-Wiener-based interpolation using dual MMSE estimator scheme, *Proceedings of the 19th International Conference on Digital Signal Processing (19th DSP2014)*, August, 20–23, 2014, Hong Kong, pp. 748–753, 2014.

27. Huang, J.-J., and Siu, W.-C., Fast image interpolation with decision tree, *Proceedings of the 2015 IEEE International Conference on Acoustics, Speech and Signal Processing (ICASSP'2015)*, April 19–24, 2015, Brisbane, Australia, pp. 1221–1225, 2015a.

28. Huang, J.-J., and Siu, W.-C., Practical application of random forests for super-resolution imaging, *Proceedings of the IEEE International Symposium on Circuits and Systems (ISCAS'2015)*, May 24–27, 2015, Lisbon Portugal, pp. 2161–2164, 2015b.

29. Hung, K.-W., and Siu, W.-C., Improved image interpolation using bilateral filter for weighted least square estimation, *Proceedings of the IEEE*

International Conference on Image Processing (ICIP 2010), September 26–29, 2010, Hong Kong, pp. 3297–3300.

30. Hung, K.-W., and Siu, W.-C., Robust soft-decision interpolation using weighted least squares, *IEEE Trans. Image Process.*, vol. 21, no. 3, pp. 1061–1069, 2012a.

31. Hung, K.-W., and Siu, W.-C., Single-image super-resolution using iterative Wiener filter, *Proceedings of the IEEE International Conference on Acoustics, Speech, and Signal Processing (ICASSP 2012)*, March 25–30, 2012, Kyoto, Japan, pp. 1269–1272, 2012b.

32. Hung, K.-W., and Siu, W.-C., Hybrid DCT-Wiener-based interpolation via learnt Wiener filter, *Proceedings of the IEEE International Conference on Acoustics, Speech and Signal Processing (ICASSP'2013)*, May 26–31, 2013, Vancouver, Canada, pp. 1419–1423, 2013.

33. Hung, K.-W., and Siu, W.-C., Block-adaptive DCT-Wiener image up-sampling, *Proceedings of the 2014 IEEE International Conference on Acoustics, Speech and Signal Processing (ICASSP'2014)*, May 04–09, 2014, Florence, Italy, pp. 5850–5854, 2014a.

34. Hung, K.-W., and Siu, W.-C., Novel DCT-based image up-sampling using learning-based adaptive k-NN MMSE estimation, *IEEE Trans. Circuits Syst. Video Technol.*, vol. 24, no. 12, pp. 2018–2033, 2014b.

35. ITU-T and ISO/IEC JTCI, Rec. H.264-ISO/IEC 14496-10 AVC, 2003, Advanced video coding for generic audiovisual services.

36. Keys, R. G., Cubic convolution interpolation for digital image processing, *IEEE Trans. Acoust., Speech, Signal Process.*, vol. ASSP-29, no. 6, pp. 1153–1160, 1981.

37. Kwok, S. H., Siu, W. C., and Constantinides, A. G., Adaptive temporal decimation algorithm with dynamic time window, *IEEE Trans. Circuits Syst. Video Technol.*, vol. 8, no. 1, pp. 104–111, 1998.

38. LogiCORE IP Video Scaler v.7.00.a, Product Guide, PG009, October 2012.

39. Lun, D. P. K., and Siu, W. C., An analysis for the realisation of an in-place an in-order prime factor algorithm, *IEEE Trans. Signal Process.*, vol. 41, no. 7, pp. 2362–2370, 1993.

40. Malvar, H. S., Low-complexity length-4 transform and quantization with 16-bit arithmetic, Doc. VCEG-N44, September 2001.

41. McClellan, J. H., and Rader, C. M., *Number Theory in Digital Signal Processing*, Prentice Hall, Inc., 1979.

42. Min, L., and Nguyen, T. Q., Markov random field model-based edge-directed image interpolation, *IEEE Trans. Image Process.*, vol. 17, no. 7, pp. 1121–1128, 2008.

43. Mitra, S. K., *Digital Signal Processing: A Computer-based Approach*, 3rd ed., 2010 or the newest version, McGraw-Hill International Ed.

44. Nguyen, N., Milanfar, P., and Golub, G., Efficient generalized crossvalidation with applications to parametric image restoration and resolution enhancement, *IEEE Trans. Image Process.*, vol. 10, no. 9, pp. 1299–1308, September 2001.

45. Nussbaumer, H. J., *Fast Fourier Transform and Convolution Algorithms*, Springer-Verlag, 1981.

46. Oppenheim, A. V., and Schafer, R. W., *Digital Signal Processing*, Prentice-Hall Inc., 1975.

47. Park, H. W., Park, Y. S., and Oh, S. K., L/M-fold image resizing in block-DCT domain using symmetric convolution, *IEEE Trans. Image Process.*, vol. 12, no. 9, pp. 1016–1034, 2003.

48. Peled, A., and Liu, B., *Digital Signal Processing, Theory, Design, and Implementation*, John Wiley & Sons, 1975.

49. Pollard, J. M., *The Fast Fourier Transform in a Finite Field*, Math. Comput., vol. 25, pp. 365–374, 1971.

50. Proakis, J. G., and Manolakis, D. G., *Digital Signal Processing*, Pearson Prentice-Hall, Inc., 2007.

51. Rader, C. M., Discrete Fourier transforms when the number of data samples is prime, *Proc. IEEE* , vol. 56, pp. 1107–1108, 1968.

52. Rader, C. M., Discrete convolutions via Mersenne transforms, *IEEE Trans. Comput.*, vol. C-21, pp. 1269–1273, 1972.

53. Rayner, P. J. W., Number theoretic transforms, *Proceedings of the NATO Advanced Study Institute*, September 1976, Italy, pp. 333–351.

54. Siu, W. C., Number theoretic transform and its applications to digital signal processing, *Proceedings of the IERE H.K. Section Workshop on Adv. Micro. and D.S.P.*, Hong Kong, September 1982, pp. 76–101, 1982.

55. Siu, W.-C., and Constantinides, A. G., Very fast discrete Fourier transform using number theoretic transform, *IEE Proceedings, Pt. G, Electron. Circuits Syst.*, vol. 130, no. 5, pp. 201–204, 1983.

56. Siu, W.-C., and Constantinides, A. G., Hardware realisation of Mersenne number transforms for fast digital convolution, *Proceedings of the IEEE International Conference on Acoustic, Speech and Signal Processing, ICASSP'84*, San Diego, U.S.A., March 1984, pp. 41A2, 1984a.

57. Siu, W.-C., and Constantinides, A. G., On the computation of discrete Fourier transform using Fermat number transform, *IEE Proceedings, Pt. F, Commun. Radar Signal Process.*, vol. 131, no. 1, pp. 7–14, 1984b.

58. Siu, W.-C., and Constantinides, A. G., Some new results on the computation of discrete Fourier transforms using Mersenne number transforms, *Proceedings, IEEE International Symposium on Circuits and System (ISCAS'84)*, May 1984, Montreal, Canada, pp. 53–56, 1984c.

59. Siu, W.-C., and Constantinides, A. G., Fast Mersenne number transforms for the computation of discrete Fourier transform, *Signal Process.*, vol. 9, no. 2, pp. 125–131, 1985.

60. Sun, J., Xu, Z., and Shum, H. Y., Gradient profile prior and its applications in image super-resolution and enhancement, *IEEE Trans. Image Process.*, vol. 20, no. 6, pp. 1529–1542, 2011.

61. Tekalp, A. M., *Digital Video Processing*, Prentice-Hall, 1995.

62. Wang, Q., and Ward, R. K., A New orientation-adaptive interpolation method, *IEEE Trans. Image Process.*, vol. 16, no. 4, pp. 889–900, 2007.

63. Winograd, S., Some bilinear forms whose multiplicative complexity depends on the field of constants, IBM Thomas J. Watson Research Centre, N. Y., U.S.A., IBM Rev. Rep., RC5669, 1975.

64. Wong, K.-L., and Siu, W.-C., Routing networks for systolic/pipeline realisation of prime factor mapping, *IEEE Trans. Comput.*, vol. 40, no. 8, pp. 1072–1074, 1991.

65. Wong, C.-W., and Siu, W.-C., Transform kernel selection strategy for the H.264, *Proceedings of the 2009 APSIPA Annual Summit and Conference (APSIPA-ASC'2009)*, October 4–7, 2009, Sapporo Convention Center, Sapporo, Japan, pp. 64–70, 2009.

66. Wong, C.-W., and Siu, W.-C., Analysis on dyadic approximation error for hybrid video codecs with integer transforms, *IEEE Trans. Image Process.*, vol. 20, no. 10, pp. 2780–2787, 2011a.

67. Wong, C.-W., and Siu, W.-C., Transform kernel selection strategy for the H.264/AVC and future video coding standards, *IEEE Trans. Circuits Systems Video Technol.*, vol. 21, no. 11, pp. 1631–1645, 2011b.

68. Woods, N. A., Galatsanos, N. P., and Katsaggelos, A. K., Stochastic methods for joint registration, restoration, and interpolation of multiple undersampled images, *IEEE Trans. Image Process.*, vol. 15, no. 1, pp. 201–203, 2006.

69. Wu, Z. , Yu, H., Chen, C. W., A new hybrid CT-Wiener-based interpolation scheme for video intra frame up-sampling, *IEEE Signal Process. Lett.*, vol. 17, no. 10, pp. 827–830, 2010.

70. Yang, S., Kim, Y., and Jeong, J., Fine edge-preserving technique for display devices, *IEEE Trans. Consumer Electron.*, vol. 54, no. 4, pp. 1761–1769, 2008.

71. Zhang, W., Men, A., and Chen, P., Adaptive inter-layer intra prediction in scalable video coding, *IEEE International Symposium on Circuits and Systems, 2009 (ISCAS 2009)*, Taipei, Taiwan, May 24–27, 2009, pp. 876–879, 2009.

72. Zhang, L., and Wu, X., An edge-guided image interpolation algorithm via directional filtering and data fusion, *IEEE Trans. Image Process.*, vol. 15, no. 8, pp. 2226–2238, 2006.

PART III

SIGNAL PROCESSING

Chapter 8

Ramanujan-Sums and the Representation of Periodic Sequences

Palghat P. Vaidyanathan

California Institute of Technology, Pasadena, CA 91125, USA
ppvnath@systems.caltech.edu

8.1 Introduction

In planning a chapter for this book celebrating the career achievements of Professor Tony Constantinides, we spent some time wondering what might be best liked by Tony. Some reflection reminded us that throughout his career Tony has conducted his research based on solid classical roots, while at the same time always bringing in fresh daisy-like novelty into his work, to suit modern applications. You will see this combination in all his work, whether it is on allpass filters or neural networks, adaptive filtering or video coding. In keeping with this glorious spirit, we have therefore decided to write about something that is at once old and new. The topic we have chosen has the charm of good old classical number theory. At the same time, it offers the excitement of a novel periodic decomposition to suit the analysis of highly structured signals.

Trends in Digital Signal Processing: A Festschrift in Honour of A. G. Constantinides
Edited by Yong Ching Lim, Hon Keung Kwan, and Wan-Chi Siu
Copyright © 2016 Pan Stanford Publishing Pte. Ltd.
ISBN 978-981-4669-50-4 (Hardcover), 978-981-4669-51-1 (eBook)
www.panstanford.com

To set the stage, let us for a moment switch our minds back to the corridors of the early 20th century number-theory. In 1918 the famous Indian mathematician S. Ramanujan, who at that time was visiting G. H. Hardy in Cambridge, defined a sequence $c_q(n)$ today known as the Ramanujan sum (Ramanujan, 1918). This sum is an integer-valued sequence defined for all integers $q \geq 1$. It was used by Ramanujan (and later by many other number theorists) to analyze number theoretic functions such as the Möbius function $\mu(n)$, Euler's totient function $\phi(n)$, the von Mangoldt function $\Lambda(n)$, and the Riemann-zeta function $\zeta(s)$ (Hardy and Wright, 2008).[a] (No worries—you need not know about these to read on!)

Nearly hundred years later, it has been recognized by some signal processing researchers that Ramanujan's sums can actually be used for the analysis of periodic signals in a way that is quite different from the use of conventional Fourier transforms (Planat, 2002; Planat, et al., 2009; Mainardi, et al., 2008). Subsequent to this, in a very recent work, we showed that any finite duration signal with duration N can be decomposed into a sum of orthogonal periodic components, with periods q_i equal to the K divisors of N (Vaidyanathan, 2014a,c). This decomposition is based on Ramanujan's sums, and has been shown to be useful to identify hidden periodic components in signals. The beauty is that the periodic components can be identified simply by performing essentially integer-valued orthogonal projection operations on the original signal. This is based on (a) the fact that Ramanujan's $c_q(n)$ is integer-valued, and (b) some new algebraic properties of Ramanujan sums proved in Vaidyanathan (2014b).

The problem of period-identification is different from standard spectral estimation problems, as evidenced clearly from some early publications (Sethares and Staley, 1999). For this reason, algorithms such as MUSIC (Schmidt, 1986; Stoica and Nehorai, 1989), or modern spectral compressive sensing methods (Duarte and Baraniuk, 2013) may not be appropriate without considerable

---

[a]An insightful connection between Ramanujan sums and the proof of the famous *twin-prime conjecture* was established by Gadiyar and Padma (Gadiyar and Padma, 1999) based on the possibility of a Wiener-Kintchine like formula for Ramanujan expansions. The conjecture itself has been proved recently by Yitang Zhang in a famous paper (Zhang , 2013).

modifications. For a detailed discussion of this issue, please see (Vaidyanathan, 2014c). Some readers might notice that examining the difference $x(n) - x(n - K)$ for $1 \leq K \leq N - 1$ should reveal the period. This works as long as there is only one periodic component, and there is no noise; see Tenneti and Vaidyanathan (2014) for details.

In this chapter we have the pleasure of sharing these recent results with our readers. We review Ramanujan's sum and the new periodic decompositions. A number of interesting properties of these decompositions will be revealed in the process. We will conclude with some applications and examples. For detailed proofs the interested reader should study the references mentioned at appropriate places in the chapter.

In Section 8.2 we review some limitations of the discrete Fourier transform (DFT) in the analysis of periodic signals. We review Ramanujan sums in Section 8.3, and consider the problem of representing FIR signals as linear combinations of Ramanujan sums. In Section 8.4 we study Ramanujan subspaces, originally introduced in (Vaidyanathan, 2014b), which are very useful in the analysis of periodic signals. Section 8.5 discusses the representation of arbitrary FIR signals as linear combinations of signals belonging to Ramanujan subspaces, and examples of applications are presented in Section 8.6. Finally in Section 8.7 we briefly discuss the use of dictionary based approaches for representing and identifying periodic components.

8.1.1 *Notations*

For convenience we summarize below some of the definitions and notations used:

(1) A sequence $x(n)$ is said to have period q if q is the **smallest** positive integer such that $x(n) = x(n + q)$ for all n. If $x(n)$ has finite support $0 \leq n \leq N - 1$ this has to hold only for all n such that $0 \leq n < n + q \leq N - 1$.

(2) $W_q = e^{-j2\pi/q}$ is the qth root of unity, and $\mathbb{C}^q$ the q-dimensional space of complex vectors. For a matrix $\mathbf{A}$, the transpose,

conjugate, and transpose-conjugate are denoted as $\mathbf{A}^T$, $\mathbf{A}^*$ and $\mathbf{A}^\dagger$ respectively.

(3) The abbreviations lcm and gcd stand for least common multiple and greatest common divisor, respectively.

(4) The notation (k, q) represents the gcd of the integers k and q. So $(k, q) = 1$ means that k and q are *coprime*, that is, they have no common factor other than unity.

(5) The quantity $\phi(q)$ is the *Euler's totient function* (Hardy and Wright, 2008). It is equal to the number of integers k in $1 \leq k \leq q$ satisfying $(k, q) = 1$. For example if $q = 10$, then the integers 1, 3, 7 and 9 are coprime to q, so $\phi(10) = 4$.

(6) The notation $q_i | q$ means that q_i is a divisor of q (i.e., a factor of q). We say q_i is a proper divisor of q if it is a divisor of q and $q_i < q$. For example, if $q = 10$, the divisors are $q_1 = 1, q_2 = 2, q_3 = 5$, and $q_4 = 10$ whereas the proper divisors are $q_1 = 1, q_2 = 2$, and $q_3 = 5$.

(7) $\mathcal{S}_q$ denotes the Ramanujan subspace associated with the integer q (to be defined in Section 8.4).

(8) Finite duration sequences $x(n)$ are often referred to as FIR signals. This is an accepted misnomer, since FIR actually stands for *finite impulse response*.

8.2 Periodic Signals and DFT

Consider a finite-duration signal $x(n)$, $0 \leq n \leq N - 1$ (i.e., an FIR signal). We know this can be represented using the DFT coefficients $X[k]$ in the form

$$x(n) = \frac{1}{N} \sum_{k=0}^{N-1} X[k] e^{j(2\pi k/N)n} \tag{8.1}$$

The component $e^{j(2\pi k/N)n}$ is unchanged if n is replaced with $n + N$. So each term in (8.1) is periodic, with period N or a divisor of N. Recall here that the period is defined to be the *smallest* repetition interval. Writing k/N in irreducible rational form, that is,

$$\frac{k}{N} = \frac{k_i}{q_i}, \tag{8.2}$$

where k_i and q_i are coprime, we see that the term $e^{j(2\pi k/N)n}$ has period q_i where q_i is a divisor of N. We therefore see that the DFT expresses $x(n)$ as a sum of period-q_i signals, where q_i are divisors of N. For example if $N = 10$ then the divisors are 1, 2, 5 and 10, so the DFT sees only these periods. Thus, if

$$x(n) = x(n + q), \quad 0 \le n < n + q \le N - 1, \qquad (8.3)$$

where q is a divisor of N, only those DFT coefficients $X[k]$ in (8.1), for which $k/N = \widehat{k}/q$ for some $\widehat{k}$, will be nonzero. In this sense, the DFT will be sparse. However, if the period q is not a divisor of N, the DFT is not sparse. These are demonstrated in Fig. 8.1, which shows 32-point signals with periods 8 and 9, and their 32-point DFTs.

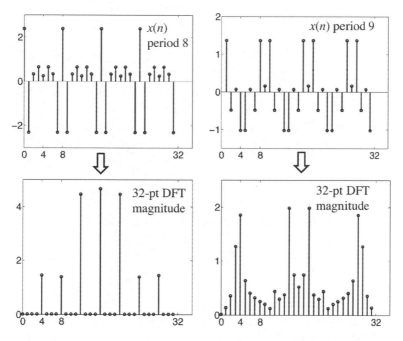

Figure 8.1   Left: a period-8 signal and its DFT (magnitude). Right: a period-9 signal and its DFT (magnitude). The DFT on the left is sparse, while that on the right is not.

8.3 Ramanujan Sums

So the first idea that comes to mind is that, for finite-duration signals which have internal periods that are not divisors of the duration, a basis different from the DFT ought to be able to give a better representation. For example, consider the representation

$$x(n) = \sum_{q=1}^{N} a_q c_q(n), \quad 0 \le n \le N - 1, \tag{8.4}$$

where $c_q(n)$ are linearly independent signals with q denoting the period of $c_q(n)$. Thus, each period q is given a presence in the set $\{c_q(n)\}$ unlike the DFT basis W_N^{kn} which gives a presence only to periods which are divisors of N. It appears that (8.4) ought to work better for FIR signals with arbitrary internal periods. In this section we will elaborate on one such basis.

In 1918 Ramanujan introduced a trigonometric summation of the form

$$c_q(n) = \sum_{\substack{k=1 \\ (k,q)=1}}^{q} e^{j2\pi kn/q} \tag{8.5}$$

which today is called the Ramanujan sum (Ramanujan, 1918). Here the notation (k, q) denotes the greatest common divisor (gcd) of k and q. Thus $(k, q) = 1$ means that k and q are coprime. For example, if $q = 6$, the coprime values of k are $k = 1, 5$ so that

$$c_6(n) = e^{j2\pi n/6} + e^{j10\pi n/6} \tag{8.6}$$

and similarly for $q = 5$

$$c_5(n) = e^{j2\pi n/5} + e^{j4\pi n/5} + e^{j6\pi n/5} + e^{j8\pi n/5} \tag{8.7}$$

From the definition (8.5) we see that the DFT of $c_q(n)$ is

$$C_q[k] = \begin{cases} q & \text{if } (k, q) = 1 \\ \\ 0 & \text{otherwise,} \end{cases} \tag{8.8}$$

which can also be taken as the defining property of Ramanujan sums. Clearly the Ramanujan sum (8.5) has period q in the argument n. It can be shown that

$$c_q(n) = \sum_{\substack{k=1 \\ (k,q)=1}}^{q} \cos\frac{2\pi kn}{q}, \tag{8.9}$$

which in fact was Ramanujan's original definition. So $c_q(n)$ is symmetric within a period, that is $c_q(q - n) = c_q(n)$. The following properties are easily verified:

$$c_q(0) = \phi(q), \quad |c_q(n)| \le \phi(q), \quad \sum_{n=0}^{q-1} c_q^2(n) = q\phi(q), \quad (8.10)$$

and $\sum_{n=0}^{q-1} c_q(n) = 0$ for $q > 1$. Here are the first few Ramanujan sums (one period shown):

$$c_1(n) = 1$$
$$c_2(n) = 1, -1$$
$$c_3(n) = 2, -1, -1$$
$$c_4(n) = 2, 0, -2, 0$$
$$c_5(n) = 4, -1, -1, -1, -1$$
$$c_6(n) = 2, 1, -1, -2, -1, 1$$
$$c_7(n) = 6, -1, -1, -1, -1, -1, -1$$
$$c_8(n) = 4, 0, 0, 0, -4, 0, 0, 0$$
$$c_9(n) = 6, 0, 0, -3, 0, 0, -3, 0, 0$$
$$c_{10}(n) = 4, 1, -1, 1, -1, -4, -1, 1, -1, 1 \quad (8.11)$$

It can be shown that for prime q, the first period of $c_q(n)$ has the form

$$\{q - 1, -1, -1, \dots, -1\} \quad (8.12)$$

Unlike sines and cosines, the quantity $c_q(n)$ is always *integer valued*, which is often an attractive property. Ramanujan proved this by establishing a relation between $c_q(n)$ and the Möbius function. An independent proof is given in Vaidyanathan (2014b), where many other properties of Ramanujan sums are reviewed.

What was Ramanujan's original purpose in introducing this sum? Basically he showed that many standard arithmetic functions in the theory of numbers can be expressed as linear combinations of $c_q(n)$, that is,

$$x(n) = \sum_{q=1}^{\infty} \alpha_q c_q(n), \quad n \ge 1. \quad (8.13)$$

The fact that $c_q(n)$ is a periodic signal with small integer values bounded by $\phi(q)$ has inspired signal processing researchers to use an expansion of the form (8.13) to look for periodic components in a signal $x(n)$ (Planat, 2002; Planat, et al., 2009; Chen, et al., 1997; Samadi, et al., 2005; Pei and Chang, 2007; Sugavaneswaran, et al., 2012; Mainardi, et al., 2008). Typically the coefficients α_q are calculated using the following formula usually attributed to Carmichael (Carmichael, 1932; Gadiyar and Padma, 1999; Planat, 2002)):

$$\alpha_q = \frac{1}{\phi(q)} \left(\lim_{M \to \infty} \frac{1}{M} \sum_{n=1}^{M} x(n) c_q(n) \right) \tag{8.14}$$

Based on the above references and the personal experience of the author, it can be said that the infinite-sum representation (8.13) has had only limited success in identifying periodic components in finite (short) duration signals. There are a number of reasons for this. First, since each term $c_q(n)$ in (8.13) or (8.4) is only one of many possible period-q signals (including, for example, sines and cosines), there is no reason to believe that that this yields a sparse representation. Furthermore, as shown in Vaidyanathan (2014a), the use of (8.14), while appropriate for infinite-duration sequences, poses some mathematical difficulties for FIR signals. The second difficulty can be overcome by resorting to a direct computation of the N coefficients a_q from (8.4) (Vaidyanathan, 2014a). For this let us return to Eq. (8.4) and rewrite it in matrix form as follows:

$$\underbrace{\begin{bmatrix} x(0) \\ x(1) \\ \vdots \\ x(N-1) \end{bmatrix}}_{\mathbf{x}} = \mathbf{A}_N \underbrace{\begin{bmatrix} a_1 \\ a_2 \\ \vdots \\ a_N \end{bmatrix}}_{\mathbf{a}} \tag{8.15}$$

where the qth column of the $N \times N$ matrix $\mathbf{A}_N$ has the first period of $c_q(n)$ repeated until we get N rows. That is,

$$\mathbf{A}_N = \begin{bmatrix} \mathbf{c}_1 & \mathbf{c}_2 & \mathbf{c}_3 & \dots & \mathbf{c}_N \end{bmatrix}, \tag{8.16}$$

where

$$\mathbf{c}_m = \begin{bmatrix} c_m(0) & c_m(1) & c_m(2) & \dots & c_m(N-1) \end{bmatrix}^T. \tag{8.17}$$

It can be shown (Vaidyanathan, 2014b) that the $N \times N$ matrix (8.16) has full rank, and the unique coefficients a_k can be computed by direct inversion of (8.15) instead of using (8.14). Thus $c_q(n)$, $1 \leq q \leq N$ forms an *integer* basis for $\mathbb{C}^N$.

However, even if $x(n)$ has one single period $q < N$, the sequence a_k is not necessarily sparse. For example, consider a simple truncated sinusoid of the form $x(n) = \cos(2\pi n/M)$, $0 \leq n \leq N - 1$, with $N = 256$, and period $M < N$. When the period is $M = 4$, the magnitudes of the coefficients a_k in the Ramanujan sum representation (8.15) are shown in Fig. 8.2a. We see that the sequence $\{a_k\}$ is very sparse (≈ 0 for all k except $k = 4$). So, the period can be identified readily. On the other hand, when the period $M = 8$, the coefficients a_k are as shown in Fig. 8.2b. This shows that the cosine cannot be represented by a single Ramanujan sum. More important, from the plot we cannot even conclude that $x(n)$ is a signal with one periodic component.

Next consider the example where $x(n) = c_{30}(n)$, that is the signal to be analyzed is itself one of the Ramanujan sums, with period 30.

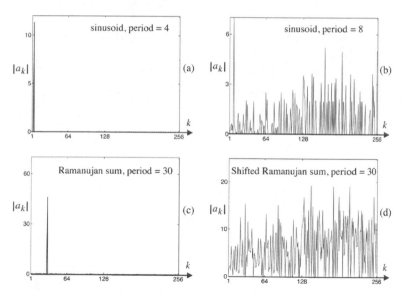

Figure 8.2 The coefficients a_k (absolute values) in the first Ramanujan FIR representation (8.4) (i.e., (8.15)), for four FIR signals with support $0 \leq n \leq 255$. (a) Sinusoid $\cos(2\pi n/4)$, (b) the sinusoid $\cos(2\pi n/8)$, (c) the Ramanujan sum $c_{30}(n)$, and (d) the circularly shifted Ramanujan sum $c_{30}(n - 1)$.

In this case, $a_k = 0$ except when $k = 30$ as expected. (Fig. 8.2c). But suppose we consider a circularly shifted example $x(n) = c_{30}(n-1)$. It turns out that this cannot be sparsely represented, as it requires many nonzero coefficients a_k (Fig. 8.2d). In fact, Planat et al. (Planat, et al., 2009) have observed the sensitivity of the representation (8.13)–(8.14) to shifts.

8.4 Ramanujan Subspaces

The reason why (8.4) does not always produce a sparse representation for periodic signals (as seen from Fig. 8.2b,d) is because each period q is represented by a one-dimensional space (i.e., the single column $c_q(n)$ in Eq. (8.16)). To alleviate this problem we introduced the concept of a Ramanujan subspace in (Vaidyanathan, 2014a), (Vaidyanathan, 2014b). For each integer q, this is a space constructed from $c_q(n)$, and it has dimension $\phi(q) > 1$ (where $\phi(q)$ is Euler's totient, see Section 8.1.1). Such a subspace captures a broader class of period-q signals and has an integer basis consisting of $c_q(n)$ and its shifted relatives.

We first explain the construction of this subspace. Starting from $c_q(n)$ define the $q \times q$ integer circulant matrix shown below:

$$
\mathbf{B}_q = \begin{bmatrix}
c_q(0) & c_q(q-1) & c_q(q-2) & \cdots & c_q(1) \\
c_q(1) & c_q(0) & c_q(q-1) & \cdots & c_q(2) \\
c_q(2) & c_q(1) & c_q(0) & \cdots & c_q(3) \\
\vdots & \vdots & \vdots & \ddots & \vdots \\
c_q(q-2) & c_q(q-3) & c_q(q-4) & \cdots & c_q(q-1) \\
c_q(q-1) & c_q(q-2) & c_q(q-3) & \cdots & c_q(0)
\end{bmatrix}
$$

(8.18)

Here, every column is obtained by a circular downward shift of the previous column. Notice the following: (a) The 0th row is the time-reversed Ramanujan sum $c_q(q-n)$. (b) Since $c_q(q-n) = c_q(n)$, we see that $\mathbf{B}_q$ is symmetric, that is, $\mathbf{B}_q^T = \mathbf{B}_q$, in fact, Hermitian (since real).

The column space of $\mathbf{B}_q$ will be called the Ramanujan subspace $\mathcal{S}_q$. Since any circulant matrix can be diagonalized by the DFT matrix, it can be shown in particular that

$$\mathbf{B}_q \mathbf{W} = \mathbf{W} \Lambda_q \tag{8.19}$$

Here Λ_q is the diagonal matrix

$$\Lambda_q = \begin{bmatrix} C_q[0] & 0 & \cdots & 0 \\ 0 & C_q[1] & \cdots & 0 \\ \vdots & \vdots & \ddots & \vdots \\ 0 & 0 & \cdots & C_q[q-1] \end{bmatrix} \tag{8.20}$$

and $\mathbf{W}$ is the $q \times q$ DFT matrix whose kth row is $\begin{bmatrix} 1 & W_q^k & W_q^{2k} & \cdots & W_q^{(q-1)k} \end{bmatrix}$. Equation (8.19) says that the columns of $\mathbf{W}$ are the eigenvectors of $\mathbf{B}_q$, with corresponding eigenvalues $C_q[k]$. The following results are proved in Vaidyanathan (2014b):

(1) $\mathbf{B}_q$ has rank $\phi(q)$, hence $\mathcal{S}_q$ has dimension $\phi(q)$. Since $\mathbf{B}_q$ is Hermitian with nonnegative eigenvalues $\in \{0, q\}$, it is positive semidefinite.

(2) $\mathbf{B}_q$ can be factorized as

$$\mathbf{B}_q = \underbrace{\mathbf{V}}_{q \times \phi(q)} \underbrace{\mathbf{V}^\dagger}_{\phi(q) \times q}, \tag{8.21}$$

where $\mathbf{V}$ is a submatrix of the DFT matrix $\mathbf{W}$ obtained by retaining the "coprime columns", i.e., columns numbered k_i such that $(k_i, q) = 1$. So the column space of $\mathbf{B}_q$ is spanned by the $\phi(q)$ columns of the DFT matrix given by

$$\begin{bmatrix} 1 \\ W^{k_1} \\ W^{2k_1} \\ \vdots \\ W^{(q-1)k_1} \end{bmatrix}, \begin{bmatrix} 1 \\ W^{k_2} \\ W^{2k_2} \\ \vdots \\ W^{(q-1)k_2} \end{bmatrix}, \dots, \begin{bmatrix} 1 \\ W^{k_{\phi(q)}} \\ W^{2k_{\phi(q)}} \\ \vdots \\ W^{(q-1)k_{\phi(q)}} \end{bmatrix}, \tag{8.22}$$

where $W = e^{-j2\pi/q}$ and $(k_i, q) = 1$.

(3) The Ramanujan sum $c_q(n)$ and its $\phi(q) - 1$ consecutive circular shifts (i.e., the first $\phi(q)$ columns of the circulant matrix $\mathbf{B}_q$) constitute a (typically nonorthogonal) integer basis for the Ramanujan space $\mathcal{S}_q \subset \mathbb{C}^q$. In fact, any set of $\phi(q)$ consecutive columns of the matrix $\mathbf{B}_q$ form a basis for $\mathcal{S}_q$.

Thus $x(n) \in S_q$ if and only if it can be expressed in either one of the following equivalent forms:

$$x(n) = \sum_{l=0}^{\phi(q)-1} \beta_l c_q(n-l) = \sum_{\substack{1 \leq k \leq q \\ (k,q)=1}} \alpha_k W_q^{kn} \qquad (8.23)$$

Whereas the $\phi(q)$ circularly shifted Ramanujan sequences $\{c_q(n-l)\}$ form an integer basis for the Ramanujan space S_q, the $\phi(q)$ sequences W_q^{kn} (with $(k,q) = 1$) form a complex orthogonal basis.

For visualization we sometimes regard the elements of S_q as period-q sequences. Moreover we will sometimes need to define matrices which are repetitions of rows of $\mathbf{C}_q$. If there are r repetitions then the column space of this matrix is a subspace of $\mathbb{C}^{qr}$. We shall continue to refer to this as the space S_q, and the sizes of the vectors (e.g., qr) are usually clear from the context.

8.4.1 Properties of Ramanujan subspaces

Before we leave this section, it is important to summarize some of the crucial properties of Ramanujan subspaces. These are proved in Vaidyanathan (2014b).

(1) $S_q \subset \mathbb{C}^q$ is a circularly shift-invariant space, that is, if $x(n) \in S_q$, then $x(n-k) \in S_q$ where the shift is circular (modulo q).

(2) *Periodicity.* Given an arbitrary sum of the form

$$x(n) = \sum_{k=1}^{q} a_k W_q^{kn} \qquad (8.24)$$

it is clear that $x(n) = x(n+q)$ because $W_q^{kn} = W_q^{k(n+q)}$ for each k. But the period of $x(n)$ can in general be q or a divisor $< q$. When $(k, q) = 1$, the component W_q^{kn} has period exactly q (and not a divisor of q). Starting from this and some other ideas, it can be shown (Vaidyanathan, 2014b) that the Ramanujan sum (8.5), and more generally the sums (8.23), have period exactly equal to q.

(3) *Period of sum.* Furthermore, if we add two signals $x_1(n) \in S_{q_1}$ and $x_2(n) \in S_{q_2}$, the result has period exactly equal to the lcm of q_1 and q_2 (it cannot be smaller).

(4) *Orthogonality.* If $x_{q_1}(n) \in \mathcal{S}_{q_1}$ and $x_{q_2}(n) \in \mathcal{S}_{q_2}$, then these signals are orthogonal over appropriate intervals, or more precisely,

$$\sum_{n=0}^{m-1} x_{q_1}(n)x_{q_2}^*(n) = 0, \quad q_1 \neq q_2. \tag{8.25}$$

where m is any common multiple of q_1 and q_2.

(5) We know a square matrix $\mathbf{P}$ is a projection if $\mathbf{P}^2 = \mathbf{P}$, and an orthogonal projection if it is also Hermitian. Using this we can show that

$$\mathbf{P}_q = \frac{\mathbf{B}_q}{q} \tag{8.26}$$

is the orthogonal projection matrix onto the Ramanujan space $\mathcal{S}_q$. Given an arbitrary vector $\mathbf{x} \in \mathbb{C}^q$, this projection can be calculated as

$$\mathbf{x}_q = \mathbf{P}_q\mathbf{x} = \frac{\mathbf{B}_q\mathbf{x}}{q}, \tag{8.27}$$

Since $\mathbf{B}_q$ has integer elements bounded by $c_q(0) = \phi(q)$ the projection $\mathbf{P}_q\mathbf{x}$ can be calculated by simple integer operations (binary shifts and adds) on the (possibly complex) elements of $\mathbf{x}$ and dividing the result by q. This is especially useful when analyzing finite duration signals in terms of their periodic components.

In the next section, we show how we can combine some of the Ramanujan subspaces to form a basis for $\mathbb{C}^N$.

8.5 A Second Ramanujan Sum Basis Using Subspaces $\mathcal{S}_{q_i}$

Given an integer N (length of the signal $x(n)$ to be analyzed), let $q_1, q_2, \ldots, q_K$ be the K divisors of N. It is proved in (Vaidyanathan, 2014c) that any length N sequence $x(n)$ can be represented as a linear combination of the Ramanujan sums $c_{q_i}(n)$ and their circularly shifted versions. More precisely $x(n)$ can be expressed as

$$x(n) = \sum_{q_i|N} \underbrace{\sum_{l=0}^{\phi(q_i)-1} \beta_{il}c_{q_i}(n-l)}_{x_{q_i}(n)}, \quad 0 \leq n \leq N-1, \tag{8.28}$$

Note that the right hand side contains only those periods q_i that are divisors of N, just as in the DFT representation. However, we will see that this representation does have some advantages over the earlier FIR representation (8.4). Since it is well-known (Hardy and Wright, 2008) that

$$\sum_{q_i|N} \phi(q_i) = N \qquad (8.29)$$

the number of functions $c_{q_i}(n - l)$ on the right hand side of (8.28) is precisely N. The main result is that these N sequences are linearly independent. Thus for any length-N FIR signal $x(n)$ (or equivalently for $\mathbb{C}^N$), the set of N sequences $\{c_{q_i}(n - l)\}$ provides an *integer basis*. It is also shown in Vaidyanathan (2014c) that this is an orthogonal basis if and only if N is a power of two.

8.5.1 *Properties of the Representation (8.28)*

Before we proceed with examples, we want to summarize the main properties of the new representation (8.28). Let us rewrite this in simple language as follows:

$$x(n) = \sum_{q_i|N} x_{q_i}(n), \qquad 0 \le n \le N - 1 \qquad (8.30)$$

Since $x_{q_i}(n) = \sum_{l=0}^{\phi(q_i)-1} \beta_{il} c_{q_i}(n-l)$ it follows that these components belong to the Ramanujan subspaces $\mathcal{S}_{q_i}$, and they have period exactly q_i. Thus, we have decomposed an arbitrary signal $x(n)$ of length N into a sum of K periodic components belonging to the K Ramanujan subspaces $\mathcal{S}_{q_i}$, one corresponding to each divisor q_i of N. Since N is a multiple of any pair of divisors q_i and q_j, it follows that $x_{q_i}(n)$ and $x_{q_m}(n)$ are orthogonal for $q_i \ne q_m$ (Section 8.4.1):

$$\sum_{n=0}^{N-1} x_{q_i}(n) x_{q_m}^*(n) = 0 \qquad (8.31)$$

Thus, $x(n)$ has been decomposed into orthogonal, periodic, components which belong to Ramanujan subspaces. Unlike the Fourier decomposition, each periodic component has an integer basis

$$\{c_{q_i}(n - l)\}, \qquad 0 \le l \le \phi(q_i) - 1 \qquad (8.32)$$

Furthermore, the component $x_{q_i}(n)$ can be regarded as an *orthogonal projection* of $x(n)$ onto the subspace $\mathcal{S}_{q_i} \subset \mathbb{C}^N$. With $x(n)$ and

$x_{q_i}(n)$ regarded as N-component vectors $\mathbf{x}$ and $\mathbf{x}_{q_i}$, this projection can be calculated using Eq. (8.27).

This projection computation is very efficient because, as explained in Section 8.4.1, $\mathbf{P}_q$ is an integer matrix (except for the factor q). Please see Vaidyanathan (2014c) for even more efficient ways to compute these projections.

8.5.2 *Finding Period Using Decomposition (8.28)*

Suppose $x(n)$ has an internal period q_m which is a divisor of N, that is $x(n + q_m) = x(n)$ and q_m is the smallest such integer. Then there is a very simple way to identify q_m from the measurements $x(n)$ as follows: compute the projections $x_{q_i}(n)$ for all q_i which are divisors of N. Let $x_{q_{i_k}}(n)$ be the nonzero projections. Then by properties of the subspaces $\mathcal{S}_{q_i}$ summarized in Section 8.4.1, the period of $x(n)$ is the lcm of these q_{i_k}.

Figure 8.3 shows a 256-point signal $x(n)$. Since the divisors of N are $q_i = 2^m$, $0 \le m \le 8$, there are nine periodic components $x_{q_i}(n) \in \mathcal{S}_{q_i}$ in the decomposition (8.28). If we compute the projections $x_{q_i}(n)$

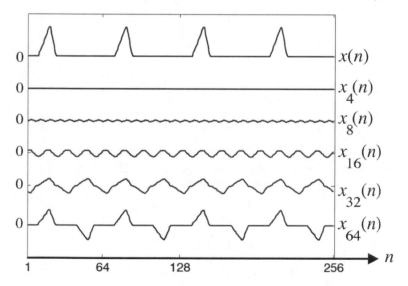

Figure 8.3 A 256-point signal $x(n)$ with period 64. The significant periodic components $x_4(n)$, $x_8(n)$, $x_{16}(n)$, $x_{32}(n)$, and $x_{64}(n)$ (projections onto Ramanujan spaces) are also shown.

as above, we find that $x_{q_i}(n) = 0$ for $q_i = 128$ and 256. Since the lcm of the integers q_i with $x_{q_i}(n) \neq 0$ is 64 it follows that the period is 64. Figure 8.3 shows plots of the significant periodic components $x_{q_i}(n)$ of $x(n)$ in this example (the constant component $x_1(n)$ is not shown; $x_2(n)$ happens to be negligibly small and is not shown.).

8.5.3 Justification of the Representation (8.28)

Here is how the representation (8.28) comes about. (The impatient reader can skip this section and come back to it later.) For each divisor q_i of N, let $\mathbf{c}_{q_i}$ be a $N \times 1$ vector containing the Ramanujan sum $c_{q_i}(n)$ (repeated N/q_i times), and define the matrix

$$\mathbf{G}_{q_i} = \begin{bmatrix} \mathbf{c}_{q_i} & \mathbf{c}_{q_i}^{(1)} & \cdots & \mathbf{c}_{q_i}^{(\phi(q_i)-1)} \end{bmatrix} \tag{8.33}$$

where $\mathbf{c}_{q_i}^{(k)}$ represents circular downshifting by k. This is a $N \times \phi(q_i)$ matrix. For example, when $N = 6$ and $q_i = 3$ we have

$$\mathbf{G}_{q_i} = \begin{bmatrix} 2 & -1 \\ -1 & 2 \\ -1 & -1 \\ 2 & -1 \\ -1 & 2 \\ -1 & -1 \end{bmatrix} \tag{8.34}$$

because $\phi(q_i) = 2$. With such a matrix $\mathbf{G}_{q_i}$ defined for each divisor q_i of N, now define a matrix

$$\mathbf{F}_N = \begin{bmatrix} \mathbf{G}_{q_1} & \mathbf{G}_{q_2} & \cdots & \mathbf{G}_{q_K} \end{bmatrix} \tag{8.35}$$

where K is the number of divisors of N. This has N rows and $\sum_{q_i \mid N} \phi(q_i)$ columns. However, since (8.29) is true, the matrix $\mathbf{F}_N$ has size $N \times N$. When $N = 6$, the divisors $q_1 = 1$, $q_2 = 2$, $q_3 = 3$, and $q_4 = 6$ have $\phi(q_1) = 1$, $\phi(q_2) = 1$, $\phi(q_3) = 2$, $\phi(q_4) = 2$, so that

$$\mathbf{F}_6 = \begin{bmatrix} 1 & 1 & 2 & -1 & 2 & 1 \\ 1 & -1 & -1 & 2 & 1 & 2 \\ 1 & 1 & -1 & -1 & -1 & 1 \\ 1 & -1 & 2 & -1 & -2 & -1 \\ 1 & 1 & -1 & 2 & -1 & -2 \\ 1 & -1 & -1 & -1 & 1 & -1 \end{bmatrix} \tag{8.36}$$

which is a 6×6 matrix indeed. It is shown in Vaidyanathan (2014c) that the matrix $\mathbf{F}_N$ constructed as above is nonsingular for any N, and furthermore it is orthogonal if and only if N is a power of two. This proves that any $N \times 1$ vector $\mathbf{x}$ can be represented in the form

$$\mathbf{x} = \mathbf{F}_N \mathbf{b} \tag{8.37}$$

Thus $\mathbf{F}_N$ defines an *integer basis* for $\mathbb{C}^N$. With the elements of $\mathbf{x}$ regarded as the samples $x(n)$, we therefore get the representation (8.28) where the coefficients β_{il} are the elements of the vector $\mathbf{b}$ in (8.37) in some order.

8.6 Examples of Use of Ramanujan Representations

In Section 8.5.2 we showed how the internal period of an FIR signal $x(n)$ can be identified from the decomposition (8.28): the period is equal to the lcm of the indices q_{i_k} of the nonzero projections $x_{q_{i_k}}(n)$. This works if there is only one internal period *and* it is a divisor of N, and is therefore of limited use.

If $x(n)$ is a sum of two or more internal periods which are also divisors of N, an appropriate modified method can be applied. Thus, suppose $x(n) = x_1(n) + x_2(n)$ where $x_1(n)$ and $x_2(n)$ have periods N_1 and N_2 (both $< N$). If the data length $N \leq \mathrm{lcm}(N_1, N_2)$, the periodicity cannot be seen in the plot (see Fig. 8.4c). In this sense, N_1 and N_2 are the *hidden periods*. In the example shown $N_1 = 16$ and $N_2 = 12$ respectively, and the lcm of the individual periods is 48 which is also the length N of $x(n)$.

Now let us use the decompositions (8.4) and (8.28) to see if the hidden periods can be gleaned. Figure 8.5a shows the Ramanujan coefficients a_k (absolute values) in the first Ramanujan FIR representation (8.4). The plot does not reveal anything about the hidden periods. But consider the second Ramanujan representation (8.28). The divisors of $N = 48$ are $\{1, 2, 3, 4, 6, 8, 12, 16, 24, 48\}$, so there are 10 Ramanujan subspaces $\mathcal{S}_{q_k}$. Figure 8.5b shows the coefficients b_k (absolute values) in the expansion (8.37) (or equivalently β_{il} in (8.28) in appropriate order), and Fig. 8.5c shows the energies of the orthogonal projections $x_{q_i}(n)$ in (8.28). The

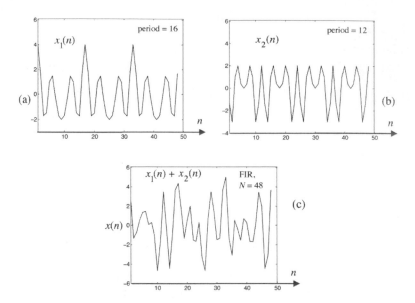

Figure 8.4 (a), (b) Periodic signals with periods 16 and 12, and (c) their sum $x(n)$.

projections are nonzero for S_3, S_4, S_{12} and S_{16}, and zero for the remaining 6 subspaces.

Now, if we examine the indices $\{3, 4, 12, 16\}$ corresponding to nonzero projections, we see that there are only two integers, namely 12 and 16 which are *not* divisors of other integers. This shows that there are two hidden periods, one corresponding to $\{4, 16\}$ and the other to $\{3, 4, 12\}$. The lcm of $\{4, 16\}$ is 16, which determines the first period. The lcm of $\{3, 4, 12\}$ is 12, which determines the second period. Thus the second Ramanujan FIR representation (8.28) can be used to identify the hidden periods. Since the two sets have some overlap, it is not possible to separate out $x_1(n)$ and $x_2(n)$, for, we have no information as to how to allocate the period-4 harmonic between the two. But the individual periods, 16 and 12, can indeed be identified.

If $x(n)$ has an arbitrary internal period (not a divisor of N) these methods do not apply, but there are other ways to handle that situation, as described in the next section.

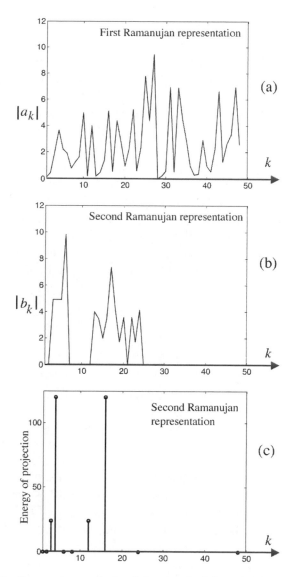

Figure 8.5 Ramanujan analysis of the signal $x(n)$ in Fig. 8.4c, which has two hidden periods. (a) The Ramanujan coefficients a_k (absolute values) corresponding to the first Ramanujan representation (8.4) (i.e., (8.15)). (b) The Ramanujan coefficients b_k (absolute values) corresponding to the second Ramanujan representation (8.28) (i.e., (8.37)). (c) Energies of the orthogonal projections x_{q_k} onto the Ramanujan subspaces $\mathcal{S}_{q_k}$.

8.7 Dictionary Approaches

So far we have considered three approaches to the representation of periodic signals, namely the DFT (Section 8.2), the first Ramanujan sum approach (Section 8.3), and the second Ramanujan sum approach (Section 8.5). The main goal is to obtain a sparse representation regardless of data length, which will help us to identify small hidden periodicities efficiently.

The DFT approach has the problem that unless the periodic components are divisors of the data length N, the representation is not sparse. This was demonstrated in Section 8.2. The first Ramanujan sum method (Eq. (8.4)) tends to alleviate this problem by including all periods in the range $1 \leq q \leq N$, but does not solve the problem entirely for various reasons: the basis is not orthogonal and furthermore each period is represented by a one-dimensional space which is not sufficient. Its inadequacy was demonstrated by the examples in Section 8.3.

It is true that the second Ramanujan decomposition (8.28) based on Ramanujan subspaces has some beautiful mathematical properties as elaborated in Section 8.5.1. It represents each period with a subspace of dimension $\phi(q_i)$, but the periods q_i are again restricted to be divisors of N, like the DFT. However, unlike the DFT, the periodic components can now be estimated by using integer projections. When we are looking for hidden periods in streaming real-time data, this is very attractive: we can repeat this projection process for a number of values of N in a given range (depending on the range in which we want to search for a period). If we were to perform such a search using the DFT, that would be less convenient: for arbitrary N in the range of search, the FFT can be slow, because N is in general not a power of two (it may even be a prime). On the other hand, since the integer-based Ramanujan-space projections are computationally more efficient than computing DFTs of arbitrary lengths, they are more attractive. Further detailed discussions about the relative merits of the three approaches can be found in Vaidyanathan (2014c).

An altogether different approach to representation (and extraction) of periodic signals is to use a dictionary of periodic atoms

(Vaidyanathan and Pal, 2014). A dictionary is simply a fat matrix $\mathbf{A}$ of size $N \times M$ where $M >> N$. Each of the M columns is a periodic signal, and is called a (periodic) atom. Given an N-vector $\mathbf{x}$ (signal $x(n)$ with N samples), the representation takes the form

$$\mathbf{x} = \underbrace{\mathbf{A}}_{N \times M} \mathbf{d} \tag{8.38}$$

Since $M >> N$, columns with all periods in the range $1 \le q \le N$ can be accommodated in the dictionary, as in the first Ramanujan sum representation (Eq. (8.4)). Furthermore, for each period q, we can accommodate a number of columns in $\mathbf{A}$ representing that period. Thus an entire subspace can be used to represent each period as in the second Ramanujan sum representation (8.28). In short, the dictionary approach effectively combines the advantages of the first and the second Ramanujan sum methods.

Since $M >> N$ in Eq. (8.38), the solution $\mathbf{d}$ for a given $\mathbf{x}$ is not unique. But there are many approaches to force it to be unique. The simplest would be to impose a sparsity constraint on $\mathbf{d}$ and look for the sparsest solution as in (Vaidyanathan and Pal, 2014). The standard theory and procedures for sparse recovery can be used in this case (Candes and Tao, 2005; Chen, et al., 2001; Wainwright, 2009; Tropp, 2004). Other approaches to find the unique $\mathbf{d}$, more suited to the goal of extracting periodicity information, are introduced in Tenneti and Vaidyanathan (2014).

Another important issue is, how to design the periodicity dictionary $\mathbf{A}$. There are many possible choices, and they have their pros and cons. The dictionary used in Vaidyanathan and Pal (2014) is called a Farey dictionary. Here, the dictionary atoms are Vandermonde vectors of the form

$$\begin{bmatrix} 1 \\ W_q^k \\ W_q^{2k} \\ \vdots \\ W_q^{(N-1)k} \end{bmatrix} \tag{8.39}$$

for each q in the range $1 \le q \le N$. For each q, the values of k are such that $(k, q) = 1$. So there are $\phi(q)$ atoms representing period q,

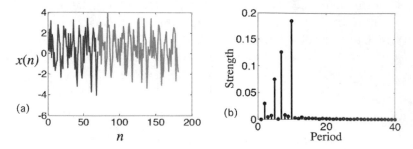

Figure 8.6 (a), (b) A signal $x(n)$ with period 70 and $N = 181$. The signal is a sum of period 7 and period 10 signals. (b) Result of using the dictionary approach to estimate the periods. See text.

and the total number of atoms is

$$\Phi(N) \triangleq \sum_{q=1}^{N} \phi(q). \tag{8.40}$$

For example, if $N = 6$, then

$$\Phi(6) = \phi(1) + \phi(2) + \phi(3) + \phi(4) + \phi(5) + \phi(6)$$
$$= 1 + 1 + 2 + 2 + 4 + 2 = 12. \tag{8.41}$$

It is shown in Vaidyanathan and Pal (2014) that the Farey dictionary has full Kruskal rank.[a] The Farey dictionary is by no means the only choice. The fundamental principles behind dictionary design for the periodicity problem are presented in Tenneti and Vaidyanathan (2014), along with many other useful choices for the dictionary. This also unifies and extends Ramanujan representations, DFT, and other periodic representations such as the one given in Sethares and Staley (1999).

Figure 8.6a shows an example generated by using one of the methods reported in Tenneti and Vaidyanathan (2014). Here $N = 181$ and $x(n)$ is a sum of two periodic components with periods 7 and 10 (plus some noise, with SNR about 5.5 dB). Since the lcm of 7 and 10 is 70, the signal has period 70. If we use one of the dictionary

---

[a]This is a necessary condition to ensure that the sparsest solution **d** is unique. The Kruskal rank ρ of a matrix is the largest integer such that any set of ρ columns is linearly independent. It is well known (Donoho and Elad, 2003) that if the Kruskal rank is ρ then we can solve uniquely for **d** from (8.38) as long as **d** has sparsity (number of nonzero elements) $s \leq \rho/2$.

approaches introduced in Tenneti and Vaidyanathan (2014) we get the plot shown in part (b). Here the "strength" for any period q refers to $\sum_k |d(k)|^2$ in the solution vector **d** where the sum is over all indices for which the atoms in the dictionary have period q. We see that the energy is concentrated in periods 2, 5, 10, and 7. Since 10 is the lcm of $\{2, 5, 10\}$, it follows that one of the periods is 10, and the other is 7. Thus, both hidden periods are neatly identified.

In this example, a Ramanujan dictionary was used. It was constructed starting from Ramanujan sums $c_q(n)$, $1 \leq q \leq N$, and using $\phi(q)$ shifted repetitions $c_q(n - l)$ of each of these. A convex program (different from traditional l_1 minimizers which promote sparsity) was used to identify the optimal solution **d** in this case. For detailed explanation of these new techniques please refer to Tenneti and Vaidyanathan (2014).

8.8 Concluding Remarks

In this chapter, we took the view that traditional tools used for spectrum analysis such as the DFT and subspace algorithms (e.g., MUSIC) are not very appropriate if the goal is only to identify hidden periodic components in signals. We then reviewed some new techniques based on the Ramanujan sum, which has its origin in the theory of numbers. We concluded by arguing that dictionary based approaches which promote sparsity or other appropriate measures work very well for this problem.

It is quite fascinating to know that number theoretic concepts do have some beautiful applications in signal processing. Many decades ago, the mathematician Hardy commented that truly deep, great, mathematics cannot have any "applications" (Hardy, 1940). According to him, branches such as applied mathematics and engineering mathematics are less distinguished cousins of pure mathematics. He also felt that no respectable pure mathematician should consider (or aspire for) their work to be "useful."

Today we see that this viewpoint stands corrected. In the last several decades, engineers have found applications of deep number-theoretic concepts in signal processing (McClellan and Rader, 1979), coding and digital communications (Blahut, 1983), cryptography

(Diffie and Hellman, 1976), periodicity analysis, and even theoretical physics (Chen, et al., 1997; Maddox, 1990). This is quite satisfying indeed!

Acknowledgements

This work was supported in parts by the ONR grant N00014-11-1-0676, and the Information Science and Technology (IST) initiative at Caltech. The author also wishes to thank Prof. Bhaskar Ramamurthi, Director of the Indian Institute of Technology, Chennai, for drawing his attention to Gadiyar and Padma (1999) (and to Planat (2002), Planat, et al. (2009)) via Dr. Gadiyar of the Vellore Institute of Technology). Subsequent enthusiastic remarks on this work from Dr. Gadiyar and Dr. Padma (VIT) are gratefully acknowledged.

References

1. T. M. Apostol, *Mathematical Analysis,* Addison-Wesley Publ. Co., 1974.
2. R. E. Blahut, *Theory and Practice of Error Control Codes,* Addison-Wesley Publ. Co., 1983.
3. E. J. Candes and Terence Tao, Decoding by Linear Programming, *IEEE Transactions on Information Theory*, vol. 51, No. 12, pp. 4203–4215, 2005.
4. R. D. Carmichael, Expansions of arithmetical functions in infinite series, *Proceedings of the London Mathematical Society*, 1932.
5. N.-X. Chen, Z.-D. Chen, and Y.-C. Wei, Multidimensional inverse lattice problem and a uniformly sampled arithmetic Fourier transform, *Physical Review E*, vol. 55, no. 1, 1997.
6. S. S. Chen, D. L. Donoho, and M. A. Saunders, Atomic decomposition by basis pursuit, *SIAM Review*, vol. 43, No. 1, pp. 129–159, 2001.
7. W. Diffie and M. E. Hellman, New directions in cryptography, *IEEE Transactions on Information Theory*, vol. 22, no. 6, pp. 644–654, 1976.
8. D. L. Donoho, and Michael Elad. Optimally sparse representation in general (nonorthogonal) dictionaries via l1 minimization, *Proceedings of the National Academy of Sciences*, vol. 100, no. 5, pp. 2197–2202, 2003.

9. M. F. Duarte and R. G. Baraniuk, Spectral compressive sensing, *Applied and Computational Harmonic Analysis*, vol. 35, issue 1, pp. 111–129, 2013.

10. H. G. Gadiyar and R. Padma, Ramanujan-Fourier series, the Wiener-Khintchine formula, and the distribution of prime numbers, *Physica A*, vol. 269, pp. 503–510, 1999.

11. G. H. Hardy, *A Mathematician's Apology,* Cambridge University Press (Reissue edition), 2012 (originally published by Hardy in November 1940).

12. G. H. Hardy, Note on Ramanujan's trigonometrical function $c_q(n)$, and certain series of arithmetical functions, Proceedings of the Cambridge Philosophical Society, vol. 20, pp. 263–271, 1921 (reprinted in *Collected papers of G. H. Hardy,* vol. II, Oxford University Press, 1967, pp. 320–328.)

13. G. H. Hardy and E. M. Wright *An Introduction to the Theory of Numbers,* Oxford University Press, Inc., New York, 2008.

14. J. Maddox, Möbius and problems of inversion, *Nature*, vol. 344, no. 29, p. 377, 1990.

15. L. T. Mainardi, M. Bertinelli, and R. Sassi, Analysis of T-wave alternans using the Ramanujan Transform, Computers in Cardiology, vol. 35 pp. 605–608, 2008.

16. J. H. McClellan and C. M. Rader, *Number Theory in Digital Signal Processing,* Prentice Hall, Inc., Englewood Cliffs, N.J., 1979.

17. A. V. Oppenheim and R. W. Schafer, *Discrete Time Signal Processing,* Prentice Hall, Inc., Englewood Cliffs, N.J., 2010.

18. S.-C. Pei and K.-W. Chang, Odd Ramanujan sums of complex roots of unity, *IEEE Signal Processing Letters*, vol. 14, pp. 20–23, 2007.

19. M. Planat, Ramanujan sums for signal processing of low frequency noise, *IEEE International Frequency Control Symposium and PDA Exhibition*, pp. 715–720, 2002.

20. M. Planat, M. Minarovjech, and M. Saniga, Ramanujan sums analysis of long-periodic sequences and $1/f$ noise, *EPL Journal*, vol. 85, pp. 40005: 1–5, 2009.

21. S. Ramanujan, On certain trigonometrical sums and their applications in the theory of numbers, *Transactions of the Cambridge Philosophical Society*, vol. XXII, no. 13, pp. 259–276, 1918.

22. S. Samadi, M. Omair Ahmad, and M. N. S. Swamy, Ramanujan sums and discrete Fourier transforms, *IEEE Signal Processing Letters*, vol. 12, pp. 293–296, 2005.

23. R. O. Schmidt, Multiple emitter location and signal parameter estimation, *IEEE Transactions on Antennas and Propagation*, vol. 34, no. 3, 1986.

24. W. A. Sethares and T. W. Staley, Periodicity transforms, *IEEE Transactions on Signal Processing*, vol. 47, pp. 2953–2964, 1999.

25. M. R. Schroeder, The unreasonable effectiveness of number theory in science and communication, *IEEE ASSP Magazine*, pp. 5–12, Jan. 1988.

26. P. Stoica and A. Nehorai, MUSIC, maximum likelihood, and Cramer-Rao Bound, *IEEE Transactions on Acoustics, Speech, and Signal Processing*, vol. 37, no. 5, 1989.

27. L. Sugavaneswaran, S. Xie, K. Umapathy, and S. Krishnan, Time-frequency analysis via Ramanujan sums, *IEEE Signal Processing Letters*, vol. 19, pp. 352–355, 2012.

28. S. Tenneti and P. P. Vaidyanathan, Dictionary approaches for identifying periodicities in data, Proceedings of the IEEE Asilomar Conference on Signals, Systems, and Computers, Monterey, CA, November 2014.

29. J. A. Tropp, Greed is good: Algorithmic results for sparse approximation, *IEEE Transactions on Information Theory*, vol. 50, pp. 2231–2242, 2004.

30. P. P. Vaidyanathan, *Multirate Systems and Filter Banks*, Prentice Hall, Englewood Cliffs, N.J., 1993.

31. P. P. Vaidyanathan, Ramanujan-sum expansions for finite duration (FIR) sequences, Proceedings of the IEEE International Conference on Acoustics, Speech, and Signal Processing, Florence, Italy, 2014a.

32. P. P. Vaidyanathan, Ramanujan sums in the context of signal processing: Part I: fundamentals, IEEE Transactions on Signal Processing, vol. 62, no. 16, pp. 4145–4157, August, 2014b.

33. P. P. Vaidyanathan, Ramanujan sums in the context of signal processing: Part II: FIR representations and applications, *IEEE Transactions on Signal Processing*, vol. 62, no. 16, pp. 4158–4172, August, 2014c.

34. P. P. Vaidyanathan and P. Pal, The Farey-dictionary for sparse representation of periodic signals, *Proceedings of the IEEE International Conference on Acoustics, Speech, and Signal Processing*, Florence, Italy, 2014.

35. P. P. Vaidyanathan, S.-M. Phoong, and Y.-P. Lin, *Signal Processing and Optimization for Transceiver Systems*, Cambridge University Press, 2010.

36. M. J. Wainwright, Sharp thresholds for high-dimensional and noisy sparsity recovery using ℓ_1 constrained quadratic programming (Lasso), *IEEE Transactions on Information Theory*, pp. 2183–2202, 2009.

37. Y. Zhang, Bounded gap between primes, Annals of Mathematics, 2013.

Chapter 9

High-Dimensional Kernel Regression: A Guide for Practitioners

Felipe Tobar[a] and Danilo P. Mandic[b]

[a] *University of Cambridge, UK*
[b] *Imperial College London, UK*
fat25@cam.ac.uk, d.mandic@imperial.ac.uk

We provide a rigorous account of high-dimensional kernels (HDK), and illuminate their theoretical and practical advantages in nonlinear regression of multivariate signals. Our emphasis is on signal processing applications, supported by deep insight into the existence of higher-dimensional feature spaces, including complex, quaternion, and vector-valued reproducing kernel Hilbert spaces. Next, these existence conditions are used to elucidate the ability of kernel regression algorithms to extract rich relationships from available data. Practical examples of the advantages of the HDK paradigm include multimodal wind prediction, body sensor trajectory tracking, and nonlinear function approximation.

9.1 Introduction

Nonlinear estimation of multivariate data is a backbone of many modern signal processing applications but is highly non-trivial

Trends in Digital Signal Processing: A Festschrift in Honour of A. G. Constantinides
Edited by Yong Ching Lim, Hon Keung Kwan, and Wan-Chi Siu
Copyright © 2016 Pan Stanford Publishing Pte. Ltd.
ISBN 978-981-4669-50-4 (Hardcover), 978-981-4669-51-1 (eBook)
www.panstanford.com

and requires flexible and accurate estimation algorithms capable of learning data relationships from a large volume of available measurements. Models for nonlinear estimation are therefore a pre-requisite for a number of emerging applications (robotics, renewable energy, bioengineering), the growth of which is facilitated by rapid advances in sensor technology that have made the recording of structurally complex, multivariate and multimodal data a routine. Despite the vast amount of available data, information about the signal generating model is typically scarce; therefore, understanding the multiple-data relationships from the available observations can be regarded as a universal function approximation task. This opens the opportunity to design data-driven techniques such as neural networks, support vector machines and Gaussian processes, which are well equipped to bridge the gap between the very large dimensionality of the measured data and the typically low dimensionality of the estimated processes (see Zhang and Constantinides, 1992). For example, body sensor networks typically use six three-dimensional body sensors to estimate only a single scalar quantity—e.g. speed or pace length—analogously to the MISO problem (Biglieri et al., 2010).

The volume of research on kernel-based adaptive filtering and machine learning has been steadily growing over the last decade (Cristianini and Shawe-Taylor, 2000; Scholkopf and Smola, 2001; Liu et al., 2010; Kung, 2014), and several well-established algorithms already exist. For signal processing applications, the focus of kernel learning has been on learning strategies (e.g. least squares, least mean square and recursive least squares), and sparsification criteria (e.g. approximate linear dependence and coherence). However, results on non-homogeneous function estimation, whereby the functions to be estimated assume different forms in different regions of the input (regressor) space, are only emerging.

Our aim is to illuminate that high-dimensional kernels (i.e. hypercomplex- and vector-valued kernels (Tobar, 2014)) are perfectly equipped to fill this void in the open literature on non-homogeneous function estimation. We also establish the extent to which such multivariate mappings provide enhanced learning capability over standard, single-kernel, approaches.

This chapter is organised as follows: Section 9.2 provides an overview on kernel estimation, from the concept of reproducing kernel Hilbert spaces to different learning strategies and sparsification criteria. Sections 9.3 and 9.4 present respectively complex- and quaternion-valued kernels, their associated feature spaces and simulations on real-world data. Section 9.5 introduces vector-valued kernels from a feature-space point-of-view and illustrates their enhanced estimation capabilities through both synthetic and real-world examples. Section 9.6 concludes this chapter.

9.2 Background on Kernel Estimation

Support vector regression algorithms approximate nonlinear functions by mapping the input space to a higher-dimensional feature space; the output is then a linear transformation of the feature samples. In the supervised-learning setting considered in this chapter, the coefficients of this linear transformation, referred to as the *mixing parameters*, are calculated based on the observed input-output data.

9.2.1 *Support Vector Regression*

Consider the sets $X \subseteq \mathbb{R}^n$ and $D \subseteq \mathbb{R}$, related by the many-to-one *unknown* mapping[a]

$$f : X \longrightarrow D$$
$$\mathbf{x} \longmapsto y = f(\mathbf{x}) \tag{9.1}$$

and the set of N input-output pairs

$$S_N = \left\{ (\mathbf{x}_i, y_i) \in \mathbb{R}^{n \times 1} \text{ s.t. } y_i = f(\mathbf{x}_i) \right\}_{i=1:N}. \tag{9.2}$$

The function $f(\cdot)$ can then be approximated by mapping the input space X onto the infinite-dimensional feature space $\mathcal{H}$, according to $\phi : \mathbf{x} \in X \mapsto \phi_{\mathbf{x}} \in \mathcal{H}$, to yield the estimate in the

---

[a]For simplicity, we introduce only the scalar-output case. The vector-valued case is then equivalent to an ensemble of scalar-valued mappings. We denote vectors by boldface letters (e.g. $\mathbf{x}$).

form of an inner product in $\mathcal{H}$, given by

$$\widehat{f}(\mathbf{x}) = \langle A, \phi_{\mathbf{x}} \rangle \tag{9.3}$$

where $A \in \mathcal{H}$ and $\langle \cdot, \cdot \rangle$ denotes the inner product in $\mathcal{H}$.

The mixing parameters $A \in \mathbb{H}$ can now be approximated by their projection onto the so-called empirical feature space spanned by the features of the training set S_N, given by

$$H = \left\{ \phi \in \mathcal{H}, \text{ s.t. } \phi = \sum_{i=1}^{N} c_i \phi_{\mathbf{x}_i}, c_i \in \mathbb{R}, \mathbf{x}_i \in S_N \right\}. \tag{9.4}$$

This allows us to approximate A by $\hat{A} = \sum_{i=1}^{N} a_i \phi_{\mathbf{x}_i}$ for some coefficients $a_i \in \mathbb{R}$, and therefore to express the estimate of the unknown function f as

$$\widehat{f}(\mathbf{x}) = \left\langle \sum_{i=1}^{N} a_i \phi_{\mathbf{x}_i}, \phi_{\mathbf{x}} \right\rangle = \sum_{i=1}^{N} a_i \langle \phi_{\mathbf{x}_i}, \phi_{\mathbf{x}} \rangle. \tag{9.5}$$

Notice that the inner product in eq. (9.5) is a function of the mapping ϕ and the samples $\mathbf{x}_i, \mathbf{x}_j$, that is, $K(\mathbf{x}_i, \mathbf{x}_j) = \langle \phi_{\mathbf{x}_i}, \phi_{\mathbf{x}_j} \rangle$. Consequently, the estimate takes the form

$$\widehat{f}(\mathbf{x}) = \sum_{i=1}^{N} a_i K(\mathbf{x}_i, \mathbf{x}). \tag{9.6}$$

Observe that the design of the estimator no longer requires explicit knowledge of the feature samples $\phi_{\mathbf{x}}$, but only of their inner products, or equivalently, the function K. This class of functions is referred to as **reproducing kernels** and their properties are formalised in the following definition.

Definition 9.1 (Reproducing kernel (Mercer, 1909)).

A reproducing kernel is a continuous, symmetric, positive-definite function $K : X \times X \longrightarrow \mathbb{R}$, $X \subseteq \mathbb{R}^n$ (or $\mathbb{C}^n$), which admits the expansion

$$K(\mathbf{x}_i, \mathbf{x}_j) = \langle \phi_{\mathbf{x}_i}, \phi_{\mathbf{x}_j} \rangle, \tag{9.7}$$

*where $\phi : \mathbf{x} \in X \mapsto \phi_{\mathbf{x}} \in \mathcal{H}$ is a suitable static nonlinear mapping. The space spanned by these expansion functions is referred to as the **reproducing kernel Hilbert space (RKHS)** generated by the reproducing kernel K.*

Based on the Moore–Aronszajn theorem (Aronszajn, 1950), which states that for every reproducing kernel there is a unique RKHS, an estimator can be designed by choosing only the function K rather than the infinite-dimensional mapping ϕ, a much harder task.

The distinguishing advantage of such an estimator is that is does not require the calculation of inner products in the infinite-dimensional space $\mathcal{H}$, but only to evaluate the generating kernel K. This result is known as the *kernel trick* (Aizerman et al., 1964) and is shown to provide significant advantages in classification and nonlinear function estimation (Scholkopf and Smola, 2001; Liu et al., 2010; Kung, 2014). Consequently, many core signal processing algorithms, such as PLS, PCA, LMS and RLS have been re-introduced within the kernel framework, this procedure is referred to as *kernelisation*. These algorithms operate in higher-dimensional feature spaces but only require performing algebraic operations in the input space.

9.2.2 *Sparsification Criteria*

One caveat of online kernel algorithms is that, by virtue of including all the available samples $\mathbf{x}_{i=1:N}$ (referred to as *support vectors*) into the kernel estimator, the computational complexity of SVR increases without necessarily improving the estimate and calls for sparsification procedures. We next present the concept of dictionary and review three standard sparsification approaches for online kernel learning, these are designed with the aim to build a set of physically-meaningful support vectors in a recursive fashion.

Definition 9.2 (Dictionary). *The set of support vectors is referred to as dictionary and is denoted by $D = \{\mathbf{s}_i\}_{i=1:N}$.*

Sparsification criterion 1: Approximate linear dependence (ALD) (Engel et al., 2002). The ALD includes the observation $\mathbf{x}$ into the dictionary $D = \{\mathbf{s}_i\}_{i=1:N}$ when its feature sample $\phi(\mathbf{x})$ **does not** fulfil the condition

$$\delta = \min_{\mathbf{b} \in \mathbb{R}^N} \|[\phi(\mathbf{s}_1), \ldots, \phi(\mathbf{s}_N)]\,\mathbf{b} - \phi(\mathbf{x})\|^2 \le \eta \qquad (9.8)$$

for some $\eta > 0$.

In other words, if a feature sample is *approximately linearly dependent* with respect to the current dictionary, its inclusion would be redundant and the associated computational cost would not justify the (marginal) increase in performance.

Sparsification criterion 2: The novelty criterion (Platt, 1991). This sparsification criterion includes a sample $\mathbf{x}$ only if: (i) the norm of the predicted error is larger than a predefined threshold δ_e and (ii) the distance between the sample $\mathbf{x}$ and the dictionary $d(\mathbf{x}, D) = \min_{\mathbf{s}_i \in D} \|\mathbf{s}_i, \mathbf{x}\|$ is greater than some predefined threshold δ_d. This can be summarised as

$$\left\| y_i - \widehat{f}(\mathbf{x}) \right\| \geq \delta_e \tag{9.9}$$
$$\min_{\mathbf{s}_i \in D} \|\mathbf{s}_i - \mathbf{x}\| \geq \delta_d.$$

A kernel-specific variant of the novelty criterion is the so-called coherence criterion proposed in (Richard et al., 2009), which gives the relationship (9.9) in terms of kernel evaluations.

Sparsification criteria 3: Presence-based online sparsification (Tobar et al., 2014). This sparsification criterion consists of two steps: (i) an *acceptance/rejection* stage based on the novelty criterion (Platt, 1991; Richard et al., 2009), and (ii) an *elimination* stage based on a measure of the contribution of each dictionary sample in time. This instantaneous contribution is assessed by the *presence* of a dictionary sample $\mathbf{s}$ at time t, and is given by

$$p_t(\mathbf{s}) = K_G(\mathbf{s}, \mathbf{x}_t), \ t = 1, 2, \dots, \tag{9.10}$$

where K_G is a user-defined Gaussian kernel.

The acceptance/rejection and elimination stages ensure not only **a consistent dictionary**, but also that such a dictionary is representative of the active region within the input space and is neither redundant nor contains irrelevant information.

9.2.3 *Finding the Optimal Mixing Parameters: Ridge Regression and Least Mean Square*

The kernel ridge regression (KRR) algorithm. The KRR estimate is given by the regularised least-squares parameters $\mathbf{a} = [a_1, \dots, a_N]^T$ and can be found via the minimisation of the quadratic cost function

$$J = \frac{1}{2} \sum_{j=1}^{N} \left(y_j - \sum_{i=1}^{N} a_i K(\mathbf{x}_i, \mathbf{x}_j) \right)^2 + \frac{\rho}{2} \sum_{i=1}^{N} a_i^2, \qquad (9.11)$$

where $\{(\mathbf{x}_i, y_i)\}_{i=1,\dots,N}$ is a set of training pairs[a] and $\rho > 0$ is the regularisation parameter.

Setting $\frac{\partial J}{\partial \mathbf{a}} = \mathbf{0}$ and solving for $\mathbf{a}$, we obtain the optimal weight vector

$$\mathbf{a} = (\mathbf{K}^T \mathbf{K} + \rho \mathbf{I})^{-1} \mathbf{K}^T \mathbf{Y}, \qquad (9.12)$$

where $\mathbf{Y} = [y_1, \dots, y_N]^T$, $\mathbf{I}$ is the identity matrix, and $\mathbf{K}$ is the Gram matrix evaluated on the set of training samples, that is

$$\mathbf{K} = \begin{bmatrix} K(\mathbf{x}_1, \mathbf{x}_1) & \cdots & K(\mathbf{x}_1, \mathbf{x}_N) \\ \vdots & \ddots & \vdots \\ K(\mathbf{x}_N, \mathbf{x}_1) & \cdots & K(\mathbf{x}_N, \mathbf{x}_N) \end{bmatrix}. \qquad (9.13)$$

The kernel ridge regression algorithm provides enhanced offline learning capability and, via the regularisation parameter ρ, allows for trading estimation accuracy for a reduction in overfitting and enhanced generalisation ability.

The kernel least mean square (KLMS) algorithm. A natural adaptive extension to the kernel ridge regression is the KLMS algorithm. Denote the kernel estimator at time t by $\hat{y}_t = \sum_{i=1}^{N_t} a_{t,i} K(\mathbf{s}_i, \mathbf{x}_t)$, the weights vector $\mathbf{a}_t = [a_{t,1}, \dots, a_{t,N_t}]$, and the number of support vector at time t, N_t; the KLMS weight update is then given by

$$\mathbf{a}_{t+1} = \mathbf{a}_t + \mu e_{t+1} \mathbf{h}_t(\mathbf{x}_{t+1}), \qquad (9.14)$$

where $e_{t+1} = y_{t+1} - \sum_{i=1}^{N_t} a_{t,i} K(\mathbf{s}_i, \mathbf{x}_{t+1})$ and $\mathbf{h}_t(\mathbf{x}_{t+1}) = [K(\mathbf{s}_1, \mathbf{x}_{t+1}), \dots, K(\mathbf{s}_{N_t}, \mathbf{x}_{t+1})]$.

This update rule is obtained by searching for the optimal weight (in the feature space) via a gradient-based minimisation of the instantaneous square error. Additionally, Eq. (9.14), can be thought of as an optimisation procedure in the finite dimensional space of kernel mixing parameters $\mathbf{a}$, where, for a fixed dictionary, the kernel estimate **becomes parametric**. The sparsification criteria are crucial to prevent the KLMS update from becoming a prohibitively computationally-expensive estimator.

---

[a]For simplicity and without loss of generality, in this section we assume that all training samples are support vectors, that is, $\mathbf{s}_i = \mathbf{x}_i$, $\forall i$.

For more detail on the KLMS algorithm, as well as its normalised version, see Liu et al. (2008) and Richard et al. (2009).

9.3 Complex-Valued Kernels

We shall next introduce our first higher-dimensional kernel approach, which is based on complex-valued kernels. The standard RKHS theory (Mercer, 1909; Aronszajn, 1950) was initially established to cater for both real- and complex-valued RKHS, thus giving theoretical support for the implementation of complex-valued kernel algorithms. However, most of the real-world applications, from the original classification applications to more recent signal processing ones, only rely on real-valued kernels such as the polynomial or Gaussian kernels. Furthermore, the use of complex-valued kernels not only allows for enhanced modelling owing to their higher degrees of freedom, but also (in the bivariate case) for the existence of a feature space that is constructed upon the algebraic field where the input data resides, that is, the complex field $\mathbb{C}$. This makes it possible to take full advantage inherent to the topology of complex spaces (Mandic and Goh, 2009).

As the standard RKHS theory admits the use of complex-valued kernels, the design of complex kernel algorithms boils down to the design of complex-valued kernels. We now review the standard complex-valued Gaussian kernel and present a procedure for generating complex-valued kernels from real-valued ones.

9.3.1 *Complexification of Real-Valued Kernels*

The standard complex extension of the Gaussian kernel (Steinwart et al., 2006) is defined as

$$K_{\mathbb{C}}(\mathbf{x}, \mathbf{z}) = \exp\left(-\frac{(\mathbf{x} - \mathbf{z}^*)^T (\mathbf{x} - \mathbf{z}^*)}{\sigma^2}\right), \qquad (9.15)$$

where the symbol $(\cdot)^*$ denotes the complex conjugation operator.

The kernel in (9.15) has several interesting properties. As the argument of the exponential is a complex number, the kernel itself is complex-valued. Observe that by denoting $\mathbf{e}_r = \Re\{\mathbf{x} - \mathbf{z}^*\}$,

$\mathbf{e}_i = \Im\{\mathbf{x} - \mathbf{z}^*\}$, where the operators $\Re$ and $\Im$ denote, respectively, the real and imaginary part of a complex number, we can rewrite (9.15) as

$$K_{\mathbb{C}}(\mathbf{x}, \mathbf{z}) = \exp\left(-\frac{\mathbf{e}_r^T \mathbf{e}_r - \mathbf{e}_i^T \mathbf{e}_i + j 2\mathbf{e}_r^T \mathbf{e}_i}{\sigma^2}\right)$$

$$= \exp\left(\frac{\|\mathbf{e}_i\|^2 - \|\mathbf{e}_r\|^2}{\sigma^2}\right)\left(\cos\left(\frac{2\mathbf{e}_r^T \mathbf{e}_i}{\sigma^2}\right) - j\sin\left(\frac{2\mathbf{e}_r^T \mathbf{e}_i}{\sigma^2}\right)\right).$$

This reveals that the complex exponential kernel grows exponentially with $\|\mathbf{e}_i\|^2 - \|\mathbf{e}_r\|^2$. As a consequence, in gradient-based learning algorithms the magnitude of $K_{\mathbb{C}}$ boosts the learning stage; however, as the kernel grows unbounded when $\|\mathbf{e}_i\|^2 >> \|\mathbf{e}_r\|^2$, the kernel estimate will deviate considerably for the inputs that reside in some of the regions that are not yet learned. Another disadvantage is that, despite its enhanced estimation capability, it is rather difficult to find a physically-meaningful interpretation of $K_{\mathbb{C}}(\mathbf{x}, \mathbf{z})$ in terms of the samples $\mathbf{x}, \mathbf{z}$ unlike its real-valued counterpart $K_G = \exp(-\|\mathbf{x} - \mathbf{z}\|^2/\sigma^2)$. Figure 9.1 shows a contour plot for $K_{\mathbb{C}}(0, \mathbf{x})$, $\mathbf{x} \in \mathbb{C}$, using $\sigma^2 = 10^3$.

Another family of complex-valued kernels introduced in Tobar et al. (2012), termed *independent complex kernels*, can be defined by considering an arbitrary real-valued mapping defined over the

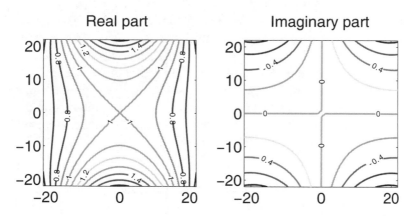

Figure 9.1 Contour plot of real and imaginary parts of the complex Gaussian kernel $K_{\mathbb{C}}$.

sample set $X \subseteq \mathbb{R}$

$$\phi : X \longrightarrow H \tag{9.16}$$

$$\mathbf{x} \longmapsto \phi_{\mathbf{x}},$$

where H is a real-valued RKHS. We can then define a complex-valued mapping over the complex set $\overline{X} = \{\mathbf{x}_r + j\mathbf{x}_i : \mathbf{x}_r, \mathbf{x}_i \in X\}$ by

$$\Phi : \overline{X} \longrightarrow \overline{H} \tag{9.17}$$

$$\mathbf{x}_r + j\mathbf{x}_i \longmapsto \phi_{\mathbf{x}_r} + j\phi_{\mathbf{x}_i},$$

where $\overline{H} = \{\phi_1 + j\phi_2, s.t. \ \phi_1, \phi_2 \in H\}$ is an RKHS of complex-valued functions. This makes it possible, through the kernel trick, to introduce a corresponding kernel given by

$$
\begin{aligned}
K_{i\mathbb{C}}(\mathbf{x}, \mathbf{z}) &= \left\langle \Phi_{\mathbf{x}_r + j\mathbf{x}_i}, \Phi_{\mathbf{z}_r + j\mathbf{z}_i} \right\rangle \\
&= \left\langle \phi_{\mathbf{x}_r} + j\phi_{\mathbf{x}_i}, \phi_{\mathbf{z}_r} + j\phi_{\mathbf{z}_i} \right\rangle \\
&= \left\langle \phi_{\mathbf{x}_r}, \phi_{\mathbf{z}_r} \right\rangle + \left\langle \phi_{\mathbf{x}_i}, \phi_{\mathbf{z}_i} \right\rangle + j \left(\left\langle \phi_{\mathbf{x}_i}, \phi_{\mathbf{z}_r} \right\rangle - \left\langle \phi_{\mathbf{x}_r}, \phi_{\mathbf{z}_i} \right\rangle \right) \\
&= K(\mathbf{x}_r, \mathbf{z}_r) + K(\mathbf{x}_i, \mathbf{z}_i) + j \left(K(\mathbf{x}_i, \mathbf{z}_r) - K(\mathbf{x}_r, \mathbf{z}_i) \right),
\end{aligned}
\tag{9.18}
$$

where K is the generating kernel associated with ϕ.

Remark 9.1. By choosing K to be a real Gaussian kernel K_G, the independent complex-valued kernel $K_{i\mathbb{C}}$ in (9.18) has an associated physical meaning: its real part accounts for the magnitude of the deviation of the samples while its imaginary part conveys a notion of the phase of such deviation.

As a consequence, for any arbitrary real kernel $K(\mathbf{x}, \mathbf{z})$ which provides a measure of deviation (*cf.* similarity) of its arguments $\mathbf{x}$ and $\mathbf{z}$, the independent complex kernel $K_{i\mathbb{C}}$ in (9.18) inherits this property and can thus be considered a generic complex-valued extension of K. Figure 9.2 shows the contour plot of an independent complex version of the real Gaussian kernel using $\sigma^2 = 10^3$, and illustrates that this kernel has a meaningful physical interpretation — its real part account for sample deviation, while its imaginary part models the phase between samples.

9.3.2 *Online Wind Prediction Using Complex-Valued Kernels*

We now illustrate the estimation ability of both complex Gaussian (CKLMS) and independent complex Gaussian (iCKLMS) kernels,

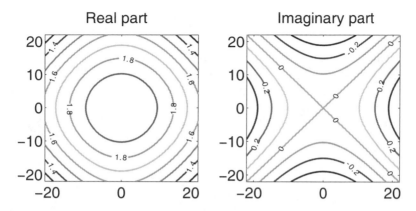

Figure 9.2 Independent complex Gaussian kernel in Eq. (9.15) with kernel width $\sigma^2 = 10^3$.

within an LMS-based update rule for the kernel mixing parameters, and benchmark them against the standard real-valued Gaussian kernel (RKLMS). The performances of these kernel algorithms were assessed for a prediction of 2D wind speed and direction. For this experiment, the coherence sparsification criterion was used (Richard et al., 2009), and a learning rate of $\mu = 0.05$. See Section 9.2.3 for detail on KLMS learning and sparsification criteria, (Tobar et al., 2012) for additional experiments, and (Bouboulis et al., 2012) for further applications of the complex Gaussian kernel.

The measurements represent the wind speed in the north-south (V_N) and east-west (V_E) directions, which admits a complex-valued representation in the form:

$$V = V_N + jV_E \qquad (9.19)$$

giving a non-circular and non-stationary complex signal (Mandic and Goh, 2009). The wind speed readings were taken[a] with a 2D ultrasonic anemometer at 50 [Hz]. The KLMS algorithms were used to predict the wind speed using six consecutive measurements (a regressor vector) from a signal consisting of 1000 samples. The quantitative performance measure was the steady-state logarithm of the mean-square error (MSE), $10 \log_{10}(\text{MSE})$, and is given

[a]The data is publicly available in http://www.commsp.ee.ic.ac.uk/mandic/research/wind.htm.

Table 9.1   MSE for wind prediction (last 500 samples)

	RKLMS	iCKLMS	CKLMS
$10\log_{10}(\mathrm{MSE})$	-21.1853	-22.5284	-23.5473

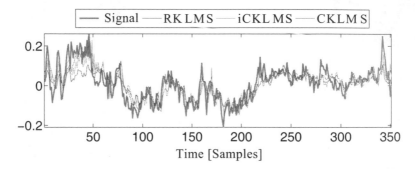

Figure 9.3   Original north-south wind speed component and KLMS estimates.

in Table 9.1 for each kernel. In addition, Fig. 9.3 shows the operation of all three KLMS algorithms for the first 350 samples when estimating the north-south component, also illustrating the convergence properties of the KLMS approach.

In terms of the average performance, observe that, due to its enhanced dimensionality, the complex kernels provided more accurate estimates than the real-valued one. Furthermore, the complex Gaussian kernel outperformed the independent complex one owing to its exponential dependence on the sample deviation that boosts the learning performance.

9.4 Quaternion-Valued Kernels

The use of complex-valued kernels in estimation applications has shown a clear advantage over real-valued kernels for bivariate signals. This motivates the extension to quaternion-valued kernels, in order to allow for the estimation of 3D and 4D signals while taking advantage of the quaternion ring as a division algebra. Unlike the complex case, where the existence of complex RKHS is guaranteed by the well-established theory, the design of quaternion-valued kernel algorithms requires a novel RKHS theory that accounts for quaternion-valued feature spaces. We next focus on the construction of these quaternion-valued RKHS, in order to use it as feature space in 3D and 4D kernel regression.

9.4.1 *Quaternion Reproducing Kernel Hilbert Spaces*

The construction of a quaternion RKHS (QRKHS) suitable for the implementation of kernel estimation algorithms requires a revised definition of quaternion Hilbert spaces, in order to verify that key results such as the Riesz representation and Moore-Aronszajn theorems also hold for the quaternion case.

Based on the non-commutativity of the quaternion division ring $\mathbb{H}$, we use the left vector spaces (Jacobson, 2009) to define both the quaternion Hilbert space and quaternion RKHS.

Definition 9.3 (Quaternion left Hilbert space). *A complete left vector space $\mathcal{H}$ is called a quaternion left Hilbert space if there is a quaternion-valued function $\langle \cdot, \cdot \rangle : \mathcal{H} \times \mathcal{H} \longrightarrow \mathbb{H}$ with the following properties $\forall \mathbf{u}, \mathbf{v}, \mathbf{z} \in \mathcal{H}$, and $p, q \in \mathbb{H}$:*

(1) $\langle \mathbf{u}, \mathbf{v} \rangle = \langle \mathbf{v}, \mathbf{u} \rangle^*$
(2) $\langle p\mathbf{u} + q\mathbf{v}, \mathbf{z} \rangle = p \langle \mathbf{u}, \mathbf{z} \rangle + q \langle \mathbf{v}, \mathbf{z} \rangle$
(3) $\langle \mathbf{u}, p\mathbf{v} + q\mathbf{z} \rangle = \langle \mathbf{u}, \mathbf{v} \rangle p^* + \langle \mathbf{u}, \mathbf{z} \rangle q^*$
(4) $\langle \mathbf{u}, \mathbf{u} \rangle \geq 0$ *and* $\langle \mathbf{u}, \mathbf{u} \rangle = 0 \iff \mathbf{x} = 0.$

With Definition 9.3 and the properties for the inner product in quaternion Hilbert spaces, we can now define both quaternion RKHS and quaternion kernels in a way analogous to the real and complex cases. These definitions are necessary requirements to establish the relationship between quaternion kernels and QRKHS.

Definition 9.4 (Quaternion reproducing kernel Hilbert space). *A quaternion left Hilbert space $\mathcal{H}$ of functions $\psi : X \rightarrow \mathbb{H}$ is a quaternion reproducing kernel Hilbert space (QRKHS) if the linear evaluation functional $L_\mathbf{x}(\psi) = \psi(\mathbf{x})$ is bounded $\forall \psi \in \mathcal{H}, \mathbf{x} \in X.$*

Definition 9.5 (Positive semidefinite kernel). *A Hermitian kernel* K, *i.e.* $K(\mathbf{x}, \mathbf{y}) = K^*(\mathbf{y}, \mathbf{x})$, *is positive semidefinite on* X *iff for any square-integrable function* $\theta : X \to \mathbb{H}, \theta \neq 0$, *it obeys*

$$\int_X \int_X \theta^*(\mathbf{x}) K(\mathbf{x}, \mathbf{y}) \theta(\mathbf{y}) d\mathbf{x} d\mathbf{y} > 0.$$

The above definitions allow the derivation of quaternion counterparts of key results of standard (real and complex) kernel learning algorithms. In particular, a quaternion extension of the Moore-Aronszajn theorem guarantees that for any QRKHS there exists a unique reproducing kernel, hence simplifying the construction of the QRKHS into the choice of a (quaternion) positive kernel. Furthermore, the quaternion Riesz representation theorem allows us to express inner products as kernel evaluations and therefore to use of the kernel trick in quaternion kernel estimation. For a full derivation of these theorems and a discussion on QRKHS, see Tobar and Mandic (2014).

Most existing quaternion kernel estimation approaches consider the quaternion-valued Gaussian kernel (Shilton and Lai, 2007) given by

$$K_{\mathbb{H}}(\mathbf{x}, \mathbf{y}) = \exp\left(-\frac{(\mathbf{x} - \mathbf{y}^*)^T (\mathbf{x} - \mathbf{y}^*)}{\sigma^2}\right). \qquad (9.20)$$

Observe that this kernel is equivalent to the real (complex) Gaussian kernel when the input is real (complex) valued.

9.4.2 *Body Motion Tracking Using Quaternion Kernels*

Real- and quaternion-valued Gaussian kernels were implemented within a ridge-regression setting to perform nonlinear multivariate prediction of real-world 3D inertial body sensor data. For results using a linear quaternion kernel, see Tobar and Mandic (2013).

Four accelerometers (placed at wrists and ankles) recorded the three Euler angles (Fig. 9.4), giving a total of 12 signals $\{\theta_s\}_{s=1,\dots,12}$ with the values in the range $[-\pi, \pi]$. To avoid discontinuities close to borders of the signals range, each signal θ_s was transformed via the invertible mapping $\theta_s \mapsto (\sin\theta_s, \cos\theta_s)$. The resulting body motion signal was a 24-dimensional real signal, or equivalently, a **a six-channel quaternion signal**.

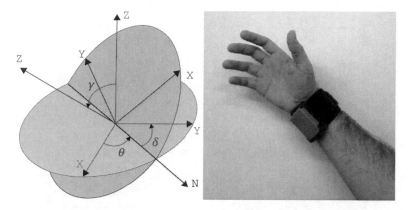

Figure 9.4 Inertial body sensors. (Left) Fixed coordinate system (red), sensor coordinate system (blue) and Euler angles (green). (Right) Body sensor placed at the right wrist.

Two regressors were considered to perform a one-step ahead prediction, so that the input and output pairs were respectively elements of $\mathbb{H}^{12}$ and $\mathbb{H}^6$; the training and validation sets were different Tai Chi sequences. The kernel width and the regularisation parameter were set to $\sigma^2 = 100$ and $\rho = 10^{-3}$ respectively.

Figure 9.5 shows the averaged prediction MSE and its standard deviation as a function of the number of support vectors for five independent 250-sample trials, for which the training samples were randomly chosen without repetition. Figure 9.6 shows the original

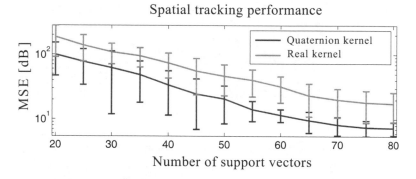

Figure 9.5 MSE and standard deviation for kernel algorithms as a function of the number of support vectors.

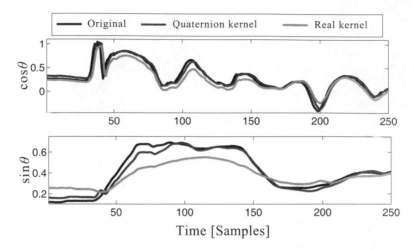

Figure 9.6 Original signals $\cos\theta$ (top) $\sin\theta$ (bottom) and their kernel estimates using 50 support vectors and 100 training samples.

values of $\cos\theta$, $\sin\theta$ and the kernel estimates for the case of 80 training samples, and the signal corresponding to the angle θ in Fig. 9.4.

Observe the superior performance of the quaternion-valued kernel algorithm. For the same number of support vectors it achieved considerably lower MSE compared to its real-valued counterpart. This highlights the enhanced function approximation capability of the four-dimensional full quaternion over real vectors. This is in line with the background theory, as quaternions exhibit advantage over real numbers in rotation and orientation modelling (the very purpose of inertial body sensors) and have thus become a standard in computer graphics.

9.5 Vector-Valued Kernels

Hypercomplex extensions of kernel regression algorithms have proven successful compared to single-kernel ones, however, they constrain the dimension of the feature space to be just bivariate (complex) or quadrivariate (quaternion) functions. The feature space approach to nonlinear estimation relies on a **sufficiently high-dimensional space** where the data relationship can be learned, therefore, multivariate kernel estimation will undoubtedly benefit from increasing the dimension of the feature space considered. We next introduce a general multiple-kernel approach which allows the kernels to be vector-valued (i.e. not constrained to two or four dimensions), the components of which can be independently chosen so as to account for different nonlinear properties.

From the RKHS perspective, the derivation of multi-kernel algorithms requires (i) a feature space of vector-valued functions, (ii) a kernel trick generalisation that yields the vector kernel, and (iii) a component-wise design of the kernels suited for the application at hand. For a comprehensive study on the derivation of vector-valued RKHS, see Tobar et al. (2014).

9.5.1 *A Vector-Valued Reproducing Kernel Hilbert Space*

Consider the input sample set $X \in \mathbb{R}^n$, a collection of M real-valued RKHS over X, $\{\mathcal{H}_i\}_{i=1:M}$, and define the set $\mathcal{H}$ containing the vector representation of the elements in $\mathcal{H}_i$, that is

$$\mathcal{H} = \{\mathbf{f} : X \longmapsto \mathbb{R}^M, \mathbf{f} = [f_1, \ldots, f_M]^T, f_i \in \mathcal{H}_i\}. \qquad (9.21)$$

This definition allows us to express the evaluation of $\mathbf{f} \in \mathcal{H}$ as

$$\mathbf{f}(\mathbf{x}) = \begin{bmatrix} f_1(\mathbf{x}) \\ \vdots \\ f_M(\mathbf{x}) \end{bmatrix} \in \mathbb{R}^M. \qquad (9.22)$$

We now need to demonstrate that the vector-valued space $\mathcal{H}$ in (9.21) has RKHS properties and that the expression $\mathbf{f}(\mathbf{x})$ in (9.22) admits an inner product decomposition that will allow for the use of the kernel trick and to identify the reproducing kernel of $\mathcal{H}$.

To prove that $\mathcal{H}$ is a vector-valued RKHS we must show that (i) it is a Hilbert space and (ii) for $\mathbf{f} \in \mathcal{H}$, the evaluation of $\mathbf{f}(\mathbf{x})$ is bounded $\forall \mathbf{x} \in X$. By construction, $\mathcal{H}$ is a complete vector space with both the inner product and norm inherited from the RKHS $\mathcal{H}_i$. Indeed,

$$\langle \mathbf{f}, \mathbf{g} \rangle = \sum_{i=1}^{M} \langle f_i, g_i \rangle_{\mathcal{H}_i}$$

$$\|\mathbf{f}\| = \sqrt{\langle \mathbf{f}, \mathbf{f} \rangle} = \sqrt{\sum_{i=1}^{M} \langle f_i, f_i \rangle_{\mathcal{H}_i}} = \sqrt{\sum_{i=1}^{M} \|f_i\|_{\mathcal{H}_i}^2},$$

where $\mathbf{f} = [f_1, \ldots, f_M]^T$, $\mathbf{g} = [g_1, \ldots, g_M]^T \in \mathcal{H}$, and $\langle \cdot, \cdot \rangle_{\mathcal{H}_i}$ and $\|\cdot\|_{\mathcal{H}_i}$ denote respectively the inner product and norm in $\mathcal{H}_i$.

For the Hilbert space $\mathcal{H}$ to be an RKHS we need to show that $\mathbf{f}(\mathbf{x})$ is bounded. This is achieved by considering

$$\|\mathbf{f}(\mathbf{x})\|^2_{\mathbb{R}^M} = \sum_{i=1}^{M} \|f_i(\mathbf{x})\|^2_{\mathbb{R}} \le \sum_{i=1}^{M} b_i^2 \|f_i\|^2_{\mathcal{H}_i}$$

$$\le \max_{i=1:M}\{b_i^2\} \sum_{i=1}^{M} \|f_i\|^2_{\mathcal{H}_i} = b^2 \|\mathbf{f}\|^2_{\mathcal{H}}, \quad (9.23)$$

where the inequalities $\|f_i(\mathbf{x})\|_{\mathbb{R}} \le b_i \|f_i\|_{\mathcal{H}_i}$ follow from the RKHS properties of $\mathcal{H}_i$ and $b = \max_{i=1:M}\{b_i\}$.

We shall now show that $\mathcal{H}$ has a reproducing property. Denote the *subkernels*, i.e. the kernels of the RKHS $\mathcal{H}_i$, by K_i and the subkernel functions by $K_i(\mathbf{x}) = K_i(\mathbf{x}, \cdot)$. The evaluation functional $\mathbf{f}(\mathbf{x})$ can then be expressed as

$$\mathbf{f}(\mathbf{x}) = \begin{bmatrix} f_1(\mathbf{x}) \\ \vdots \\ f_M(\mathbf{x}) \end{bmatrix} = \begin{bmatrix} \langle f_1, K_1(\mathbf{x}) \rangle \\ \vdots \\ \langle f_M, K_M(\mathbf{x}) \rangle \end{bmatrix} = \left[\begin{bmatrix} f_1 \\ \vdots \\ f_M \end{bmatrix}, \begin{bmatrix} K_1(\mathbf{x}) \\ \vdots \\ K_M(\mathbf{x}) \end{bmatrix} \right],$$

where the operator $[\cdot, \cdot]$ denotes the element-wise inner product, a vector-valued extension of the inner product, and the identities $\langle f_i(\mathbf{x}) \rangle = \langle f_i, K_i(\mathbf{x}) \rangle$ follow from the RKHS properties of $\mathcal{H}_i$. As a consequence, we can write the reproducing property in $\mathcal{H}$ as $\mathbf{f}(\mathbf{x}) = \left[\mathbf{f}, \vec{K}(\mathbf{x}) \right]$, where $\vec{K} = [K_1, \ldots, K_M]^T$ is the reproducing kernel of $\mathcal{H}$ and $\vec{K}(\mathbf{x}) = \vec{K}(\mathbf{x}, \cdot)$ is the kernel function.

The so-introduced multidimensional RKHS and its properties are analogous to the standard single-kernel learning paradigm. In particular, due to the multilinear construction of $\mathcal{H}$, a choice of a vector-valued kernel $\vec{K}$, with positive definite subkernels K_i, guarantees the existence of the corresponding RKHS $\mathcal{H}$ via the Moore–Aronszajn theorem. This is a key result for multikernel estimation where, in analogy to the standard theory, the implementation of vector-kernel estimation algorithms requires only the choice of a suitable set of subkernels.

To illustrate how the vector-valued kernels can be used in multiple kernel estimation, consider the support vectors $\{\mathbf{s}_i\}_{i=1:N}$

and the vector-kernel estimator

$$\widehat{y} = \sum_{i=1}^{N} \mathbf{a}_i \, \vec{K}\,(\mathbf{s}_i, \mathbf{x}) = \sum_{i=1}^{N} \sum_{j=1}^{M} \mathbf{a}_{i,j} K_j(\mathbf{s}_i, \mathbf{x}). \qquad (9.24)$$

The multikernel estimation can then be interpreted as a procedure for placing a different kernel, $\sum_{j=1}^{M} \mathbf{a}_{i,j} K_j(\mathbf{s}_i, \cdot)$, on each support vector, $\mathbf{s}_i$. As a consequence, the multikernel approach not only offers accurate estimation due to its higher number of degrees of freedom but also provides localised function approximation by combining different kernels in different regions of the input space, to fully account for observed data relationships.

9.5.2 *Nonlinear Function Approximation Using Multikernel Ridge Regression*

Multikernel learning benefits from large training sets. We now illustrate the learning capability of the multikernel concept on the estimation of a piecewise-differentiable continuous function. The function and the support vectors are shown in Fig. 9.7; all samples were considered for training.

We considered the Gaussian kernel, for which the optimal (least squares) width σ was found by exhaustive search, as this optimisation cannot be performed in closed form due to the nonlinear dependency of the kernel evaluation $K_G(\mathbf{x}, \mathbf{y}) = \exp(-\sigma^{-2} \|\mathbf{x} - \mathbf{y}\|^2)$ on σ. Fig. 9.8 shows the estimation error for the considered support vectors as a function of the kernel width; the global minimum is highlighted. This reveals that the best single-kernel estimate has an associated error of 3.11 (for $\sigma = 1.48$).

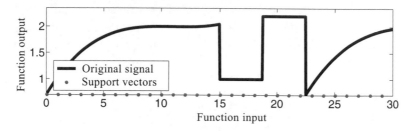

Figure 9.7   A nonlinear function and support vectors.

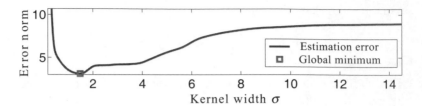

Figure 9.8   Norm of the training error for different values of the kernel width. The global minimum has the value of 3.11 and is reached for $\sigma = 1.48$.

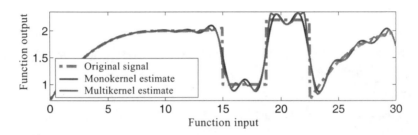

Figure 9.9   Nonlinear function estimation using mono- and multi-kernel ridge regression algorithms.

We next implemented a monokernel algorithm using $\sigma = 1.48$ and a two-kernel multikernel algorithm using two Gaussian kernels of widths $\sigma_1 = 1.48$ and $\sigma_2 = 0.24$. The parameter σ_2 was found by analysing the residual of the monokernel estimate. The estimates for both KRR algorithms are shown in Fig. 9.8 and the norm of the estimation error in Table 9.2.

Observe from Fig. 9.9 that multikernel estimation provided both reduced overshoot around $x = 15$ and suppressed oscillations in $x \in [25,30]$. Additionally, in terms of overall performance, the multikernel estimate was 8.7% more accurate than its monokernel counterpart. This experiment also reveals the ability of the

Table 9.2   Estimation error for mono- and multi-kernel ridge regression algorithms

Algorithm	Monokernel	Multikernel
‖Error‖	3.11	**2.86**

multikernel algorithm to provide a more localised estimation, a direct benefit from larger training sets, and also to assign tailored kernel combinations to each region of the input space.

9.6 Discussion

After revisiting the standard support vector regression framework, we have reviewed three approaches to higher-dimensional kernels (HDK): complex-, quaternion-, and vector-valued kernels. For each of these cases, we have discussed their theoretical requirements and have illuminated how their feature spaces allow for the design of kernel estimation algorithms. We have also shown that the HDK concept is flexible, as it admits different learning strategies and sparsification criteria. The enhanced estimation capability of the HDK approach has been demonstrated through real-world applications and benchmarked against their single-kernel counterparts.

Learning data relationships in higher-dimensional feature spaces has shaped up much of the research on universal function approximation in the 20th century. It is our firm conviction that HDKs are a fertile ground for both researchers and practitioners alike to undertake a quantum step forward to perform signal estimation using kernels, even when the underlying mappings are non-homogeneous and time-varying.

References

1. Aizerman, A., Braverman, E. M., and Rozoner, L. I. (1964). Theoretical foundations of the potential function method in pattern recognition learning, *Automation and Remote Control* **25**, pp. 821–837.
2. Aronszajn, N. (1950). Theory of reproducing kernels, *Transactions of the American Mathematical Society* **68**, 3, pp. 337–404.
3. Biglieri, E., Calderbank, R., Constantinides, A., Goldsmith, A., Paulraj, A. and Poor, H. V. (2010). *MIMO Wireless Communications* (Cambridge University Press).
4. Bouboulis, P., Theodoridis, S., and Mavroforakis, M. (2012). The augmented complex kernel LMS, *IEEE Transactions on Signal Processing* **60**, 9, pp. 4962–4967.

5. Cristianini, N., and Shawe-Taylor, J. (2000). *An Introduction to Support Vector Machines and Other Kernel-Based Learning Methods* (Cambridge University Press).

6. Engel, Y., Mannor, S., and Meir, R. (2002). Sparse online greedy support vector regression, in *Proceedings of the 13th European Conference on Machine Learning*, pp. 84–96.

7. Jacobson, N. (2009). *Basic Algebra I* (Dover).

8. Kung, S.-Y. (2014). *Kernel Methods and Machine Learning* (Cambridge University Press).

9. Liu, W., Pokharel, P. P., and Principe, J. C. (2008). The kernel least-mean-square algorithm, *IEEE Transactions on Signal Processing* **56**, 2, pp. 543–554.

10. Liu, W., Principe, J. C., and Haykin, S. (2010). *Kernel Adaptive Filtering: A Comprehensive Introduction* (Wiley).

11. Mandic, D. P., and Goh, S. L. (2009). *Complex Valued Nonlinear Adaptive Filters: Noncircularity, Widely Linear and Neural Models* (John Wiley & Sons).

12. Mercer, J. (1909). Functions of positive and negative type, and their connection with the theory of integral equations, *Philosophical Transactions of the Royal Society of London (A)* **209**, pp. 415–446.

13. Platt, J. (1991). A Resource-allocating network for function interpolation, *Neural Computation* **3**, 2, pp. 213–225.

14. Richard, C., Bermudez, J. C. M., and Honeine, P. (2009). Online prediction of time series data with kernels, *IEEE Transactions on Signal Processing* **57**, 3, pp. 1058–1067.

15. Scholkopf, B., and Smola, A. (2001). *Learning with Kernels: Support Vector Machines, Regularization, Optimization, and Beyond* (MIT Press, Cambridge, MA, USA).

16. Shilton, A., and Lai, D. (2007). Quaternionic and complex-valued support vector regression for equalization and function approximation, in *Proceedings of IJCNN*, pp. 920–925.

17. Steinwart, I., Hush, D., and Scovel, C. (2006). An explicit description of the reproducing kernel Hilbert spaces of Gaussian RBF kernels, *IEEE Transactions on Information Theory* **52**, 10, pp. 4635–4643.

18. Tobar, F. (2014). *Kernel-Based Adaptive Estimation: Multidimensional and State-Space Approaches*, Ph.D. thesis, Imperial College London.

19. Tobar, F., Kuh, A., and Mandic, D. (2012). A novel augmented complex valued kernel LMS, in *Proceedings of the 7th IEEE Sensor Array and Multichannel Signal Processing Workshop*, pp. 473–476.

20. Tobar, F., Kung, S.-Y., and Mandic, D. (2014). Multikernel least mean square algorithm, *IEEE Transactions on Neural Networks and Learning Systems* **25**, 2, pp. 265–277.

21. Tobar, F., and Mandic, D. (2013). The quaternion kernel least squares, in *Proceedings of IEEE ICASSP*, pp. 6128–6132.

22. Tobar, F., and Mandic, D. (2014). Quaternion reproducing kernel Hilbert spaces: Existence and uniqueness conditions, *IEEE Transactions on Information Theory* **60**, 9, pp. 5736–5749.

23. Zhang, S., and Constantinides, A. (1992). Lagrange programming neural networks, *IEEE Transactions on Circuits and Systems II: Analog and Digital Signal Processing* **39**, 7, pp. 441–452, doi:10.1109/82.160169.

Chapter 10

Linear Microphone Array TDE via Generalized Gaussian Distribution

Theodoros Petsatodis and Fotios Talantzis

Athens Information Technology, Greece

tpet@ait.edu.gr, fota@ait.gr

10.1 Introduction

Time delay estimation (TDE) algorithms are embedded in many applications related to localization and tracking of sources, as part of direction-of-arrival (DOA) estimating systems. Applications of interest include voice tracking, sonar and radars [1–3]. For the acoustic (voice) source tracking scenario that we will examine here, the problem is approached by employing distant microphone arrays for the collection of data in frames, so that the current TDE estimate can be provided. DOA estimation relies on identifying the relative delay between pairs of microphones using some statistical measure that returns a peak at the correct DOA of the source. Such systems are relevant in smart systems and critical infrastructure monitoring [4, 5].

Trends in Digital Signal Processing: A Festschrift in Honour of A. G. Constantinides
Edited by Yong Ching Lim, Hon Keung Kwan, and Wan-Chi Siu
Copyright © 2016 Pan Stanford Publishing Pte. Ltd.
ISBN 978-981-4669-50-4 (Hardcover), 978-981-4669-51-1 (eBook)
www.panstanford.com

The generalized cross-correlation (GCC) algorithm, proposed by Knapp and Carter [6], is generally considered the baseline method for TDE [7]. The typical limitation of GCC is that if the system is used in reverberant and noisy environments, the maximum cross-correlation could occur in an erroneous time-delay due to the reverberation of the room. Alternative methods have been proposed to overcome those issues, like multichannel cross-correlation coefficient (MCCC) [8], that takes advantage of the redundant information from multiple sensor pairs. However, for non-Gaussian source signals or with limited number of sensors, it is still not any better than GCC.

More recently, the information-theoretic metric of mutual information (MI) was employed in order to improve TDE [9]. Based on characterizing the speech source as Gaussian, the marginal MI measure was used for TDE. In addition, in order to overcome reverberation problems more effectively, the MI scheme was modified to encapsulate information about reflections, improving significantly the robustness of the estimator against reverberation. Nevertheless, for the algorithms above, it is assumed that the source is Gaussian distributed (GD), which is not accurate for speech. As depicted in [10–12] for several feature domains including time, Fourier transform (DFT), discrete cosine transform (DCT), and Karhunen Loeve transform (KLT), distributions of clean speech, can be better approximated by Laplacian (LD) and gamma distributions (ΓD).

On top of that, when far-field microphones are used instead of the conventional close-talking, reverberation effects, competitive sound sources, and speaker movement can alter the distribution of captured speech. It is thus apparent that speech cannot be expected to be solely GD, LD, or ΓD distributed, given its non-stationarity in time and its dependence on external interferences. Thus, speech processing systems relying solely on the Gaussian assumption fail to perform adequately under varying conditions.

Toward the direction of embedding super-Gaussian distributions for TDE, the authors in [13] worked on modelling speech with a Laplacian distribution. The relative delay was estimated via minimizing the joint entropy of the multiple microphone output signals. A comparison study [15] presenting performance differences when employing either Laplacian or Gaussian modelling on the information theoretical TDE of [9] was performed showing similar performance for both systems with in fact the Gaussian one performing marginally better. Although, the Laplacian framework presented in [13] was based on empirical approximations, in order to evaluate the expectations involved in TDE estimation and the multivariate LD, not allowing for a solid comparison.

In this chapter, we study information-theoretical time delay estimation for linear microphone arrays, using speech shaped distributions. To this end, the generalized Gaussian distribution (GGD) has been employed, allowing the investigation of the problem under a wider range of distributions, ranging from Gaussian to gamma with a more generalized view. The analysis performed, depicts that the employed marginal MI criterion TDE proposed in [9] does not depend on the underlying assumption for the distribution of speech as long as it belongs to the GGD. To extend the theoretical analysis, closed forms of the multivariate and univariate differential entropies for the GGD are derived for multiple equispaced microphones to take advantage of the additional information, encapsulating the entropies of other well known distributions like GD, LD and ΓD.

The chapter is organized as follows: In Section 10.2, the signal model and the statistical properties of speech in time and frequency domain are discussed along with the effects of noise and reverberation on the distribution of captured speech with far-field microphones. Section 10.3 reviews the employed mutual information based TDE scheme. The proposed generalized Gaussian based TDE is discussed in Section 10.4, along with the analysis showing that the mutual information TDE scheme is independent of the underlying assumption for the distribution modelling speech. Section 10.5 summarizes the chapter findings.

10.2 System Model Description

Speech signals captured within reverberant enclosures using far-field microphones are subject to superposition of reflected versions of the source signal. Additionally, the captured signal can be highly affected by competitive sound sources, background noise and possible movement of the source (e.g., walking speaker). Assuming a single speaker, the speech signal captured by a distant microphone array, bearing M microphones, at time t is

$$x_m(t) = h_m(t) * s(t) + n_m(t), \qquad (10.1)$$

where x_m denotes the signal captured by the mth microphone $s(t)$ the source speech signal at time t, $h_m(t)$ the corresponding acoustic impulse response, $n_m(t)$ the additive noise, and $*$ denotes convolution. $h_m(t)$ is a filter that contains not only the effect of the time in samples τ_m that it takes for the source signal to reach the mth microphone (direct path) but also that of several other delays created by the reverberant paths.

It has been shown that, pdf of source speech samples (assumed to be anechoic and noiseless) in the time domain and short-time frequency domain is much better modelled by a LD or a ΓD density function than a GD one [10–12].

The histogram of the source speech amplitude in both time and frequency domain is given in Figs. 10.1a and 10.1b, respectively. The histograms in this section have been derived from source speech signal segments, taken from a series of recordings performed using a close-talking microphone in the Anechoic Chamber of Aalborg University as described in [12, 16]. For taking STFT of the source, speech has been segmented using a time window of 40 msec and 75% overlap at $f_s = 16$ kHz.

As noise intensity and reverberation increase, the distribution of captured speech is expected to change. Figure 10.2a shows that in the presence of 0 dB of AWGN, the distribution of speech becomes GD. The effect of AWGN on the statistics of the amplitude of captured speech in the frequency domain is similar: the more the SNR increases, the more their distribution becomes GD-shaped. For 20 dB of AWGN, the distributions of higher-frequency amplitudes of captured speech are being shaped to LD (Fig. 10.2b), whereas for 15 dB, this is also what appears to happen with the amplitude of mid-frequency components. Further reduction of SNR transforms of low and mid-frequency amplitudes. Reverberation effect on the statistics of captured speech has been examined via the *Image Model for Small Room Acoustics* [17] for an increasing rate of reverberation time T_{60} on source speech signal [18]. The distribution of amplitudes

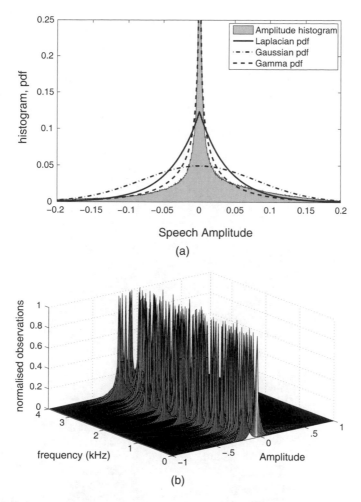

Figure 10.1 Time and frequency speech distribution. (a) Typical speech distribution histogram with three theoretical distributions fitted. (b) Speech frequency distribution histogram. Histograms are normalized to their maximum value per frequency bin.

for reverberant speech in time and frequency domain is depicted in Figs. 10.3a and 10.3b, respectively.

As the reverberation time increases over $T_{60} > 0.3$ sec, the distribution of time amplitude of captured speech tends to become LD. Similarly, the distribution of frequency amplitudes is also

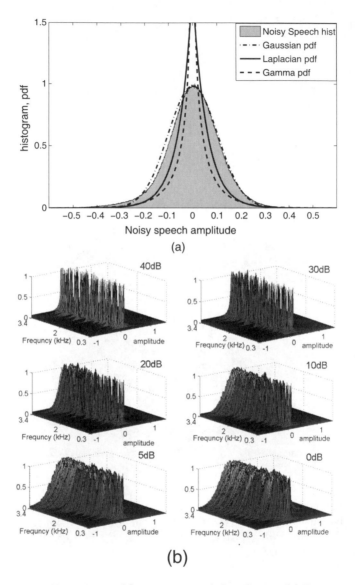

Figure 10.2 Noisy time and frequency speech distribution. (a) Noisy speech amplitude distribution for SNR = 0 dB and the three fitted theoretical pdfs. (b) Noisy speech amplitude distribution in frequency domain. Histograms have been normalized to their maximum value. The distributions of frequencies tend to be better approximated by GD as noise intensity increases. Higher frequencies are affected more than the lower ones due to less energy.

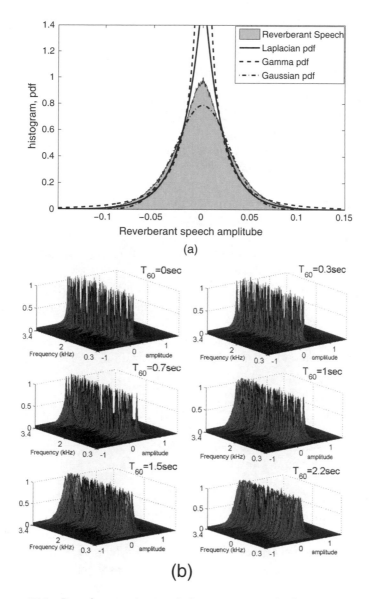

Figure 10.3 Reverberant time and frequency speech distribution. (a) Reverberant Speech Amplitude Distribution $T_{60} = 2.2$ sec and the three fitted theoretical distributions. (b) Effect of reverberation on the spectral amplitude of captured speech for various values of T_{60}. Histograms have been normalized to their maximum value.

affected by reverberation. Contrary to the case of AWGN though, the effect of reverberation on captured speech is evident only for high values of T_{60}. Only for reverberation times greater than 0.7 sec, the distribution of most of the captured reverberant speech frequency amplitudes is better modelled by a LD.

Reverberation usually coexists with additive noise sources in the same enclosure and thus, such distribution alterations are enhanced. Even low reverberation times (T_{60}) when combined with additive noise can have malicious effects on the performance of speech processing systems. This has been illustrated in [12] quantified in terms of Kolmogorov–Smirnov test [19].

10.3 Information Theoretical Time Delay Estimation

In general, GCC [6] and its variants like the GCC-PHAT [7] are the most common methods for TDE. They have the property of exhibiting a global maximum at the lag value that corresponds to the correct sample delay τ that is syncing the microphone recordings. The corresponding delay τ can be converted to the source's DOA angle θ by using

$$\theta = \arcsin\left[\frac{\tau c}{f_s d}\right],\tag{10.2}$$

where f_s is the sampling frequency of the recording system, and c is the speed of sound. Thus, the DOA can be obtained by estimating the TDE τ.

The problem of the GCC family algorithms is that they cannot perform adequately within reverberant environments described by the model of (10.1), failing to return accurate estimates of the relative delay τ. This becomes even more evident for relatively high T_{60} values.

10.3.1 *Mutual Information-Based TDE*

In order to overcome this drawback, some researchers steered their focus on methods employing information theory, aiming to remain robust under adverse conditions. One of them is Mutual Information, a measure of how much information one random variable contains about another random variable. Without loss of generality, we may consider the signals $x_1, x_2, \ldots, x_m$ and captured by two distant microphones $m_1, m_2, \ldots, m_m$ to be stationary stochastic processes, for which the MI between them is defined as [20]

$$I = H[x_1] + H[x_2(\tau)] + \ldots + H[x_m(\tau(m-1))]$$
$$- H[x_1, x_2(\tau), \ldots, x_m(\tau(m-1))], \tag{10.3}$$

where $H[x_m]$ is the differential entropy of x_m, and $H[x_1, x_2(\tau), \ldots, x_m(\tau(m-1))]$ is the joint entropy of the captured signal x_1 and the delayed by τ samples $x_2(\tau)$ and the delayed by $\tau(m-1)$ samples $x_m(\tau(m-1))$. In the scope of TDE, the problem of finding the correct relative delay between microphone signals is equivalent to finding the delay τ that maximizes (10.3). This practically means that when we determine this delay and synchronize the microphone signals, the information that one microphone signal has about the other will be maximum.

If we let x_n be an observation vector of a random variable, with density function $p(x_n)$, the differential entropy is defined as

$$H(x_n) = - \int p(x_n) \ln p(x_n) dx = -E\{\ln p(x_n)\}, \tag{10.4}$$

where $E\{\cdot\}$ denotes mathematical expectation.

If we now consider N observation vectors of random variables

$$x = [x_1 \quad x_2 \quad \ldots \quad x_N]^T \tag{10.5}$$

with joint density $p(x)$ their joint entropy will be

$$H(x) = - \int p(x) \ln p(x) dx = -E\{\ln p(x)\}. \tag{10.6}$$

Assuming that the random variables $x_1, x_2, \ldots, x_N$ are Gaussian distributed signals their multivariate normal distribution with zero mean and covariance matrix

$$R = E\{xx^T\} = \begin{bmatrix} \sigma_{x_1}^2 & r_{x_1x_2} & \cdots & r_{x_1x_N} \\ r_{x_1x_2} & \sigma_{x_2}^2 & \cdots & r_{x_2x_N} \\ \vdots & \vdots & \ddots & \vdots \\ r_{x_1x_N} & r_{x_2x_N} & \cdots & \sigma_{x_N}^2 \end{bmatrix} \tag{10.7}$$

will be given by

$$p_G(\mathbf{x}) = \frac{1}{\left(\sqrt{2\pi}\right)^N [\det(\mathbf{R})]^{\frac{1}{2}}} \exp^{-\frac{1}{2}\mathbf{x}^T\mathbf{R}^{-1}\mathbf{x}}. \qquad (10.8)$$

By substituting (10.8) into (10.6) we compute the joint multivariate Gaussian entropy

$$
\begin{aligned}
H_G^m(\mathbf{x}) &= -\int p_G(\mathbf{x})\ln p_G(\mathbf{x})d\mathbf{x} \\
&= \ln\left\{\left(\sqrt{2\pi}\right)^N [\det(\mathbf{R})]^{\frac{1}{2}}\right\} \int p_G(\mathbf{x})d\mathbf{x} + \frac{1}{2}\int p_G(\mathbf{x})\mathbf{x}^T\mathbf{R}^{-1}\mathbf{x}d\mathbf{x} \\
&= \frac{1}{2}\ln\left\{(2\pi)^N \det(\mathbf{R})\right\} + \frac{1}{2}E\left\{\mathbf{x}^T\mathbf{R}^{-1}\mathbf{x}\right\}.
\end{aligned}
\qquad (10.9)
$$

In order to evaluate the expectation $E\left\{\mathbf{x}^T\mathbf{R}^{-1}\mathbf{x}\right\}$ the trace property is employed so that $E\left[U^T V U\right] = E\left[tr(U^T V U)\right] = tr(V E\left[U U^T\right]) = tr(I) = N$ where N the size of the identity matrix [20].

Thus the joint multivariate Gaussian entropy will be

$$
\begin{aligned}
H_G^m(\mathbf{x}) &= \frac{1}{2}\ln\left\{(2\pi)^N \det(\mathbf{R})\right\} + \frac{1}{2}E\left\{\mathbf{x}^T\mathbf{R}^{-1}\mathbf{x}\right\} \\
&= \frac{1}{2}tr\left\{E\left[\mathbf{R}^{-1}\mathbf{x}\mathbf{x}^T\right]\right\} + \frac{1}{2}\ln\left\{(2\pi)^N \det(\mathbf{R})\right\} \\
&= \frac{1}{2}\ln\left\{(2\pi e)^N \det(\mathbf{R})\right\}
\end{aligned}
\qquad (10.10)
$$

Intuitively, the corresponding univariate entropy for any of the random variables $\mathbf{x_1}, \mathbf{x_2}, \ldots, \mathbf{x_N}$ is given by

$$H_G^u(x_n) = \frac{1}{2}\ln\left\{2\pi e\sigma_{x_n}^2\right\} \qquad (10.11)$$

If we assume that the source signal is zero-mean Gaussian distributed, the MI of (10.3) will be equal to [20]

$$I = -\frac{1}{2}\ln\frac{\det[\mathbf{C}(\tau)]}{C_{11}C_{12}\cdots C_{mm}} \qquad (10.12)$$

with $det[\cdot]$ the determinant operator and $\mathbf{C}(\tau)$ the joint covariance matrix of the microphone signals. For large frame size L (ideally $L \to \infty$) $\mathbf{C}(\tau)$ can be approximated as

$$
\mathbf{C}(\tau) \approx
\begin{bmatrix}
\mathbf{x_1} \\
\mathbf{x_2}(\tau) \\
\vdots \\
\mathbf{x_m}(\tau(m-1))
\end{bmatrix}
\begin{bmatrix}
\mathbf{x_1} \\
\mathbf{x_2}(\tau) \\
\vdots \\
\mathbf{x_m}(\tau(m-1))
\end{bmatrix}^{T}
$$

$$
=
\begin{bmatrix}
C_{11} & C_{12}(\tau) & \cdots & C_{1m}(\tau(m-1)) \\
C_{21}(\tau) & C_{22} & \cdots & C_{2m}(\tau(m-2)) \\
\vdots & \vdots & \ddots & \vdots \\
C_{m1}(\tau(m-1)) & C_{m2}(\tau(m-2)) & \cdots & C_{mm}
\end{bmatrix}.
$$

$$(10.13)$$

Note that C_{11}, C_{22} and C_{mm} are time-shift independent variables. The relative delay is obtained as that delay that maximizes (10.12) through the evaluation of $\hat{\tau} = \arg\max_\tau \{I\}$.

As described in [9], given the theoretical equivalence between maximizing the MI in (10.12) and the GCC algorithm, which is in fact the time-domain interpretation of the basic form of the GCC method, the MI-based estimator suffers from the same limitations of GCC and its PHAT variant, i.e. it would not be robust enough in multi-path environments. Thus, the MI calculation of (10.12) is not representative enough in the presence of reverberation.

In the anechoic case of (10.3), only a single delay is present in the microphone signals and thus, the measurement of the information contained in a sample l of x_1 is only dependent on the information contained in sample $l - \tau$ of $x_2(\tau)$. Nevertheless, within multi-path environments, the information of sample l of x_1 is also contained in neighbouring samples of sample $l - \tau$ of $x_2(\tau)$ due to the convolution operator in (10.1).

In order to estimate the information between the microphone signals, we use the marginal MI that considers jointly neighbouring samples and can be formulated as follows [9]:

$$
\begin{aligned}
I_{N(G)} = {} & H_G^u[\mathbf{x_1}] + H_G^u[\mathbf{x_1}(1)] + \ldots + H_G^u[\mathbf{x_1}(D)] + H_G^u[\mathbf{x_2}(\tau)] \\
& + H_G^u[\mathbf{x_2}(\tau+1)] + \ldots + H_G^u[\mathbf{x_2}(\tau+D)] + \ldots \\
& + H_G^u[\mathbf{x_m}(\tau(m-1))] + H_G^u[\mathbf{x_m}(\tau(m-1)+1)] + \ldots \\
& H_G^u[\mathbf{x_m}(\tau(m-1)+D)] - H_G^m[\mathbf{x_1}, \mathbf{x_1}(1), \ldots, \\
& \mathbf{x_1}(D), \mathbf{x_2}(\tau), \mathbf{x_2}(\tau+1), \ldots, \mathbf{x_2}(\tau+D), \ldots, \mathbf{x_m}(\tau(m-1)), \\
& \mathbf{x_m}(\tau(m-1)+1), \ldots, \mathbf{x_m}(\tau(m-1)+D)],
\end{aligned}
$$

$$(10.14)$$

which reduces to the following expression for the Gaussian distributed signals

$$I_{N(G)} = -\frac{1}{2}\ln\frac{\det[\mathbf{C}(\tau)]}{\det[\mathbf{C}_{11}]\det[\mathbf{C}_{22}]\cdots\det[\mathbf{C}_{mm}]} \tag{10.15}$$

with the joint covariance matrix

$$\mathbf{C}(\tau) \approx \begin{bmatrix} \mathbf{x}_1 \\ \mathbf{x}_1(1) \\ \vdots \\ \mathbf{x}_1(D) \\ \mathbf{x}_2(\tau) \\ \mathbf{x}_2(\tau+1) \\ \vdots \\ \mathbf{x}_2(\tau+D) \\ \vdots \\ \mathbf{x}_m(\tau(m-1)) \\ \mathbf{x}_m(\tau(m-1)+1) \\ \vdots \\ \mathbf{x}_m(\tau(m-1)+D) \end{bmatrix} \begin{bmatrix} \mathbf{x}_1 \\ \mathbf{x}_1(1) \\ \vdots \\ \mathbf{x}_1(D) \\ \mathbf{x}_2(\tau) \\ \mathbf{x}_2(\tau+1) \\ \vdots \\ \mathbf{x}_2(\tau+D) \\ \vdots \\ \mathbf{x}_m(\tau(m-1)) \\ \mathbf{x}_m(\tau(m-1)+1) \\ \vdots \\ \mathbf{x}_m(\tau(m-1)+D) \end{bmatrix}^T$$

$$= \begin{bmatrix} C_{11} & C_{12}(\tau) & \cdots & C_{1m}(\tau(m-1)) \\ C_{21}(\tau) & C_{22} & \cdots & C_{2m}(\tau(m-2)) \\ \vdots & \vdots & \ddots & \vdots \\ C_{m1}(\tau(m-1)) & C_{m2}(\tau(m-2)) & \cdots & C_{mm} \end{bmatrix}. \tag{10.16}$$

If D is chosen to be greater than zero, the elements of $\mathbf{C}(\tau)$ are now themselves matrices. In fact, for any value of τ, the size of $\mathbf{C}(\tau)$ is always $m(D+1) \times m(D+1)$ where $N = m(D+1)$. We call D the order of the tracking system.

10.4 Employing Generalized Gaussian Distribution

A Gaussian random variable has the highest entropy of all random variables for a given variance. Hence, a Gaussian random variable is, in some sense, the least predictable of all, which is why the GD is usually associated with noise. Information-bearing signals contain structures that make them more predictable than GD random variables [21]. Those characteristic structures directly affect the distributions of such signals which deviate significantly from GD. Thus, given that speech is fundamentally an information-bearing signal, one should look for more accurate representation of its distribution.

Furthermore, when it comes to acoustic environments, where the signal of interest is typically speech, GD modelling can be accurate only under specific conditions of reverberation and noise as was shown in Section 10.2. Thus, under the rough and inaccurate assumption of GD speech for TDE, performance reduction should be expected. Towards the direction of substituting the Gaussian entropy assumption with entropies the distributions of which fit better speech characteristics, the authors in [13] worked on the derivation of the Laplacian Entropy. Simulations performed under various reverberant conditions demonstrated that employing GD models results in performing similarly or slightly better than employing LD for TDE. Nevertheless, the Laplacian framework proposed includes several approximations that do not allow for a solid comparison (i.e. the multivariate LD, empirical approximations for the expectations) something that can possibly explain the reduced performance of LD contrary to one's expectations.

To examine how distributions of higher super-Gaussianity affect the performance of information theoretical TDE, the output changes of (10.14) have to be evaluated as we employ different underlying distributions. In order to deal with such comparisons along a wider set of distributions, we take advantage of the properties of the multivariate generalized Gaussian distribution (MGGD) [14].

The generalized Gaussian distribution represents an extension of the standard Gaussian distribution which comprises of three parameters, mean, variance and the shape parameter. The latter is a measure of the peakedness of the pdf, and allows the GG to approximate a large class of statistical distributions, including the Gaussian, the Laplacian, and the gamma distributions which are very close to the distribution of speech.

The N-dimensional zero-mean generalized Gaussian (GG) distribution for $x_1, x_2, \ldots, x_N$ is defined as [22]

$$p_{GG}(\mathbf{x}) = \frac{[\det(R)]^{-1/2}}{[Z(\beta)A(\beta)]^N} \exp\left\{-\frac{1}{2}[\mathbf{x}^T\mathbf{R}^{-1}\mathbf{x}]^{\frac{\beta}{2}}\right\}, \tag{10.17}$$

where β is the shape parameter. $Z(\beta) = \frac{2}{\beta}\Gamma\left(\frac{1}{\beta}\right)$ and $A(\beta) = \sqrt{\frac{\Gamma(1/\beta)}{\Gamma(3/\beta)}}$ with Γ the gamma function. The Gamma, Laplacian, Gaussian and uniform distributions are special cases of the GGD, with $\beta = \frac{1}{2}, \beta = 1, \beta = 2$ and $\beta = \infty$ respectively.

Through the GGD all multivariate expressions of distributions can be represented in a closed form avoiding the usage of approximations like in [13] that can potentially result in performance degradation.

The joint entropy for the generalized Gaussian random variables $\mathbf{x_1}, \mathbf{x_2}, \ldots, \mathbf{x_N}$ is given by

$$H_{GG}^m(\mathbf{x}) = -\int p_{GG}(\mathbf{x}) \ln p_{GG}(\mathbf{x})d\mathbf{x}$$

$$= -\int p_{GG}(\mathbf{x}) \ln\left[\frac{[\det(R)]^{-1/2}}{[Z(\beta)A(\beta)]^N} \exp\left\{-\frac{1}{2}[\mathbf{x}^T\mathbf{R}^{-1}\mathbf{x}]^{\frac{\beta}{2}}\right\}\right]d\mathbf{x}$$

$$= -\int p_{GG}(\mathbf{x}) \left[\ln\left\{\frac{[\det(R)]^{-1/2}}{[Z(\beta)A(\beta)]^N}\right\} - \frac{1}{2}[\mathbf{x}^T\mathbf{R}^{-1}\mathbf{x}]^{\frac{\beta}{2}}\right]d\mathbf{x}$$

$$= \int p_{GG}(\mathbf{x}) \left[-\ln\left\{\frac{[\det(R)]^{-1/2}}{[Z(\beta)A(\beta)]^N}\right\} + \frac{1}{2}[\mathbf{x}^T\mathbf{R}^{-1}\mathbf{x}]^{\frac{\beta}{2}}\right]d\mathbf{x}$$

$$= \frac{1}{2}\int p_{GG}(\mathbf{x}) [\mathbf{x}^T\mathbf{R}^{-1}\mathbf{x}]^{\frac{\beta}{2}} d\mathbf{x}$$

$$\quad - \ln\left\{\frac{[\det(R)]^{-1/2}}{[Z(\beta)A(\beta)]^N}\right\} \int p_{GG}(\mathbf{x})d\mathbf{x}$$

$$= \frac{1}{2}E\left\{[\mathbf{x}^T\mathbf{R}^{-1}\mathbf{x}]^{\frac{\beta}{2}}\right\} - \ln\left\{\frac{[\det(R)]^{-1/2}}{[Z(\beta)A(\beta)]^N}\right\}. \tag{10.18}$$

The expectation $E\left\{[\mathbf{x}^T\mathbf{R}^{-1}\mathbf{x}]^{\frac{\beta}{2}}\right\}$ in the left part of (10.18) cannot be evaluated through the *trace* property as for the case of multivariate Gaussian entropy in (10.9). The methodology proposed in [13] for evaluating the expectations for the Laplacian joint entropy could be followed instead. Nevertheless, using such approximations will result in an instant input dependent system, something definitely not beneficial for comparing TDE systems based on different distribution assumptions.

The specific expectation $E\left\{\left[\mathbf{x}^T\mathbf{R}^{-1}\mathbf{x}\right]^{\frac{\beta}{2}}\right\}$ is actually a Dirichlet integral of type 1 [14, 22, 23]. We note that the expectations over the whole parameter space $\mathfrak{R}^N$ of a function $\phi(\mathbf{x}^T\mathbf{R}^{-1}\mathbf{x}) = \phi(\mathbf{z}^T\mathbf{z}) \equiv \phi(u)$ with $u > 0$ for $\mathbf{x} \neq 0$ can be reduced to integrals over $\mathfrak{R}^+$ (for non-negative functions $\phi(u)$). Thus, for $\phi(u) = u^{(\beta/2)}$ the expectation becomes

$$
\begin{aligned}
E\left\{\left[\mathbf{x}^T\mathbf{R}^{-1}\mathbf{x}\right]^{\frac{\beta}{2}}\right\} &= \int_{\mathfrak{R}^N}\left[\mathbf{x}^T\mathbf{R}^{-1}\mathbf{x}\right]^{\frac{\beta}{2}} p_{GG}(\mathbf{x})d\mathbf{x} \\
&= \frac{[\det(R)]^{-1/2}}{[Z(\beta)A(\beta)]^N}\int_{\mathfrak{R}^N}\left[\mathbf{x}^T\mathbf{R}^{-1}\mathbf{x}\right]^{\frac{\beta}{2}}\exp^{\left\{-\frac{1}{2}\left[\mathbf{x}^T\mathbf{R}^{-1}\mathbf{x}\right]^{\frac{\beta}{2}}\right\}}d\mathbf{x} \\
&= \frac{[\det(R)]^{-1/2}}{[Z(\beta)A(\beta)]^N}\int_{\mathfrak{R}^N}\phi\left(\mathbf{x}^T\mathbf{R}^{-1}\mathbf{x}\right)\exp^{\left\{-\frac{1}{2}\left[\mathbf{x}^T\mathbf{R}^{-1}\mathbf{x}\right]^{\frac{\beta}{2}}\right\}}d\mathbf{x} \\
&= \frac{\beta}{\Gamma\left(\frac{N}{\beta}\right)2^{\left(\frac{N}{\beta}+1\right)}}\int_{\mathfrak{R}^+}\phi\left(u\right)u^{\frac{N}{2}-1}\exp^{\left(-\frac{1}{2}u^{\frac{\beta}{2}}\right)}du \\
&= \frac{\beta}{\Gamma\left(\frac{N}{\beta}\right)2^{\left(\frac{N}{\beta}+1\right)}}\int_{\mathfrak{R}^+}u^{\frac{\beta}{2}+\frac{N}{2}-1}\exp^{\left(-\frac{1}{2}u^{\frac{\beta}{2}}\right)}du \\
&= \frac{\beta}{\Gamma\left(\frac{N}{\beta}\right)2^{\left(\frac{N}{\beta}+1\right)}}\frac{2^{2+\frac{N}{\beta}}\Gamma\left(\frac{\beta+N}{\beta}\right)}{\beta} = \frac{2\Gamma\left(\frac{\beta+N}{\beta}\right)}{\Gamma\left(\frac{N}{\beta}\right)}.
\end{aligned}
$$

$$(10.19)$$

By substituting the expectation of (10.18) with (10.19) we get

$$
\begin{aligned}
H_{GG}^m(\mathbf{x}) &= -\int p_{GG}(\mathbf{x})\ln p_{GG}(\mathbf{x})d\mathbf{x} \\
&= \frac{2\Gamma\left(\frac{\beta+N}{\beta}\right)}{\Gamma\left(\frac{N}{\beta}\right)} - \ln\left\{\frac{[\det(R)]^{-1/2}}{[Z(\beta)A(\beta)]^N}\right\}.
\end{aligned}
$$

$$(10.20)$$

Given that β has to be $0.5 \leq \beta \leq 2$, (10.20) reduces to

$$
H_{GG}^m(\mathbf{x}) = \frac{N}{\beta} - \ln\left\{\frac{[\det(R)]^{-1/2}}{[Z(\beta)A(\beta)]^N}\right\}
$$

$$(10.21)$$

For the univariate case of the generalized Gaussian distributed variable x_n the entropy is

$$H_{GG}^u(x_n) = \frac{1}{\beta} + ln\left[2\Gamma\left(1 + \frac{1}{\beta}\right)\sigma_{x_n}\sqrt{\frac{\Gamma(1/\beta)}{\Gamma(3/\beta)}}\right] \qquad (10.22)$$

The theoretical solutions of (10.22), (10.21), derived through the evaluation of Dirichlet integrals match exactly the theoretically evaluated multi- and univariate entropies presented in (10.11), (10.10), for $\beta = 2$, and at the same time provide the multi- and univariate entropies over a wider family set of distributions that can be represented through the GGD.

Based on the evaluated expressions for generalized Gaussian Entropies the marginal MI (10.14) has been modified and used with the GG assumption to estimate the sample delay between signals received by a two-omni microphone array. The evaluation has been conducted for values of β in the range $0.5 \leq \beta \leq 2$ that correspond to distributions ranging from Gaussian, to gamma shaped. The resulting MI is depicted in Fig. 10.4.

The system's response is identical for the different values of β resulting in exactly the same sample delay estimation regardless of the assumed underlying distribution. Those results actually

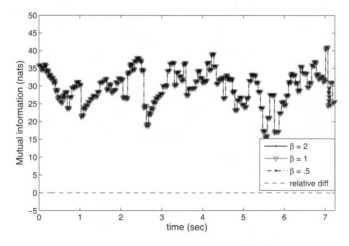

Figure 10.4 Marginal MI estimated for different values of the shape parameter β employing GGD and their sum of absolute relative differences.

indicate that the estimation of marginal MI does not depend on the underlying distribution.

Indeed, by substituting (10.21) and (10.22) in the estimation of the marginal MI (10.14) we have

$$I_{N(GG)} = H^u_{GG}[\mathbf{x_1}] + H^u_{GG}[\mathbf{x_1}(1)] + \ldots + H^u_{GG}[\mathbf{x_1}(D)] + H^u_{GG}[\mathbf{x_2}(\tau)]$$
$$+ H^u_{GG}[\mathbf{x_2}(\tau+1)] + \ldots + H^u_{GG}[\mathbf{x_2}(\tau+D)] + \ldots$$
$$+ H^u_{GG}[\mathbf{x_m}(\tau(m-1))] + H^u_{GG}[\mathbf{x_m}(\tau(m-1)+1)] + \ldots$$
$$H^u_{GG}[\mathbf{x_m}(\tau(m-1)+D)] - H^m_{GG}[\mathbf{x_1}, \mathbf{x_1}(1), \ldots,$$
$$\mathbf{x_1}(D), \mathbf{x_2}(\tau), \mathbf{x_2}(\tau+1), \ldots, \mathbf{x_2}(\tau+D), \ldots, \mathbf{x_m}(\tau(m-1)),$$
$$\mathbf{x_m}(\tau(m-1)+1), \ldots, \mathbf{x_m}(\tau(m-1)+D)]$$

$$= \frac{2(D+1)}{\beta} + \ln\left\{\left[2\Gamma\left(1+\frac{1}{\beta}\right)\sqrt{\frac{\Gamma(1/\beta)}{\Gamma(3/\beta)}}\right]^{2(D+1)}\right.$$

$$\left. \times\sqrt{\det[\mathbf{C_{11}}]\det[\mathbf{C_{22}}]\cdots\det[\mathbf{C_{mm}}]}\right\}$$

$$- \frac{2(D+1)}{\beta} - \ln\left\{\left[\frac{2}{\beta}\Gamma\left(\frac{1}{\beta}\right)\sqrt{\frac{\Gamma(1/\beta)}{\Gamma(3/\beta)}}\right]^{2(D+1)}\right.$$

$$\left. \times\sqrt{\det[\mathbf{C}]}\right\}$$

$$= \ln\frac{\beta\Gamma\left(1+\frac{1}{\beta}\right)\sqrt{\det[\mathbf{C_{11}}]\det[\mathbf{C_{22}}]\cdots\det[\mathbf{C_{mm}}]}}{\Gamma\left(\frac{1}{\beta}\right)\sqrt{\det[\mathbf{C}]}}$$

$$= -\frac{1}{2}\ln\frac{\det[\mathbf{C}(\tau)]}{\det[\mathbf{C_{11}}]\det[\mathbf{C_{22}}]\cdots\det[\mathbf{C_{mm}}]}. \tag{10.23}$$

The result is identical to the closed form marginal MI of (10.15) estimated for Gaussian assumed signals. This indicates that the evaluation of marginal MI is distribution independent, verifying the results depicted in Fig. 10.4. The outcome directly exploits MI invariance property that implies that if $\acute{X} = F(X)$ and $\acute{Y} = G(Y)$ are homeomorphisms, then $I(X, Y) = I(\acute{X}, \acute{Y})$ [24]. The underlying distribution assumption for the marginal MI estimation is a function of the β, shaping factor i.e. a linear invertible transformation. Thus, MI will be the same regardless of the β value for the given distribution family of GGD for the same covariance matrix. Although the invariance property is numerically extremely useful, it would not hold in general for other interdependence measures. Entropy for example, changes in general under a homeomorphism.

Furthermore, the solution shows that the illustrated difference in performance results in [15] indicating that the Laplacian based TDE in [13] is surpassed by the Gaussian case, emerges from the approximations used for the Laplacian multivariate distribution employed by the authors in [13] and the proposed empirical approximation for the evaluation of $E\left\{\left[\mathbf{x}^T\mathbf{R}^{-1}\mathbf{x}\right]^{\frac{\beta}{2}}\right\}$.

10.5 Conclusions

The advent of marginal mutual information TDE significantly improved the performance of DOA estimation systems in reverberant environments, compared to the baseline approaches such as GCC. Given that when captured by far-field microphones, the distribution of speech cannot be adequately modelled solely by Gaussian distribution, due to its highly varying nature and dependence on the noise and reverberation conditions, research steered its focus toward switching the underlying Gaussian distribution with a Laplacian to further improve the performance of this TDE criterion.

In this chapter we investigated how the performance of this robust information-theoretical TDE algorithm changes, as we switch between different underlying assumptions for the distribution of speech. By employing the generalized Gaussian distribution we investigate the problem under a wide range of super-Gaussian distributions ranging from Gaussian to Gamma. Moreover, we develop the framework of marginal Mutual Information TDE for multiple equispaced microphones of a linear array in order to take advantage of the additional information delivered with the increasing number of microphones.

The analysis performed, indicates that the examined marginal MI criterion for TDE is not dependent on the underlying assumption, for the distribution of speech, when it belongs to the family of generalized Gaussian distribution, with the same covariance matrix. This outcome directly exploits the invariance property of MI. To support the analysis, closed forms of the multivariate and univariate differential entropies for the generalized Gaussian distribution were derived, encapsulating the entropies of other well-known distributions like Gaussian, Laplacian and Gamma. Finally, it turns out that TDE enhancement utilising marginal mutual information can only be achieved by employing additional microphones as encapsulating speech shaped distributions results in the same outcome.

References

1. F. Talantzis, An acoustic source localization and tracking framework using particle filtering and information theory, *IEEE Transactions on Audio, Speech, and Language Processing* **18**, 1806–1817 (2010).

2. J. Li and R. Wu, An efficient algorithm for time delay estimation, *IEEE Transactions on Signal Processing* **46**, 2231–2235 (1998).

3. G. Carter, Time delay estimation for passive sonar signal processing, *IEEE Transactions on Acoustics, Speech and Signal Processing* **29**, 463–470 (1981).

4. ARGOS FP7-SEC-2012-1, Advanced pRotection of critical buildinGs by Overall anticipating System, (2012), URL http://www.argos-project.eu/(date last viewed 14/4/15).

5. DIRHA FP7-ICT-2011-7, Distant-speech Interaction for Robust Home Applications, (2012), URL https://dirha.fbk.eu/(date last viewed 14/4/15).

6. C. Knapp and G. Carter, The generalized correlation method for estimation of time delay, *IEEE Transactions on Acoustics, Speech and Signal Processing* **24**, 320–327 (1976).

7. M. Brandstein and D. Ward, *Microphone Arrays: Signal Processing Techniques and Applications* (Springer Verlag, Berlin Heidelberg), pp. 157–167 (2001).

8. J. Chen, J. Benesty, and Y. Huang, Robust time delay estimation exploiting redundancy among multiple microphones, *IEEE Transactions on Speech and Audio Processing* **11**, 549–557 (2003).

9. F. Talantzis, A. Constantinides, and L. Polymenakos, Estimation of direction of arrival using information theory, *Signal Processing Letters, IEEE* **12**, 561–564 (2005).

10. R. Martin, Speech enhancement using MMSE short time spectral estimation with gamma distributed speech priors, in *booktitle2002 IEEE International Conference on Acoustics, Speech, and Signal Processing (ICASSP)*, vol. 1, 253–256 (2002).

11. S. Gazor and W. Zhang, Speech probability distribution, *Signal Processing Letters, IEEE* **10**, 204–207 (2003).

12. T. Petsatodis, C. Boukis, F. Talantzis, Z.-H. Tan, and R. Prasad, Convex combination of multiple statistical models with application to VAD, *IEEE Transactions on Audio, Speech, and Language Processing* **19**, 2314–2327 (2011).

13. J. Benesty, Y. Huang, and J. Chen, Time delay estimation via minimum entropy, *Signal Processing Letters, IEEE* **14**, 157–160 (2007).

14. T. Petsatodis, F. Talantzis, C. Boukis, Z.-H. Tan, and R. Prasad, Exploring super-Gaussianity toward robust information-theoretical time delay estimation, *The Journal of the Acoustical Society of America* **133**, 1515–1524, number3 (2013).

15. F. Wen and Q. Wan, Robust time delay estimation for speech signals using information theory: A comparison study, *EURASIP Journal on Audio, Speech, and Music Processing*, 3 (2011).

16. E. Department, Aalborg university small anechoic room, (2012), URL http://doc.es.aau.dk/labs/acoustics/facilities/anechoic room small/ (date last viewed 5/30/12).

17. J. Allen and D. Berkley, Image method for efficiently simulating small-room acoustics, *Journal of Acoustical Society of America* **65**, pp. 943–950 (1979).

18. L. Kinsler, A. Frey, A. Coppens, and L. Sanders, *Fundamentals of Acoustics*, 4th ed. (John Wiley & Sons Inc. New York), pp. 336–338 (1999).

19. A. Glen, L. Leemis, and D. Barr, Order statistics in goodness-of-fit testing, *IEEE Transactions on Reliability* **50**, 209–213 (2001).

20. T. Cover, J. Thomas, J. Wiley, *Elements of Information Theory*, vol. 6 (John Wiley & Sons Inc. New York), pp. 542 (1991).

21. K. Kumatani, J. McDonough, B. Rauch, D. Klakow, P. Garner, and W. Li, Beamforming with a maximum negentropy criterion, *IEEE Transactions on Audio, Speech, and Language Processing* **17**, 994–1008 (2009).

22. G. Verdoolaege and P. Scheunders, On the geometry of multivariate generalized Gaussian models, *Journal of Mathematical Imaging and Vision* 1–14 (2011).

23. K. Fang and Y. Zhang, *Generalized Multivariate Analysis* (Science Press Beijing, Springer-Verlag Berlin Heidelberg), pp. 48–55 (1990).

24. A. Kraskov, H. Stögbauer, and P. Grassberger, Estimating mutual information, *Physical Review E* **69**, 066138 (2004).

Chapter 11

Recognition of Human Faces under Different Degradation Conditions

Soodeh Nikan and Majid Ahmadi

Electrical and Computer Engineering Department, University of Windsor,
401 Sunset Avenue, Windsor, Ontario, N9B 3P4, Canada
nikan@uwindsor.ca

Face recognition is considered as an effective biometric identification technique that is used in a wide range of applications such as video surveillance and law enforcement. In real-world scenarios, dramatic degradation occurs by illumination variation, facial expression, occlusion, head pose, aging effect, blur, and low resolution. In this chapter, the effect of illumination and occlusion, as two challenging appearance changes in unconstrained environment, on the face recognition algorithms is evaluated.

11.1 Introduction

Face recognition is one of the most remarkable image analysis and biometric identification techniques that is utilized in a wide range of applications such as human–computer interaction, law enforcement, video surveillance, and forensic investigation. An

Trends in Digital Signal Processing: A Festschrift in Honour of A. G. Constantinides
Edited by Yong Ching Lim, Hon Keung Kwan, and Wan-Chi Siu
Copyright © 2016 Pan Stanford Publishing Pte. Ltd.
ISBN 978-981-4669-50-4 (Hardcover), 978-981-4669-51-1 (eBook)
www.panstanford.com

automatic face recognition system has a significant capability in distinguishing individuals from their face images without the human cooperation requirement. It is composed of three main stages: image preprocessing, employed in order to enhance the appearance of face image and reduce the irrelevant effects, which might lead to misclassification of the image; feature extraction, which is carried out by utilizing an image descriptor to derive distinctive characteristics of image; and classification, which attributes the most probable identity label, among a large number of subject classes, to an unknown individual [12]. Although there exist many commercial face recognition algorithms that are highly accurate in constraint environment, it is still an extremely challenging computer vision research area due to the sensitivity of identification accuracy to the appearance variations that occur in uncontrolled conditions, such as illumination and head pose variation, facial expression, partial occlusion, blur and low resolution problem, and aging effect. In this chapter, illumination variation and partial occlusion will be addressed in detail, which are very crucial problems in real-world applications and mislead the face recognition algorithm considerably.

11.2 Illumination Variation Challenge

Illumination variation has a remarkable effect on the face appearance and the intra-subject changes in the images belonging to one person at different lighting conditions might be more significant than the inter-personal differences between two various individuals [1]. Therefore, it can reduce the accuracy of face recognition system substantially. Within the past few decades, different strategies have been applied in order to cope with the image degradation caused by lighting condition, which are divided into three categories: (i) illumination-insensitive image processing, which utilizes gray level transformations or gradient image to reduce the illumination effect, or extracts the reflection component and removes the lighting effect, (ii) illumination invariant image descriptors to extract image features that are insensitive to lighting effect and (iii) block-based pattern recognition techniques, which reduce the influence of degraded image sub-regions on the identification process [12, 28], where combination of all categories improves the recognition performance.

11.2.1 *Illumination-Insensitive Image Processing*

There exist a variety of image processing approaches to normalize the face image and remove the lighting influence. These techniques are divided into three categories as follows.

11.2.1.1 Intensity-level transformation

In this category of illumination-insensitive image processing, a linear or non-linear transformation is applied on the gray level images to map the intensity and correct the illumination effect to some extent [12]. Gamma correction (GC) [27] and histogram equalization (HE) [24] are two examples of non-linear gray-level transformations that correct the uneven intensity distribution of lighting effect in the image [12]. In GC, each image pixel is replaced with its gray value to the power of γ as follows [27]:

$$I = \begin{cases} I^\gamma & \text{for } \gamma > 0 \\ \log(I) & \text{for } \gamma = 0 \end{cases}, \quad \text{where} \quad \gamma \in [0, 1]. \qquad (11.1)$$

HE is a nonlinear transformation of the image intensity values, I, which enhances the image contrast by spreading the intensity distribution of image in order to create a new image with flat histogram [24] as follows:

$$T(I) = \text{floor}(L-1) \sum_{n=0}^{I} h(n), \qquad (11.2)$$

where $h(n)$ is image histogram and L is the maximum intensity level.

In order to further reduce the effect of lighting, the modified version of HE in the form of an orientated local histogram equalization (OLHE) was proposed in [17], where the illumination-insensitive face representation is captured while the rich face information on the edge orientations are preserved.

Difference of Gaussian (DoG) [18] is another gray scale transformation methods that is a band-pass filter, consisting of two low-pass filters with standard deviations σ_1 and σ_2, to enhance the edges in image. DoG at pixel position (xy) is as follows:

$$\text{DoG}\,(x,\,y) = \frac{1}{2\pi\sigma_1^2} e^{-\frac{x^2+y^2}{2\sigma_1^2}} - \frac{1}{2\pi\sigma_2^2} e^{-\frac{x^2+y^2}{2\sigma_2^2}}. \qquad (11.3)$$

11.2.1.2 Gradient-based techniques

Gradient-based preprocessing techniques find the illumination invariant representation of image using the fact that the illumination component of image, $L(x,\,y)$, changes slowly, in comparison with the abrupt variations in the reflection component, $R\,(x,\,y)$ [12]. In [40], based on the reflection image model, the illumination-insensitive representation of the face image, I, is derived using the arctangent of the ratio between directional derivatives of the face image, which is called gradient face (GF).

$$I\,(x,\,y) = R\,(x,\,y) \times L(x,\,y). \qquad (11.4)$$

$$\text{GF} = \tan^{-1}\left[\frac{\frac{\partial I(x,y)}{\partial y}}{\frac{\partial I(x,y)}{\partial x}}\right] = \tan^{-1}\left[\frac{L\,(x,\,y) \times \frac{\partial R(x,y)}{\partial y}}{L\,(x,\,y) \times \frac{\partial R(x,y)}{\partial x}}\right] = \tan^{-1}\left[\frac{\frac{\partial R(x,y)}{\partial y}}{\frac{\partial R(x,y)}{\partial x}}\right]. \qquad (11.5)$$

The authors improved their technique [37] by extracting the ratio of wavelet filtering of y-derivative of image over the x-derivative to obtain the multi-resolution illumination invariant analysis of the image.

The psychological law that was proposed by Ernst Weber in 1834 implies that the ratio between a noticeable variation in a stimulus and its original value is a constant [14]. Based on Weber's law, Wang et al. calculated the illumination-insensitive image representation by using the tangent inverse of the ratio between the local intensity variation, which is computed using the Laplace operator, and is called "Weber-face" (WF) [35].

$$WF = \tan^{-1}\left[\alpha \sum_{i\in A}\sum_{j\in A} \frac{I\,(x,\,y) - I\,(x - i\,\Delta x,\,y - j\,\Delta y)}{I\,(x,\,y)}\right]$$

$$= \tan^{-1}\left[\alpha \sum_{i\in A}\sum_{j\in A} \frac{L\,(x,\,y)\,.\,[R(x,\,y) - R(x - i\,\Delta x,\,y - j\,\Delta y)]}{L\,(x,\,y)\,.\,R(x,\,y)}\right]. \qquad (11.6)$$

Subspace learning-based approaches are also very popular techniques in illumination-insensitive image preprocessing. Tzimiropoulos et al. proposed principal component analysis (PCA) [32], linear discriminant analysis (LDA) [4], locally linear embedding (LLE) [25], and Laplacian Eigenmaps (LE) [5] learning methods to obtain a robust image representation against illumination variation based on the gradient orientations of image instead of the pixel gray values. The cosine kernel is employed to calculate the image correlation, which leads to robustness versus noise and outliers [33].

11.2.1.3 Reflection component estimation

Another category of illumination invariant preprocessing techniques is based on the estimation of reflectance component of the image [12]. Self-quotient image (SQI), proposed by Wang et al. [34], is the ratio between the input image and its smoothed version, using a smoothing kernel S, based on the concept of quotient method.

$$\text{SQI} = \frac{I}{\hat{I}} = \frac{I}{S.I}. \tag{11.7}$$

Wavelet transform has been used as a viable technique for illumination invariant image processing. Cao et al. [7] applied a denoising method on the high-frequency coefficients of the wavelet transform and the reflectance component has been considered as noise. Thresholding was proposed to remove noise; thus the luminance component was obtained and subtracted from the logarithmic image to extract illumination invariant component.

The luminance and reflection components were separated using the reflection model in logarithmic form in the proposed algorithm in [3].

$$\log\left(I\left(x, y\right)\right) = \log\left(R\left(x, y\right)\right) + \log\left(L\left(x, y\right)\right). \tag{11.8}$$

However, the authors utilized a normalized form of logarithm function to enhance the illumination, which can be tuned by two parameters, ξ and ϵ, as follows:

$$\hat{I}_{\text{pro}} = \xi \frac{\log\left(I\left(x, y\right)\right)}{\sqrt{\log\left(I\left(x, y\right)\right) - \epsilon}}. \tag{11.9}$$

In order to remove the illumination effect, they employed a double-density dual-tree complex wavelet transform (DD-DTCWT) with 32 directional wavelets to decompose the frequency sub-bands of the illumination-enhanced image and the high-frequency components are thresholded by the minimum frequency coefficient in every row of the high-frequency sub-bands. If the values of the frequency coefficients are greater than the threshold value, they are set to zero. The luminance component is preserved by thresholding the high-frequency sub-bands and reconstructing by inverse DD-DTCWT. The reconstructed image is subtracted from the logarithmic image to extract the reflection component. In order to further reduce the effect of illumination, low-pass filtering and edge amplifying were also applied on the reconstructed image. DD-DTCWT is utilized in this stage to extract the features of the illumination-insensitive image and extreme learning machine is applied as the classification technique [3]. Because of the poor scalability and slow learning of feed forward neural networks, extreme learning machine [13] is used. Therefore, the iterative weight adjustment is not required and it is extremely faster than feed forward neural network [13].

Discrete cosine transform (DCT) is another image transformation to separate the frequency sub-bands. Chen et al. applied DCT on the image logarithm [9] and by eliminating the low frequency DCT coefficients, which are related to lighting effect, the illumination variation was compensated. The authors applied the logarithmic form of reflection model as follows:

$$
\begin{aligned}
\log\left(I\left(x, y\right)\right) &= \log\left(R(x, y)\right) + \log\left(L\left(x, y\right)\right) \\
&= \log\left(R(x, y)\right) + \log(\hat{L}) + \epsilon\left(x, y\right), \quad (11.10)
\end{aligned}
$$

where $L(x, y)$ is the incident illumination component and $\hat{L}$ is the desired uniform illumination, which affects the image pixels uniformly, and $\epsilon(x, y)$ is the compensation term, which is the difference between normalized and original illumination effects. Due to the fact that luminance component varies slowly compared to the reflectance, it is the low frequency component of image [9].

The authors employed images containing only the face area since hair is a low frequency image component and varies by time changing, thus is not a stable feature. DCT is a redundancy reduction

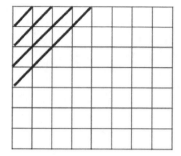

Figure 11.1   The manner in which the DCT coefficients are discarded.

based on a set of orthogonal cosine functions [9].

$$D\left(p,q\right) = \alpha\left(p\right)\alpha\left(q\right)\sum_{m=0}^{R-1}\sum_{n=0}^{C-1} I\left(m,n\right)\cos\left[\frac{\left(2m+1\right)p\pi}{2R}\right]$$

$$\times\cos\left[\frac{\left(2n+1\right)q\pi}{2C}\right], \tag{11.11}$$

where

$$\begin{cases} \alpha\left(p\right) = 1/\sqrt{R} & \text{if} \quad p = 0. \\ \alpha\left(p\right) = \sqrt{2}/R & \text{if} \quad p = 1, 2, \ldots, R. \\ \alpha\left(q\right) = 1/\sqrt{C} & \text{if} \quad q = 0. \\ \alpha\left(q\right) = \sqrt{2}/C & \text{if} \quad q = 1, 2, \ldots, C. \end{cases} \tag{11.12}$$

In order to discard the illumination effect the authors applied DCT on the logarithmic image and set the low frequency coefficients to zero. DCT of image results in a matrix of frequency coefficients of the same size as image. In [9] the authors illustrated that the coefficients with large values of standard deviation, corresponding to the low frequency components, are located in the top left corner of DCT coefficients matrix. Thus, an appropriate number of coefficients, in the manner shown in Fig. 11.1, are discarded to reduce the illumination effect on the image [9].

11.2.2 *Illumination-Invariant Image Descriptor*

Local binary pattern (LBP) is a histogram-based illumination-insensitive image descriptor [2]. Due to the comparison between the intensity values of the neighbor pixels, this technique is robust

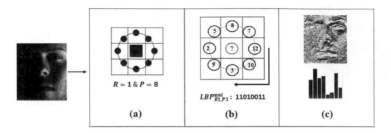

Figure 11.2 LBP. (a) Selecting neighborhood size, (b) comparing each pixel and its neighbors, (c) utilizing pixels decimal values to make image histogram.

against monotonic image variations with fast and easy execution and no learning requirement [2, 22]. As shown in Fig. 11.2, LBP extracts texture features of image by comparing each pixel with its neighbors, where R is radius of neighborhood region and P is the number of pixels in that region to compare with the centre pixel. Therefore, a P-bit binary pattern for each image pixel is constructed as illustrated in Fig. 11.2 and the corresponding decimal values are utilized to make the image histogram.

However, utilizing the combination of illumination-insensitive image processing and illumination invariant feature extraction techniques could lead to better performance. In the approach proposed by Tan and Triggs [30], a series of preprocessing techniques consists of GC [27], DoG filtering [18], masking and equalization of image contrast using HE [24], were utilized along with a kernelized illumination-insensitive local descriptor, which is the modification of LBP, called local ternary pattern (LTP).

11.2.3 *Block-Based Illumination-Invariant Pattern Recognition*

Holistic-based approaches, compared with block-based image analysis have less stability against intra personal variations. By employing the whole face image, appearance changes that occur in some regions of the image might influence all of the extracted features.

However, lighting effect may influence certain areas of human face. In such cases, local-based strategies are more adequate to cope

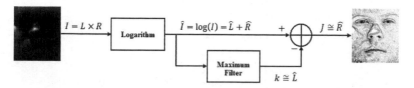

Figure 11.3 Illumination-insensitive image representation using Max filter [21].

with the local appearance changes where local face characteristics are extracted separately. Thus, degraded regions of face affect only the features of the corresponding sub-region. In addition, despite the stability of local-based approaches against intensity asymmetry caused by shadow in side-lighting, holistic-based methods do not tackle that problem properly [12]. Nabatchian et al. proposed a Max filtering technique on the logarithmic reflection model of image [21] in order to extract the luminance component. The output of maximum filter is subtracted from the logarithm image, which results in the illumination-insensitive image representation as shown in Fig. 11.3. The authors applied a local-based technique by dividing the illumination-insensitive image into non-overlapping image partitions and principal component analysis (PCA) was utilized to extract local features from different sub-blocks. Support vector machine (SVM) [6] was applied as the local classifier to assign class labels to the image partitions and they employed majority voting scheme to combine local decisions to find the best match in the gallery set for the corresponding probe image. Subsequently, the same feature extraction and classification techniques were applied on the whole face area as a holistic-based face recognition and its result was taken into account in the voting scheme. In order to vary the contribution of different sub-blocks in the classification of the probe image, the authors assigned an adaptive weight to each sub-block. The adaptive weight is the fusion of three different weights. First, the difference between the mean intensity value of pixels in each sub-block of the probe image and the corresponding sub-block in the canonical image is calculated, which shows the influence of illumination on that sub-region. The canonical image is the mean image of all gallery samples that have a good level of illumination. Smaller difference shows better illumination condition of the probe image sub-block, which means its local result should have more effect on the majority voting.

$$d_{sb}^P = m_{sb}^P - m_{sb}^{canonical}, \tag{11.13}$$

where m_{sb}^P and $m_{sb}^{canonical}$ are the mean gray value of the sub-block in the probe and canonical images, respectively [21]. The second proposed weight is based on the entropy or the information property of the probe image sub-block, which is calculated as follows:

$$En_{sb}^P = - \sum_{i=1}^{N_t} p_i \log (p_i) \tag{11.14}$$

where N_t shows the total number of gray levels in the probe image sub-block and p_i is probability of the ith intensity level [21]. The third proposed weight in [21] is calculated using the mutual information between the sub-block of the probe image and the corresponding sub-region in the reference image. The reference image is the mean image of the available gallery samples for the class of subject that is assigned to the sub-block of the probe image. The larger value of the mutual information indicates the greater similarity between two images. The mutual information of two random variables X and Y with marginal probability distribution functions, $p_1(x)$ and $p_2(y)$ and joint probability distribution function $p(x, y)$, is calculated as follows [21]:

$$\mu I (X, Y) = \sum_{x \in X} \sum_{y \in Y} p(x, y) \log \left(\frac{p(x, y)}{p_1(x) \cdot p_2(y)} \right) \tag{11.15}$$

The adaptive weight that is assigned to each sub-block in the probe image is calculated by combining the aforementioned local weights, which are normalized between 0 and 1 [21].

$$AWG_{sb}^P = \mu I_{sb}^P \times (En_{sb}^P)^2 \times (d^{max} - d_{sb}^P). \tag{11.16}$$

Figure 11.4 illustrates some images of the Yale B (YB) database [11], which contains 5760 images for 10 individuals with 576 viewing conditions (9 poses and 64 illumination conditions per pose). Their illumination-insensitive representations using the aforementioned techniques, DCT [9], DoG [18], gradient faces [40], LBP [2], maximum filter [21], SQI [34], Weber faces [35] and wavelet denoising [7], are shown in Fig. 11.4.

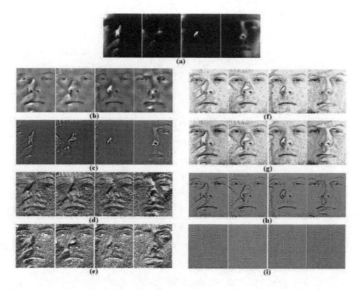

Figure 11.4 Samples of YB database: (a) Original images, and illumination-insensitive images using: (b) DCT [9], (c) DoG [18], (d) gradient faces [40], (e) LBP [2], (f) Max filter [21], (g) SQI [34], (h) Weber faces [35], and (i) wavelet denoising [7].

Moreover, the database is divided into five subsets corresponding to the angle between the light source and the camera axis, α; subset 1 consists of 7 images per subject, $(\alpha < 12°)$ and subsets 2 to 5 contain 12, 12, 14, and 19 images per subject, with $(20° < \alpha < 25°)$, $(35° < \alpha < 50°)$, $(60° < \alpha < 77°)$, and $(\alpha > 78°)$, respectively. Table 11.1 shows the recognition accuracies of the above methods when subset 1 is used as the gallery set and subsets 2–5, are employed as four probe sets [21].

11.3 Partial Occlusion Challenges

Occlusion is another crucial challenge in face recognition that occurs in real-world applications such as video surveillance in security controlling systems where the criminals try to cover some parts of their faces or occlusion caused by other people or objects in a crowded scene. Thus, the face area is occluded by an obstacle such

Table 11.1   Accuracy of the face identification algorithms for subsets 2–5 of the YB database (%)

Method	Subset 2	Subset 3	Subset 4	Subset 5
LBP [2]	100	97.6	65.2	44.4
DoG [18]	100	97.4	98.7	93.4
Weberface [35]	100	100	96.4	96.8
SQI [34]	100	100	96.4	97.9
DCT [9]	100	100	99.82	98.29
Gradientfaces [40]	100	100	99.28	100
Max+PCA/SVM+WVS [21]	100	100	99.29	100
Wavelet denoising [7]	100	100	100	100

as sunglasses, scarf, hat, or another face or object [8]. Therefore, some parts of facial information are lost, which can affect the accuracy of face identification and depending on the regions that are occluded and the size and texture of occlusion, accuracy reduction is different. In some cases, the non-occluded portion of image does not contain sufficient distinctive information and the face identification is difficult or impossible [29]. In holistic-based face description techniques such as PCA [32] and LDA [4], the whole face is applied to extract features and the occluded region of the face can affect the whole feature vector [26]. While, partial occlusion corrupts some areas of face and local-based descriptors are good alternatives in order to tackle the partial occlusion problem where the face image is divided into small patches and local degradation affects the local features of the corresponding occluded regions. The effect of occluded areas on the recognition system can be reduced by detecting the occlusion [26]. Occluded image partitions can be determined by training the face recognition system using both occluded and non-occluded sample. Gabor filter [10], with PCA as a dimensionality reduction technique, was applied in [26] to extract the characteristics of image sub-regions and train the face recognition system by occluded and non-occluded sample. SVM [6] was utilized to attribute the occluded or non-occluded labels to sub-regions of the probe image and LBP [2] extracted features of non-occluded partitions. However, in real-world and uncontrolled situations, the available database does not contain occluded image samples and in some cases we have only one training sample per individual available. In such cases, we need to apply an information theory technique in order to detect the occluded parts according to the information content of the image partitions. As soon as we categorize the image patches as occluded or non-occluded, there are two categories of face recognition approaches available to deal with partially occluded images. In the first group, we can reconstruct the corrupted parts by a reconstruction technique and apply a face recognition technique on the repaired image. Second category consists of methods where the occluded parts are excluded from the identification process and face recognition is carried out using the information extracted from the non-occluded areas, or local weights are assigned to image sub-regions and the influence of corrupted regions, on the face recognition process, is reduced by devoting lower weights those regions [16]. In this chapter, the second category of identification approaches is considered.

11.3.1 *Excluding Occluded Face Regions or Reducing Their Effect*

In this category of occluded face recognition techniques, the image completion or reconstruction is not carried out due to the fact that it is not fast enough and computationally cost effective and requires a large set of training samples. Therefore, the recognition is based on a local-based technique and excluding the occluded pixels or minimizing their effect on the recognition algorithm [16]. A local probabilistic subspace method was used by Martinez [20] for occluded face recognition with one sample per subject by dividing image into sub-blocks and finding the subspace for each sub-region in order to project the sub-blocks in the training set to the eigenspaces. For a probe image, the kth sub-block, P_{sb}^k, was projected to the corresponding eigenspace and the local probability for each sub-region was calculated using the projected sub-block of probe image, $\hat{P}_{\text{sb}}^k$, and mean, $\mu_{j,k}$, and covariance, $\Psi_{j,k}$, of the subspace as follows:

$$\text{LocProb}_{j,k} = \left(\hat{P}_{\text{sb}}^k - \mu_{j,k}\right) \cdot \Psi_{j,k} \cdot \left(\hat{P}_{\text{sb}}^k - \mu_{j,k}\right), \quad (11.17)$$

where $k = 1, 2, \ldots, N_{\text{sb}}$ and $j = 1, 2, \ldots, N_C$. N_{sb} and N_C are the number of sub-blocks and number of classes, respectively. The local probabilities were taken into account and summed up and the maximum of its argument calculated as the class label of probe image [20].

$$\text{Class} = \text{argmax}_j \left\{ \sum_{k=1}^{N_{\text{sb}}} \text{LocProb}_{j,k} \right\}. \tag{11.18}$$

J. Kim et al. proposed a local-based face recognition algorithm [23] by dividing image into a finite number of non-overlapping sub-blocks and the occluded sub-regions were detected using a nearest neighbor classifier on the PCA sub-space and then identification based on a selective local non-negative matrix factorization (LNMF) was carried out. LNMF bases in the occluded regions are detected by calculating the portion of total energy that belongs to an occluded region for each LNMF, as follows:

$$E_i = \frac{\sum_{x,y \in W} B_i^2(x, y)}{\sum_{x=1}^{R} \sum_{y=1}^{C} B_i^2(x, y)}, \quad i = 1, 2, \ldots, N_b, \tag{11.19}$$

where $B_i(r, c)$ is the value of the ith LNMF at (x, y) image coordinate, W is the detected occluded face region, $R \times C$ is the size of image and N_b is the total number of LNMF bases. If the energy value is greater than a threshold, that basis is considered as an occluded LNMF. Data projection is carried out using only the non-occlude bases, the energy value of which is smaller than the threshold. For a probe image the set of corresponding occlusion-free bases is $B = [b_1, b_2, \ldots, b_M]$, where its pseudo inverse, B^{PI}, is used to project the probe image and gallery set to the occlusion-free LNMF subspace [23].

$$\hat{P} = B^{\text{PI}} \times P. \tag{11.20}$$

$$\hat{G}_i = B^{\text{PI}} \times G_i, \tag{11.21}$$

where P and G_i are probe and i^{th} gallery images, respectively, and $\hat{P}$ and $\hat{G}_i$ are their projection coefficients in the LNMF subspace [23]. Coefficients of the probe and gallery images are compared to find the closest match.

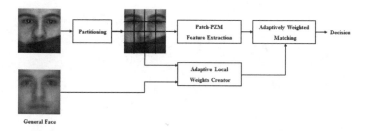

Figure 11.5 Block diagram of the proposed algorithm in [15].

Kanan et al. in [15] proposed pseudo Zernike moment (PZM), to extract features of image sub-regions. As shown in Fig. 11.5, the sample face image of size $M \times M$ pixels from the AR database, which contains 3536 facial images of 136 people (76 men and 60 women) affected by partial occlusion (scarf or sunglasses) [19], is partitioned into equal-sized and non-overlapping sub-blocks of $w \times w$ resolution. Each sub-region is bounded inside a unit circle and the sub-block coordinates, x_i and y_j, are mapped to the polar form.

$$\begin{cases} x_i = -\frac{\sqrt{2}}{2} + \frac{\sqrt{2}}{w-1}i, & i = 0, 2, \ldots, w-1. \\ y_j = +\frac{\sqrt{2}}{2} - \frac{\sqrt{2}}{w-1}j, & j = 0, 2, \ldots, w-1. \end{cases} \tag{11.22}$$

The PZMs, based on a set of orthogonal pseudo Zernike polynomials, are extracted from image sub-block, $I_{r,c}(x_i, y_j)$, at location (r, c) as follows [15]:

$$\mathrm{PZM}_{p,q}^{r,c}\left(I(x_i, y_j)\right) = \frac{p+1}{\pi \lambda(w)} \sum_{j=0}^{w-1} \sum_{i=0}^{w-1} Z_{p,q}^*(x_i, y_j)$$
$$\times I\left(w(r-1) + x_i, w(c-1) + y_j\right) \tag{11.23}$$

where $r, c = 1, 2, \ldots, M/w \lambda(w) = \frac{w^2}{2}$ is the normalization factor employed for mapping to the unit circle and $Z_{p,q}^*(x, y)$ is the complex conjugate of the pseudo Zernike polynomial. Finally, the feature vector of the face image is constructed by concatenating the local PZMs of image sub-blocks. The distance between the probe and gallery images, P and G, respectively, is as follows [15]:

$$D(P(r, c), G(r, c)) = \sum_{r=1}^{M/w} \sum_{c=1}^{M/w} \text{AWM}_{r,c}(a, b)$$

$$\times \left\{ \sum_{p=0}^{p_{\max}} \sum_{q=0}^{p} [|\text{PZM}_{p,q}^{r,c}(P(x_i, y_j))| \right.$$

$$\left. - |\text{PZM}_{p,q}^{r,c}(G(x_i, y_j))|]^2 \right\} \qquad (11.24)$$

$$\text{AWM}_{r,c}(a, b) = (\text{AOM}_{r,c}(a, b))^2 \cdot \text{CM}_{r,c}(a, b), \quad a, b = 1, 2, \ldots, W, \tag{11.25}$$

where $\text{AOM}_{r,c}(a, b)$ is the adaptive occlusion map that shows the difference between PZM features of the sub-region in the probe image and the corresponding sub-region in the general image, where the general image is the average of all gallery samples. Also, $\text{CM}_{r,c}(a, b)$ is the contribution map of the probe image sub-block according to the information content of that sub-region, which is obtained by calculating the local entropy value in the image sub-block using (11.14). The values of CM and AOM are normalized and between 0 and 1 [15].

A sparse representation was proposed by Wright and et al. [36], where the choice of feature transformation is not critical anymore but it requires many sample images per class. A general classification was proposed based on sparse representation. The probe sample can be represented sparsely as a linear combination of gallery samples of the same class [36]. The matrix of gallery samples is as follows:

$$\bar{G} = [\bar{G}_1, \bar{G}_2, \bar{G}_3, \ldots, \bar{G}_N]. \tag{11.26}$$

$$\bar{G}_i = [G_1^i, G_2^i, G_3^i, \ldots, G_{N_{\bar{G}_i}}^i], \tag{11.27}$$

where $\bar{G}_i$ is the matrix of gallery samples of the ith class and G_k^i is the feature vector of the kth sample in $\bar{G}_i$. N_C and $N_{\bar{G}_i}$ are the number of classes and gallery samples per i^{th} class, respectively. A probe image can be represented as follows [36]:

$$\bar{P} = \bar{G} \times \bar{C}. \tag{11.28}$$

$\bar{C} = [0, 0, \ldots, 0, c_1^i, c_2^i, \ldots, c_L^i, 0, 0, \ldots, 0]$, where c_j^i is the jth coefficient associated with the ith class and L is the number of gallery samples per i^{th} class. In order to find the coefficient vector of the corresponding probe image, we need to solve the l_1-minimization problem as follows:

$$(l_1): \quad \hat{C}_1 = \text{argmin} \left\| \bar{C} \right\|_1 \quad \text{while } \bar{P} = G \times C. \tag{11.29}$$

The authors showed the important factor to recover the sparse representation and correctly assign the class label to the probe image is the dimension of the feature space, which should be large enough and the l_1-norm solution being sufficiently sparse, thus the selection of feature space is not considerable. The robustness versus occlusion was undertaken by the assumption that the error occurred by partial occlusion has a sparse basis due to the fact that it affects just a fraction of image pixels. Therefore, the linear model in (11.28) is extended as follows [36]:

$$\bar{P} = \left(\bar{G} \times \bar{C} \right) + e, \tag{11.30}$$

where e is the error vector and a small portion of its elements are nonzero. The location and magnitude of error that is caused by occlusion is unknown. The equation (11.30) is modified and the sparsest solution is found by solving the l_1-minimization as follows [36]:

$$\bar{P} = [\bar{G}, \, I] \begin{bmatrix} \bar{C} \\ e \end{bmatrix} = \hat{G} \times V, \tag{11.31}$$

$$(l_1): \quad \hat{V}_1 = \text{argmin} \left\| V \right\|_1 \quad \text{while } \bar{P} = \hat{G} \times V, \tag{11.32}$$

where $\hat{V}_1 = \left[\hat{C}_1, \hat{e}_1 \right]$ and the occlusion is removed by setting $\bar{P}_r = \bar{P} - \hat{e}_1$.

Nikan and Ahmadi proposed a local-based face recognition under occlusion by using one gallery sample per individual in the database [22]. Figure 11.6 illustrates the block diagram of their proposed algorithm. The face image is partitioned into equal-sized and non-overlapping sub-blocks. The accuracy of the face recognition algorithm can be affected by the size of image sub-blocks. Utilizing very large sub-blocks is not computationally cost effective and does not satisfy the block-based idea. However, very

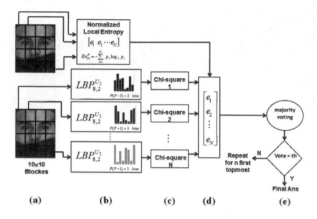

Figure 11.6 Proposed algorithm in [22]. (a) Image sub-division, (b) LBP on each sub-block, (c) local nearest neighbor classifiers, (d) local entropy calculation, (e) majority voting scheme and thresholding maximum vote to find final decision.

small image partitions cannot provide satisfactory discriminative information [31]. LBP descriptor, which is robust to rotation, scaling, and illumination variation, is applied on the image sub-blocks to extract local texture features. LBP procedure is carried out on each image partition and binary patterns are employed to construct local histograms for image sub-blocks. In order to reduce the feature dimensionality, the authors took only uniform binary patterns into account [22]. The binary code is uniform if there are at most two bitwise transitions from 0 to 1 or 1 to 0. Each local histogram contains $P\,(P-1)+2$ bins for uniform and 1 bin for all non-uniform patterns [2]. Local histograms of probe image sub-regions are compared with the histograms of corresponding sub-blocks in the gallery samples and classified using local Chi-square-based nearest neighbor classifier, which is one of the most accurate histogram similarity metrics as follows [2, 18]:

$$X^2\left(P^{\text{sb}}, G^{\text{sb}}\right) = \sum_{i=1}^{P(P-1)+3} \frac{\left(h_j^{P^{\text{sb}}} - h_j^{G^{\text{sb}}}\right)^2}{h_j^{P^{\text{sb}}} + h_j^{G^{\text{sb}}}}, \qquad (11.33)$$

where P^{sb} and G^{sb} are the sub-blocks of the probe and gallery images, and $h_j^{P^{\text{sb}}}$ and $h_j^{G^{\text{sb}}}$ are the jth histogram bins of the probe and gallery sub-blocks, respectively.

The main advantage of the local-based face recognition techniques is their capability to reduce the influence of occluded image partitions on the recognition result by assigning lower weights to the occluded regions, since they are ineffective in differentiating between facial images of different individuals, and emphasizing on the sub-blocks containing discriminative information [22]. Local entropy, (11.14), was proposed in [22], which provides weights based on the information property of image sub-blocks. Local classifiers' decisions were combined and identity of the corresponding probe image was determined by adopting a decision fusion strategy. The authors [22] utilized weighted majority voting approach, which is straightforward without learning requirement. The majority of sum of calculated local weighted votes gives the final class label.

Zhang et al. proposed LBP on the magnitude of Gabor features as the local Gabor binary pattern histogram (LGBPH) technique [38]. Representation of 2-D Gabor filter is similar to the human visual system. Gabor extracts image features at different scales and orientations, which is the multiplication of a sinusoid function by a Gaussian kernel as follows [10]:

$$\psi_{s,o}(x,y) = \frac{f_s^2}{\pi \delta \theta} \times e^{-\left[\left(\frac{f_s^2 \hat{x}^2}{\delta_x^2}\right)+\left(\frac{f_s^2 \hat{y}^2}{\delta_y^2}\right)\right]} \times e^{-(j2\pi \cdot f_s \cdot \hat{x})}, \qquad (11.34)$$

$$\begin{cases} s = 0, 1, 2, \ldots, S_{\max}-1 \\ o = 0, 1, 2, \ldots, O_{\max}-1 \\ \hat{x} = +x\cos(\beta_o) + y\sin(\beta_o) \\ \hat{y} = -x\sin(\beta_o) + y\cos(\beta_o), \end{cases} \qquad (11.35)$$

where $S_{\max}$ and $O_{\max}$ are the maximum number of scale and orientation, respectively. $\beta_o = (o\pi)/8$, $f_s = f_{\max}/(\sqrt{2})^s$, $f_{\max}$ is the maximum frequency of the filters, and δ_x and δ_y are the sharpness of the x- and y-axes, respectively. In order to obtain Gabor images, the image is convolved with a filter bank of $S_{\max} \times O_{\max}$ filters. As shown in Fig. 11.7, Gabor images are divided into small sub-blocks and LBP histograms are extracted from each sub-region and concatenated to make the feature vector of the image [38].

Zhang et al. also proposed another face recognition algorithm, with robustness against occlusion, using the same LGBPH technique

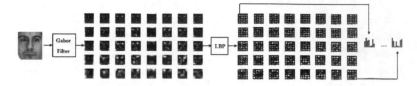

Figure 11.7 Proposed face recognition approach in [38].

as in [38] and employed the Kullback–Leibler divergence (KLD)-based method in order to assign weighs to the local histograms in the concatenation stage and reduce the effect of occluded image partitions by assigning lower weights to those regions [39]. KLD between the histograms of occluded sub-regions and the mean histogram of gallery sub-blocks is calculated as follows:

$$\text{KLD}_j = \sum_{i=1}^{N_b} H_j^P(i) \times \log\left(\frac{H_j^P(i)}{\hat{H}_j(i)}\right) \qquad j = 1, 2, \ldots, N_b, \tag{11.36}$$

$$\hat{H}_j = \frac{1}{N_G} \sum_{i=1}^{N_G} H_j^{G_i}, \tag{11.37}$$

where H_j^P and $H_j^{G_i}$ are the histograms of jth sub-block in the probe and i^{th} gallery images and N_b and N_G are the number of histogram bins and non-occluded gallery images, respectively. Probability of occlusion in the image sub-blocks is obtained by comparing the local KLD's with a threshold [39].

Table 11.2 shows recognition accuracies of mentioned occlusion-robust face recognition techniques on AR database [19] with 50 random subjects and for each individual only the first sample with neutral expression in session 1 is used in the gallery set and images with sunglasses and scarves in session 1 and 2 are employed in four probe sets [22].

11.4 Conclusion

The performance of commercial face recognition systems is extremely degraded in real-world applications such as law enforcement and security surveillance due to lighting variation, partial

Table 11.2 Accuracy of the face identification algorithms for AR database (%)

Method	Session 1		Session 2	
	Sunglasses	Scarf	Sunglasses	Scarf
Loc-Pb[20]	80	82	54	48
LGBPH[38]	80	98	62	96
KL-LGBPH[39]	84	100	80	96
AWPPZM[15]	70	72	59	60
LBP-MV[22]	100	100	100	100

occlusion, facial expression, blur, effect or head pose. In this chapter, a variety of state of the art face recognition strategies to deal with the appearance changes caused by illumination variation and partial occlusion are studied. Illumination-insensitive face recognition methods are divided into three groups: illumination-insensitive preprocessing, illumination invariant descriptors, and block-based pattern recognition. Moreover, partial occlusion corrupts some portion of discriminative facial information. Local-based techniques are applied where the effect of occluded regions, on the identification performance, is excluded or reduced.

References

1. Adini, Y., Moses, Y., and Ullman, S. (1997) Face recognition: The problem of compensating for changes in illumination direction, *IEEE Trans. Pattern Anal. Mach. Intell*, 19, pp. 721–732.

2. Ahonen, T., Hadid, A., and Pietikainen, M. (2004) Face recognition with local binary patterns, *Lect. Notes. Comput. Sc.*, **3021**, pp. 469–481.

3. Baradarani, A., Wu, Q. M. J., and Ahmadi, M. (2013) An efficient illumination invariant face recognition framework via illumination enhancement and DD-DTCWT filtering, *Pattern Recogn.*, **46**, pp. 57–72.

4. Belhumeur, P. N., Hespanha, J. P., and Kriegman, D. J. (1997) Eigenfaces vs. Fisherfaces: Recognition using class specific linear projection, *IEEE Trans. Pattern Anal. Mach. Intell.*, **19**, pp. 711–720.

5. Belkin, M., and Niyogi, P. (2003) Laplacian eigenmaps for dimensionality reduction and data representation, *Neural Comput.*, **15**, pp. 1373–1396.

6. Burges, C. J. C. (1998) A tutorial on support vector machines for pattern recognition, *P. Soc. Photo Opt. Ins.*, **2**, pp. 121–167.

7. Cao, X., Shen, W., Yu, L. G., Wang, Y. L., and Yang, J. Y. (2012) Illumination invariant extraction for face recognition using neighboring wavelet coefficients, *Pattern Recogn.*, **45**, pp. 1299–1305.

8. Charoenpong, T. (2010) A survey of face occlusion detection for visual surveillance system, *Proc. Int. Conf. Knowl. Smart Tech.*, KST, pp. 24–25.

9. Chen, W., Er, M. J., and Wu, S. (2006) Illumination compensation and normalization for robust face recognition using discrete cosine transform in logarithm domain, *IEEE Trans. Syst. Man. Cyb.*, **36**, pp. 458–466.

10. Daugman, J. (1988) Complete discrete 2-d Gabor transform by neural networks for image analysis and compression, *IEEE Trans. Acoust. Speech Signal. Process.*, **36**, pp. 1169–1179.

11. Georghiades, S., Belhumeur, P. N., and Kriegman, D. J. (2001) From few to many: Illumination cone models for face recognition under variable lighting and pose, *IEEE Trans. Pattern Anal. Mach. Intell.*, **23**, pp. 643–660, The YaleB face database, Available (online) at: http://cvc.yale.edu/projects/yalefacesB/yalefacesB.html.

12. Han, H., Shan, S., Chen, X., and Gao, W. (2013) A comparative study on illumination preprocessing in *face recognition, Pattern Recogn.*, **46**, pp. 1691–1699.

13. Huang, G. B., Zhu, Q. Y., and Siew, C. K. (2006) Extreme learning machine: Theory and applications, *Neurocomputing*, **70**, pp. 489–501.

14. Jain, A. K. (1989) *Fundamentals of Digital Signal Processing* (Englewood Cliffs, NJ: Prentice-Hall).

15. Kanan, H. R., Faez, K., and Gao, Y. (2008) Face recognition using adaptively weighted patch PZM array from a single exemplar image per person, *Pattern Recogn.*, **41**, pp. 3799–3812.

16. Kim, T. Y., Lee, K. M., Lee, S. U., and Yim, C. H. (2007) Occlusion invariant face recognition using two-dimensional PCA, *Comm. Com. Inf. Sc.*, **4**, pp. 305–315.

17. Lee, P. H., Wu, S. W., and Hung, Y. P. (2012) Illumination compensation using oriented local histogram equalization and its application to face recognition, *IEEE Trans. Image Process.*, **21**, pp. 4280–4289.

18. Lian, Z. C., Er, M. J., and Li, J. (2011) A novel face recognition approach under illumination variations based on local binary pattern, *Proc. Int. Conf. Comp. Anal.*, CAIP, pp. 89–96.

19. Martinez, A., and Benavente, R. (1998) The AR face database, *Technical Report CVC 24 Purdue Univ.*, Available (online) at: http://www2.ece.ohio-state.edu/~aliex/ARdatabase.html.

20. Martinez, A. (2002) Recognizing imprecisely localized, partially occluded and expression variant faces from single sample per class, *IEEE Trans. Pattern Anal. Mach. Intell.*, **24**, pp. 748–763.

21. Nabatchian, A., Abdel-Raheem, E., and Ahmadi, M. (2011) Illumination invariant feature extraction and mutual information based local matching for face recognition under illumination variation and occlusion, *Pattern Recogn.*, **44**, pp. 2576–2587.

22. Nikan, S., and Ahmadi, M. (2012) Human face recognition under occlusion using LBP and entropy weighted voting, in: *Proc. Int. Conf. Pattern Recogn.*, ICPR, pp. 1699–1702.

23. Oh, H. J., Lee, K. M., and Lee, S. U. (2008) Occlusion invariant face recognition using selective local non-negative matrix factorization basis images, *Image Vision Comput.*, **26**, pp. 1515–1523.

24. Pizer, S. M., Amburn, E. P., Austin, J. D., Cromartie, R., Geselowitz, and et. al. (1987) Adaptive histogram equalization and its variations, *Lect. Notes. Comput. Sc.*, **39**, pp. 355–368.

25. Roweis, S. T., and Saul, L. K. (2000) Nonlinear dimensionality reduction by locally linear embedding, *Science*, **290**, pp. 2323–2326.

26. Rui, M., Hadid, A., and Dugelay, J. (2011) Improving the recognition of faces occluded by facial accessories, *Proc. IEEE Int. Conf. Autom. FGR.*, AFGR, pp. 442–447.

27. Shan, S., Gao, W., Cao, B., and Zhao, D. (2003) Illumination normalization for robust face recognition against varying lighting conditions, *Proc. IEEE. Int. Wksp. Anal. Mod.*, AMFG, pp. 157–164.

28. Solar, J. R., and Quinteros, J. (2008) Illumination compensation and normalization in eigenspace-based face recognition: A comparative study of different preprocessing approaches, *Pattern. Recogn. Lett.*, **29**, pp. 1966–1979.

29. Storer, M., Urschler, M., and Bischof, H. (2010) Occlusion detection for ICAO compliant facial photographs, *Proc. IEEE. Comp. Soc. CVPR. Wksp.*, CVPRW, pp. 122–129.

30. Tan, X., and Triggs, B. (2010) Enhanced local texture feature sets for face recognition under difficult lighting conditions, *IEEE Trans. Image Process.*, **19**, pp. 1635–1650.

31. Topc, B., and Erdogan, H. (2010) Decision fusion for patch-based face recognition, *Proc. IEEE Int. Conf. Pattern Recogn.*, ICPR, pp. 1348-1351.

32. Turk, M., and Pentland, A. (1991) Eigenfaces for recognition, *J. Cogn. Neurosci.*, **3**, pp. 71–86.

33. Tzimiropoulos, G., Zafeiriou, S., and Pantic, M. (2012) Subspace learning from image gradient orientations, *IEEE Trans. Pattern Anal. Mach. Intell.*, **34**, pp. 2454–2466.

34. Wang, H., Li, S. Z., and Wang, Y. (2004) Face recognition under varying lighting conditions using self quotient image, *Proc. IEEE Int. Conf. Autom. FGR.*, AFGR, pp. 819–824.

35. Wang, B., Li, W., Yang, W., and Liao, Q. (2011) Illumination normalization based on Weber's law with application to face recognition, *IEEE Signal Process. Lett.*, **18**, pp. 462–465.

36. Wright, J., Yang, A. Y., Ganesh, A., Sastry, S. S., and Ma, Y. (2009) Robust face recognition via sparse representation, *IEEE Trans. Pattern Anal. Mach. Intell.*, **31**, pp. 210–227.

37. Xu, B., Zhang, T. P., and Shang, Z. W. (2012) Multi-scale invariant abstracted under varying illumination, *Proc. IEEE Int. Conf. Wavelet. Anal. Pattern Recogn.*, ICWAPR, pp. 28–32.

38. Zhang, W., Shan, S., Gao, W., Chen, X., and Zhang, H. (2005) Local Gabor binary pattern histogram sequence (LGBPHS): A novel non-statistical model for face representation and recognition, *Proc. IEEE Int. Conf. Comp. Vis.*, ICCV, pp. 786–791.

39. Zhang, W., Shan, S., Chen, X., and Gao, W. (2007) Local Gabor binary patterns based on Kullback–Leibler divergence for partially occluded face recognition, *IEEE Signal Process. Lett.*, **14**, pp. 875–878.

40. Zhang, T., Tang, Y. Y., Fang, B., and Shang, Z. (2009) Face recognition under varying illumination using gradientfaces, *IEEE Trans. Image Process.*, **18**, pp. 2599–2606.

Chapter 12

Semantic Representation, Enrichment, and Retrieval of Audiovisual Film Content

Alexandros Chortaras, Stefanos Kollias, Kostas Rapantzikos, and Giorgos Stamou

School of Electrical and Computer Engineering,
National Technical University of Athens,
Zografou 15780, Athens, Greece
achort@cs.ntua.gr, stefanos@cs.ntua.gr, rap@image.ntua.gr, gstam@cs.ntua.gr

12.1 Introduction

Searching audiovisual content for specific information has been a key issue in the development of multimedia technologies. Accessing huge amounts of video, television documentaries, or films and looking for specific categories of objects, events, or concepts over the Web is still one of the main challenges in multimedia analysis and multimedia search.

Digital evolution of the cultural heritage field has grown rapidly the last few years, with massive digitization and annotation activities taking place all over Europe and the United States. The

Trends in Digital Signal Processing: A Festschrift in Honour of A. G. Constantinides
Edited by Yong Ching Lim, Hon Keung Kwan, and Wan-Chi Siu
Copyright © 2016 Pan Stanford Publishing Pte. Ltd.
ISBN 978-981-4669-50-4 (Hardcover), 978-981-4669-51-1 (eBook)
www.panstanford.com

heavy involvement of companies, like Google, and the positive reaction of the European Union have led to a variety of, rather converging, actions towards multimodal and multimedia cultural content generation from all possible sources, such as galleries, libraries, archives, museums and audiovisual archives. The creation and evolution of Europeana,[a] as a unique point of access to European Cultural Heritage, has been one of the major achievements in this procedure. More than 34 million objects, expressing the European cultural richness, are currently accessible through the Europeana portal, with the target pointing to double this number within the next five years. As a consequence of the above, research in digital cultural heritage (DCH) is rapidly becoming data intensive, in common with the broader humanities, social, life and physical sciences. Despite the creation of large bodies of digital material through mass digitization programmes, estimates suggest that only a small proportion of all cultural heritage material has been digitized to date, and there is significant commitment to further digitization at national and institutional levels across Europe.[b] A vast amount of data (around 77 million books, 358 million photographs, 24 million hours of audiovisual material, 75 million of works of art, 10.5 billion pages of archives) is still to be digitized.

On the other hand, semantic Web technologies and respective knowledge structures, such as ontologies, have been identified as one of the main tools to achieve interoperability and management of these great amounts of diverse content types, providing effective and efficient access to content and answering user queries in an appropriate and engaging way. The Web has evolved in recent years, from a global information space of linked documents to one where both documents and data are linked.[c] The use of ontologies in data access is based on semantic query answering, i.e., on answering user queries expressed in terms of a terminology (that is connected to the data) and usually represented in the form of conjunctive queries (CQs) [30]. The main restriction of the applicability of the specific approach is that the problem of answering CQs in terms

---

[a]www.europeana.eu.
[b]For details, see the NUMERIC project final report at http://cordis.europa.eu/fp7/ict/telearn-digicult/numeric-study_en.pdf.
[c]http://linkeddata.org/research.

of ontologies represented in description logics (the underlying framework of the W3C's Web Ontology Language—OWL) has been proved to be difficult, suffering from very high worst-case complexity (higher than other standard reasoning problems) that is not relaxed in practice [16]. This is the reason that methods and techniques targeting the development of practical systems either reduce the ontology language expressivity used for the representation of CQs vocabulary, or sacrifice completeness of the CQ answering process, providing as much expressivity as possible. The query posed by the user through the query processing interface is analyzed with the aid of the ontologies and expanded into a set of conjunctive queries, using all the constrains provided by the ontologies. Then, the CQs of the above set are processed with traditional query answering methods on databases or triple stores, where the actual data reside.

In this chapter, we combine semantic content search and enrichment with state-of-the-art visual content analysis, presenting a novel system for semantic and content-based access to audiovisual information. The proposed approach includes, on the one hand, analysis of the metadata and text accompanying films for detection of relevant objects or events, as well as enrichment of these through various thematic thesauri and ontologies, providing results based not only on the explicitly stated data, but also on implicit ones which are found by reasoning on the schema of each ontology. On the other hand, we use local visual feature detectors, which build on edge-based local features, extended with color features, detecting—through visual similarity—frames that show historic locations and monuments. The experimental results of the application of the system on a small number of films that include references to historic places, locations, and monuments illustrate the good performance of the proposed approach.

Figure 12.1 shows the general architecture of the proposed system. Its main component is the *Knowledge Base* that includes the film videos, metadata information about the films (structural and descriptive information about the film content in XML format) and the semantic description that follows the film timelines. This semantic description is based on the terminological definitions of the domain represented in a description logics' (DL) ontological

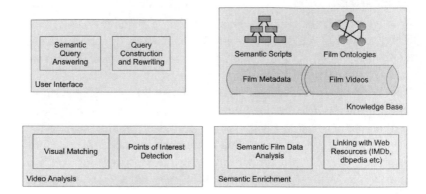

Figure 12.1   System Architecture.

axioms (*Film Ontologies*), including definitions of concepts like actors, titles, genres, etc., descriptions and restrictions of the film structure (definition of scenes, shots, etc.), object and event characterizations, like actions, dialogs, points of interests, persons, characters, places, etc. The above terminology is used for the formal semantic script description of the film (*Semantic Scripts*) that is represented as a hierarchical timelined ABox of the above ontology, including individual definitions and characterizations of each film content, with timecode information. Semantic Scripts are enriched using standard DL reasoning services that extract implicit knowledge and Web resources information linking (with the aid of the *Semantic Enrichment*), and, moreover, through the *Video Analysis* process, that extract points of interest based on visual matching. Finally, the used interface is supported by state-of-the-art semantic query answering services that provide the user with sophisticated semantic query construction using the rich ontological terminology.

The present chapter is organized as follows. Following the introduction, the adopted film data description, with reference to the metadata and scripts that are used is presented in Section 12.2. The knowledge-based representation of the film data, including the semantic technologies used and the respective ontologies is given in Section 12.3. Presentation of the visual analysis subsystem follows in Section 12.4. The film enrichment procedure is presented in Section 12.5, while experimental results and evaluation of the application of the proposed approach within a semantic query answering framework is given in Section 12.6. Conclusions and suggestions for further work are provided in Section 12.7.

12.2 Film Data Description

12.2.1 *Metadata*

A film is usually delivered by a production company in some digital format together with a few standard metadata, such as *title*, *duration*, *year of production*, *genre*, *director*, participating *actors*, *plot summary*, etc. These were the kind of metadata included in the dataset we used in our system, in an XML structured format like the one shown in Fig. 12.2.

```
<Movie ID="3713" Year="2007" Duration="97'"
                                AspectRatio="16:9/2.40:1">
    <Title>Death Defying Acts</Title>
    <Categories>
        <Category>Mystery</Category>
    </Categories>
    <Directors>
        <Director>Gillian Armstrong</Director>
    </Directors>
    <Actors>
        <Actor>Guy Pearce</Actor>
        <Actor>Catherine Zeta-Jones</Actor>
    ...
</Movie>
```

Figure 12.2   Metadata in XML format.

However, nowadays there are several specialized databases available on the Web, which offer considerably richer metadata about films. The most comprehensive and popular such online database is the Internet Movie Database (IMDb),[a] which provides dozens of metadata and other information about millions of films and

---

[a]http://www.imdb.com/.

TV programs, including information about the cast, the production crew, parental guides, trivia, etc. In fact, the provided information is much more extensive than traditional metadata, and contains rich details about many aspects of a film, including dynamic, user-contributed elements, such as keywords, ratings, comments, etc.

The use of metadata in its simplest form allows the development of a traditional information retrieval system, in which the stored objects are characterized by their metadata; the metadata are the searchable fields on which the users pose their queries. Some metadata may be also keyword searchable, such as the titles and the plot summaries. Metadata may contain extensive information about the content of an object that has been obtained after its manual or semi-automatic processing; an example are the rich keyword characterizations that accompany the films in IMDb, which allow a significantly more in-depth, content-oriented retrieval of visual objects such as films. However, this information still works as a global content characterization, and does not allow, for example, the retrieval of particular scenes of a film for which a particular keyword is relevant.

12.2.2 *Scripts and Post-Production Scripts*

Most commercial films are produced based on a script, which is a document that describes every visual, aural, behavioral and lingual element of the film. Typically, a script divides a film into a series of scenes, which in turn consist of series of shots. There are some general guidelines for producing script documents, which define the basic formatting strategies and some abbreviations for commonly used keywords [9]. So, each new scene is introduced by a new *scene heading* that tells the reader where exactly the scene takes place. It also tells whether the scene is an indoor or outdoor scene, it provides the name of the location, and usually also the time of the day. The scene heading is followed by the *action* part, which is a description of the setting of the scene, and introduces the characters that take part in the scene. Actions are short descriptions, typically a couple of lines long. An action may be followed by one or more *dialogues*. In each dialogue, the *character name* of the speaker is first provided, which may be an actual name, a description, or an occupation. The character name is followed by the exact dialogue text. A dialogue may contain also a *parenthetical*, which is a remark about the attitude or the facial expression of the speaker, or about the addressee of the dialogue. A dialogue may contain also an *extension* which is a technical note about the way in which the character's voice is heard, saying, e.g., that an off-screen voice or a narration (voice over) is heard. In transitions between actions or scenes, a *transition* element may be included, which tells how the transition is done, whether, e.g., a fade-in or a fade-out occurs. Finally, at the beginning of an action description, a *shot* element may be included which informs the reader about the focal point of the camera within the scene, and may be, e.g., a close-up, a moving shot, an overhead shot, a low angle shot, etc. The appearance of a shot element establishes the change of the camera position and hence the beginning of a new shot; a shot may consist of several alternating actions and dialogues.

An enriched form of scripts are post-production scripts, which are produced after the production of a film, and provide exact timing information for each scene, shot, or dialogue. Traditionally, timing is given in timecodes that represent locations within reels, and are given in units of feet and frames within each film reel. Given the film type (e.g., 35 mm) and the film speed (e.g., 24 frames/sec), timing in terms of time units can be computed. An indicative excerpt of a post-production script from our dataset for the film of Fig. 12.2 is shown in Fig. 12.3. It consists of three external (outdoor) night scenes. The first two consist of a single action element, while the third shot contains alternating actions and dialogues. The WS, MS (wide shot, medium shot, respectively) abbreviations are specific shot elements, declaring that the camera position has changed. It follows that the third scene consists of two shots, the first one of which coincides with the scene opening. In all descriptions, character names are typed uppercase. Each scene/shot is accompanied by a starting timecode, and each dialogue by a starting, ending and duration timecode, and a serial number.

The richness of the information contained in a production script can obviously be used for the development of a film content retrieval system that goes beyond standard metadata-based information retrieval systems. It can provide real context-based search for prominently visual objects such as films, and it can, furthermore, be combined with image analysis techniques for further enriching the returned results. In addition, a very significant benefit from

| 1078.12 | 40. | EXT. | EDINBURGH - PRINCES ST GARDENS | NIGHT | 40. |

WS Tilt down from Edinburgh Castle, perched high on the dark crags, to BENJI, hurrying through the Princes Street Gardens. She runs home. She's in love!

| 1102.12 | 41. | EXT. | EDINBURGH ALLEY | NIGHT | 41. |

MS Heart racing, BENJI clatters down the steps of the cobbled alley.

| 1113.14 | 42. | EXT. | BOTHY, ENCAMPMENT | NIGHT | 42. |

MS BENJI skips through the graveyard.

> BENJI [sings]

| 1115.12 | 6.07 | 381 | I met Houdini! I met Houdini! |
| 1122.03 |

1122.04   WS BENJI skips to her mother, waiting by the door.

> BENJI

| 1124.08 | 1.14 | 382 | I met him, ma! |
| 1126.06 |

| 1127.00 | 5.00 | 383 | He's got these eyes that just burn through to |
| 1132.00 | | | the back of your head! |

Figure 12.3   Post-production script extract.

using the script information is that the search within films can be more fine-grained: the searchable objects are not entire films, but scene and shots within films, even frames, where particular words are uttered, or particular actions take place, or where particular objects, places or persons appear. If the information extracted from the scripts is coupled with the metadata information, and the information extracted by analysis of the visual content of a film, a powerful content-based retrieval system for films can be built.

Since one of the main sources of data for the proposed system are scripts, a significant preliminary task is processing the script files in order to extract the contained information and convert it into a structured representation. Unfortunately, although general formatting guidelines for writing scripts exist, so that all the above-described elements are easily recognizable within a script document, and despite the fact that some proposals have been made towards defining a markup language for scripts [37], there is yet no such standard language. Currently, script processing programs mostly export scripts in some HTML or other simple layout markup format, ignoring the semantics of the script structure. Moreover, scripts produced by different programs or companies have slightly or substantially different formats, occasionally also misformation errors, which makes their automatic processing problematic. In the following, we focus on post-production scripts in Microsoft Word and Adobe PDF formats. Due to the diversity in their formatting, for the extraction of content from the layout information, its conversion into a structured content and then into a semantic representation in terms of the ontological models described later in the chapter, a different data extraction program was coded for each script.

12.3 Knowledge-Based Representation of Data

In this section, we discuss the details of building the knowledge base of the proposed film content retrieval system. Since our purpose is to build a semantic knowledge base with inference capabilities, for the modeling of the data we use several of the technologies that have been recently developed in the context of the Semantic Web. The general idea behind these technologies is to make data available in a structured form that conveys information about their meaning. Such structured data can then be used in conjunction with relevant domain knowledge descriptions in order to perform inferences, and hence obtain new implicit information. We will start the description of our data representation model by a brief introduction to the semantic technologies.

12.3.1 *Semantic Technologies*

In the context of the Semantic Web, an elementary piece of information (e.g., an object, a concept, a relation) is a resource, and any resource that needs to be described is assigned a URI. Because URIs may represent both real-world objects (e.g., a person) and digital objects (e.g., a document), they do not necessarily enable access to the respective resource; they are resource identifiers. Using this approach, we can first define, e.g., a concept for representing film scripts and assign it the URI http://image.ntua.gr/ontologies/so/Script, another concept for representing scenes with URI http://image.ntua.gr/ontologies/so/Scene, and use the predefined URI http://purl.org/dc/terms/isPartOf for modeling inclusions relations; then, let us assign to the script object shown in Fig. 12.3 the URI http://image.ntua.gr/data/mv/SR3713; finally, let us assign the URI http://image.ntua.gr/data/mv/SR3713SC0042 to an object representing the first scene of that script. To improve readability and efficiency, instead of full URIs we can use *namespaces*, i.e., abbreviate http://image.ntua.gr/ontologies/so/, http://image.ntua.gr/data/mv/, and http://purl.org/dc/terms/ to the namespace prefixes so, mv, and dc respectively. Then, the above URIs can be written as so:Script, so:Scene, dc:isPartOf, mv:SR3713, and mv:SR3713SC0042, respectively. Since so:Script, so:Scene and dc:isPartOf express abstract concepts and relations (which technically are called *classes* and *properties*, respectively), while mv:SR3713 and mv:SR3713SC0042 represent actual objects, the next thing we would like to be able to express is to declare that mv:SR3713 is a particular script, i.e., an *instance* of the so:Script class, that mv:SR3713SC0042 is an instance of so:Scene, and that mv:SR3713SC0042 is a part of so:SR3713. These statements form a very simple *knowledge base*. Resource Description Framework (RDF) [36] is the Semantic Web technology that allows the declaration of such statements. In its simplest form, such a statement is a subject-predicate-object triple, called an RDF triple. Thus, our knowledge consists of the three triples mv:SR3713 rdf:type so:Script, mv:SR3713SC0042 rdf:type so:Scene, and mv:SR3713SC0042 dc:isPartOf so:SR3713, where rdf:type is a predefined property which denotes that a particular resource is an instance of a class. While subjects and predicates in an RDF triple must be resource URIs, the object may as well be a string, numerical or other data value. We need such values to declare, e.g., that mv:SR3713SC0042 dc:description "BOTHY, ENCAMPMENT". This makes dc:description a *data property*, and dc:isPartOf an *object property*. A collection of RDF triples like the above forms an RDF graph and is usually stored in a triple store; for querying the graph in order to retrieve triples that satisfy certain patterns, the SPARQL language [38] has been developed.

The RDF triple model described above allows us to create statements about relations between resources. The definition of the vocabulary which is used in the statements is very important, since semantic interpretation of the statements derives from it. For instance, we have already seen that `rdf:type` is used to declare instances of a class. In fact, `rdf:type` is part of RDF Schema [35], a commonly used vocabulary for expressing facts about resources, which, however, is rather limited and lacks the rigid semantics needed by logic-based reasoning systems. In order to model domain knowledge having both rich expressive capabilities and rigid semantics, an *ontology* language is needed. In general, an ontology contains *axioms*, which describe formally a domain of related concepts and their relationships. In this way, ontologies provide formal semantics for the underlying data, and since these semantics are described using logical formalisms, they allow automatic inferencing over the underlying datasets. An ontology describing the films domain may state, e.g., that `so:NightScene` is a subclass of `so:Scene`, which means that every *explicit* `so:NightScene` instance is *inferred* to be also an *implicit* `so:Scene` instance. The standard ontology language in the Semantic Web is OWL (its current version is OWL2 [26]), and has its roots in the Description Logics formalism [6]. Using these formalism, the above axiom would, e.g., be written as `so:NightScene ⊑ so:Scene`. Ontologies may of course contain more complex axioms; assuming existence of the necessary vocabulary and data model, we may state, e.g., that a film that has a scene in which some violent action takes place, is a film suitable only for viewers over 13 years old: `cc:PG13Film ⊑ cc:Film ⊓ ∃dc:isPartOf⁻.(so:Scene ⊓ ∃cc:takesPlace.cc:ViolentAction)`. The type of axioms that are allowed by an ontology language determine its expressivity. Ontologies that lack axioms, essentially define a *vocabulary* for describing a domain. Two such commonly used vocabularies are Dublin Core and FOAF (for which we will use, respectively, the already defined namespace dc, and the namespace foaf for http://xmlns.com/foaf/0.1/). There are several ways to serialize OWL ontologies, one of which uses the RDF model, and decomposes each axiom into a series of RDF triples. In the context of OWL, the statement that an object is instance of a concept is called an *assertion* and can be serialized using a single RDF triple as was discussed above.

Ontologies can be used to answer semantic queries. Such queries are usually conjunctive queries, in which the user, using the ontology vocabulary, asks for objects that have certain properties. For example, if in the above context the user wants to retrieve all nights scenes of PG13 films, he should pose the following query: `Q(?y) <- cc:PG13Film(?x),dc:isPartOf(?y,?x),so:NightScene(?y)`. In order to perform such *ontology-based query answering*, a simple lookup in the set of explicit assertions (i.e., by querying the underlying triple store by directly converting the above query to a SPARQL query) is not enough, and some *reasoning* needs to take place in order to take into account the implicit knowledge, which results, e.g., from the axioms defining the `cc:PG13Film` and `so:NightScene` classes. Although rich in modeling capabilities, expressive ontology languages suffer of high computational complexity when reasoning is required, and are, therefore, in general unsuitable for applications that process large amounts of data and where real-time responsiveness is required. For this reason, OWL declares several sub-languages, called OWL profiles, which offer a varying level of modeling expressivity.

The ability provided by Semantic Web technologies to define simple vocabularies or complex ontologies to model a domain and then to assign to objects unique URIs and declare them to be instances of the entities defined in the relevant domain ontologies or vocabularies, provides the ability to make available online a knowledge base about any domain, and link it (using appropriate URIs) with any other such online knowledge base. This has given rise to the Linked Open Data (LOD) cloud, and several knowledge bases are already available online. One of the most important and largest members of the LOD is DBpedia,[a] which provides structural information about millions of resources that represent real-world objects. It provides also a quite extensive general-purpose ontology that defines some general taxonomies and relations.

---

[a]http://dbpedia.org/About.

12.3.2 *Overview of the Semantic Representation*

The semantic technologies outlined in the above section provide the technological framework within which we will develop the proposed semantic representation of film content. In order to set up, however, the exact representation model, we need to consider, at an abstract level, the nature of the data we our modeling. For the proposed system, a film has three different aspects: it is a creative work, which has some metadata providing general information about its overall content; it is a particular digital object with some encoding (e.g., the MPEG-4 encoded film file, stored in the filesystem); and it is also an abstract (independent of encoding) video object that, for the purpose of image analysis, can be considered to consist of a series of images (frames).

In parallel to these, there are also the film scripts, which essentially impose some structure on the sequence of frames that make up each film, by grouping them into scenes and shots, providing some textual description of them, and defining also subsequences of frames in which a particular action or dialogue takes place. However, a film script is itself a standalone object, which should have its own representation, independently of the video object to which it refers.

Thus, for the ontological representation of the data we need:

- A vocabulary to model the overall properties a film, seen as a creative work. These properties are obtained from the film metadata. The provided metadata may be further enriched from external data sources such as IMDb. In the concrete world, each film is instantiated by a particular digital object with a particular encoding.
- A vocabulary to model the contents of the digital object that corresponds to a film, seen as a video object, i.e., as a sequence of frames.
- A vocabulary to model the structural and content information of a film, as obtained from the corresponding script. Since this information refers to particular fragments of a film, it should be linked to the corresponding elements of the respective video object.

- A vocabulary to model additional, non-structural, but content information, obtained by the analysis of the textual content of scripts, and the film frames. As described later, such information may be named entities, word hypernyms, landmarks, points of interest, etc. Again, this information should be linked to the elements of the video object to which it refers.

We will discuss the vocabulary for the first three items in detail in the following subsections. In relation to the last item, we define here a simple vocabulary that allows us to describe in a general way the results of any content analysis, applied either on the textual information contained in the scripts or on the frames of a video object. Although the extraction process may greatly vary (ranging from the detection of named entities in a text to the identification of a landmark in an image), we assume that the result itself is always a resource of the LOD cloud. For this purpose we define the namespace voc as http://image.ntua.gr/ontologies/voc/, and the following:

- voc:ExtractedObject: The class of objects that have been extracted by applying a content analysis algorithm on some data. We also define the subclasses voc:NamedEntity, voc:TextWord and voc:ImagePOI.
- voc:extraction: An object property that relates an object (on which content analysis has been performed) with a voc:ExtractedObject.
- voc:linksTo: An object property that relates a voc:ExtractedObject with a URI that represents the extracted object in the LOD cloud.

Finally, before proceeded to describing the specific vocabulary for the representation of metadata, video and script content, we note that in order to be able to model either a video object or a script we need a way to model sequences of objects (of images, and of scenes/shots, respectively) that may in addition have inclusion relations between them. For this reason we define also the following general-purpose vocabulary:

- `voc:isNextOf`: An object property that relates an object that belongs to a sequence, with the immediately preceding object. The object can be a frame, a shot, etc.
- `dc:isPartOf`: An object property that models an inclusion relation between objects. It is borrowed from the Dublin Core vocabulary.
- `voc:isFirstPartOf`: A subproperty of `dc:isPartOf` that declares that a particular object that is a part of some other object is in fact the first element in a sequence of included objects.

12.3.3 *Film Ontologies and Metadata Representation*

As already mentioned, technically, a film is a media resource that can be seen both as a creative work and as a multimedia object. Depending on the modeling level of abstraction, different concepts and properties may be more relevant for modeling the metadata of a film, and several general or specialized ontologies offering a vocabulary that can be used for describing them exist (e.g., Dublin Core, EBUCore, MPEG-7). In this respect, Media Ontology [25] is a W3C recommendation for an ontology that provides a vocabulary whose purpose is to bridge the various existing descriptions and provide a core set of descriptive properties, without distinguishing between the several levels of abstraction. So, Media Ontology defines, e.g., the classes `ma:MediaResource` (with subclasses `ma:Image` and `ma:MediaFragment`), and `ma:Agent` (with subclasses `ma:Organization` and `ma:Person`), some high-level data and object properties such as `ma:title`, `ma:duration`, `ma:hasCreator`, `ma:hasGenre`, `ma:hasRating`, `ma:hasKeyword`, as well as `ma:playsIn`, and also some technical properties referring to the digital object such as `ma:frameHeight`, `ma:framRate`, and `ma:sampligRate` (in the above `ma` is the namespace http://www.w3.org/ns/ma-ont#). Other general purpose ontologies that have emerged in order to cover a wide range of the content publishable in the Semantic Web cover also the media resources domain. Schema.org[a] is one of them, and defines `schema:Movie` as a subclass of `schema:CreativeWork` with several relevant properties

---

[a]http://schema.org/.

such as `schema:headline`, `schema:duration`, `schema:creator`, `schema:genre`, `schema:aggregateRating`, `schema:keywords`, `schema:actor`, that correspond roughly to the Media Ontology concepts. However, having a special film concept, Schema.org defines some specialized properties such as `schema:director`, and `schema:trailer`. Moreover, in Schema.org it is possible to distinguish a film seen as a creative work from a film seen as a digital media object; the technical details of a particular video object corresponding to an abstract film object can be modeled by linking a `schema:Movie` object to an instance of `schema:VideoObject` using the `schema:encoding` property, and then using appropriate properties such as `schema:videoFrameSize`, `schema:bitrate`, etc. (In the above, `schema` is the namespace http://schema.org/)

Due to the increased modeling flexibility offered by the Schema.org ontology, we use it for describing film metadata in the proposed system. Fig. 12.4 shows the set of assertions (as RDF triples) generated for the metadata of Fig. 12.2 using the Schema.org vocabulary. Note that the classes of some objects are not defined. For example, `mv:PS0017` is not declared to be a `schema:Person`; this is not necessary because the Schema.org ontology defines as range of the `schema:director` property the class `schema:Person` and hence the type of `mv:PS0017` can be inferred.

12.3.4 *Video Content Representation*

For the proposed system, it suffices to model a video object content as a simple sequence of frames. So, we define the `vr:Frame` class to represent individual frames (using the namespace `vr` for http://image.ntua.gr/ontologies/vr/), and use the vocabulary defined in Section 12.3.2 to model the ordering relations between them. We also define the `vr:startTime` data property to link a frame with its relative appearing time within the video object.

Using the above vocabularies, Fig. 12.5 shows how the contents of the video object referred to in Fig. 12.4 for the film "Death Defying Acts" are modeled. As it can be verified by converting script timecodes to true timestamps, frame `mv:MV3713V01FR045069` corresponds to the starting frame of scene 42 in Fig. 12.3.

mv:MV3713	rdf:type	schema:Movie
mv:MV3713	schema:headline	"Death Defying Acts"
mv:MV3713	schema:datePublished	"2007"
mv:MV3713	schema:encoding	mv:MV3713V01
mv:MV3713V01	rdf:type	schema:VideoObject
mv:MV3713V01	schema:contentUrl	"file:///data/mv3713.mpeg4"
mv:MV3713V01	schema:videoFrameSize	"16:9/2.40:1"
mv:MV3713V01	schema:duration	mv:MV3713DU1
mv:MV3713DU1	schema:name	"PT1H37M"
mv:MV3713	schema:genre	"Mystery"
mv:MV3713	schema:director	mv:PS0017
mv:MV3713	schema:actor	mv:PS0018
mv:MV3713	schema:actor	mv:PS0019
mv:PS0017	schema:name	"Gillian Armstrong"
mv:PS0018	schema:name	"Guy Pearce"
mv:PS0019	schema:name	"Catherine Zeta-Jones"

Figure 12.4 Metadata assertions.

12.3.5 *Script Representation*

In order to semantically describe the structural information extracted by processing post-production scripts, we developed an appropriate ontology, named the Script Ontology. Script Ontology defines the following vocabulary:

- so:Script: The class of film script objects.
- so:Scene: The class of scenes into which a script is divided. The so:Scene concept has several more specific subclasses, which correspond to the standard scene types appearing in scripts: a scene may be a so:ExternalScene or a so:InternalScene, and also a so:DayScene, a so:DawnScene, a so:MorningScene, a so:EveningScene, a so:AfternoonScene, or a so:NightScene. If a scene has a special transition feature, this is captured by appropriate subclasses such as so:FadeInScene, so:FadeOutScene, so:DissolveToScene, so:BackToScene, etc.
- so:Shot: The class of shots into which a scene is divided. There are several types of shots that are defined to

```
mv:MV3713V01FR000001    rdf:type            vr:Frame
mv:MV3713V01FR000001    voc:isFirstPartOf   mv:MV3713V01
mv:MV3713V01FR000001    vr:startTime        "00:00:00.000"
mv:MV3713V01FR000002    rdf:type            vr:Frame
mv:MV3713V01FR000002    dc:isPartOf         mv:MV3713V01
mv:MV3713V01FR000002    voc:isNextOf        mv:MV3713V01FR000001
mv:MV3713V01FR000002    vr:startTime        "00:00:00.040"
                            ...
mv:MV3713V01FR045069    rdf:type            vr:Frame
mv:MV3713V01FR045069    dc:isPartOf         mv:MV3713V01
mv:MV3713V01FR045069    voc:isNextOf        mv:MV3713V01FR045068
mv:MV3713V01FR045069    vr:startTime        "00:30:02.760"
mv:MV3713V01FR045070    rdf:type            vr:Frame
mv:MV3713V01FR045070    dc:isPartOf         mv:MV3713V01
mv:MV3713V01FR045070    voc:isNextOf        mv:MV3713V01FR045069
mv:MV3713V01FR045070    vr:startTime        "00:30:02.800"
```

Figure 12.5 Video content assertions.

be subclasses of `so:Shot`. For example, a shot may be a `so:CloseUpShot`, a `so:WideAngleShot`, a `so:MediumShot`, a `so:MovingShot`, a `so:HighAngleShot`, etc. These correspond to the standard shot types commonly used in scripts.

- `so:Event`: The class of events that are contained in shots.
- `so:Action`: Subclass of `so:Event` representing an action description.
- `so:Dialogue`: Subclass of `so:Event` representing a dialogue, with subclasses `so:VoiceOverDialogue` and `so:OffScreen Dialogue`.
- `so:Character`: The class of characters that take part in the action of a script.
- `so:script`: An object property used to relate an instance of `schema:Movie` or `schema:VideoObject` to an instance of `so:Script`.
- `dc:description`: A data property that represents the textual description of a `so:Scene`, `so:Shot`, or `so:Event`. The value is a string and is meant to be the exact text provided by

the respective script part. The property is borrowed from Dublin Core.

- `so:performedBy`: An object property that relates a `so:Dialogue` with the `so:Character` that performs it.
- `so:addressedTo`: An object property that relates a `so:Dialogue`, with the instances of `so:Character` it is addressed to.
- `so:parenthetical`: A data property that provides a parenthetical description for a `so:Dialogue`.
- `foaf:name`: A data property that represents the name of a `so:Character`. It is borrowed from FOAF.
- `so:hasCharacter`: An object property that relates a `so:Script` with the instances of `so:Character` that take part in the action.
- `so:takesPlaceIn`: An object property that relates a `so:Event` with the `so:Shot` it takes place in.
- `so:startFrame`. An object property that provides the starting frame within a video object, for a script object that lasts one or more frames. This can be a scene, a shot, a dialogue, etc.
- `so:endFrame`. An object property that provides the ending frame for a script object that has a duration.
- `so:duration`. A data property that provides the duration (in number of frames) for a script object that has a duration.

As already mentioned, in order to generate the semantic representation of each film in terms of the Script Ontology, we have created several script processing programs. Figure 12.6 shows a representative extract of the assertions generated for the script extract of Fig. 12.3.

Using the above-described script representation, Table 12.1 shows the starting frames for a sequence of shots, starting from the shot of the first scene of the script extract of Fig. 12.6.

In Section 12.3.4 we discussed how a video object is modeled as a sequence of frames, whereas in this section we discussed how a script is modeled as a sequence of scenes, which in turn are modeled as sequences of shots. Hence, at the video level we can consider the frame as the smallest building element, and also consider the shot as the smallest building element of a script. Although shot and frames are linked by the `so:startFrame` property,

mv:MV3713	so:script	mv:SR3713
mv:SR3713	rdf:type	so:Script
...		
mv:SR3713SC0042	rdf:type	so:ExternalScene
mv:SR3713SC0042	rdf:type	so:NightScene
mv:SR3713SC0042	dc:isPartOf	mv:SR3713
mv:SR3713SC0042	dc:description	"BOTHY, ENCAMPMENT"
mv:SR3713SC0042	voc:isNextOf	mv:SR3713SC0041
mv:SR3713SC0042	so:startFrame	mv:SR3713FR045069
mv:SR3713SH0406	rdf:type	so:MediumShot
mv:SR3713SH0406	voc:isFirstPartOf	mv:SR3713SC0042
mv:SR3713SH0406	voc:isNextOf	mv:SR3713SH0405
mv:SR3713SH0406	so:startFrame	mv:SR3713FR045069
mv:SR3713EV0352	rdf:type	so:Action
mv:SR3713EV0352	so:takesPlaceIn	mv:SR3713SH0406
mv:SR3713EV0352	dc:description	"BENJI skips through the graveyard."
mv:SR3713EV0353	rdf:type	so:Dialogue
mv:SR3713EV0353	so:takesPlaceIn	mv:SR3713SH0406
mv:SR3713EV0353	dc:description	"I met Houdini! I met Houdini!"
mv:SR3713EV0353	so:parenthetical	"sings"
mv:SR3713EV0353	so:performedBy	mv:SR3713RL0
mv:SR3713EV0353	so:startFrame	mv:SR3713FR045099
mv:SR3713EV0353	so:endFrame	mv:SR3713FR045202
mv:SR3713EV0353	so:duration	"103"
...		
mv:SR3713	so:hasCharacter	mv:SR3713RL0
mv:SR3713RL0	foaf:name	"BENJI"

Figure 12.6 Script content assertions.

which links a shot to its starting frame, it is also desirable to model the inverse relation so as to be able to find the shot a frame belongs to. This is useful for user queries, since in general the conceptually interesting element of a film is the shot rather than the frame, but the video analysis algorithms work at the frame level. For this reason, we aligned the assertions generated by the

Table 12.1 Starting frames for a sequence of shots

video and the script contents, by post-processing them based on the timing information, and generating additional assertions of the form `mv:SR3713FR045069 dc:isPartOf mv:SR3713SH0406` and `mv:SR3713FR045070 dc:isPartOf mv:SR3713SH0406`, etc., for all frames of a video object.

12.4 Visual Analysis

12.4.1 *The Analysis Subsystem*

In this section, we focus on the enrichment of film content with additional—to existing metadata—information that will provide effective navigation and search capabilities. The visual analysis part of the proposed method includes the following: First, an off-line process, which identifies points of interest (POIs) like buildings, landmarks, and famous squares in the video. Then, an online process, through a Web interface, which allows temporal navigation based on the detected POIs and gives access to relevant information (e.g., Wikipedia links). Analysis is based on a collection of a large number of related Flickr images accompanied by metadata such as title, tags, and geo-locations. Based on this collection, we enable rapid retrieval of visually similar images and propagate their metadata to the unknown ones (frames with a detected landmark), thus enriching existing content metadata and semantic information.

12.4.2 *The Main Components*

12.4.2.1 Local visual characteristics and descriptors

The latest techniques that retrieve totally or partially identical images from large collections are based on local features. In this context, the image is represented by a set of features or regions accompanied by position, scale, orientation information and a structural descriptor. Among the most widespread local features and descriptors are affine invariant areas, i.e., areas that "follow" affine image transformations and remain relatively invariant to viewpoint, illumination changes and partial occlusion. According to Mikolajczyk et al. [23], the MSER [21] and Hessian-affine [23] detectors perform best in standard benchmarks. Efforts to develop computationally more efficient detectors and descriptors resulted in BRIEF [8], BRISK [20], and SURF [7], with the latter remaining the most widespread. Recently we proposed detectors that achieve a good trade-off between statistical performance and computational efficiency [4] [42]. Under the framework of this work, we also exploit the MPEG-7 features that have been widely used for categorizing images, detecting high-level concepts and retrieving images/sequences [10]. They are composed of a set of color, shape, and texture descriptors. Specifically, the Dominant Color Descriptor (DCD—a set of dominant colors in a region or the whole image), the Color Structure Descriptor (CSD—a set of global and local color features), the Color Layout Descriptor (CLD—a resolution invariant descriptor in the YCbCr color space), the Scalable Color Descriptor (SCD—a Haar transformed color histogram), the Region-Based Shape descriptor (RSD—a descriptor of pixels' spatial distribution within a region), the Homogeneous Texture Descriptor (HTD—a quantitative texture descriptor based on directional filters) and the Edge Histogram Descriptor (EHD—an edge distribution descriptor).

12.4.2.2 Quantization and codebook

In order to achieve computational efficiency without compromising performance, the bag-of-words (BoW) model has been proposed [39] and successfully used for large-scale image retrieval. BoW facilitates indexing by descriptor quantization and enables rapid retrieval [27] by exploiting techniques from the text community, like inverted files. The centers of the quantized descriptors define the visual codebook and each centre is called a visual word. Recent techniques improve the creation and/or indexing of the codebook either by appropriate grouping of visual words [44] or by hierarchical scoring and soft assignment [24]. Recently, we have proposed a relevant method to effectively quantize features with automatic calculation of the number of centers [2].

12.4.2.3 Visual matching and geometry

Although the BoW model considerably boosts large-scale image retrieval, it is currently not sufficient due to the fast growth of available data. A successful method that leads to significant performance improvement is the geometry consistency check of the retrieved images. The goal is to compute a reliable geometrical transformation between the query image and the retrieved ones. Philbin et al. achieves this by using a RANSAC-type algorithm for the complete set of the first 1000 retrieved images [27]. In this direction, Perdoch et al. [28] and Jegou et al. [18] suggest solutions for integrating the local shape of regions in the index. Most recently, Tolias et al. suggest a successful and computationally more efficient technique for geometric verification [40].

12.4.3 *The Visual Analysis Scheme*

Our goal is to successfully identify POIs, such as known buildings and landmarks without compromising computational performance. Each film/scene/shot sequence is regarded as a sequence of still images, i.e., frames, and the analysis is performed on a subset of those images based on temporal sampling. Similarity computation between the query frames and the dataset is achieved by extracting and using local visual features, which are invariant to common transformations. For this purpose we have created a collection of 2,791,240 photos from 45 cities (worldwide), which have been posted by users on Flickr.[a] The photos are accompanied by metadata such as title, description, comments, tags, and geographic locations. Each image is decomposed into a set of local features, which are then quantized and encoded based on the visual codebook, as shown in Fig. 12.7. The codebook is constructed by unsupervised learning from a subset of the given collection; an inverted file is then created, making similarity computation and retrieval efficient. The same analysis is performed for all sampled frames. The structure of the inverted file, as shown in Fig. 12.8, allows rapid retrieval of similar images from the given collection, in descending order of similarity. At this point, similarity is based solely on the quantized visual descriptors and not on the geometry (position, scale and orientation). Nevertheless, geometry is crucial for retrieval accuracy of the retrieval, especially on a large scale basis. As shown in Fig. 12.9, we check for geometric consistency between the query image and each of the retrieved ones. The result is the set of retrieved images reordered based on spatial geometry. Using the metadata of the retrieved images and specifically the geo-location, title and tags, identification of POIs is achieved by searching relevant databases such as Geonames[b] and Wikipedia[c] that combine reliable text information (e.g., identity of the landmark) and verified geo-location. The combination of visual similarity, geographic proximity and metadata similarity provides identification with extremely high accuracy. In this way, each video sequence is enriched with

---

[a] http://www.flickr.com.
[b] http://www.geonames.org.
[c] http://www.wikipedia.org.

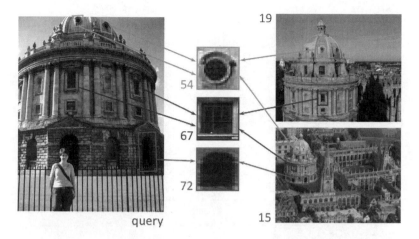

Figure 12.7 Local feature matching based on visual codebook.

additional information, i.e., by the monuments, sights, squares that appear in it. The user is therefore able to navigate through the visual corpus based on semantic content, as defined by the POIs it contains. Furthermore, the accompanying geo-locations allow for the visualization of those points on the world map. The analysis process is conducted off-line. The result is a new set of metadata for each recognized POI in the film/trailer that includes the corresponding time of occurrence and all the propagated metadata.

In the above procedure, we have managed to improve quality and speed of the matching algorithms used, based on local features/descriptors, focusing on sub-linear large-scale indexing/retrieval. According to the BoW model, the visual codebook encodes the appearance of features in the descriptors' space and sub-linear indexing is made possible by exploiting the sparse representation caused by the oversized codebook/dictionary. Particular issues which are significant in this procedure are discussed next.

12.4.3.1 Constructing visual dictionaries

The construction of visual codebooks scaling up to the order of 10^6 visual words is so far limited to variants of the k-means algorithm. We have created a new method, namely Approximates Gaussian Mixtures (AGM) [2], which is based on a mixture model

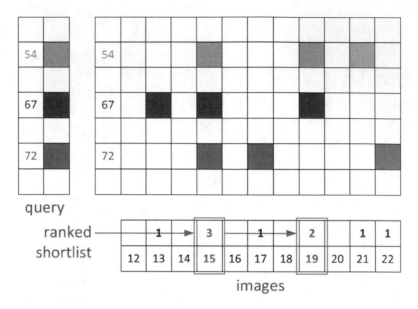

Figure 12.8 Inverted file indexing. Each row (column) represents a visual word (image). For each visual word a sparse list is created with the images that contain it.

of normal distributions (Gaussian mixture model, GMM) on this scale by applying approximate nearest neighbor search to the EM algorithm, making the complexity linear in the number of samples. The size of the dictionary is dynamically estimated, resulting in fewer parameters and superior performance, with a cost that is similar to the approximate k-means.

12.4.3.2 Geometry consistency checking

Verification of geometric similarity among the retrieved images is—typically—a sequential process of spatial verification that is slow and is applied only to a short list of the most relevant images. Recently, there has been a growing interest in geometric indexing to compensate for those shortcomings. Existing methods are either not invariant to geometric transformations or limited to local ones. Taking advantage of the shape of local features, we use the feature map hashing method (FMH) [5] that is the first to encode the overall

Figure 12.9 Geometric consistency between the query image and one of the retrieved images.

geometry in the index, while remaining invariant. FMH has been evaluated on a set of 50K images, with retrieval time at the scale of milliseconds. In practice, retrieval time depends only on spatial verification. Taking this into consideration, we developed the Hough Pyramid Matching (HPM) method [40], a very simple generic model for spatial matching. HPM can address multiple surfaces or non-rigid objects with improved statistical performance. In the worst case, the complexity of existing models is at least square to the number of matches, while HPM is linear, achieving thousands of image matches per second.

12.4.3.3 Feature selection

A popular way to reduce the space required for the index is feature selection via multiple viewpoint matching of the same object or scene. We developed a new method of feature selection based on an alignment measure [5] that can be shown to use FMH for up to 1 million and the traditional BoW for up to 10 million images. We also applied the HPM method for the same purpose:

namely, we introduced the SymCity method [41], the first one that selects features from single viewpoint by detecting symmetries and repeating patterns with a runtime of a few milliseconds.

12.4.3.4 Geo-location exploitation

Images derived from social networks such as Flickr, are usually accompanied by supplementary information like tags or geo-tags. Furthermore, they often include repetitive information, e.g., tourists' pictures in cities taken from diverse viewpoints. Grouping or clustering such images is a popular workaround of repetitive or unnecessary information, but visual matching in pairs can be prohibitive in large-scale (millions of images). Most of the existing methods are limited to sets of popular landmarks' images. In [3] we exploit the geo-tags and apply sub-linear indexing to group one million images in just a few hours on a single processor. We use the *kernel vector quantization* method that ensures the preservation of even single-element clusters and that all images in a cluster have at least one common rigid-object or surface with a specific reference image. We then construct a scene map [19] for each group (cluster) by projecting the images to a common plane. Indexing of such maps—instead of the individual images—not only saves space, but also improves recall. The results are similar to query expansion methods, but in our case the procedure is off-line and retrieval time is not affected.

12.4.3.5 Feature extraction

At the core of all methods discussed so far lies the extraction of a sparse set of local features. The matching performance is highly affected by invariance of features to changes in illumination or viewpoint. While most existing detectors consider features as elliptical shaped regions, we propose a detector of arbitrarily shaped regions and scale starting from unstable single-scale edges [34]. With the same input, our WaSH detector uses weighted a-shapes and provides improved performance over state-of-the-art detectors in retrieval and matching experiments [42]. Generalizing the previous result and starting from single-scale derivatives, we compute the exact weighted distance transform and the corresponding weighted medial axis and decompose the image similarly to the watershed transform. The medial feature detector (MFD) [4] has similar performance to WaSH, but provides features at pixel accuracy.

12.5 Film Metadata and Content Enrichment

The assertions of Fig. 12.6 generated by processing the film scripts, model the structural information of the film, but have actually little to say about its content. This is because textual descriptions contained in scripts about all settings and actions, as well as all dialogue texts are captured by the `dc:description` datatype property and hence are modeled as simple strings. However, this very rich source of information, upon adequate processing may dramatically increase the available information about the actual content of a film, and provide extended capabilities of answering complex semantic queries on the film content. The same holds for the video analysis process described in 12.4; the results of the analysis should be incorporated in the film representation so that they can be used at query time. Moreover, by examining the assertions of Fig. 12.4 and 12.6 we notice that there is a significant missing link between them. By using the metadata we have obtained information about the actors that play in a film, and by using the scripts we get information about the characters that take part in the film action. Since each actor playing in a film enacts a character, it would be desirable to include in the knowledge base also such a link, since it will widen the range of interesting queries that can be answered; this information is not, however, available either from the provided film metadata, or from the scripts.

In this section, we extend the knowledge base constructed in the previous sections by considering the above issues. We start the discussion from the latter.

12.5.1 *Using IMDb Data*

In order to overcome the difficulty of interlinking actors appearing in film metadata and characters appearing in scripts, we resort to IMDb, which among the extended set of metadata that makes available for each film, provides also a mapping between the actors of a film and the character they enact. As already mentioned, IMDb does not use a publicly available vocabulary or ontology to model its data that would make it part of the LOD Cloud, neither does it provide a public data retrieval API. Nevertheless, most of the data can be downloaded in the form of compressed plain text files, which can then be processed by third party tools. One such tool is IMDbPy,[a] which converts the text files into a relational database, thus enabling easy access to the entire IMDb dataset.

Although such a relational database is easily accessible through SQL queries, a knowledge-based system models the world at a different level of abstraction than a relational database does, and, as we have already discussed, considers the data as instances of ontology concepts and relations between instances. Databases handle the data in their raw form without imposing any semantics. Thus, in order to provide ontology-based data access, a kind of mapping between the data residing in the database and the objects handled by the ontologies needs to be defined [30]. A language for expressing such a mapping from relational databases to RDF datasets, called R2RML, has become a W3C recommendation [32], while Direct Mapping [13] is also a W3C recommendation for converting an entire relational database automatically into an RDF representation. Mappings essentially are custom construction instructions for converting selected database data to assertions in the form of RDF triples, and consist of a template describing the structure of the generated triples, and an SQL query for retrieving the data to be applied on the template. Once defined, such mappings can either be materialized, i.e., executed and generate an actual set of assertions that is stored in a RDF triple store, or used as a virtual assertion set and be generated dynamically only when necessary, e.g., at query answering time.

Cast information is not part of the standard film metadata, and this is reflected in the fact that Schema.org does not make any provision for it. Thus in order to construct the relevant assertions from the IMDb data and the mappings, we first need the

---

[a]http://imdbpy.sourceforge.net/.

schema:Movie(imdb:ID@1)	SELECT title.id, title.title
schema:headline(imdb:ID@1,"@2")	FROM title
schema:Person(imdb:ID@1)	SELECT case_info.person_id, name.name
schema:name(imdb:ID@1,"@2")	FROM cast_info, name
	WHERE cast_info.person_id = name.id
	SELECT cast_info.person_role_id,
so:Character(imdb:ID@1)	char_name.name
foaf:name(imdb:ID@1,"@2")	FROM cast_info,char_name
	WHERE cast_info.person_role_id =
	char_name.id
	AND cast_info.role_id IN (1,2)
so:character(imdb:ID@1,imdb:ID@2)	SELECT cast_info.movie_id,
	cast_info.person_role_id
	FROM cast_info
	WHERE cast_info.role_id IN (1,2)
so:isPlayedBy(imdb:ID@1,imdb:ID@2)	SELECT cast_info.person_role_id,
	cast_info.person_id
	FROM cast_info
	WHERE cast_info.role_id IN (1,2)

Figure 12.10 IMDb mapping definitions

vocabulary to describe the relevant entities. So, as an extension of our vocabularies so far, we define two additional object properties: so:isPlayedBy relates a so:Character to the schema:Person that enacts it, and so:character relates a schema:Movie to a so:Character that is enacted by an actor that features in it.

Figure 12.10 shows the mappings that have been defined for constructing the assertions from the relational database generated by IMDbPy. The first column provides the templates based on which assertions are created after execution of the SQL queries provided in the second column. For constructing URIs we defined the namespace imdb to be http://www.image.ntua.gr/imdb/. The result of an SQL query is considered to be a table, and its columns are referenced by @1, @2, etc. For each row in the SQL query result table, a new assertion for each relevant template is created. An indicative set of the assertions that resulted from the materialization of the mappings in Fig. 12.10 are shown in Fig. 12.11.

Now, in the assertion set there are two types of instances, one generated from the available metadata and the scripts, and the other from IMDb data. This is reflected in the different namespaces; we

```
imdb:ID2004003      rdf:type           schema:Movie
imdb:ID2004003      schema:headline    "Death Defying Acts"
imdb:ID2688536      rdf:type           schema:Person
imdb:ID2688536      schema:name        "Ronan, Saoirse"
imdb:ID3104898      rdf:type           so:Character
imdb:ID3104898      foaf:name          "Benji McGarvie"
imdb:ID2004003      so:character       imdb:ID3104898
imdb:ID3104898      so:isPlayedBy      imdb:ID2688536
```

Figure 12.11   Materialized mappings.

have used mv for the first and imdb for the second. This was done because the two kinds of data were obtained from independently developed and unrelated between each other sources, without prior knowledge of the potential equivalences between some of the constructed instances. For example, in the assertions obtained from IMDb, an instance for each film character is constructed and is assigned a name; the same is done for the assertions constructed from the scripts. Although clearly there exists an equivalence relation between these objects, this is not immediately identifiable and has to be inferred by comparing character names. The task is not trivial, because the same character may be given a full name in the one source and a short name in the other (cf. the character names "Benji McGarvie" and "BENJI" in Figs. 12.11 and 12.6, respectively), or because different writing conventions and abbreviations may be used by the two sources. In our case, by applying substring matching on the film titles and character names, we extracted the necessary equivalences between identical objects that allow a unified view of all data. Equivalences between instances are declared using the predefined in the OWL language owl:sameAs predicate, so as to get, e.g., the triples imdb:ID2004003 owl:sameAs mv:MV3713, and imdb:ID3104898 owl:sameAs mv:SR3713RL0.

12.5.2 *Named Entity Recognition*

An important piece of information that may be contained in film scripts are named entities, i.e., names of persons, organizations, locations, etc., whose detection in a text is traditionally called

mv:MV3713SH0404	voc:extraction	mv:MV3713NE067
mv:MV3713NE067	rdf:type	voc:NamedEntity
mv:MV3713NE067	rdfs:label	"Edinburgh Castle"
mv:MV3713NE067	voc:linksTo	dbpedia:Edinburgh_Castle
mv:MV3713SH0404	voc:extraction	mv:MV3713NE068
mv:MV3713NE068	rdf:type	voc:NamedEntity
mv:MV3713NE068	rdfs:label	"Princes Street Gardens"
mv:MV3713NE067	voc:linksTo	dbpedia:Princes_Street_Gardens

Figure 12.12   Assertions resulting from named entity recognition.

named entity recognition. Named-entity recognition is a subfield of information extraction, has a long research tradition, and current state-of-the art systems for the English language can offer near-human performance.

Recognizing that certain film scripts contain references to real locations and persons, we performed named entity recognition on all textual descriptions included in the film scripts. For this purpose we used the statistical-based engine ([12]) of DBpedia Spotlight.[a] DBpedia Spotlight a not a traditional named entity recognition tool in that after recognizing the named entities in the text, it does not simply annotate them using the traditional, relatively poor named entity categorization scheme (which consists of a small number of very wide categories such as person, location, organization, etc.), but following a disambiguation phase, it annotates them by providing links to the most probable corresponding entities of DBpedia. In DBpedia resources are of course identified by their URI, and these are the links provided by DBpedia Spotlight. In our modeling, we represent each extracted entity as an instance of the voc:NamedEntity class, and using the voc:linksTo property, we link them with the respective DBpedia resources. Figure 12.12 shows the assertions that were generated for the first scene of the script extract shown in Fig. 12.3.

Having available the URIs of the extracted entities, we make further use of the LOD Cloud by querying DBpedia in order to

---

[a]https://github.com/dbpedia-spotlight/dbpedia-spotlight/wiki.

retrieve the classes to which the identified objects belong. DBpedia offers a rich categorization of its objects using several vocabularies of the LOD Cloud; for simplicity, we keep only the classes that are part of the DBpedia ontology. For example, in relation to the assertions of Fig. 12.12, we got that for DBpedia dbpedia:Edinburgh_Castle is an instance of dbpedia-owl:MilitaryStructure, so we included in our assertions set the triple dbpedia:Edinburgh_Castle rdf:type dbpedia-owl:MilitaryStructure. Then, by reasoning we can infer, e.g., that dbpedia:Edinburgh_Castle is also an instance of the dbpedia-owl:Building, dbpedia-owl:ArchitecturalStructure, and dbpedia-owl:Place classes, since dbpedia-owl:MilitaryStructure is a subclass of all of the above classes in the DBpedia ontology.

12.5.3 *Linking to WordNet*

The textual descriptions included in the scripts contain much more information apart from the named entities, since they describe every aspect of what is happening in a film. Even a traditional keyword-based search on these texts would allow the retrieval of scenes or shots where particular words are mentioned. However, WordNet [15, 22] can greatly enhance this capability. WordNet is a "large lexical database of English, in which nouns, verbs, adjectives and adverbs are grouped into sets of cognitive synonyms (called *synsets*), each expressing a distinct concept." A very useful feature of WordNet is that each concept provides a set of hypernym concepts, which are more general concepts, including semantically the concept in question. Thus, by exploiting this hierarchy, one can go gradually from a lower-level concept to more high-level concepts and use this information to allow more powerful semantic search. For example, if one is interested in retrieving scenes of films where mammals are shown, it is very unlikely to retrieve anything by just searching for keyword mammal. By using the hypernymity hierarchies of WordNet, however, scenes whose description includes the word horse or elephant can be retrieved by searching for mammals, since horse and elephant are hyponyms of mammal.

An RDF version of the entire WordNet knowledge base is available online,[a] which we use in the proposed system. Our aim

---

[a]http://semanticweb.cs.vu.nl/lod/wn30/.

is to match all words in the available textual descriptions with the respective WordNet concepts, so as to obtain all semantic characterizations of each word. However, since each word may have several meanings, automatically determining what its meaning is in a particular context, is a hard, AI-complete problem, called Word Sense Disambiguation (WSD). In order to perform WSD, we used WordNet::SenseRelate [29],[a] which is a Perl tool that takes a text document as an its input, and provides in the output an enriched version of the text, in which each word is annotated with the respective WordNet synset with which the disambiguation process has associated it.

Using WordNet::SenseRelate, we associated each word in the textual descriptions of the scripts to a WordNet synset, and subsequently retrieved all hypernym synsets. Given that each word may have several distinct meanings, in order to reduce false meaning identification, in all cases we kept only the most common hypernym of each synset. As an example, consider the word "crags" mentioned in the first scene of the script in Fig. 12.3, which gave rise to the assertions shown in Fig. 12.13.

```
mv:MV3713SH0404    voc:extraction    mv:MV3713TW0390
mv:MV3713TW0390    rdf:type          voc:TextWord
mv:MV3713TW0390    rfds:label        "crag"
mv:MV3713TW0390    voc:linksTo       wn30:synset-crag-noun-1
mv:MV3713TW0390    voc:linksTo       wn30:synset-cliff-noun-1
mv:MV3713TW0390    voc:linksTo       wn30:synset-geological_
                                     formation-noun-1
mv:MV3713TW0390    voc:linksTo       wn30:synset-physical_
                                     entity-noun-1
mv:MV3713TW0390    voc:linksTo       wn30:synset-entity-noun-1
mv:MV3713TW0390    voc:linksTo       wn30:synset-object-noun-1
```

Figure 12.13 Assertions linking text words to the WordNet.

Each of the WordNet synsets that are retrieved carries an rdfs:label that provides in text the word that it represents, so that

---

[a]http://senserelate.sourceforge.net/.

```
{ "id": "3713",
  "title": "Death Defying Acts",
  "results": [ {
     "time": 943000,
     "images": [ {
        "uri": "http://farm4.static.flickr.com/
                             3058/2866620780
                             _d47efbea14_m.jpg",
        "id": 638017,
        "location": { "latitude": 51.508598,
                     "longitude": -0.128767 },
        "similarity": "8.071",
        "inCluster": false,
        "title": "WestminsterAbbey",
        "deleted": 0 }, ... ]
     "location": { "latitude": 51.5137, "longitude":
                  -0.100196 },
     "landmarks": [ {
        "wikiID": 0,
        "name": "St Paul's Cathedral",
        "link": "http://en.wikipedia.org/wiki/
                     St_Paul's_Cathedral",
        "location": { "latitude": 51.5138, "longitude":
                     -0.098  },
        "city": "London",
        "type": "landmark",
        "similarity": 0.94999998807907,
        "count": 1 }, ... ],
     "city": "London"
  } ]
}
```

Figure 12.14 Video analysis results.

text-based search can be performed. For example, the constructed knowledge base contains also the assertion `wn30:synset-cliff-noun-1` `rdfs:label "cliff"@en`.

Table 12.2 Frame with detected POI and matching Flickr images

12.5.4 *Visual Analysis Results*

The last kind of analysis results that we have to incorporate into the knowledge base are the video analysis result. As discussed in detail in 12.4.3, the video analysis procedure resulted in the identification of some POIs for each film. In its simplest form, a POI is characterized only by the location coordinates and a city name, but in most cases a set of one or more matching landmarks is also provided, with a link to the respective Wikipedia resource. Links to the Flickr images which led to the detection of the POI are also provided.

The detected POIs are represented in a JSON format, a small extract of which for the film of Fig. 12.2 is shown in Fig. 12.14. Furthermore, the top of Table 12.2 shows the frame in which the particular POI was detected, and the bottom of the same table shows the matching Flickr images.

For incorporating the video analysis results in the semantic representation of the film contents, the essential information are the timecode of the appearance of each POI within the film (which allows the computation of the corresponding frame), the city name,

```
mv:MV3713V01FR023575    voc:extraction    mv:MV3713IMG1

mv:MV3713IMG1           rdf:type          voc:ImagePOI

mv:MV3713IMG1           voc:linksTo       dbpedia:St_Paul's_Cathedral
```

Figure 12.15   Assertions for a detected POI.

and the Wikipedia URI (which is changed to the corresponding DBpedia URI) of the corresponding landmarks, when available. The resulting assertions for the POI of Fig. 12.14 are shown in Fig. 12.15.

12.6 Query Answering

The semantic knowledge base whose construction was described in detail in the preceding sections was done in order to enable us to pose semantic queries on it, so as to be able to retrieve, e.g., shots of films where a certain landmark appears. As already mentioned, answering semantic queries over OWL ontologies is in general a difficult task due to the high computational complexity that is a result of the high expressivity of OWL. Systems that solve this task, even using several optimization, cannot handle efficiently large volumes of data. In order to enable the development of practical systems with reasonable response times, several lower expressivity sublanguages of OWL have been proposed. One such language is DL-Lite, which is also the theoretical base of OWL QL. There are also some more expressive sublanguages which may behave reasonably well in practical problems; these are based on the $\mathcal{EL}$ description language, and underpin the OWL EL profile. Several practical systems that resolve the query answering programs over ontology languages of restricted expressivity have been developed, such as QuOnto [1], Presto [33], Nyaya [17], IQAROS [43], which support the expressivity of DL-Lite; Requiem [31] and Rapid [11], that support the expressivity of $\mathcal{ELHI}$, and Clipper [14] that supports the even more expressive Horn-$\mathcal{SHIQ}$ language.

12.6.1 *Query Rewriting*

One of the most prominent approaches in query answering with low expressivity ontology languages such as DL-Lite is query rewriting. According to this approach, the given query is processed in conjunction with the provided ontology in order to produce an expanded query that can be managed be existing data access techniques. The expanded query may be, e.g., a union of conjunctive queries, that can be transformed into an SQL or SPARQL query and executed on a relational database system or a triple store respectively, or it may be a datalog program that requires a deductive database system to be executed. The process of producing the expanded query essentially involves the performance of all possibly inferences between the used query and the ontological knowledge, so that the extended query is an encoding of all knowledge that was implicit in the user query and modeled in the ontological knowledge.

The simplest illustrative example is the case of a taxonomical knowledge and a user that asks for all instances of a high level concept. Consider, for instance, a user that wants to retrieve all shots of a film where a well-known building appears. In our system, such buildings may have been detected by the named entity recognition or by the video analysis module. In either case the result are assertions about the recognized buildings in terms of the DBpedia ontology. So the user query should ask for all shots that are linked to a `dbpedia-owl:Building`. However, the buildings may have been recognized, e.g., as `dbpedia-owl:MilitaryStructure`, `dbpedia-owl:ReligiousBuilding` or `dbpedia-owl:Hotel` buildings. Given that all of these classes are subclasses of dbpedia-owl:Building, in order to retrieve all relevant shots, the initial user query asking for `dbpedia-owl:Building` has to be expanded into a union of queries, one for each subclass of `dbpedia-owl:Building`. These queries can then be executed directly over the underlying triple store and get all answers. Of course, in practice when the knowledge is not a simple taxonomy, the inferences that give rise to the expanded query are much more complex.

12.6.2 *Evaluation*

In this section, we discuss some examples of queries posed on the knowledge base that we have constructed. The corpus generated in the national project acknowledged in the paper contained more than 100 films, their trailers and scripts, and some Greek documentaries. The results presented in this section refer to a knowledge base constructed from a subcorpus of 10 films, which have been analyzed semantically and content-based, as described above.

In the system implementation we adopted the query rewriting approach, and as reasoning engine for answering user queries we used the Rapid system [11], which is highly efficient for DL-Lite ontologies. The reasoning required for the rewriting was performed using the ontologies defined in Section 12.3, whose expressivity falls within the DL-Lite expressivity, as well as the DL-Lite fragment of the DBpedia ontology. The results of the query rewriting were translated into the corresponding SPARQL queries, which were then executed on the knowledge base which was constructed in Sections 12.3 and 12.5.

(1) *Find all internal night scenes of a particular film.* A query like this offers the user the possibility to get some kind of visual overview of a film, considerably more focused than the sequence of shots shown in Table 12.1. In order to be answered, only the structural information obtained from the scripts is required. The query, for the film "Death Defying Acts" is formulated as follows:

```
Q1(?time,?descr) <- schema:Movie(?film),
                    schema:headline(?film,"Death Defying
                         Acts"@en),
                    so:script(?film,?script),
                    dc:isPartOf(?scene,?script),
                    so:InternalScene(?scene),
                    so:NightScene(?scene),
                    so:startFrame(?scene,?frame),
                    vr:startTime(?frame,?time),
                    dc:description(?scene,?descr).
```

The first 8 results are shown in Table 12.3. The results are the first shot of the matching scenes and accompanied by the timestamp, and scene description.

Table 12.3   Results for query Q1

1. Death Defying Acts, 00:07:10.40
MCTAVISH'S PALACE MUSIC HALL

2 .Death Defying Acts, 00:13:16.56
STAR PICTURE THEATRE

3. Death Defying Acts, 00:22:08.32
RECEPTION, SCOTTISH LION HOTEL

4. Death Defying Acts, 00:23:32.96
HOUDINI'S DRESSING ROOM

5. Death Defying Acts, 00:24:14.56
HOUDINI'S DRESSING ROOM

6. Death Defying Acts, 00:26:31.56
THEATRE ROYAL

7. Death Defying Acts, 00:29:36.64
BACKSTAGE – THEATRE ROYAL

8. Death Defying Acts, 00:30:26.36
BOTHY

(2) *Find shots where a weapon appears.* Since "weapon" is a general term for referring to an object that is used for fighting or attacking someone, it is more likely that in the textual descriptions contained in the scripts particular types of weapons such as guns, bombs, etc. will be mentioned. Thus, the ability to answer this query, relies on the linking of the textual descriptions with the WordNet synset hierarchies. The query is formulated as follows:

```
Q2(?title,?time,?word) <- schema:Movie(?film),
                          schema:headline(?film,?title),
                          so:script(?film,?script),
                          dc:isPartOf(?scene,?script),
                          dc:isPartOf(?shot,?scene),
                          so:startFrame(?shot,?frame),
                          vr:startTime(?frame,?time),
                          voc:extraction(?shot,?ex),
                          voc:TextWord(?ex),
                          rdfs:label(?ex, ?word),
                          voc:linksTo(?ex,?link),
                          rdfs:label(?link,"weapon"@en).
```

Some indicative results are shown in Table 12.4. The results are the matching shots and they are accompanied by the title of the film, the timestamp, and the actual word of the script which caused each shot to be retrieved. As expected, most of the results are retrieved because a particular type of weapon appears in the respective shots.

(3) *Find shots where a well-known building appears.* Within the film content, a well-known building may have been detected either from the image analysis of the video content, or from the named entity recognition procedure applied in the scripts. In either case the knowledge base will provide a triple that links a film shot with the DBpedia URI of the building that has been detected to appear in it. Hence, the query for retrieving the results obtained from script content analysis is

Table 12.4 Results for query Q2

1. Youth Without Youth, 00:57:46.77
pistol

2 .Bangkok Dangerous, 00:02:21.40
bullet

3. Bangkok Dangerous, 00:02:33.76
rifle

4. Bangkok Dangerous, 00:21:50.64
gun

5. Bangkok Dangerous, 01:23:22.56
weapon

6. In Her Line of Fire, 00:11:38.91
bullet

7. In Her Line of Fire, 00:12:28.95
gun

8. In Her Line of Fire, 00:14:15.51
machete

```
Q3(?title,?time,?resource) <- schema:Movie(?film),
                               schema:headline(?film,?title),
                               so:script(?film,?script),
                               dc:isPartOf(?scene,?script),
                               dc:isPartOf(?shot,?scene),
                               so:startFrame(?shot,?frame),
                               vr:startTime(?frame,?time),
                               so:extraction(?shot,?ex),
                               voc:linksTo(?ex,?resource),

                               dbpedia:Building(?resource).
```

while to retrieve the results that come from image analysis we have to match the frame where a building has been detected, to the respective movie shot. The query is the following:

```
Q4(?title,?time,?resource) <- schema:Movie(?film),
                               schema:headline(?film,?title),
                               schema:encoding(?film,?video),
                               dc:isPartOf(?frame,?video),
                               dc:isPartOf(?frame,?shot),
                               so:Shot(?shot),
                               so:startFrame(?shot,?sframe),
                               vr:startTime(?sframe,?time),
                               so:extraction(?frame,?ex),
                               voc:linksTo(?ex,?resource),

                               dbpedia:Building(?resource).
```

Some indicative results are shown in Tables 12.5 and 12.6, respectively. Each result is accompanied by the title of the film, the timestamp, and the URI to the respective DBpedia object.

All the above examples illustrate the capability of the proposed approach to provide semantic searching in semantically enriched audiovisual film content.

12.7 Conclusions

The design and implementation of intelligent semantic analysis and retrieval of multimedia content has been a key issue in the last decade, following the development of the MPEG and Semantic

Table 12.5 Results for query Q3

1. In Her Line of Fire, 00:20:11.80
http://dbpedia.org/resource/
White_House

2. In Her Line of Fire, 01:10:10.70
http://dbpedia.org/resource/
White_House

3. Death Defying Acts, 00:37:24.60
http://dbpedia.org/resource/
Edinburgh_Castle

4. Death Defying Acts, 01:05:21.24
http://dbpedia.org/resource/
Edinburgh_Castle

Web standards. Of specific importance in this framework is the development of systems that are able to semantically analyze and answer user queries. In particular, semantic query answering refers to construction of answers to queries posed by users, based not only on string matching over data that are stored in databases, but also on the implicit meaning that can be found by reasoning. In this way, content metadata can be terminologically described, semantically connected and used in conjunction with other, useful, possibly complementary information, independently published on the Web. In this chapter we have proposed and developed a system which, on the one hand, is able to semantically represent, enrich and retrieve audiovisual, specifically film, content, and on the other hand, includes a powerful visual analysis subsystem, able to identify points of interest in the film content and retrieve the parts of it that match the query content. An experimental study has been presented which illustrates the improvement achieved

Table 12.6   Results for query Q4

| 1. In Her Line of Fire, 00:00:56.77
http://dbpedia.org/resource/
White_House | 2. In Her Line of Fire, 01:20:34.79
http://dbpedia.org/resource/
White_House |

| 3. Death Defying Acts, 00:15:38.44
http://dbpedia.org/resource/
St_Paul's_Cathedral | 4. Five Minarets in New York, 01:22:41.00
http://dbpedia.org/resource/
Sultan_Ahmed_Mosque |

by exploiting both semantic and visual aspects of audiovisual film content. Since the amount of audiovisual and cultural content being digitized and searchable through the Web continuously increases, this type of content is a characteristic type of big data. We are currently extending the presented approach and the developed system so as to handle large amounts of audiovisual, specifically film, data, by interweaving the semantic and content based search methodology with a machine learning framework. In particular, Support Vector Machines constitute a well known method which is based on kernel functions to efficiently induce classifiers that work by mapping visual features, and the corresponding items, onto an embedding space, where they can be discriminated by means of linear classifiers. As such, they can be used for effectively exploiting the extracted visual features, as well as metadata information, and classify the film content in different concept categories that are included in the formal knowledge, reducing the search space and being able to deal with big amounts of data.

Acknowledgments

This work is partially funded by the Greek GSRT-funded project 09SYN-72-922 "IS-HELLEANA: Intelligent System for HELLEnic Audiovisual National Aggregator," and by the European Commission Best Practice Network "Europeana Space" under Contract No 621037. All presented script excerpts and frames come from films provided by Ausiovisual SA within the above-mentioned IS-HELLEANA project. We thank them for this.

References

1. Andrea Acciarri, Diego Calvanese, Giuseppe De Giacomo, Domenico Lembo, Maurizio Lenzerini, Mattia Palmieri, and Riccardo Rosati. Quonto: Querying ontologies. In *AAAI*, pages 1670–1671, 2005.
2. Yannis Avrithis and Yannis Kalantidis. Approximate gaussian mixtures for large scale vocabularies. In *Computer Vision–ECCV 2012*, pages 15–28. Springer, 2012.
3. Yannis Avrithis, Yannis Kalantidis, Giorgos Tolias, and Evaggelos Spyrou. Retrieving landmark and non-landmark images from community photo collections. In *Proceedings of the International Conference on Multimedia*, pages 153–162. ACM, 2010.
4. Yannis Avrithis and Konstantinos Rapantzikos. The medial feature detector: Stable regions from image boundaries. In *Computer Vision (ICCV), 2011 IEEE International Conference on*, pages 1724–1731. IEEE, 2011.
5. Yannis Avrithis, Giorgos Tolias, and Yannis Kalantidis. Feature map hashing: sub-linear indexing of appearance and global geometry. In *Proceedings of the International Conference on Multimedia*, pages 231–240. ACM, 2010.
6. Franz Baader, Diego Calvanese, Deborah L. McGuinness, Daniele Nardi, and Peter F. Patel-Schneider, editors. *The Description Logic Handbook: Theory, Implementation, and Applications*. Cambridge University Press, New York, NY, USA, 2003.

7. Herbert Bay, Tinne Tuytelaars, and Luc Van Gool. Surf: Speeded up robust features. In *Computer Vision–ECCV 2006*, pages 404–417. Springer, 2006.

8. Michael Calonder, Vincent Lepetit, Christoph Strecha, and Pascal Fua. Brief: Binary robust independent elementary features. In *Computer Vision–ECCV 2010*, pages 778–792. Springer, 2010.

9. Hillis Cole. *The Complete Guide to Standard Script Formats*. CMC Pub, North Hollywood, Calif, 1988.

10. Shih-Fu Chang, Thomas Sikora, and A Purl. Overview of the mpeg-7 standard. *Circuits and Systems for Video Technology, IEEE Transactions on*, 11(6):688–695, 2001.

11. Alexandros Chortaras, Despoina Trivela, and Giorgos B. Stamou. Optimized query rewriting for OWL 2 QL. In *CADE*, pages 192–206, 2011.

12. Joachim Daiber, Max Jakob, Chris Hokamp, and Pablo N. Mendes. Improving efficiency and accuracy in multilingual entity extraction. In *I-SEMANTICS*, pages 121–124, 2013.

13. A Direct Mapping of relational data to RDF. http://www.w3.org/TR/2012/CR-rdb-direct-mapping-20120223/.

14. Thomas Eiter, Magdalena Ortiz, Mantas Simkus, Trung-Kien Tran, and Guohui Xiao. Query rewriting for horn-shiq plus rules. In *AAAI*, 2012.

15. C. Fellbaum. *WordNet: An Electronic Lexical Database*. Language, Speech and Communication. Mit Press, 1998.

16. Birte Glimm, Carsten Lutz, Ian Horrocks, and Ulrike Sattler. Conjunctive query answering for the description logic SHIQ. *Journal of Artificial Intelligence Research*, 31:157–204, 2008.

17. Georg Gottlob, Giorgio Orsi, and Andreas Pieris. Ontological queries: Rewriting and optimization. In *ICDE*, pages 2–13, 2011.

18. Herve Jegou, Matthijs Douze, and Cordelia Schmid. Hamming embedding and weak geometric consistency for large scale image search. In *Computer Vision–ECCV 2008*, pages 304–317. Springer, 2008.

19. Yannis Kalantidis, Giorgos Tolias, Evaggelos Spyrou, Phivos Mylonas, and Yannis Avrithis. Visual image retrieval and localization. In *7th International Workshop on Content-Based Multimedia Indexing, Greece*, 2009.

20. Stefan Leutenegger, Margarita Chli, and Roland Yves Siegwart. Brisk: Binary robust invariant scalable keypoints. In *Computer Vision (ICCV), 2011 IEEE International Conference on*, pages 2548–2555. IEEE, 2011.

21. Jiri Matas, Ondrej Chum, Martin Urban, and Tomás Pajdla. Robust wide-baseline stereo from maximally stable extremal regions. *Image and Vision Computing*, 22(10):761–767, 2004.

22. George A. Miller. Wordnet: A lexical database for english. *Communications of the ACM*, 38(11):39–41, November 1995.

23. Krystian Mikolajczyk and Cordelia Schmid. Scale & affine invariant interest point detectors. *International Journal of Computer Vision*, 60(1):63–86, 2004.

24. David Nister and Henrik Stewenius. Scalable recognition with a vocabulary tree. In *Computer Vision and Pattern Recognition, 2006 IEEE Computer Society Conference on*, volume 2, pages 2161–2168. IEEE, 2006.

25. Ontology for Media Resources 1.0. http://www.w3.org/TR/mediaont-10/.

26. Ontology Web Language. http://www.w3.org/TR/owl2-overview/.

27. James Philbin, Ondrej Chum, Michael Isard, Josef Sivic, and Andrew Zisserman. Object retrieval with large vocabularies and fast spatial matching. In *Computer Vision and Pattern Recognition, 2007. CVPR'07. IEEE Conference on*, pages 1–8. IEEE, 2007.

28. Michal Perd'och, Ondrej Chum, and Jiri Matas. Efficient representation of local geometry for large scale object retrieval. In *Computer Vision and Pattern Recognition, 2009. CVPR 2009. IEEE Conference on*, pages 9–16. IEEE, 2009.

29. Ted Pedersen and Varada Kolhatkar. Wordnet::senserelate::allwords: A broad coverage word sense tagger that maximizes semantic relatedness. NAACL-Demonstrations '09, pages 17–20, Stroudsburg, PA, USA, 2009. Association for Computational Linguistics.

30. Antonella Poggi, Domenico Lembo, Diego Calvanese, Giuseppe De Giacomo, Maurizio Lenzerini, and Riccardo Rosati. Linking data to ontologies. *Journal on Data Semantics*, 10:133–173, 2008.

31. Héctor Pérez-Urbina, Boris Motik, and Ian Horrocks. Tractable query answering and rewriting under description logic constraints. *Journal of Applied Logic*, 8(2):186–209, 2010.

32. R2RML: RDB to RDF Mapping Language. http://www.w3.org/TR/r2rml/.

33. Riccardo Rosati and Alessandro Almatelli. Improving query answering over dl-lite ontologies. In *KR*, 2010.

34. Konstantinos Rapantzikos, Yannis Avrithis, and Stefanos Kollias. Detecting regions from single scale edges. In *Trends and Topics in Computer Vision*, pages 298–311. Springer, 2012.

35. RDF Schema. http://www.w3.org/TR/rdf-schema/.

36. Resource Description Framework. http://www.w3.org/RDF/.

37. Dieter Van Rijsselbergen, Barbara Van De Keer, Maarten Verwaest, Erik Mannens, and Rik Van de Walle. Movie script markup language. In *ACM Symposium on Document Engineering*, pages 161–170, 2009.

38. SPARQL query language for RDF. http://www.w3.org/TR/rdf-sparql-query/.

39. Josef Sivic and Andrew Zisserman. Video google: A text retrieval approach to object matching in videos. In *Computer Vision, 2003. Proceedings. Ninth IEEE International Conference on*, pages 1470–1477. IEEE, 2003.

40. Giorgos Tolias and Yannis Avrithis. Speeded-up, relaxed spatial matching. In *Computer Vision (ICCV), 2011 IEEE International Conference on*, pages 1653–1660. IEEE, 2011.

41. Giorgos Tolias, Yannis Kalantidis, and Yannis Avrithis. Symcity: feature selection by symmetry for large scale image retrieval. In *Proceedings of the 20th ACM International Conference on Multimedia*, pages 189–198. ACM, 2012.

42. Christos Varytimidis, Konstantinos Rapantzikos, and Yannis Avrithis. Wαsh: weighted α-shapes for local feature detection. In *Computer Vision–ECCV 2012*, pages 788–801. Springer, 2012.

43. Tassos Venetis, Giorgos Stoilos, and Giorgos B. Stamou. Query extensions and incremental query rewriting for owl 2 ql ontologies. *Journal on Data Semantics*, 3(1):1–23, 2014.

44. Junsong Yuan, Ying Wu, and Ming Yang. Discovery of collocation patterns: from visual words to visual phrases. In *Computer Vision and Pattern Recognition, 2007. CVPR'07. IEEE Conference on*, pages 1–8. IEEE, 2007.

Chapter 13

Modeling the Structures of Complex Systems: Data Representations, Neural Learning, and Artificial Mind

Tetsuya Hoya

Department of Mathematics, College of Science & Technology, Nihon University,
1-8-14, Kanda-Surugadai, Chiyoda-Ku, Tokyo, Japan 101-8308
hoya@math.cst.nihon-u.ac.jp

Complex architectures can be decomposed into their constituents that can be straightforward, as well as analytically tractable, and reconstructed in reverse, yielding a holistic representation that is fully descriptive in an elegant and uniform manner using mathematical modeling tools. This kind of approach is what Prof. Anthony G. Constantinides inspired the author to explore when he was under his supervision during the PhD period at Imperial (1994–1997). Since then, the author has engaged in a number of topics—graph theoretic representation of image data, data pruning, models of learning by neural networks, and proposal of artificial mind system. The Festschrift reviews the author's research activities so far relevant to modeling complex systems, with a reminiscence of the days in the past, and suggests some future directions.

Trends in Digital Signal Processing: A Festschrift in Honour of A. G. Constantinides
Edited by Yong Ching Lim, Hon Keung Kwan, and Wan-Chi Siu
Copyright © 2016 Pan Stanford Publishing Pte. Ltd.
ISBN 978-981-4669-50-4 (Hardcover), 978-981-4669-51-1 (eBook)
www.panstanford.com

13.1 Introduction

The year 1994 was an important turning point in my life, as studying abroad unexpectedly came up as a possibility; it was one day in late January of that year while I was working as a teaching assistant for some laboratory experiments, when Prof. Yoshihisa Ishida, the author's supervisor for his master's thesis at the Department of Electronics and Communication Engineering of Meiji University, spoke to me and out of the blue suggested a further study by joining the signal processing laboratory led by Prof. Constantinides at Imperial College. Just before the author's enrollment of the master's course at Meiji, Prof. Ishida had been on his sabbatical leave to Perth, where Prof. Constantinides was also present and they soon came to know each other. In those days, I was not fully convinced of what to do next, though the vast majority of graduate students from the master's course went straight into industry upon completing the degree without any apparent hesitation, and I could very well have followed the same path as theirs. All around me, no story was heard about continuing their studies for a higher degree, nor studying abroad. However, I decided to follow my supervisor's advice and soon after sent an international fax to the number printed on the card that was personally given to me by Prof. Ishida, in which I included an introduction of myself and inquiries regarding how to make an application for the PhD course at Imperial. That was the first contact I made with Tony. Soon after that, I received a kind response from him and later received an official letter of conditional offer from Imperial. In September 1994, I flew to London and for the very first time met him in person and told him about how I had been studying both adaptive filtering and speech recognition areas, as well as investigating the feasibility of incremental training by multi-layered perceptron-type neural networks (MLP-NNs). Then I told him that I was interested in joining his laboratory for the PhD degree. It was rather surprising to me, when I was immediately told that he would accept me as a PhD student in his lab, only after having heard my clumsy explanation in English; I had imagined that to get into his laboratory there must be a series of checkpoints to pass, from improving my IELTS score by means of attending a pre-sessional course in English, to sitting eventually for a formal oral examination in the presence of many pedants to demonstrate my research abilities.

I used to approach the Kensington Gardens from Lancaster Gate or Queensway tube station and then walk down to the south of the Gardens to come out in the busy Kensington Rd., walking on the pleasant evergreen lawns between the grids of trees. On the way, it was a real joy when I would pass by a host of swans together with their offspring around the man-made Round Pond between (if my memory is correct) the spring to early summer periods, or, in winter, when from time to time I had to keep my head straight up against the chilly and strong head wind, under the leaden, murky sky. The sign of "Imperial College of Science, Technology, and Medicine" would finally be visible at the T-junction of Prince Consort Rd. and Exhibition Rd. The Electrical Engineering building can be accessed via the Exhibition Rd., on the eighth floor of which is situated Tony's laboratory. Inside the lab were several partitioned and small-squared rooms, one of which was at the center of the EE building and, as far as I remember, shared by some visitors from the mainland China, a tall British man working for BT, Lambo (Prof. Sangarapillai Lambothoran of Loughborough University) sitting on the other side from me, and myself. In that space, I was given a large, wooden desk that was wide enough to pile up several bunches of papers on as well as some books, while still providing extra surface area to place a working paper or laptop on. The room was almost always kept relatively tidy and quiet enough for us all to hear someone typing on the keyboard or snoring in their sleep from some other separated room(s).

My first year of the PhD program went by rather hectically, as it was mandatory for every PhD candidate in the lab to take a few MSc taught courses and pass the exams, on top of carrying on with their own research; the two lectures on digital filters by Tony and neural networks were somewhat similar to the ones that I had taken at Meiji, but the other one, i.e., the one on the probability theory, was really tough; I had never studied it before coming to the UK, although I later learned that it is an inevitable subject in order to understand the signal processing domain in depth. On the research side, the professor suggested to me a book chapter to read through, i.e., the chapter on the location of centers in graphs, in a book [1] written by Prof. Nicos Christofides (of the Department of Management Science of Imperial College). At the time, it was not obvious to me at all how the materials in the chapter, which are all relevant to graphs, can be useful to solve the problem I was working on, i.e., performing robustly an incremental training by MLPs, nor did he explain in detail how to fulfill the objectives. But soon afterwards, the professor proposed to me another fascinating research topic, i.e., that the algorithms of finding absolute centers in graphs might be employed to prune the data sets used for training NNs. (Later, I realized that this manner of teaching students is tremendously important for those who eagerly wish to develop their own creativity: not giving the instructions I could think of all the time but rather urging students to contemplate the problem they are faced with for themselves, with only a few words, and waiting for their own solutions to pop out.) In parallel to this, I had engaged in studying edge-detection of an image by applying the shortest path algorithm by Dijkstra, the algorithm of which also appears in another chapter of Nicos' monograph. Both the studies eventually led to the successful MPhil to PhD transfer, which took place in my second year. Subsequently, the PhD viva was held during my third year, i.e., in the winter of 1997, soon after the recovery from a terrible flu. As far as I remember, the viva itself did not take longer at all than I expected (later, I have heard from my colleagues that it indeed was unusually quite short one), where both Profs. Constantinides and Christofides (at that moment Prof. Christofides kindly served as another examiner of my thesis) were present. In the viva, I was asked to describe concisely each of the topics studied during the past three years, using a somewhat small whiteboard, and did my best to answer all the relevant technical questions raised during the viva.

It was around that period of time when the decision to embark upon a career as a research scientist naturally came to my mind. Coincidentally, there was a job opening for a postdoc within the same group, just before the completion of my PhD thesis. The job was on the three-year basis of the project funded by the EPSRC (Engineering and Physical Sciences Research Council, UK), under the direction by both Jonathon (Prof. Jonathon A. Chambers of Loughborough

University) and Dr. Patrick A. Naylor. Although the topic of interest, i.e., acoustic echo cancellation and noise reduction in speech signals, was to a certain extent shifted from the main study during the PhD period, I thought it would be a very good opportunity to broaden my knowledge toward different directions, while extending the stay in the UK on my own earnings. Eventually, my hope came true; soon after, I was chosen among several candidates and became able to spend another three years in London, while studying further the signal processing areas. (Later, I happened to know that Prof. Constantinides supported strongly my application during the selection process, which eventually led to another important turning point in my life, and I am thus deeply indebted to him in this respect, too.)

13.2 Holistic Representation of Complex Data Structures—by Way of Graph Theoretic Methods

13.2.1 *Edge Detection of an Image*

On digital computers, an image is typically represented by a myriad of finite values, called *pixels*, each value of which varies according to its intensity. Applying a graph theoretic algorithm to an image enables us to reveal its underlying meaningful structures in a uniform and rigorous manner, which may not be at a first glance apparent, and re-visualize it via the reintegration of the image in various forms. In such an approach, all the pixels of an image are converted into some form of a graph that is composed by a set of vertices and their weighted links. Morris, et al. [2] showed that segmentation and edge detection of an image are interrelated and that both the problems can be uniformly treated by means of shortest-spanning tree (SST) of a graph. In their method, an SST of a grid-shaped graph, i.e., a four-way connected weighted graph (called the dual-graph), is formed for the edge detection, in which each link is given a negative value of the difference between two adjacent pixels.

In the thesis [3], another method by means of applying a shortest path algorithm is presented. In the method, *N*-shortest paths are first found on a modified dual-graph. The modified dual-graph has a pair of artificially terminated vertices, each connected to all the vertices lying on either the top/left or bottom/right edge of the graph, and the N-disjoint shortest paths are iteratively searched in both the directions of top-to-down and left-to-right. Since the edges of an image are considered to lie on some portions of the shortest paths so found, an edge image can be eventually obtained by mapping the portions (i.e., $L(<N)$ least costly links from them) back onto the respective pixels. It was empirically shown that, though the resultant edge images are almost identical to those obtained using the SST, images with thinner edges than the case of SST can be generated by applying a masking function; all the links in the vicinity of the shortest paths (the range of which is specified by the masking function) found up to the last search will be skipped during the next.

For edge detection of an image, the approach by applying a local derivative operator is probably most well known, as represented by the work of Marr and Hildreth [4]. In contrast, the two edge detection methods described above are in principle based upon a global search algorithm that has a firm mathematical background in graph theory. As aforementioned, these approaches yield a holistic and hierarchical representation of an entire image, which can be useful for various purposes. What would be more interesting is to figure out some biological correspondence with these mathematical principles. For instance, analyzing the way how a slime mold forms an efficient network may give us a clue toward this direction [5].

13.2.2 *Pruning the Dataset Used for Training Neural Networks*

In the engineering domain, the term neural network (NN) normally stands for a mathematically modeled network of real neurons in the brain (namely, *artificial neural networks*, or ANNs, in short), and thus NNs are regarded as biologically motivated (or inspired) functions to fulfill various objectives. In order to get them to work as expected, the internal parameters normally need to be adjusted in advance, by means of the so-called *training* algorithm, using a set of training data and target response pairs. In practice, however, it quite often becomes crucial to reduce the amount of the data set for training.

This is not simply because the computational load can be relaxed via removing the redundant data contained in the original training set, but because degradation in the generalization capability due to the excessive training can be avoided. For this purpose, a data clustering algorithm, such as k-means or learning vector quantization (LVQ), is commonly employed.

There is another approach based upon the graph theory; during the PhD period, the author developed three graph theory-oriented methods for the data pruning [3, 6], namely the vertex-chain, list-splitting, and SST-splitting methods. In the approach, a nondirected tournament graph is formed, in which each vertex represents the corresponding training pattern, while the link between a pair of the vertices denotes the distance (i.e., Euclidean) between the two distinct pattern data. Each of the three methods follows the same steps; (1) partition the tournament graph into a certain number of its disjoint subgraphs, (2) find the absolute center on each subgraph, and (3) convert the location of each center to the corresponding pattern (a.k.a. "representative pattern"), the collection of which eventually constitutes a pruned version of the entire training set. In contrast, they differ from each other, in their manners of forming subgraphs; the original tournament graph is recursively partitioned into its subgraphs in both the list-splitting and SST splitting methods (i.e., in the list splitting, the operation of recursive splitting is performed on an ordered list of the distances between the dominant and other remaining vertices in the original graph, whereas an SST is used, instead of a list, for the SST splitting method), whereas in the vertex-chain, as the name stands, p multiple pairs of chains consisting of the vertices in the original graph are first created in an iterative fashion, and the 2^p vertex chains so obtained are then transformed to the respective subgraphs.

Similar to the edge detection methods as described in the previous subsection, the three graph theoretic data pruning methods equivalently exploit the holistic representation of data, resulting in preservation of a well-balanced data structure during the pruning. In [3, 6], the efficacy of the three graph theoretic data pruning methods, in comparison with the k-means and LVQ, is also reported by showing the simulation study using a couple of the data sets for speech recognition tasks.

13.3 Incremental Training Using a Probabilistic Neural Network

In the machine learning context, *incremental learning* is often referred to as a capability of a learning mechanism, in which new incoming data can be learned without the need for retraining from scratch, whereas the already-formed data representation remain intact. Such a capability can be compared to that of our brain; we can usually remember the things memorized in the past, even after we acquire some new information. During the master's period, the author experienced limited success in performing the incremental learning using an MLP-NN and, since then, had been searching for other connectionist approaches to realize this. In general, performing an incremental training using MLP-NNs is not straightforward, due to its distributed data representation spread through the entire network architecture. Also, a problem still resides in the training itself; training the network parameters of an MLP-NN is typically performed using an iterative, steepest descent-type algorithm. Such an iterative manner of training requires exhaustive computational load, whereas the training data set is normally very large in practice. Moreover, there is another inherent numerical instability problem known as local minima.

It was not until near the graduation from Imperial that the author revisited another type of ANN, i.e., radial basis function neural network (RBF-NN) and was convinced that an RBF-NN can do a good job for the incremental learning, when he came across a mathematical note on the incremental learning procedure using an RBF-NN in the article by Orr [7], while surfing the Web; similar to MLP-NNs, an RBF-NN is a three-layered, feed-forward type network: (1) input layer (i.e., each unit receiving the corresponding element in the incoming pattern vector), (2) hidden layer consisting of the RBFs (i.e., the units represented by Gaussian distribution functions), each functioning as a similarity measurement between the incoming and its *centroid* vector (i.e., interpreted as the representative data held within the unit) , and (3) output layer of the units that integrate the activations in the second layer and eventually emit the weighted linear sum value for the respective classes.

A class of RBF-NNs is known as probabilistic neural network (PNN) due to Specht [8], in which its weight vectors between the hidden and output layers are fixed as the respective target vectors, unlike ordinary RBF-NNs or MLPs. This essentially benefits from its local representation of data. Then, it becomes clear that performing an incremental training of PNN can be quite straightforward, without resting on an arduous iterative network parameter tuning; all need is simply to allocate a new RBF (i.e., with setting the centroid vector of the hidden layer unit) during the training, where required, and then to establish a connection (i.e., with giving a unity weight value) between the new hidden unit and the output unit representing the class to which the RBF belongs.

13.3.1 *A Pattern Correction Scheme Using a PNN*

Soon after graduation, the author proposed a unified scheme for on-line pattern correction of misclassified patterns [9] as a practical implementation of incremental learning using a PNN. Within the scheme, both network growing and shrinking are considered; in the growing phase, a subset of the misclassified patterns in the incoming training data set is added into the PNN (i.e., by newly creating the RBFs with their centroid vectors identical to the respective pattern vectors) until there is no classification error given the entire incoming data. After the network growing, the shrinking mechanism is exerted, in order to reduce the redundancy in the learned data (or to avoid the effect of excessive training). This shrinking mechanism takes a cognitively-inspired, dual-stage approach, and the reduction is performed in both short-term and long-term wises; the RBFs with less contributions to the overall generalization performance are simply removed from the PNN after the network growing (namely, short-term memory leakage), whereas a data-pruning algorithm is applied to update periodically all the remaining centroid vectors of the RBFs within the PNN (thus corresponding to the long-term memory update).

In the late summer in 1998, a part of the work above was presented at a workshop held at both the Isaac Newton Institute and Robinson College in Cambridge (i.e., the 1998 IEEE Workshop on Neural Networks for Signal Processing, and Prof. Constantinides was one of the co-organizers), where the author met in person for the very first time Prof. Andrzej Cichocki, who has led the Laboratory for Advanced Brain Signal Processing (Lab. ABSP) at the Brain Science Institute of RIKEN (BSI-RIKEN) and later kindly gave the author the opportunity to work with after the three-year postdoc period in London.

13.3.2 *Accommodation of New Classes within a PNN*

The aforementioned intriguing network configuration property, namely that training of a PNN can be performed incrementally in a straightforward manner, without requiring an iterative learning, can be exploited further; in [10], the author empirically showed that accommodating new classes by a PNN can be also performed via a simple instance-based incremental learning procedure, while causing little deterioration in the generalization performance of previously learned classes. In practice, such a property is quite attractive, as this can lead to the design of more sophisticated learning machines, e.g., with a capability of defining autonomously a new classification task by themselves in the course of adapting them to some yet to be observed situations.

13.4 The Concept of Kernel Memory

In the summer in the second millennium (2000), the contract of three-year postdoc terminated. In the October of the same year, the author went back to Japan and joined the lab headed by Prof. Cichocki at BSI-RIKEN, as a fulltime research scientist. At that time, one of the groups within the BSI was referred to as the "creating the brain" group, which was composed by several independent laboratories and had focused upon the direction toward realization of various brain mechanisms by way of man-made machines. The Lab. ABSP also belonged to the group. There, the author started engaging in the analysis of brain data using signal processing methods, in parallel to modeling the mechanisms of brain. Similar to the lab at Imperial, the Lab. ABSP comprised an international society, which made the author somewhat feel comfortable, and was quite well equipped for performing various experiments relevant to brain data analysis. Each full-time lab member was allowed to occupy a partitioned square of a large room, and inside was placed one or two desktop computers (plus a notebook on the desk), depending upon the researcher's need (which was then enough to let the daily race in getting one slip away completely from the author's memory, apart from the annual update of the maximum five-years contract).

In the early years after joining the new lab, the useful features of PNN described in the previous section were still sticking in the author's head, which eventually led to the proposal of a novel neural network paradigm, i.e., the kernel memory concept [12]. The term *kernel* derived from a kernel function, which had come to appear almost invariably in the statistical learning literature, and was rephrased in the context of connectionism; a node having a kernel function (thus, a kernel unit) that represents locally some data space. Hence, kernel memory was coined to represent the memory architecture composed by the network of kernel units. (In an alternative view, such a network can be thought to be an extension of conventional symbolic approaches such as knowledge line concept, or K-line, due to Minsky [11], with each node having a capability to transform the input into some other form(s) and emit eventually its output.)

In the context of kernel memory, a kernel unit can have any type of output function in response to the input data given. This enables a flexible network configuration; units with different kernel functions can coexist within a unified, single network. In this regard, a PNN can be regarded as a particular case of kernel memory; it is a two-layered feed-forward network composed by two types of kernel units – the first layer consists of the units, each uniformly with a Gaussian kernel that transforms non-linearly the input vector (which is uniform to all the first layer units) into a single output value. On the other hand, each unit in the second layer gathers all the output values of the first layer units falling into a particular class and outputs the linear sum value. In the case of PNN, a kernel function for the units in both the layers is represented in a general form:

$$K(\mathbf{x}) = K(\mathbf{x}, \mathbf{t}), \tag{13.1}$$

where x and t are the input and so-called the *template* vector, respectively, the representation of which is then considered to be useful for various pattern classification problems. For the i-th kernel in the first layer,

$$h(i) = K_i(\mathbf{x}, \mathbf{t}_i^1) = \exp\left(\frac{\|\mathbf{x} - \mathbf{t}_j^1\|_2^2}{\sigma^2}\right), \qquad (13.2)$$

where σ is the radius and $\|\cdot\|_2$ denotes $L2$-norm. Then, each first layer kernel yields a non-linear similarity metric between the input and template vector. In contrast, the second layer kernels can be uniformly represented by using (13.1) with an inner-product operator

$$\begin{aligned}
o(j) &= K(\mathbf{x}_j^2, \mathbf{t}_j^2) = \mathbf{x}_j^2 \cdot \mathbf{t}_j^2, \\
\mathbf{x}_j^2 &= [h(i_1^j), h(i_2^j), \dots, h(i_{N_j}^j)], \\
\mathbf{t}_j^2 &= \underbrace{[1, 1, \dots, 1]}_{N_j}{}^T
\end{aligned} \qquad (13.3)$$

where the elements of input vector $\mathbf{x}_j^2$ for the j-th kernel in the second layer are the respective N_j values of activation obtained from the first layer kernel that belong to class j.

In the kernel memory context, it is also possible to configure a network that can deal with multiple-domain input (i.e., taking into account the multiple input data with different dimensions for the respective kernel units) at the same time. By exploiting this property, a kernel network that simultaneously processes, e.g., both auditory and visual sensory data can be configured. Besides this, the notion of connection between a pair of nodes in kernel memory is extended from that of conventional ANN models; (1) the introduction of *link weight* connections and, where appropriate, (2) their directional links. For (1), lateral connections are allowed between the nodes. Moreover, a kernel unit can be excited *without* the input given directly but externally by the transfer of activation from other unit(s) via the link weight(s). The introduction of link weights also removes the topological constraint of a network structure, as in conventional ANN models. For (2), the connection between a kernel unit pair can be established via either a uni- or bi-directional link weight. In the unidirectional case, the transfer of activation occurs only in a single direction, which can be utilized to model an excitatory/inhibitory synapse in the neurophysiological context.

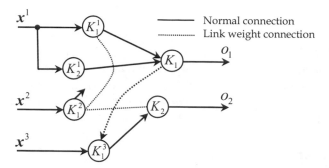

Figure 13.1 An example of kernel memory. This kernel network deals with three different domain input data x^1, x^2, and x^3 and eventually yields two network outputs, o_1 and o_2.

Generally, a network of kernel memory is not necessarily fully connected but can be self-organized; the link weight connection between a pair of kernel units can be established via a simple rule [12]:

> When a pair of kernels K_A and K_B is simultaneously excited (repeatedly), a new link weight w_{AB} between the pair is formed.

The connection rule above was motivated from Hebb's neuropsychological postulate between a pair of cells [14], and it is considered that a variety of modifications to the above are possible, dependent upon the application (e.g., [12, 13, 15]). For instance, the value w_{AB} can also be increased, rather than using a fixed value if such a simultaneous excitation occurs intermittently, or decreased otherwise if such an excitation has not occurred in a certain period.

As an example, a network represented by the kernel memory is illustrated in Fig. 13.1. In this case, the network can simultaneously process the three different domain input data x^1, x^2, and x^3, where both the kernel units K_1^1 and K_2^1 (K_i^j; i-th kernel unit for the j-th domain data) receive the first domain data x^1 as the input to their kernel functions, whereas K_1^2 and K_1^3 the second and third domain data x^2 and x^3, respectively. In contrast, the units without a superscript, i.e., K_1 and K_2, do not receive any direct domain input. In the figure, the kernel K_2 receives the activation from K_1^3 as the direct input to its kernel function, while it can be excited by the external input via the link weight due to the activation transfer from K_1^2. Then, the network eventually yields the two outputs o_1 and o_2. This example also implies that the activation transfer from K_1 to K_1^3 is only allowed to occur, due to the unidirectional link weight lying in between. Moreover, even an intricate cyclic data flow of $x^3 \rightarrow K_1^3 \rightarrow K_2 \rightarrow K_1^2 \rightarrow K_1^1 \rightarrow K_1 \rightarrow K_1^3$, can be considered to occur in this example, which models a Hopfield-type recurrent network architecture [16].

13.4.1 *Simultaneous Pattern Classification and Association by Kernel Memory*

As a more concrete application of the link weight connections, a network of kernel memory, which simultaneously performs pattern classification $K_A K_B x(n) o_1 z^{-1} K_2 o_2 x(n - 1) K_1$ and association of multi-domain data, was proposed in [15].

The network construction is carried out through a self-structuring process using a simplified version of the training algorithm for resource allocating networks [17]. In the approach, both the kernel (i.e., Gaussian kernel) units and link weights in between are added by a one-shot incremental learning procedure; first, a total of M (say) sub-networks, each responsible for pattern classification of the corresponding domain data, are independently constructed by the self-structuring algorithm. Then, lateral connections across some parts of the distinct sub-networks (i.e., represented by the link weights between some numbers of kernel units that co-excited during the presentation of multi-domain data) are established, which can eventually be used to perform pattern association; during the testing phase, while ordinary pattern classification is performed, activation of kernel units in some particular sub-network(s) can also occur. This may happen even without the direct inputs given, due to the transfer of activation from the kernels within other sub-networks (provided that these kernels are connected via the link weights). Such a process can be compared to performing a task of mental imagery in the cognitive sense; a particular modality of sensory data can invoke some other following perceptual processes. (For instance, consider a situation that a portrait image of one's

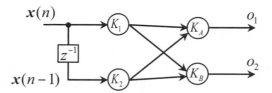

Figure 13.2 A simple kernel network that can handle a temporal data processing. In the network, K_A detects the activation sequence of $K_1 \to K_2$, whereas K_B does $K_2 \to K_1$ (adapted from [12]).

grandmother, passed away many years ago, can still remind one of the voice, without actually hearing it.)

13.4.2 *Temporal Data Processing by Way of Kernel Memory*

The notion of template data within a kernel unit can be exploited further for performing a temporal data processing. For instance, consider a network consisting of the four kernel units as shown in Fig. 13.2. Suppose that each of the kernels K_A and K_B has a kernel function to perform a certain kind of pattern matching with the corresponding template matrix, which is alternative to the vector representation in (13.1), i.e.,

$$\mathbf{T}_A = \begin{pmatrix} 1 & 0 \\ 0 & 1 \end{pmatrix}, \quad \mathbf{T}_B = \begin{pmatrix} 0 & 1 \\ 1 & 0 \end{pmatrix}, \tag{13.4}$$

where the element at the i-th row and j-th column of the matrices

$$t_{ij} = \begin{cases} 1 \, ; K_i \text{ is activated at time index } (n + j - 2) \\ 0 \, ; \text{otherwise} \end{cases},$$

the kernel K_A can detect the activation sequence of $K_1 \to K_2$, whereas K_B does the sequence occurred in the counter-wise, i.e., $K_2 \to K_1$.

13.4.3 *Application of Kernel Units for Detecting Sequential Patterns to Spoken Word Recognition*

As an alternative to the matrix representations in (13.4), the template vectors

$$\mathbf{t}_A = [1, 2], \mathbf{t}_B = [2, 1] \tag{13.5}$$

can be also exploited for the sequence detection, provided that each element in (13.5) represents the corresponding kernel index. Then, by regarding each element as a character and concatenating all the elements in the vector to form a string (i.e., "12" or "21"), the detection of activation sequence can be alternatively achieved in terms of the string matching, by applying, e.g., an edit distance-type algorithm (e.g., see [18]).

The principle of the aforementioned sequence detection was successfully exploited in the kernel network for spoken word recognition [19] (i.e., cascaded neuro-computational, viz. CNC, model). In speech processing, a spoken word can be generally represented by multiple frame data consisting of mel-frequency cepstral coefficients (MFCC). Then, multiple frame data are treated as a certain sequence pattern of characters, namely a string, within the CNC model, and thereby word recognition is performed. In the CNC model, there are three layers of kernel units (with no lateral connections within each layer), and all the three layers are arranged in a cascading manner. At a glance, this manner of network formation seems to be nothing more than a typical multi-layered neural net (such as MLPs). The CNC model is, however, not necessarily a fully connected network. Moreover, the forwarding manner of activations from the previous layer to the next is different from that of conventional NNs; the first layer of a CNC model, called the pre-lexical layer, is composed by Gaussian kernels (as in ordinary RBF-NNs/PNNs), each of which yields its activation corresponding to a segment of spoken word (i.e., represented by a single frame of MFCC). Then, unlike typical NNs, the first layer eventually yields the ID of a winning kernel as the input to the second layer (i.e., lexical layer), rather than the activation value. This process is continued till the end of the frame data for a spoken word, and thus a set of such IDs (i.e., a serial-order of activations) can be eventually obtained. Then, provided that each unit in the second layer has the template vector of the form in (13.5) and performs the aforementioned string matching, it can detect the serial-order pattern of a particular single word. In other words, each unit in the second layer is connected only to the first units that appear in the template vector. From a different point of view, the explicit distinction between pre-lexical and lexical layers of the CNC model agrees with the architectural stance of the connectionist models proposed in cognitive linguistics-oriented studies (see, e.g., [20, 21]), though many of these models dealt no more than with artificial speech inputs. The third layer units gather all the activations from the second layer corresponding to the respective classes (i.e., words), and the final recognition result can be obtained from the third layer by taking the ordinary winner-takes-all strategy.

Unlike many of the cognitive models proposed previously, the construction of a CNC model is not determined *a priori*, but grown dependent upon the training data given. Similar to the work [15], a CNC model is constructed through a self-structuring process; initially, there is only a single unit within the first layer and no other units within both the second and third layers. All the units but the very first one in the first layer, as well as the interlayer connections, are added in to the corresponding layers, where appropriate, by using the Hebbian motivated, one-shot incremental learning algorithm as described in Section 13.4.1.

In [19], an extensive simulation study shows that for digit voice recognition tasks the classification rates comparable to that using the state-of-the-art approach of hidden Markov model (HMM) can be obtained by the CNC model.

13.5 Artificial Mind System: Toward Drawing a Blueprint of Artificial Intelligence

Having spent about three years since joining the lab at BSI-RIKEN, the author came to ponder how the kernel memory concept could fit into modeling a variety of the cognitive faculties, each of which is essential to depict a holistic picture of artificial intelligence. While engaging in the development of signal processing techniques to analyze brain-wave related data, such as electroencephalography (EEG), he was able to find time in completing the first monograph on artificial mind system (AMS) [12] (I am really grateful to Prof. Cichocki very much, for his generous approval of my writing; the publication of the first monograph eventually brought me to the current working environment at Nihon University). In the monograph, the kernel memory concept is described as a fundamental connectionist paradigm to model various mechanisms relevant to the AMS.

13.5.1 *A Hierarchical Network Model of Short- and Long-Term Memory, Attention, and Intuition*

It was on the day of arrival at the hotel in Salt-Lake City in May 2001 for attending a huge signal processing-oriented conference (i.e., International Conference on Acoustics, Speech, and Signal Processing, ICASSP-2001), when the author suddenly hit upon an idea; the data processing between the short-term memory (STM) and long-term memory (LTM), as well as both the cognitive faculties of attention and intuition, can be modeled in terms of multiple kernel networks arranged in a hierarchical manner [22]. Figure 13.3 depicts the model (cf. [12, 22]) that embodies the four cognitive faculties of STM, LTM, attention, and intuition. As shown in the figure, the model consists of two major components, i.e., STM and LTM, whereas the two psychological modalities of attention and intuition are considered to function as the accompanying data processing/structure with these memory components. It is assumed that the model receives simultaneously a total of N_s different domain input data (denoted X_{in}) from the respective sensors. When the learning is completed, there will be a single kernel network within the STM (hence, called the "STM" network), whereas multiple independent (but interrelated to each other) kernel networks responsible for the LTM (i.e., Kernel Net 1-L) will be eventually constructed within the architecture. Once the formation is done, the units in LTM, however, do not remain intact, and the contents (i.e., in the form of the template vectors) can be dynamically varied during the memory reconfiguration stage.

In the STM network, two groups of kernel units coexist; the "attentive kernel units" are copied at a certain period from the LTM nets, due to the operation by the selection mechanism involved with the STM, and then will be activated more likely by a particular set of domain input data than others. This can be compared to the situation, where the system is given a priority to process only a set of sensory data (thus, the system being *attentive* to, e.g., some objects), while receiving (as well as processing) concurrently other sensory data, in order to perform a certain privileged task. In a more schematic point of view, it is noticeable that the output from the STM net (denoted by O_{STM} in Fig. 13.3) can be regarded as a *filtered*

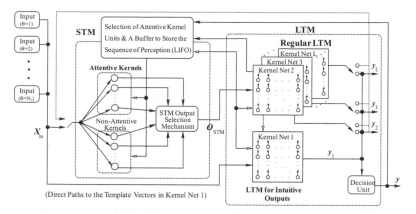

Figure 13.3 A hierarchical network model of short- and long-term memory, attention, and intuition by means of kernel memory representation (adapted from [12, 23]).

version of the original input domain data, since it is represented by a collection of multiple template vectors obtained from a set of winning kernel units (i.e., regardless of the domain data, due to the STM output selection mechanism). Then, the STM output is given as the input to the LTM nets.

The formation of regular LTM networks reflects the cognitive postulate of hierarchical memory system in LTM, and the accessibility of the memory contents depends upon the *level*, viz. the contents stored in the form of kernels within Kernel Net 2 can be more accessible than those in Kernel Net 3. (More concretely, Kernel Net 2 is composed by a collection of N_2, say, mostly activated kernel units during the learning phase, and less activated units are stored within Kernel Net 3, 4, and so forth.) Each kernel net in LTM yields the output vectors y_i ($i = 1, 2, ..., L$) of dimension N_s, with each element given as the output value of the mostly activated kernel unit within the LTM net corresponding to the domain input data. The decision unit then gathers all the weighted output vectors from these LTM nets and eventually emits the network output vector y (again, of dimension N_s) by applying a simple winner-takes-all strategy to each domain. While the regular LTM nets (i.e., Kernel Net 2-L) process the output data from STM network (i.e., O_{STM}), Kernel Net 1 receives the direct input X_{in}, without the intervener by the STM. Moreover, the weight values for each element of y_1 are set relatively larger than those for the regular LTM nets. Such a formation facilitates the generation of relatively strong activations from the units in Kernel Net 1 for a particular set of input data, the notion of which can be interpreted as the cognitive sense of *intuition* [12, 22]. During the learning phase, the units in Kernel Net 1 are given as a collection of the most strongly activated kernel units within the regular LTM networks.

13.5.2 *The Artificial Mind System*

The artificial mind system (AMS) [12] was proposed to be a holistic model of artificial intelligence. Macroscopically, its architecture can be viewed as an augmented model of Fig. 13.3; in addition to the four cognitive faculties of STM, LTM, attention, and intuition, the AMS incorporates six other faculties of emotion, intention, instinct/innate structure, language, primary output (behavior, motion, and endocrine), semantic networks/lexicon, and thinking. In the AMS context, the LTM can be divided further in functional wise into the two modalities of explicit and implicit LTM, whereas the input and output of the model are interpreted as sensation and perception (secondary output), respectively. The classification into these faculties agrees adequately well with the taxonomy due to Hobson [24], based upon the psychological account of mind modularity principle [25]; each module (i.e., corresponding to the cognitive faculty under the same name) is generally considered to operate independently from others. In [12], the concept of kernel memory is described as a substrate to model each module of the AMS, as well as their mutual data processing. Then the structure of AMS eventually exhibits a much larger-scaled version of the composite kernel network model, in comparison with that in Fig. 13.3. The following is a brief summary of the aforementioned six faculties that constitute a part of the AMS:

(1) Emotion: This module functions in parallel with the three other modules of instinct/innate structure, LTM, and primary output. Within the module, there are several kernel units representing

the respective emotional states (e.g., corresponding to pleasure, anger, grief, joy, and so forth), which have the link weight connections established with the units in the LTM modules or prewired ones with the instinct/innate structure module. Their activations may directly affect the current internal states of the AMS/body.

(2) Instinct/Innate structure: This can be regarded as a particular kind of LTM and modeled as a series of pre-defined values (albeit represented in the form of kernel units) describing the physical limitations/properties of the body, which can considerably affect the entire data processing within the AMS.

(3) Intention: The module functions to hold temporarily (but in a relatively longer period than that in the attention module) the resultant states (i.e., in the form kernel units) reached during the operation of thinking module and greatly affect the memory search process by the STM/working memory module. Unlike the attention module, the states within the module are rather immune to the abrupt change in the contents of the incoming data arrived at the STM/working memory module.

(4) Language: The kernel networks within the module represent a set of grammatical rules that may be acquired in the LTM during the learning process (or preset ones, but, if so, still reconfigurable) and thus regarded as the constituents of the language module. It is utilized as the means to perform the data processing (i.e., verbal reasoning or thinking process) by the thinking module.

(5) Primary output: The faculty is viewed as the final way out to the physical devices (and the mechanism(s) to cause internal activities) connected to the AMS. In the kernel memory representation, this module may be modeled as a set of gating networks, and their states are monitored by the STM/working memory module via the associated link weight connections.

(6) Semantic networks/Lexicon: The module exhibits the semantic part of the explicit LTM module and consists of the kernel networks (of rather symbol-based units) that represents, so to speak, the mental lexicon.

13.5.3 *Ongoing Research Activities Relevant to the Artificial Mind System*

One of the salient features equipped with humans is, needless to say, the ability to communicate with other individuals via the use of language. Since the publication of the first monograph, the author has become more inclined to exploring the AMS/kernel memory concept in the direction of modeling various mechanisms of the language faculty. This is partly because the author considers that the language-oriented tasks involve many of the modules within the AMS and thus can eventually lead to a thorough justification of the original proposal.

In the linguistic community, simulating various aspects of human language acquisition by way of connectionist models is a matter of long debate. Among such is how inflection of verbs in past tense from the original forms can be represented by a connectionist model; e.g., work $\rightarrow$ worked (i.e., regular), whereas steal $\rightarrow$ stole (irregular). The previous work [26] attempted to give an account for this by using an MLP-NN, but it has later been claimed that the model does not generalize well some novel regular verbs [27]. In addition to the linguistic view in [27], another possible reason for such a failure would be due to the inherent numerical instability during the learning.

The author then suggested a different approach for the related issue to this, i.e., inflection of nouns in their plural forms (e.g., bird $\rightarrow$ birds versus mouse $\rightarrow$ mice), in terms of the interactive data processing between the STM/working memory and LTM modules of AMS [28]. In brief, after performing the pattern recognition tasks of noun-specific sensory data arrived at the STM/working memory, the winner of the two kernel networks (i.e., the one responsible for regular inflection and the other for irregular, both consisting of the kernel units for sequence detection as described in Section 13.4.2) within the LTM (i.e., a certain part of the explicit/implicit LTM, language, and semantic networks/lexicon module) yields the final result of inflection.

Another related issue currently under investigation is the extension of CNC model (described in Section 13.4.3) to perform continuous speech recognition tasks; an augmented version of the CNC model that can deal with both the coarticulation effect and silent periods between the spoken words might be constructed by exploiting the interactive processing between the STM/working memory and LTM modules, in a similar way to the aforementioned case of inflections.

13.6 Conclusion

In this festschrift, a review of the author's research activities so far relevant to modeling complex systems has been given. In the early years (i.e., during the PhD period), the author had focused upon the application of graph theoretic methods to edge detection of an image and development of data pruning algorithms. In this direction, complex data structures are analyzed and then reconstructed, rather dependent heavily upon the global information of available data. In contrast, the AMS, a holistic model of artificial intelligence, can be descriptive by means of kernel memory. The kernel memory concept has been proposed as a novel connectionist framework, and the establishment of connections ascribes to the original Hebbian principle [14], which exploits the local information of two adjacent kernel units (cf. Section 13.4). Hence, the construction of modules (i.e., represented by kernel networks) within the AMS is not governed by a certain ruling agent or such (as compared to the "homunculus") but, rather, organized/formed by themselves during the mutual data processing.

Although it is already almost twenty years since the author arrived in London and joined the signal processing laboratory at Imperial, the memory of the exciting days there is still not blurred. It is then quite an honorable moment for me to contribute an article to the Festschrift for the 70th anniversary of Prof. Anthony G. Constantinides (my sincere gratitude goes to both the classmates, Prof. Danilo P. Mandic and Dr. Yong-Qin Zeng, for their recommendations).

References

1. Christofides, N. (1975). *Graph Theory: An Algorithmic Approach* (Academic Press, London).

2. Morris, O. J., Lee, M. de J., and Constantinides, A. G. (1986). Graph theory for image analysis: An approach based on the shortest spanning tree, *IEE Proc. F—Commun. Radar Signal Process.* **1332**, pp. 146–152

3. Hoya, T. (1997). *Graph Theoretic Methods for Data Partitioning* (PhD thesis, Imperial College, UK).

4. Marr, D., and Hildreth, E. (1980). Theory of edge detection, *Proc. Royal Soc. London*, **B-207**, pp. 187–217.

5. Tero, A., Takagi, S., Saigusa, T., Ito, K., Bebber, D. P., Fricker, M. D., Yumiki, K., Kobayashi, R., and Nakagaki, T. (2010). Rules for biologically inspired adaptive network design, *Science*, **327**, pp. 439–442.

6. Hoya, T. (1998). Graph theoretic techniques for pruning data and their applications, *IEEE Trans. Sig. Proc.*, **46-9**, pp. 2574–2579.

7. Orr. M. J. L. (1996). Introduction to radial basis function networks, on-line article available at www.cns.ed.ac.uk (Centre for Cognitive Science, University of Edinburgh).

8. Specht, D. F. (1990). Probabilistic neural networks, *Neural Netw*, **2**, 568–576.

9. Hoya, T., and Chambers, J. A. (2001). Heuristic pattern correction scheme using adaptively trained generalized regression neural networks, *IEEE Trans. Neural Netw*, **12-1**, pp. 91–100.

10. Hoya, T. (2003). On the capability of accommodating new classes within probabilistic neural networks, *IEEE Trans. Neural Netw*, **14-2**, pp. 450–453.

11. Minsky, M. (1985). *The Society of Mind* (Simon & Schuster, New York).

12. Hoya, T. (2005). *Artificial Mind System: Kernel Memory Approach* (Springer-Verlag, Heidelberg).

13. Hoya, T. (2004). Self-organising associative kernel memory for multi-domain pattern classification *Proceedings of the IFAC Workshop on Adaptation and Learning in Control and Signal Processing (ALCOSP2004)*, pp. 735–740.

14. Hebb, D. O. (1949). *Organization of Behavior* (Wiley, New York).

15. Hoya, T., and Washizawa, Y. (2007). Simultaneous pattern classification and multidomain association using self-structuring kernel memory networks, *IEEE Trans. Neural Netw*, **18-3**, pp. 732–744.

16. Hopfield, J. J. (1982). Neural networks and physical systems with emergent collective computational abilities. *Proc. Nat. Acad. Sci. U.S.A.* **81**, pp. 3088–3092.

17. Platt, J. (1991). A resource-allocating network for function interpolation, *Neural Comput.*, **3-2**, pp. 213–225.

18. Duda, R. O., Hart, P. E., and Stork, D. G. (2001). *Pattern Classification* (2nd ed., Wiley, New York).

19. Hoya, T., and van Leeuwen, C. (2010). A cascaded neuro-computational model for spoken word recognition, *Connect. Sci*, **22-1**, pp. 87–101.

20. Morton, J. (1969) Interaction of information in word recognition, *Psychol. Rev.*, **76**, pp. 165–178.

21. McClelland, J. L. and Elman, J.L. (1986) The TRACE model of speech perception, *Cognit. Psychol.*, **18**, pp. 1–86.

22. Hoya, T. (2004). Notions of intuition and attention modeled by a hierarchically arranged generalized regression neural network, *IEEE Trans Syst, Man, Cybern—Part B: Cybern.*, **34-1**, pp. 200–209.

23. Hoya, T. (2003). A kernel based neural memory concept and representation of procedural memory and emotion, *Proceedings of the International Symposium on Artificial Life and Robotics (AROB-03)*, pp. 373–376.

24. Hobson, J. A. (1999). *Ishiki-To-Nou (Consciousness and Brain)* (Tuttle-Mori Agency, Inc. Tokyo & W. H. Freeman and Company New York).

25. Fodor, J. A. (1983). *The Modularity of Mind: An Essay on Faculty Psychology* (The MIT Press, Cambridge).

26. Rumelhart, D. E., McClleland, J. L., and the PDP Research Group (1986). *Parallel Distributed Processing: Explorations in the Microstructure of Cognition—Vol. 1. Foundations* (MIT Press, Cambridge).

27. Pinker, S. (2000). *Words and Rules: The Ingredients of Language* (Perennial).

28. Hoya, T. (2006). Artificial intelligence and language acquisition—an example of a new approach—solution to the "WUG-test" interpreted within the artificial mind system context, *Proceedings of the 8th Annual International Conference of the Japanese Society for Language Sciences*, pp. 169–174.

PART IV

COMMUNICATIONS

Chapter 14

Markov Chain Monte Carlo Statistical Detection Methods for Communication Systems

Behrouz Farhang-Boroujeny

Department of Electrical and Computer Engineering, University of Utah, USA
farhang@ece.utah.edu

14.1 Introduction

Code division multiple access (CDMA) and multiple-input multiple-output (MIMO) communication systems are two different, but fundamentally very similar communication techniques. In CDMA a number of users simultaneously transmit information symbols, with each user being identified by a spreading code (Viterbi, 1995; Verdù, 1998). In MIMO, on the other hand, a data stream is separated into a parallel set of streams, which are then transmitted through separate antennas (Foschini, 1996; Telatar, 1999). The key point here is that the multiuser data, in a CDMA system, as well as the parallel data streams, in a MIMO system, are transmitted in the same frequency band. Hence, the system capacity increases

Trends in Digital Signal Processing: A Festschrift in Honour of A. G. Constantinides
Edited by Yong Ching Lim, Hon Keung Kwan, and Wan-Chi Siu
Copyright © 2016 Pan Stanford Publishing Pte. Ltd.
ISBN 978-981-4669-50-4 (Hardcover), 978-981-4669-51-1 (eBook)
www.panstanford.com

with the number of users/transmit antennas. Joint detection has to be carried out at the receiver to harness this potential capacity of the multiuser/MIMO systems. Suboptimum receivers, such as decorrelating and minimum mean square error (MMSE) detectors, can only realize a fraction of the capacity (Verdù, 1998). The full channel capacity can only be harnessed through the optimum detector that jointly detects data streams (Verdù, 1996). The optimum detector, unfortunately, has a complexity that grows exponentially with the number data streams.

In this chapter, we present a class of low-complexity detectors whose complexity grows nearly linear with the number of data streams, yet performs very close to their optimum counterparts. The presented algorithms make use of Markov chain Monte Carlo (MCMC) simulation technique to search for a subset of important samples from the data signal space whose use is sufficient for a near optimum performance of the receiver. We also discuss implementation of the MCMC detectors. The results presented in this chapter summarizes a line of research of the author in the past 10 years. Selected publications of the author that report various aspects of this research are Farhang-Boroujeny et al. (2006), Zhu et al. (2005), Chen et al. (2010), and Peng et al. (2010).

This chapter is organized as follows. The discussion begins with introduction of a channel model in Section 14.2. The concept of iterative multiuser/MIMO receiver is laid out in Section 14.3. Section 14.4 presents an overview of Monte Carlo statistical methods. Monte Carlo integration, importance sampling, MCMC simulation, and Gibbs sampler (a tool for effective implementation of MCMC simulator) are introduced in this section. The Monte Carlo statistical methods are applied to multiuser/MIMO detectors in Section 14.5. We call these, MCMC detectors. A hardware structure for effective implementation of MCMC detectors is presented in Section 14.6.

Throughout this chapter, the following notations are adhered to. Vectors are denoted by lowercase bold letters. All vectors are in column form. Matrices are denoted by uppercase bold letters. The ij-th element of a matrix, say, **A**, is denoted by a_{ij}. The superscript T is used to denote matrix or vector transpose. Integer subscripts are used to distinguish different users, in CDMA, or the data streams transmitted through different antennas, in MIMO channels. We use $P(\cdot)$ and $p(\cdot)$ to refer to probability mass distribution and probability density distribution, when the underlying random variables are discrete and continuous, respectively.

14.2 Channel Model

We consider a flat fading channel model whose input and output, for each instant of channel use, are related according to the equation

$$\mathbf{y} = \mathbf{Hd} + \mathbf{n}, \tag{14.1}$$

where $\mathbf{d}$ is the vector of transmit symbols, $\mathbf{n}$ is the channel additive noise vector, $\mathbf{y}$ is the received signal vector, and $\mathbf{H}$ is the channel gain matrix. In the case of a MIMO channel, the elements of $\mathbf{H}$ are the channel gains between transmit and receive antennas. In the case of a CDMA system, on the other hand, the columns of $\mathbf{H}$ contain the spreading code of the users scaled by the respective channel gains. We assume that $\mathbf{H}$ has M rows and N columns. This implies that, in the case of a MIMO system, there are N transmit and M receive antennas and, in the case of a CDMA system, there are N users with spreading codes of length M.

It may be noted that in broadband communications where orthogonal frequency division multiplexing (OFDM) is used for signaling, each subcarrier has a channel model similar to (14.1). Here, without any loss of generality, we limit our discussion to a single equation like (14.1).

14.3 Iterative Multiuser/MIMO Receiver

Figure 14.1 presents a block diagram of an iterative receiver. The multiuser/MIMO detector takes the received signal vector $\mathbf{y}$ (for each instant of channel use) and any available *a priori* information, λ_2^e, about data symbols, i.e., the elements of $\mathbf{d}$, and generates the soft/log-likelihood information λ_1 of the data symbols. After subtracting the *a priori* information λ_2^e, the new (called *extrinsic*) soft information $\lambda_1^e = \lambda_1 - \lambda_2^e$ is formed. The extrinsic soft information

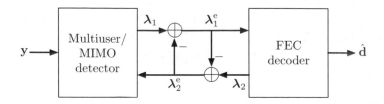

Figure 14.1 Iterative receiver.

collected from a number of channel uses, corresponding to one (set of) code word(s) are passed to the forward error correction (FEC) decoder(s). The FEC decoder(s) uses (use) the information that relate the coded bits to generate additional extrinsic information, λ_2^e, about data symbols. These are then passed to the multiuser/MIMO detector, to start the next iteration. The exchange of extrinsic information between the two blocks (multiuser/MIMO detector and FEC decoder) continues for a number of iterations until the receiver converges. The final decision about information symbols, $\hat{\mathbf{d}}$, (equivalently, information bits) is then made.

To proceed, we use d_1 through d_N to denote the elements of the data symbol vector $\mathbf{d}$. Also, for convenience of the discussion here we assume that data symbols are binary, taking values of $+1$ and -1, however, we note that, in general, the data symbols may be selected from a QAM alphabet of size L, with each symbol carrying $\ell = \log_2 L$ bits. Each symbol information is quantified by the log-likelihood ratios (LLR), or L-values,

$$\lambda_1(d_k) = \ln \frac{P(d_k = +1|\mathbf{y}, \lambda_2^e)}{P(d_k = -1|\mathbf{y}, \lambda_2^e)}, \tag{14.2}$$

and

$$\lambda_2(d_k) = \ln \frac{P(d_k = +1|\lambda_1^e, \text{decoding})}{P(d_k = -1|\lambda_1^e, \text{decoding})}. \tag{14.3}$$

The L-values in (14.3) are obtained by following a standard decoding algorithm; e.g., a soft Viterbi, a turbo, or a low-density parity check (LDPC) decoder. The major problem is finding the values of $\lambda_1(d_k)$ in a computationally efficient manner. To see this difficulty, one may expand $P(d_k = +1|\mathbf{y}, \lambda_2^e)$ as

$$P(d_k = +1|\mathbf{y}, \lambda_2^e) = \sum_{\mathbf{d}_{-k}} P\left(d_k = +1, \mathbf{d}_{-k}|\mathbf{y}, \lambda_2^e\right)$$

$$= \sum_{\mathbf{d}_{-k}} P(d_k = +1|\mathbf{y}, \mathbf{d}_{-k}, \lambda_2^e)P(\mathbf{d}_{-k}|\mathbf{y}, \lambda_2^e), \quad (14.4)$$

where the second identity follows by applying the chain rule, $\mathbf{d}_{-k}$ $= [d_1 \ldots d_{k-1}\ d_{k+1} \cdots d_N]^{\mathrm{T}}$, and the summation is over all possible values of $\mathbf{d}_{-k}$. The number of combinations that $\mathbf{d}_{-k}$ takes grows exponentially with $(N - 1) \times \ell$, where, as defined above, ℓ is the number of bits carried by each data symbols. As an example, consider the case where $N = 8$ and $\ell = 6$ (i.e., 64-QAM symbols are transmitted). For this example $(N-1)\times\ell = 42$ and, thus, the number of combinations of $\mathbf{d}_{-k}$ will be $2^{42} = 4.4 \times 10^{12}$. This prohibitive complexity can be avoided by adopting the Monte Carlo statistical methods that are reviewed in the next section.

14.4 Monte Carlo Statistical Methods

14.4.1 *Monte Carlo Integration*

Consider the generic problem of evaluating the weighted mean of a function $h(x)$ of the random variable X, given by

$$E_f[h(X)] = \int_{\mathcal{X}} h(x)f(x)dx, \quad (14.5)$$

where $\mathcal{X}$ is the domain of X and $f(\cdot)$ is a proper density function, i.e., $f(x) \geq 0$ for $x \in \mathcal{X}$ and $\int_{\mathcal{X}} f(x)dx = 1$. According to the classical Monte Carlo integration (Hammersley and Handscomb, 1964; Fishman, 1996), an estimate of (14.5) is obtained by evaluating the empirical average

$$\bar{h} = \frac{1}{N_s} \sum_{n=1}^{N_s} h(x_n), \quad (14.6)$$

where x_n's are a set of samples from the distribution $f(x)$. Clearly, the accuracy of this estimate improves with increasing the number of samples. This is often measured by the variance of $\bar{h}$ which is given by (Fishman, 1996),

$$\sigma_{\bar{h}}^2 = \frac{1}{N_s(N_s - 1)} \sum_{n=1}^{N_s} |h(x_n) - \bar{h}|^2. \tag{14.7}$$

Here, x may be a scalar or a vector variable. When x is a vector, the integral in (14.5) is a multiple integral whose direct computation will grow exponentially with number of integrals and may soon become prohibitive as the dimension of x increases. An interesting observation that is made through (14.7) is that the accuracy of the estimate (14.6) reduces with the square of the number of sample points. This, in turn, implies to obtain a relatively good estimate of the desired weighted mean, a medium size N_s, that does not necessarily grows exponentially with the dimension of x, may be sufficient.

14.4.2 *Importance Sampling*

In the method of importance sampling, $E_f[h(X)]$ is evaluated by performing the empirical average (Fishman, 1996):

$$E_f[h(X)] \approx \frac{1}{N_s} \sum_{n=1}^{N_s} \frac{f(x_n)}{f_a(x_n)} h(x_n), \tag{14.8}$$

where the samples x_n are chosen from the auxiliary distribution $f_a(x)$. Equation (14.8) follows from the alternative representation of (14.5)

$$E_f[h(X)] = \int_{\mathcal{X}} \frac{f(x)}{f_a(x)} h(x) f_a(x) dx, \tag{14.9}$$

and performing the integral using the regular Monte Carlo integration based on the distribution $f_a(x)$.

A practical approximation that has been motivated from the importance sampling and usually results in a better approximation than (14.8) is (Robert and Casella, 1999),

$$\bar{h} = \frac{\sum_{n=1}^{N_s} \frac{f(x_n)}{f_a(x_n)} h(x_n)}{\sum_{n=1}^{N_s} \frac{f(x_n)}{f_a(x_n)}}, \tag{14.10}$$

Many choices of $f_a(x)$ can be made. Some lend themselves to a simple/convenient implementation, others, for a given number of samples N_s, lead to a more accurate estimate of $E_f[h(x)]$. In the problem of interest in this chapter, the choice of a uniform distribution over the range that $f(x)$ is both convenient and, according to the simulations presented in Farhang-Boroujeny et al. (2006), gives in accurate result based on a relatively small number of samples, N_s. When $f_a(x)$ is uniformly distributed, (14.11) reduces to

$$\bar{h} = \frac{\sum_{n=1}^{N_s} f(x_n) h(x_n)}{\sum_{n=1}^{N_s} f(x_n)}. \tag{14.11}$$

14.4.3 *Connection with LLR Computation*

Comparing (14.4) and (14.5), one will immediately find that the multi-dimensional summation in (14.4) is similar to the multidimensional integral in (14.5). The former is obtained from the latter, if $P(d_k = +1|\mathbf{y}, \mathbf{d}_{-k}, \lambda_2^e)$ is treated as $h(x)$, $P(\mathbf{d}_{-k}|\mathbf{y}, \lambda_2^e)$ as $f(x)$, $\mathbf{d}_{-k}$ as x, and the summations and integrals are considered as equivalent. The key point is to obtain a set of important samples for approximations such as (14.6) and (14.11) to perform accurately. Methods of obtaining such important sets are discussed in the sequel.

14.4.4 *MCMC Simulation and Gibbs Sampler*

MCMC simulation is a statistical method that allows generation of samples of a random process when such process could be modeled as a Markov chain (Robert and Casella, 1999; Häggström, 2002). Here, we use MCMC to generate samples of $\mathbf{d}$ from the distribution $P(\mathbf{d}|\mathbf{y}, \lambda_2^e)$. Accordingly, we define a Markov chain in which each state corresponds to one selection of $\mathbf{d}$. A common method of generating samples of a Markov chain is Gibbs sampling (Robert and Casella, 1999; Häggström, 2002). The Gibbs sampler that we use here is summarized as follows:

- Initialize $\mathbf{d}^{(-N_b)}$ (randomly),
- for $n = -N_b + 1$ to N_s

  draw sample $d_1^{(n)}$ from $P(d_1 | d_2^{(n-1)}, \ldots, d_K^{(n-1)}, \mathbf{y}, \lambda_2^e)$

$$\texttt{draw sample } d_2^{(n)} \texttt{ from } P\left(d_2 | d_1^{(n)}, d_3^{(n-1)}, \ldots, d_K^{(n-1)}, \mathbf{y}, \lambda_2^{\text{e}}\right)$$

$$\vdots$$

$$\texttt{draw sample } d_K^{(n)} \texttt{ from } P\left(d_K | d_1^{(n)}, \ldots, d_{K-1}^{(n)}, \mathbf{y}, \lambda_2^{\text{e}}\right)$$

Here, $\mathbf{d}^{(-N_{\text{b}})}$ is initialized randomly, possibly taking into account the *a priori* information λ_2^{e}. The 'for' loop examines the state variables, d_k's, in order, $N_{\text{b}} + N_{\text{s}}$ times. The first N_{b} iterations of the loop, called *burn-in* period, is to let Markov chain converge to near its stationary distribution. The samples used for LLR computations are those of the last N_{s} iterations, i.e., $\mathbf{d}^{(n)} = [d_1^{(n)} \ d_2^{(n)} \ \ldots \ d_K^{(n)}]^{\text{T}}$, for $n = 1, 2, \cdots, N_{\text{s}}$.

14.4.5 *Symbol-wise and Bit-wise Gibbs Samplers*

The Gibbs sampler procedure that is presented above may be referred to as symbol-wise Gibbs sampler. In each step, a new symbol value is drawn from the respective distribution. Note that, in general, each symbol carrier multiple bits. In particular, when data symbols are taken from an alphabet of size $L = 2^{\ell}$, each symbol carries ℓ bits. Gibbs samplers may also be designed to draw samples by examining one bit at a time. In terms of performance both bit-wise and symbol-wise Gibbs samplers lead to the same receiver performance (Chen et al., 2010). However, bit-wise Gibbs sampler lends itself to a simpler implementation in hardware (Laraway and Farhang-Boroujeny, 2009). Here, we continue our derivations based on symbol-wise Gibbs sampler, as this lends itself to a more straightforward presentation.

14.5 Implementation of Multiuser/MIMO Detector

In this section, we apply the results of previous section to present methods of evaluating the L-values $\lambda_1(d_k)$ of (14.2). From (14.4), we note that exact evaluation of (14.2) requires a summation over all possible choices of $\mathbf{d}_{-k}$, for each k. As noted earlier, this may soon lead to a prohibitive complexity as N and the data constellation size, L, grows. MCMC simulation/Gibbs sampler allows us to resolve this problem by searching over a small (but, important) subset of the choices of $\mathbf{d}_{-k}$. We divide our discussion into two subsections. In Subsection 14.5.1, the approximations (14.6) and (14.11) are adopted and the corresponding expressions for the multiuser/MIMO detector are presented. In Subsection 14.5.2, numerical procedures involved in the computation of the extrinsic information are derived. Statistical inference, an alternative approach for computation of extrinsic information is introduced in Subsection 14.5.3. The max-log approximation, a method that significantly reduces the complexity, at a cost of negligible loss in performance, is mentioned in Subsection 14.5.4. Finally, a discussion on the findings of the section is presented in Subsection 14.5.5.

14.5.1 *Monte Carlo Summations*

To obtain a summation similar to (14.6) for computation of $P(d_k = +1|\mathbf{y}, \lambda_2^e)$, we treat $P(\mathbf{d}_{-k}|\mathbf{y}, \lambda_2^e)$ as the density function, $f(x)$, and $P(d_k = +1|\mathbf{y}, \mathbf{d}_{-k}, \lambda_2^e)$ as the function whose weighted sum is to be obtained, $h(x)$. An estimate of $P\left(d_k = +1|\mathbf{y}, \lambda_2^e\right)$ is thus obtained by evaluating the empirical average

$$P\left(d_k = +1|\mathbf{y}, \lambda_2^e\right) \approx \frac{1}{N_s} \sum_{n=1}^{N_s} P\left(d_k = +1|\mathbf{y}, \mathbf{d}_{-k}^{(n)}, \lambda_2^e\right), \quad (14.12)$$

where $\mathbf{d}_{-k}^{(n)}$ are the samples that are chosen from the distribution $P(\mathbf{d}_{-k}|\mathbf{y}, \lambda_2^e)$.

Starting with (14.11), we treat $P(\mathbf{d}_{-k}|\mathbf{y}, \lambda_2^e)$ as $f(x)$, and $P(d_k = +1|\mathbf{y}, \mathbf{d}_{-k}, \lambda_2^e)$ as $h(x)$. This gives

$$P(d_k = +1|\mathbf{y}, \lambda_2^e) \approx \frac{\sum_{n=1}^{N_s} P(d_k = +1|\mathbf{y}, \mathbf{d}_{-k}^{(n)}, \lambda_2^e) P(\mathbf{d}_{-k}^{(n)}|\mathbf{y}, \lambda_2^e)}{\sum_{n=1}^{N_s} P(\mathbf{d}_{-k}^{(n)}|\mathbf{y}, \lambda_2^e)},$$

$$(14.13)$$

where the samples $\mathbf{d}_{-k}^{(n)}$ are chosen from a uniform distribution. These samples should be uniformly distributed over the choices of $\mathbf{d}_{-k}$ that belong to the significant part(s) of the probability distribution $P(\mathbf{d}_{-k}|\mathbf{y}, \lambda_2^e)$. They can be obtained by running the Gibbs sampler that was introduced earlier and removing the repetitions of $\mathbf{d}^{(n)}$; see Farhang-Boroujeny et al. (2006) for details.

14.5.2 *Computation of L-Values*

Here, we develop couple of numerical procedures for computation of the extrinsic *L*-value

$$\lambda_1^e(d_k) = \lambda_1(d_k) - \lambda_2^e(d_k). \qquad (14.14)$$

The estimates (14.12) and (14.13) are treated separately.

14.5.2.1 Computation based on (14.12)

Here, we need to evaluate $P(d_k = +1 | \mathbf{y}, \mathbf{d}_{-k}^{(n)}, \boldsymbol{\lambda}_2^e)$, for $n = 1, 2, \cdots,$ N_s. For this, we define

$$\lambda_1^{(n)}(d_k) = \ln \frac{P(d_k = +1 | \mathbf{y}, \mathbf{d}_{-k}^{(n)}, \boldsymbol{\lambda}_2^e)}{P(d_k = -1 | \mathbf{y}, \mathbf{d}_{-k}^{(n)}, \boldsymbol{\lambda}_2^e)}, \qquad (14.15)$$

and expand it as

$$\lambda_1^{(n)}(d_k) = \ln \frac{p(\mathbf{y} | \mathbf{d}_{-k}^{(n)}, d_k = +1) P(\mathbf{d}_{-k}^{(n)}, d_k = +1 | \boldsymbol{\lambda}_2^e)}{p(\mathbf{y} | \mathbf{d}_{-k}^{(n)}, d_k = -1) P(\mathbf{d}_{-k}^{(n)}, d_k = -1 | \boldsymbol{\lambda}_2^e)}$$

$$= \ln \frac{p(\mathbf{y} | \mathbf{d}_{-k}^{(n)}, d_k = +1)}{p(\mathbf{y} | \mathbf{d}_{-k}^{(n)}, d_k = -1)} + \lambda_2^e(d_k)$$

$$= \frac{1}{2\sigma_n^2} \left(|\mathbf{y} - \mathbf{H}_{-k}\mathbf{d}_{-k}^{(n)} + \mathbf{h}_k|^2 - |\mathbf{y} - \mathbf{H}_{-k}\mathbf{d}_{-k}^{(n)} - \mathbf{h}_k|^2 \right)$$

$$+ \lambda_2^e(d_k)$$

$$= \frac{2}{\sigma_n^2} \Re\{\mathbf{h}_k^H (\mathbf{y} - \mathbf{H}_{-k}\mathbf{d}_{-k}^{(n)})\} + \lambda_2^e(d_k)$$

$$= \frac{2}{\sigma_n^2} \Re \left\{ y_k^{MF} - \sum_{\substack{l=1 \\ l \neq k}}^{K} \rho_{kl} d_l^{(n)} \right\} + \lambda_2^e(d_k), \qquad (14.16)$$

where $\Re\{\cdot\}$ denotes the real part of, $\mathbf{H}_{-k}$ is $\mathbf{H}$ with its kth column, $\mathbf{h}_k$, removed, $y_k^{MF} = \mathbf{h}_k^H \mathbf{y}$ is the matched filter output for the kth user/stream and $\rho_{kl} = \mathbf{h}_k^H \mathbf{h}_l$ is the cross-correlation between users/streams k and l. Moreover, the second line follows from the fact that, because of interleaving effect, the extrinsic information provided by each element of $\boldsymbol{\lambda}_2^e$ is independent of those provided by its other elements, and we assume that the elements of **d** are independent of one another. This implies

$$\ln \frac{P(\mathbf{d}_{-k}^{(n)}, d_k = +1|\lambda_2^e)}{P(\mathbf{d}_{-k}^{(n)}, d_k = -1|\lambda_2^e)} = \ln \frac{P(\mathbf{d}_{-k}^{(n)}|\lambda_{2,-k}^e)}{P(\mathbf{d}_{-k}^{(n)}|\lambda_{2,-k}^e)} + \ln \frac{P(d_k = +1|\lambda_2^e(d_k))}{P(d_k = -1|\lambda_2^e(d_k))}$$

$$= \ln \frac{P(d_k = +1|\lambda_2^e(d_k))}{P(d_k = -1|\lambda_2^e(d_k))} = \lambda_2^e(d_k), \quad (14.17)$$

where $\lambda_{2,-k}^e$ is λ_2^e with $\lambda_2^e(d_k)$ dropped from it and the last identity follows from the definition of L-value. The third line in (14.16) follows since $p(\mathbf{y}|\mathbf{d}) = \frac{1}{(2\pi\sigma_n^2)^{N/2}} e^{-|\mathbf{y}-\mathbf{Hd}|^2/2\sigma_n^2}$.

Once $\lambda_1^{(n)}(d_k)$ is obtained, recalling that

$$P(d_k = -1|\mathbf{y}, \mathbf{d}_{-k}^{(n)}, \lambda_2^e) = 1 - P(d_k = +1|\mathbf{y}, \mathbf{d}_{-k}^{(n)}, \lambda_2^e)$$

and solving (14.15) for $P(d_k = +1|\mathbf{y}, \mathbf{d}_{-k}^{(n)}, \lambda_2^e)$, we obtain

$$P(d_k = +1|\mathbf{y}, \mathbf{d}_{-k}^{(n)}, \lambda_2^e) = \frac{1}{1 + \exp(-\lambda_1^{(n)}(d_k))}. \quad (14.18)$$

This is used in (14.12) for computation of $P(d_k = +1|\mathbf{y}, \lambda_2^e)$. Next, we calculate $\lambda_1(d_k) = \ln \frac{P(d_k = +1|\mathbf{y}, \lambda_2^e)}{1 - P(d_k = +1|\mathbf{y}, \lambda_2^e)}$ and substitute in (14.14) to obtain $\lambda_1^e(d_k)$.

14.5.2.2 Computation based on (14.13)

Here, we begin with evaluating the L-value

$$\lambda_1(d_k) = \ln \frac{P(d_k = +1|\mathbf{y}, \lambda_2^e)}{P(d_k = -1|\mathbf{y}, \lambda_2^e)}. \quad (14.19)$$

Substituting (14.13) and its dual when $d_k = -1$ in (14.19), we obtain

$$\lambda_1(d_k) = \ln \frac{\sum_{n=1}^{N_s} P(d_k = +1|\mathbf{y}, \mathbf{d}_{-k}^{(n)}, \lambda_2^e) P(\mathbf{d}_{-k}^{(n)}|\mathbf{y}, \lambda_2^e)}{\sum_{n=1}^{N_s} P(d_k = -1|\mathbf{y}, \mathbf{d}_{-k}^{(n)}, \lambda_2^e) P(\mathbf{d}_{-k}^{(n)}|\mathbf{y}, \lambda_2^e)}. \quad (14.20)$$

We note that

$$P(\mathbf{d}_{-k}^{(n)}|\mathbf{y}, \lambda_2^e) = \frac{p(\mathbf{d}_{-k}^{(n)}, \mathbf{y}|\lambda_2^e)}{p(\mathbf{y}|\lambda_2^e)}$$

$$= \frac{p(\mathbf{y}|\mathbf{d}_{-k}^{(n)}, \lambda_2^e) P^e(\mathbf{d}_{-k}^{(n)})}{p(\mathbf{y}|\lambda_2^e)}, \quad (14.21)$$

where $P^{\mathrm{e}}(\mathbf{d}_{-k}^{(n)})$ is short-hand notation for $P(\mathbf{d}_{-k}^{(n)}|\lambda_2^{\mathrm{e}})$, i.e., the probability of $\mathbf{d}_{-k} = \mathbf{d}_{-k}^{(n)}$ given the available extrinsic information. Also, using the Bayes rule, we obtain

$$P(d_k = +1|\mathbf{y}, \mathbf{d}_{-k}^{(n)}, \lambda_2^{\mathrm{e}}) = \frac{p(\mathbf{y}|\mathbf{d}_{-k}^{(n)}, d_k = +1)P^{\mathrm{e}}(d_k = +1)}{p(\mathbf{y}|\mathbf{d}_{-k}^{(n)}, \lambda_2^{\mathrm{e}})}.$$

$$(14.22)$$

Substituting (14.22), the dual of (14.22) with $d_k = +1$ replaced by $d_k = -1$, and (14.21) in (14.20), we get

$$\lambda_1(d_k) = \ln \frac{\sum_{n=1}^{N_s} p(\mathbf{y}|\mathbf{d}_{-k}^{(n)}, d_k = +1)P^{\mathrm{e}}(\mathbf{d}_{-k}^{(n)})}{\sum_{n=1}^{N_s} p(\mathbf{y}|\mathbf{d}_{-k}^{(n)}, d_k = -1)P^{\mathrm{e}}(\mathbf{d}_{-k}^{(n)})} \cdot \frac{P^{\mathrm{e}}(d_k = +1)}{P^{\mathrm{e}}(d_k = -1)}$$

$$= \ln \frac{\sum_{n=1}^{N_s} p(\mathbf{y}|\mathbf{d}_{-k}^{(n)}, d_k = +1)P^{\mathrm{e}}(\mathbf{d}_{-k}^{(n)})}{\sum_{n=1}^{N_s} p(\mathbf{y}|\mathbf{d}_{-k}^{(n)}, d_k = -1)P^{\mathrm{e}}(\mathbf{d}_{-k}^{(n)})} + \lambda_2^{\mathrm{e}}(d_k). \quad (14.23)$$

Recalling that $\lambda_1^{\mathrm{e}}(d_k) = \lambda_1(d_k) - \lambda_2^{\mathrm{e}}(d_k)$, from (14.23), we obtain

$$\lambda_1^{\mathrm{e}}(d_k) = \ln \frac{\sum_{n=1}^{N_s} p(\mathbf{y}|\mathbf{d}_{-k}^{(n)}, d_k = +1)P^{\mathrm{e}}(\mathbf{d}_{-k}^{(n)})}{\sum_{n=1}^{N_s} p(\mathbf{y}|\mathbf{d}_{-k}^{(n)}, d_k = -1)P^{\mathrm{e}}(\mathbf{d}_{-k}^{(n)})}. \quad (14.24)$$

14.5.3 *Statistical Inference*

In the works prior to Farhang-Boroujeny (2006), researchers considered using the statistical inference to obtain *L*-values, e.g. see Gatherer et al. (2000) and Chen (2002). In this approach, $P(d_k = +1|\mathbf{y}, \lambda_2^{\mathrm{e}})$ is obtained by collecting samples of d_k through a Gibbs sampler and then evaluating the statistical average

$$P(d_k = +1|\mathbf{y}, \lambda_2^{\mathrm{e}}) \approx \frac{1}{N_s} \sum_{n=1}^{N_s} \delta(d_k^{(n)} = +1), \quad (14.25)$$

where $\delta(\cdot)$ is an indicator function that takes value of 1 if its argument is true and value of 0 otherwise.

To compare the approach of (14.25) and the detection approaches that were proposed earlier, we note that (14.12) may be viewed as a *Rao-Blackwellization* (Robert and Casella, 1999) of (14.25). We thus refer to the L-value estimates based on (14.12) as Markov chain Rao-Balckwellization (MCRB) estimate. We also refer to the estimates based on (14.13) as MCRB with uniform sampling (MCRB-U). MCRB reduces the variance of the estimates when additional side information is available; see page 311 of Robert and Casella (1999). This follows from the identity var(U) = var($E[U|V]$) + $E[\text{var}(U|V)]$, which implies that var($E[U|V]$) $\leq$ var(U). Note that, here, var($\cdot$) denotes the variance of the argument. The desired result is obtained if we replace U by the estimate (14.25), i.e., $\frac{1}{N_s}\sum_{n=1}^{N_s}\delta(d_k^{(n)} = +1)$ and V by ($\mathbf{y}$, $\mathbf{d}_{-k}^{(n)}$, λ_2^e) and note that

$$P(d_k = +1|\mathbf{y}, \mathbf{d}_{-k}^{(n)}, \lambda_2^e) = E[\delta(d_k = +1)|\mathbf{y}, \mathbf{d}_{-k}^{(n)}, \lambda_2^e].$$

14.5.4 *Max-log Approximation*

It is well-known that log ratios, such as (14.24), could be approximated as (Robertson, 1995)

$$\lambda_1^e(d_k) \approx \ln \frac{\max_n p(\mathbf{y}|\mathbf{d}_{-k}^{(n)}, d_k = +1)P^e(\mathbf{d}_{-k}^{(n)})}{\max_n p(\mathbf{y}|\mathbf{d}_{-k}^{(n)}, d_k = -1)P^e(\mathbf{d}_{-k}^{(n)})} \tag{14.26}$$

without any significant loss in the receiver detection performance. This, which is known as max-log approximation, simplifies the MCRB-U algorithm with two respects. Firstly, it avoids the summations in (14.24). Secondly, and more importantly, it avoids the process of looking for repetitions of $\mathbf{d}^{(n)}$. This can be a great saving, since the number of comparisons required for deleting repetitions grows with the square of N_s.

14.5.5 *Discussion*

Three methods of estimating the bit/symbol probabilities $P(d_k = +1|\mathbf{y}, \lambda_2^e)$, and, accordingly, the respective L-values, were presented: (i) Statistical inference; (ii) MCRB; and (iii) MCRB-U. Extensive computer simulations presented in Farhang-Boroujeny et al. (2006) have revealed that a satisfactory performance of the statistical inference requires a very large number of samples. On the other hand, MCRB-U is more stable than MCRB and, in general, has a superior performance. Additional studies that have been performed by the author and his co-workers, e.g., Zhu et al. (2005) and Chen et al. (2010), have revealed that MCMC always outperforms other candidate choices in the literature. The choices that have been

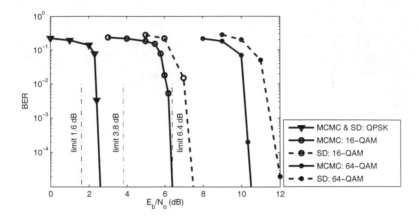

Figure 14.2 BER results of the MCMC detector and list sphere decoding. Courtesy of Farhang-Boroujeny (2006).

considered are the soft-in soft-out list sphere decoding (LSD) and the soft-in soft-out minimum mean square error (MMSE) detectors. From these LSD outperforms MMSE detector.

Here, we present a sample example from Farhang-Boroujeny (2006). This example compares MCRB-U and LSD in a MIMO setup with 8 transmit and 8 receive antennas. It is assumed that the channel matrix **H** has elements that are complex Gaussian and independent of one another. The channel code is rate 1/2 turbo code and each code word consists of 9216 information bits. The bit-error-rate (BER) curves versus bit energy over noise power, E_b/N_0, for the cases of QPSK, 16-QAM and 64-QAM modulated symbols are presented in Fig. 14.2. The vertical lines at 1.6 dB, 3.8 dB, and 6.4 dB the capacity limits for QPSK, 16-QAM, and 64-QAM constellations, respectively.

14.6 Implementation of MCMC Detector

In Laraway and Farhang-Boroujeny (2009), it has been shown that MCMC detector can be implemented in a hardware architecture that lends itself to a low complexity implementation. In this section, we present a summary of the hardware architecture that has been suggested in Laraway and Farhang-Boroujeny (2009).

14.6.1 *Reformulation of the Channel Model*

The realization of the MCMC detection algorithms that were discussed above is greatly simplified if we rearrange (14.1) in terms of real and imaginary parts of the underlying variables and coefficients. Such rearrangement is straightforward and leads to the equation

$$\mathbf{x} = \mathbf{Ac} + \mathbf{v}, \tag{14.27}$$

where

$$\mathbf{x} = \begin{bmatrix} \Re\{\mathbf{y}\} \\ \Im\{\mathbf{y}\} \end{bmatrix}, \quad \mathbf{A} = \begin{bmatrix} \Re\{\mathbf{H}\} & -\Im\{\mathbf{H}\} \\ \Im\{\mathbf{H}\} & \Re\{\mathbf{H}\} \end{bmatrix},$$

$$\mathbf{c} = \begin{bmatrix} \Re\{\mathbf{d}\} \\ \Im\{\mathbf{d}\} \end{bmatrix}, \quad \mathbf{v} = \begin{bmatrix} \Re\{\mathbf{n}\} \\ \Im\{\mathbf{n}\} \end{bmatrix}.$$

$\Re\{\cdot\}$ and $\Im\{\cdot\}$ denote the real and imaginary parts of the arguments. We note that when the elements of $\mathbf{d}$ are from an square L-QAM constellation, the elements of $\mathbf{c}$ are from an $\sqrt{L}$-ary pulse amplitude modulated (PAM) alphabet. We also note that with the sizes specified above, $\mathbf{x}$ and $\mathbf{v}$ are of length $2M$, $\mathbf{c}$ is of length $2N$, and $\mathbf{A}$ is an $2M$-by-$2N$ matrix.

14.6.2 *Bit-wise Gibbs Sampler*

The Gibbs sampler that was introduced earlier, in Section 14.4.4, draws samples of data symbols, one at a time. The Gibbs sampler may be also implemented to operate on finer grain of drawing one bit at time. To put together a set of equations that formulate such a Gibbs sampler, we assume that each element of $\mathbf{d}$ carries ℓ bits, and define the bit vector $\mathbf{b} = [b_1 \ b_2 \ \cdots \ b_{\ell M}]$. Each choice of $\mathbf{b}$ is mapped to $\mathbf{d}$ or, equivalently, to $\mathbf{c}$, and the subsequent calculations are performed following to (14.1) or (14.27).

To draw $b_k^{(n)}$ in the Gibbs sampler, one needs to obtain $P(b_k = +1|b_1^{(n)}, \cdots, b_{k-1}^{(n)}, b_{k+1}^{(n-1)}, \cdots, b_{\ell M}^{(n-1)}, \mathbf{x}, \lambda_2^e)$. To derive an equation for this probability, we define

$$\mathbf{b}_{-k}^{(n)} \triangleq [b_1^{(n)} \ \cdots \ b_{k-1}^{(n)} \ b_{k+1}^{(n-1)} \ \cdots, \ b_{\ell M}^{(n-1)}]^{\mathrm{T}} \tag{14.28}$$

and note that
$$P(b_k = +1|\mathbf{x}, \mathbf{b}_{-k}^{(n)}, \lambda_2^e) =$$

$$\frac{P(b_k = +1|\mathbf{x}, \mathbf{b}_{-k}^{(n)}, \lambda_2^e)}{P(b_k = +1|\mathbf{x}, \mathbf{b}_{-k}^{(n)}, \lambda_2^e) + P(b_k = -1|\mathbf{x}, \mathbf{b}_{-k}^{(n)}, \lambda_2^e)}. \tag{14.29}$$

In (14.29) and other equations that follow $\mathbf{b}_{-k}^{(n)}$ is the short hand notation for $\mathbf{b}_{-k} = \mathbf{b}_{-k}^{(n)}$. We also note that

$$P(b_k = +1|\mathbf{x}, \mathbf{b}_{-k}^{(n)}, \lambda_2^e) = \frac{p(\mathbf{x}|\mathbf{b}_{k+}^{(n)}, \lambda_2^e) P(\mathbf{b}_{k+}^{(n)}|\lambda_2^e)}{p(\mathbf{x}, \mathbf{b}_{-k}^{(n)}|\lambda_2^e)} \tag{14.30}$$

and

$$P(b_k = -1|\mathbf{x}, \mathbf{b}_{-k}^{(n)}, \lambda_2^e) = \frac{p(\mathbf{x}|\mathbf{b}_{k-}^{(n)}, \lambda_2^e) P(\mathbf{b}_{k-}^{(n)}|\lambda_2^e)}{p(\mathbf{x}, \mathbf{b}_{-k}^{(n)}|\lambda_2^e)} \tag{14.31}$$

where $\mathbf{b}_{k+}^{(n)} = \left[b_1^{(n)} \cdots b_{k-1}^{(n)}, +1, b_{k+1}^{(n-1)} \cdots b_{\ell M}^{(n-1)}\right]^{\mathrm{T}}$ and $\mathbf{b}_{k-}^{(n)} = \left[b_1^{(n)} \cdots b_{k-1}^{(n)}, -1, b_{k+1}^{(n-1)} \cdots b_{\ell M}^{(n-1)}\right]^{\mathrm{T}}$. Moreover, $p(\mathbf{x}|\mathbf{b}_{k+}^{(n)}, \lambda_2^e) = p(\mathbf{x}|\mathbf{b}_{k+}^{(n)})$ and $p(\mathbf{x}|\mathbf{b}_{k-}^{(n)}, \lambda_2^e) = p(\mathbf{x}|\mathbf{b}_{k-}^{(n)})$, since when the data vector $\mathbf{b}$ is fully specified the extrinsic information become irrelevant. Using these and substituting (14.30) and (14.31) in (14.29), after deleting the common terms, we obtain
$$P(b_k = +1|\mathbf{x}, \mathbf{b}_{-k}^{(n)}, \lambda_2^e) =$$

$$\frac{p(\mathbf{x}|\mathbf{b}_{k+}^{(n)}) P^e(b_k = +1)}{p(\mathbf{x}|\mathbf{b}_{k+}^{(n)}) P^e(b_k = +1) + p(\mathbf{x}|\mathbf{b}_{k-}^{(n)}) P^e(b_k = -1)} \tag{14.32}$$

where $P^e(b_k = i) \triangleq P(b_k = i|\lambda_2^e(b_k))$, for $i = \pm 1$, and we have assumed that the elements of $\mathbf{b}$ are independent of each other, hence,
$$P(\mathbf{b}_{k+}^{(n)}|\lambda_2^e) = P^e(b_1 = b_1^{(n)}) \cdots P^e(b_{k-1} = b_{k-1}^{(n)})$$

$$\times P^e(b_k = +1) P^e(b_{k+1} = b_{k+1}^{(n-1)}) \cdots P^e(b_{\ell M} = b_{\ell M}^{(n-1)}) \tag{14.33}$$

and
$$P(\mathbf{b}_{k-}^{(n)}|\lambda_2^e) = P^e(b_1 = b_1^{(n)}) \cdots P^e(b_{k-1} = b_{k-1}^{(n)})$$

$$\times P^e(b_k = -1) P^e(b_{k+1} = b_{k+1}^{(n-1)}) \cdots P^e(b_{\ell M} = b_{\ell M}^{(n-1)}). \tag{14.34}$$

When $\mathbf{A}$ is known and the noise vector $\mathbf{v}$ is Gaussian and satisfies $E[\mathbf{v}\mathbf{v}^{\mathrm{H}}] = \frac{1}{2}\sigma_n^2 \mathbf{I}$, we have

$$p(\mathbf{x}|\mathbf{b}_{k+}^{(n)}) = \frac{1}{(\pi \sigma_n^2)^{N/2}} e^{-||\mathbf{x} - \mathbf{A}\mathbf{c}_{k+}^{(n)}||^2/\sigma_n^2}, \tag{14.35}$$

and

$$p(\mathbf{x}|\mathbf{b}_{k-}^{(n)}) = \frac{1}{(\pi\sigma_n^2)^{N/2}} e^{-||\mathbf{x}-\mathbf{A}\mathbf{c}_{k-}^{(n)}||^2/\sigma_n^2}, \tag{14.36}$$

where $\mathbf{c}_{k+}^{(n)}$ and $\mathbf{c}_{k-}^{(n)}$ are the vectors of transmit symbols obtained through mapping from $\mathbf{b}_{k+}^{(n)}$ and $\mathbf{b}_{k-}^{(n)}$, respectively. Direct substitution of (14.35) and (14.36) in (14.32) results in a procedure that is computationally involved and sensitive to numerical errors. A log-domain implementation similar to those in the log-MAP turbo decoders avoids this problem.

Defining

$$\gamma_{k+} \triangleq \ln(P^{\mathbf{e}}(b_k = +1)) - \frac{||\mathbf{x}-\mathbf{A}\mathbf{c}_{k+}^{(n)}||^2}{\sigma_n^2} \tag{14.37}$$

$$\gamma_{k-} \triangleq \ln(P^{\mathbf{e}}(b_k = -1)) - \frac{||\mathbf{x}-\mathbf{A}\mathbf{c}_{k-}^{(n)}||^2}{\sigma_n^2}, \tag{14.38}$$

and using (14.35) and (14.36), (14.32) may be rearranged as

$$P(b_k = +1|\mathbf{x}, \mathbf{b}_{-k}^{(n)}, \lambda_2^e) = \frac{1}{1 + e^{-(\gamma_{k+} - \gamma_{k-})}}. \tag{14.39}$$

Using (14.37) and (14.38), we obtain

$$\gamma_{k+} - \gamma_{k-} = \lambda_2^e(b_k) - \frac{||\mathbf{x}-\mathbf{A}\mathbf{c}_{k+}^{(n)}||^2 - ||\mathbf{x}-\mathbf{A}\mathbf{c}_{k-}^{(n)}||^2}{\sigma_n^2} \tag{14.40}$$

where $\lambda_2^e(b_k) = \ln\frac{P^{\mathbf{e}}(b_k=+1)}{P^{\mathbf{e}}(b_k=-1)}$. Noting that $\mathbf{c}_{k+}^{(n)}$ and $\mathbf{c}_{k-}^{(n)}$ differ only in one term, straightforward manipulations leads to

$$\gamma_{k+} - \gamma_{k-} = \lambda_2^e(b_k) - \frac{1}{\sigma_n^2}\left(\left(c_{k+,p}^{(n)}\right)^2 - \left(c_{k-,p}^{(n)}\right)^2\right) r_{pp}$$

$$+ \frac{2}{\sigma_n^2}\left(c_{k+,p}^{(n)} - c_{k-,p}^{(n)}\right)\left(y_p^{\mathrm{mf}} - \sum_{q=1, q\neq p}^{K} r_{pq}c_q^{(n)}\right), \tag{14.41}$$

where $x_p^{\mathrm{mf}} = \mathbf{a}_p^T\mathbf{x}$, $\mathbf{a}_p$ is the pth column of $\mathbf{A}$, r_{pq} is the pqth element of $\mathbf{R} = \mathbf{A}^T\mathbf{A}$, $c_q^{(n)}$ is the qth element of $\mathbf{c}^{(n)}$, $c_{k+,p}^{(n)}$ and $c_{k-,p}^{(n)}$ are the pth element of $\mathbf{c}_{k+}^{(n)}$ and $\mathbf{c}_{k-}^{(n)}$, respectively, and we assume b_k is mapped to $c_p^{(n)}$. Equation (14.41) may be further rearranged as

$$\gamma_{k+} - \gamma_{k-} = \lambda_2^e(b_k) - \kappa_1 r_{pp}' + \kappa_2\left(x_p'^{\mathrm{mf}} - \sum_{q=1, q\neq p}^{2M} r_{pq}'c_q^{(n)}\right), \tag{14.42}$$

where $\kappa_1 = \frac{1}{2} \left(\left(c_{k^+,p}^{(n)} \right)^2 - \left(c_{k^-,p}^{(n)} \right)^2 \right)$, $\kappa_2 = \left(c_{k^+,p}^{(n)} - c_{k^-,p}^{(n)} \right)$, $x_p'^{\text{mf}} =$ $\frac{2}{\sigma_n^2} x_p^{\text{mf}}$ and $r_{pq}' = \frac{2}{\sigma_n^2} r_{pq}$. We note that $x_p'^{\text{mf}}$ and r_{pq}' can be calculated prior to starting the Gibbs sampler and thus are treated as inputs to it.

Finally, we argue that since, in practice, each c_k is an $\ell/2$ bit binary number and $\ell/2$ is typically small (4 or smaller), the multiplications involved in (14.42) may be handled trivially through a few addition and subtraction operations for each. That is, we will have a multiplier-free implementation.

14.6.3 *L-Values Calculator*

As noted earlier L-values computation based on (14.13) is superior to the other methods. Accordingly, we follow this approach here.

The bit-wise equivalent to (14.26), finds the following form:

$$\lambda_1^e(b_k) = \ln \frac{\sum_{n=1}^{N_s} p(\mathbf{x}|\mathbf{b}_{-k}^{(n)}, b_k = +1) P^e(\mathbf{b}_{-k}^{(n)})}{\sum_{n=1}^{N_s} p(\mathbf{x}|\mathbf{b}_{-k}^{(n)}, d_k = -1) P^e(\mathbf{b}_{-k}^{(n)})}, \tag{14.43}$$

where $P^e(\mathbf{b}_{-k}^{(n)}) = P^e(b_1 = b_1^{(n)}) \cdots P^e(b_{k-1} = b_{k-1}^{(n)}) P^e(b_{k+1} = b_{k+1}^{(n-1)}) \cdots P^e(b_{\ell M} = b_{\ell M}^{(n-1)})$.

To avoid numerical instability and to develop an efficient implementation, we follow the same line of derivations that led to (14.39). To this end, we define

$$\eta_{k^+}^{(n)} \triangleq \ln P^e(\mathbf{b}_{-k}^{(n)}) - \frac{||\mathbf{x} - \mathbf{Hc}_{k^+}^{(n)}||^2}{\sigma_n^2} \tag{14.44}$$

and

$$\eta_{k^-}^{(n)} \triangleq \ln P^e(\mathbf{b}_{-k}^{(n)}) - \frac{||\mathbf{x} - \mathbf{Hc}_{k^-}^{(n)}||^2}{\sigma_n^2} \tag{14.45}$$

and note that (14.43) can be rearranged as

$$\lambda_1^e(b_k) = \ln \left(\sum_{n=1}^{N_s} e^{\eta_{k^+}^{(n)}} \right) - \ln \left(\sum_{n=1}^{N_s} e^{\eta_{k^-}^{(n)}} \right). \tag{14.46}$$

In order to avoid the computationally expensive exponent evaluations, we adopt the Jacobian logarithm, *viz.*,

$$\max{}^*(x, y) \triangleq \ln(e^x + e^y) = \max(x, y) + \ln(1 + e^{-|x-y|}). \tag{14.47}$$

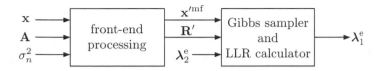

Figure 14.3 Top-level block diagram of the MCMC detector.

We also adopt a max-log-MAP type approach and use the following approximation:

$$\lambda_1^e(b_k) \approx \max_n \eta_{k+}^{(n)} - \max_n \eta_{k-}^{(n)}. \tag{14.48}$$

This approximation significantly simplifies the implementation of the detector. If (14.46) is to be implemented, each new sample has to be compared with all the previous samples and deleted if it is a repeat sample. When N_s is large this may be a complexity burden. Implementation of (14.48), on the other hand, can be trivial. As samples of **b** are generated, the respective values $\eta_{k+}^{(n)}$ and $\eta_{k-}^{(n)}$ are computed. Each of these are then compared to their counterpart from the previous Gibbs samples and replaced if they are larger or discarded if they are smaller.

14.6.4 *Hardware Architectures*

Figure 14.3 presents a top-level block diagram of the MCMC detector. It consists of two distinct parts: (i) the front-end processing; and (ii) the Gibbs sampler and LLR calculator block. The front-end processing takes **x**, **A** and σ_n^2 as inputs and calculates $\mathbf{x}'^{\mathrm{mf}} = \frac{2}{\sigma_n^2}\mathbf{A}^{\mathsf{T}}\mathbf{x}$ and $\mathbf{R}' = \frac{2}{\sigma_n^2}\mathbf{A}^{\mathsf{T}}\mathbf{A}$. The Gibbs sampler/LLR calculator takes $\mathbf{x}'^{\mathrm{mf}}$, $\mathbf{R}'$ and λ_2^e from the channel decoder and generates λ_1^e.

To develop a complete architecture for Gibbs sampler and LLR calculator, we first take note of (14.39) which should be performed once $\gamma_{k+} - \gamma_{k-}$ is calculated according to (14.42). Since exponential computation in (14.39) is costly to implement in hardware, a look-up table is often used to obtain a rough estimate of the right-hand side of it. An alternative approximation that has been suggested in Laraway and Farhang-Boroujeny (2009) uses the following equation.

$$\frac{1}{1+e^{-x}} \approx \begin{cases} \dfrac{x}{2^3} + \dfrac{1}{2}, & -4 < x < 4 \\ 1, & x \ge 4 \\ 0, & x \le -4 \end{cases} \tag{14.49}$$

Substituting (14.42) in (14.49), we get, when $-4 < \gamma_{k^+} - \gamma_{k^-} < 4$,

$$P(b_k = +1|\mathbf{x}, \mathbf{b}_{-k}^{(n)}, \lambda_2^e)$$

$$\approx \frac{1}{2} + \frac{\lambda_2^e(b_k) - \kappa_1 r'_{pp} + \kappa_2 \left(x_p'^{\mathrm{mf}} - \sum_{q=1, q \ne p}^{2M} r'_{pq} c_q^{(n)} \right)}{2^3}. \tag{14.50}$$

In the Gibbs sampler, the next choice of b_k is made by selecting $b_k = +1$ with the probability $P(b_k = +1|\mathbf{x}, \mathbf{b}_{-k}^{(n)}, \lambda_2^e)$. To realize this in hardware, a random variable, v, with uniform distribution in the interval 0 to 1 is generated, and b_k is set equal to +1 if $P(b_k = +1|\mathbf{x}, \mathbf{b}_{-k}^{(n)}, \lambda_2^e) - v > 0$, otherwise b_k is set equal to -1. Alternatively, and more conveniently here, we may write the latter inequality as $2^3(P(b_k = +1|\mathbf{x}, \mathbf{b}_{-k}^{(n)}, \lambda_2^e) - 0.5) - u > 0$, where $u = 2^3(v - 0.5)$ is a random variable with uniform distribution in the interval -4 to $+4$. The random variable u can be easily generated using a linear feedback shift register (LFSR) circuit that acts as a random number generator with statistically independent outputs. Putting these together, the circuit shown in Fig. 14.4 may be proposed. This is self-explanatory. It follows from (14.50) and other relevant equations in the previous section. Without any loss of generality, here we have presented an implementation when $2M = 4$. $\mathbf{R}''$ is $\mathbf{R}'$ with its diagonal elements forced to zero. Also, as noted earlier, since in practice c_k's are from a small alphabet and accordingly the number of possible values of κ_1 and κ_2 are small, each multiplier in Fig. 14.4 can be performed with a few addition and subtraction operations. Hence, the Gibbs sampler of Fig. 14.4 is effectively a multiplier-free realization.

Next, we develop a circuit for computation of L-values. This is done by using (14.48) and applying proper approximations wherever possible. We note that the computation of $\eta_{k+}^{(n)}$ and $\eta_{k-}^{(n)}$ requires computation of $\ln P^e(\mathbf{b}_{-k}^{(n)})$, $\frac{||\mathbf{x} - \mathbf{Ac}_{k+}^{(n)}||^2}{\sigma_n^2}$ and $\frac{||\mathbf{x} - \mathbf{Ac}_{k-}^{(n)}||^2}{\sigma_n^2}$. We also

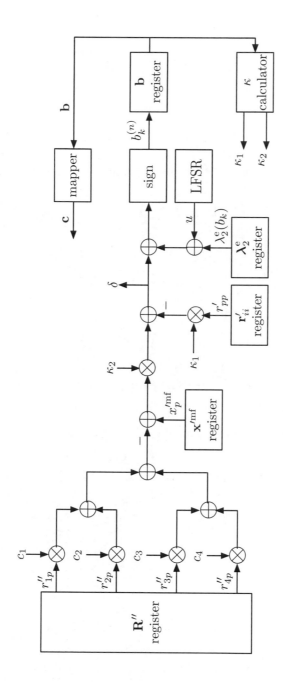

Figure 14.4 Gibbs sampler circuit.

note that, for $i = \pm 1$,

$$
\begin{aligned}
\ln P^e(b_k = i) &= \ln \frac{1}{1 + e^{-i\lambda_2^e(b_k)}} \\
&= -\max{}^*(0, -i\lambda_2^e(b_k)) \\
&\approx -\max(0, -i\lambda_2^e(b_k)) \\
&= \min(0, i\lambda_2^e(b_k)).
\end{aligned}
\tag{14.51}
$$

Using $\psi_k^{(n)}$ to denote the approximation, and assuming that the elements of the bit vector **b** are independent, we obtain

$$
\psi_k^{(n)} = \sum_{l=1}^{k} \min(0, b_l^{(n)}\lambda_2^e(b_k)) + \sum_{l=k+1}^{KL} \min(0, b_l^{(n-1)}\lambda_2^e(b_k)). \tag{14.52}
$$

We propose the following procedure for updating $\psi_k^{(n)}$:

if $b_k^{(n)} \neq b_k^{(n-1)}$: $\psi_k^{(n)} = \psi_{k-1}^{(n)} - b_k^{(n-1)}\lambda_2^e(b_k)$
else: $\psi_k^{(n)} = \psi_{k-1}^{(n)}$.

Here, we have noted that

$$
\psi_k^{(n)} = \psi_{k-1}^{(n)} - \min(0, b_k^{(n-1)}\lambda_2^e(b_k)) + \min(0, b_k^{(n)}\lambda_2^e(b_k))
$$

and that this simplifies to $\psi_k^{(n)} = \psi_{k-1}^{(n)} - b_k^{(n-1)}\lambda_2^e(b_k)$ when $b_k^{(n)} \neq b_k^{(n-1)}$. One can calculate $\ln P^e(\mathbf{b}_{-k}^{(n)})$ by removing the contribution of $b_k^{(n-1)}$ from $\psi_{k-1}^{(n)}$, viz.,

$$
\ln P^e(\mathbf{b}_{-k}^{(n)}) = \psi_{k-1}^{(n)} + \max(0, -b_k^{(n-1)}\lambda_2^e(b_k)). \tag{14.53}
$$

The above results lead to the circuit shown in Fig. 14.5. We note that ψ is insensitive to a bias since the subtraction of the two terms

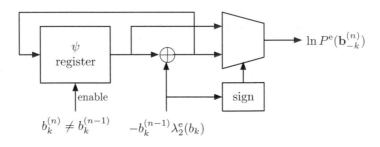

Figure 14.5 ψ circuit: to compute $\ln P^e(\mathbf{b}_{-k}^{(n)})$.

on the right-hand side of (14.48) removes such a bias. Hence, ψ can be assigned any arbitrary initial value.

Next, we develop a circuit for computation of $\xi_{k+}^{(n)} = \frac{||\mathbf{x}-\mathbf{Ac}_{k+}^{(n)}||^2}{\sigma_n^2}$ and $\xi_{k-}^{(n)} = \frac{||\mathbf{x}-\mathbf{Ac}_{k-}^{(n)}||^2}{\sigma_n^2}$. We note that the difference $\xi_{k+}^{(n)} - \xi_{k-}^{(n)} = \delta$ is available from the Gibbs sampler of Fig. 14.4. Accordingly, we propose the following procedure for updating the $\xi_{k+}^{(n)}$ and $\xi_{k-}^{(n)}$:

if $b_k^{(n)} \neq b_k^{(n-1)}$
    if $b_k^{(n)} = +1$
        $\xi_{k+}^{(n)} = \xi + \delta$; $\xi_{k-}^{(n)} = \xi$; $\xi = \xi + \delta$
    else
        $\xi_{k+}^{(n)} = \xi$; $\xi_{k-}^{(n)} = \xi - \delta$; $\xi = \xi - \delta$
    else
    if $b_k^{(n)} = +1$
        $\xi_{k+}^{(n)} = \xi$; $\xi_{k-}^{(n)} = \xi - \delta$
    else
        $\xi_{k+}^{(n)} = \xi + \delta$; $\xi_{k-}^{(n)} = \xi$.
end.

Using this procedure, Fig. 14.6 presents a circuit that may be used to compute $\xi_{k+}^{(n)}$ and $\xi_{k-}^{(n)}$.

Finally, combining the circuits in Figs. 14.5 and 14.6, the circuit presented in Fig. 14.7 is proposed for computation of the L-values. The inputs to Fig. 14.7 are generated by the Gibbs sampler of

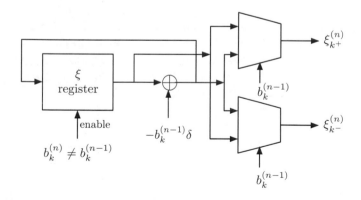

Figure 14.6 ξ circuit: to compute $\xi_{k+}^{(n)}$ and $\xi_{k-}^{(n)}$.

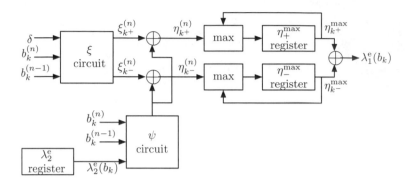

Figure 14.7   Circuit for computation of the L-values.

Fig. 14.4. Hence, combining Figs. 14.4 and 14.7, we obtain a complete implementation of the Gibbs sampler/L-value calculator.

References

1. R. Chen, J. S. Liu, and X. Wang (2002), Convergence analyses and comparisons of Markov chain Monte Carlo algorithms in digital communications, *IEEE Trans. Signal Process.*, vol. 50, no. 2, pp. 255–270, February 2002.

2. R.-R. Chen, R.-H. Peng, A. Ashikhmin, B. Farhang-Boroujeny (2010), Approaching MIMO capacity using bitwise Markov chain Monte Carlo detection, *IEEE Trans. Commun.*, vol. 58, no. 2, 2010, pp. 423–428.

3. B. Farhang-Boroujeny, H. Zhu, and Z. Shi (2006), Markov chain Monte Carlo algorithms for CDMA and MIMO communication systems, *IEEE Trans. Signal Process.*, vol. 54, no. 5, pp. 1896–1909, May 2006.

4. G. Fishman (1996), *Monte Carlo: Concepts, Algorithms and Applications*, Springer-Verlag, New York, 1996.

5. G. J. Foschini (1996), Layered space-time architecture for wireless communication in a fading environment when using multi-element antennas, *Bell Labs Tech. J.*, vol. 1, pp. 41–59, August 1996.

6. T. M. Gatherer, A. X. Wang, and R. Chen (2000), Interference cancellation using the Gibbs sampler, *IEEE VTS-Fall VTC 2000*, vol. 1, pp. 429–433, September 24–28, 2000.

7. O. Häggström (2002), *Finite Markov Chains and Algorithmic Applications.* Cambridge University Press, 2002.

8. J. Hammersley and D. Handscomb (1964), *Monte Carlo Methods. Methuen*, New York, 1964.

9. S. A. Laraway and B. Farhang-Boroujeny (2009), Implementation of a Markov Chain Monte Carlo Based Multiuser/MIMO Detector, *IEEE Trans. Circuits Syst.,* vol. 56, no. 1, Jan. 2009, pp. 246–255.

10. R.-H. Peng, R-R. Chen, and B. Farhang-Boroujeny (2010), Markov chain Monte Carlo detectors for channels with intersymbol interference, *IEEE Trans. Signal Process.,* vol. 58, no. 4, 2010, pp. 2206–2217.

11. C. P. Robert and G. Casella (1999), *Monte Carlo Statistical Methods.* Springer-Verlag, New York, 1999.

12. P. Robertson, E. Villebrun, P. Hoeher (1995), A comparison of optimal and sub-optimal MAP decoding algorithms operating in the log domain. *IEEE International Conference on Communications,* ICC 95, vol. 2, pp. 1009–1013, Seattle, June 18–22, 1995.

13. E. Telatar (1999), Capacity of multi-antenna Gaussian channels, *European Trans. Telecomm.,* vol. 10, no. 6, pp. 585–595, November–December 1999.

14. S. Verdú (1996), Minimum probability of error for asynchronous Gaussian multiple-access channels, *IEEE Trans. Inform. Theory*, vol. 32, pp. 85–96, January 1986.

15. S. Verdù (1998), *Multiuser Detection.* Cambridge University Press.

16. A. J. Viterbi (1995), *CDMA : Principles of Spread Spectrum Communication.* Prentice Hall.

17. H. Zhu, B. Farhang-Boroujeny, and R.-R. Chen (2005), On performance of sphere decoding and Markov chain Monte Carlo detection methods, *IEEE Signal Process. Lett.,* October 2005, pp. 669–672.

Chapter 15

Multiple Antennas for Physical Layer Secrecy

Jiangyuan Li[a] and Athina P. Petropulu[b]

[a]*South China University of Technology, China*
[b]*Rutgers—The State University of New Jersey, USA*
eejyli@aliyun.com, athinap@rutgers.edu

15.1 Physical Layer Secrecy

Due to the broadcast nature of the wireless channel, information transmitted over a wireless network can be accessed by unauthorized users, also referred to as eavedroppers. Ensuring that only the legitimate receiver will be able to decipher the transmitted information has been traditionally achieved by cryptographic approaches operating at various layers of the network protocol stack, e.g., WEP (LAN, 1990), at the link layer, SET (SET, 1997), at the application layer, IPSec (IPSec, 2000), at the network layer, TLS/SSL (SSL, 1996), and WTLS (WAP, 2002) at the transport layer. However, cryptographic protocols, mainly developed for wireline networks, impose significant challenges to wireless devices, which typically have limited resources. They require significant storage

Trends in Digital Signal Processing: A Festschrift in Honour of A. G. Constantinides
Edited by Yong Ching Lim, Hon Keung Kwan, and Wan-Chi Siu
Copyright © 2016 Pan Stanford Publishing Pte. Ltd.
ISBN 978-981-4669-50-4 (Hardcover), 978-981-4669-51-1 (eBook)
www.panstanford.com

overhead (Liu et al., 2006) and computational power, thus impacting battery life (Potlapally et al., 2006). Further, they rely on secret keys, and key distribution and management over wireless networks is difficult and expensive (NIST Report, 2009). It should be noted that a cryptographic approach does not prevent an unauthorized user from receiving the transmitted packet; it just makes it computationally difficult for the unauthorized user to decrypt the message contained in the packets.

Physical (PHY) layer approaches have recently received significant attention as means of achieving secure wireless communications without relying on cryptography. By exploiting the characteristics of the wireless channel, PHY layer approaches provide the packet to the unauthorized user under such conditions, that the unauthorized user would not be able to recover the message in the packet even if he knew the encoding/decoding scheme of the transmitter/receiver. The objective is to maximize the rate of reliable information from the source to the intended receiver, with the unauthorized user being kept as ignorant of that information as possible. This line of work was pioneered by Wyner, who, in the context of wireline communications, introduced the wiretap channel and established the possibility of creating perfectly secure communication links without relying on private (secret) keys (Wyner, 1975). Wyner showed that when an eavesdropper's channel is a degraded version of the main source-destination channel, the source and destination can exchange messages in perfect secrecy at a non-zero rate, while the eavesdropper cannot infer much about the messages based on his observations. A rate at which information can be transmitted secretly from the source to its intended destination is termed an achievable *secrecy rate*, and the maximal achievable secrecy rate is named the *secrecy capacity*. The secrecy capacity of the scalar Gaussian wire-tap channel was studied in Leung and Hellman (1978), while Wyner's approach was generalized to the transmission of confidential messages over broadcast channels in (Csiszár and Körner, 1978). Recently, there has been considerable interest in generalizing Wyner's results to the wireless fading channel and to multi-user scenarios (see, e.g., Chapters 6–8 in Liang et al. (2009) for an overview).

The feasibility of PHY layer secrecy approaches based on single antenna systems is hampered by channel conditions. In cases of no feedback, when the single-input single-output source-destination channel is worse than the source-eavesdropper channel, the secrecy rate is typically zero (Wyner, 1975; Leung and Hellman, 1978). Some recent works have been proposed to overcome this limitation by employing multiple antennas at the source and/or destination (Khisti and Wornell, 2010a,b; Oggier and Hassibi, 2011; Bustin et al., 2009; Liu and Shamai, 2009; Oggier and Hassibi, 2007). Indeed, the use of multiple antennas can ensure positive secrecy rate even if when the single antenna systems fail to do so.

In the following, we address the secrecy capacity of the MIMO wiretap channel.

15.2 Secrecy Capacity Concept of the Wiretap Channel

Let us first introduce some terminology for the most basic physical layer model, as first introduced by Wyner (Wyner, 1975) (see Fig. 15.1). According to that model, a transmitter wishes to transmit a message to a legitimate receiver, while keeping the message as secret as possible from an eavesdropper. The eavesdropper is assumed to be a passive receiver, i.e., he does not transmit signals over the channel.

A source message W, drawn from the index set $\{1, 2, \cdots, M\}$, is encoded to signal $X^n(W)$, which is transmitted over a discrete memoryless channel (DMC), resulting in the output sequences Y^n and Z^n at the destination and the eavesdropper, respectively.

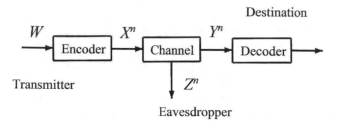

Figure 15.1 Illustration of the wiretap channel.

The destination and the eavesdropper estimate the index W, respectively. Formally, an (M, n) code for the main channel consists of the following:

1. An index set $\{1, 2, \cdots, M\}$.
2. An encoding function $f: \{1, 2, \cdots, M\} \rightarrow \mathcal{X}^n$ yielding codewords $x^n(1), x^n(2), \cdots, x^n(M)$ where $\mathcal{X}$ is the channel input alphabet and n is the number of channel uses for transmitting the message. The set of codewords is called the codebook.
3. A decoding function $g : \mathcal{Y}^n \rightarrow \{1, 2, \cdots, M\}$ yielding an estimate $\hat{W}$ of W.

The rate R of an (M, n) code is defined by $R = \frac{1}{n} \log_2 M$. The reliability of the transmission is measured by the probability of error $P_e^{(n)} = \Pr\{\hat{W} \neq W\}$. The security of the transmission is measured by the equivocation rate, defined by $R_e^{(n)} = \frac{1}{n} H(W|Z^n)$, where $H(X|Y)$ denotes the conditional entropy of X given Y. A rate-equivocation pair (R, R_e) is achievable if there exists an $(2^{nR}, n)$ code such that $P_e^{(n)} \rightarrow 0$ as $n \rightarrow \infty$ and the equivocation rate R_e satisfies $R_e \leq \liminf_{n \to \infty} R_e^{(n)}$. Please see Chapter 2 in Liang et al. (2009) for more details.

R_e indicates the eavesdropper's uncertainty about the message. The rate-equivocation pair (R, R_e) indicates the confidential rate R achieved at a secrecy level R_e. *Perfect secrecy* refers to the case in which $R = R_e$. The *secrecy capacity* C_s is defined as the largest rate achievable with perfect secrecy, i.e.,

$$C_s = \max_{(R, R) \in \mathbb{C}} R, \qquad (15.1)$$

where the capacity-equivocation region, $\mathbb{C}$, is defined to be the closure of the set that consists of all achievable rate-equivocation pairs (R, R_e).

The intuition behind the secrecy capacity is that by transmitting on the main link at rate $R \leq C_s$, there exists a code that can achieve perfect secrecy, that is, the eavesdropper's information about the entire source message will be zero (Carleial and Hellman, 1977). The secrecy capacity C_s is the maximal amount of information that can be sent not only reliably but also confidentially. In Chapter 4 of Liang et al. (2009), several coding schemes achieving perfect secrecy for the wire-tap channel are addressed.

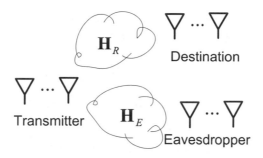

Figure 15.2 Illustration of the MIMO wiretap channel.

15.3 Secrecy Capacity of MIMO Wiretap Channels

Consider a MIMO wiretap channel, as shown in Fig. 15.2; the transmitter is equipped with $n_T \geq 2$ antennas, and the legitimate receiver and an eavesdropper have n_R and n_E antennas, respectively. Flat channel fading is assumed, and the eavesdropper is a passive receiver.

The received signals at the legitimate receiver and the eavesdropper can be expressed as

$$\mathbf{y}_R = \mathbf{H}_R\mathbf{x} + \mathbf{n}_R \tag{15.2}$$

$$\text{and } \mathbf{y}_E = \mathbf{H}_E\mathbf{x} + \mathbf{n}_E, \tag{15.3}$$

where $\mathbf{H}_R$ ($n_R \times n_T$), $\mathbf{H}_E$ ($n_E \times n_T$) are, respectively, the channel matrices between the transmitter and the legitimate receiver, and between the transmitter and the eavesdropper; $\mathbf{x}$ is the $n_T \times 1$ transmitted signal vector. It is assumed that $\mathbf{x}$ has zero mean and covariance matrix $P\mathbf{Q}$ where P is the transmit power and $\mathbf{Q}$ is a positive semi-definite matrix ($\mathbf{Q} \succeq 0$) with $\text{Tr}(\mathbf{Q}) \leq 1$; $\mathbf{n}_R$ and $\mathbf{n}_E$ are Gaussian noise vectors with zero mean and covariance matrices $\sigma^2\mathbf{I}_{n_R}$ and $\sigma^2\mathbf{I}_{n_E}$, respectively, where $\mathbf{I}_n$ denotes an identity matrix of size $n \times n$.

The following fundamental result (Khisti and Wornell, 2010b); (Oggier and Hassibi, 2011) establishes the secrecy capacity of the MIMO wiretap channel.

Proposition 15.1 *When both $\mathbf{H}_R$ and $\mathbf{H}_E$ are perfectly known, the secrecy capacity of the MIMO wiretap channel is defined as*

$$C_s \triangleq \max_{\mathbf{Q} \succeq 0,\ Tr(\mathbf{Q}) \leq 1} C_s(\mathbf{Q}), \qquad (15.4)$$

where

$$C_s(\mathbf{Q}) = \log \det(\mathbf{I} + \rho \mathbf{H}_R \mathbf{Q} \mathbf{H}_R^\dagger) - \log \det(\mathbf{I} + \rho \mathbf{H}_E \mathbf{Q} \mathbf{H}_E^\dagger) \qquad (15.5)$$

and $\rho = P/\sigma^2$.

For a general MIMO channel, finding C_s via a polynomial time algorithm is still an open problem and requires a global optimization technique such as the branch-and-bound algorithm (Liu et al., 2009).

15.3.1 *Conditions for Positive Secrecy Capacity, Convexity, and Solution*

An important question is when the secrecy capacity is positive, as this is the case of interest in most applications. As it turns out, the condition for $C_s > 0$ depends entirely on the quantity $\mathbf{H}_R^\dagger \mathbf{H}_R - \mathbf{H}_E^\dagger \mathbf{H}_E$, as stated in the following proposition.

Proposition 15.2 *The sufficient and necessary condition for $C_s > 0$ is that $\mathbf{H}_R^\dagger \mathbf{H}_R - \mathbf{H}_E^\dagger \mathbf{H}_E$ has at least one positive eigenvalue* (Li and Petropulu, 2011).

Intuitively, Proposition 15.2 suggests that positive secrecy capacity is achieved when there is at least one eigendirection along which the legitimate channel is stronger than the eavesdropper's channel.

Another interesting question is when can the secrecy capacity be found as the solution of a convex problem, as convex problems can usually be solved effectively. It is well-known that $\log \det(\mathbf{X})$ is a concave function of $\mathbf{X}$ (p. 74, Boyd and Vandenberghe, 2004). Thus, $C_s(\mathbf{Q})$ of (15.4) is the difference of two concave functions, and the problem of maximizing $C_s(\mathbf{Q})$ is referred to as DC (difference of convex functions) programming. A difference of two convex functions is in general not a convex function. However, under some conditions, $C_s(\mathbf{Q})$ is a concave function of $\mathbf{Q}$.

Proposition 15.3 *$C_s(\mathbf{Q})$ is a concave function of $\mathbf{Q}$ when $\mathbf{H}_R^\dagger \mathbf{H}_R - \mathbf{H}_E^\dagger \mathbf{H}_E \succeq 0$* (Khisti and Wornell, 2010b).

Intuitively, if $\mathbf{H}_R^\dagger \mathbf{H}_R - \mathbf{H}_E^\dagger \mathbf{H}_E \succeq 0$ the legitimate channel is stronger than the eavesdropper's channel along all eigendirections.

If $\mathbf{H}_R^\dagger \mathbf{H}_R - \mathbf{H}_E^\dagger \mathbf{H}_E \not\succeq 0$, it is easy to show that $C_s(\mathbf{Q})$ is not a concave function of $\mathbf{Q}$ and hence the problem of maximizing $C_s(\mathbf{Q})$ is in general difficult. For such cases one needs to analyze the problem, look for effective algorithms and study their theoretical properties. The Karush-Kuhn-Tucker (KKT) conditions can be the basic tool for these purposes (Khisti and Wornell, 2010b; Li and Petropulu, 2010a,b). Based on the results in Li and Petropulu (2010a,b), the KKT conditions (with Lagrange multipliers) are equivalent to a set of conditions without Lagrange multipliers.

Proposition 15.4 *The following conditions are equivalent to the KKT conditions:*

$$\mathbf{Q} \succeq 0, \tag{15.6}$$

$$\mathbf{\Theta Q} = Tr(\mathbf{\Theta Q})\mathbf{Q}, \tag{15.7}$$

$$and \; \lambda_{\max}(\mathbf{\Theta}) = Tr(\mathbf{\Theta Q}) \tag{15.8}$$

where

$$
\begin{aligned}
\mathbf{\Theta} &= \rho \mathbf{H}_R^\dagger (\mathbf{I} + \rho \mathbf{H}_R \mathbf{Q} \mathbf{H}_R^\dagger)^{-1} \mathbf{H}_R - \rho \mathbf{H}_E^\dagger (\mathbf{I} + \rho \mathbf{H}_E \mathbf{Q} \mathbf{H}_E^\dagger)^{-1} \mathbf{H}_E \\
&= \mathbf{S}_R (\mathbf{I} + \mathbf{Q} \mathbf{S}_R)^{-1} - \mathbf{S}_E (\mathbf{I} + \mathbf{Q} \mathbf{S}_E)^{-1} \\
&= (\mathbf{I} + \mathbf{S}_R \mathbf{Q})^{-1} \mathbf{S}_R - (\mathbf{I} + \mathbf{S}_E \mathbf{Q})^{-1} \mathbf{S}_E \tag{15.9}
\end{aligned}
$$

with $\mathbf{S}_R = \rho \mathbf{H}_R^\dagger \mathbf{H}_R$ and $\mathbf{S}_E = \rho \mathbf{H}_E^\dagger \mathbf{H}_E$. Moreover, any $\mathbf{Q}$ satisfying (15.6), (15.7), and (15.8) has the following properties:

i) *$\mathbf{Q}$ and $\mathbf{\Theta}$ commute (i.e., $\mathbf{\Theta Q} = \mathbf{Q\Theta}$) and hence have the same eigenvectors (simultaneously unitarily diagonalizable) (p. 239, Davis and Thomson, 2000), (p. 235, Horn and Johnson, 1990), i.e., there exists a unitary matrix $\mathbf{V}$ such that $\mathbf{\Lambda} = \mathbf{V}^\dagger \mathbf{\Theta V}$ and $\mathbf{D}_q = \mathbf{V}^\dagger \mathbf{QV}$ are both diagonal matrices;*

ii) *$\mathbf{Q}(\mathbf{S}_R - \mathbf{S}_E)\mathbf{Q} \succeq 0$.*

When $\mathbf{H}_R^\dagger \mathbf{H}_R - \mathbf{H}_E^\dagger \mathbf{H}_E \succeq 0$, the KKT conditions of Proposition 15.4 are sufficient and necessary for the corresponding convex problem. When $\mathbf{H}_R^\dagger \mathbf{H}_R - \mathbf{H}_E^\dagger \mathbf{H}_E \not\succeq 0$, the problem of finding the secrecy capacity is in general non-convex and may have several local maxima. For a non-convex problem, the $\mathbf{Q}$ that satisfies the KKT conditions may be global optimum, local optimum, or saddle point. However, for some special MIMO systems, as shown in the following proposition, the KKT conditions of Proposition 15.4 are sufficient for a global optimum.

Proposition 15.5 *For MISO wiretap channels (i.e., $n_R = n_E = 1$), the KKT conditions are sufficient and necessary for global optimality, i.e., any $\mathbf{Q}$ satisfying the conditions in Proposition 15.4 will be globally optimal* (Li and Petropulu, 2010b).

Remarks: There are some other non-convex cases in which the KKT conditions in Proposition 15.4 are sufficient and necessary for globally optimality, such as $n_T = 2$, or when $\mathbf{H}_R^\dagger \mathbf{H}_R - \mathbf{H}_E^\dagger \mathbf{H}_E$ has exactly one positive eigenvalue. The proof is based on the KKT conditions and can be done along the lines of Li and Petropulu (2010b, 2011).

15.3.2 MISO Wiretap Channels

For the MISO wiretap channel, the secrecy capacity can be obtained in closed form (Li and Petropulu, 2010a,b) as shown below. Since in this case $n_R = n_E = 1$, the channel matrices $\mathbf{H}_R$ and $\mathbf{H}_E$ collapse into vectors $\mathbf{h}_R^\dagger$ and $\mathbf{h}_E^\dagger$, respectively.

Proposition 15.6 *The secrecy capacity of the MISO wiretap channel equals*

$$C_s = \log \frac{b + \sqrt{b^2 - 4ac}}{2a} \tag{15.10}$$

where $a = 1 + \rho\|\mathbf{h}_E\|^2$, $b = 2 + \rho\|\mathbf{h}_R\|^2 + \rho\|\mathbf{h}_E\|^2 + \rho^2(\|\mathbf{h}_R\|^2\|\mathbf{h}_E\|^2 - |\mathbf{h}_R^\dagger \mathbf{h}_E|^2)$ and $c = 1 + \rho\|\mathbf{h}_R\|^2$.

The closed form expression of (15.10) is particularly convenient for studying the properties of MISO wiretap channels. One of the properties is the condition for positive secrecy capacity. It can be seen that, if $\mathbf{h}_R \neq \xi\mathbf{h}_E$ for any complex number ξ, then it holds that $b > a + c$, and hence, $C_s > 0$. Thus, if $\mathbf{h}_R \neq \xi\mathbf{h}_E$ for any complex ξ, the MISO wiretap channels always has a positive secrecy capacity. Moreover, if $\mathbf{h}_R$ and $\mathbf{h}_E$ are drawn from independent Gaussian distributions, $\mathbf{h}_R \neq \xi\mathbf{h}_E$ for any complex ξ holds with probability 1 (p. 82 (Muirhead, 2005)).

The second property is the rate at which the secrecy capacity scales with $\log \rho$, also referred to as secrecy degree of freedom $(s.d.o.f.)$ (Liang et al., 2007). If $\mathbf{h}_R \neq \xi \mathbf{h}_E$ for any complex number ξ, then under high SNR, it follows from (15.10) that

$$C_s(\rho) = \log \rho + \log(\|\mathbf{h}_R\|^2 - |\mathbf{h}_R^\dagger \mathbf{h}_E|^2 / \|\mathbf{h}_E\|^2 + O(1/\rho)) \quad (15.11)$$

where $O(\cdot)$ is the big-O notation. The secrecy degree of freedom then equals (Li and Petropulu, 2010b)

$$s.d.o.f \triangleq \lim_{\rho \to \infty} \frac{C_s(\rho)}{\log \rho} = 1. \quad (15.12)$$

Let us compare the MISO capacity to that of the SISO for which $n_T = n_R = n_E = 1$. Based on Proposition 15.6, the SISO secrecy capacity equals $C_s = \log(1 + \rho|h_R|^2) - \log(1 + \rho|h_E|^2)$, and as $\rho \to \infty$, $C_s \to \log \frac{|h_R|^2}{|h_E|^2}$. The corresponding secrecy degree of freedom is hence zero. This confirms the claim that the use of multiple antennas at the source benefits secrecy.

15.3.3 *Single-Antenna Eavesdropper*

When the eavesdropper is equipped with a single antenna, i.e., $n_E = 1$, the secrecy capacity problem can be converted into a problem of one variable (Li and Petropulu, 2012). In this case, $\mathbf{H}_E$ collapses into a vector $\mathbf{h}_E^\dagger$, and the problem of (15.4) becomes

$$\max_{\mathbf{Q}} \log \det(\mathbf{I} + \rho \mathbf{H}_R \mathbf{Q} \mathbf{H}_R^\dagger) - \log(1 + \rho \mathbf{h}_E^\dagger \mathbf{Q} \mathbf{h}_E) \quad (15.13)$$

$$\text{s.t.} \quad \mathbf{Q} \succeq 0, \ \text{Tr}(\mathbf{Q}) = 1.$$

Let $z = \mathbf{h}_E^\dagger \mathbf{Q} \mathbf{h}_E$. The range of z is $0 \leq z \leq \|\mathbf{h}_E\|^2$. Let

$$f(z) \triangleq \max_{\mathbf{Q}} \log \det(\mathbf{I} + \rho \mathbf{H}_R \mathbf{Q} \mathbf{H}_R^\dagger) \quad (15.14)$$

$$\text{s.t.} \quad \mathbf{Q} \succeq 0, \ \text{Tr}(\mathbf{Q}) = 1, \ \mathbf{h}_E^\dagger \mathbf{Q} \mathbf{h}_E = z.$$

This is a convex problem, which can be effectively solved. The problem of (15.13) is equivalent to a problem of one variable:

$$\max_{z} \ f(z) - \log(1 + \rho z) \quad (15.15)$$

$$\text{s.t.} \quad 0 \leq z \leq \|\mathbf{h}_E\|^2.$$

An one-dimensional algorithm can be used to solve this problem.

15.3.4 *Two-Antenna Transmitter*

In Shafiee et al. (2009), the case $(n_T, n_R, n_E) = (2, 2, 1)$ was analyzed and it was shown that under certain assumptions on the channels, beamforming is the optimal transmission scheme, in other words rank$(\mathbf{Q}) = 1$. In Oggier and Hassibi (2007), the $(2, 2, 2)$ case was studied under equality power constraint and the positive definiteness assumption for the Gram matrix of the eavesdropper's channel matrix.

In Li and Petropulu (2013), the more general $(n_T = 2, n_R, n_E)$ was studies, and it was shown that the secrecy capacity can be derived in closed form. The expression involves the largest real root of a quartic equation, which can be found in closed form (p. 87, King, 1996), and is given in the following proposition.

Proposition 15.7 *The wiretap channel with $n_T = 2$ admits a secrecy capacity*

$$C_s = log\tau_1, \qquad (15.16)$$

where τ_1 is the largest real root of the quartic equation

$$(-\tau^2 q_2 + \tau p_2 - q_5)^2$$
$$-4(-\tau^2 q_1 + \tau p_1 - q_4)(-\tau^2 q_3 + \tau p_3 - q_6) = 0 \quad (15.17)$$

such that

$$0 < -\frac{-\tau_1^2 q_2 + \tau_1 p_2 - q_5}{2(-\tau_1^2 q_1 + \tau_1 p_1 - q_4)} < 1, \qquad (15.18)$$

where $p_1 = -b_1^* b_2 - b_1 b_2^* - (1 + a_1)(a_2 c_2 - |b_2|^2) - (1 + a_2)(a_1 c_1 - |b_1|^2)$, $p_2 = 2b_1^* b_2 + 2b_1 b_2^* + (1 + a_1)(a_2 - c_2 + a_2 c_2 - |b_2|^2) + (1 + a_2)(a_1 - c_1 + a_1 c_1 - |b_1|^2)$, $p_3 = (1 + a_1)(1 + c_2) + (1 + a_2)(1 + c_1) - b_1^* b_2 - b_1 b_2^*$, $q_1 = -a_2(c_2 + a_2 c_2 - |b_2|^2)$, $q_2 = a_2 - c_2 + a_2^2 + |b_2|^2 + a_2(a_2 c_2 - |b_2|^2)$, $q_3 = 1 + a_2 + c_2 + a_2 c_2 - |b_2|^2$, $q_4 = -a_1(c_1 + a_1 c_1 - |b_1|^2)$, $q_5 = a_1 - c_1 + a_1^2 + |b_1|^2 + a_1(a_1 c_1 - |b_1|^2)$, $q_6 = 1 + a_1 + c_1 + a_1 c_1 - |b_1|^2$, and $a_1, b_1, c_1, a_2, b_2, c_2$ are entries of $\mathbf{S}_R = \rho \mathbf{H}_R^\dagger \mathbf{H}_R$ and $\mathbf{S}_E = \rho \mathbf{H}_E^\dagger \mathbf{H}_E$, i.e.,

$$\mathbf{S}_R = \begin{pmatrix} a_1 & b_1 \\ b_1^* & c_1 \end{pmatrix}, \quad \text{and} \quad \mathbf{S}_E = \begin{pmatrix} a_2 & b_2 \\ b_2^* & c_2 \end{pmatrix}.$$

If $\mathbf{H}_E^\dagger \mathbf{H}_E$ is full rank, i.e., $\text{rank}(\mathbf{H}_E^\dagger \mathbf{H}_E) = 2$, the secrecy degree of freedom (see (15.12)) for this case is

$$s.d.o.f = \lim_{\rho \to \infty} \frac{C_s(\rho)}{\log \rho} = 0. \qquad (15.19)$$

The proof for (15.19) is as follows. First, if $\text{rank}(\mathbf{Q}) = 2$, then $\mathbf{Q}\mathbf{H}_E^\dagger \mathbf{H}_E$ is non-singular, and as $\rho \to \infty$, one may write (15.5) as follows (see Eq. (10), Li and Petropulu, 2011; Eq. (54), Li and Petropulu, 2010a):

$$C_s(\mathbf{Q}) = \log \det \left(\mathbf{I} + (\mathbf{I} + \rho \mathbf{Q}\mathbf{H}_E^\dagger \mathbf{H}_E)^{-1} \rho \mathbf{Q}(\mathbf{H}_R^\dagger \mathbf{H}_R - \mathbf{H}_E^\dagger \mathbf{H}_E) \right)$$

$$\to \log \det \left(\mathbf{I} + (\mathbf{Q}\mathbf{H}_E^\dagger \mathbf{H}_E)^{-1} \mathbf{Q}(\mathbf{H}_R^\dagger \mathbf{H}_R - \mathbf{H}_E^\dagger \mathbf{H}_E) \right) \qquad (15.20)$$

On the other hand, if $\text{rank}(\mathbf{Q}) = 1$ (beamforming), it holds that (Li and Petropulu, 2012)

$$\lim_{\rho \to \infty} C_s(\mathbf{Q})_{\text{rank}(\mathbf{Q})=1} = \log \left(\lambda_{\max} \left\{ (\mathbf{H}_E^\dagger \mathbf{H}_E)^{-1}(\mathbf{H}_R^\dagger \mathbf{H}_R) \right\} \right) \qquad (15.21)$$

and (15.19) follows from (15.20) and (15.21).

Summarizing, if $\mathbf{H}_E^\dagger \mathbf{H}_E$ is full rank, the two-transmit antenna wiretap channel is always capacity-limited. In other words, the secrecy capacity has an upper bound even if infinite power is used. For example, when $\mathbf{H}_E$ is drawn from standard Gaussian distribution, $\mathbf{H}_E^\dagger \mathbf{H}_E$ is full rank with probability 1 as long as $n_E \geq n_T$ (p. 82, Muirhead, 2005). In that case, if the eavesdropper has two or more antennas, the wiretap channel with two transmit antennas is capacity-limited.

On the other hand, if $\mathbf{H}_E^\dagger \mathbf{H}_E$ is low rank (rank one), there exists a 2×1 vector $\mathbf{h}_E$ such that $\mathbf{H}_E^\dagger \mathbf{H}_E = \mathbf{h}_E \mathbf{h}_E^\dagger$. There are two cases. If $\mathbf{H}_R^\dagger \mathbf{H}_R$ is low rank (rank one), there exists a 2×1 vector $\mathbf{h}_R$ such that $\mathbf{H}_R^\dagger \mathbf{H}_R = \mathbf{h}_R \mathbf{h}_R^\dagger$. This case is equivalent to the MISO system of Section 15.3.2, according to which, if $\mathbf{h}_R \neq \xi \mathbf{h}_E$ for any complex number ξ, the secrecy degree of freedom equals

$$s.d.o.f = \lim_{\rho \to \infty} \frac{C_s(\rho)}{\log \rho} = 1. \qquad (15.22)$$

For the second case, if $\mathbf{H}_E^\dagger \mathbf{H}_E$ is low rank and $\mathbf{H}_R^\dagger \mathbf{H}_R$ is full rank, and if beamforming is used (i.e., $\text{rank}(\mathbf{Q}) = 1$), it holds that (Li and Petropulu, 2012) (see also Section 15.3.5)

$$\lim_{\rho \to \infty} \frac{C_s(\mathbf{Q})_{\text{rank}(\mathbf{Q})=1}}{\log \rho} = 1. \qquad (15.23)$$

It is easy to further show that for this case it holds that $s.d.o.f = 1$. The proof is as follows. If $\text{rank}(\mathbf{Q}) = 2$, one can write

$$C_s(\mathbf{Q}) = \log\det(\mathbf{I} + \rho\mathbf{H}_R^\dagger\mathbf{H}_R\mathbf{Q}) - \log(1 + \rho\mathbf{h}_E^\dagger\mathbf{Q}\mathbf{h}_E)$$
$$= \log(1 + \rho\lambda_1) + \log(1 + \rho\lambda_2) - \log(1 + \rho\mathbf{h}_E^\dagger\mathbf{Q}\mathbf{h}_E), \quad (15.24)$$

where λ_1, λ_2 are the two non-zero eigenvalues of $\mathbf{H}_R^\dagger\mathbf{H}_R\mathbf{Q}$. On the other hand, $\mathbf{h}_E^\dagger\mathbf{Q}\mathbf{h}_E \neq 0$ since $\text{rank}(\mathbf{Q}) = 2$. Thus, it holds that

$$\lim_{\rho\to\infty} \frac{C_s(\mathbf{Q})_{\text{rank}(\mathbf{Q})=2}}{\log\rho} = 1. \quad (15.25)$$

$s.d.o.f = 1$ follows from (15.23) and (15.25).

The above suggests that for two transmit antenna case, if $\mathbf{H}_E^\dagger\mathbf{H}_E$ is low rank, the wiretap channel is not capacity-limited and can benefit by increasing the transmit power.

15.3.5 $\mathbf{H}_R^\dagger\mathbf{H}_R - \mathbf{H}_E^\dagger\mathbf{H}_E$ Has Exactly One Positive Eigenvalue

The following result was proposed in Li and Petropulu (2010a, 2011, 2012).

Proposition 15.8 *When $\mathbf{H}_R^\dagger\mathbf{H}_R - \mathbf{H}_E^\dagger\mathbf{H}_E$ has exactly one positive eigenvalue, beamforming (rank($\mathbf{Q}$) = 1) is the best transmission strategy. The corresponding secrecy capacity C_s^{bf} and optimal input covariance matrix $\mathbf{Q}_{bf}$ are*

$$\mathbf{Q}_{bf} = \mathbf{u}_0\mathbf{u}_0^\dagger, \quad (15.26)$$
$$C_s^{bf} = \log\lambda_0 \quad (15.27)$$

where λ_0 and $\mathbf{u}_0$ are the largest eigenvalue and corresponding unit-norm eigenvector of $(\mathbf{I} + \rho\mathbf{H}_E^\dagger\mathbf{H}_E)^{-1}(\mathbf{I} + \rho\mathbf{H}_R^\dagger\mathbf{H}_R)$.

Some simple scenarios in which the condition in Proposition 15.8 is met are the following (Li and Petropulu, 2011, 2012):

- $n_R = n_E = 1$ (Lemma 1, (Li and Petropulu, 2010b));
- $n_R = 1$
  Since $\mathbf{H}_E^\dagger\mathbf{H}_E \succeq 0$ and $\mathbf{H}_R\mathbf{H}_R^\dagger$ has exactly one positive eigenvalue, $\mathbf{H}_R\mathbf{H}_R^\dagger - \mathbf{H}_E^\dagger\mathbf{H}_E$ has at most one positive eigenvalue (p. 181, Horn and Johnson, 1990);

- $n_T = 2, n_E = 1, \mathbf{H}_R^\dagger \mathbf{H}_R \succ 0, \mathbf{H}_E^\dagger (\mathbf{H}_R^\dagger \mathbf{H}_R)^{-1} \mathbf{H}_E \geq 1$
  Let $\mathbf{A} = \mathbf{H}_R^\dagger \mathbf{H}_R - (1/(\mathbf{H}_E^\dagger (\mathbf{H}_R^\dagger \mathbf{H}_R)^{-1} \mathbf{H}_E)) \mathbf{H}_E \mathbf{H}_E^\dagger$ which is 2×2.
  One can show that $\det \mathbf{A} = 0$ (p. 475, Meyer, 2000). Thus, $\mathbf{A}$ has
  a zero eigenvalue and hence has at most one positive eigenvalue.
  On the other hand, since $\mathbf{H}_E^\dagger (\mathbf{H}_R^\dagger \mathbf{H}_R)^{-1} \mathbf{H}_E \geq 1$, it holds that $\mathbf{A} \succeq$
  $\mathbf{H}_R^\dagger \mathbf{H}_R - \mathbf{H}_E \mathbf{H}_E^\dagger$. Thus, $\mathbf{H}_R^\dagger \mathbf{H}_R - \mathbf{H}_E \mathbf{H}_E^\dagger$ has at most one positive
  eigenvalue (p. 181, Horn and Johnson, 1990);
- $n_T = n_R = 2, n_E = 1$ (Shafiee et al., 2009).

Next we address the secrecy degree of freedom. According to Li
and Petropulu (2012), when $\mathbf{H}_E^\dagger \mathbf{H}_E$ is full rank, the secrecy degree of
freedom is

$$s.d.o.f \triangleq \lim_{\rho \to \infty} \frac{C_s(\rho)}{\log \rho} = 0. \tag{15.28}$$

In fact, according to Proposition 15.8, as $\rho \to \infty$,

$$(\mathbf{I} + \rho \mathbf{H}_E^\dagger \mathbf{H}_E)^{-1}(\mathbf{I} + \rho \mathbf{H}_R^\dagger \mathbf{H}_R) \to (\mathbf{H}_E^\dagger \mathbf{H}_E)^{-1}(\mathbf{H}_R^\dagger \mathbf{H}_R), \tag{15.29}$$

$$C_s^{bf} \to \log \left(\lambda_{\max} \{ (\mathbf{H}_E^\dagger \mathbf{H}_E)^{-1}(\mathbf{H}_R^\dagger \mathbf{H}_R) \} \right) \tag{15.30}$$

which leads to (15.28). When $\mathbf{H}_E^\dagger \mathbf{H}_E$ is not full rank, one can derive
the secrecy degree of freedom in direct and simple fashion. Let
$\text{rank}(\mathbf{H}_E^\dagger \mathbf{H}_E) = n_T - r$ and let $\mathbf{H}_E^\dagger \mathbf{H}_E$ have an eigen-decomposition
$\mathbf{U}_E \text{blkdiag}(\mathbf{D}_E, 0_r) \mathbf{U}_E^\dagger$ where $\mathbf{D}_E$ is a $(n_T - r) \times (n_T - r)$ diagonal
matrix with all positive diagonal entries, 0_r is a $r \times r$ zero matrix,
and $\text{blkdiag}(\cdot)$ is block diagonal operation. Let

$$\mathbf{U}_E^\dagger \mathbf{H}_R^\dagger \mathbf{H}_R \mathbf{U}_E = \begin{pmatrix} \mathbf{A} & \mathbf{B} \\ \mathbf{B}^\dagger & \mathbf{S}_r \end{pmatrix}, \tag{15.31}$$

where $\mathbf{S}_r$ is a $r \times r$ positive semidefinite matrix. If $\mathbf{S}_r \neq 0$, the secrecy
degree of freedom is

$$s.d.o.f \triangleq \lim_{\rho \to \infty} \frac{C_s(\rho)}{\log \rho} = 1. \tag{15.32}$$

In fact, let $\mathbf{u}_0$ $(r \times 1)$ be the unit-norm eigenvector associated with
the largest eigenvalue of $\mathbf{S}_r$, and let $\mathbf{Q}_0 = \text{blkdiag}(0, \mathbf{u}_0 \mathbf{u}_0^\dagger)$. We may
write

$$\begin{aligned} C_s(\mathbf{Q}_0) &= \log \det(\mathbf{I} + \rho \mathbf{Q}_0 \mathbf{H}_R^\dagger \mathbf{H}_R) - \log \det(\mathbf{I} + \rho \mathbf{Q}_0 \mathbf{H}_E^\dagger \mathbf{H}_E) \\ &= \log(1 + \rho \mathbf{u}_0^\dagger \mathbf{S}_r \mathbf{u}_0) \\ &= \log(1 + \rho \lambda_{\max}(\mathbf{S}_r)), \end{aligned} \tag{15.33}$$

which leads to

$$\lim_{\rho \to \infty} \frac{C_s(\mathbf{Q}_0)}{\log \rho} = 1; \tag{15.34}$$

One may write (15.5) as (see Eq. (10), Li and Petropulu, 2011; Eq. (54), Li and Petropulu, 2010a)

$$\begin{aligned}
C_s(\mathbf{Q}) &= \log \det \left(\mathbf{I} + (\mathbf{I} + \rho \mathbf{Q} \mathbf{H}_E^\dagger \mathbf{H}_E)^{-1} \rho \mathbf{Q} (\mathbf{H}_R^\dagger \mathbf{H}_R - \mathbf{H}_E^\dagger \mathbf{H}_E) \right) \\
&\leq \log \det \left(\mathbf{I} + (\mathbf{I} + \rho \mathbf{Q} \mathbf{H}_E^\dagger \mathbf{H}_E)^{-1} \rho \mathbf{Q} \lambda_1 \mathbf{u}_1 \mathbf{u}_1^\dagger \right) \\
&= \log(1 + \rho \lambda_1 \mathbf{u}_1^\dagger (\mathbf{I} + \rho \mathbf{Q} \mathbf{H}_E^\dagger \mathbf{H}_E)^{-1} \mathbf{Q} \mathbf{u}_1) \tag{15.35}
\end{aligned}$$

where λ_1 is the unique positive eigenvalue of $\mathbf{H}_R^\dagger \mathbf{H}_R - \mathbf{H}_E^\dagger \mathbf{H}_E$, $\mathbf{u}_1$ is the corresponding unit-norm eigenvector. Clearly $\lambda_1 \mathbf{u}_1 \mathbf{u}_1^\dagger \succeq \mathbf{H}_R^\dagger \mathbf{H}_R - \mathbf{H}_E^\dagger \mathbf{H}_E$. Thus, it follows from (15.35) that

$$\lim_{\rho \to \infty} \frac{C_s(\mathbf{Q})}{\log \rho} \leq 1, \tag{15.36}$$

and (15.32) follows from (15.34) and (15.36).

$\mathbf{H}_R^\dagger \mathbf{H}_R - \mathbf{H}_E^\dagger \mathbf{H}_E$ is an important quantity describing the properties of MIMO wiretap channels. In Loyka and Charalambous (2012), it is shown that

$$\text{rank}(\mathbf{Q}) \leq n_{++}(\mathbf{H}_R^\dagger \mathbf{H}_R - \mathbf{H}_E^\dagger \mathbf{H}_E), \tag{15.37}$$

where $n_{++}(\mathbf{A})$ denotes the number of positive eigenvalues of matrix $\mathbf{A}$. When $\mathbf{H}_R^\dagger \mathbf{H}_R - \mathbf{H}_E^\dagger \mathbf{H}_E$ has exactly one positive eigenvalue, which is the case considered in this subsection.

15.3.6 *Conditions for Optimality of Beamforming*

Beamforming is a simple signaling scheme, which limits the rank of the input covariance matrix to unity, i.e., $\text{rank}(\mathbf{Q}) = 1$. In practice, beamforming simplifies the system design, since it reduces a MIMO system into a SISO one, for which scalar codec technology can be used. The beamforming solution can be obtained in closed form which translates to very low computational complexity. At low signal-to-noise ratio (SNR), the beamforming solution gives close to optimal results. This can be seen as follows. Using the fact $\det(\mathbf{I} + \rho \mathbf{A}) \approx 1 + \text{Tr}(\rho \mathbf{A})$ for a small ρ and a positive semi-definite matrix $\mathbf{A}$, it holds that $C_s(\mathbf{Q}) \approx \log(1 + \text{Tr}(\mathbf{Q} \mathbf{S}_R)) - \log(1 + \text{Tr}(\mathbf{Q} \mathbf{S}_E))$. It can be easily shown that beamforming is optimal for the objective function $\log(1 + \text{Tr}(\mathbf{QS}_R)) - \log(1 + \text{Tr}(\mathbf{QS}_E))$.

The beamforming solution was given in Proposition 15.8. A sufficient condition for the optimality of beamforming was given in Section 15.3.5, i.e., $\mathbf{H}_R^\dagger\mathbf{H}_R - \mathbf{H}_E^\dagger\mathbf{H}_E$ has exactly one positive eigenvalue.

Here we address sufficient and necessary conditions for optimality of beamforming (Li and Petropulu, 2013).

Proposition 15.9 *For wiretap channel with $n_T = 2$, the sufficient and necessary conditions for beamforming to be the optimal transmission strategy are the following:*

$$\tau_{bf}^2 q_2 - \tau_{bf} p_2 + q_5 \geq 0, \tag{15.38}$$

$$(\tau_{bf}^2 q_1 - \tau_{bf} p_1 + q_4) + (\tau_{bf}^2 q_2 - \tau_{bf} p_2 + q_5) \geq 0, \tag{15.39}$$

and

$$2\tau_{bf} q_1 - p_1 \leq 0, \ or$$
$$2\tau_{bf} q_2 - p_2 \geq 0, \ or$$
$$2\tau_{bf} q_2 - p_2 \leq -2(2\tau_{bf} q_1 - p_1), \ or$$
$$(2\tau_{bf} q_2 - p_2)^2 - 4(2\tau_{bf} q_1 - p_1)(2\tau_{bf} q_3 - p_3) \leq 0 \tag{15.40}$$

where the quantities p_1, p_2, p_3, q_1, q_2, q_3, q_4, q_5, q_6 can be found in Proposition 15.7, and $\tau_{bf} = (p_3 + \sqrt{p_3^2 - 4q_3 q_6})/(2q_3)$. Under those conditions, the secrecy capacity $C_s = \log \tau_{bf}$.

For general cases, the necessary conditions for beamforming to be optimal can be obtained from the KKT conditions. If beamforming is the solution, the optimal beamforming vector $\mathbf{u}_0$ (see Proposition 15.8) should satisfy the KKT conditions. According to Proposition 15.4, the conditions can be expressed as

$$\mathbf{\Theta}_0\mathbf{u}_0\mathbf{u}_0^\dagger = \text{Tr}(\mathbf{\Theta}_0\mathbf{u}_0\mathbf{u}_0^\dagger)\mathbf{u}_0\mathbf{u}_0^\dagger, \tag{15.41}$$

$$\text{and } \lambda_{\max}(\mathbf{\Theta}_0) = \text{Tr}(\mathbf{\Theta}_0\mathbf{u}_0\mathbf{u}_0^\dagger) \tag{15.42}$$

where $\mathbf{\Theta}_0 = \mathbf{S}_R(\mathbf{I} + \mathbf{u}_0\mathbf{u}_0^\dagger\mathbf{S}_R)^{-1} - \mathbf{S}_E(\mathbf{I} + \mathbf{u}_0\mathbf{u}_0^\dagger\mathbf{S}_E)^{-1}$. In fact, (15.41) holds. Thus, the necessary condition for beamforming to be optimal is only (15.42) which can be written explicitly as

$$\lambda_{\max}\left(\mathbf{S}_R(\mathbf{I} + \mathbf{u}_0\mathbf{u}_0^\dagger\mathbf{S}_R)^{-1} - \mathbf{S}_E(\mathbf{I} + \mathbf{u}_0\mathbf{u}_0^\dagger\mathbf{S}_E)^{-1}\right)$$

$$= \frac{1}{1+\mathbf{u}_0^\dagger\mathbf{S}_E\mathbf{u}_0} - \frac{1}{1+\mathbf{u}_0^\dagger\mathbf{S}_R\mathbf{u}_0}. \tag{15.43}$$

Moreover, we also know that if (15.43) holds, then the beamforming solution is a KKT point (stationary point).

15.3.7 *Algorithms for General Non-Convex Cases*

Except for the above cases and the convex case, for the general non-convex case, finding a polynomial time algorithm to obtain the solution is still an open problem.

As pointed out in Section 15.3.1, the secrecy capacity problem is a DC programming problem. The DC algorithm of (An and Tao, 2005) can be used. The DC algorithm of (An and Tao, 2005) in general converges to stationary points (KKT points).

In Li and Petropulu (2010a), a fixed-point algorithm is addressed without a proof of convergence, although in numerical simulations, the fixed-point algorithm and the DC algorithm always converge to the same solution.

References

1. L. T. H. An and P. D. Tao, The DC (difference of convex functions) programming and DCA revisited with DC models of real world nonconvex optimization problems, *Annals of Operations Research*, vol. 133, pp. 23–46, 2005.
2. S. Boyd and L. Vandenberghe, *Convex Optimization*, Cambridge University Press, UK, 2004.
3. R. Bustin, R. Liu, H. V. Poor, and S. Shamai (Shitz), An MMSE approach to the secrecy capacity of the MIMO Gaussian wiretap channel, in *Proceedings of the IEEE International Symposium on Information Theory (ISIT)*, Seoul, Korea, June–July 2009.
4. A. B. Carleial and M. E. Hellman, A note on Wyner's wiretap channel, *IEEE Trans. Inform. Theory*, vol. 23, no. 3, pp. 387–390, May 1977.
5. I. Csiszár and J. Körner, Broadcast channels with confidential messages, *IEEE Trans. Inform. Theory*, vol. 24, no. 3, pp. 339–348, May 1978.
6. H. T. Davis and K. T. Thomson, *Linear Algebra and Linear Operators in Engineering*, Academic Press, 2000.
7. R. A. Horn and C. A. Johnson, *Matrix Analysis*, Cambridge University Press, UK, 1990.

8. IPSec Working Group, http://www.ietf.org/html.charters/ipsec-charter.html, 2000.

9. A. Khisti and G. Wornell, Secure transmission with multiple antennas-I: The MISOME wiretap channel, *IEEE Trans. Inform. Theory*, vol. 56, no. 7, pp. 3088–3104, July 2010.

10. A. Khisti and G. Wornell, Secure transmission with multiple antennas-II: The MIMOME wiretap channel, *IEEE Trans. Inform. Theory*, vol. 56, no. 11, pp. 5515–5532, November 2010.

11. R. Bruce King, *Beyond the Quartic Equation*, Birkhäuser, Boston, 1996.

12. *LAN Standards Committee of the IEEE CS*, Wireless LAN, Medium Access Control (MAC) and Physical Layer (PHY) Specification: IEEE standard 802.11, 1990.

13. S. K. Leung-Yan-Cheong and M. E. Hellman, The Gaussian wire-tap channel, *IEEE Trans. Inform. Theory*, vol. 24, no. 4, pp. 451–456, July 1978.

14. J. Li and A. P. Petropulu, Transmitter optimization for achieving secrecy capacity in Gaussian MIMO wiretap channels, [Online]. Available: http://arxiv.org/pdf/0909.2622.pdf, 2010.

15. Jiangyuan Li and A. P. Petropulu, Optimal input covariance for achieving secrecy capacity in Gaussian MIMO wiretap channels, in *Proc. Int. Conf. Acoustics, Speech, Signal Processing (ICASSP)*, Dallas, TX, pp. 3362–3365, March 14–19, 2010.

16. J. Li and A. P. Petropulu, On beamforming solution for secrecy capacity of MIMO wiretap channels, in *Global Communications Conference (Globecom) Workshops*, Houston, Texas, December 5–9, 2011.

17. J. Li and A. P. Petropulu, Optimality of beamforming for secrecy capacity of MIMO wiretap channels, in *IEEE International Workshop on Information Forensics and Security (WIFS)*, Tenerife, Spain, December 2–5, 2012, pp. 276–281.

18. J. Li and A. P. Petropulu, Optimality of beamforming and closed form secrecy capacity of MIMO wiretap channels with two transmit antennas, in *Proceedings of the 16th International Symposium on Wireless Personal Multimedia Communications (WPMC)*, Atlantic City, New Jersey, USA, 2013.

19. Y. Liang, G. Kramer, H. V. Poor, and S. Shamai (Shitz), Compound wiretap channels, in *Proceedings of the 45th Annual Allerton Conference on Communication, Control and Computing*, Monticello, IL, USA, September 2007.

20. Y. Liang, H. V. Poor, and S. Shamai (Shitz), *Information Theoretic Security*, Now Publishers, Delft, The Netherlands, 2009.

21. J. Liu, Y. Hou, and H. D. Sherali, Optimal power allocation for achieving perfect secrecy capacity in MIMO wire-tap channels, in *Proceedings of the 43rd Annual Conference on Information Sciences and Systems (CISS)*, pp. 606–611, March 2009.

22. W. Liu, W. Lou, Y. Fang, and Y. Zhang, Securing mobile ad hoc networks with certificateless public keys, *IEEE Trans. Dependable Secure Comput.*, vol. 3, no. 4, pp. 386–399, October–December 2006.

23. T. Liu and S. Shamai (Shitz), A note on the secrecy capacity of the multi-antenna wire-tap channel, *IEEE Trans. Inform. Theory*, vol. 55, pp. 2547–2553, June 2009.

24. S. Loyka and C. D. Charalambous, On optimal signaling over secure MIMO channels, in *Proceedings of the IEEE International Symposium on Information Theory (ISIT)*, MA, USA, July 2012.

25. C. D. Meyer, *Matrix Analysis and Applied Linear Algebra*, SIAM, Philadelphia, 2000.

26. R. J. Muirhead, *Aspects of Multivariate Statistical Theory*, John Wiley and Sons, New Jersey, 2005.

27. NIST Internal Report 7609: Cryptographic Key Management Workshop, http://csrc.nist.gov/publications/nistir/ir7609/nistir-7609.pdf, 2009.

28. F. Oggier and B. Hassibi, The secrecy capacity of the 2×2 MIMO wiretap channel, in *Proceedings of the 45th Annual Allerton Conference on Communication, Control and Computing*, Monticello, IL, USA, September 26-28, 2007.

29. F. Oggier and B. Hassibi, The secrecy capacity of the MIMO wiretap channel, *IEEE Trans. Inform. Theory*, vol. 57, no. 8, pp. 4961–4972, August 2011.

30. N. R. Potlapally, S. Ravi, A. Raghunathan, and N. K. Jha, A study of the energy consumption characteristics of cryptographic algorithms and security protocols, *IEEE Trans. Mobile Comput.*, vol. 5, no. 2, pp. 128–143, February 2006.

31. SET Secure Electronic Transaction Specification (V1.0), http://www.maithean.com/docs/, 1997.

32. S. Shafiee, N. Liu, and S. Ulukus, Towards the secrecy capacity of the Gaussian MIMO wire-tap channel: The 2-2-1 channel, *IEEE Trans. Inform. Theory*, vol. 55, no. 9, pp. 4033–4039, September 2009.

33. SSL 3.0 Specification, http://wp.netscape.com/eng/ssl3/, 1996.

34. Wireless Application Protocol 2.0—Technical White Paper, http://www.wapforum.org/, January 2002.

35. A. D. Wyner, The wire-tap channel, *Bell System Tech. J.*, vol. 54, pp. 1355–1387, October 1975.

Chapter 16

Radio Frequency Localization for IoT Applications

Antonis Kalis and Anastasis Kounoudes

SignalGeneriX, Cyprus
akal@signalgenerix.com, tasos@signalgenerix.com

16.1 Indoor Localization Challenges and Applications

In recent years, radio frequency localization has become as common as GPS (global positioning system) devices. The benefits of localization have become evident by the emergence of an ever-increasing number of applications, ranging from consumer location-based services like weather forecasts and advertisements, to fleet management and logistics. Although GPS has acted as a significant driver of such applications, emerging ideas and technologies like wireless sensor networks which implement the "Internet of Things" (IoT) have revealed the limitations of this satellite-based localization system.

In the emerging vision of a world of "smart objects", GPS poses two main barriers that need to be over passed by new localization systems. The first one is that as a satellite-based system,

Trends in Digital Signal Processing: A Festschrift in Honour of A. G. Constantinides
Edited by Yong Ching Lim, Hon Keung Kwan, and Wan-Chi Siu
Copyright © 2016 Pan Stanford Publishing Pte. Ltd.
ISBN 978-981-4669-50-4 (Hardcover), 978-981-4669-51-1 (eBook)
www.panstanford.com

it cannot provide location information in indoor environments. And indoor environments provide great potential for location-based services. For example, one of the most promising technological areas for achieving the goal for a sustainable human environment is the development of smart buildings, capable of reducing their own energy footprint, and of providing information for predictive maintenance actions, without compromising habitants' comfort and safety. The development of smart buildings is based on a number of innovative technologies like wireless sensor networks, sensor and actuator systems, intelligent data processing and fusion techniques, innovative decision support processes, low powered microelectronics and digital signal processing algorithms [1]. Of all the aforementioned systems, the wireless sensor network technologies are there to equip buildings with a digital nervous system capable of providing the necessary information for all other functions [2]. One of the most helpful information that such a network could provide is localization data. The latter act as the corner stone for many algorithms that require information on building usage, climate control, air quality control, energy footprint reduction, safety, security etc.

A second barrier for embedding radio frequency localization systems into the larger vision of the IoT is cost. Namely, when the targeted application requires for the deployment of hundreds to thousands of "smart dust" nodes, the cost for each device is critical, and in many cases ruling out a GPS-based solution. A recent example comes from the maritime transportation sector [3]. Despite the huge investment in maritime technology today, there is a significant drawback in onboard systems used for safe evacuation of people in large cruise vessels. Technologies which enable real-time localization and tracking of all persons onboard or overboard a ship during a real emergency evacuation have been for long considered inefficient. This inefficiency, which puts a great strain on the officers and crew when faced with a real emergency, comes mainly from the fact that the industry cannot afford GPS-based solutions that would increase the cost of life-saving equipment to 5 to 10 times their current price, especially when the number of life jackets onboard a cruise ship could be in the order of several thousands.

Based on these observations, it is evident that radio frequency-based localization systems need to be redesigned if they are to meet challenges of new application areas. And any redesign of a localization system would have to reconsider the same basic limitations that the wireless environment imposes upon any radio frequency system. Two main characteristics should always be considered for the design of such systems:

- ***Accuracy:*** The accuracy requirements of a localization system depend on the application needs. For some applications (e.g. location-based advertising, indoor climate control, etc.) an accuracy of several meters would suffice. In others, high precision would be required (e.g. for smart factories, or automated warehouses). In all cases, the wireless environment affects RF localization accuracy, due to the multi-path effect. The latter is an inherent characteristic of any wireless channel, causing multiple copies of a single transmitted RF signal to appear at the receiver. This effect is more severe in indoor environments, mostly considered by IoT applications.
- ***Bandwidth:*** The available bandwidth for RF localization largely dictates the accuracy of the system. However, bandwidth in wireless systems is a scarce resource, which must be contended for by both localization and communication systems in the area.

Localization systems are often faced with the need to make trade-offs between these two main characteristics in order to satisfy the requirements of a given application. The following section reviews a number of such basic methods, before focusing on the specific requirements of novel applications for satisfying the greater vision for an Internet of Things.

16.2 Basic Measurement-Based Methods

In general, localization involves finding the coordinates of a device in a coordinate system. The goal of any localization method is to create

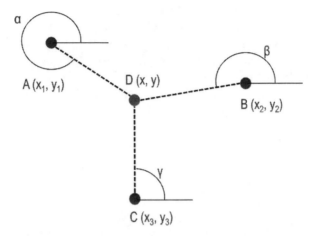

Figure 16.1 RF measurement-based localization.

a set of equations that will enable us to find the coordinate values of the device's location. In the example shown in Fig. 16.1, should we want to find the location of a device in a two dimensional space, we would rely on a set of equations involving either the measured distances between the device and known locations A, B and C, or the measured relative angles α, β, and γ.

In range-based methods, the location of a node can be determined from the following set of simple equations. Let (x, y) be the node coordinates and (x_i, y_i) the anchor coordinates. Assuming that range measurements are available from n anchors, the circle equations

$$\begin{bmatrix} (x_1 - x)^2 + (y_1 - y)^2 \\ (x_2 - x)^2 + (y_2 - y)^2 \\ \cdots \\ (x_n - x)^2 + (y_n - y)^2 \end{bmatrix} = \begin{bmatrix} r_1^2 \\ r_2^2 \\ \cdots \\ r_n^2 \end{bmatrix}$$

yield the following system to solve:

$$\mathbf{Ax} = \mathbf{b}$$

$$\text{where } \mathbf{A} = \begin{bmatrix} 2(x_n - x_1) & 2(y_n - y_1) \\ 2(x_n - x_2) & 2(y_n - y_2) \\ \cdots \\ 2(x_n - x_{n-1}) & 2(y_n - y_{n-1}) \end{bmatrix}$$

$$\text{and } \mathbf{b} = \begin{bmatrix} r_1^2 - r_n^2 - x_1^2 - y_1^2 + x_n^2 + y_n^2 \\ r_2^2 - r_n^2 - x_2^2 - y_2^2 + x_n^2 + y_n^2 \\ \cdots \\ r_n^2 - r_{n-1}^2 - x_{n-1}^2 - y_{n-1}^2 + x_n^2 + y_n^2 \end{bmatrix}$$

In the case of square matrices, the system can be solved as

$$\mathbf{x} = (A^T A)^{-1} A^T \mathbf{b}.$$

In the ideal case, solving the equation above would result in a single solution, resembling a single point. However, measured values contain errors and a least-squares system must be used.

In RF localization, RF waves are used as a means of measuring the aforementioned values. Depending on the characteristic of the transmitted RF wave that is measured, the methods are divided into three main categories: Time-of-flight measuring methods, received signal strength measuring methods and angle of arrival measuring methods.

16.2.1 Time-of-Flight Measuring Methods

Time-of-flight measuring methods are quite common in RF localization. The main idea is to measure the time that it takes for an RF signal to cover the distance from a transmitter to a receiver. Since the propagation speed of waves in the air is known, the distance can be computed by multiplying the propagation speed with the measured time.

Depending on the exact implementation of the propagation time measurement, these methods are divided into time-of-flight (TOF) methods and round-trip-time-of-flight (RTOF). The former requires for the transmitter and receiver to have the same time reference, as shown in Fig. 16.2. This is quite difficult to achieve, and is one of the disadvantages of the method. In GPS, where a form of TOF method is used (namely a method called time-difference of arrival—TDOA), satellites that act as the known locations are equipped with very accurate and expensive clocks. However, such a solution is not always feasible in cost sensitive applications.

Round-trip time-of-flight methods mitigate the problem of synchronization by transferring the TOF computation from the receiver to the transmitter as shown in Fig. 16.3. In these methods,

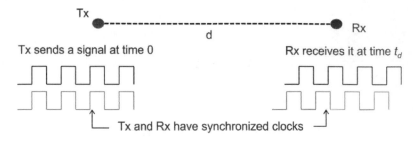

Figure 16.2   Time-of-flight methods.

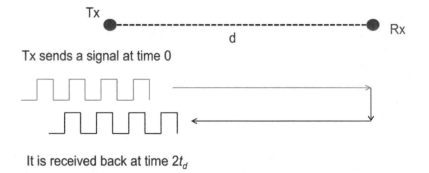

Figure 16.3   Round-trip time-of-flight methods.

the receiver simply sends the RF signal back to the transmitter. Since the signal reception and processing is performed at the transmitter, there is no need for synchronization of the transmitter and receiver clocks.

Recently, this method has been used in an indoor radar implementation that has taken advantage of the low complexity requirements of the receiver hardware, in order to reduce the receiver complexity to a bare minimum. This implementation, called the Frequency Modulated Constant Wave (FMCW) radar, was developed under the European FP6 project RESOLUTION[a] [4],

---

[a]In RESOLUTION, a team of engineers under A. G. Constantinides in SignalGeneriX Ltd. were responsible for implementing the base station hardware that executed the baseband signal processing algorithms of the FMCW radar.

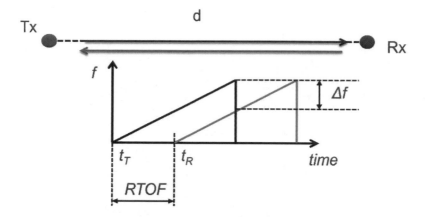

Figure 16.4   The FMCW radar principle.

targeting smart factory applications that have very high accuracy requirements.

The FMCW radar consists of two separate electronic systems, a base station and a reflector. The base station sends out a signal resembling a frequency ramp, called a chirp signal. This is a signal which changes its frequency with respect to time. When received at the reflector, the chirp signal is immediately sent back to the base station. Due to the time it takes for the electromagnetic wave to travel from the base station to the reflector and back, the received chirp signal will have a frequency difference Δf with respect to the original signal, as shown in Fig. 16.4.

Through the frequency difference, the distance to the reflector is calculated using the following:

$$d = \frac{c \cdot T_r \cdot \Delta f}{4 \cdot \text{BW}}$$

Although in this set-up the reflector might as well be implemented as a passive backscattering device, in order to meet the range requirements of smart factory applications the reflector was actually an active device, based on a periodically switched voltage controlled oscillator (VCO), which regenerates and amplifies the chirp signal, sending it back to the base station.

When the chirp signal reaches back to the base station, it is multiplied in the IF stage with the original signal. The resulting

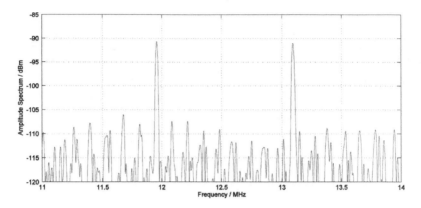

Figure 16.5 Snapshot of the frequency spectrum of mixed signal at the base station.

mixed signal is then sampled and fed into the baseband stage of the base station. A snapshot of the frequency response of such a signal is shown in Fig. 16.5. Clearly, if we perform a fast Fourier transform (or apply a super resolution technique like MUSIC, if a higher accuracy is required) on the received complex time-domain signal, a response with two peaks will be created. The distance between these two peaks is the Δf of the transmitted and received waveforms.

Therefore, by extracting the frequency difference between the two peaks in the spectrum of Fig. 16.5, the distance to the object can be calculated by the following equation:

$$d = \frac{c \cdot T_r \cdot \Delta f}{4 \cdot \text{BW}} - \frac{c \cdot T_{on}}{4},$$

where c is the speed of light in vaccum, T_r is the round trip time of flight, Δf is the measured frequency difference between two peaks of the spectrum, BW is the signal bandwidth and T_{on} is the duration of the frequency ramp. The FMCW system has demonstrated that accuracies in the centimetre level can be achieved with minimum complexity on the device level. However, since the accuracy is proportional to the duration and bandwidth of the chirp signal, reaching such accuracy levels would be prohibitive for most wireless sensor network applications. Furthermore, since the bandwidth occupied by FMCW system is dedicated to the distance measuring process, interoperability issues arise when additional wireless bandwidth is required for communication purposes. Finally, the aforementioned system calls for the deployment of customized hardware components of high complexity on the base station side.

Such issues are not unique in the FMCW concept, but are rather common in TOF systems. If you think, for example, of GPS, it has a dedicated spectrum, it does not allow communication on the same frequency band, and is based on a dedicated hardware platform. On the other hand, in most wireless sensor network applications, bandwidth is scarce and mainly used for communication. Furthermore, the need for additional node hardware is preferably avoided, especially for large area, large node density applications. For these reasons, some of the most popular localization algorithms for wireless sensor networks are based on measurements of the received signal strength of packets that are already used for data communication. This is a family of localization algorithms that are described in the following paragraph.

16.2.2 *Received Signal Strength-Based Measurements*

Receive signal strength indicator (RSSI)-based localization has attracted much attention because it is a simple technique making use of measurements that are already available in the network, requiring no additional hardware. This is because most (if not all) RF communication hardware chipsets provide an indication of the received signal strength with every received data packet. Since the power at which the RF signals are received is largely dependent on the distance between transmitter and receiver, nodes can use this information for location estimation purposes.

Although attractive for wireless sensor network applications, this method suffers from extremely low accuracy, especially in indoor environments where the multi-path effect is dominant. As described above, the multi-path effect causes multiple images of the same signal to appear in the vicinity of the receiver. The vector sum of these signals has an amplitude that can be modelled as a random process, meaning that significant ambiguity is introduced when trying to translate received power to distance. To make matters worse, since most wireless environments are time varying, errors in distance and location estimation are also time varying.

Due to the stochastic nature of the multi-path environment, distance estimation is normally based on statistical models. Whether in outdoor or indoor radio channels, the most widely used model is assuming a Gaussian distribution of the received power, with a mean value that is logarithmically decreasing with distance. Therefore, the received power at a distance d from a source can be characterized as follows:

$$P(d) \sim N(\overline{P}(d), \sigma_{dB}^2)$$

$$\overline{P}(d) = P_0 - n_p \log\left(\frac{d}{d_0}\right),$$

where $\bar{P}(d)$ is the mean received power at distance d (in dBm) and P_0 the received power at reference distance d_0.

Therefore, distance d is given in terms of P (or RSS):

$$d = d_0 10 \frac{(P_0 - P)}{(10 n_P)}$$

In practice, d_0 is 1 m and P_0 and n_p are determined based on experimental values. However, this model is far from accurate when considering indoor environments, where multi-path propagation is dominant. As shown in Fig. 16.6, estimating distance from RSSI values could lead to significant errors, which could be in the order of several meters or tens of meters.

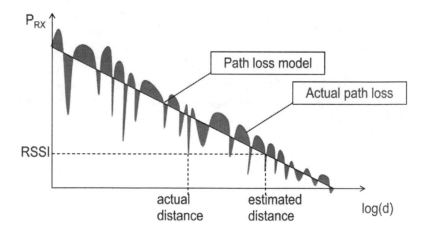

Figure 16.6 Error of RSSI-based measurements due to multi-path.

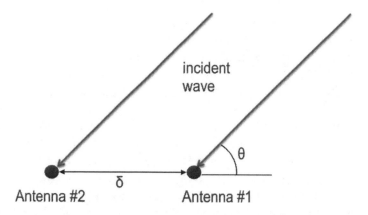

Figure 16.7 AoA estimation using multiple antennas.

16.2.3 *Angle of Arrival-Based Measurements*

Angle of arrival (AoA) methods are based on the estimation of the incident angle of the incoming wave at the receiver. As shown in Fig. 16.1, if angles α, β, and γ are measured using the AoA method, then the position of the node under test can be accurately estimated using a simple triangulation algorithm.

Traditionally, AoA is estimated using multiple antenna elements at the receiver. Consider, for example, the use of a simple antenna array consisting of two antenna elements, as shown in Fig. 16.7. When an incident plane wave hits the array, it arrives at the different antenna elements at different time instances. The difference in the time of arrival depends on the distance δ between antenna elements (which is known by design), and the cosine of the incident angle θ. Since the signals used in wireless communications are sine waves, this delay corresponds to a phase difference between the signals received at the different antenna elements. This phase difference can be measured either on the RF/IF stage or using baseband signal processing, and the AoA can be estimated.

This method comes with significant advantages. First, it does not require significant signal bandwidth to operate. The concept described above can be applied to a single carrier wave, as well as to an information signal. Consequently, AoA estimations can be extracted from any packet used for communication, without burdening the wireless network with specialized packets. Finally, AoA estimations are quite immune to multi-path, provided that a dominant line-of-sight (LOS) path exists between transmitter and receiver.

On the other hand, the integration of multiple antenna elements with adequate inter-element space δ, and the need for specialized signal processing hardware, is often considered an overkill for wireless sensor network applications. It could be argued that such implementations could be restricted to the base stations of the localization system. Still, traditional AoA estimation methods would need significant processing power in order to be of useful accuracy. However, their clear advantages make them a significant candidate for localization estimation in IoT applications.

16.3 The Special Case of Wireless Sensor Networks

In the previous sections, we have reviewed the main methods for estimating the location of an RF signal source. These methods have been widely used in many applications, each of which has sets a different trade-off between the two main competing parameters of accuracy and bandwidth. However, as already implied in previous comments, the integration of localization systems in wireless sensor networks, and especially for IoT applications, is bound by additional constraints:

- *Cost:* When networks of hundreds to thousands of nodes have to be deployed in order to meet the vision for an Internet of Things, node cost becomes quite significant. Since cost is a function of production volume, custom and application-specific solutions that would not utilize standard protocols and chipsets are not preferable.
- *Power Consumption:* Wireless sensor nodes deployed in large numbers are usually powered by batteries of limited capacity, which are hard to replace. Therefore, wireless sensor networks are required to have large lifetimes, spanning over periods of years or more. As a consequence, hardware implementations and algorithms

should be as power efficient as possible in order to meet this requirement.

- **Complexity:** Largely due to the two aforementioned constraints, sensor nodes have very limited processing power and memory. Therefore, any algorithms developed for IoT applications should be of low complexity and require low processing speeds and memory sizes.
- **Size:** As the name suggests, the Internet of Things describes a vision of creating a vast network of smart objects, equipped with electronic devices. This vision stretches the size requirements of the embedded electronic systems.

It is evident that localization systems present a significant challenge when applied in WSN that have significant limitations in energy consumption, communication range, bandwidth and cost. These limitations impede the integration of complex digital signal processing algorithms on sensor nodes, and the use of distributed localization algorithms that require the exchange of significant amount of information among nodes. Therefore, current WSN solutions for localization are based on simple received signal strength indicators [5], or on algorithms that do not require range measurements [6]. Some of these propositions are summarized below:

Centroid Algorithm

This is a simple, range-free, base station (or "anchor")-based, distributed algorithm, assuming that the radio propagation is the same in all directions and that all nodes transmit with identical power [7 , 8]. The anchor nodes are deployed in a regular mesh and transmit periodic beacon signals containing their respective coordinates. The one-hop nodes that receive these coordinates estimate their own location by calculating the centroid of the received coordinates. Experimental results show that, in an outdoor 10 m × 10 m area with four anchor nodes at the corners, this algorithm achieves a mean localization error of about 2 m and maximum error of 4 m. However, the radio model approximation is not appropriate for indoor environments where reflection, multipath fading and other RF anomalies are common.

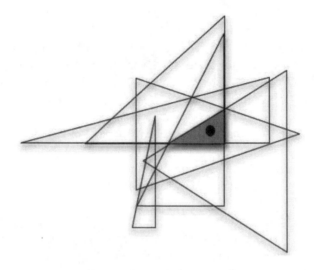

Figure 16.8   Area-based APIT algorithm.

Approximate Point-in-Triangulation (APIT)

APIT [6] is a range-free and anchor-based localization algorithm that divides the environment into triangular regions between the anchors, which beacon their coordinates. Each node chooses three anchors from all audible ones and tests with RSSI measurements whether it is inside or outside of the triangular regions formed by these anchors. The node position is the centre of gravity of the intersection of all triangles in which the node lies, as shown in Fig. 16.8. As noted, although this method does not make direct use of RSSI to measure distances, it does assume that the received signal strength decreases monotonically with distance. This may be true in an outdoor environment, but this assumption does not hold in indoor environments due to the reflection and multi-path fading. In addition, APIT causes additional communication overhead and requires a certain node and anchor densities.

Ad hoc Positioning System (APS)—DV-HOP

APS [9] is a decentralized, range-free, anchor-based algorithm, also assuming that the wireless transmissions are isotropic. Each anchor floods the network with a beacon message containing its location and a distance counter. In the DV-HOP version the distance is a hop counter, incremented at every intermediate hop. Each regular node maintains the minimum hop count per anchor, which it forwards, ignoring any other beacons originating from this anchor. Once an anchor node obtains the number of hops separating it from all other anchors, it estimates the average distance for one hop, given the fact that each anchor node knows the coordinates (and by consequence, the Euclidean distance) of the other anchor nodes. The average hop distance calculated by each anchor node is flooded as a correction to the network. With this correction, each node (regular and anchor nodes) can estimate its Euclidean distance to all the anchor nodes, which can be used to perform a triangulation.

Multi-Dimensional Scaling
Multi-dimensional Scaling (MDS) [10–12] is a range-based algorithm that attempts to arrange nodes in a space with a particular number of dimensions so as to reproduce the distances reported by network nodes. It is much like trying to create a mechanical beam constellation with given beams, without stressing the structure. MDS uses a function minimization algorithm that evaluates different configurations with the goal of maximizing the goodness-of-fit (or minimizing "lack-of-fit"). The most common measure that is used to evaluate how well (or poorly) a particular configuration reproduces the observed distance matrix is a so-called "stress" measure or cost function. The goal is then to minimize this cost function. There are many types of MDS techniques: MDS Classic, MDS-MAP, distributed weighted multi-dimensional scaling (dwMDS), etc. They require a large amount of computation power. In theory, they perform well but, in practice, they are difficult to implement.

Monte Carlo-Based Localization Algorithms
Monte Carlo Localization (MCL) [5, 13] is a distributed, range-free and anchor-based algorithm that was originally proposed to solve the global localization problem of a mobile robot. In wireless sensor networks, MCL and its more recent improved version, Monte Carlo Boxed (MCB), use a recursive Bayes filter to estimate the a posteriori distribution of the possible locations of a node, using a set of weighted samples. The algorithms can be applied to free space or unmapped terrain, with various network topologies and they can

work with low anchor density. The algorithms assume that anchors and nodes may move at a known maximum speed. The anchors periodically transmit beacon messages with their coordinates. To find its location, each regular node chooses a random set of N samples (called particles) in the deployment area, and, for each time interval t, and for each particle at time $t - 1$, it proceeds through the two following phases:

- *Prediction:* It randomly chooses possible particle positions at time t, based on the particle position at time $t - 1$ and on the maximum motion speed.
- *Filtering:* It filters out those positions that are not compatible with the new observations from the anchors (taking into consideration one-hop and two-hop anchors and an assumed radio hop range value).

This process continues until N new locations are obtained for time t. The position of the node at time t is the average of the positions of the N particles. The authors of MCL recommend $N = 50$ for good accuracy, but this value actually depends on anchor density. These algorithms generally perform well but require a large amount of resources.

RF fingerprinting and proximity detection (*k*-nearest neighbour)
RF fingerprinting [14] offers an alternative to distance estimations. The main idea is to buind an RSSI map of the deployment area, in order to be able to match sampled points with the mapped ones. Such algorithms require a training phase, during which a data set of RSSI values from n beacon nodes is stored in an n-dimensional space. During normal operation, the RF signal strengths of a mobile node are compared to the training data set in order to find the k nearest matching records. This algorithm is used by RADAR [15], a localization system based on 802.11 technology.

16.4 Smart Antennas for WSN

As stated above, RSSI-based localization methods have little reliability in severe multi-path indoor environments, while range-free methods as the ones summarized in the previous paragraph suffer from reduced accuracy. Recently [16] a method based on AoA measurements was proposed, which overcomes these problems by introducing a simple distributed localization algorithm, which is less affected from multi-path effects and provides higher accuracy than other non-range-based methods.

The proposed scheme is based on a new generation of miniature low-power wireless sensor nodes which have been introduced in [17], and utilize advanced smart antenna technology for continuous monitoring, localization and tracking of events in the network environment. The nodes, called WiseSPOT nodes, propose an innovative system architecture, which utilizes directional antennas able to be selected via antenna switching. This system architecture is motivated by the considerable advantages that the use of smart antennas has shown in wireless ad-hoc networks [17, 18]. These advantages, which include range increase, power consumption decrease, and interference cancellation at the network level [19], are quite attractive for WSN applications where range, node power consumption and interference largely dictate the overall lifetime of the network. The WiseSPOT wireless node, illustrated in Fig. 16.9, is based on the M2110 MEMSIC's IRIS OEM Edition module, and provides a functional integration of the microprocessor, memory and the wireless transceiver. The latter is compatible to the 2.4 GHz Zigbee standard, which is widely used in wireless sensor

Figure 16.9 WiseSPOT node with two integrated directional fractal Yagi antennas.

network applications [20, 21]. The WiseSPOT node utilizes two printed fractal antennas and optionally, two external antennas. The algorithms work well not only in the full system configuration with four antennas, but have been tested to provide very good accuracies with the standard configuration with only two antennas. In the latter, two back-to-back directional antennas are used, pointing towards opposite directions.

The node is designed in such a way so that the two radiation patterns are mirror images of each other, and switching between radiation patterns is done through a simple SPDT switch, that is controlled by the node's microcontroller. This approach was followed in order to avoid the modification of the physical layer and MAC layer standards, thus reducing the cost and increasing the interoperability of the proposed solution.

The mirror radiation patterns are produced by high-gain, wide-bandwidth fractal array antennas. The array antennas cover the whole bandwidth between 2.40 GHz and 2.50 GHz frequencies on which the sensor node transceiver works. The return loss of the antennas is lower than -10 dB for the entire bandwidth while the antennas maximum gain reaches 6 dBi. This translates to a beamwidth of $120°$ 3 dB azimuth beamwidth and a front to back ratio of -14 dB.

The proposed algorithm is based on the use of WiseSPOT nodes, taking advantage of their unique use of switched beam arrays which provide a low-cost solution for determining the angle of arrival of incoming signals, as described in the next paragraph.

16.4.1 *Direction Finding*

The direction finding algorithms of the WiseSPOT system architecture combines RSSI and AOA techniques in order to utilize the four directional antennas. WiseSPOT nodes are used as the anchors of the localization system, with their location known upon deployment. Mobile nodes that use these anchors can be simple nodes with a single omni-directional antenna each. Upon communication between the wireless nodes and the anchors, the latter switch between their beams, and record the RSSI values for each received packet and antenna used. Once this information is

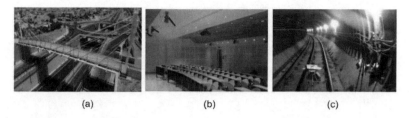

Figure 16.10 WiseSPOT testing environments with different levels of multi-path effect severity: (a) Outdoor localization scenario, (b) indoor mild multi-path scenario, (c) indoor severe multi-path scenario.

available, the WiseSPOT nodes can compute the ratio between the two RSSI values corresponding to the antennas used for receiving packets from the same wireless node. As previously described in [22], if there is dominant LOS signal between transmitter and receiver, then the direction of arrival of the incoming signal may be computed from the ratio of the RSSI values with adequate accuracy, even in multi-path environments. This observation is backed up by tests performed in many different environments with different levels of multi-path.

As shown in Fig. 16.10, three such sites were considered. The first was used for testing performance in an outdoor environment with mild multi-path effects, performed in collaboration with the Department of Civil Engineering and Geomatics of the Cyprus University of Technology at the Agios Athanasios steel cable-stayed footbridge. The second resembles an indoor environment with mild multi-path effects, conducted in an amphitheatre of Athens Information Technology. The third site was used for testing the performance of the algorithm in indoor environments with severe multi-path effects, in collaboration with the Signal processing and Communication Group of the Electrical and Electronic Engineering Department at Imperial College London. From these tests, it was shown that in environments with mild multi-path effects, the antenna directionality can be effectively exploited to determine the general direction of a transmitting device.

In order to mitigate the effects of multi-path, statistical data analysis was used during deployment for system calibration, so that the ratios of RSSI values between the two antennas for two

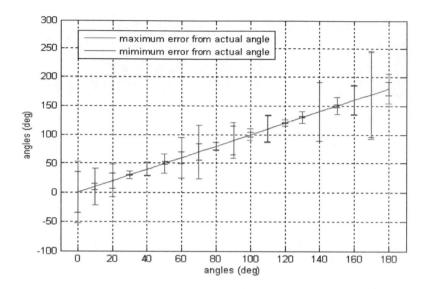

Figure 16.11 WiseSPOT measured error in AoA estimation.

consecutive packets were mapped to actual angles of arrival of the signal. Using this analysis, it was shown that the average error deviation with the WiseSPOT system utilizing two antennas was around 20°. Minimum and maximum error values of this system are shown in Fig. 16.11, where it is evident that errors below 15° are quite common. Therefore, although the method itself is RSSI based, the actual AoA estimation is less susceptible to multi-path fading effects, since the ratio of RSSI measurements rather than the actual RSSI values are considered.

16.4.2 *Localization*

A straightforward method for using the AoA information provided by the WiseSPOT nodes, using the process described in the previous paragraph, is to run a simple triangulation algorithm. As described in Fig. 16.12, in the absence of error the target location would be on the intersection of the angles of arrival measured by the anchor nodes. In the realistic case, where the AoA estimation has errors, then the AoA lines would create a polygon. In that case, which is the case of

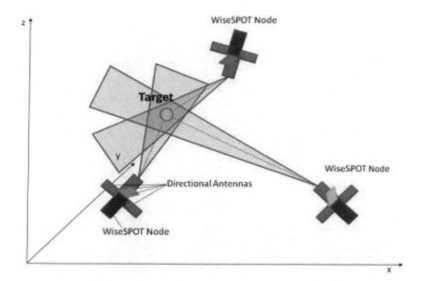

Figure 16.12   WiseSPOT localization using AoA estimations.

the WiseSPOT implementation, the target location is assumed to be on the centre of gravity of this polygon.

This simple algorithm has been tested in an indoor environment with mild multi-path effects, showing impressive accuracies of 40 cm mean error, clearly outperforming RSSI methods. Actually, the performance of the system is comparable to that of expensive TOF methods, utilizing only a fraction of the bandwidth, and without the need for integrating customized hardware on the targeted nodes.

A second approach to indoor localization using WiseSPOT nodes has also been proposed [23]. This approach would need minimal amount of information to be exchanged among anchors. The method proposes that the localization algorithm is performed centrally, using a single bit of information per anchor and target.

For this method, we assume that the anchors of the network are placed at known locations, and that the orientation of their antennas is known. Consider, for example, the network described in Fig. 16.13, where the antenna beams are aligned on the north-south axis. Gateway nodes are presented to be placed on a rectangular grid, which would be a typical case for many indoor applications. Using this configuration, each gateway node may locally compute

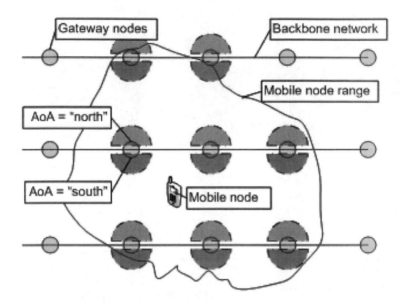

Figure 16.13 The simplified WiseSPOT localization method.

the AoA of the signals received from mobile nodes in range, as described in the previous paragraph. Instead of transmitting full AoA information, gateways just need to send a single bit per user, depending on whether the mobile node is detected towards their "north" beam, or their "south" beam. This information is collected in a central station, which knows the gateway coordinates and their antenna orientation. From this information, the central station will be able to derive estimations on each user's location in the following way: by detecting the grid row where the AoA changes from "north" to "south", it may find the exact row that the user lies in. Moreover, by calculating the centre of gravity of the overlapping area of the active gateways' beams within this row, the central station can provide an estimation of the location of the mobile node.

The proposed algorithm resembles a "presence detection" algorithm, which is well known in wireless sensor networks for its low complexity and low communication overhead. However, by using the advantages provided by the use of smart antennas, the accuracy of the proposed scheme is much higher, as shown by extensive simulations.

For these simulations, a 10×10 rectangular grid of such anchor nodes was considered, forming a network of 100 active nodes with known locations and antenna orientation. Mobile nodes using simple omni-directional antennas are placed randomly within the grid and are localized using the algorithm described above. The performance of the proposed scheme is compared against other low-bandwidth localization schemes that do not make use of the angular information that sensor nodes equipped with smart antennas can provide. We therefore consider as a benchmark an equivalent set-up that would use RSSI measurements to determine whether the mobile node is within each gateway's range. This information, which can also be coded into a single bit, is transmitted and processed centrally, in order to produce location estimations.

The performance of the proposed scheme was evaluated taking into consideration two key parameters: detection beamwidth, and mobile node range. Detection beamwidth stands for the angle range within which a gateway node will activate a transmission of a detection bit towards the central station. For example, if the detection beamwidth is $100°$, then a gateway node sends information to the central station only when the AoA of the incoming signal is within $40°$ to $140°$ (sending "north") or $-40°$ to $-140°$ (sending "south"). If the AoA is detected to be within $-40°$ to $40°$ or $140°$ to $-140°$, no information is sent towards the central station. It is noted here that the detection beamwidth is not the antenna beamwidth. It is a parameter of the algorithm, which is utilized after the AoA detection process described in the previous paragraph.

All errors and ranges are expressed as a fraction of the distance d between two consecutive gateways on the grid, which is a defining parameter of the system performance. In Fig. 16.14, the error of the proposed scheme is computed with respect to the detection beamwidth, and compared against the omni-directional case. It is evident that the larger the detection angle, the larger the error, since more distant gateways are involved in the computation of the location within the same row. Moreover, large localization errors are produced for small detection angles. This quite interesting result has the following explanation. When the detection angle is small, then the gateways that have the smaller distance to the mobile node, will not activate detection messages towards the

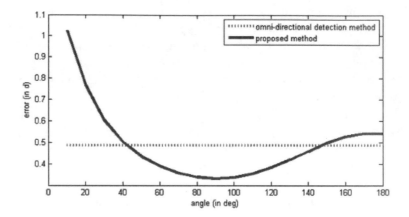

Figure 16.14   Estimation error in respect to detection beamwidth.

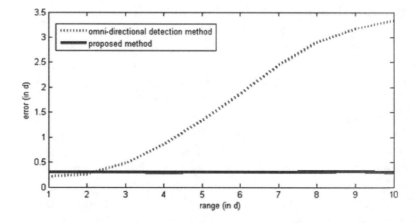

Figure 16.15   Estimation error in respect to mobile node range.

central station. Only distant gateways will generate such messages, resulting in large estimation errors. The smallest error is evidently produced for detection beamwidths equal to 90°, and these are significantly smaller than the errors produced by the benchmark method. Although this result was produced for a mobile node range of 3d, it is shown in Fig. 16.15 that this small error remains unaffected by the node range, as opposed to the omni-directional detection method.

16.5 Summary

In the emerging "Internet of Things" vision, RF localization is expected to play a key role in enhancing the services and applications provided to users. Although RF localization in itself is not a new field of engineering, requirements set by this new range of applications make us revisit old solutions, re-evaluate them under the strict constraints of low-power, low-cost devices, and find new solutions that would seem out of place at a first glance. This chapter was full of such examples: We revisited TOA methods, which are considered inappropriate for low-cost applications, showing that if the complexity of the algorithms are moved from the targeted devices to the base stations, the former can become as simple as RFID tags. We showed cases where bandwidth-consuming, low-accuracy RSSI measurements can be bypassed through range-free algorithms that depend only on hop-counts in multi-hop networks. Finally, we reviewed the concept of integrating smart antennas in wireless sensor networks, a feature that seems out of place at a first glance, showing that simple switched antennas can be at the same time small, low-cost, and provide location estimation at high accuracy, without the need for extensive bandwidth use, or additional hardware on the targeted nodes. In essence, the field of RF localization for IoT applications is full of examples that show how "out of the box" thinking may find new solutions that pave the way to new visions.

References

1. Los Alamos National Laboratory Report, A Review of Structural Health Monitoring Literature 1996–2001, LA-013976-MS, 2004.
2. J. P. Lynch, An overview of wireless structural health monitoring for civil structures, *Phil. Trans. R Soc. A*, vol. 365 no. 1851, pp. 345–372, 2007.
3. http://www.lynceus-project.eu/.
4. P. Traggas, et al., RESOLUTION: Reconfigurable systems for mobile local communication and positioning, *Mobile and Wireless Communications Summit*, 2007.

5. L. Hu and D. Evans, Localization for mobile sensor networks, in *Proceedings of Tenth Annual International Conference on Mobile Computing and Networking*, 2004.

6. T. He, C. Huang, B. Blum, J. Stankovic, and T. Abdelzaher, Range-free localization schemes in large scale sensor networks, in *Proceedings of the ACM/IEEE 9th Annual International Conference on Mobile Computing and Networking (MobiCom'03)*, 2003.

7. N. Bulusu, J. Heidemann, and D. Estrin, GPS-less low cost outdoor localization for very small devices, *IEEE Pers. Commun.* (Special Issue on Smart Spaces and Environments), vol. 7, no. 5, pp. 28–34, 2000.

8. N. Bulusu, J. Heidemann, D. Estrin, and T. Tran, Self-configuring localization systems: Design and experimental evaluation, *ACM Trans. Embedded Comput. Syst.*, vol. 3, no. 1, pp. 24–60, 2004.

9. D. Niculescu, and B. Nath, Ad hoc positioning system (APS), in *Proceedings of the IEEE GLOBECOM'01*, November 2001.

10. I. Borg and P. J. F. Groenen, *Modern Multidimensional Scaling: Theory and Applications*, pp. 614, Springer, New York, NY, 2005.

11. Y. Shang, W. Ruml, Y. Zhang, and M. P. J. Fromherz, Localization from mere connectivity, in *Proceedings of the Mobihoc'03*, June 1–3, 2003, Annapolis, Maryland, USA, pp. 201–212, 2003.

12. N. Patwari, J. N. Ash, S. Kyperountas, A. O. Hero III, R. L. Moses, and N. S. Correal, Locating the nodes, *IEEE Signal Processing Magazine July*, 2005.

13. A. Baggio and K. Langendoen, Monte Carlo localization for mobile wireless sensor networks, in I. F. Akyldiz (ed.), *Ad Hoc Networks 6*, pp. 718–733, Elsevier, 2008.

14. R. Zekavat, et al., Fundamentals of received signal strength-based position location, in *Handbook of Position Location: Theory, Practice and Advances*, pp. 359–394, Wiley-IEEE Press, 2012.

15. P. Bahl and V. N. Padmanabhan, RADAR: An in-building RF-based user location and tracking system, in *Proceedings of the IEEE INFOCOM '00*, March 2000.

16. A. Kounoudes, T. Onoufriou, A. Kalis, Ph. Traggas, A. G. Constantinides, M. Milis, and R. Votsis, WiseSPOT, a novel approach for wireless localisation of damages in bridges, in *6th International Conference on Bridge Maintenance, Safety and Management*, 2012, Stresa, Lake Maggiore, 2012.

17. D. Leang and A. Kalis, Smart sensor DVBs: Sensor network development boards with smart antennas, in *Proceedings of IEEE International*

Conference on Communications, Circuits and Systems (ICCCAS 2004), June 2004, vol. 2, pp. 1476–1480, 2004.

18. E. Navarro, J. Blanes, J. A. Carrasco, and C. Reig, Yagi-like printed antennas for wireless sensor networks, in *International Conference on Sensor Technologies and Applications. SensorComm 2007*, October 2007, pp. 254–259, 2007.

19. P. Baronti, P. Pillaia, et al., Wireless sensor networks: A survey on the state of the art and the 802.15.4 and ZigBee standards, *Comput. Commun.*, vol. 30, no. 7, pp. 1655–1695, 2007.

20. J. A. Gutierrez, M. Naeve, E. Callaway, M. Bourgeois, V. Mitter, and B. Heile, IEEE 802.15.4: A developing standard for low-power low-cost wireless personal area networks, *IEEE Netw.*, vol. 15, no. 5, pp. 12–19, 2001.

21. A. Kalis and T. Dimitriou, Fast routing in wireless sensor networks using directional transmissions, *Int. J. Mobile Netw. Des. Innovation*, vol. 1, pp. 63–69, 2005.

22. S. Preston V. Thiel, T. Smith, S. O'Keefe, and J. Lu, Base-station tracking in mobile communications using a switched parasitic antenna array, *IEEE Trans. Antennas Propagat.*, vol. 46, no. 6, pp. 841–844, 1998.

23. A. Kalis, M. Milis, A. Kounoudes, and A. G. Constantinides, Bandwidth efficient localization for sustainable and safe building environments, *2013 Proceedings of the 21st European Signal Processing Conference (EUSIPCO)*, 2013.

Chapter 17

Classification and Prediction Techniques for Localization in IEEE 802.11 Networks

Kelong Cong and Kin K. Leung

Imperial College London, UK
kc1212@imperial.ac.uk, kin.leung@imperial.ac.uk

IEEE 802.11 (Wi-Fi) networks have been widely deployed in many countries. Information about user locations in indoor environments can be very useful to both businesses and consumers. For example, in a shopping centre, the owner may want to identify popular areas or paths that customers often take. With this information, the owner will be able to optimize the shop and product locations and/or shop rental fees to maximize profit and improve customer experiences.

In this chapter, we investigate several classification and prediction techniques for a popular localization method called "fingerprinting" in the IEEE 802.11 environment. These techniques are based on the idea of machine learning, each of which consists of the offline training and online location-prediction phases. We study the techniques by using data generated from simulations and data collected in a real office environment. Among the techniques under consideration, it has been found that the Support Vector Machine classifier and the k-Nearest Neighbour classifier perform well in all our tests. Furthermore, all techniques under study demonstrate

Trends in Digital Signal Processing: A Festschrift in Honour of A. G. Constantinides
Edited by Yong Ching Lim, Hon Keung Kwan, and Wan-Chi Siu
Copyright © 2016 Pan Stanford Publishing Pte. Ltd.
ISBN 978-981-4669-50-4 (Hardcover), 978-981-4669-51-1 (eBook)
www.panstanford.com

diminishing improvement in the probability of correct location prediction as the number of measurements used for training or prediction increases. Our results also reveal that with a moderate number of measurements, several of the techniques can provide correct location prediction with a probability above 90%.

17.1 Introduction

Wi-Fi and GPS enable smartphone and tablet sales have grown significantly in the past few years, to the point where the worldwide smart-phone population exceeded one billion in 2013 [1]. Thus, location-based services (LBS) such as navigation, social networking and weather forecast became exceedingly popular. Technology giants such as Google, Microsoft and Apple as well as start-ups all make use of location-based services in their products.

Knowing the location of customers has enormous business value. For example, in a shopping centre, the owner may want to identify popular areas or paths that customers often take. With this information, the shopping centre owner will be able to optimize the shop locations and/or rental fees to maximize profit and improve customer experience.

Outdoor localization technologies are well developed. The Global Positioning System (GPS) is widely used. Its accuracy is often within 1 metre [11], which is enough for most civilian applications. However, GPS signals cannot reach indoor environments.

Determining the location of a user in an indoor environment has been an active topic of research for more than a decade [2, 3, 8, 14, 15]. Many methods were developed during this period but the fingerprinting method is widely considered to be the most robust solution [9]. However, very little was published on comparisons between classification algorithms.

We would like to present a study on different machine learning algorithms for indoor localization applications, as well as the effect on those algorithms after changing the characteristics of the input data. Moreover, an open-source implementation of the classification algorithms—"scikit-learn" will be used. This gives reproducible results and more confidence in the correctness of the algorithms.

The remainder of this chapter is organized as follows. First, the background and existing work is introduced, which is followed by the methodology section presenting details on the setup of the simulation and experiment. Finally the key findings are discussed in the results section.

17.2 Background

17.2.1 *Path-Loss and Log-Normal Shadowing*

Path-loss is the attenuation of an electromagnetic wave as it propagates through space. It is caused by propagation mechanisms such as reflection, diffraction and scattering. The path-loss model is used to estimate the received signal strength and signal-to-noise ratio (SNR) as a function of distance. It is an empirical model that slowly emerged over time as experiments of more data from different environments became available.

The log-distance path-loss model (17.1) is a path-loss model that predicts the signal propagation loss in outdoor or indoor environments, where n is the path-loss exponent which indicates the rate of change of path-loss with respect to distance in the given radio environment. In free space n is generally taken to be 2. d_0 is the reference distance near the transmitter, $\overline{PL}(d_0)$ is the signal strength measured in dBm[a] at d_0. Finally d is the transmitter–receiver (T–R) separation distance measured in metres.

$$\overline{PL}(d) = \overline{PL}(d_0) + 10n \log \frac{d}{d_0} \qquad (17.1)$$

The surrounding environments may have many obstacles, this will cause the received signal strength indicator (RSSI) measurements to be different at two different locations that have the same T–R separation. In other words the RSSI measurements will be different than the average value predicted by (17.1). To capture this randomness, the log-normal shadowing model shown in (17.2)

---

[a]dBm or dBmW is the power ratio in dB (a dimensionless unit) of the measured power referenced at one milliwatt, i.e. 0 dBm = 1000 μW, −1 dBm = 794 μW, −30 dBm = 1 μW and −60 dBm = 1 nW.

can be used. Note that it is simply the log-distance path-loss model with an additional variable X_σ, where X_σ is a normally distributed random variable in dB with a mean that equals to zero and a standard deviation of σ. Value σ varies for different radio environments.

$$\overline{PL}(d) = \overline{PL}(d_0) + 10n \log \frac{d}{d_0} + X_\sigma \qquad (17.2)$$

17.2.2 *Location Estimation: Fingerprinting*

Overall, there are two common methods to estimate the location using RSSI measurements: triangulation and fingerprinting. The fingerprinting technique was found to be more accurate than triangulation [9]. Note that these methods need not be applied in Wi-Fi networks.

Fingerprinting techniques avoid the modelling of complex indoor radio environments by constructing a radio map[a] of RSSI measurements at known locations. Then a localization algorithm makes use of the radio map to determine the user's location. Fingerprinting techniques generally use two types of devices: monitor and fingerprinter. The monitor collects RSSI measurements from all the Wi-Fi enabled devices. Fingerprinters are Wi-Fi enabled devices with a known location. The fingerprinting technique for location estimation consists of two phases:

(1) The first phase is the offline training phase. Here the radio map is built using RSSI measurements collected by the monitors from fingerprinters located around the area of interest using a classification algorithm.
(2) The second phase is the online position determination phase. Here the system will use the radio map built previously to determine the location of an unknown Wi-Fi enabled device.

Figure 17.1 shows an example of the fingerprinting system. Every monitor continuously collects RSSI measurements from every fingerprinter over time. For example, at time t, the reading from

---

[a]A radio map is some data that describes the collected RSSI measurements from all the fingerprinters.

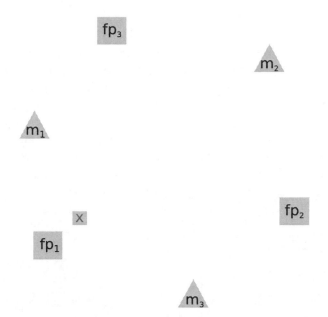

Figure 17.1 This is an example of a simple fingerprinting system. It has three monitors (m_1, m_2 and m_3) and three fingerprinted locations (fp_1, fp_2 and fp_3). The location of the user is marked by x.

fp_1, fp_2 and fp_3 measured by m_1 is (P_{11}^t, P_{12}^t, P_{13}^t) or $\mathbf{P}_1^t$. Therefore measurements at m_1 from $t = 1$ to $t = n$ is

$$\overrightarrow{\mathbf{P}_1} = \mathbf{P}_1^1, \mathbf{P}_1^2, \dots, \mathbf{P}_1^n \qquad (17.3)$$

Using the fingerprints and the measurements from device x, that is $\overrightarrow{\mathbf{P}_1}$, $\overrightarrow{\mathbf{P}_2}$, $\overrightarrow{\mathbf{P}_3}$, $\overrightarrow{\mathbf{P}_x}$, and a localization algorithm, it is possible to determine device x's location. In this work, if x is determined to be at fp_1, then we can say the localization algorithm performed a correct prediction, because that is the closest fingerprinted location to x.

Fingerprinting techniques are especially suitable for GSM and Wi-Fi networks where the frequency range is approximately between 850 MHz to 2.4 GHz due to two reasons [12]. First, the signal strength at those frequencies demonstrates an important spatial variability. Second, it has good consistency in time regardless of the variations caused by large and small-scale fading [12].

17.2.3 *Machine Learning*

Machine learning is a branch of artificial intelligence (AI). It is a technique that enables systems to "learn" or "study" data to detect or extrapolate patterns [16]. We will be using machine learning algorithms to perform the classification. The terms "feature" and "class" are often used in machine learning. For this problem, "features" are signal strength readings from different monitors and "classes" are the fingerprinted locations. Since fingerprinting localization techniques is a two step process as previously mentioned, supervised machine-learning algorithms such as naive Bayes or support vector machines are highly suitable for the task.

17.2.4 *Existing Work*

17.2.4.1 RADAR and Horus

The authors of the RADAR system [2] investigated two methods of determining the location of the user. Fingerprinting was their first method, and they were able to achieve distance errors of 2 to 3 metres on an office floor that is 22.5 metres × 43.5 metres. In the second method they used a propagation model (triangulation). However, the accuracy was poor; the distance errors were generally over 5 metres. During their experiment, some important discoveries were made:

- RSSI is a stronger indicator of location than SNR. The latter is impacted by random fluctuations in the noisy process.
- RSSI varies significantly (by up to 5 dBm) depending on the user's orientation. Water affects signal propagation and the human body is mostly made up of water. If a human body is blocking the T–R link, then RSSI will be heavily affected.

The work is one of the first published indoor localization systems that used the fingerprinting method. The discoveries and results of this system influenced much future indoor localization work.

The Horus system [15] is based on the RADAR system. The author took the ideas from RADAR and made it more accurate at a reduced computational cost. This system was able to decrease the distance error by more than 58% by applying probabilistic techniques. The number of (computer) operations used per location estimate was also reduced.

17.2.4.2 COMPASS

COMPASS [8] is a localization method that applies probabilistic methods and investigate the human body blocking issue. The authors discovered that when the person is completely blocking the line of sight between the transmitter and receiver, the RSSI measurements were relatively stable, the standard deviation was less than 5 dBm. It was also found that the RSSI increased by nearly 15 dBm when the person was not blocking, and more than 5 dBm when the person is only partially blocking.

Their system makes use of a digital compass equipped on the user's mobile device. With this extra piece of information and Bayesian inference, COMPASS was able to achieve an average error of 1.65 metres or less in an experimental environment of 312 square metres.

17.2.4.3 Ekahau

Ekahau [7] is one of the first commercial solutions for indoor localization. Not a lot of data is published as it is a proprietary system. However, it is known that it uses the IEEE 802.11 b/g network and infra-red sensors. Probabilistic modelling and filtering mechanisms are used to perform localization. It is capable of identifying different floors, which is an improvement over the other systems. The accuracy is typically 1 to 3 metres. However, Ekahau requires dedicated hardware.

17.3 Methodology

We start our analyses using a simulation and then move on to a real environment. In this section, we describe how our simulation and experiment are set up and carried out.

17.3.1 *Simulated Data Generation*

To gain a good understanding on how the algorithms may perform under different data characteristics, various analyses on simulated data were carried out before experimenting on a real environment. Using simulated data is advantageous as we can perform the analyses on different arrangements of fingerprinted locations, monitor locations, radio environments, etc., without physically rearranging the testbed.

For most of our simulations, we have used the arrangement as shown in Figure 17.2 because this setup shares some similarities to the real-life environment which we will experiment on later. There are nine fingerprinted locations (fp_1 to fp_9) placed in a 3×3 grid. Four monitors (m_1 to m_4) are scattered around the nine finger-printed locations, such that the RSSI readings collected by those four monitors would uniquely represent nine different locations. The distance between neighbouring fingerprinted locations for example fp_1 and fp_2 was set to 3 metres by default.

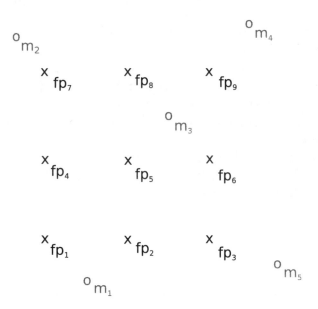

Figure 17.2 Arrangement of fingerprinted locations and monitors for most of the simulations that were carried out in this work.

The RSSI measurements received by every monitor were calculated (in dBm) using the log-distance path-loss equation discussed in (17.2). We used $n = 3.5$ (path-loss exponent) and $\sigma = 4$ (standard deviation of X_σ) for the simulations as they are the most common parameters for an indoor environment [4].

17.3.2 *Experimental Testbed*

The real-life experiment has been performed in an office environment at Imperial College. The office is more than 200 square metres. It consists of approximately 20 cubicles; computers, chairs and various objects can be found inside each cubicle. This gives us a mixture of shadowing, multipathing and line-of-sight radio environments. An environment like this is likely to occur in practical applications.

Figure 17.3 shows the annotated floor-plan of our testbed. There are 10 fingerprinted locations (fp_1 to fp_{10}) and 4 monitors (m_1 to m_4). Raspberry-Pi's connected with WiPi's were used as monitors. WiPi's are Wi-Fi dongles designed to be used with Raspberry-Pi's. Using monitors that can receive RSSI reliably is important in this experiment. Fortunately, our WiPi's were found to be excellent monitors. A Samsung Galaxy S3 was used to perform the fingerprinting. The position of the antenna on the Galaxy S3 smart phone has an effect on RSSI, and unknown readings may not always have the same orientation as the fingerprinted readings. Therefore we wanted to increase the variation in RSSI reading for every fingerprinted location; this was achieved by using four

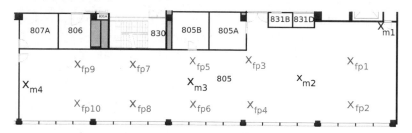

Figure 17.3 Arrangement of fingerprints and monitors in the EEE building at Imperial College.

different orientations at 90° from each other to produce a single fingerprint.

17.3.3 *Data Collection and Processing*

It is important to obtain a robust Wi-Fi device for our experiments. WiPi was one of the most suitable dongles we tested. Other dongles such as "TP-Link TL-WN772NC" did not produce consistent RSSI readings with respect to distance even though it was the most popular dongle on Amazon.co.uk at the time of purchase. The operating mode for the WLAN interface must be switched to "monitor" to enable monitoring. By default, the WLAN interface is set to "managed" mode. In this mode, the interface connects to a network composed of many access points. This is the mode to use if we want to connect to the internet for example. We used the Airmon-ng script from the Aircrack-ng software to switch the operating mode. Aircrack-ng is highly popular for wireless networking work, as it is described as "a set of tools for auditing wireless networks" [6].

After the Wi-Fi dongle was set to the correct operating mode, we could start to collect network traffic. This was done using a Python script and a software called TShark. TShark "lets you capture packet data from a live network" [17]. The packet information can be saved on text files or uploaded to a database. Finally, we transform the data to an appropriate form and pass them to a classifier.

17.3.4 *Classification Algorithms*

17.3.4.1 Input data

The input data must be transformed into a certain format before it can be used by the classification algorithms shown below, where N is the total number of measurements, M is the number of monitors.

$$\text{data} = [N \times M]$$
$$\text{target} = [N \times 1]$$

The data matrix stores all the RSSI measurements and the target matrix stores the fingerprinted location identifier for every corresponding row in the data matrix.

17.3.4.2 Algorithms and their implementation

Five machine-learning classification algorithms were employed in this experiment: Mean Classifier, Naive Bayes (NB), k-Nearest Neighbours (kNN), Support Vector Machine (SVM) and Decision Trees (DT).

The mean classifier is not a classifier that is used in practice. It is a classifier created to act as a baseline for the purposes of this work. It uses the same form of input data as all the other classifiers. During the training phase, the mean classifier will calculate the average value that is recorded in the data array for every class (fingerprinted location) and then store the results into an internal array. During the testing phase, for every test data, the Euclidean distance will be calculated between the test data and every element of the previously calculated average value array. Then the algorithm will attempt to find the smallest Euclidean distance and return the corresponding class (fingerprint location) as the result.

Naive Bayes classifier is a simple probabilistic classifier based on the Bayes' theorem often used in practice. The final classification rule is shown in (17.4); where C represents the class (fingerprinted location), and F represents the feature (RSSI readings from different monitors). We assume the relationship between every pair of features is independent and the likelihood to be Gaussian.

$$\hat{C} = \arg\max_{C} P(C) \prod_{i=1}^{n} P(F_i|C) \qquad (17.4)$$

The kNN classifier is another simple classifier used in practice. During the training phase, it stores all the data into an internal table. During the testing phase the algorithm will compute the distances of k (a user specified value) nearest neighbouring points. Typically the distances are measured using Minkowski distance or L^p norm [16, chap. 18.8]. Unlike the methods mentioned previously, kNN requires an input parameter k. We used grid search to obtain the optimal value of k, by running the classifier many times using a variety of k values.

SVM is one of the most robust classifiers, which has attractive properties such as excellent generalization, ability to learn from non-linear data, resistance to over-fitting and so on [16, chap. 18.8]. We used the radial basis function (RBF) as our kernel function as it generalizes well for non-linear problems. Two parameters C and γ are required to use the RBF kernel, where C defines the amount of slack and γ defines the amount influence a single training data can have. As before, we used a grid search to obtain the optimal values for C and γ.

The last classifier we tested was DT. It is generally used for discrete-valued classes (e.g. age, gender); however, it has been successful in a wide range of subject areas [10]. As the name suggests, this classifier uses a tree type data-structure. A tree consists of nodes, brunches and leaves. During the training phase, the algorithm will attempt to construct a suitable tree. During the testing phase, the algorithm will simply traverse down the tree according to the unclassified feature value. The leaf which the algorithm ends on will be the final classification. We can control variables such as maximum depth of the tree or minimum number of samples required to split an internal node such that an optimal tree can be built. These variables are again computed by running a grid search.

All the algorithms except the mean classifier were implemented using the scikit-learn library, the mean classifier was implemented from scratch in Python. scikit-learn is a free and open-source machine learning library primarily written in C but uses Python as its interface. It is suitable for small to medium machine learning problems [13]. Code used to perform the grid search is also a part of the scikit-learn library.

17.4 Results

17.4.1 *Analysis on Simulated Data*

17.4.1.1 Analysis on the number of measurements per fingerprinted location used in the training phase

This analysis will help understand the approximate number of RSSI measurements per fingerprinted location to collect in order to accurately perform the prediction. Not enough measurements led to poor accuracy, but too many of them are a waste of computational resources.

The simulation was run for all the algorithms discussed in Section 17.3.4 using the parameters below. We use N_{train} to denote the number of measurements per fingerprinted location used in the training phase, and N_{predict} to denote the number of measurements used to perform a single prediction. Further, n is the path-loss exponent, σ is the standard deviation of X_σ and d is the distance between neighbouring fingerprinted locations as discussed in Section 17.3.1.

$$n = 3.5, \quad \sigma = 4, \quad d = 3$$
$$N_{\text{train}} = \{5, 10, 15, 20, 30, 40, 50, 60, 70, 80, 90, 100\}$$
$$N_{\text{predict}} = 1$$

The data was learned and one unclassified measurement was predicted. This process was repeated 5000 times at every N_{train} to achieve an appropriate statistical significance. All the simulations in this chapter used a sample size that is well above the required sample size to achieve at least 95% confidence interval.

Figure 17.4 shows the probability of correct location prediction versus the number of measurements per fingerprinted location used in the training phase. The probability of correct location prediction is the number of correctly classified measurements over the total number of measurements. We can see that initially the probability of correct prediction is relatively low, with most of the algorithm being below 80%. However as the training size is increased, correct localization probability also increases, but only up to a certain point (approximately $N_{\text{train}} = 50$). After that, most of the algorithm except DT stabilized at 85%.

The mean classifier performed just as well as the other classifiers was because we had perfect RSSI measurements as a perfectly symmetrical normal distribution was used to generate X_σ. On the other hand, DT classifier was significantly underperforming. Due to the tree type data-structure, if the data is non-linear or has unclear boundaries between different classes, then the optimal tree becomes difficult to find, and the classifier will either over-fit or under-fit the data and produce poor results.

When the simulation was repeated using a different d (the distance between neighbouring fingerprinted locations) namely $d = 5$, while keeping other parameters the same, the overall accuracy

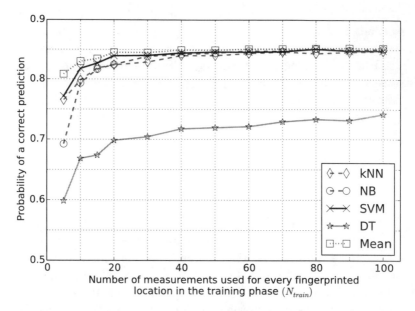

Figure 17.4 Probability of correct prediction versus number of measurements per fingerprinted location used in the training phase, using $d = 3$.

increased to 90% while the graph still followed the same shape. That is, except for DT, all the other algorithms converged at approximately $N_{\text{train}} = 50$.

In conclusion, for indoor environments where the RSSI measurements measured in dBm are normally distributed, we need at least 50 measurements per fingerprinted location to achieve convergence on the probability of correct location prediction using k-nearest neighbour, naive Bayes, support vector machine, and mean classifier. Due to the effect of diminishing return, the correct prediction probability is unlikely to increase further when more than 50 measurements are used for this type of environment.

17.4.1.2 Analysis on the number of measurements used to perform a single prediction

In this simulation, rather than predicting the location using a single measurement, we predicted the location using multiple measurements. We assumed those measurements all came from a single location. If this was a real-life application, the measurements would have been collected while the Wi-Fi device is stationary. If the RSSI measurements are time-stamped, it is easy to determine whether a set of RSSI measurement came from a stationary Wi-Fi device. For instance, if five samples were collected during a 1 second period, then it is unlikely for the device to have moved a significant distance.

The classification was determined using a majority vote. For example, if three measurements were acquired from the same location, two of them are classified to be location 2 and the other one is classified to be location 1, the final class will be location 2. We used the following parameters for this experiment:

$$n = 3.5, \quad \sigma = 4, \quad d = 3$$
$$N_{\text{train}} = 100$$
$$N_{\text{predict}} = \{1, 3, 5, 7, 9, 11\}$$

Figure 17.5 shows probability of correct prediction as a function of N_{predict}. It is clear that the probability of correct localization increases as prediction size increases. Since the standard deviation is relatively low, the RSSI measurement is unlikely to "overlap",[a] the probability of correct prediction converges to 1.0 as N_{predict} approaches 11 for all the algorithms except DT.

If the standard deviation of shadowing (σ) is increased, the probability of correct prediction will become lower. This is expected because when the standard deviation is higher, there is more "overlap" between fingerprinted locations. We repeated the experiment using $\sigma = 6$ dB, the probability was about 0.66 at $N_{\text{predict}} = 1$ and 0.95 at $N_{\text{predict}} = 11$.

From the results above, it was determined that the required number of measurements used to perform a single prediction depends on the characteristics of the RSSI measurement. If a group of RSSI measurements are known to be at the same location, then that group should be used as a whole to perform the classification to maximize prediction correctness. Probability of correct localization is expected to slowly converge to 1 as N_{predict} is increased.

---

[a] If different groups of RSSI measurements can be represented by probability density functions, then overlap occurs when the probability density functions lie on top of each other.

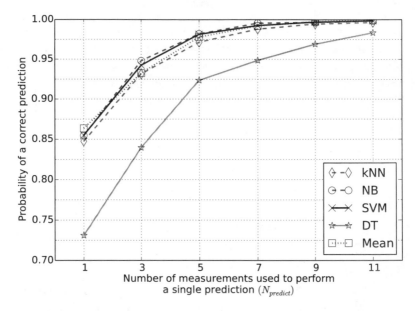

Figure 17.5 Probability of correct prediction versus the number of measurements used to perform a single prediction, using $\sigma = 4$.

17.4.2 *Analysis on Real Data*

17.4.2.1 Analysis on the number of measurements per fingerprinted location used in the training phase

In this experiment, we collected on average 200 measurements per fingerprinted location. Unlike the simulated experiment, the measurements were collected on four different orientations: north, south, east and west, that is, 50 measurements per orientation. Using randomly selected subsets of the collected measurement, we were able to plot Fig. 17.6. This is the same as the first analysis on simulated data. The x-axis is the number of measurements per fingerprinted location used as training data (N_{train}), and the y-axis is the probability of correct prediction. The train-test phase was repeated 2000 times for every N_{train}. One measurement was used to perform the prediction ($N_{\text{predict}} = 1$).

Unlike the results from Fig. 17.4, there were a lot more variation between the different classifiers when real data was used.

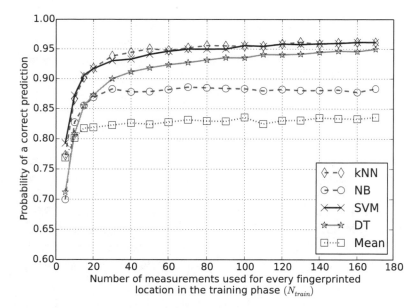

Figure 17.6 Prediction size analysis using real data in an office environment.

The mean classifier has the lowest percentage of correct localization, this was expected because the collected measurements often do not follow a normal distribution. Naive Bayes has the second lowest percentage of correct localization. This may be due to two reasons. First, the likelihood is calculated using the Gaussian probability density function on data that might not strictly follow a Gaussian distribution. Second, the conditional independence assumption is not always true, this is the more likely reason out of the two.

DT was performing a lot better here than in Section 17.4.1.1. We found that the number of unique RSSI measurements in the real data was 12, and the number of unique RSSI measurements in the fictitious data was 30. Less variation in the data will cause the chance of over-fitting to decrease, hence the improvement in performance.

The DT classifier was not as good as kNN or SVM. Both performed exceptionally well on almost all N_{train}, having a correct localization probability above 95% at maximum N_{train}. The overall probability of correct prediction was increasing, which agrees with the results from the analysis on simulated data. We did not run an analysis using different values of $N_{predict}$ for the same training and testing data because a high probability of correct prediction was already achieved using $N_{predict} = 1$.

17.4.2.2 Monitor subset analysis using confusion matrix

Using fewer monitors is likely to decrease the probability of correct prediction, we attempted to identify where the misclassification will occur using confusion matrices and the results are discussed below.

Confusion matrix is a common way to visualize the performance of a machine learning algorithm. For this analysis, we used SVM as it is one of the most popular algorithms [5], and it also performed exceptionally well in our tests. Figure 17.7 is the confusion matrix constructed using 80% of all the available for the training phase

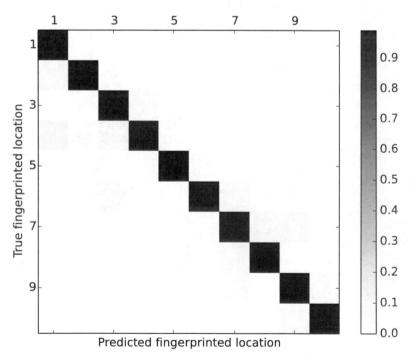

Figure 17.7 Confusion Matrix constructed using SVM classifier with monitors $m_{1,2,3,4}$.

and the remaining data for the testing phase when all four monitors are turned on. The y-axis represents the true fingerprinted location (m_1 to m_{10}) and the x-axis represents the predicted fingerprinted location. If all the predictions are perfect, i.e. the true fingerprinted location is equal to the predicted fingerprinted location, then we expect the diagonal squares to all be black. The advantage of this matrix is that, when misclassification occurs, we are able to visually identify which fingerprinted location is causing it. With this information, it will be possible to adjust the fingerprint and/or monitor locations accordingly to improve accuracy. When all four monitors were used, all the classes had an accuracy above 90%, and there was no significant misclassification for any particular fingerprinted location.

Next, monitors 2 were 3 were removed, and the classification was performed again but using monitors 1 and 4 only, the result is shown in Fig. 17.8. The majority of the unknown data from

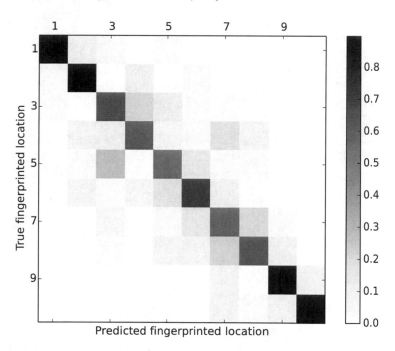

Figure 17.8 Confusion Matrix constructed using SVM classifier with monitors $m_{1,4}$.

fingerprinted locations 1, 2, 9 and 10 were classified correctly. This is likely due to their proximity to monitors 1 and 4. However, a lot of the remaining data were misclassified. From the position of the gray squares, we can see that the misclassification occurred mainly between neighbouring fingerprinted locations. There was very little or no misclassification between fingerprinted locations that were far away, for example between fp_1 and fp_{10}. We repeated the same analysis for other combinations of monitors and the same results were observed.

Two discoveries were made in this section: (1) Probability of correct localization is expected to decrease for fingerprinted locations at regions that are far away from any monitor. (2) In those regions, the classifier is more likely to get confused between neighbouring fingerprinted locations.

17.5 Conclusion

We tested four popular classification algorithms: Naive Bayes, k-Nearest Neighbours, Support Vector Machines and Decision Trees for Wi-Fi localization in indoor environments.

Naive Bayes classifier is one of the simplest classifiers. Since the RSSI measurements often follow a Gaussian distribution, the likelihood is calculated using the Gaussian probability density function. It does not require any user-defined parameters therefore grid search is not needed prior to executing the algorithm. Its performance was decent on all our tests that used fictitious data since those data strictly followed a Gaussian distribution. This is also its weakness, if the input data has an arbitrary distribution or the data is not conditionally independent, naive Bayes may not perform as well as the alternatives. It is a good candidate to try first as it is easy to implement, has short execution time and does not require any parameters. However, to maximize the probability of correct prediction, we recommend using an alternative classifier.

K-Nearest Neighbours is the second algorithm we investigated. kNN needs a user-supplied parameter: k. It is an excellent classifier in all the radio environments investigated in this work. However, great care must be taken when using it on large applications since it is required to store all the data internally to build the model.

SVM is another classifier that performed well in all our experiments. Like kNN, it requires some user supplied parameters. Unlike kNN, it is likely to scale up to bigger problem sizes because it keeps a memory efficient internal model. However, understanding theory behind SVM may not be a trivial task.

The final algorithm we tested was the Decision Tree classifier. Due to over-fitting problems, its performance was significantly lower than all the other algorithms when used on fictitious data. However, this problem did not occur on real data because there were fewer unique readings. We do not recommend DT classifier because it may not work well certain radio environments.

Some important discoveries were made that are not specific to the algorithms. We identified the importance of the number of training data. We also identified that increasing the prediction size can increase the probability of correct localization. Diminishing return has an effect on both of those two properties. Furthermore, understanding was attained on the effect of using a less than optimal number of monitors, consequently fingerprinted locations at regions that are far away from the monitors is likely to be misclassified.

Although new insights were acquired in this work, there are still a lot of questions waiting to be answered for indoor localization problems. There may be ways to optimize the monitor placements to improve probability of correct prediction. There are many other classification algorithms that we have not investigated, e.g. artificial neural networks, adaptive boosting. Finally, all our tests were done on a flat plane, but Wi-Fi signals can penetrate ceilings and floors which makes 3D fingerprinting an interesting possibility.

Acknowledgements

The authors would like to thank Athanasios Gkelias for his helpful discussion. Kin Leung is partly supported by the EPSRC Pathways to Impact funding scheme.

References

1. Analytics, S. (2012). Strategy analytics: Worldwide smartphone population tops 1 billion in Q3 2012, http://www.businesswire.com/news/home/20121017005479/en/Strategy-Analytics-Worldwide-Smartphone-Population-Tops-1.

2. Bahl, P. and Padmanabhan, V. N. (2000). Radar: An in-building RF-based user location and tracking system, in *IEEE INFOCOM 2000. Nineteenth Annual Joint Conference of the IEEE Computer and Communications Societies. Proceedings. IEEE*, vol. 2 (IEEE), pp. 775–784.

3. Bolliger, P. L. (2011). *Robust Indoor Positioning through Adaptive Collaborative Labeling of Location Fingerprints*, Ph.D. thesis, ETH Zurich.

4. Bose, A. and Foh, C. H. (2007). A practical path loss model for indoor wifi positioning enhancement, in *Information, Communications & Signal Processing, IEEE 6th International Conference on*, pp. 1–5.

5. Data Mining Algorithms in R/Classification/SVM (2013). Wikibooks, https://en.wikibooks.org/wiki/Data_Mining_Algorithms_In_R/Classificatio% n/SVM.

6. d'Otreppe, T. (2013). Aircrack-ng, http://www.aircrack-ng.org.

7. Ekahau, I. (2012). Ekahau, http://www.ekahau.com/.

8. King, T., Kopf, S., Haenselmann, T., Lubberger, C. and Effelsberg, W. (2006). Compass: A probabilistic indoor positioning system based on 802.11 and digital compasses, in *Proceedings of the ACM 1st International Workshop on Wireless Network Testbeds, Experimental Evaluation & Characterization*, pp. 34–40.

9. Martin, E., Vinyals, O., Friedland, G. and Bajcsy, R. (2010). Precise indoor localization using smart phones, in *Proceedings of the International Conference on Multimedia* (ACM, New York, NY, USA), pp. 787–790.

10. Mitchell, T. (1997). *Machine Learning* (McGraw Hill).

11. National Coordination Office for Space-Based Positioning, Navigation, and Timing (2013). The global positioning system, http://www.gps.gov/systems/gps/.

12. Otsason, V., Varshavsky, A., LaMarca, A. and De Lara, E. (2005). Accurate GSM indoor localization, in *UbiComp 2005: Ubiquitous Computing* (Springer), pp. 141–158.

13. Pedregosa, F., Varoquaux, G., Gramfort, A., Michel, V., Thirion, B., Grisel, O., Blondel, M., Prettenhofer, P., Weiss, R., Dubourg, V., Vanderplas, J., Passos, A., Cournapeau, D., Brucher, M., Perrot, M. and Duchesnay, E.

(2011). Scikit-learn: Machine learning in Python, *Journal of Machine Learning Research* **12**, pp. 2825–2830.

14. Rai, A., Chintalapudi, K. K., Padmanabhan, V. N. and Sen, R. (2012). Zee: Zero-effort crowdsourcing for indoor localization, in *Proceedings of the ACM 18th Annual International Conference on Mobile Computing and Networking,* pp. 293–304.

15. Rehim, M. A. A. A. Y. A. (2004). *Robust Indoor Positioning through Adaptive Collaborative Labeling of Location Fingerprints*, Ph.D. thesis, University of Maryland.

16. Russell, S. J. and Norvig, P. (2010). *Artificial Intelligence: A Modern Approach*, 3rd edn. (Pearson Education), ISBN 0-13-207148-7.

17. The Wireshark team (2013). Tshark, http://www.wireshark.org/docs/man-pages/tshark.html.

PART V

FINALE

Chapter 18

Our World Is Better Served by DSP Technologies and Their Innovative Solutions

Paulina Chan

Imperial College London,
South Kensington Campus, London SW7 2AZ, UK
paulina.chan@alumni.imperial.ac.uk

18.1 Synopsis

DSP is embedded in almost all communications devices, systems, and networks. DSP technologies offer many and novel solutions to satisfy personal needs and industry requirements. Our social values have changed and so have the business practices. Development of DSP applications addresses many topical areas of world interests and challenges. Healthcare technology and availability to all, information access management and control, transborder data flows and privacy, intelligent mobility, environmental protection, ecology and resource development are on the list of priority. Our quality of life is improving. Let us celebrate the innovations of DSP which is a

Trends in Digital Signal Processing: A Festschrift in Honour of A. G. Constantinides
Edited by Yong Ching Lim, Hon Keung Kwan, and Wan-Chi Siu
Copyright © 2016 Pan Stanford Publishing Pte. Ltd.
ISBN 978-981-4669-50-4 (Hardcover), 978-981-4669-51-1 (eBook)
www.panstanford.com

significant influence and a major contributor to the dynamic digital economy.

18.2 DSP Offers Solutions to Societal Needs and Sets Technology Trends

The goals are set for the initiation and development of DSP (digital signal processing)—in theories and with applications. Technologies and applications of DSP offer solutions to societal needs and set technology trends in intelligent data and image processing. DSP technologies expressed in complex symbols and sophisticated simulations cover a wide spectrum of core components in hardware and software systems. The fields of digital filtering techniques and complicated transformation equations, large varieties and many variations in signal processing, and the huge cloud in communications networks of people, data and things are major achievements in building and sustaining the DSP framework. DSP technologies are embedded in the development of new products and new services across industry segments. DSP is the pivotal change agent that has made great contribution to impact world economy and life styles.

Wide coverage and fast tempo in global pursuit of digital economy have ignited a large variety and many variations in R&D as well as an influx of new products and new services. Very intelligent devices, novel communications systems, smart gadgets and advanced networks and services are introduced very rapidly and regularly to the world markets. The benefits of all great solutions bring instant and easy access to information, improved quality of life, universal and available healthcare, and energy and resource conservation, among others. These emerging phenomena present many opportunities for new product and service development. They also require the user communities—individuals and businesses alike to generate, learn and adapt to a new set of practices. Rural and urban communities are facing the same challenges. R&D professionals, engineers, industry partners and business enterprises are committed to fulfil their societal responsibilities while they are inventing the science and technology of DSP and delivering their applications. Original algorithms and complex methodologies of DSP and their applications are keys to open many doors of innovations and global initiatives. DSP is indispensable in all the intelligent designs. The technology is a strategic yet a low-key partner in all big networks and small nanochips, in local neighbourhoods and at the worldwide webs.

Core team members of DSP are cross-disciplinary. Topical DSP solutions are designed in partnership with the healthcare industry, ICT providers, construction industry, energy resource management, smart communities, and governments. The list is expanding.

Applications of DSP are being developed along an evolving path in high speed to satisfy computing and communications demands in the digital economy. The development should benefit all stakeholders, including consumers, industries, and governments of the world. DSP adds value to the paradigm shift in many centres of excellence. DSP solutions generate business revenues, assist in disaster recoveries, support crisis management, and champion the spirit of technology innovations.

The applications and solutions of DSP technologies in four topical areas of global interests have experienced paradigm shifts:

1. Universal and Personalised Healthcare
2. Internet of Data/Things/People in Communications
3. Smart Cities Applications and Sustainable Ecology
4. Green Technologies and Renewable Energy

18.3   Area 1: Universal and Personalised Healthcare

Public and private spending in healthcare is growing rapidly and tremendously. Reference to the World Health Organization (WHO), the total expenditure on health (2010) as percentage of GDP was: 17.6% of the USA, 9.6% of the UK, and 5% of China. The statistics re Per Capita of Government Expenditure on Health were (in USD): $4,000 in the USA, $2,900 in the UK, and $200 in China.

DSP applications in I-Healthcare.

The market for world healthcare is expected to grow from $99.6 billion in 2010 to $162.2 billion in 2015, at a CAGR (Compund Annual Growth Rate) of 10.2%. The needs to counter environmental challenges, cut healthcare costs, enhance clinical/administrative workflow of hospitals, and huge demand for faster, error-free, efficient healthcare delivery, are driving public and private healthcare providers to invest in advanced technologies. Information technologies and engineering are the business operation and management aids in Intelligent Healthcare (I-Healthcare), a movement of Healthcare Reform.

I-Healthcare involves extensive applications of DSP solutions. Deployments of the DSP solutions enhance the service features and reduce the costs in healthcare systems and management. Special priority is given to universal and personalised healthcare to all, healthcare technology for silver age, and assistive technology healthcare. The current state-of-the-art healthcare systems aim to improve significantly the clinical benefits of drugs and healthcare management in order to serve an expanded patient population. The president and premier of China announced in 2014 that healthcare reform was the top priority for "social harmony".

China has emergent needs for I-Healthcare products and services. Reference to the China Ministry of Health: healthcare spending is projected to be US$1 trillion in 2020 (i.e. a 10-fold increase in ten years.) With a population of 1.4 billion (i.e. 4 times of that in the USA,) the market size and business opportunity of universal and personalised healthcare in China are among the world's most attractive, and by far the fastest-growing of all the large emerging countries. Current state-of-the-art medical-device and-equipment companies, such as GE Healthcare and Philips, have annual revenues of more than US$1 billion in the China market and are growing.

Universal healthcare requires cross-disciplinary cooperation and active involvement among governments, R&D organisations, and industries. For example, China has organised cross-ministerial development among their Ministries of Health, Science & Technology, and Industry & Information Technology. All participate collectively in developing the electronic-biomedical industry.

In the UK, universities and industries have formulated cross-departmental collaborations among the departments of medicine, bioengineering, electrical and electronic engineering, chemistry, computing, mathematics, and the business school to do research, develop and market DSP-based biomedical equipment and systems for the futuristic healthcare industry. Most is done through partnerships in R&D and manufacturing.

18.3.1 *The Synergy of Engineering and I-Healthcare in Global Healthcare Innovation*

On a multidisciplinary team to solve complex health problems, engineering provides DSP technology platforms for I-Healthcare products and services, e.g. robotic surgery, digital image processing, equipment and system designs as a synergy.

18.3.2 *Big Data for I-Care Systems*

There is also an emergent need and market for some Big Data for the Intelligent-Care Systems (I-Care). This is a significant example of large-scale DSP-embedded solutions. When it is compiled, systems alike Care data in the UK will be a giant database of medical records showing how individuals have been cared for across the physicians and hospital sectors. The information will be vital in helping healthcare providers and the various ministries to assess diseases, examine new drugs and new treatments on the market, as well as identify infection outbreaks. The information is management aids to monitor the performance of the multi-tier healthcare in towns and countries. The data is solid information for planning national service deployment to the wide spreading population in many municipalities and across nations.

It is noted that privacy issues and personal data on public records would be a concern to many. Intelligent healthcare systems are efficient and effective for the identified region especially in crisis management and many exceptional circumstances, such as during an epidemic outbreak, at earthquake rescue and recovery. DSP offers fundamental technologies to the core competence of universal healthcare initiatives that add value to people.

18.3.3 *I-Training and Education*

Products and services of I-Healthcare would assist in training and continued education of physicians and other medical personnel, locating the availability of effective drugs that patients can trust, and the founding of integrated networks of primary and tertiary institutions to manage patient flows effectively.

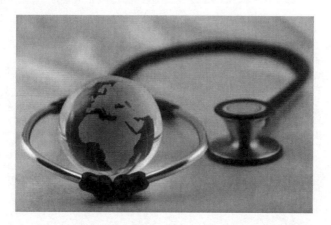

DSP solutions, systems and devices would also assist in better and earlier diagnoses, higher rates of treatment and compliance with therapies. Examples of DSP-assisted medical technologies are: endovascular robotics, energy based devices, human factors and ergonomics, point of care diagnostics, venous disease, robotic cardiac surgery, and personalised medicine.

There are also examples in collaborations between academic R&D and those of the pharmaceutical industry. The Phenome Research Centre in the UK is in partnership with GlaxoSmithKline, inheriting the anti-doping facilities used to test samples during the 2012 Olympic and Paralympic Games.

18.3.4 *Apply Omics Science to Clinical Applications*

At Imperial College London, there is a development in the translation of omics science to clinical applications for predictive and diagnostic biotechnology and engineering. Professor Jeremy Nicholson, head of the Department of Surgery and Cancer, is the champion of the team. The team designs mega data bases for futuristic medical applications. Cyber technologies and treatments have been developed for many clinical and diagnostic deployments.

Imperial College London in collaboration with Waters researchers, led by Dr Zoltan Takats (Medicine), have developed an intelligent knife that can tell surgeons immediately whether the tissue they are cutting is cancerous or not.

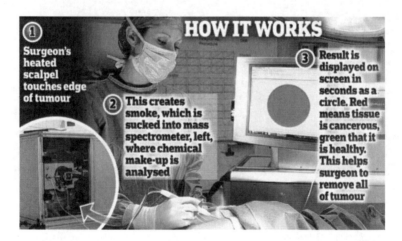

In the first study to test the invention in the operating theatre, the "iKnife" diagnosed tissue samples from 91 patients with 100% accuracy, instantly providing information that ordinarily takes up to half an hour to reveal using laboratory tests.

18.4 Area 2: Internet of Data/Things/People in Communications

One significant DSP-based information portal is information and computing technology (ICT). ICT ignited Smart Revolution from material movement to digital economy. At the midst of the Smart Revolution, the DSP-based portals are free for supporters, open to the public, and they are big in size and widespread in coverage. Information technologies have updated themselves and have begun to deliver for the global trend on demand to all in absolute "smartness" and total availability.

Expertise in DSP technologie has the current state-of-the-art and know-how to build complex structures of intelligence in the ICT portals. The smart deliverables rely on cyberspace that is also resilient, intrinsically safe and secure.

18.4.1 *DSP in ICT Industry*

The market potential of DSP applications in the ICT industry is huge. Reference to the consolidated view of: ITU (International Telecommunication Union, Switzerland), IDC (International Data Corporation, USA), McKenzie Group Consultant (UK), AT&T and IBM,

the global spending on the revolutionary multimedia ICT was US$3.6 trillion (2011) with a CAGR (compound annual growth rate) of 18.4%.

DSP technologies are integral to the innovation-driven economies. DSP solutions cover a number of related disciplines: from semiconductor design and production, through hardware manufacture (mainframes, servers, intelligent devices for end users), to software, data storage, backup and retrieval, networking, and the Internet.

18.4.2 *Making the Digital Economy Smarter*

Technology is moving fast. DSP products and services prepare updates and support the Digital Economy. DSP applications, such as 5-G Mobile Networks, Internet of Things (IoT), Big Data and cloud computing, and Internet of People are in demand with very promising growth patterns.

18.4.2.1 Fifth-Generation Mobile Networks and Systems

Reference to the NGMN Alliance (Next Generation Mobile Networks Alliance): By 2020, 5G networks will be deployed to support new applications such as the Internet of Things, broadcast quality services, emergency communications in time of natural disaster. Major requirements of 5G are: the increase of communications bandwidth available to transmit very big information files, reduction in power consumption and infrastructure costs, improvement in spectral efficiency, and increase in the resilience of the network. 5G networks adopt new technologies such as mesh networking which is also DSP-based. Mesh networking allows devices to communicate with each other directly without relying on signal transfers through the bay-stations on the network. Advanced and accurate signalling support data rate at several tens of Mb/s for tens of thousands of users, 1 Gbit/s to be offered simultaneously to tens of workers on the same office floor, several hundreds of thousands of simultaneous connections for massive sensor deployments.

18.4.2.2 Internet of Things

Internet of Things (IoT) was first documented by Kevin Ashton, a British visionary, in 1999. IoT is the network of physical objects or "things" embedded with electronics, software, sensors and connectivity. DSP technology is embedded in these "things" and devices and covers a variety of protocols, domains, and applications. Examples of Things in the IoT could be a wide variety of devices such as heart monitoring implants, biochip transponders on farm animals, electric clams in coastal waters, automobiles with built-in sensors, or field operation devices that assist fire-fighters in search and rescue, smart thermostat systems and washer/dryers that utilize Wi-Fi for remote monitoring. These devices collect useful data with the help of DSP technologies and then autonomously flow the data between other devices.

IoT enables smart things and the network to achieve greater value and service by exchanging data with the manufacturer, users, operators, and other connected smart things and smart devices. Each thing is uniquely identifiable through its embedded DSP technology but is able to interoperate within the existing internet infrastructure. This wide variety of smart objects and smart devices is in automation, in nearly all fields.

18.4.2.3 Internet of Big Data and Cloud Computing

IoT is also expected to generate a large amount of data from diverse locations that is aggregated very quickly, thereby increasing the need to better index, store and process such data.

Big Data is able to process and analyse data sets at ever greater orders of magnitudes. For example, Big Data has the capacity in transforming science from genome sequencing to the search for the Higg's boson.

Big Data technology and solutions were predicted (2014) to grow at a 27% CAGR to US$32.4 billion through 2017, i.e. about six times the growth rate of the overall ICT market. There is a wide range of applications for Big Data, with examples including the analysis of sentiment on social media and the calculation of house prices based on factors such as traffic levels and crime rates.

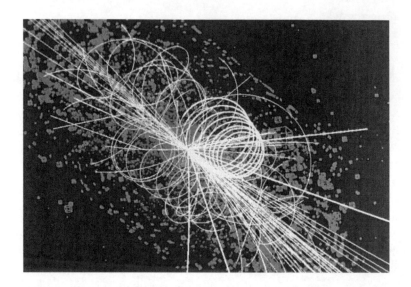

Cloud computing has been a major item in corporate spending considering that "the cloud" encompasses DSP technologies in servers, storage, networking, and application services. Spending on cloud computing is predicted to increase four times faster than traditional ICT spending overall. Worldwide spending on "public cloud" services was US$74 billion in 2010 with 20% CAGR. The spending will reach US$177 billion in 2015. The growth of "cloud infrastructure" has the highest CAGR of 49% through 2017.

Cloud computing changes business practices and contributes to cost reduction. For example, a significant amount of data that can be described as Big Data in the datacentres will either get disposed of or archived to the cloud, which will result in cost reduction in traditional storage at the datacentres.

18.4.2.4 Internet of People and Online Gaming

People are spending much time in online communications and online games. The online habit and online leisure have become an ever-more-important sector of the information technology market. For example, global spending on gaming was US$74 billion in 2011 with 10.4% CAGR. The eco-system of Internet of People comprises high-end intelligent devices and the virtual environment for online systems and online games.

The industry of personal communications and computing gaming is growing along the penetration rate of DSP-embedded intelligent devices and telecommunications networks, e.g. smartphones, iPads, notebooks, and internets. The ITU has published a world average of 95% global penetration of cellular phones and other end-user intelligent devices. The anticipated growth of products and applications in virtual reality and artificial intelligence for leisure and at work is here and now.

Besides technologies, personal communications and computer gaming projects must consider the psychological aspect for general acceptance by the public and the changes of social behaviours and life styles. This is a remarkable phenomenon and a huge research area in many business schools and departments of social science in the world.

18.5 Area 3: Smart City Applications and Sustainable Ecology

The definition varies on "What makes a city smart?" The European Innovation Partnership on Smart Cities and Communities (EIP-SCC) said that "smart cities are defined by their innovations, their ability to solve problems, and use of communication technologies to improve this capacity."

As business skills are used to deliver sustainable economic development and a higher quality of life, engaging citizens and managing natural resources are as essential.

DSP technologies support the intelligence-systems which are major enablers to build smart communities, smart buildings, and smart planet. Cities and countries in Europe are pioneers of Smart Societies. Sweden, Vienna, Verona, Amsterdam, Eindhoven, Lyon, Malaga, Malta are all good examples of smart cities, smart regions and smart districts.

Advancement in DSP makes smart cities smarter so they are ready to provide for a strong increase in urban migration. As projected by the WHO, for the first time ever, the majority of the world's population resides in a city. The proportion continues to grow from 20% to 40% of the global population who moved to live in cities in the last century, to more than half of all people lived in an urban area in 2010, and then the proportion of city dwellers is expected to rise to 70% by 2050. There are great needs for better city planning, efficient use of natural resources, and effective use of intelligent technologies. More smart cities are needed to serve the urban population.

The market opportunity is rich for all suppliers who build smart cities. It is also a great incentive to do focus R&D on smart living with all kinds of smart technologies, in particular smart power grids.

18.5.1 *Smart Grids*

Intelligent electricity networks–Smart Grids are a key component in the energy strategy. Smart Grid projects have been growing with great results in smart energy utilization and effective distribution.

Smart grid integrates utility Information Technology (IT) with Operational Technology (OT) in Sweden.

The EcoGrid System in island Bornholm, Sweden, is a sustainable energy demonstration project debuted in 2013. Through this project, the utility Østkraft is integrating onto one power grid: electricity transmitted from the mainland via cable with locally generated energy from wind, solar, biomass, and biogas. The EcoGrid also provides 10% of the business accounts with information on power pricing and availability. Residential participants are equipped with demand response devices/appliances using gateways and smart controllers to control electric heating, water heaters, battery storage and heat pumps. This enables flexible, customer-programmed, automated demand response to real-time price signals.

At a time when the world is experiencing slower economic growth, building smart cities will be a significant driving force for not only the information industry but also related frugal industries.

China is a growing market for smart cities where IT infrastructure and communications are used to make life more convenient. At the Smart City Expo (2014) the market size of smart cities in China alone is expected to reach US$165 billion.

The opportunities in building smart cities in Africa are tremendous. With no to minimal installed base, many countries are in the process of building fundamental infrastructure from civil and mechanical engineering projects to high-tech communications networks. New development could all be "smart" from the start. The urbanisation movement is phenomenal because the African populations in many countries are migrating to the cities for work and to live. International countries are supporting the African Union in many joint projects adopting and applying intelligence-technologies.

18.5.2 *Modelling Some Smart Applications in Smart Cities in the USA and at Imperial College London*

Different applications of DSP technologies in smart cities are summarized in Boston, Seattle, Scottsdale (Arizona), and at Imperial College London. Members in partnerships include Massachusetts Institute of Technology, University of Washington's School of Medicine, Imperial College London, Microsoft, NEC, The Boeing Co., Sheraton Hotel, U.S. Department of Energy, U.S. Economic Development Administration, and numerous city governments.

The partnerships ensure a list of objectives: innovative applications, better planning, a more participatory approach, higher energy efficiency, better transport solutions, and intelligent use of intelligent tools such as Big Data, mobile networks, web portals, sensors and tracking systems, social media. The solutions bring tangible benefits such as enhancing quality of life, improving government processes, and reducing energy consumption to the cities and people.

18.5.2.1 A Wireless Mesh Network to monitor Traffic

One smart city is Scottsdale, Arizona. The city has been using a wireless mesh network (since 2013) which links to more than 300 traffic signal controllers and 110 high-definition video cameras to monitor traffic flow, as well as 36 electronic signs that inform drivers in real time about traffic congestion and collisions. A fibre optic network leverages wireless mesh radios for the last mile.

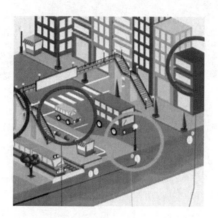

The Traffic Management Center and the Arizona Department of Transportation analyse movement patterns and model transit demand. The results help create a route design that maximizes ridership while minimizing cost and average commute time. The ability to view live video feeds from heavy traffic areas allows officials to make fast decisions on how to prevent or reduce congestion, improve information given to drivers via the signs and actively manage traffic affected by special events, weather and emergency.

18.5.2.2 The All Traffic Solutions

The Boston Transportation Department has launched All Traffic Solutions which is designed to proactively improve traffic flow in the city's Innovation District. The program includes the use of electronic Time-to-Destination message signs. A cloud-based application will be accessed to generate the signs which provide drivers with accurate, constantly updated travel times to key destinations across multiple routes.

The goals are to reduce traffic snarls and help get travellers to their destinations faster; the city will monitor the impact the signage has on those goals through driver surveys.

There are 330 Smart Parking sensors installed in the neighbour-hood that work with free mobile app to provide drivers with real-time data about available on-street parking spaces. The city expects the sensors to reduce traffic congestion caused by drivers circling around looking for open parking spots.

Street Bump is another effort involving technology to enhance quality of life in Boston in partnership with utility companies. It aims at helping residents improve neighbourhood streets. As users drive, a mobile application with built-in GPS running on a smartphone collects data about the smoothness of the ride and reports obstacles e.g. sunken manhole covers. Data provides the city with real-time information that it uses to fix problems and plan long-term investments in road construction.

18.5.2.3   A High-Performance Building Programme

In July 2013, Seattle launched its High-Performance 2030 Building Program that allows real-time tracking of energy efficiency to help

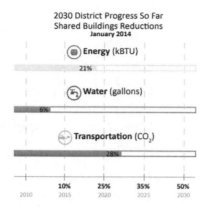

reduce both costs and carbon emissions. The "smart buildings" partnership is formulated among the city, Microsoft's CityNext initiative and a public-private collaborative of downtown Seattle property owners. The program creates "building information systems" to capture and centralize real-time data from the equipment that runs buildings' heating, cooling and lighting systems. The systems analyse data to identify and report items that could lead to inefficient equipment performance and energy waste. Building staff can use this data to adjust elements in each room of a building—such as lighting, temperature and the position of window shades—to maximize energy efficiency. The project aims to reduce power consumption through real-time data analyses. The program uses analytic software and Cloud services to gain deeper insight from data generated by building management systems, sensors, controls and meters. Building managers can monitor building energy usage and efficiency.

18.5.2.4 At Imperial College London

Note that Imperial College London and the telecommunication company NEC Corporation established a Smart Water Systems Lab at the College. The Lab develops new technologies to monitor the UK's Victorian water infrastructure and optimize how it is managed. In this 5-year collaboration, researchers at the Lab will pioneer smart sensors and data analysis tools engineered to monitor and control water flow and pressure in pipes. The research will draw on the expertise from across the College, in the departments of Civil and Environmental Engineering, and Computing.

18.6 Area 4: Green Technologies and Renewable Energy

Also known as clean technology, green technology refers to the use of technology that makes products and processes more environmentally friendly, for example, by reducing CO_2 emissions or by making products more biodegradable. Overall, green technology aims at contributing to environmental sustainability.

—Financial Times

There are prominent green technologies that give us hope for a sustainable future. DSP technologies are applied in the exploration, designs and constructions of infrastructures, operation analyses, assessment and review process of green technologies in the green field.

Green industry is also a multidisciplinary sector which covers the technologies and expertise in chemical engineering, chemistry, civil and environmental engineering, earth science, electrical and electronic engineering, life sciences, materials, mathematics, mechanical engineering, and physics. Exemplary subject areas of green technology are green chemistry, green IT and green housing. "Green technology" is also used to describe sustainable energy generation technologies such as photovoltaics, wind turbines, bioreactors, etc.

Multinational corporations and governments have committed to investing in a sustainable future, e.g. a contract (2014) between the Royal Dutch Shell and the UK government which funds £100 million on a carbon capture and storage programme at a power plant in Aberdeenshire. The goal is to provide 500,000 homes with clean energy by capturing 10 million tons of carbon dioxide emissions.

General Electric invested US$5 billion in the first five years in the R&D of clean technology and generated US$70 billion in ecomagination revenues. The company launched the "ecomagination initiative" in 2005 on R&D in solar energy, hybrid locomotives, lower-emission aircraft engines, lighter and stronger durable materials, efficient lighting, and water purification technology.

Venture capitalists are also active in searching for innovations to commit themselves in green tech sectors. Some prominent green technologies are thriving, and some of them are yet not in the mainstream but are expected to be soon.

18.6.1 *Multidisciplinary Teams at Imperial College London on Green*

18.6.1.1 Wind Turbine Industry Analysis at the Business School

Currently in the UK 7.5% of the nation's electricity is generated by over 4000 individual wind turbines deployed across 531 wind farms. The UK is one of the best locations for wind power in the world and is considered to be the best in Europe.

Researchers at Imperial College London are doing extensive analyses using data from NASA over a twenty year period to measure the wind speed at the exact site of each onshore wind farm in the UK. Researchers developed a formula to calculate how wear and tear of the machinery affects the performance of the turbine to help determine the life span of newer wind farms for a favourable return of economic benefits. The results showed that the turbines will last their full life of about 25 years before they need to be upgraded. This is comparable to the performance of gas turbines used in power stations. The IC team says this makes a strong business case for further investment in the wind farm industry, as directed by Dr Iain

Staffell and Professor Richard Green, Head of the Department of Management, IC Business School.

18.6.1.2 The Energy Futures Lab at the Engineering Faculty

The Energy Futures Lab at Imperial College London is a multidisciplinary unit. It is focus on cross-faculty research initiatives designed to meet broader energy challenges and facilitate the transition to a sustainable energy economy. Its overarching aim is to produce an integrated view of future energy supply, demand and distribution that encompasses technological, environmental, economic, and security aspects. It develops highly skilled professionals in cross-cutting energy analysis and technologies.

The Lab has developed research networks to enable communication between departments and particular technological groupings on: solar, electric and hybrid vehicles and carbon capture and storage. It also has strong links with industry and a constantly evolving project portfolio. The Lab is directed by Professor Tim Green, Professor of Electrical Power Engineering. It has collaborated with Alstom, BP, Shell, E.ON UK, EDF Energy, Scottish Power (Iberdrola), BG Group and Geothermal International.

 Energy Futures Lab

18.6.2 *Green Architecture in the UK*

Green architecture is the most widely implemented and environment friendly structure in construction spaces. The goal is to control the use of natural resources and to make urban expansion more sustainable. Green buildings are constructed to make the best use of natural light and insulation to increase energy efficiency and reduce energy consumption. Other features of green architecture include sourcing of materials from landfills and urban waste, reduced waste production and aiming for zero levels of emissions, water waste, energy waste etc. DSP-based technologies are embedded in all intelligent sensors, devices, construction designs, analysis and communications hardware and software systems.

BedZED is located in the suburb of London, UK. It is designed to have minimal ecological impact in both construction and operation. It was built with materials from recycled or renewable sources within a 56 km distance from the site; and aims at generating most of the energy it needs from renewable sources that include 777 m^2 of solar panels. Houses face south to maximize exposure to sunlight, and are fitted with good thermal insulation and triple-glazed windows to reduce heat transfer. Appliances chosen are low-energy and low-water, and use recycled water as much as possible. There are facilities to collect rain water for reuse, as well as recycling provisions at all garbage collection points.

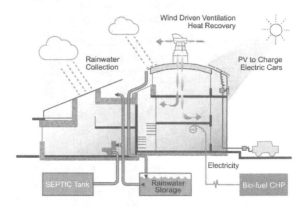

BedZED residents are encouraged to walk, cycle and use public transport. Parking space is limited to discourage driving, and come with charging stations for electric cars. An on-site car club allows homeowners to use a vehicle when they need one.

As a result of these practices, BedZED homeowners have a smaller carbon footprint than the local average. They consume 45% less electricity and 81% less heat (from gas), use over 50% less water from the public system, and have 65% fewer fossil-fuel car miles driven.

18.6.3 *Green Mobility in the USA*

While electric cars have seen an emergence in recent years, internal combustion engines are expected to continue to run most vehicles across the world, but in a new eco-friendly avatar. In the US, the EPA (Environmental Protection Agency) has been encouraging more fuel-efficient and carbon emission controlled engine designs especially in the heavy duty vehicle sector. China has stated a greater focus on energy saving engines that will account for 60% of the total engines used by 2015. Electric engines should be more robust to variation in fuel, deliver high peak efficiency rather than elastic power delivery and also be able to be produced in high volume to control costs.

For example, electric car-maker Tesla in California, USA, uses a liquid-cooled AC motor at a capacity of 16,000 rpm, and powered by 85 kWh lithium-ion battery pack to produce 362 horsepower and 325 pound-feet of torque. The electric vehicle is on the best seller icon, meeting a BMW owner's definition of a sports sedan. Recently, it is reported that two of the world's most innovative companies

Tesla and Apple may have discussed collaboration, according to a *San Francisco Chronicle* report.

18.6.4 *Solar Farms and Solar Grids*

18.6.4.1 Sahara Desert: The Source of Solar Energy

If just 0.3% of the Saharan Desert was used for a concentrating solar plant, it would produce enough power to provide all of Europe with clean renewable energy.

—Time Magazine

Twenty multinational corporations led by German companies discuss plans and investments to create the Dessertech Industrial Innovation Initiative, proposing to erect 100 GW of concentrating solar power plants throughout Northern Africa. The Sahara renewable energy belt is estimated to be worth US$555 billion.

The Sahara Solar Breeder Project (Japan) turns Desert into Energy Source. The project uses the world's biggest desert as its main energy source. The initiative is to build silicon manufacturing and solar power plants in the desert, in turn using the power generated from these plants to build even more silicon and power plants in a "breeding" process.

Scientists are hoping that such plants will be able to supply energy worldwide through DC power lines using high-temperature superconductors. While the project is still in its research stages, they have already set a target goal of providing 50% of the world's energy by 2050.

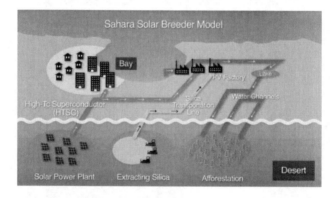

Solar technologies continue to be the most accessible green technology that homeowners and commercial spaces can employ to reduce dependence on limited energy resources. Its implementation depends on the sunlight potential of each specific area. Solar Farms and Solar Energy Grids are widespread deployed in Spain, Italy, Germany and Thailand with solar buy-back programmes of the governments. Rooftop solar systems are installed in California (with 200,000 rooftop solar systems), Colorado, Delaware, New York, Washington, Utah and Hawaii.

18.6.4.2 Manufacturing Solar Panels in China

China is the biggest manufacturer of solar panels. Strong solar constituencies and solar-friendly policies are in place in many countries to encourage large-scale installations of solar technology.

Well-designed systems can reduce peak demand of energy, shift usage time to off-peak hours, enhance sustainability and keep fossil fuel prices low, besides having other advantages.

18.6.5 *Waste Water to Electricity Generation*

A new hybrid electricity generator is developed at the Oregon State University, USA. The generator uses two different technologies: reverse electro dialysis and microbial fuel cells to create a system that generates electricity from waste water. The generator will be able to power water treatment while contributing significantly to the main power grid.

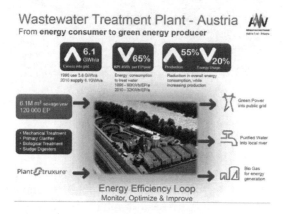

18.7 A Path from R&D to Product and Service Releases for DSP

The development of DSP has leapfrogged because DSP is the embedded technology and the core competence of a wide range of emerging intelligent products and new services. DSP applications are supporting many emerging demands in the very topical areas of world interests. They are intelligent-healthcare systems and services, advent mobile communications networks, Internet of Things, big data and cloud computing, smart cities and smart world, and green technology development.

Certain criteria are suggested to assess social responsibility and sustainable growth of DSP innovations. The criteria are resource availability, technical expertise, operational readiness, market opportunities and economic outlook, political sentiment, scheduling and cultural compatibility.

A model is suggested to illustrate along the path from development to commercialisation:

Entering a Transitioning Process

Original ideas and advanced methodologies are generated and developed in the laboratories—a technology nursery. An incubator test bed, a launch pad may be set up to help prospective entrepreneurs form and grow start-up companies.

Building an Entrepreneurial Community from Classroom to Marketplace

The tangible benefits of academic research are extraordinary from ideas to product releases. Intellectual properties of DSP could be transferred among small businesses and niche subsidiaries of many big businesses for manufacturing. There are frequently the people, many times with faculty, who bring the innovations to market in the form of a small company that, in turn, hires employees.

Partnering and Serving Clients Big and Small, the Local Communities and the World

Development of DSP brings together the research, the entrepreneurs, the companies, and the products and services. These nano-technology, biotechnology, high-tech materials, intelligent systems, and other businesses help provide an anchor for growth.

DSP applications also promote global participation.

Evolving DSP Applications in Financial Segment

The fundamental technologies in DSP, the algorithms and simulation methodologies are integral in the designs, analyses, and development of moving communications signals in most advanced intelligent networks and things. Similar profiles and patterns may also be applicable to exploration in the financial sector to process market signals and market movement.

We are only confined by our own imagination!

Source and Reference

The content in this chapter is based on personal experience, dialogue with colleagues and friends in industries and governments, published literature and pamphlet across multiple information platforms. All graphics are from the Internet. All statistics are quotations and consolidated data from publications of the World Health Organization, International Telecommunication Union, Market Analysis of CM Market Research, Boston Consulting Group, the Gartner Reports, International Data Group, McKenzie Group Consultant, and Annual Reports of many public companies and corporations.

Acknowledgements

I wish to pay the very special tribute to Professor A. G. Constantinides.

Tony is my dear friend and always my teacher—in generating original ideas and turning challenges into opportunities, at Imperial and in life. Many thanks to Tony for his enlightenment and continued encouragement!

I would also like to express my gratitude to Professor Lim Yong Ching, Professor Hon Keung Kwan, and Professor Siu Wan-chi. Yong Ching and Hon Keung are my friends at Imperial and valued colleagues in my doctoral research. Thanks to Wan-chi for his insights in our discussion on the education of DSP. The three professors entrust me to contribute this chapter in the most precious Festschrift in honour of Professor A. G. Constantinides. I am very honoured.

Photo taken with Professor A. G. Constantinides and Professor Peter Cheung, Head of EEE Department at Imperial College London.

The Author

This chapter is written from a personal perspective of Dr Paulina Chan, an alumna who studied Electrical and Electronic Engineering at Imperial College London. Being Imperial College Ambassador, and the Principal and CEO of an international consortium on multinational technology business, Paulina works with trans-disciplinary professionals across continents to foster collaborations in innovative technologies, intelligent infrastructures and green energies.

Her career includes Managing Directors and expatriates of AT&T/Lucent Technologies in the US, Asia/Pacific Region, and the EU; Project Director of Exxon/Mobil Corporation Headquarters, New York NY; China Regional General Manager and expatriate of ICO Global Communications London and Beijing; and Senior Adviser of the EU for Hungary.

Paulina has chaired special sessions and published in many professional conferences, including the IEEE - ICC, NCC, and INFOCOM. She is also the Champion of the Imperial College Mentoring Programme to guide young scientists/technologists/engineers/managers-in-training to develop career paths and personal growth.

Closing Remarks

Lajos Hanzo

University of Southampton, UK

lh@ecs.soton.ac.uk

It is a privilege to write the closing remarks for this exquisite anthology in celebrating the pioneering contributions of Professor Anthony Constantinides, who has tirelessly promoted the development of digital signal processing over a period close to fifty years.

As an inspirational scientist, research leader, educator and prolific PhD advisor, he influenced generations of signal processing enthusiasts with his shrewd long-term vision, charisma and boundless energy. The celebratory colloquium organized to mark his seventieth birthday was a true testimony to the global influence he enjoyed, which brought back a large cohort of his 140 or so former PhD students to London, many of whom now hold posts of high esteem and global influence. While I am writing these lines, dear Colleagues, a tingling feeling shivers down my spine, as I reminisce...

Indeed, I reminisce along numerous lines. I got to know him as a prolific scientist through his influential publications, a little later as a much respected leading academic of the British, European as well as global signal processing community. He is widely known as a colourful, knowledgeable person. It is the ancient Greek terminology of 'polyhistor' that describes him best, which is in plain English "someone gifted or learned in multiple disciplines", as it is eloquently detailed in more depth at Wikipedia.

If I may indulge in science for a moment, this volume nicely wraps up the past few decades of advances in digital signal processing, indicating both the direct and indirect influence Professor Constantinides has had on this burgeoning field. The structure of the book mirrors these trends with its three-pronged approach of considering filtering and transforms, the broader aspects of sophisticated contemporary signal processing and, finally, communications. The sheer achievement of the contributors in bringing this volume together is admirable. There is a coherent progression from classic filtering-related issues, which hallmarked his early career, towards his more recent interests in signal processing for communications.

To elaborate a little further on the three core sections of the book following its introductory part, one of the critical elements of digital signal processing is the analogue/digital converter, which is touched upon at the beginning of Part II. This is followed by the portrayal of a range of wideband filters designed for contemporary software-defined radios that are capable of processing the radio signal of several standards with the aid of sophisticated reconfiguration techniques. Furthermore, an in-depth survey of digital all-pass filters is provided, which is complemented by a range of recent advances in carefully optimized bespoke finite impulse response filters. A suite of sparse models conceived for echo cancellation are also portrayed in the volume—after all, echo cancellation is a rich classic subject closely linked to adaptive filtering. It has found its way into our daily lives, since every single desk-phone has one built into it. However, it is also finding a host of hitherto unexplored applications, for example, in full-duplex wireless relays, that constitutes a hot research subject at the time of writing. The first part of the book is rounded off by a treatise on salient transform domain processing techniques conceived for diverse applications, including video signal processing.

Part III is related to a broader range of advanced signal processing techniques, commencing with an in-depth discussion on the specialist subjects of Ramanujan sums and the representation of periodic sequences as well as on high-dimensional kernel regression. These detailed discussions are then followed by a selection of audiovisual subjects, touching upon microphone arrays, on the recognition of human faces under realistic practical conditions as well as on the semantic representation, enrichment and retrieval of audiovisual film content. This part of the anthology is then concluded with a detailed treatise on the modelling of complex systems, on their data representations and on neural learning, with an outlook to the artificial mind. Isn't it fascinating, what has been achieved by this dedicated community of signal processing scientists?

Finally, Part IV of this volume is dedicated to an impressively diverse spectrum of achievements in the applied signal processing subject area of telecommunications. Specifically, it covers advanced subjects, exemplified by the Markov Chain Monte Carlo detection technique, which is capable of approaching the performance of the 'brute-force' full-search based detectors at the cost of a substantially reduced number of cost-function evaluations in a diverse range of applications. The topic of physical-layer security is also addressed in the book, which exploits the simple plausible fact that provided the capacity of the channel between the source and destination is higher than that between the source and an eavesdropper, then perfect secrecy can be achieved. In this context, the employment of multiple antennas further improves the attainable grade of secrecy by improving the capacity of the desired link. The final two chapters of the book deal with the subject of radio frequency localization and prediction techniques, which are particularly promising in the context of indoor application scenarios, where the global positioning system is unable to provide adequate coverage.

The Finale of the book eloquently augments our understanding of how digital signal processing changed the world we live in throughout the exquisite career of Professor Constantinides.

Having surveyed this inspiring journey of discovery hallmarking the career of Professor Constantinides and his distinguished associates, I feel that tingle again—sincere thanks to you all for taking me with you on this journey of discovery!

Index